ADVERTISING

ADVERTISING

Dorothy Cohen

Hofstra University

SCOTT, FORESMAN AND COMPANY

Glenview, Illinois
Boston
London

To: Morris, Richard, Susan, Fred, and Marc

23456-RRW-939291908988

Library of Congress Cataloging-in-Publication Data

Cohen, Dorothy.
Advertising.
Includes bibliographical references and index.
  1. Advertising   I. Title.
HF5821.C56   1988   659.1   87-15933
ISBN 0-673-18255-X

PREFACE

ADVERTISING is a new text that examines the business of advertising as a function of marketing and a way of communication. It takes three main approaches: a *managerial* approach, examining advertising as an effective marketing tool; a *production* approach, revealing both the inspirational and the practical sides of creativity; and a *public policy* approach, showing how advertising reflects and affects our environment.

Advertising has become a fact of our culture. Given its omnipresence, students come to the course with many opinions and a good deal of interest. Advertising is an exciting subject whose study begins well before the classroom and continues in the workplace. Practitioners of years' standing—account executives, product managers, copywriters, and art directors—have often emphasized how in each campaign is found something new to learn. Business people know they need advertising and want to integrate it efficiently and effectively into their marketing plans. For both purposes, a comprehensive analysis of the basics of the discipline, well-organized and accessible, is the best a course—and a book—can offer. *Advertising* is meant to be a solid resource book for the basics of the discipline.

ORGANIZATION

The book follows a four-part format. By defining different kinds of advertising and outlining a historical perspective, Part I lays the groundwork for study by really explaining *why* people advertise. In defining the field's primary concepts and purposes, we can begin to position advertising as an integral part of our economy. The business side of advertising is as much a part of our environment as advertising's effects. Part II details advertising as a business function, both within the firm that advertises and the agency that serves the advertiser. Organizational structure, budget, managerial activity, control, and planning take many forms in many firms, yet advertising touches them all.

Part III is an extensive examination of advertising from the perspective of its communication and creative functions. Five separate sections within this part focus on how strategic efforts drive the preparation, development, execution, and evaluation of the *advertising campaign*, the backbone of the advertising industry. Situation analysis, creative strategy, media strategy, and research fill out, start to finish, the campaign structure. Strategic efforts come together in an illustration of an actual advertising campaign, followed by a look at the campaign applied to special markets, including the international realm.

Part IV covers public policy, describing advertising's role as a socio-economic force. It discusses the mechanisms society has formed to resolve conflicts generated by advertising's effects upon our environment. Government and industry regulation provide answers to many of the public's concerns.

SPECIAL FEATURES

Each part and section of the book showcases award-winning and effective advertisements, with light narration to tie the images to central messages of the text. For example, the process of how ads reach their target markets is clarified with over twenty fresh examples in one photo essay; in another the reader moves visually through an advertising agency and through agency services, stopping to look at a client meeting, a photo shoot, and a presentation—at both the business and creative aspects of the profession.

Opening each chapter is a description of a real-life incident that illustrates how a concept to be explored in that chapter operates in the business world. Objectives for learning are presented on the first page of every chapter to pose a challenge to the student.

Questions for discussion and review, key terms, and a experiential exercise conclude the chapters. Cases prepared from actual business experiences appear at the end of every part and section in the book.

A page-referenced glossary provides a quick resource for the student who needs to check definitions of important terms. In addition to a Subject Index, a separate Name Index for authors, practitioners, and researchers appears.

The text is supported with a strong base in consumer behavior insights and touches on the important contributions of computer technology to advertising decision making. New concepts and theories in advertising research and evaluation keep the book relevant to advertising today.

SUPPLEMENTS TO THE TEXT

An *Instructor's Manual* provides help in course planning and lists general resources in advertising (casebooks, journal articles, books) in addition to the core features. There are additional class projects and a complete *Test Bank* with over one thousand items.

The *Study Guide and Activities Workbook* helps students organize course material and test their understanding through developing and applying advertising concepts.

Overhead *Color Transparencies* are designed to be a lecture strong point, supplementing the text's illustration program with an extra fifty labeled advertisements.

ACKNOWLEDGMENTS

I owe a debt of gratitude to the many professionals, academicians, business people, and students whose knowledge, expertise, and enthusiasm has contributed to this project. My appreciation extends to the numerous agencies, firms, and organizations that supplied illustrations and exhibits—BBDO, Burrell Advertising, Hal Riney & Partners, Foote, Cone & Belding, Chiat/Day, Procter & Gamble, the Coca-Cola Company, Anheuser-Busch, the American Cancer Society, Kameny Communications, the New York State Department of Commerce, and Wells, Rich, Greene, Inc., to name only a few. I am deeply grateful to Romare Bearden whose outstanding artistic creativity has been a continuing source of pleasure and inspiration. I would also like to offer a special note of thanks to Thomas Kinnear for his support, and to Carol Karton and Ann-Marie Buesing for their significant aid in editing and project management. Acknowledgment is also due to the following people who provided input: Richard F. Beltramini, Arizona State Universtiy; Cathy Goodwin, Georgia State University; Shanna Greenwalt, Southern Illinois University; Thomas C. O'Guinn, University of Illinois; and Edward A. Riordan, Wayne State University.

In closing, I would like to thank the many students I have taught over the years who encouraged me to undertake this project through their statements that my advertising course has helped them in their different vocations. Special appreciation goes to my husband Morris and to the rest of my family, Richard, Susan, Fred, and Marc. Throughout the development of the book, they have been there always for continuing support, encouragement, and understanding.

Dorothy Cohen
Hofstra University

TABLE OF CONTENTS

ADVERTISING

I

The Basics of Advertising

ADVERTISING is designed to give students a broad overview of a dynamic and complex subject. The text is divided into four parts to provide a workable framework for study. Part One, consisting of Chapters 1 and 2, prepares the groundwork by providing explanations of advertising's most important areas and concepts; it goes on to outline the history of advertising and its development as a major institution in our economy.

1

What Is Advertising?

CHAPTER OBJECTIVES

— To define *advertising*

— To classify advertising according to its sources, targets, objectives, and media

— To explain the plan of this book

One day, in the late 1800s, a soapmaker at Procter & Gamble left his machine running during his lunch period and returned to find a whipped soap that, when made into bars, was buoyant. The company capitalized on this mistake by proclaiming, "Ivory Soap—It Floats." Although the focus of the campaign has changed from that first advertising effort, over 100 years later the soap is still advertised and Procter & Gamble is still a perennial leader in advertising expenditures.

It is reported that whenever Milton S. Hershey spotted a Hershey-bar wrapper on the ground, he always checked to see if the Hershey name was up. If it wasn't, he would carefully pick up the wrapper, smooth it out, and place it back on the ground with the name clearly visible. This was Hershey's idea of an advertising campaign.

Inroads into its market from competitors eventually caused the company to change its strategy. In 1970, 66 years into its corporate life, Hershey began advertising and, in the 1980s, Hershey has become one of the one hundred largest advertisers in the country.

Today it is difficult to find major organizations that do not advertise, but why firms advertise, how they advertise, and how this extensive advertising effort affects us and our society are some of the significant issues that need to be examined. Before we can begin the discussion, however, it is necessary to explain what is meant by the term *advertising*.

DEFINING ADVERTISING

Although it is difficult to concretely define this complex concept, there are some widely quoted definitions of advertising that can suggest some limits. At the turn of the century a well-known advertising copywriter named John E. Kennedy remarked that advertising was "salesmanship in print." This often-repeated saying indicates that the ultimate objective of advertising is to sell.

In 1948, the Definitions Committee of the American Marketing Association developed what is, to this day, the most widely quoted definition of advertising:

> *Advertising is any paid form of nonpersonal presentation and promotion of ideas, goods, or services by an identified sponsor.*[1]

This definition presents an explanation of what advertising is, while at the same time it offers insights into what advertising is not. The key words describing advertising are *presentation* and *promotion*. *Presentation* refers to an offering; *promotion* involves communication and persuasion; therefore, advertising is designed to offer people ideas, goods, or services and persuade them of the benefits, utility, and desirability.

The terms *nonpersonal, paid form* and *identified sponsor* point out what advertising is not. Advertising is not personal selling, for it does not use individual face-to-face communications. Referring to advertising as *word of mouth* is also incorrect, since this, too, suggests the use of a human agency. Advertising is not publicity since unlike publicity, it is paid for and identifies the sponsor of the message.

The AMA definition is limited and does not suggest the persuasive and creative aspects of advertising or indicate its functions and responsibilities. Therefore the author offers the following utopian definition:

> *Advertising is a business activity, employing creative techniques to design persuasive communications in mass media that promote ideas, goods, and services in a manner consistent with the achievement of the advertiser's objectives, the delivery of consumer satisfactions, and the development of social and economic welfare.*

ADVERTISING CLASSIFICATIONS

There is not one clear, all-embracing term to describe the complex character and multiple, interrelated functions of advertising, but, because it is a form of communication, it is frequently described in terms of the sources, audiences, and objectives of its communications, as well as by the mass media through which its messages are delivered. While these classifications are neither precise nor mutually exclusive, they are helpful in providing a clearer explanation of advertising efforts.

---

[1]"Report of the Definitions Committee," *Journal of Marketing*, Vol. 13, No. 2 (1948), p. 205.

EXHIBIT 1.1
Commercial Advertising

Advertising Sources

Both individuals and groups can originate messages. John Smith might want to let people know about the one-cents sale at his hardware store; Sears, Roebuck and Company might advertise its financial services department; the National Cancer Society might want to communicate to the public-at-large facts about smoking. These sources are designated by the function of their advertising as either commercial advertisers or noncommercial advertisers.

Commercial Advertisers
Manufacturers and producers often advertise a product or service, while resellers, wholesalers, and retailers frequently call attention to the place where the product may be bought. Advertising from these sources is called *commercial advertising*—a term that indicates not only the source of the message but the purpose of the ads (see Exhibit 1.1).

Noncommercial Advertisers
There has been a significant increase in recent years in *noncommercial advertising*, that advertising by religious and philanthropic organizations, politicians, labor unions, and the government that promotes ideas

What's Old,
What's New
in Advertising

Many American companies have been advertising for decades. Both similarities and differences in style and appeal can be seen in some of these campaigns through the years.

Coca-Cola has advertised consistently since the soft drink's introduction at an Atlanta drugstore soda fountain in 1886.

1986

1905

1912

The pause that refreshes

1929

Thru 50 years...1886 to 1936
The pause that refreshes

1936

1946

1953

1964

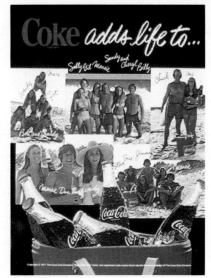

1976

1982

1986

Procter & Gamble has used the same appeal to advertise Ivory Soap for about one hundred years—an emotional appeal linking purity of ingredients, childcare, and soft skin. Deviations from this appeal have been interlaced throughout the years. Men have been targeted in the workplace as well as in the bath, and advice on beauty has been given.

1898

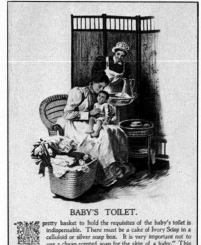

1901

1929

1929

1930

1955

1987

The company continues to use an appeal very similar to the original one, now positioning the soap as a classic product.

Singer: Hershey Bar. One of the
All-Time Greats.

Music

Music

Music

Music

Singer: Hershey's

Unlike Coca-Cola and Ivory, it took Hershey Foods sixty-six years to begin advertising. Company founder, Milton S. Hershey's own form of advertising was to smooth out and replace, name-up, any Hershey bar wrappers he found on the street. Today the company is one of the nation's top one hundred advertisers.

Colgate-Palmolive is a long-time advertiser. Children have frequently appeared in the company's campaigns as users of the products.

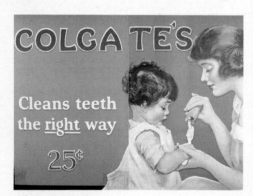

COLGATE'S

Cleans teeth the *right* way

25¢

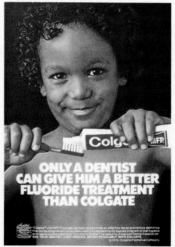

ONLY A DENTIST
CAN GIVE HIM A BETTER
FLUORIDE TREATMENT
THAN COLGATE

MILES AHEAD

A Publication by Miles Laboratories, Inc., for Retail Druggists

HE'LL BE SELLING FOR YOU IN '52!

"SPEEDY"
Alka-Seltzer
FEATURED IN

BIG
COLOR ADS
IN
WOMEN'S MAGAZINES

Alka-Selzer has been advertised by Miles Laboratories since the 1930s. "Speedy" was a familiar trade character of the 1950s; here he is introduced to pharmacists and druggists on the cover of a company-published trade journal. Today the product still is heavily advertised in broadcast media.

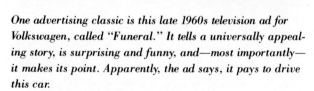

One advertising classic is this late 1960s television ad for Volkswagen, called "Funeral." It tells a universally appealing story, is surprising and funny, and—most importantly—it makes its point. Apparently, the ad says, it pays to drive this car.

> Open on a funeral procession of limousines each containing the beneficiaries of a will.
>
> *Male voiceover:*
> I, Maxwell E. Snavely, being of sound mind and body, do bequeath the following:
>
> To my wife Rose, who spent money like there was no tomorrow, I leave $100 and a calendar.
>
> To my sons Rodney and Victor, who spent every dime I ever gave them on fancy cars and fast women, I leave $50 in dimes.
>
> To my business partner Jules, whose motto was "spend, spend, spend," I leave nothing, nothing, nothing. And to my other friends and relatives who also never learned the value of a dollar, I leave . . . a dollar.
>
> Finally, to my nephew, Harold, who oft time said, "A penny saved is a penny earned." And who also oft time said: "Gee, Uncle Max, it sure pays to own a Volkswagen". . . I leave my entire fortune of one hundred billion dollars.

Creative Characters

Animated spokespersons—cartoon characters—have been employed in advertising since the 1950s. Today they can add warmth and interest to products and services that may be seen as cold or nebulous—those actually selected for salient features or price but not on the basis of emotional appeal.

"The Peanuts characters were appropriate because they're thoughtful people with adult philosophical problems with unique solutions—in general, they're very intellectual," said the copywriter of these advertisements for Metropolitan Life Insurance Company.

"It's hard to hate a bunny," explained the creative director of the Sony Betamax campaign for which Bugs Bunny spoke. The underlying creative concept was to promote a sharper video picture through the endorsement of the "most famous carrot eater of all."

"He's a fat cat that loves to be pampered," stated an art director for the Embassy Suites account that hired Garfield.

"It's not often you see a computer with Mickey Mouse," emphasized the art director who helped publicize the famous mouse's role as a system expert for Sperry (now Unisys). It's not often you see Mickey Mouse in advertising at all. Walt Disney Productions has been very careful about their family of characters not becoming overexposed.

Source: excerpts from "Creative Concepts: Snoopy Meets Madison Avenue," *Marketing and Media Decisions*, May, 1986. Copyright © 1986 Decisions Publications Inc. Reprinted by permission.

or institutions. The government, for example, has become a heavy advertiser in campaigns to encourage army enlistments (see Exhibit 1.2).

Approximately $150 million was spend on television advertising in 1984 to elect a president, thirteen governors, and numerous members of Congress and the Senate.[2] Some of this promotion was criticized as excessively negative, a concern that eventually led to the proposal for the passage of a "Clean Campaign Act."

Advertising Targets

The nature of advertising, and the use of mass media as its method of transmission, suggests that audiences are generally large groups or masses of people. However, the choice of medium can serve to widen or to reduce the market selected for a specific advertisement. For example, the use of network television generally gives a message extensive exposure, while direct mail advertising can limit receipt of the message to a smaller, selected group of people. The basic target groups in advertising are most frequently classified geographically—national and local— or according to their primary characteristics—consumer or business.

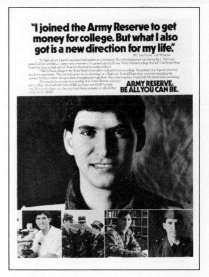

EXHIBIT 1.2
The Government as an Advertiser

National Advertising
National advertising has more than a geographic connotation; it refers to the source of the advertisement as well as the target. Although it implies that the market is national rather than local, the term may be misleading because the market may be only regional or local. *National advertising* more precisely serves to indicate that a manufacturer is promoting his or her own *brand,* as distinguished from a reseller who may be promoting his or her own *label.*

Local Advertising
The term *local advertising* is advertising serving the needs of a particular limited area, and, although it is frequently initiated by retailers in that area, it may also originate with national producers, local producers, and local service organizations. *Retail advertising,* often used interchangeably with *local advertising,* indicates the source of the message rather than its target and suggests that the advertisement originated from a retail store.

There are significant differences between retail advertising and national advertising. Retail advertising (1) covers a less extensive territory, (2) has a closer relationship to the customer, (3) attracts reader interest on a more regular basis, (4) expects customers to visit a specific store rather than any store, and (5) features price much more frequently as an integral part of the advertisement.[3]

[2]Edwin Diamond and Stephen Bates, "30-Second Elections," *New York* (October 1, 1984), p. 46.

[3]Charles M. Edwards, Jr. and Russel A. Brown, *Retail Advertising and Sales Promotion* (Englewood Cliffs, N.J.: Prentice-Hall, Inc., 1959), pp. 25–31.

Consumer Advertising

Consumer advertising is designed to reach anyone who does not remake or resell a product, or more specifically, the ultimate consumer. It is the largest target market for products and services, comprising over 230,000,000 people in the United States alone.

Producers of raw materials, semifabricated goods, and component parts may also advertise to final consumers in an effort to encourage them to look for or request elements from these specific companies in their final purchases. Extensive consumer advertising emanates from E. I. DuPont de Nemours and United States Steel, although these companies do not sell their products to final consumers.

Business-to-Business Advertising

Business-to-business advertising has increased both in volume and scope in recent years. The term relates to advertising that is directed to industrial users (steel advertised to automobile manufacturers), resellers, and professionals.

Industrial advertising is the advertising of raw materials, semimanufactured goods, equipment, supplies, and services to the agricultural, extractive (mining) and manufacturing industries (see Exhibit 1.3). *Trade advertising* promotes to *resellers* rather than *reusers* of the product. A manufacturer advertises to wholesalers, retailers, and various other institutions in his channel of distribution, to encourage them to purchase his merchandise, to reorder, to display it extensively, to sell it aggressively, or to service it adequately.

Professional advertising refers to the promotional efforts designed to reach professional groups such as physicians, dentists, and pharmacists who may use the advertiser's equipment, or products in servicing patients. This activity should be distinguished from advertising by professionals—ads directed to the ultimate consumer by doctors, lawyers, and other professionals—a promotional activity that has gained momentum since the Supreme Court decisions permitted such advertising.

Advertising Objectives

There are numerous reasons for advertising, and a complete discussion of these objectives is presented in Chapter 7. The discussion here is limited to defining several broad classifications: product and institutional (also called corporate) advertising, primary demand and selective demand advertising, comparative advertising, public service advertising and advocacy advertising.

Product Advertising
The major portion of advertising expenditures are spent on *product advertising*, the presentation and promotion of new products, old products, and revised products. When General Electric extols the virtues of its refrigerators or washing machines this is clearly product advertising. Product advertising encompasses services as well. Hertz advertises the speed of its auto rental service, while Citibank promotes its twenty-four-hour availability.

Corporate Advertising
When an advertisement shows General Electric's role in the development of the oil-drilling business, thus talking about the company and not the product, this is *corporate advertising*. The term clarifies that it is the firm which is advertised. Several other terms distinguish among corporate advertising efforts: *image advertising* and *public relations advertising*.

Most corporate advertising is designed to create a favorable image for a company and its products; however, *image advertising* specifically denotes a corporate campaign that highlights the superiority or desirable characteristics of the sponsoring corporation. A company may use such advertising to change its image, to indicate its change in direction, or to make itself appear more modern.

As with many advertising classifications it is sometimes difficult to distinguish between a firm's image and its public relations advertising. Generally, however, when the corporate ad focuses on the public interest, but has some relationship to the product or service provided by the firm, it is considered a form of *public relations advertising*. An example is the Shell "Answer Man" campaign which is not directly related to Shell gasoline or the services provided by Shell service stations, but helps consumers solve their automobile problems and encourages safe driving.

EXHIBIT 1.3
Industrial Advertising

Anaconda Wire & Cable Company aired this humorous TV spot indicating that its cable increased mine productivity in western Virginia, lower West Virginia, and eastern Kentucky, where half the nation's 2000 underground mines are located.

EXHIBIT 1.4
A Primary Demand Campaign

The decline in meat consumption is due to several factors. In part the reason is economic; retail prices of meat have risen 110 percent in the past decade. Health considerations, including the desire to reduce the amount of saturated fat and cholesterol in diets, have led to a decline in meat purchases. This decline has been accelerated by changing social patterns—increases in the numbers of "singles" who tend to consume less meat than family members, working women who have less time to cook or roast, and people who are more apt to "snack" through the day than eat regular meals.

To reverse the decline in meat consumption, various trade associations in the meat industry are engaging in primary demand campaigns (see Exhibit 1.4). The Beef Industry Council is attempting to overcome a health stigma with the slogan "Beef Gives Strength." The National Pork Products Council is using the theme "America, you're leaning on pork!" This is intended to convey the double meaning that pork is slimming as well as inexpensive. The American Sheep Producers Council is trying to reach the slightly more than half of the population in the United States that has never had lamb as a family meal. Their campaign—"Experience Lamb"—suggests new ways to prepare lamb for the family.

Source: Bernice Kanner, "On Madison Avenue, the Ways of All Flesh," *New York* (November 22, 1983), pp. 20–22.

Primary Demand and Selective Demand Advertising

A major portion of the advertising effort is designed to increase the demand for a product or service. There are two kinds of demand: primary and selective. *Primary demand* refers to the demand for the generic product, such as a television set. *Selective demand* is designed to gain acceptability for a particular manufacturer's brand—a Zenith television set.

Primary Demand Advertising

If a product is in its introductory stage, the best promotional strategy may be to use advertising that is designed to gain acceptability for a product group rather than extol the virtues of a particular manufacturer's brand. This primary demand advertising was used in the early days of television when the consumer had little experience with, and little faith in, "the black box with knobs." Television set manufacturers were much more concerned with gaining acceptance of the entire product class, rather than with carving out a share of the market for their specific brands. The industry believed that, by increasing the total demand for this new product concept, each manufacturer's share would increase as well. Accordingly, attempts to differentiate among the different brands were at a minimum. Advertising appeals stressed the general feasibility and workability of the mechanism, rather than competitive attributes.

Frequently primary demand advertising is conducted by an industry group or trade association in order to promote a product. There are a

EXHIBIT 1.5
A Primary Demand Campaign to Overcome a Stigma

number of reasons why a particular industry may decide to promote a product under the generic name:

1. To reverse a declining primary demand.
2. To overcome a stigma (see Exhibit 1.5).
3. To combat the effect of substitutes.
4. To suggest new uses.

Selective Demand Advertising

Relatively few completely new products appear on the market; thus most new product introductions today are accompanied by selective demand advertising, which promotes a specific manufacturer's brand. It comprises the bulk of advertising effort and is the major focus of this text. A company that considers increasing the primary demand for the product group as an important objective must nonetheless engage in some selective demand advertising, if only to notify consumers what the product is called and where it can be purchased.

When a product has become accepted and is exhibiting a favorable primary demand, each manufacturer can direct his or her efforts to increasing market share. For example, the phenomenal growth of the jeans industry led to a proliferation of many brands each of which was promoted through selective demand advertising. The various coffee companies invest in heavy advertising of their individual brands. General Foods promotes its Maxwell House using a commercial directed at the youth on MTV, the music video station.[4] Efforts to promote individual coffee brands have involved the use of personalities such as Mrs. Olson, Robert Young, Joe DiMaggio, Danny Thomas, and Lauren Bacall.

Florence Henderson, star of stage, screen, TV

"I was nearly deaf until I got help."

Florence Henderson, one of Hollywood's busiest television personalities, almost went deaf a few years ago. But for the sake of her family, her happiness, and her career, she did something about it.

Florence is one of millions who overcame hearing loss. Yet millions of others still suffer from uncorrected hearing disorders. Most could be helped—medically, surgically, or through amplification.

If you or someone close to you doesn't hear well, don't hide it. Get help. Arrange for a hearing checkup.

For more information about hearing loss and available hearing help write: Hearing, Box 1840, Washington, D.C. 20013.

You should hear what you're missing!

 Better Hearing Institute
1430 K Street, N.W., Suite 600, Washington, D.C. 20005

EXHIBIT 1.6
Public Service Advertising

Public Service Advertising

Public service advertising is designed to operate in the public interest and promote the public welfare. Public service advertisements emanate from various organizations, commercial and noncommercial. The Heart Association, medical and dental groups, and a variety of professional organizations have devised campaigns (see Exhibit 1.6). A cigarette company has introduced a public interest campaign to discourage young people from smoking (see Exhibit 1.7). While this is a form of public relations advertising for the cigarette firm, it is more specifically defined as a public service ad since its objective is to discourage use of the advertiser's product.

A major source of public service advertising is an organization formed in World War I, composed of representatives from advertising agencies, the media, and the industry. *The Advertising Council*, as it is now called, has prepared public service advertising urging people to

---

[4]Aimie Stern, "General Foods' Strategy for Tomorrow," *Dun's Business Month* (May 1985), p. 52.

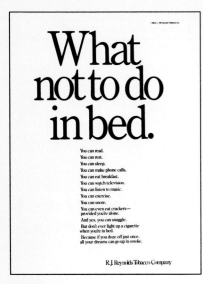

EXHIBIT 1.7
Public Service Ad by Commercial Advertiser

EXHIBIT 1.8
Advocating for Wildlife Conservation

register to vote, to stop polluting, to prevent forest fires, to reduce juvenile automobile theft, to continue education, and to contribute to worthy causes. Many of the campaigns have been effective both in attracting attention and generating responses. Besides Smokey the Bear the best known Advertising Council campaign symbol is Iron Eyes Cody, the crying Indian.

Advocacy Advertising

Advocacy advertising, also called *issue advertising*, is concerned with the propagation of ideas and the clarification of controversial social issues of public importance.[5] In some respects it resembles public service or public relations advertising; however, it is different from these efforts because the message represents an advertiser's point of view that, in many cases, is controversial. For example, USX (formerly U.S. Steel) ads advocated creating a more favorable tax structure to provide for more investment capital.

A growing number of firms have applied advertising strategies to social causes such as conserving wildlife (see Exhibit 1.8) or to influencing consumers' viewpoints—for example, that big business needs big profits.

Advocacy advertising was given significant support by a Supreme Court ruling stating that corporations may use advocacy advertising for political issues, even though these issues do not directly affect the corporation's own business interests.[6] Such advertising on the part of corporations is a controversial issue. Its use indicates that the business community is vocal and forthcoming in stating its corporate mind and much less worried about offending one constituency or another. A firm not only can advocate a point of view favorable to its needs; it may deter the passage of unfavorable regulations.

To some, the result of this kind of advertising by business is a much greater public understanding of the role of business in our society.[7] Others are concerned with the financial strength of corporations to advocate their views. Unless there are provisions for funding of contrasting views, there may be one-sided discussions in the political arena.

Comparative Advertising

Comparative advertising compares specific product attributes with competitors' brands (see Exhibit 1.9). Comparative advertising has been used widely by automobile companies, those who produce and sell pain relievers, as well as computer manufacturers. Prior to the 1970s adver-

---

[5] S. Prakash Sethi, "Institutional Advertising and Idea/Issue Advertising as Marketing Tools: Some Public Policy Issues," *Journal of Marketing*, Vol. 43 (January 1979), pp. 68–78.
[6] *First National Bank of Boston* v. *Bellotti*, 98 S. Ct. 1407 (1978).
[7] "Comment," *Journal of Marketing*, Vol. 43 (January 1979) p. 79.

EXHIBIT 1.9
A Comparative Ad

tising was rarely used for this purpose. Advertisers considered it undesirable to present competitors' brand names in their own advertisements believing they were offering "free advertising" to the competition. Negative comments concerning competitors in such advertisements were viewed as ranging from "unprofessional" to "unethical."

Comparative advertising was encouraged in the early seventies by the success of Schick's Flexamatic advertising, which reportedly increased Schick's market share from 8 percent to 24 percent at the expense of its competitors.[8] Subsequently, it was further encouraged by the FTC which considered comparative advertising an important tech-

---

[8]William L. Wilkie and Paul W. Farris, "Comparison Advertising: Problems and Potential," *Journal of Marketing*, Vol. 39 (October 1975), pp. 7–15.

nique for increasing competition in the marketplace, since it is specifically directed toward, and actually names, competitors' brands.

Several researchers have examined the effects of comparative advertising. Wilkie and Farris indicated that it may increase awareness of a brand through the novelty effect. Levine's research indicated that such advertising may generate greater sponsor misidentification and so benefits the named competitor.[9] Recommendations for comparative advertising have included suggestions that the comparison be made to the industry leader. In a recent study, Murphy and Amundsen, however, concluded that noncomparative appeal is more effective than comparative appeals for new brands which are competing with the dominant brand in their product category.[10]

There is currently little agreement as to the desirability and effectiveness of comparative advertising. Defenders declare it provides consumers with more information, forces manufacturers to strive for product improvement to avoid unfavorable comparisons, and that the novelty may enhance the attention capabilities of the ads. Critics declare that comparative ads overload the consumer with information, may tend to result in confusion and, therefore, misidentification of the compared brands, and may be used in an unscrupulous manner by advertisers, generating litigation and tarnishing the reputation of advertising in general.[11] Union Underwear, makers of Fruit of the Loom, the Number-One seller of lower-priced men's and boy's underwear, is suing Hanes for its comparative ads which feature Inspector 12 showing company trainees that laundered Hanes T-shirts shrink "38 percent less" than Fruit of the Loom laundered shirts. The lawsuit is pending, and although a District Judge failed to grant a preliminary injunction and stop broadcasts of the ad, he did note that the ad may make viewers think Fruit of the Loom leaves "one's midsection improperly covered after five washings."[12]

Advertising Media

Advertising is frequently transmitted through channels that permit the message to reach vast audiences simultaneously. These channels are called *mass media* and are broadly classified as print or broadcast.

Newspapers, magazines, and direct mail are considered *print media*. Outdoor and transit media, which include posters and displays,

[9]Philip Levine, "Commercials That Name Competing Brands," *Journal of Advertising Research*, Vol. 16 (December, 1976), pp. 7–14.

[10]John H. Murphy, II and Mary S. Amundsen, "The Communications Effectiveness of Comparative Advertising for a New Brand on Users of the Dominant Brand," *Journal of Advertising*, Vol. 10, No. 1 (1981), pp. 14–20.

[11]Stephen B. Ash and Chow-Hou Wee, "Comparative Advertising: A Review with Implications for Future Research," in *Advances in Consumer Research*, Vol. X, eds. Richard P. Bagozzi and Alice M. Tybout (Ann Arbor: Association for Consumer Research, 1983), pp. 370–76.

[12]Ronald Alsop, "Hanes Riles Underwear Firms with Feisty Comparative Ads," *The Wall Street Journal* (September 18, 1986), p. 35.

while basically dependent on print for transmission of the message, are sometimes differentiated from other print media because the message appears outdoors. They are therefore called *out-of-home media.*

Radio and television traditionally are designated as *broadcast media;* however, new technologies have created additional electronic facilities such as cable and video text. Some of these are considered "narrowcasting" since they are designed to reach specialized, rather than mass, audiences.

Advertisers use numerous other methods for relaying their messages—through the medium of motion pictures, the use of directories, or at point of purchase. These channels are usually referred to as *supplementary,* a term that refers to novel means of presenting messages, ranging from the use of Beetle Boards (the old Beetle Volkswagens used to display information) to, more recently, messages appearing on stamps.

In 1986 media expenditures surpassed $100 billion. The largest share of advertising expenditures is allocated to newspapers; however, the largest expenditures for national advertising occur in television. Direct mail is the third largest medium in terms of advertising expenditures.

THE FUNCTIONS OF ADVERTISING

Definitions and classifications only provide a common language in which to develop an understanding of advertising. One also needs to explore advertising's numerous interrelated functions and to view it from various perspectives.

Advertising performs a *business function;* it is one of the methods by which a firm may conduct its marketing activities. More precisely, advertising is one alternative among various promotional tools as discussed in Part Two.

The *communication function* of advertising is accomplished through the selection of the target market, and the choice of appropriate mass media for sending messages to these target groups. An effective communication process requires *creativity*—which is not only originality, but the ability to achieve results—and a means for evaluating these results. Integration of the various communication elements requires the formulation of advertising strategies and the creation of an advertising campaign, as described in Part Three.

Advertising involves more than a specific ad, advertiser, or campaign. It is considered an entire *institution.* According to Nicosia, the advertising institution is "the set of all activities of individuals and organizations as they relate to the sending and the seeking/receiving of 'economic' information via mass media."[13] The institution thus includes such classes as the senders of ads; the advertising agencies; the mass

---

[13]Francesco M. Nicosia, *Advertising, Management, and Society, A Business Point of View* (New York: McGraw-Hill Book Company, 1974), p. 153.

media; the seekers or receivers of messages; legislators, regulatory agencies, and courts; and the messages that flow throughout the institution.

The performance of advertising as an institution influences an entire socioeconomic system. It is irretrievably intertwined with many business decisions that ultimately affect the economy, including those of production, distribution, and resource allocation. From a social perspective, advertising's creative process develops style and pinpoints fashion, while its communication network provides information, molds opinions, and establishes standards. These issues are examined in Part Four.

SUMMARY

A clear understanding of advertising, therefore, requires familiarity with its various classifications.

Advertising can be considered a communication process and is frequently classified by its sources, targets, objectives, and media. Advertising sources include commercial advertisers such as business institutions and noncommercial advertisers such as politicians, philanthropic organizations, and the government. Advertising targets can be classified by geographic areas—national or local—or according to specific groups—consumers, trade, or industry.

There are many specific objectives for advertising campaigns; but, in a broad sense, advertising promotes a product or a firm. The latter activity is called *institutional* or *corporate advertising*.

The purpose of advertising may be to increase the demand for a product, either by primary demand or selective demand advertising. Primary demand advertising promotes a product class, while selective demand advertising promotes a specific manufacturer's brand.

Public service advertising operates in the public interest and promotes the public welfare. It emanates from various organizations including The Advertising Council, a group formed by members of the advertising community.

Advocacy or issue advertising propagates ideas and clarifies controversial social issues. The extent to which commercial corporations should engage in such advertising to present their points of view is itself a controversial issue.

Comparative advertising is a relatively new technique that names competitors for the purpose of comparing specific product attributes. There is controversy concerning the desirability and effectiveness of this kind of advertising.

Media classifications for advertising include print media (magazines, newspapers, and direct mail), broadcast media (television and radio), and out-of-home media (outdoor and transit).

QUESTIONS FOR DISCUSSION

1. Should an advertisement attempt to reach the largest possible group of people? Explain.
2. Define *national, retail,* and *local advertising* and explain the differences among these terms.
3. Select some examples of institutional advertising and explain each firm's purpose for presenting these ads.
4. If you were asked to initiate an advertising campaign for moon travel would you recommend primary demand or selective demand advertising? Why?
5. Provide an example of primary demand advertising and explain the objectives of the campaign.
6. How effective is public service advertising? Suggest a public interest or public welfare issue that would benefit from such a campaign.
7. What is meant by *advocacy advertising?* Do you believe corporations should be encouraged to engage in it? Why or why not?
8. Under what circumstances would you recommend comparative advertising for a firm? What is your opinion about such advertising?
9. What are the major advertising media? Which medium do you think will be most important in the future? Why?
10. What is your general view of advertising?

KEY TERMS

commercial advertising
noncommercial advertising
national advertising
local advertising
retail advertising
consumer advertising
business-to-business advertising
industrial advertising
trade advertising
professional advertising

product advertising
corporate advertising
primary demand advertising
selective demand advertising
comparative advertising
public service advertising
advocacy advertising
image advertising
public relations advertising

AD PRACTICE

Find examples of the following types of advertising in two major, general magazines:

industrial advertising
product advertising
corporate advertising
primary-demand advertising

selective-demand advertising
public service advertising
advocacy advertising
comparative advertising

Which type of advertising appears most frequently? Least frequently? What reasons can you offer for these variations?

2

The History of Advertising

For many years scholars had tried, without success, to unlock the key to the inscriptions on Egyptian temples, tombs, and manuscripts. In 1799, French engineers accompanying Napoleon's army in Egypt discovered the Rosetta stone, a basalt tablet dating from the year 136 B.C. The priesthood had erected many of these basalt tablets throughout the land, telling the story of Ptolemy Epiphanes, the ruler of Egypt, who had remitted some taxes to them. Each tablet bore a eulogy of the king in three languages—Greek, hieroglyphics, and Coptic—and advertised Ptolemy as "the true Son of the Sun, the Father of the Moon, and the Keeper of the Happiness of Men." Only the Rosetta stone survived, and, by the aid of this poster, the hieroglyphic system was recovered, permitting the study of thirty centuries of Egyptian history. It appears that we owe our knowledge of hieroglyphics to an advertisement.

According to Henry Sampson, an advertising historian, "Almost as long as there has been a world . . . there have been advertisements." The medium through which advertisements are communicated, their manner of presentation, and the messages they deliver reflect social, economic, and technological changes over time. The theories, concepts, and activities that emerged throughout its evolutionary period have had a significant impact on advertising as it is practiced today.

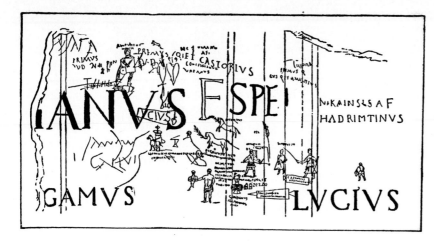

EARLY HISTORY

The first advertisements appear some three thousand years B.C. as stenciled inscriptions on bricks made by the Babylonians. These bricks carried the names of the temples in which they were used and the kings who built them. The kings were actually conducting institutional or corporate advertising campaigns for themselves and their dynasties.[1]

The ruins of Pompeii revealed early advertising, dating from 79 A.D. *Graffiti* appeared on the walls of houses and buildings and included, besides scribblings, notices urging the election of a particular candidate for a specific office. There were a variety of painted announcements, mostly of theatrical performances, sports, and baths, but especially ones for gladiatorial exhibitions (see Exhibit 2.1).

While evidence of the earliest forms of advertising is written, the earliest advertising medium was vocal, its appeal aural. Thousands of years ago the Greeks used criers to announce the sale of slaves and cattle as well as to intone new state edicts, make public announcements, or to chant advertising appeals for facial cosmetics.[2]

From Greek and Roman times through the Middle Ages advertising did not develop beyond the primitive stages of pictorial signboards and public cries. A goat was a sign for a dairy; a mule driving a mill was the designation of a bakery; a coat of arms was the sign of an inn. With few exceptions the function of this kind of advertising was simply to identify places, tradespeople, and artisans, and to inform the public where to find certain goods and services. Even the calls of the public criers—these alone contained what is now known as "selling appeal"—became stereotyped and served merely as reminders that wine, fish, or bread was for sale.

EXHIBIT 2.1
Advertising Found in the Ancient Ruins of Pompeii

These advertisements for gladiators and poets appeared on the excavated walls of Pompeii. A translation of one of them reads: *The Troops of Gladiators of the Aedil Will Fight on the 31st of May There will be Fights with Wild Animals And an Awning to Keep Off the Sun.* Examples of signboards found in the ruins of Pompeii (bottom). The grain mill designated the bakery and the goat indicated the dairy.

---

[1]Frank S. Presbrey, *The History and Development of Advertising* (New York: Doubleday, Doran & Co., Inc., 1929), p. 2.

[2]James Playsted Wood, *The Story of Advertising* (New York: The Ronald Press Co., 1958), p. 18.

Early English Advertising

Printed advertising began to make its appearance when, after the general illiteracy of the Middle Ages, people began to learn to read and write again. The Chinese had invented paper, the Turks had introduced it to Europe in the 1100s, and Europe had its first paper mill by 1276. By 1438 Johann Gutenberg had developed printing from movable type, which was the most significant development in the early history of advertising. Initially it led to the printing of handbills and, later, to the publication and printing of newspapers containing advertisements.

An early English periodical, the *Mercurius Britannicus*, carried on the back page of the issue for February 1, 1625, what is considered the first newspaper advertisement:

> *An excellent discourse concerning the match between our most Gracious and Mightie Prince Charles, Prince of Wales, and Lady Henrietta Maria, daughter of Henry the Fourth, late King of France . . . with a lively picture of the Prince and lady cut in Bronze.*[3]

Newspaper advertising became more important when Richard Steele and Joseph Addison created the *Spectator*, which began daily publication in 1711. Its chief support came from advertising. There were eight advertisements in the first issue, and the number grew as the circulation increased. There was advertising for tea, coffee, chocolate, auction sales, lotteries, wigs, cosmetics, tobacco, and even assignations. It was directed to a limited circle, generally the frequenters of coffee houses, where the newspapers were read.

Early American Advertising

The first issue of a successful newspaper in the American colonies, *The Boston News-Letter* (published April 24, 1704) contained a notice soliciting advertising. The May 1–8 issue contained three entries under the word *Advertising*. Two advertisements offered rewards for the capture of thieves and the third was an advertisement for the sale of real estate at Oyster Bay on Long Island, New York.

Not until it received the skillful ministrations of the "patron saint of American advertising," however, did advertising begin to flower. Benjamin Franklin's *Pennsylvania Gazette* contained an advertisement for "choice hard soap, very reasonable," in its first edition in 1729. Franklin subsequently advertised everything from runaway servants, slaves, and ships' sailings to things he sold in his own shop: books, paper, ink, quills, Spanish wine, lampblack, tea, coffee, chocolate, cheese, cloth, spectacles, compasses, lumber, scales, and sundries.

In the 1830s Americans first began to hear the name of a young Connecticut original—Phineas T. Barnum, that "rogue elephant" of ad-

---

[3]E. S. Turner, *The Shocking History of Advertising* (New York: E. P. Dutton & Co., Inc., 1953), p. 22.

vertising. Barnum formulated a philosophy of advertising which was set out in his autobiography, published in 1850. "You may advertise a spurious article and induce many people to call and buy it once, but they will gradually denounce you as an imposter."[4] If a man has not the pluck to keep on advertising, said Barnum, all the money he has already spent is lost.

Growth of Brand Advertising

By the mid-nineteenth century advertising was vigorous and thriving. Men like Barnum, the English Holloway, a patent medicine manufacturer who was opening the United States as a market for his Carter's Little Liver Pills, and Dr. J. C. Ayer, whose Cherry Pectoral, sarsaparilla, and many other remedies brought him millions and the distinction of having a Massachusetts town named in his honor, were advertising heavily. Most of the advertising of these names was to retailers who seemed to value the products more than consumers.

In the 1870s and early 1880s, patent medicine advertisers promoted their products as cures for all ailments (see Exhibit 2.2). Bogeles, owner of St. Jacobs Oil, an ointment, began advertising extensively to ultimate consumers by promoting the brand name. "There was hardly a township in the United States in which the words *St. Jacob's Oil for Rheumatism* or just *St. Jacob's Oil* were not carried on barns, fences, trees, or anywhere they could be placed, and hardly a newspaper that did not have the small but ever-present advertisement."[5] During this period Castoria was also advertised in magazines and on outdoor signs, using the phrase "children cry for it."

Slogans and Trade Characters

Along with the promotion of brand names came slogans and trade characters. Ivory Soap has been 99 and 44/100s percent pure since 1882 when Harley Procter, sales manager of the Cincinnati soapmaking firm his father had founded, decided on the mathematical limitations of this new product's purity. Eastman, who invented and coined the name *Kodak* for his portable camera in 1888, the first year spent $25,000 advertising "You press the button, we do the rest." (See Exhibit 2.3.) H. J. Heinz decided 57 was a lucky figure and proceeded to offer more than 57 varieties of foods, all of which were advertised with this number.

Animals and people have been used as trade characters from the late 1800s to today. The very first trademark registered by the U.S. Patent Office on October 25, 1870, was the eagle, the symbol of the Averill Chemical Paint Company of New York. In London in the 1890s an artist, Francis Barraud, noticed that his fox terrier, Nipper, was listening to the wax cylinder recording on the small phonograph. Barraud painted his interpretation of the scene and sold the picture to the Gramophone Company, Ltd., in London. The Victor Talking Machine Company was founded in the United States in 1901 and acquired the picture

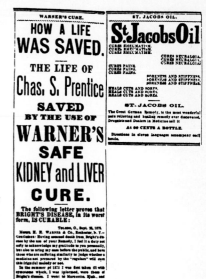

EXHIBIT 2.2
Patent Medicine Advertising

---

[4]E. S. Turner, *The Shocking History of Advertising*, p. 131.
[5]Frank S. Presbrey, *The History and Development of Advertising* (New York: Doubleday, Doran & Company, 1929), pp. 389–90.

EXHIBIT 2.3
An Early Kodak Ad

Today's Polaroid "One Step" ads stress the same theme—ease of performance.

New Kodak Cameras.

" *You press the button,*
  we do the rest."

(OR YOU CAN DO IT YOURSELF.)

Seven New Styles and Sizes

ALL LOADED WITH

Transparent Films.

For sale by all Photo. Stock Dealers.   *Send for Catalogue.*

THE EASTMAN COMPANY, Rochester, N. Y.

of "His Master's Voice" which, since 1928, has belonged to RCA. It was recently resurrected as an active trademark.

Morton Salt's small girl under a big umbrella, Aunt Jemima, the famous Campbell Soup Kids, and the Fisk boy, along with "His Master's Voice," "Chases Dirt," "When It Rains It Pours," and "Time to Re-Tire," were early trade characters and slogans that have been used for many years. The fashion that began in the 1880s and 1890s continued into the early twentieth century with "Say It With Flowers," and Bon Ami's "Hasn't Scratched Yet" (see Exhibit 2.4).

HOW THE ADVERTISING AGENCY GREW UP

At the beginning of the eighteenth century the newspaper became the primary medium for advertising by local concerns. As the volume of advertising increased, the direct relationship between merchant and newspaper became difficult and complex, and there arose the need for a middleman. The advertising specialist assisted in the buying and selling of newspaper space. The newspapers themselves provided the first advertising agents of any prominence in the United States.[6]

The Newspaper Advertising Agency

The first advertising agency opened in Philadelphia in 1841 when a gentleman by the name of Volney B. Palmer announced that he represented a select and exclusive list of newspapers for which he was prepared to

---

[6]Ralph M. Hower, *The History of an Advertising Agency* (Cambridge, Mass.: Harvard University Press, 1949), p. 26.

sell space to advertisers. Mr. Palmer was a space salesman. He did not plan or create the advertising, but merely contacted potential advertisers, to whom he sold space; for this service he received a 25-percent commission from the newspapers. By 1861 there were about 30 agencies selling newspaper space.

The Space Wholesaler

Immediately after the Civil War a new type of agent appeared. He was the space wholesaler, who dominated the period between 1865 and 1880. The space wholesaler purchased space in bulk from publishers, as cheaply as possible, and resold it to advertisers and other agents in small lots for more money. George P. Rowell initiated this plan in 1865 and was the most influential advertising agent for many years.

While Rowell was becoming successful in space wholesaling for newspapers, J. Walter Thompson was offering retailing magazine space to advertisers and other agents. Up to this time literary magazines did not carry advertising; however, Thompson had convinced a number of them to open their pages.

The Advertising Contract

Shortly after the Civil War, F. W. Ayer founded a Philadelphia agency named after his father, N. W. Ayer. He initiated a proposal that was to serve as the basis for the advertising agency of the future: the advertising contract. Along with Rowell, Ayer felt that the competitive bid system should be eliminated. He proposed that the agent and advertiser agree, by contract, to work together for an extended period of time. The advertiser was to pay a commission to Ayer, which varied from 12½ percent to 8 percent to 15 percent. Although the Ayer plan for a commission to be paid by the *advertiser* rather than the *publisher* was not accepted by the rest of the industry, the idea of a contract between advertisers and agencies was adopted. A commission rate of 15 percent was eventually deemed fair by most media.

It wasn't until the 1890s that the advertising agency finally came into its own as a service organization. Prior to this time, it had been a fairly general practice for agencies to assist in the mechanical production of their clients' advertising messages. In fact, such extended services were replacing the competitive bid as ways to win or hold accounts, but little, if any, creative help was offered. Instead, the large national advertisers hired expensive freelance copywriters or set up their own advertising departments. Eventually agents began to offer ideas to prospects as additional incentives to sign on as accounts, and it was inevitable that one day the advertiser would ask the agency, "Why don't you write this ad?"[7]

EXHIBIT 2.4
Slogans and Trade Characters

"It isn't just for breakfast any more," heard in today's ads, echoes "Did you think Bon Ami was only for cleaning windows?"—the lead sentence in the ad above, which ran in 1911.

---

[7]Paul C. Harper, "The Advertising Agency," p. 84.

The Expansion of Creative Services

The backbone of the typical advertising agency's business in the nineteenth century was patent medicine. The Ayer firm advertised sure cures for cancer, for consumption, for fits, for stuttering. It advertised "Compound Oxygen," which cured almost every human ailment, "Kennedy's Ivory Tooth Cement," which made "everyone his own dentist!" and "Dr. Case's Liver Remedy and Blood Purifier," which would supplant the doctor entirely. There was also the Pino-Palmine mattress which introduced "into every home, wherever situated, the VERY AROMA WHICH MEDICATES AND TONES FLORIDA AIR and expels rheumatic and neuralgic pains from the body."[8]

A significant change in advertising occurred when Albert D. Lasker joined the Lord & Thomas Agency in 1898. Lasker then hired John E. Kennedy, an advertising copywriter whose remark about advertising being "salesmanship in print" impressed Lasker, and George C. Hopkins whose magic formula involved the use of "Reason Why" copy, text offering reasons why a product was superior and should be purchased by consumers. The Lord & Thomas team was responsible for informing the public that Puffed Wheat and Puffed Rice were "shot from guns," and Schlitz beer was pure because Schlitz cleaned its bottles with steam. They sold the idea of "the hard sell" in strong, all-out campaigns for quick results. Lasker, Kennedy, and Hopkins made copywriting a central function of an agency.[9]

The 1920s were considered formative years for ad agencies. Because of the Depression and clients demanding greater efficiency, the burden of creating and maintaining markets fell to advertising. Many agencies began to extend their services based on factors such as advertising philosophy, client requirements, and resources. During the Depression the agencies learned a great deal about the consumer-research and independent-research firms which developed from a need to have consumer and market information on a national scale. In effect, except for extensions and refinements of service, and the entry of television, the agencies of today differ very little from those of the late 1920s and 1930s.[10]

According to Lasker, by the 1930s only three things of major importance had ever happened in the history of the advertising agency business: the Ayer contract, Lasker's hiring of John Kennedy and the subsequent development of copy as the most important advertising element in an agency, and the injection of sex into advertising (when J. Walter Thompson dreamed up "The Skin You Love to Touch" for Woodbury's Soap).[11]

----

[8]Ralph M. Hower, *The History of an Advertising Agency*, p. 44.
[9]James Playsted Wood, *The Story of Advertising* (New York: The Ronald Press Co., 1958), p. 293.
[10]Paul C. Harper, "The Advertising Agency," p. 92.
[11]James Playsted Wood, *The Story of Advertising*, p. 295.

EARLY TWENTIETH-CENTURY ADVERTISING

Two significant changes occurred in advertising in the late nineteenth century: Mass circulation magazines became an important advertising medium and the invention of the bicycle brought forth a new kind of promotion—competitive advertising.

The literary, and literate, monthly magazines such as *Atlantic*, *Harper's*, and *North American* were the primary and powerful advertising media at the turn of the century. However, they soon toppled with the proliferation of cheaper magazines addressed to a greater reading public. These cheaper magazines, made financially possible by the Postal Act of 1879 granting favorable mailing privileges to magazines because of their educational natures, soon began to climb to high positions of journalistic and commercial influence. The most important ones were *Ladies Home Journal* (1883), *Cosmopolitan* (1886), *Munsey's* (1889), and *McClures* (1893).

In 1885 the English successfully marketed the bicycle, and its subsequent introduction to the United States wrought a small revolution in industrial and social spheres and a large one in advertising. The bicycle seized the imagination of Americans and changed their mode of life. Between 1890 and 1896 Americans spent $100 million for bicycles. Bicycle advertising flourished and unlike other advertising, it was strongly competitive, rather than informative.

Bicycle advertising promoted the idea of spending a considerable sum of money for a pleasure vehicle. Installment payments were now acceptable for purchases of durable merchandise. When the bicycle craze dwindled, its manufacturers found the public receptive to purchasing automobiles. The Stanley was a bicycle before it became a steam automobile.

Automobile Advertising

The first advertisement for an automobile appeared in the original issue of *Horseless Age*, November, 1895.[12] The car makers discovered they had to demonstrate both the speed and durability of their products to break down the prejudice and envy heard in the derisive taunt "Get a horse!" All manufacturers found it necessary to advertise for one very practical reason—most of the companies making or assembling automobiles were very shakily financed and often needed the cash from the sale of one car in order to build the next.

In 1900, the *Saturday Evening Post* presented its first automobile advertisements and the magazine quickly became the leading national advertising medium for the automobile. In fact, the automobile soon

---

[12]James Playsted Wood, *The Story of Advertising*, p. 300.

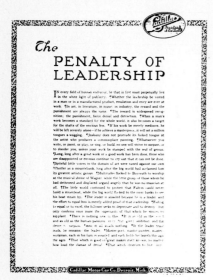

EXHIBIT 2.5
A "Classic" Ad for Cadillac in 1915

became the bulwark of all national advertising. By 1911 automobiles were taking up an estimated one-eighth of all advertising space in nationally circulated magazines.[13]

Probably the best-known automobile advertisement in the United States appeared in the *Saturday Evening Post*, January 2, 1915. It was written for Cadillac by Theodore Francis McManus, owner of McManus Inc. Under the headline "The Penalty of Leadership" was, "In every field of human endeavor, he that is first must perpetually live in the white light of publicity. Whether the leadership be vested in a man or in a manufactured product, emulation and envy are ever at work. . . ." This ad (see Exhibit 2.5) appears regularly on every list of great advertisements.

In December 1927 an advertising campaign unveiling the Model "A" Ford aroused America to near hysteria. For eighteen years the famous black Model "T" had clattered its way around the world; then, Henry Ford, with deep reluctance, had decided to retool his factories in order to produce a new model that could hold its own with the multicolored Chevrolets and Chryslers. A successful policy of secrecy made the new Ford the nation's main topic of conversation. On December 2, the day of the unveiling, a million people in New York tried to view the model "A," which, by late afternoon, had to be removed from its showroom and installed in Madison Square Garden. Ford ran a five-day series of full-page advertisements in two thousand newspapers at a cost of $1,300,000. The result was a promotional triumph and, henceforth, a customer could buy a Ford in any color (so long as it was Arabian Sand, Niagara Blue, Dawn Gray, or Gun-Metal Blue).[14]

World War I

Two things happened in advertising as soon as war was declared in 1917. Many advertisers quickly canceled their contracts and declared they would do no further advertising during the war, and the representatives of advertising agencies and the advertising media formed themselves into a group and offered their services to the Council of National Defense.[15]

When the draft was promulgated, advertising people felt that the concept needed to be "sold" to the American public, who were traditionally against conscription. The military advisors disagreed, but, at the last minute, the advertising group was given permission to go ahead with its campaign. At a signal, newspapers and signs across the country declared "All Patriots Will, All Others Must Register." The advertising called forth Columbus, George Washington, Thomas Jefferson, Benjamin Franklin, and other familiar symbols of patriotic tradition to sell conservation, thrift, and Liberty Bonds.

---

[13]James Playsted Wood, *The Story of Advertising*, p. 307.
[14]E. S. Turner, *The Shocking History of Advertising*, p. 233.
[15]James Playsted Wood, *The Story of Advertising*, p. 353.

Prior to World War I there were criticisms about the excesses of outdoor display and the desecration of the countryside. Now, stirring posters, such as "Uncle Sam Wants You," exhorting patriotism, bond purchase, and enlistment appeared everywhere. In fact, it was this use by the government during World War I that gave sanction to the billboard.

Advertising in the Twenties

At the end of World War I people had money and the desire to spend it. It was a seller's market, and the advertisers made the most of it. Total advertising expenditures, which had sagged to $1,468,000,000 in 1918, leaped to $2,282,000,000 in 1919, almost touched the three billion mark in 1920, fell off slightly for two years, and soared again to almost four billion in 1929.[16]

Advertising was more than respectable now. It was glamorous, exciting, colorful, ingenious, often spectacular, and sometimes incredible. Magazines had developed high-speed, four-color printing, and advertisers and agencies used it extravagantly. New products were more quickly developed and established in the marketplace.

An ancient advertising ploy was rejuvenated—testimonial advertising. Opera stars, society women, prize fighters, and baseball players were all available at a price to sing the praises of soaps, lotions, and breakfast foods (see Exhibit 2.6). Enterprising advertisers got up lists of celebrities who would, for a consideration, endorse everything from life insurance to burial vaults.[17]

The immediate causes of this great increase in the volume of advertising expenditures during this period were (1) the obvious success of advertising in the promotion of the war effort, (2) the resumption of peacetime trade, (3) the desire of some manufacturers to increase advertising appropriations rather than pay large, federal excess-profits taxes, and (4) most important, the increasing intensity of competition that marked the postwar period.[18]

EXHIBIT 2.6
An Early Celebrity Ad

Joan Crawford appeared in this early ad selling Coca-Cola before she became chairman of the Board of Pepsi Cola.

Rise of Consumerism

On October 29, 1929, the stock market crashed, and advertising began a precipitous decline. Advertising expenditures dropped from the peak of $3,426,000,000 reached that year to $1,302,000,000 in 1933. The Depression gave swift quietus to hundreds of advertising campaigns; it

---

[16]James Playsted Wood, *The Story of Advertising*, p. 365.
[17]James Playsted Wood, *The Story of Advertising*, p. 392.
[18]Harold F. Williamson, ed., *The Growth of the American Economy*, 2nd ed. (New York: Prentice-Hall, Inc., 1951), p. 782.

EXHIBIT 2.7
A Personal Hygiene Ad

In the 1930s the top-selling soap in the United States, Lifebuoy, popularized the phrase, "Body Odor," later immortalized in ads as "B.O."

also brought a period of vulgarity to advertising. Most of the offenders were those selling products for personal hygiene. Preoccupation with bodily hygiene and functions grew steadily during the postwar years (see Exhibit 2.7). In addition, there were bogus claims, bogus testimonials, exaggerations, and offenses against decency.

The thirties provided bitter, if fertile, soil for a consumer movement to take firm root. An index of its popularity was the rise in membership of Consumers' Research, an organization involved in independent product testing, which increased from 12,000 in 1930 to 48,000 in 1936.[19] Consumer literature gave the consumer movement further impetus. Arthur Kallet and Frederick Schlink's *100,000,000 Guinea Pigs*, an attack on useless and dangerous proprietaries, became a bestseller in 1933. It was followed by other books of social criticism such as the *The Joy of Ignorance, The Popular Practice of Fraud*, and *40,000,000 Guinea-Pig Children*.

Advertising also faced an attack from the government. Passage of the Wheeler-Lea Amendment clarified the FTC's control over false and deceptive advertising. To counter these criticisms, the American Association of Advertising Agencies, in conjunction with the Association of National Advertisers, in 1932, drew up a code of ethics urging members to discountenance bogus claims and exaggerations.

Post-Depression Advertising

Restoring advertising's creditability was a slow task, but, by 1934, the worst of the Depression was over. From 1933 to 1948 advertising expenditures increased gradually. With the repeal of prohibition, liquor advertising appeared. Other familiar items on the advertising pages of the thirties were refrigerators, home movies, electric toasters, silk stockings, and brassieres. Copywriters were becoming increasingly addicted to "word magic." A line of baby talk developed to accompany pictures of food. Breakfast cereals of the *snap, crackle, pop* variety had long had a nursery nomenclature of their own; now makers of other foods began to boost their specialties as *yummy, tangy, zippy, chewy, crispy*, and *krunchy*.[20]

ADVERTISING TODAY

Advertising began to thrive again with World War II. Unlike in World War I, there were few advertisers who abolished or diminished their advertising efforts. Despite shortages and scarcity, advertisers knew the necessity of keeping their brand names prominently displayed, even when their branded products could not be bought.

[19]Joseph J. Seldin, *The Golden Fleece* (New York: The Macmillan Company, 1963), p. 32.
[20]E. S. Turner, *The Shocking History of Advertising*, p. 248.

With the war, advertising's big job suddenly changed from hard-selling to what was called "selling in reverse." Rather than encourage product consumption by the public, ads focused on a product's performance in wartime efforts. Wartime themes of conservation, patience, and dedication were quickly translated into product-identifying mechanisms. "Lucky Strike green" (the dye used to color its package) had gone to war. The great bulk of copy in ads for this product was devoted to explaining how The Product was now a vital part of an M-1 rifle or a Sherman tank.[21]

The War Advertising Council, an offshoot of the original Advertising Council, planned and engineered nationwide campaigns in support of the war effort. The Council devised campaigns for war bond sales, recruitment, conservation of rubber, paper, rope, fuel, and other scarce products and materials. In the first year of World War II the War Advertising Council got and used a hundred times as much free advertising as was donated during all of World War I. The government was now enthusiastic in its praise of advertising.

The advertising world began to recreate some of its earlier glamour. There was originality and innovation in artwork and copy. David Ogilvy created luxurious images with his "Man in the Hathaway Shirt" (see Exhibit 2.8) and "Commander Whitehead" of Schweppes, and William Bernbach devised equally expensive advertising campaigns to denote the extensive inspection and preoccupation with details that accompanies the production of the Volkswagen (see Exhibit 2.9). Humor and sex became standard advertising elements, and there was an expanded use of competitive advertising.

The man in the Hathaway shirt

EXHIBIT 2.8
Image Advertising

Advertising in the Sixties

The development of television as a major national medium brought with it the potential to have visual and aural contact with vast numbers of people simultaneously. As technology improved so did the distances it could link. Satellite television was beamed around the world, and the most phenomenal broadcast in recorded history emanated from the moon. Thirty hours of network television coverage was given to the moon landing, the culmination of which was the moon walk of Neil Armstrong and Edwin Aldrin, Jr., on July 20, 1969. It was estimated that 150,000,000 Americans were watching television at some time during that epoch-making broadcast, sponsored by many national advertisers.

Annual advertising expenditures increased substantially and by the end of the 1960s they were reaching the $19-billion mark. Science was applied to other areas of advertising; marketing research expanded, advertising models were created, computer technology was applied, and increased attention was paid to quantitative analysis and behavioral data. This was the decade when creativity and science were designated as essential components of advertising.

---

[21]Judith Dolgins, "The Copywriter," *Advertising Today-Yesterday-Tomorrow*, p. 129.

EXHIBIT 2.9
A Marketing Success

The Volkswagen advertising campaign created in the Sixties was considered by *Advertising Age* as the greatest advertising/marketing success of the past 50 years.

Advertising in the Seventies

The application of social science research to advertising accelerated significantly in the seventies. Influences from behavioral insights, learning theory, research design, and advanced statistical analysis, were adopted by advertising as a result, in part, from increased efforts of competing advertisers to be more effective and a desire to reduce the risk in advertising decision-making. Furthermore, acceleration of regulatory efforts to eliminate deceptive advertising and the requirement that advertisers substantiate many of their claims, had generated interest in research.

This scientific emphasis led to a criticism that ads tended to be less creative, duller, and, in some cases, too much alike. Whether the sameness in advertising was because of its research orientation or not, it appeared to exist—soft drinks used ads with jingles, fast foods used "happy songs," and analgesics were advertised with comparisons.[22]

Another significant change in the seventies that was certain to have repercussions in the eighties was the movement away from broadcasting to "narrowcasting." Proliferation of various broadcasting techniques provided numerous ways of reaching target markets comprised of smaller groups of people—a significant change from the early days of broadcasting with their emphasis on mass marketing.

Advertising in the Eighties

It is difficult to evaluate advertising in the eighties at this writing. It appears that the growth in advertising expenditures will decrease in the latter part of the decade. Moreover, it is clear that a number of advertisers have looked back historically and resurrected old appeals such as the "Man in the Hathaway Shirt" or Safeguard soap's claim that it reduces body odor (see Exhibit 2.10). Nevertheless several major changes have occurred which suggest new concepts may be developed and applied to advertising campaigns.

EXHIBIT 2.10
The "New" Man in the Hathaway Shirt

The sixties were called the *creative decade*, the seventies the *research decade*, and the eighties have been designated as the *media decade.* This latter designation is in response to the development of new electronic information technologies that provide many ways to disseminate messages on both television or home-terminal screens. These techniques include cable subscription television, communication satellites, superstations, direct broadcast satellites, teletext, videotex, videocassettes and videodiscs, telephone, and interactive viewdata systems which link the viewer's television set to a central data bank via telephone lines.[23] Home Shopping Network, for example, is a cable system that offers live, 24-hour-a-day, seven-day-a-week advertising. Jewelry, clothing, electronics, housewares, and novelty items are displayed on the screen and sold through WATS telephone lines.

In addition to the proliferation of communication technologies, shorter time slots are available to advertisers as a result of the Justice Department's elimination of the broadcasting association's ban on 15-second commercials. Fragmentation of audiences, the potential for advertising clutter, and the ability to "zap" out commercials through videorecorders will make media decisions increasingly difficult.

The changing nature of media has brought about a resurgence of creativity; emotional appeals and high-tech productions are suggested as a means of attracting and holding the interest of the audience. The fragmentation of the mass audience and the changing nature of consumers suggest targeting to the best potential customers and creating messages in a manner that will attract and sell those customers.

---

[22]Merle Kingman, "Who's to Blame for Sameness in Ads? Not Us: Researchers," *Advertising Age* (February 2, 1981), p. 41.

[23]Federal Trade Commission, Media Policy Session, Technology and Legal Change, FTC Office of Policy Planning and Evaluation, December 31, 1979.

Mergers among major advertisers may result in a concentration of advertising efforts. The General Foods Corporation takeover by Philip Morris is likely to generate extensive advertising expenditures by the combined organizations.

Global advertising has become an area of interest as a means of efficiently coordinating a company's worldwide advertising. While the effectiveness of global advertising is controversial, a number of advertising agencies have restructured their organizations to accommodate clients interested in global campaigns.

Greater societal concerns are reflected in increasing efforts to restrict tobacco and alcohol advertising and encourage advertising that may help prevent the use of drugs and the spread of Aids.

The history of advertising in the eighties will reflect the manner in which advertisers respond to the recent changes, not only in the population and its characteristics, but in the rapidly emerging technological developments.

SUMMARY

There is evidence that advertising existed some three thousand years B.C., but its use and applications were limited to messages scratched on walls, placed on signs, and heralded by criers. The most significant development in the early history of advertising was the invention of movable type in the fifteenth century, ultimately leading to the publication and printing of newspapers containing advertisements. Advertising in newspapers, in turn, led to the emergence, in the 1840s, of the space salesmen, whose services were ultimately expanded and refined into the advertising agency of today.

The end of the Civil War brought an upsurge in commercial and industrial expansion, and competition led to the growth and development of brand advertising. Magazines became an important advertising medium in the late nineteenth century, and the invention of the bicycle and the competitive promotion of this product gave further impetus to advertising.

Although advertising declined significantly during World War I, the end of the war brought a renewed interest in and an aura of respectability to advertising. This respectability lost ground during the depression years, but advertising began to thrive again after World War II.

The most significant development in modern times was the invention of television broadcasting which added new dimensions to the advertising message and could reach even people who could not read. With the emergence of new communication technologies and their tendencies to reach smaller and more selective audiences, there are indications that advertisements may have to be redesigned to be effective in these media.

One can only hazard a guess as to the future, but it appears certain that advertising cannot look only to its past for its successes, but has to take on new directions to meet emerging developments.

QUESTIONS FOR DISCUSSION

1. What do you see as the major differences between advertisements of the nineteenth century and those of the twentieth century?
2. What was the original purpose of branding? How did this change with the growth of brand advertising?
3. What factors do you see as most important in contributing to the changing nature of advertising over the years?
4. Cite three major developments that were significant in the history of advertising.
5. Do you think slogans and trade characters are used as much today as they were in the late nineteenth century? Why or why not?
6. What are the reasons for the development of the advertising agency?
7. How have the functions and services of the advertising agency changed from its initiation to the present?
8. What are the major socioeconomic forces that changed the nature of advertising in the twentieth century?
9. How does advertising in the eighties differ from that of the seventies?
10. What changes do you foresee in advertising in the future?

AD PRACTICE

Select a product that has been advertised for at least the last three decades. Find examples of advertising campaigns for this product in the 1960s, 1970s, and 1980s. What differences do you note in terms of the advertising strategy?

Advertising Classifications

Until the breakup of AT&T most people took their telephone service for granted. Recently, long-distance telephone users were faced with the prospect of having to select a long-distance phone company from a list that included a half dozen or more candidates. Many of the companies are advertising to attract customers to their services.

For some time AT&T had conducted an advertising campaign presenting a series of sentimental commercials that encouraged people to "Reach Out and Touch Someone." MCI Communications Corp., a major competitor, poked fun at these ads in its own advertisements which offered potential customers discounts to offset AT&T's "high prices." AT&T uses a celebrity endorser, Cliff Robertson, who declares AT&T's services cannot be copied. MCI's ads declare their service is just as good as AT&T's. Sprint stresses billing features and competent service.

The selection process for long-distance services is lengthy, and, when completed, the choices made may ultimately be changed. Because rate differences have narrowed, all of the long-distance telephone companies are designing advertising campaigns in an effort to get customers.

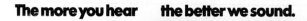

DISCUSSION QUESTIONS

1. How would you classify the type of advertising AT&T conducted for its long-distance service in the past? Explain.
2. How would you classify MCI and Sprint advertising? Explain.
3. What kinds of advertising campaigns would you suggest the telephone companies use to secure customers for their long-distance services?

Source: Francine Schwadel, "Long-Distance Phone Services May Be Missing Mark on Ads," *The Wall Street Journal* (November 14, 1985), p. 35.

CASE

Issue Advertising

In one current ad campaign for the Dow Chemical Company, a cap-and-gowned college graduate is shown thinking ". . . In two days I walk into a Dow laboratory and begin work on new ways to help grow more and better grain for those kids who so desperately need it. I can't wait." It appears, however, that Dow's intended audience isn't the current class of graduating seniors (in fact, Dow recently announced that it was laying off 2500 people), but that generation of students who came of age in the late '60s and early '70s when a critical issue in campus recruitment was the napalm and Agent Orange manufactured by Dow for military use in Vietnam.

In a recent print campaign a House of Seagram's ad contests the television networks' refusal to run a Seagram commercial showing that 12 ounces of beer, 5 ounces of wine, and 1 and ¼ ounces of whiskey all contain the same amount of alcohol. The networks maintain that the spot would violate the liquor industry's voluntary abstention from broadcast media and promote Seagram's liquor products. Seagram contends the spot would be a public service.

R. J. Reynolds is responding to the emotional secondhand smoke argument in ads appearing in magazines and newspapers by overtly discounting evidence that being exposed to someone else's cigarette smoke is harmful. Reynolds is also taking a strong postion against legislation or company policies that would limit the right to smoke. Some of the ads conclude with the line: "Brought to you in the interest of common courtesy."

DISCUSSION QUESTIONS

1. What is the difference between issue advertising and public service advertising?
2. After reading this article, would you respond any differently to the Dow Chemical, Seagram, or R. J. Reynolds ads?
3. There are at least two sides to any issue. As long as the public is aware they are seeing only one side, what could be controversial about issue advertising?
4. Why don't we see more issue advertising?

Source: John O'Toole, "Selling Ideas, Not Products," *U.S. News & World Report* (March 10, 1986), p. 54.

II

Advertising: A Micro View

P_{ART} Two, Chapters 3 through 7, looks at the nature and role of advertising from a firm's perspective. Because advertising is a business activity, it is an important element in the marketing mix. It affects the way a firm defines its corporate objectives, processes, and problems. The focus then shifts to the advertising agency as an organization that provides aid and support to advertising activities. The ad budget— a part of the method a firm uses to decide its advertising expenditures— is the subject of the closing chapter in this part.

3

Advertising and the Marketing Mix

In 1985 Procter & Gamble, America's perennial leading advertiser, reported its first earnings decline in 33 years. When management began to look at its previous decisions, it appeared that, although the company had continued to expend large sums advertising its products, money alone could not overcome marketing miscalculations.

Advertising is only one element in a firm's marketing activities. Effective advertising requires an understanding of, and coordination with, all of a firm's marketing efforts.

One of marketing's primary functions is to understand the consumer. Even though consumers were willing to pay more for diapers with greater absorbency, Procter & Gamble had continued to offer its economical, but less absorbent, Pampers diapers and lost in the marketplace to Kimberly Clark's Huggies. P&G was also slow to respond to consumers who wanted a dentifrice that came in a pump and had a gel taste. Ultimately, however, P&G demonstrated that it understood the new competitive environment, introducing several major products in rapid succession: New "Blue Ribbon" Pampers, Ultra Pampers and Luvs Baby Pants, Crest Tartar-Control Formula Toothpaste and the long-awaited pump dispensers, and several new detergent formulations under the Tide name, including Liquid Tide. By 1986 Procter & Gamble's earnings increased significantly.

DEFINING MARKETING

Various definitions of marketing have been introduced over the years. The classic definition declared that marketing was the performance of business activities that directed the flow of goods and services from producer to consumer or user.[1] In 1985 the Board of Directors of the American Marketing Association disseminated a new definition stating that marketing "is the process of planning and executing the conception, pricing, promotion, and distribution of ideas, goods, and services to create exchanges that satisfy individual and organizational objectives." A more complete explanation of marketing must examine its activities in conjunction with a firm's corporate goals—macromarketing and micromarketing.

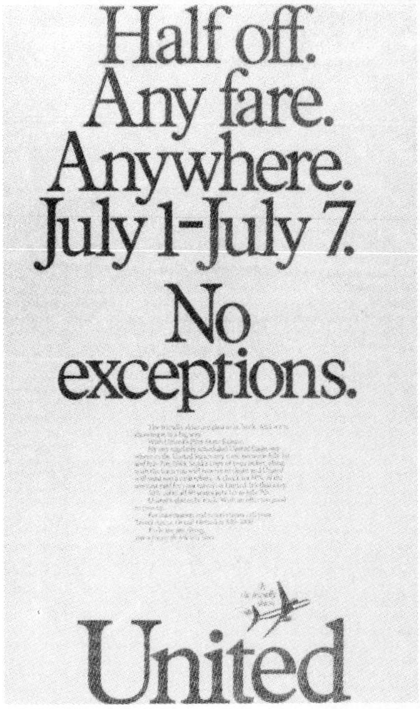

Macromarketing

A firm performs its marketing activities in a business environment which is constantly changing. External forces continually influence the organization, while internal actions and reactions affect both the firm and its environment. The external forces are generally characterized as *uncontrollable* by the firm. *Macromarketing* refers to the means by which a company *adapts itself* to the uncontrollable factors in its social, economic, cultural, political, legal, and competitive environments.

Advertising decisions may play a part in a company's response to these external forces. United Airlines' efforts to recoup losses after an extensive employee strike included an advertising campaign offering discount fares for a limited time period on all its flights (see Exhibit 3.1). On the other hand, in 1985, when Japan Air Lines suffered the worst single-plane air disaster ever, it suspended all of its advertising worldwide for at least three months.[2]

Micromarketing

Micromarketing refers to the internal micromarketing activities a firm uses to react to external forces. These are designated as *controllable* factors, since they are primarily under the direction of the firm and its marketing department. Some of these micromarketing factors are the setting of marketing objectives, selecting a target market, developing a marketing plan, and controlling the marketing effort.

EXHIBIT 3.1
An Advertising Campaign to Recover Strike Losses

---

[1]Ralph S. Alexander, "Report of the Definition Committee," *Journal of Marketing,* Vol. 12 (October 1948), pp. 202–17.
[2]Jack Burton and Dennis Chase, "JAL Grounds Ads After Crash," *Advertising Age* (August 19, 1985), p. 4.

FIGURE 3.1   Corporate Goals: Marketing Strategy and the Marketing Mix

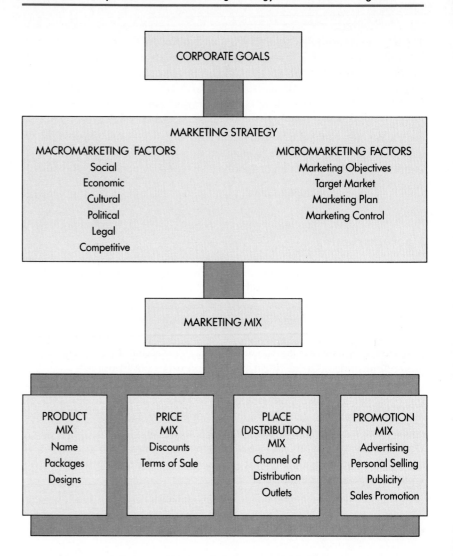

THE MARKETING MIX

The efficient business adjusts its internal capabilities to its changing environment by developing and administering a marketing mix that meets the needs and wants of particular markets at particular periods of time.

A *marketing mix* is the unique combination of marketing procedures and policies used by a firm. While the mix can contain numerous elements, the basic ingredients have been designated as *the four Ps*—what *product* is to be sold, at what *price,* in what *place* (channel of distribution), and its method of *promotion.*

The efficient organization pinpoints its marketing targets and then arranges the four Ps into a marketing mix which, hopefully, will reach these targets most effectively. This consists of all the inputs and resources utilized in the firm's marketing program.

Each of the elements, in turn, can be considered to be composed of *submixes;* that is, numerous ingredients from which marketing choices may be made. Advertising is one of the ingredients available for a promotional submix (see Figure 3.1).

A marketing mix may vary from product to product and industry to industry. For example, the marketing mix for an industrial item, such as a metalpress for making cans, may include extensive and precise product specifications, a competitive price, distribution directly or through a manufacturer-owned outlet, and a promotional mix involving personal selling combined with favorable trade publicity. A tube of toothpaste, on the other hand, may suggest a marketing mix that relies heavily on a brand name and packaging for product attributes, offers frequent price discounts, calls for indirect distribution through numerous supermarkets and drugstores, and involves a promotional mix that is heavy on television advertising and sales promotion in the form of samples.

Product Mix

A *product* is defined as an object which, when used, gives satisfaction to an individual. Product satisfactions emerge not only from the product's design and quality, but also from the brand name, the package, and the services and warranties which accompany it. A good product design communicates to the user the product's functions, its aesthetic qualities, and its appropriateness.

A major responsibility for an organization is to develop and introduce new products. A study of business history demonstrates that growth businesses have been heavily new product-oriented. The Booz, Allen & Hamilton consulting firm surveyed more than 700 manufacturers of consumer and industrial products to determine the importance of new products and the emphasis on new-product planning. These are some of the highlights of the study:[3]

— Seven new product ideas are now needed to generate one commercially successful product. In 1968, fifty-eight ideas were required.
— Thirty-five percent of new products fail.
— Within several years, one-third of total company profits will come from products not yet introduced.
— The factors most contributing to new product success are the product's fit with market needs and internal functional strengths, technology superiority, top management support, the development process, the competitive environment encountered, and the product management structure.

[3] Thomas D. Kuczmarshi and Steven J. Silver, "Strategy: The Key to Successful New Product Development," *Management Review* (July 1982), pp. 26–40.

EXHIBIT 3.2
Introducing a Product Modification
as "New"

Introducing New, Improved All Natural Manwich.

They loved it before. Now they'll love it even more.

Now Manwich is 100% natural…and it tastes
even better. It's still thick with tomatoes,
chunks of crisp bell peppers and onions, and
seasoned to perfection. Just add it to your
own fresh ground beef and you'll have one
nutritious meal they've always loved.

**Just brown some ground beef and
Have a Manwich Night.**

Hunt's
MANWICH
ORIGINAL
SLOPPY JOE SAUCE
NEW! IMPROVED
ALL NATURAL

Beatrice
Hunt's
MANWICH
ALL NATURAL
SLOPPY JOE
SEASONING MIX
ALL
NATURAL

Beatrice

© 1986 Beatrice Companies, Inc. Manwich is a registered trademark.

Advertising is an integral part of launching new products; however, such efforts can be costly. In 1985 a record 2206 new products were introduced; however, a large proportion were not expected to survive.[4]

Many companies respond to the need for product development by engaging in some product modification; that is, they change a product's physical attributes or its packaging (see Exhibit 3.2). Modifications help a company promote its offerings as new or improved, important words

---

[4]Daniel Kahn, "Perils of Pioneering Innovative Products," *Newsday* (September 15, 1986), Part III, p. 5.

in advertising. The Paper-Mate division of The Gillette Company introduced a "new" pen in 1979—Eraser Mate—an *erasable* ballpoint pen. In 1981 the "new" Eraser Mate 2 was introduced—an erasable, *disposable* ballpoint pen.

Market Segmentation

A *market segment* is a group of buyers who have similar needs and may respond to similar marketing efforts. *Market segmentation* is the process of targeting these groups and developing appropriate marketing mixes. Once this is done, advertising informing these segments of the availability of specific goods or services, is designed. Oil of Olay was targeted to an "older woman" segment with significant success. Sales of this facial lotion have gone from $10 million to $174 million annually in just over ten years.

Product Differentiation

Product differentiation is a technique that "is concerned with bending of demand to the will of supply."[5] That is, it attempts to secure a measure of control over the demand for a product by developing and promoting differences between the company's offering and the offering of competing sellers. Miller's, for example, successfully captured a large share of the beer market with its Lite beer.

Product differentiation may be achieved by developing a feature that adds to a product's performance or capability. For example, Admiral introduced its 1983 refrigerator as the first to make ice cream. Some product modifications are minor, such as individually wrapping cheese slices or "stick up" room deodorants. Other differences are created mainly through brand names and advertising, such as Jordache versus Calvin Klein jeans.

Product Positioning

Another concept in product strategy that has particular relevance to advertisers is product positioning. Positioning refers to a brand's placement (as perceived by customers) among its competitors. The relative position may involve dimensions such as the product's attributes, value, quality, performance, or image. To position its product, a company finds an "attractive space" within a range of competitive brands and places its brand there. For example, Topol successfully positioned itself as a toothpaste that removes tobacco stains.

Product positioning strategies, frequently designed to change or reinforce consumers' perceptions of a product's attributes or image, are closely related to advertising decisions. Advertising campaigns can designate a brand's position relative to its competitors' as offering *more* (more pain relief), *less* (less cholesterol), or as *free* (free from caffeine or alcohol). Sanka Brand coffee is not only positioned as "97% Caffeine Free," its better taste is guaranteed (see Exhibit 3.3).

EXHIBIT 3.3
Positioning a Product

[5]Wendell R. Smith, "Product Differentiation and Market Segmentation as Alternative Marketing Strategies," in *Managerial Marketing: Perspectives and Viewpoints*, eds. E. J. Kelley and W. Lazer (Homewood, Ill.: Richard D. Irwin, Inc., 1967), p. 200.

Frequently a firm finds it useful to reposition a product; that is, a firm will encourage consumers to perceive the product as part of a different category. Repositioning is desirable when sales in a current product category are stable or declining. 3M spent an estimated $5 million to widen the market for its Buf-Puf, repositioning it as a beauty aid instead of an acne treatment.[6]

Seven-Up has used product positioning strategies with significant success. To change the perception that it was primarily a "mixer" to be combined with other liquids, Seven-Up conducted a repositioning campaign designating itself the "Uncola." This campaign successfully placed Seven-Up in the soft-drink category and indicated that it was an alternative to the cola soft drink. Subsequently, Seven-Up was advertised as caffeine free, a benefit that differentiated it still further from other soft drinks. This led Coca-Cola and others to introduce caffeine-free products, suggesting that this "position" was important.

Developing an appropriate product mix also requires decisions concerning a product's attributes, such as its brand name or packaging. Advertising's relationship to these issues will be discussed in the section on the preparation of the advertising campaign.

The Price Mix

Pricing is one of the most important and critical tools of marketing; yet there appears to be less formalized procedures among companies for the establishment of prices than for any other marketing area. A realistic approach to pricing suggests that the marketing managers establish pricing objectives and then develop policies within the framework of these objectives that include the basic price and pricing practices.

Pricing Objectives

Pricing objectives are related to a firm's overall objectives; choosing a specific strategy depends on what the company wants to achieve. For example, if a firm wants a quick return on investment, it may use a *skimming strategy* in pricing its new product. This strategy requires a high price in the early stages of market development and may suggest large advertising expenditures to attract purchasers.

If a company is looking for stability and growth, it might choose a strategy that would maximize profits in the long run while minimizing risk. Its objectives might be stated as meeting competition, avoiding competition, or stabilizing prices.

A company's growth-oriented objectives might suggest policies to increase market share. Under these circumstances a company might use a *penetration pricing* strategy, which suggests a relatively low price in the introductory stage of a product. This is desirable if the following conditions exist: sensitivity to price, even at the early stages; substantial economies achievable through large-scale operations, and the threat of

[6]"3M's Aggressive New Consumer Drive," *Business Week* (July 16, 1984), p. 14.

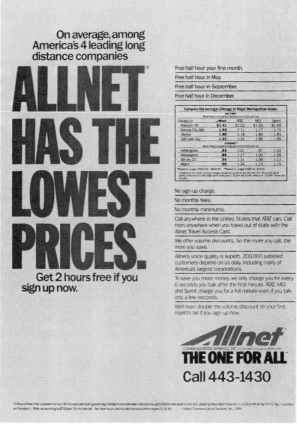

EXHIBIT 3.4a, b
Pricing Above and Below the Competition

strong potential competition. Promotional expenditures may take the form of samples and cents-off coupons rather than messages in the media.

Basic Price Determination

The actual price set by the firm requires an evaluation of a product's design and quality, the target market, the kinds of outlets in which the item will be sold, as well as the expenditures required for promoting it. The techniques for arriving at prices vary.

Using *cost-based pricing*, the marketer sets prices by computing production, overhead, distribution, and promotion expenses, and adds on a profit figure. Demand may not be included in this analysis.

In *demand-oriented pricing*, the marketer focuses on the target population to determine the price range they will accept. An analysis is made to determine whether the prices in the range are sufficient to cover costs and profits.

A marketer using *competition-oriented pricing* sets prices based on competitors' activities. This pricing policy includes such approaches as pricing above (Exhibit 3.4a), below (Exhibit 3.4b), or at the level of competitors' offerings.

Pricing Practices

In addition to determining a basic price the company must decide whether different prices should be placed on slightly different products to appeal to different segments of the market. Several pricing practices designed for consumers contain a promotional element.

One are that has been the subject of a significant amount of research is the relationship between price and consumer perception of quality. While the evidence is somewhat contradictory, numerous products are advertised as expensive as a means of indicating quality. *Prestige pricing* is using a higher price to make the product more desirable.

There is widespread use of *discount pricing* as a promotional strategy. While this may encourage purchases in some cases, a reduction may also be viewed as an indication of further cuts, so that consumers defer their buying. Furthermore, a firm that frequently advertises discount prices may develop an undesirable discount image. Discounts may also be offered to wholesalers and retailers such as quantity discounts for purchasing larger amounts, trade discounts for performing various marketing functions, and cash discounts for early payment.

In recent years various retailing establishments have instituted a strategy known as off-pricing. Like discounting *off-pricing* suggests a lower price; however, items that are off-priced are usually well-known, nationally branded products, such as designer clothing. While discount pricing generally attracts the lower- and middle-income consumer, off-pricing is used to appeal, as well, to the higher-income groups, who are searching for quality merchandise at bargain prices. Several retail chains advertise off prices, including Filene's Department stores in Boston and Caldor's in New York City.

The use of *odd pricing* is based on an assumption that a price ending in an odd number will be associated in the consumer's mind with a lower price rather than with the next higher price and, in effect, will create the illusion of a bargain. Some advertisers offer goods at prices ending in unconventional numbers (for example, 3 or 7) or in odd dollar amounts, such as $3.98, to attract increased attention. Since there is no significant research to support the effectiveness of this activity, before advertisers adopt an odd-pricing strategy they should consider the potential losses from pricing each item a little less.

The objective of *leader pricing* is to increase store traffic by creating the illusion that many other items in the store are relatively low priced. Items may be sold below the usual level or at a loss (loss leader). A nationally branded item that is frequently purchased and quickly consumed is advertised in the media so that prices can be compared. Items such as ice cream and coffee are usually used in leader pricing.

Place (Distribution) Mix

The producer's goal, in a quest for efficiency, is to make large quantities of a standardized item; the consumer, on the other hand, requires small quantities of many different varieties of goods. To meet the needs of assorting and regrouping merchandise, a number of marketing institu-

FIGURE 3.2   Channels of Distribution

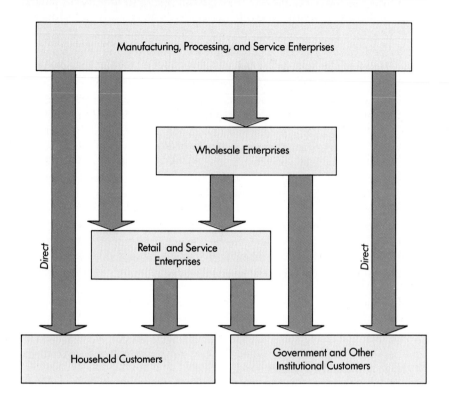

tions have developed. As the gap between the producer and consumer widened, these institutions (generally designated as *middlemen*) have become more numerous and of greater diversity.

Channels of Distribution

As part of its marketing strategy a firm has a choice of distributing its merchandise itself or selecting among middlemen to perform some of its responsibilities. The path that is selected is called a *channel of distribution*, which may fulfill several definite functions for the manufacturer. It can routinize decisions and transactions, and by operating for a number of producers at the same time, it can lower unit costs. It can provide financing, even purchasing the item from the manufacturer and, thereby, reducing the risks. The close contact with retailers and/or consumers can permit the channel to serve as an intelligence agent for the producer. It can offer efficiencies in other areas: by transporting carload quantities at carload prices; lowering storage costs by optimizing the utilization of warehouse space; lowering the per-unit cost of selling by having salespeople promote the products of a number of different manufacturers to the same customers.

To aid in the performance of the firm's marketing functions there are a number of traditional channels from which the marketing managers may select (see Figure 3.2).

Manufacturers may sell directly to consumers (door-to-door, or in manufacturer-owned outlets), they may sell indirectly through the many intermediaries currently available, or they may initiate a new or specialized route for their goods and services. The number and kinds of intermediaries chosen and the functions they are required to perform are the major ingredients of a place (distribution) mix.

Manufacturers who choose *direct channels* of distribution generally wish to exert control over the entire marketing program. Such firms are responsible for the performance of most of the marketing functions including the selling effort. While much of the selling may be conducted door-to-door, advertising, such as direct mail or television spots for records may also be used to secure a sale. Avon Products, Inc., the direct-selling cosmetics company, increased its advertising budget by 50 percent in 1985 to create a "new image" advertising campaign designed to position the company as a beauty-product specialist.[7]

Indirect channels may contain various types of middlemen that exist between the manufacturer and the final user. These middlemen are designated as wholesalers—institutions that sell primarily to resellers, or as retailers—institutions that sell primarily to consumers.

Outlet Selection

In addition to determining the path directing the flow of goods and services, manufacturers must also decide on the number of outlets to be used. These strategies are called intensive distribution, selective distribution, and exclusive distribution.

A manufacturer may decide that, on the basis of a product's characteristics, its target market, and other marketing requirements, it is desirable to have as many outlets as possible. Toothpaste manufacturers, for example, often place their product in every supermarket, grocery store, druggist, department store, and discount outlet in a particular district. This *intensive distribution* is usually accompanied by mass advertising familiarizing the public with the product and noting its availability.

For some products, particularly those considered as "shopping goods" (that is, the consumer is willing to shop and make comparisons), the decision may be to use fewer outlets. Clothing producers, for example, may emphasize pleasant shopping conditions and good personal service. Advertising still plays an important role in this *selective distribution*, featuring the product's benefits and the stores where it can be found.

In *exclusive distribution* a manufacturer severely limits the number of outlets that can offer its merchandise in order to capitalize on the product's image, as well as to secure significant channel loyalty and attention to the product and its service. Advertising for electronic components, for example, usually stresses exclusive outlets with knowledgeable personnel and adequate services.

---

[7]"Avon Is Calling a New Tune," *Dun's Business Month* (May 1985), p. 24.

The Role of Advertising in the Channel

Manufacturers must develop and maintain effective channel relations, and advertising can play an important role. *Trade advertising* persuades middlemen to carry a producer's merchandise by emphasizing its benefits to the retailer or wholesaler. *Consumer advertising* encourages customers to ask for merchandise and generates the middleman's interest in distributing the product.

The importance of the wholesaler's or retailer's own promotional effort cannot be underrated. He or she displays the merchandise, advertises it, and sells it. Frequently manufacturers offer funds or other assistance to distributors or dealers to defray part of the cost of promoting the manufacturer's specific brand. In offering such *cooperative advertising* funds the firm hopes to encourage its outlets to carry and display its brand of merchandise and to offer supplementary advertising at the local level where the item is purchased.

Promotional Mix

A sale is a measure of commercial marketing success. It is a basic element in a network of marketing activities that precedes, accompanies, and follows the exchange of goods and services for money. Although there is no best method for achieving sales, there are a variety of selling activities available to a firm. These activities, known as promotion, include advertising, personal selling, publicity, and sales promotion. Although the focus of this book is advertising, it should be noted that under certain circumstances, one of these other promotional methods may be more desirable.

Personal Selling

Personal selling is a promotional effort that offers direct, face-to-face contact between buyer and seller. A two-way communication network is set up, characterized by immediate feedback—verbal exchanges, expressions, and gestures. The salesperson can answer questions, respond to objections, and adjust the presentation to fit individual conditions. A major strength of personal selling lies in the ability of the salesperson to actually "close" (finalize) the sale.

The outstanding weakness of personal selling as a promotional effort is its high cost-per-contact. To use a sales force effectively requires not only hiring good salespeople, but enacting an extensive sales management program involving training, supervising, motivation, and compensation. Therefore, personal selling is rarely used to sell consumers a relatively inexpensive product, such as breakfast cereal, that has widespread use.

Personal selling as a promotional device is considered desirable when the market consists of few customers who are geographically concentrated and easily identified. Furthermore, where the needs are varied and the selling message must be adapted to these needs, personal selling can be more effective than advertising. Salespeople provide the

EXHIBIT 3.5
Helping Salespeople Sell

MORAL: Sales start **before** your salesman calls—with business publication advertising.

McGRAW-HILL MAGAZINES
BUSINESS•PROFESSIONAL•TECHNICAL

flexibility necessary for individual conditions. Moreover, they offer an immediate and personal reward, such as approval and good friendship, for compliance through purchasing.

Advertising and personal selling tend to reinforce each other. Advertising may be designed to secure leads for the salesperson, to create a favorable image of the company so that the sales representative is well received, or to pull items through the channel of distribution so that the salesperson's job is made easier (see Exhibit 3.5).

Personal selling has a promotional advantage in that it is able to change opinion and behavior. Therefore, it is useful in the introductory phase of a new product when it may be directed to those people who are not now using the product, but whom the firm would like to influence.[8] This initial selling effort can make subsequent mass communications more effective.

Publicity

Publicity is part of a broader function called *public relations*, which involves efforts to create and maintain favorable relationships between an organization and its numerous publics of employees, stockholders, dealers, suppliers, governmental agencies, and labor unions, as well as prospective buyers. Public relations has been defined as a "management function which evaluates public attitudes, identifies the policies and procedures of an organization with the public interest, and executes a program of action (and communication) to earn public understanding and acceptance."[9] While such activities may ultimately affect the firm's marketing efforts, many public relations programs have managerial objectives. For example, a firm may use public relations to establish a favorable climate for securing investment funds, or to communicate management's interest in employees and their families through an annual employees' picnic.

Publicity is a special form of public relations. Specifically it involves securing placement of information about a product, service, or idea in media. Publicity, like advertising, is a form of mass communication. There are, however, several basic differences. While publicity appears as information in mass media, its messages occur in the editorial sections (where stories and news are placed), not in the advertising areas. The company it mentions is not billed for space or time and in this sense, publicity is not paid for; however, the firm may have gone to considerable expense to secure this "free" publicity, including the cost of public-relations personnel.

Advantages of Publicity   Publicity has the advantage of low cost and potentially greater impact than advertising as a result of being part of the nonadvertising content of media. Publicity benefits the seller by increasing goodwill, creating a favorable attitude, attention, and awareness. It contains a strong element of believability because it is not sponsored and is read as news; it may be associated with the authority and prestige of the medium in which it appears. When a newspaper columnist wrote in his syndicated column, "A sip of the stuff is like biting into a hot fudge sundae," within nine days the A. J. Canfield company sold 1.5 million cans of its Diet Chocolate Fudge Soda around the world, more than its entire 1984 production.

Publicity may also reach and influence people not easily accessible through other promotional tools. Top management, for example, may

[8]Robert C. Brooks, Jr., "Relating the Selling Effort to Patterns of Purchase Behavior," in *Dimensions of Communication,* ed. Lee Richardson (New York: Appleton-Century-Crofts, 1969), p. 52.
[9]John E. Marson, *Modern Public Relations* (New York: McGraw-Hill Book Co., Inc., 1979), p. 6.

not read advertisements or be available to salespeople but may pay attention to news releases.

Disadvantages of Publicity   This method has some serious disadvantages, which limit its use as a promotional effort. First, it is difficult to secure the benefits of repeat exposure. Second, the medium retains complete control over the placement of publicity and the ability to change the contents of the release. Manufacturers of television sets, for example, have established favorable images through mass-media stories about their production of components for space flights. Occasionally, however, the impact of the publicity was unfavorable when a component failed during the course of a space mission.

Kinds of Publicity   In order for publicity to be successful it should be part of the total promotional strategy and integrated into the marketing plan. Like all planning activities, publicity objectives should be defined, the means to accomplish these objectives should be determined, and they should be formalized in procedures for accomplishment.

The form of publicity, whether news releases, feature articles, press conferences, tapes and films, or editorials, depends on the objectives. If the purpose is to promote a new product image, press kits and news conferences may be used. If the purpose is to disseminate information quickly, news releases do better than featured articles.

While there are no formalized procedures for handling unfavorable publicity, it is suggested that a permanent crisis-communications team be formed within a company.[10] The type and kinds of responses to the publicity depend on the situation and the extent of the problem.

Sales Promotion

Sales promotion has been defined as those promotional activities that supplement, coordinate, and render both advertising and personal selling more effective. According to the American Marketing Association, promotion includes "activities other than personal selling, advertising and publicity that stimulate consumer purchasing and dealer effectiveness, such as display, shows, exhibitions, demonstrations, and various nonrecurrent selling efforts not in the ordinary routine."[11]

Sales promotion adds an extra value to a product as an incentive for the distributor, sales force, or the ultimate consumer. The specific activities involved can be divided into *dealer and distributor stimulants*, methods to increase purchasing action on the part of marketing intermediaries, and *direct consumer stimulants*, techniques for greater consumer purchases.

[10]David P. McClure, "Publicity Should Be Integrated in the Marketing Plan," *Marketing News* (December 10, 1982), p. 6.
[11]American Marketing Association, Committee on Definitions, *Marketing Definitions, A Glossary of Terms*.

These include trade shows, point-of-purchase displays, premiums, samples, contests, sweepstakes, and many other incentive efforts. Since many of these activities are closely related to advertising they are discussed in detail in Chapter 21.

THE PROMOTIONAL/COMMUNICATION NETWORK

Promotion has been defined as the coordination of all seller-initiated efforts to set up channels of information and persuasion to facilitate the sale of a good or service, or the acceptance of an idea.[12] In accordance with this definition, the basic function of promotion is to communicate persuasively.

The simplest communication network requires three ingredients—a sender, a signal, and a receiver. The sender and receiver are participants, and the signal provides the common element. The signal may be verbal, oral, mechanical, electronic, graphic, symbolic, or in the form of gestures; however it is presented, it must exist within the frame of reference and the field of experience of both the sender and receiver.

A promotional/communication network serves various purposes. The first is to provide information to all people directly or indirectly related to the organization. The second is to persuade—the businessperson wishes to persuade nonpotential customers to become potential customers, and potential customers to purchase the product or service. A third purpose, which may, in fact, be considered a prerequisite for the other two, is to create a favorable environment conducive to the satisfactory performance of the persuasive and informative activities. To accomplish these tasks the simple communication network is expanded in terms of elements, interconnections, and complexities.

When the communication system is designed for marketing it encompasses various promotional activities. In this network the signal (or message) must be encoded so that it taps into the consumers' frames of reference and is consistent with their experiences. It is transmitted through the various channels of advertising, personal selling, publicity, and sales promotion techniques. Even though these channels are filled with "noise" in the form of competitive messages or other distractions, the message is designed to secure some kind of response ranging from awareness to purchase action. Feedback is necessary to determine the manner in which the message is decoded, and to improve the network's efficiency (see Figure 3.3).

The proper design of this network suggests that each promotional ingredient be incorporated in accordance with its capabilities, cost, and effectiveness. However there is not always time to examine every advertising decision in terms of personal selling, publicity, or sales promotion as promotional alternatives. Nonetheless it might be worthwhile

---

[12]Edward L. Brink and William T. Kelley, *The Management of Promotion* (Englewood Cliffs, N.J.: Prentice-Hall, Inc., 1963), p. 6.

FIGURE 3.3 A Promotional Communication Network

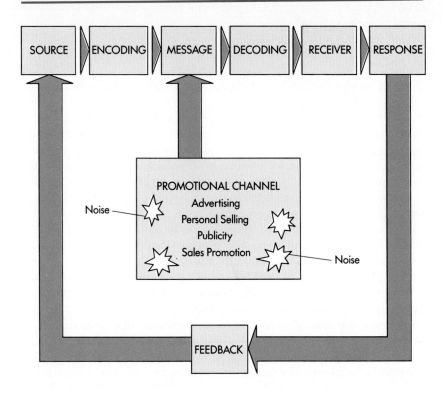

for the advertising manager to take time out occasionally to consider the possibilities of an alternative promotional mechanism which may secure the same objective more efficiently and at a lower cost.

Evaluating Promotional Alternatives

There are several promotional techniques that can be used for communications, and it is necessary to determine the extent to which personal selling, publicity, sales promotion, and/or advertising are incorporated in the marketing communication network. While there are many factors which affect these decisions, the major considerations are the company's resources, the nature of the target market, the nature of the product, and the product's stage in its life cycle.

Company Resources
Availability of funds is a primary consideration in choosing a promotional activity; however, cost itself is an inefficient criterion, since there are no precise yardsticks for measuring the efficiency of these outlays. Moreover, each promotional technique performs a different function and must be chosen not only for its cost, but also for the purpose.

Comparisons among promotional tools are frequently made in terms of cost per contact. While such costs vary from industry to industry, and from product to product, personal selling cost per contact tends to be higher than for any other promotional effort. In 1985, the cost of an average business sales call was $229.70.[13] A sales call, however, can do much more than just secure contact; it can actually secure the sale.

Advertising is a mass medium, so it is frequently expressed in cost per thousand. When this expenditure is computed in terms of individual contacts, it tends to be relatively low. Generally, the larger the circulation of a medium, the lower the cost per contact. Thus, although television dollar outlays are high, the cost per contact is very low.

It is difficult to determine the cost per contact of publicity since much of it is characterized as "free." Generally the cost of sales promotional devices cannot be allocated among many prospects, so the cost per contact remains high. However, according to the Trade Show Bureau, it cost $89.95 to reach each person who has an interest in a product or exhibit in its trade shows.[14]

Nature of the Target

Purchases by an industrial user are generally large and costly, and the consequences of a wrong decision can be disastrous. For that reason the promotional mix for industrial consumers tends to rely on salespeople, who encourage and reinforce customer decisions. Sales to wholesalers, too, emphasize personal selling, since salespeople frequently provide incentives for purchasing, such as approval and friendship.

However, the personal selling technique may not be the best one for retailers. Supermarket managers, for example, are already burdened by upwards of 15,000 separate products. Under such circumstances trade deals, rather than close personal ties, may influence a store to carry a new product or stock more of the seller's brand than the competitor's.

Advertising is an efficient way to reach customers who are distributed across all market segments. Nonetheless, some customers seek a personal atmosphere in their shopping experiences and are strongly influenced by store personnel. Others are "deal prone"; that is, they are highly motivated to purchase through sales promotional incentives, such as coupons. Still other customer targets are hard to persuade and require the credibility that comes with publicity.

Nature of the Product

Frequently the nature of the product dictates the basic ingredients of the promotional mix. Industrial products are often designed to exact specifications and require the explanation, installation, and servicing that only a personal sales effort can provide. Also, when there is no urgent need for a product, a marketing manager may choose personal selling: door-to-door encyclopedia sales are a case in point—permitting the salesperson to explain to parents the usefulness of the product for their children's education.

---

[13]"Survey: Business sales calls costing $229.70," *Marketing News* (August 1, 1985), p. 23.

[14]"Marketing Briefs," *Marketing News* (August 2, 1985), p. 23.

FIGURE 3.4   Stages in the Product
             Life-Cycle

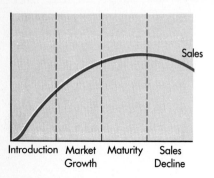

Introduction Market   Maturity   Sales
              Growth   Decline

One of Soviet Georgia's senior citizens thought
Dannon was an excellent yogurt. She ought to know.
She's been eating yogurt for 137 years.

EXHIBIT 3.6
A Primary Demand Campaign in the
Early Stages

On the other hand, convenience goods, such as milk and bread, that are bought with a minimum of effort, are heavily promoted through advertising that presells the product and notes its availability. Although goods such as furniture and refrigerators, usually subject to comparison buying, benefit from advertising, they also require sales personnel to point out competitive advantages.

Stages in the Product Life-Cycle

The lifetime sales of many products reveal particular patterns of development known as the *product life-cycle,* which is divided into the stages of introduction, growth, maturity, and sales decline (see Figure 3.4). These divisions are not necessarily related to time span; instead, they refer to stages of market acceptance. Promotional objectives and activities usually differ for these stages.

In the introductory stage the promotional mix may consist of the following: personal selling to overcome objections and secure new product acceptance; publicity, in the form of news releases, to announce the product; and press conferences and press kits, while expensive, to provide extensive product awareness. Coca-Cola, in introducing its first product extension using the Coca-Cola name (Diet Coke), spent extensively on a combined advertising and publicity campaign.

Sales promotion devices, such as samples, are also effective ways to introduce new products. When Monsanto Chemical (then a producer of industrial products) presented All, the first low-sudsing detergent for consumer use, the company contacted washing-machine manufacturers and requested that samples of its product be placed in every new washing machine.

As a product moves though its life-cycle, the firm starts to search harder for untapped needs in order to maintain or increase sales. The objectives during this stage may go beyond awareness and develop into strong competition for sales. Thus, in the growth stage, the firm tends to pursue *selective demand advertising* which highlights the features and benefits of a specific manufacturer's brand. The television industry, for example, quickly turned from primary demand to selective demand.

Yogurt, on the other hand, has been around for many years; yet it wasn't until the 1970s, when Dannon conducted an extensive campaign designed to increase primary demand for the product, that it began to gain consumer acceptance. Dannon's campaign focused on the generic product, noting its nutritional value and suggesting that it might have positively influenced the health of the long-living people from Soviet Georgia (see Exhibit 3.6). As yogurt entered the growth stage, more and more competitors entered the market and Dannon's advertising campaign had to be directed at selective demand, since each manufacturer was now noting its product's differences. Dannon began to offer "frozen yogurt on a stick," while Kraft's "LeShake" focused on consistency, emphasizing that it was "the yogurt you eat with a straw." Yoplait was addressed to members of the market segment who wanted a little "culture" in their lives.

In the mature stage of the product life-cycle, firms may turn to promotions in the form of consumer stimulants. A survey conducted among a number of companies revealed that during the introduction and growth stages of the product life-cycle they tended to rely heavily on advertising. In the maturity and decline stages they increased their sales promotion budgets.[15]

Promotional programs are generally reduced during the decline or termination stage. However, some publicity is useful at this stage to maintain favorable public relations in announcing, for example, the sale of a product line or the discontinuance of product production.

Some marketing professionals question the validity of the product life-cycle concept. They suggest that it may be a self-fulfilling prophecy; that is, if it is taken as given, marketers may discontinue efforts to maintain a product in what they consider to be the later stages of its life cycle.[16]

Moreover they note that there are differences between the *product* life-cycle and the *brand* life-cycle. Marketing efforts, including advertising, may, in fact, extend the life of a particular brand. Examples are Johnson's baby shampoo which is now recommended for all members of the family (see Exhibit 3.7); Jello, which continually suggests new recipes; and Ivory Soap, which has celebrated its one-hundredth birthday with an extensive advertising campaign, while other soaps have declined in acceptance and market share. Advertising has also been considered responsible for prolonging the life-cycle of General Foods' Brim decaffeinated coffee, General Mills' Nature Valley granola line, S.C. Johnson & Sons' Edge shave gel, and Gillette Co.'s Soft 'n Dri deodorant.[17]

It should be understood that the product life-cycle tends to describe the total industry's sales rather than those of a particular brand. While product life-cycle analysis is not to be ignored, it has to take place in the context of a well-rounded, total marketing point of view.[18]

EXHIBIT 3.7
Extending a Product's Life-Cycle

SUMMARY

A marketing mix is a combination of procedures used by a firm to achieve its marketing objectives. Advertising is only one ingredient in this mix, but its performance is closely related to the other elements of product decisions, pricing decisions, the channels of distribution selected by the firm, and all forms of promotion.

The product encompasses, besides its tangible characteristics, a cluster of satisfactions such as name, package, and color. Advertising helps promote these satisfactions. Product development strategies such as market segmentation, product differentiation, and product positioning frequently require advertising support.

[15]"Special Report, Marketing and Sales Promotion," *Sales & Marketing Management*, Vol. 121 (August 1978), pp. 51–82.

[16]Nairman Khalla and Sonia Yuspeh, "Forget the Product Life Cycle Concept," *Harvard Business Review*, Vol. 54 (January-February 1976), pp. 102–6.

[17]Nancy Giges and James F. Forkan, "Product Life Cycle Theory Thrown a Curve," *Advertising Age* (May 24, 1982), p. 56.

[18]Yoram Wind and Henry J. Claycamp, "Planning Product Line Strategies: A Matrix Approach," *Journal of Marketing*, Vol. 40 (January 1976), pp. 2–9.

Pricing the product is a major marketing decision, and the determination of how heavily the product should be advertised is an important factor in the selection of the ultimate price. In addition, price can be used with advertising in the administration and dissemination of various pricing practices such as prestige pricing, discount pricing, off-pricing, odd pricing, and leader pricing.

Channels of distribution fulfill several marketing functions for the producer, and the firm's promotional strategy serves to motivate and secure loyal marketing middlemen as well as develop and maintain these resellers' promotional support.

The various forms of promotion available to the firm include advertising, selling, publicity, and sales promotion. Advertising and publicity are forms of mass communication, personal selling offers an interpersonal exchange, and sales promotion activities supplement and support these other efforts. All of these ingredients can be incorporated into a promotional/communication network through which a firm may provide information and/or persuasion to facilitate the sale of a good or service or the acceptance of an indea.

A number of factors are relevant for determining the most efficient promotional mix in the design of a communication network. These include company resources, the nature of the target market, and the nature of the product. Of particular significance in this decision is the product's stage in its life-cycle.

CHAPTER REVIEW

QUESTIONS FOR DISCUSSION

1. What is meant by the marketing mix? Is advertising always part of this mix?
2. What role does advertising play in the product development strategies available to the firm?
3. How are pricing policy decisions supported by advertising?
4. Which of the traditional channels of distribution do you believe requires the greatest emphasis on promotion?
5. What advertising techniques can help administer and maintain effective channel relations?
6. How do the various promotional techniques differ in terms of their communication characteristics?
7. Which promotional technique would you recommend to introduce an antipollutant soap? A battery-powered automobile?
8. Discuss how the nature of the target market and the product influence the promotional choice.
9. In which stage of the product life-cycle do you believe advertising is most important? Least important?
10. Can advertising help lengthen the duration of the product life-cycle? How?

KEY TERMS

macromarketing	odd-pricing
micromarketing	leader pricing
marketing mix	intermediaries
four Ps	channel of distribution
submix	intensive distribution
product	selective distribution
market segment	exclusive distribution
market segmentation	trade advertising
product differentiation	consumer advertising
product positioning	cooperative advertising
skimming strategy	personal selling
penetration pricing	publicity
cost-based pricing	sales promotion
demand-oriented pricing	dealer and distributor stimulants
competition-oriented pricing	direct consumer stimulants
prestige pricing	product life-cycle
discount pricing	selective demand advertising
off-pricing	

AD PRACTICE

Visit several stores that feature fragrance counters and gather information relevant to the following:

1. Product Mix: use of market segmentation, product differentiation, and product positioning
2. Pricing Policies
3. Outlets Used
4. Sales Promotion Activities

4

Managing the Advertising Effort

After its sales and earnings had declined for a number of years, Beatrice Foods Company undertook a major reorganization. It consolidated into a small number of marketing-oriented business groups under the name Beatrice Companies, discarding its former decentralized management structure in favor of a tighter centralized management. The advertising function was centralized and the number of advertising agencies the firm used was cut from one hundred to less than ten. "Beatrice. You've known us all along" was the theme of the major campaign undertaken to popularize the name of the corporation.

While it will take some time to evaluate the results of this managerial reorganization, awareness of the name *Beatrice* and its connection with its products has increased significantly. Kohlberg, Kravis, Roberts & Co., a major investment firm that took over Beatrice, believed Beatrice had the potential to become an industry superpower.

Advertising is a business function, and, as such, requires efficient management. In preparation for its advertising effort the firm must design an appropriate managerial framework.

MANAGING ADVERTISING

Advertising, more than most other business functions, operates in an aura of uncertainty, due, in part, to the inability to develop universally accepted standards for measuring its effectiveness. The management of profitable advertising involves the administrative processes shown in Figure 4.1, but these steps do not necessarily occur in a prescribed order, nor are they separate and distinct stages in a process. For example, closely intertwined with the establishment of strategy is a determination of how much to spend. And the budget, which may finance a specific advertising program, is also a control element. Furthermore, measurement of results, while not always precise, does provide feedback information for the planning process. (Part III, Advertising Campaign and Strategy, examines some of these issues in greater detail.)

THE ADVERTISING ORGANIZATION

As with any business function, effective advertising requires the establishment of the appropriate organizational structure staffed by competent personnel. Creating such a structure and defining personnel roles facilitate both planning and control.

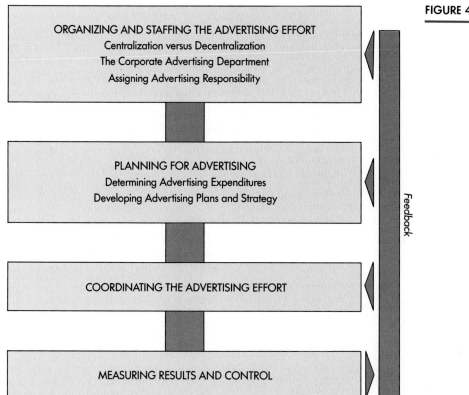

FIGURE 4.1 Managing Advertising

One option for an organization is to use an advertising agency, an external department to which the company delegates a large share of its promotional responsibilities. Client companies and their advertising agencies generally design administrative systems that include liaison personnel and close working relationships between the two organizations. This is discussed in detail in Chapter 5.

Whether or not a firm uses an advertising agency, it must have some advertising unit within the business structure. Its placement depends on the size of the firm, the multiplicity of divisions and products, the importance of advertising to the firm, the availability of advertising funds, the advertising mission, the personal involvement of top management in the advertising function, and the framework of the company's total organizational structure.[1] The placement of this advertising responsibility, moreover, has an effect on how the advertising function is administered.

In creating an advertising organizational structure several areas require managerial decisions. These include centralizing or decentralizing the advertising function; introducing a corporate advertising department; and assigning the advertising responsibility.

Centralizing the Advertising Function

A company's advertising responsibility can be centralized in one unit that services the entire organization. This happens in a functional organization structure where marketing, finance, manufacturing, and research and development are the major functions. Reporting to the marketing director are the separate promotional departments, headed by the sales manager, the advertising manager, and the sales promotion manager (see Figure 4.2).

From an advertising perspective, this centralized department serves a company best when the number of products produced by the company is sufficiently limited and the advertising effort is effectively administered by one executive. It is also useful in a company where a line of products is sold to similar markets and through similar channels. The centralized department also works well when it is advantageous to promote the product line as a family of products.

The exact position of the centralized advertising unit depends to a great extent on the importance of advertising in the company's total marketing effort, and to the extent to which top management feels it should become involved in the advertising effort. Thus the advertising manager may report to the president (in smaller companies), to the chief marketing executive, or even to various division heads (see Figure 4.3).

---

[1]Alfred R. Oxenfeldt and Carroll Swan, *Management of the Advertising Function* (Belmont, Calif.: Wadsworth Publishing Co., Inc., 1964), p. 43.

FIGURE 4.2 The Centralized Advertising Department

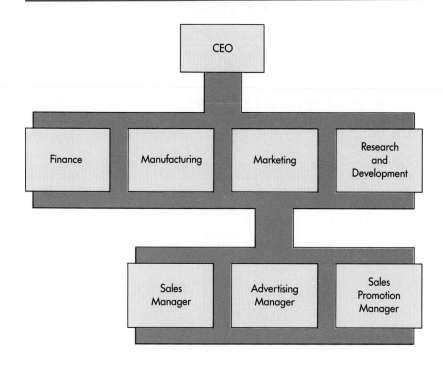

The basic advantages of a centralized advertising department are the following.

— It decreases the need for an extensive staff of personnel.
— It provides for an easier flow of communications within the organization.
— It permits uniform communications, allowing benefits to accrue through an advertising campaign with consistent, extensive repetition of the advertising message.
— The structure allows top management to participate in advertising decisions, thereby reducing the need for personnel at the lower levels.

Decentralizing the Advertising Function

Many multibrand or multidivision companies find the best arrangement for them is the decentralizing of the advertising department. When the advertising function is decentralized within a corporation arranged by divisions, final authority for the advertising function rests with the divisional head who generally has his or her own advertising staff and budget. Decentralization can be done by product, territory, division, or

FIGURE 4.3   Three Possible Ways to Centralize the Advertising Function

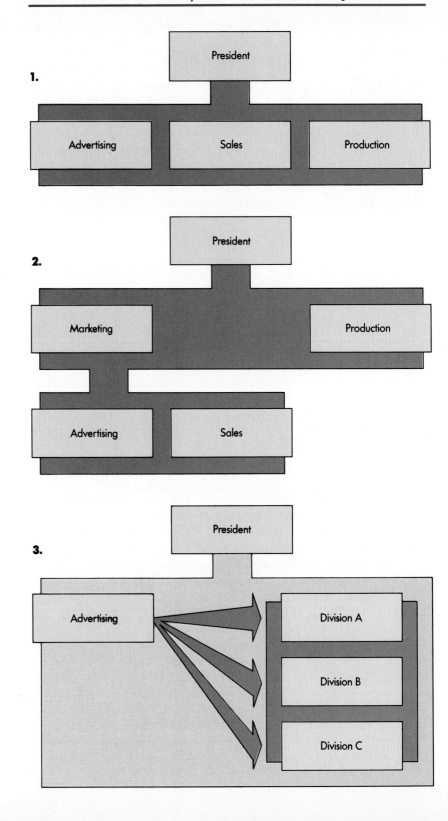

FIGURE 4.4   A Decentralized Advertising Department in a Multidivision Company

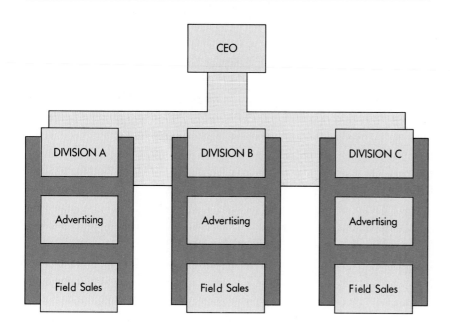

brand. Figure 4.4 represents an example of a decentralized advertising department within a multidivision company.

The advantages of a decentralized advertising department, particularly in the large multidivision company, are the following.

— It permits advertising to be geared more easily to specific needs of the division.
— It allows more flexibility in the promotional approach and permits speedier and easier changes.
— It allows independent measurement of the success of each division's advertising process.
— It provides more opportunity for innovation and a variety of approaches.
— It provides motivation and incentive for better advertising efforts by encouraging competition among divisions.

The decentralized advertising department, however, suffers from a number of deficiencies. It does not permit a uniformity of advertising through the organization which may, in turn, reduce the potential building power of repetitive advertising. It may create too much competition, to the extent that each division head is less interested in the manner in which advertising benefits the entire company and more concerned with securing the largest share of the advertising effort for the division. Rivalry tends to lead to secrecy; each division head may jealously guard innovative or successful strategies.

FIGURE 4.5   Corporate Advertising as a Staff Function

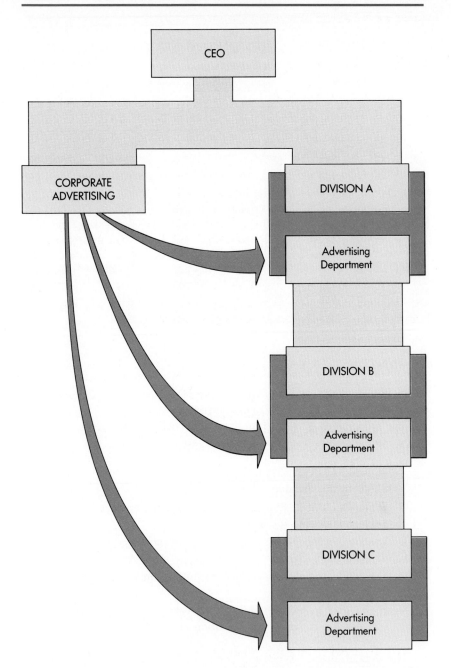

The lack of strong centralized authority reduces the ability to coordinate the advertising effort. For example, one multidivision company that decentralized its advertising function found it difficult to compel each division to use a uniform logotype, the company's standard signature, in its diverse ads. The lack of unity in the company's ads failed to bring the firm's products together as a family. In another case an automobile company found that two of its divisions had developed advertising campaigns claiming the same element of superiority, creating consumer confusion and potential legal problems.

The Corporate Advertising Department

As part of its organizational structure, a multiproduct or multidivision company frequently maintains, as a staff function, a top-level advertising manager who has the prime responsibility for corporate advertising and for coordinating the advertising effort within all divisions. Although this executive does not have direct line control over the advertising managers within each division, he or she exerts considerable control through final approval of the advertising budget (see Figure 4.5).

The corporate advertising department may exist within any organizational design, but it is particularly useful in a company that adopts a decentralized structure. Frequently, the corporate department has the authority to approve or disapprove advertising for policy reasons, such as matters of taste, ethics, and advertising to children. In a company that uses more than one advertising agency, the corporate staff performs a media coordination function in an effort to obtain optimum discounts from the various media that the separate agencies employ.

Corporate Advertising Campaign

A *corporate advertising campaign* treats the company as a product, carefully positioning it and clearly differentiating it from other companies, and basically selling it to select audiences.[2] As shown in Exhibit 4.1 corporate advertising may be designed to accomplish several objectives for the organization:

— To build better awareness for a company,
— To act as a marketing umbrella for a firm's products,
— To inform the public about what a company does,
— To improve employee morale and recruit professionals, especially in high technology industries,[3]
— To inform the public on how most efficiently to use a company's products and services,
— To improve relationships with various groups—the public as well as government regulatory bodies,
— To persuade the public to accept a company's stand on a controversial issue through "advocacy" advertisements,

[2]S. Parkash Sethi, "Institutional/Image Advertising and Idea/Issue Advertising as Marketing Tools: Some Public Policy Issues," *Journal of Marketing,* Vol. 43 (January 1979), pp. 68–78.

[3]Thomas Garbett, "When to Advertise Your Company," *Harvard Business Review* (March/April, 1982), pp. 100–106.

EXHIBIT 4.1
A Corporate Ad

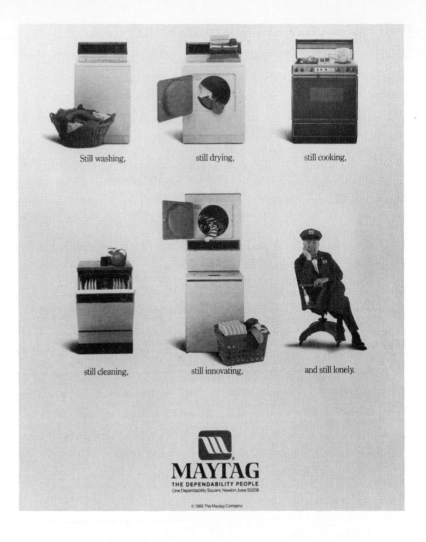

— To improve financial considerations and encourage inquiries
from potential investors, and

— To increase consumer motivation to buy a firm's product.[4]

Over one billion dollars a year has been spent on corporate advertising campaigns in the past, and there are indications that expenditures
for corporate advertising will grow. Many firms have made major commitments to their corporate advertising programs,[5] but future research
must determine whether corporate messages are more efficient than
brand/product messages in achieving a company's objectives.

ASSIGNING THE ADVERTISING RESPONSIBILITY

In most companies the advertising manager, as head of the advertising
department, has the major responsibility for the advertising effort. However, sometimes the responsibility rests with the product manager or
alternative personnel because of strategic considerations.

The Product Manager Organization

A response to organizational problems that occur when a company has too many products and brands for any executive to handle effectively is *product management,* a system that gives concentrated managerial attention to each product by designating a product (or brand) manager who has the marketing responsibility for that product or brand. Some companies have several brands of the same product in order to capture a larger share of a specific market. Furthermore, they believe it is useful to encourage competition among their own brands. Procter & Gamble has a product (or brand) manager for each of its major toothpaste products, Crest and Gleem.

Because product management is a form of decentralized organization, a major portion of the advertising responsibility is shifted from the advertising manager to the product manager. There is an assumption that an advertising department cannot develop the product and market expertise for a large number of products except at a high cost. Furthermore, the lines of communication can be shortened by having the product manager deal directly with the advertising agency. In fact, in some product management organizations, the advertising department may not be listed on the organization's chart; or, if one is there, it is usually at the corporate level and provides services common to several divisions (see Figure 4.6).

There are a number of criticisms of the product manager/advertising relationship. Product managers are generally positioned at a relatively low organizational level; consequently, they are frequently young and inexperienced. Although they have advertising responsibility, they have not been given commensurate authority. A survey of companies using this system indicated that the product manager may not be responsible for major advertising decisions about important products or strategy changes for less important products. These major decisions may still be made at the corporate or division marketing manager level. Thus, the advertising approval process goes through a hierarchy of approval levels, slows down decision making, and tends to encourage a conservative approach to creative concepts.[6]

Companies who use the product management form of reorganization are taking steps to minimize the disadvantages. The product manager's role is being redefined and clarified, the advertising decision-making point is being moved up the management ladder, and some companies are reintroducing advertising specialists to provide expert counsel for line decision-making executives.[7]

Despite the findings in a survey of product managers of 97 large corporations, where over 90 percent of the brand managers indicated

[4]Lewis C. Winters, "The Effect of Brand Advertising on Company Image: Implications for Corporate Advertising," *Journal of Advertising Research*, Vol. 26 (April, May 1986), p. 59.

[5]Charles H. Patti and John P. McDonald, "Corporate Advertising: Process, Practices, and Perspectives (1970–1989)," *Journal of Advertising*, Vol. 14, No. 1. (1985), pp. 42–49.

[6]Victor P. Buell, *Changing Practices in Advertising Decision-Making and Control* (New York: Association of National Advertisers, Inc., 1973), pp. 3, 4.

[7]*Ibid.*, p. vi.

FIGURE 4.6   A Company with Product Managers in Divisions

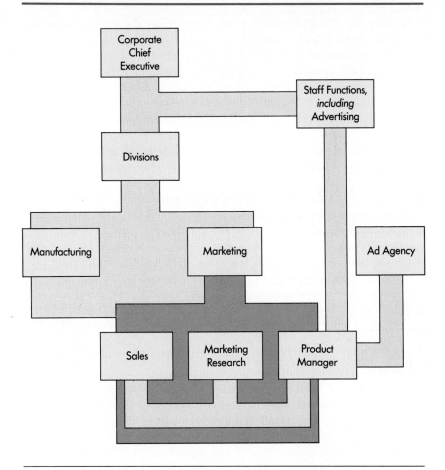

From "Changing Practices in Advertising Decision-Making and Control," Association of National Advertisers, Inc., 1973, p. 25. Copyright © 1973 by Association of National Advertisers, Inc. Reprinted by permission.

much involvement with advertising policies,[8] many large consumer product companies now have layers of marketing management to make decisions, especially when it comes to major advertising decisions. The brand manager function in this area is to assemble all the facts and make a recommendation, generally to the marketing vice-president.[9]

The brand manager of the eighties will have more available marketing information because of developments such as universal product coding and interactive cable. However, the product manager will also be faced with more complicated advertising decisions as media become

---

[8]Richard T. Hise and J. Patrick Kelly, "Product Management on Trial," *Journal of Marketing*, Vol. 42 (October 1978), pp. 28–33.

[9]"Brand Management—Boon or Boondoggle?" *Marketing and Media Decisions*, Vol. 15 (August 1980), pp. 57–59.

The Advertising Business: Inside & Outside An Agency

The advertising agency, in its present form, has only been around since the turn of the century.

Sellers seeking customers for their products and services engage advertising agencies to create and place advertising in the various media. The creative and business people who make up an ad agency are writers, artists, producers, market and media analysts, merchandisers, researchers, and salespeople.

What Ad Agencies Do

The steps in creating and placing an ad include data collection, study, analysis, planning, and the execution of the plan.

Accountant and account executive discussing the advertising budget

Tabulating media information

Data Collection and Study

A client's product or service must be studied to determine its advantages and how it compares with competitors. A product's use, price, packaging, and availability must all be taken into account.

Market researcher polling a shopper

Analysis and Planning

Who, when, where, and why are important questions that must be asked about the consumer of a product or service. Agency people must constantly reassess the industry for which the ad functions. In the planning stage, knowledge of the media and their audiences is crucial to planning advertising.

Corporate strategy meeting

Focus group research

Marketing meeting in an agency

Execution of the Plan

After the client has approved the advertising plan, the agency works to execute it.

Operating Departments

There are four operating departments within the advertising agency. The account management department works with the client to develop a strategy for the product or service to be marketed and passes the information on to the creative team. The research department does marketing and advertising research by testing consumer usage patterns and reader and viewer responses to ads. The media department then analyzes the quantitative data and presents the best solutions. Finally, the creative department works with the media department to prepare and place an ad in the advertising media. The creative department includes copywriters, art directors, and television producers. There may also be specialists such as print and broadcast production experts.

Advertising layout session at Esprit

Art director and art buyer selecting images

Graphic designer at work on print advertisement

Graphic designer and account executive reviewing a project

Presenting storyboards of a TV commercial for client approval

Illustrator presenting work for approval

Videotape editing

Retouching negatives for photoengraving

Final assembly on a printing press

Finishing Touches

Execution of an advertising plan is done through people in the creative department. They work on putting the advertisement into words and pictures. An ad for broadcast media entails work with outside experts—film producers, camera crews, and actors. An ad for print media must be converted into printing plates that are produced by outside suppliers.

Filming on location for a farm product advertisement

Sound recording technician

Recording a voiceover

Sometimes the agency does special work for an advertiser. Package design, sales research, sales training, preparation of sales and service literature, designing merchandising displays, and publicity are examples of some of the special work an agency may do.

Sales meeting at a toy company

Package design meeting

WHAT DOES A BRAND MANAGER DO?

The brand manager of Maxwell House Instant, the best-selling instant coffee in the United States, is 30 years old. It is the brand manager's responsibility to market and advertise this important product of the coffee division of General Foods and, in the large context, to promote the corporate well-being. The brand manager is expected to vanquish all comers, notably Nestlé's Nescafé and P&G's Folger's. At the same time, the marketing and advertising objectives—and the budget to achieve them—are defined by a multitude of bosses, who must weigh the needs of Maxwell House Instant Coffee against those of other General Foods coffee brands.

At General Foods there is a separate consumer promotions department that comes up with coupon ideas as well as advertising specialists within the coffee division.

Although these curb the brand manager's freedom, the Maxwell House Instant brand manager must keep a finger constantly on the market's pulse. The brand manger confers almost daily with the four regional managers for the coffee division about promotions, arguing the best rates to give the trade, and the wisdom of distributing a certain package size in a given market. He or she may talk to the consumer promotions department about ideas for coupons, and discuss strategy with the advertising agency, Ogilvy & Mather. To this extent, the position of brand manager provides an effective training ground for relatively inexperienced people in the areas of marketing and advertising.

Source: Sandra Salmans, "Brand Manager," John Susko, "Pushing the Maxwell Product at General Foods," *The New York Times* (August 16, 1982), p. 8F.

more fragmented and marketing techniques more elaborate. Moreover, major problems will still exist in terms of the short tenure which usually accompanies a particular product management position. Since advertising decisions must be made at the long-term level, placing such decisions in the hands of a product manager, who spends a short period on any one product, may not be feasible.

Strategic Organization

Corporate executives of basic industries agree that the product management system may not be appropriate in an era of slow economic growth and mature markets.[10] Product managers' decisions are likely to be based on short-term considerations, and, more specifically, on increasing market share, with little concern for the ramifications of these decisions on the entire organization. The profit-center emphasis tends to encourage product managers to compete with their company's other products, sometimes to the detriment of some products.

Many organizations have developed organizational structures that emphasize strategic planning. Kotler defines *strategic planning* as "the

---

[10]Victor P. Buell, "Firms to Modify, Abolish Product Manager Jobs Due to Sluggish Economy, Centralized Planning," *Marketing News* (March 18, 1983), Section 2, p. 8.

managerial process of developing and maintaining a strategic fit between the organization and its changing marketing opportunities. It relies on developing a clear company mission, objectives and goals, growth strategy, and product portfolio plans."[11]

An organization structure based on strategic management replaces the emphasis on product with an emphasis on strategy (see Figure 4.7). In this structure, a group director of product strategy shares responsibility with his or her immediate superior for strategy design and goals attainment and also would be responsible for the direction of programs that implement the strategies. Consumer marketing staff specialists (rather than product managers) report to this executive and are responsible for tactical implementation of the strategies and for subsidiary advertising goals such as awareness and trial levels. Advertising strategies emanating from these strategic planners have a longer range focus and would be based on total organizational needs rather than short-term returns.

ADVERTISING EXPENDITURE STRATEGY

One of the key elements in the advertising planning process is determining how much to spend on advertising. Product managers and salespeople present their budgetary needs, which are coordinated, and perhaps modified, by the corporate advertising head. The responsibility for the decision, which also acts as a control mechanism, frequently rests with the advertising manager, subject to the approval of the firm's top executive, the president or CEO. Depending on the organizational structure, other personnel, such as the vice-president of marketing or the firm's advertising agency, may be involved.

While there are many advertisers in the United States, the bulk of advertising expenditures are concentrated in the hands of relatively few. The one hundred leading national advertisers spent $26.67 billion in national advertising in 1985. See the Appendix Table in the back of the book that lists the one hundred leading advertisers by primary business.

Heavy advertisers are generally found in the food, retail department stores, motor vehicles, pharmaceuticals, toiletries and cosmetics, and soaps and cleanser industries. Procter & Gamble, the perennial leader, spent $1.6 billion on advertising in 1985. A relatively new major advertiser is the U.S. Government, where problems of voluntary enlistment have led to a decrease in the pool of potential enlistees. Sears, Roebuck & Co. was the Number Four national advertiser in 1985, and if local advertising expenditures for this company were added to its national expenditures, it would rank as the Number One advertiser. K mart and J. C. Penney have expanded their retail outlets and have turned to heavy national advertising to support this expansion and promote their insurance, real estate, and financial services.

---

[11]Philip Kotler, *Principles of Marketing* (Englewood Cliffs, N.J.: Prentice-Hall, Inc., 1980), p. 74.

FIGURE 4.7   A Strategic Management Structure

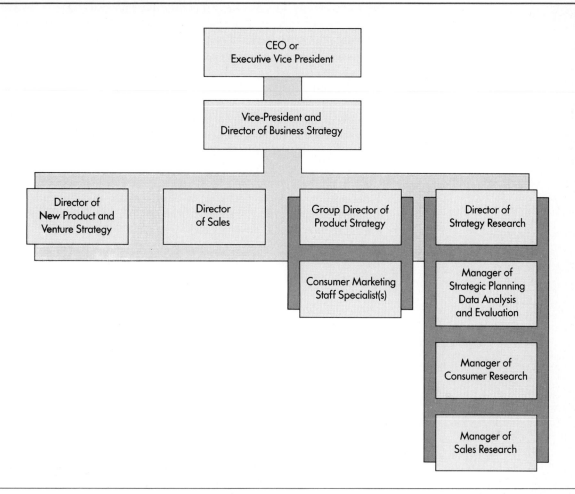

"An Organization Structure to Help You in the 80's" by Terry Haller, *Advertising Age* (August 25, 1980), p. 45. Copyright © 1980 by Crain Communications, Inc. Reprinted with permission from Advertising Age.

Ads Forecasts, an annual research report on advertising expenditures, predicted that major new industries, such as retail mobile homes and freight forwarding, will emerge as large advertising spenders in the next few years.[12]

The Selection of a Strategy

A firm's expenditure strategy must respond to changing needs. Each situation demands a different option, depending on the goals of the organization.[13]

---

[12]Ad Study uncovers spending patterns," *Advertising Age* (September 15, 1986), p. 60.

[13]R. Craig Endicott, "P & G Retains Ad-Spending Crown," *Advertising Age* (September 16, 1985), pp. 1–2.

New Corporate Management   Campbell Soup increased advertising expenditures by 71 percent, reflecting the aggressive stance of its new company president, R. Gordon McGovern. He instituted a program designed to increase acquisitions, new products, and expand lines—all supported by heavy advertising campaigns.

Introduction of New Products   Sterling Drug introduced the "world proven" Panadol in the United States in 1983 with an advertising appropriation of $25 million, representing 64 percent of the anticipated first-year sales of $39 million. Polaroid budgeted $40 million to introduce its Spectra instant camera in 1986.

Mergers and Acquisitions   R. J. Reynolds moved to Number Three in expenditures in 1985 partly as a result of its merger with Nabisco Brands. Philip Morris Companies became Number Two after inheriting a $450 million budget from its acquisition of General Foods.

To Support Troubled Brands or Product Divisions   Warner Communications increased its advertising expenditures to provide support for its Atari division when videogames declined in popularity. S. C. Johnson, to regain lost market share, reformulated and repackaged Agree and increased advertising expenditures for this product by 73 percent.

To Provide Continuing Support Against Actual and Potential Competitors   The American Dairy Association became a "top 100" advertiser in 1985 and succeeded in increasing milk consumption by 3 percent. Procter & Gamble tried to maintain its competitive position by spending $236 million on advertising 15 laundry products, 7 bar soaps, and 5 dishwashing products.

To Encourage Trade to Maintain Product Inventory   Many products were hurt by reduced retailer inventory levels in response to recessionary fears in the early eighties. Revlon's strategy to counter this was to increase its advertising and merchandising support for many of its products at the retail level.

Advertising/Sales Relationships

Advertising budgets are frequently reported as a percentage of sales. Thus, General Motors achieved the rank of fifth largest advertiser in 1985 by expending a little less than one percent of its sales revenue on advertising, and E. I. du Pont deNemours was able to maintain its position as one of the 100 leaders in advertising with 0.6 percent of its sales devoted to advertising. On the other hand, Noxell Corporation (selling Cover Girl, Noxzema, and Lestoil) spent over 32 percent of its sales revenue on advertising. While such variations reflect the disparity in income, they also reflect the extent to which advertising is considered important in a marketing mix.

A recent study identified the facts that "explain" the variations in the percent of sales spent on advertising by various businesses.[14] The study incorporated both advertising and sales promotion expenditures for various industrial and consumer manufacturing businesses. The results indicated that, with few exceptions, the same characteristics of the product, the market, and the business unit's competitive position were significantly associated with the ratio of advertising and sales promotion to sales. According to this study, which was based on correlation and multiple regression analyses, the ratio of advertising and sales promotion to sales (A&P/S) is higher when:

the product is standardized, rather than produced to order;

there are many end-users (almost all households);

the typical purchase amount is small;

auxiliary services are of some importance;

sales are made through channel intermediaries rather than direct users;

the product is premium-priced (and probably premium quality);

the manufacturer has a high contribution margin per dollar of sales;

the manufacturer has a relatively small share of market and/or has surplus production capacity; or

a high proportion of the manufacturer's sales come from new products.

These characteristics are consistent with the products of the heavy advertisers—drugs, toiletries, cosmetics, and soaps. A&P/S ratios are typically low for capital goods such as power generating equipment, which is essentially produced to order, high in unit value, and sold direct to the user through a bidding process. A detailed discussion of how companies arrive at their advertising budgetary decisions appears in Chapter 6.

THE ADVERTISING PLAN

An important tool for managing and controlling the advertising effort is the preparation and promulgation of an *advertising plan,* a statement, usually in writing, about the advertising for a company and its products. Advertising plans serve as guides for decision making, provide direction for those who are to implement them, suggest how advertising can be coordinated with other activities, and provide control devices by specifying what results are expected and how these results will be measured.

Many persons participate in the preparation of the advertising plan,

---

[14]Paul W. Farris and Robert D. Buzzell, "Why Advertising and Promotional Costs Vary: Some Cross-Sectional Analyses," *Journal of Marketing,* Vol. 43 (Fall 1979), pp. 112–22.

FIGURE 4.8   Components of an Advertising Plan

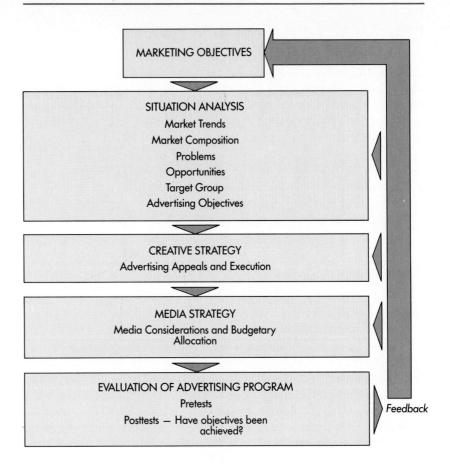

both in the client company and the advertising agency. Ordinarily, the executive responsible for managing the advertising activities within the company is also responsible for preparing the advertising plan. Normally this function is exercised by an advertising manager; however, in a growing number of instances this responsibility might rest with a product or brand manager, a marketing services manager, or a marketing director.

Typically the advertising plan is made on an annual basis and incorporates many of the components previously designated as part of the advertising management effort, such as the marketing objectives which, in turn, are translated into advertising objectives, advertising strategy, and techniques for controlling and evaluating the program (see Figure 4.8). The plan may be quite detailed, specifying the findings from situation analysis, the basis for the selecting of specific objectives, and the anticipated response of the target. It acts as a coordinating device and encourages consultation with other marketing departments to specify the other promotional efforts to be used. The advertising plan is particularly useful as a control device since advertising performance can be measured against specific objectives.

COORDINATION OF ADVERTISING WITH OTHER BUSINESS ACTIVITIES

In order to integrate advertising into the total business process, advertising decisions must be made in conjunction with, rather than separate from, other business decisions. Advertising is more than a short-run expenditure and possesses some characteristics of the manufacturer's capital outlay.

An able management has to proceed on the basis that advertising is inextricably intertwined *with all of the other elements of the business and marketing operation and that its decisions regarding advertising must be made in the light of a thorough understanding of those other elements and of the business, merchandising, and selling strategies to which it is committing the resources of the firm for the longer term.*[15]

The activities of advertising must be coordinated with all other activities of the firm, particularly among all promotional efforts. An advertising campaign should not work at cross purposes with the sales promotion activities designed to support it. Advertising should support a public relations effort designed to develop favorable public attitudes toward a company. Advertising can help secure leads for salespeople as well as help sell products, and good timing is essential for these programs to harmonize.

Wroe Alderson noted that it is useful to regard marketing processes as a flow of goods and a parallel flow of informative and persuasive messages.[16]

In these terms the design of communication facilities and channels becomes a major aspect of the creation of marketing systems. Marketing has yet to digest and apply the insights of the rapidly developing field of communication theory which in turn has drawn freely from both engineering and biological and social sciences.

Coordination between the promotion, production, and distribution departments also requires mutual planning. Advertising for a product that is behind in production schedules can become a serious waste.

---

[15]Neil H. Borden and Martin V. Marshall, *Advertising Management, Text and Cases* (New York: The Ronald Press Co., 1963), p. 4.

[16]Wroe Alderson, "The Analytical Framework for Marketing," in *Marketing and Its Environment: Some Issues and Perspectives,* Richard A. Scott and Norton E. Marks, eds. (Belmont, Calif.: Wadsworth Publishing Co., Inc., 1968), p. 21.

Moreover, in a recent national study of households, the Number One consumer complaint was that the store did not have the product it advertised for sale.[17]

More so than any other business activity, advertising uses services of agencies and groups external to the firm. Part of a company's advertising function may be performed by advertising agencies, media, production houses, and research houses, as well as institutions within its channel of distribution. This results in a fragmentation of the decision-making process, since it becomes dependent upon alternatives presented by external as well as internal organizational units. In order to cope with these multiple variables, several techniques have been developed to modify this complex decision-making procedure and select advertising strategies with the greatest probability of success. The creation of marketing information systems, the utilization of computer techniques, and the development of models are discussed in Chapter 6.

CONTROLS

Controls are devices ensuring that standards of performance set by management are met. They emanate from each of the components of advertising management, particularly from an organization structure and budgetary decisions. Furthermore, an advertising plan may specify methods for determining whether specific objectives were achieved and for applying such information as feedback in future analysis. For example, Standard Brands introduced into the market Smooth & Easy, a thickening agent which required only melting margarine and adding flour to make a thickened gravy. The flavored mixture was then formed into bars and refrigerated so that consumers could slice off as much as they needed, just like margarine. Despite an extensive advertising campaign, the product failed. While a number of factors were cited, one element in the failure was the inability of advertising to change consumers' attitudes that all commercial gravy is inferior and of little value. Exhibit 4.2 presents Standard Brand's postmortem, which diagnoses the advertising and promotion problems of Smooth & Easy, many of which relate to improper planning. These included the lack of precise marketing goals and a general agreement as to their desirability; the lack of assigning product managers at the initial stages of planning; and inadequate financial planning. The methods for determining whether the goals had been achieved were neither adequately prepared nor properly implemented. Furthermore, the plan was developed for a limited time period.

Increased efforts and new techniques are emerging for evaluating advertising effectiveness. These activities, which perform an important control function, are described in detail in Chapter 23.

---

[17]Marc A. Granier, Kathleen A. McEvoy, and Donald W. King, "Consumer Problems and Complaints: A National View," in *Advances in Consumer Research*, Vol. 6, ed. William L. Wilkie (Ann Arbor: Association for Consumer Research, 1979), p. 496.

Advertising Diagnostic
Problem: Preliminary Planning Inadequate
Why Avoidable:
— No product management assigned until after launch.
— Time constraints were judged more important than dollar efficiencies.
— Too heavy an involvement by general management in the marketing function.
— Marketing goals were imprecise and they did not have universal agreement.
— Lack of authoritative central control.
— Financial planning inadequate.

Problem: Too Much Money Spent on Introductory Advertising
Why Avoidable:
— There was a definite misunderstanding as to whether the project was a test market or not.
— Management misunderstanding of the lag-time involved in data collection for decision making.
— Inadequate media planning.
— Too heavy an involvement by management in line marketing functions.
— Inadequate financial planning.
— Lack of accountability.

Why Unavoidable:
— Volume significantly overestimated; research disregarded.

Problem: Inadequate Media Planning
Why Avoidable:
— Poor media mix selected with little investigation of cost-efficient alternatives.
— Too much reliance on newspaper.
— No trade advertising.
— Sunday supplements an afterthought.
— Radio not even considered in preliminary planning.
— Poorly defined brand positioning and copy strategy resulted in scatter buys.
— Little or no financial evaluations of media plans.

Problem: Ineffective Advertising
Why Unavoidable:
— Failure to recognize that this market has gone untapped for significant number of years and that consumers have ingrained a natural bias against commercial gravies which can not efficiently be overcome by advertising. This probably could not have been foreseen.

Problem: Brand Positioning and Copy Strategy Weak and Confused
Why Avoidable:
— Management involvement and disagreement—after we introduced the product major changes in the positioning were still being debated and implemented in a piece-meal fashion.

Promotion Diagnostic
Problem: Preliminary Planning Inadequate
Why Avoidable:
— No plans were developed beyond the four-month introductory period.
— The major fulcrum of promotion during introduction was the ability to communicate the product concept to consumers in-store via display shippers. The trade will not permit floor stands in the dairy aisle.
— Point of sale materials were not checked against actual field conditions before they were put into mass production.

Problem: Investment Excessive
Why Avoidable:
— No attempt to organize data on basis of what was affordable.
Why Unavoidable:
— Demands for merchandising pieces was great. Delivery became paramount.

Problem: Coupon Investment Ineffective
Why Unavoidable:
— Preliminary consumer predisposition unknown.

EXHIBIT 4.2
A Diagnosis of Smooth & Easy's Advertising and Promotion Problems

From "Smooth & Easy Brand's Short Life Was Anything But" by Nancy Giges, *Advertising Age* (September 10, 1979), p. 33. Copyright © 1979 Crain Communications, Inc. Reprinted with permission from Advertising Age.

SUMMARY

Effective management of advertising encompasses a number of steps. In organizing the advertising effort, two basic approaches may be used: the centralized method or the decentralized one. A centralized advertising department may decrease the need for an extensive staff of personnel and provide for an easier flow of communications within the firm. The decentralized unit permits advertising to be geared more easily to specific needs of the product or division and provides more opportunity for innovation. It tends, however, to generate rivalry and excessive secrecy which may be detrimental to the firm.

A corporate advertising department may be included in the organizational structure to coordinate the advertising effort and secure compliance from the decentralized advertising units. The corporate department also exerts control over the final advertising budget.

The product management organization is a decentralized structure which shifts the advertising responsibility from the advertising manager to the product or brand manager. It offers concentrated managerial attention to each product; frequently, however, product managers are responsible for minor rather than major advertising decisions.

The strategic organization replaces the emphasis on product management with that of strategic management. This structure is designed to emphasize the long-term needs of advertising and focuses on the total organization rather than on a particular product or division.

The advertising planning process involves a series of interrelated steps. A major decision faced by firms is how much to spend on advertising. Such expenditures vary widely among organizations; these variations are sometimes associated with the firm's market, product, or competitive position.

An important tool for managing advertising and establishing controls is the advertising plan which is a written statement about the advertising for a company and its products. The advertising effort should be coordinated with the firm's other business activities and requires control mechanisms. Such controls may emanate from the organization structure, the budgetary determination and planning procedures, and an evaluation of advertising effectiveness.

QUESTIONS FOR DISCUSSION

1. Which organization structure (centralized or decentralized) do you believe is more efficient for advertising? Why?
2. What are the functions of a corporate advertising department?
3. Discuss the corporate advertising objectives you consider most important.
4. What are the benefits and disadvantages of the product manager organization?
5. How is the product manager organization related to the performance of advertising function?
6. How may advertising decisions differ in a strategic organization from the traditional organizational structure?
7. What characteristics of the product or market are associated with heavy advertising expenditures?
8. What is the purpose of an advertising plan and what kinds of information should it contain?
9. Describe some business activities which require coordination with advertising efforts.
10. What are some of the sources of control for the advertising program?

KEY TERMS

centralization	brand manager
decentralization	corporate advertising campaign
product management	advertising plan
strategic planning	controls

AD PRACTICE

Visit a local firm and find out how its advertising organization is structured. Evaluate the organization structure and indicate the changes you would make. Specify the control mechanisms you would establish.

5

The Advertising Agency

In the late 1940s Texize, a local company that made industrial cleaning products, was approached by the owner of Henderson Advertising who suggested that Texize package its liquid cleaner in small containers and sell it to consumers. Today, Texize, as the household product division of Morton-Norwich, Chicago, has annual sales of more than $165,000,000, and successful products such as Fantastik, Glass Plus, and Spray'N'Wash. Henderson Advertising, in 1981, was selected as the Agency of the Year by *Advertising Age* for its new product development work and its contribution to the growth and success of its major clients, notably Texize.

Present-day advertisers may use an agency for its diversified background, a corps of specialists, and the discount the agency receives from media. Because a firm is limited by its own experience and knowledge of its particular product, an agency can bring a diverse background and knowledge of the markets, media, and advertising strategies. Moreover, an agency can bring an important trait to the client and its advertising—objectivity.

ADVERTISING AGENCY ORGANIZATION

To more effectively perform its advertising function a firm may employ the services of an *advertising agency,* an organization of business and creative people dedicated to making advertising succeed.[1] There are some 8000 advertising agencies in the United States, varying in size from a one-person agency with few accounts to an agency with several hundred accounts and several thousand employees in offices all over the world. Most are small businesses.

Less than 500 advertising agencies belong to a trade association called the American Association of Advertising Agencies (the 4 A's), and about half of these are considered small. However, this group conducts approximately 70 percent of advertising agency business in terms of dollar volume in the United States. The 4 A's provide services for its agency members, cooperates with other advertising groups, and offers educational services in many areas.

Agency size is usually described in terms of *billings*—the amount of the clients' money the agency spends on media and related advertising activities. Recently, the focus has been on a more appropriate designation—*gross income,* the amount of the clients' funds the agency receives for its services (generally about 15 percent of billings). Table 5.1 shows the estimated billings for the ten largest advertising agencies based on 1986 billings.

TABLE 5.1 Top Ten Agencies in World Billings

Rank	Agency	Worldwide Billings	
		1986	1985
1	Young & Rubicam	$4,191.4	$3,575.3
2	Saatchi & Saatchi Compton Worldwide	3,320.0	3,033.1
3	Ted Bates Worldwide	3,261.8	3,106.9
4	BBDO Worldwide	3,259.0	2,894.7
5	Ogilvy & Mather Worldwide	3,154.6	2,752.1
6	J. Walter Thompson Co.	3,141.5	2,899.1
7	McCann-Erickson Worldwide	2,852.7	2,464.6
8	DDB Needham Worldwide	2,557.5	2,512.9
9	D'Arcy Masius Benton & Bowles	2,258.6	2,229.5
10	Foote, Cone & Belding Communications	2,154.5	1,900.7

NOTE: Dollars are in millions.

Source: From "Agencies Gain 11.5%, Overseas Income Surges 19.2%" by R. Craig Endicott, *Advertising Age* (March 26, 1987). Copyright © 1987 by Crain Communications, Inc. Reprinted with permission from Advertising Age. All rights reserved.

---

[1]"What Advertising Agencies Are, What They Do, and How They Do It," (New York: American Association of Advertising Agencies, Inc., 1976), p. 8.

FIGURE 5.1   The Organization of a Small Agency

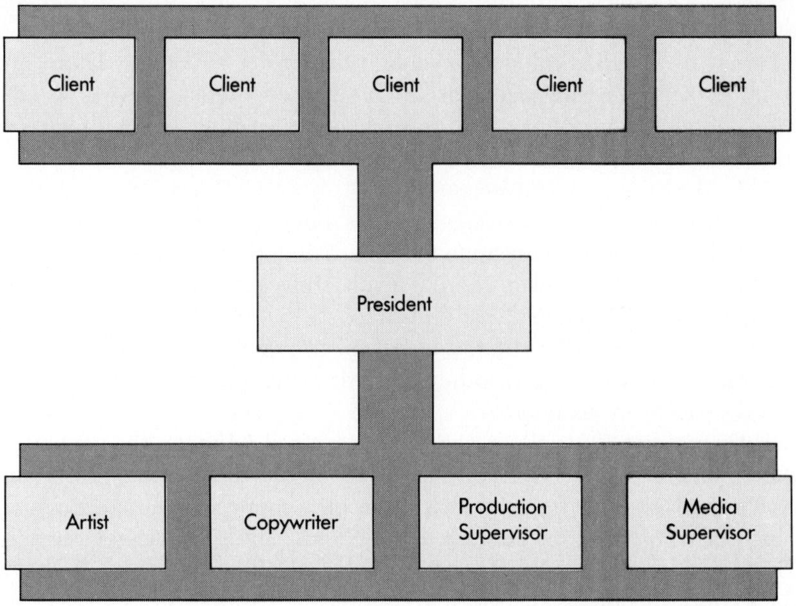

The structure of agency organization is a function of its size. A small agency may consist of three or four specialists reporting to the president, who, in turn, reports to all client companies. (Figure 5.1 presents such an organization.) The large agency, which provides many specialized services, frequently adopts an organizational structure by department or group. Some agencies combine the two structures for greater efficiency.

Organization by Department

The departmentalized or concentric agency, is divided by function rather than by client. The media department, writing department, and TV production department serves every client (see Figure 5.2).

Organization by Group

In a group agency, people are organized to handle the contact, planning, and creative work for one or more clients or products. There are centralized research, media, and print production departments, and a general planning board.

Figure 5.3 presents the organization chart for three major clients in a large advertising agency. The management supervisor has the prime

FIGURE 5.2 Advertising Agency Organization by Department

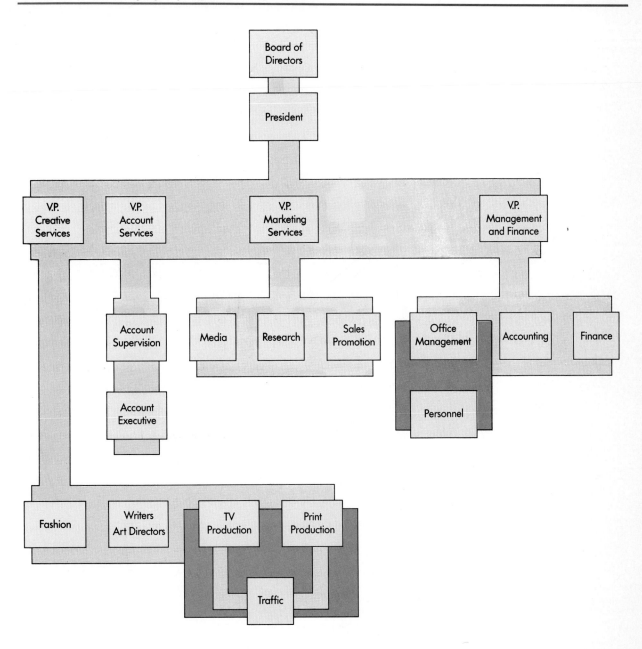

responsibility for these three accounts. Several account executives (also called account supervisors or account representatives) are assigned to help manage these accounts; in addition, a group of specialists is given the direct responsibility for servicing these specific clients.

FIGURE 5.3 Advertising Agency Organization by Group

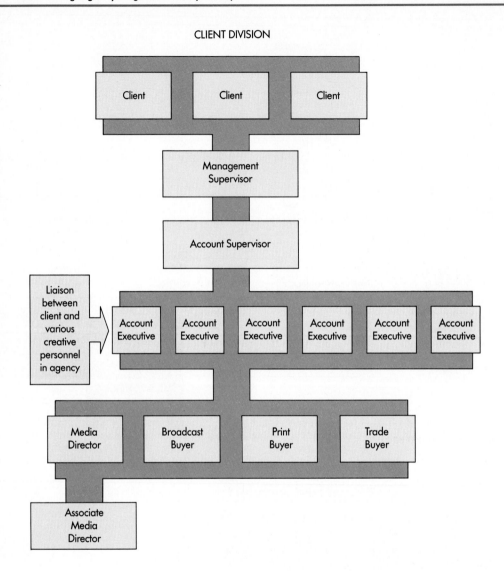

CLIENT DIVISION

KINDS OF AGENCIES AND THEIR FUNCTIONS

Advertising management is considered a shared responsibility between an advertiser and an agency. While planning, execution, and control may be shared, obviously the agency bears the major responsibility for developing, preparing, and placing advertising for sellers in advertising media.

As described in Chapter 2, the advertising agency evolved from merely a buyer of media space to a provider of many diverse services for its clients. However, in recent years, agencies have experimented with providing only specialized services for some clients, resulting in the emergence in the 1960s of "boutiques" of creative specialists, the development of independent media buying services, and the increased use of in-house agencies.

Full-Service Agency

The *full-service agency* performs a complete range of services for the advertiser. In addition to offering all research, creative, and media services, the full-service agency often becomes involved in the advertiser's marketing process. For example, an agency may provide package design, publicity, sales promotion, dealer aids, sales meeting assistance, product testing, sales forecasting, and advice on distribution and marketing strategy.

The benefits of a full-service agency include attracting and holding the very best talent, providing numerous services which may require an interrelated approach, and providing an objective examination of concepts from an outside perspective based on widespread experience. Despite the emergence of other types of agencies, it is estimated that the major proportion of national advertising media dollars are spent by advertisers who use full-service agencies.

The extent of services offered by an agency generally depends on its size and the way it is organized; it also depends on the people who make up the agency. However, most full-service agencies perform the following functions.

Planning   The most important function in agency operation is the development of an advertising plan, usually prepared in conjunction with the client company. The advertising plan is viewed as part of the overall marketing plan. An essential part of planning is budgeting, and the agency usually provides alternative budget proposals to help the client determine how much should be spent on advertising.

Research   Even prior to the formulation of the plan, an agency must do some research. The scope of research has expanded so much that, in recent years, independent specialized research organizations have been created to meet the expanded needs of both marketing and advertising research.

Creative Services   One of the earliest additions to the responsibilities of the advertising space salesperson was the writing of copy. Today copywriters frequently work in conjunction with artists in the preparation of print advertising, and copywriters, art directors, and broadcast producers usually combine their efforts in the preparation of broadcast selling messages.

Print and Broadcast Production   Print production people are responsible for converting artwork and copy into printing plates used to produce finished advertisements. Proofs of advertisements are submitted for approval to clients before final printing plates are made. Print production workers must maintain contacts with printers, typographers, typesetters, and photoengravers.

In the early days of television, broadcast productions were prepared by the advertising agency; today, shows are more frequently purchased from networks, broadcasting stations, or independent show producers. However, agency men and women still do the creative work on both radio and television commercials. They prepare the storyboards and choose (and even design) props, costumes, and scenery. The actual mechanical production of the commercial may be done by an outside producer under the supervision of an agency TV producer.

Media Selection   One of the areas where the expertise of an advertising agency may be a necessity is in media selection. Media choice involves a knowledge of each medium's characteristics and its coverage, as well as an understanding of the target market to be reached. An agency must select what it considers to be the best medium, must contact the various media, execute the contracts, and pay media bills. As an aid in the media selection process a number of advertising agencies have applied computer techniques to the creation of media models.

Traffic Control   A vital internal function of the advertising agency, particularly as it grows in size, is traffic control. It is the responsibility of traffic to see that copy, artwork, commercials, plates, and other materials for production are prepared on schedule, that client and legal approvals have been obtained, and that final material is issued to reach each medium on or before deadline. Traffic is a coordinating, as well as a control, function; it assures that the activities of the various departments are accurately intertwined.

Account Management   Since the advertising agency is an organizational unit external to the firm, some continuing and close contact must be established to promote communication and understanding between the client and agency. The advertising agency establishes a contact person to maintain this liaison. In the small agency this function may be performed by the president; the account executive performs as liaison in a larger agency, and, in some cases, there may be an account group consisting of several account executives headed by an account supervisor. The contact person must know the functions and activities of both the agency and client and must be able to interpret these satisfactorily to both organizations.

Accounting   Although accounting is of prime importance to all businesses, it has added significance to an agency. Since the agency is responsible for payment to media, it becomes particularly important to keep accurate accounts of billing, to check the appearance of advertisements, and to maintain records of payments.

New Business   Generally, a well-managed advertising agency budgets a minimum of 2 percent of its income for new business promotion, since the average tenure of accounts is approximately four to eight years. To secure new business to replace the normal mortality, some agencies hire contact people; others engage in agency "house" advertising, advertising designed to sell the agency's services to prospective clients.

Other Services   In order to provide a total marketing concept, agencies become more involved in promotional activities that are not strictly advertising. The extent of services required by clients varies; producers of consumer goods tend to place greater emphasis than industrial goods producers upon the range of an agency's service in the selection process.[2] Some agencies provide merchandising for their clients; that is, they create sales-promotional material, aid in dealer-cooperative advertising campaigns, execute point-of-purchase displays, and help develop contests. They may also offer expertise in public relations, usually on a fee basis and as an activity somewhat separate from their advertising. Some larger agencies may go beyond promotion and provide such services as sales forecasting, new product planning, and package development.

À La Carte Services

Some advertisers prefer to order *à la carte*, rather than using all of an agency's services. À la carte services can be purchased from a full-service agency or from an individual firm that specializes only in creative work, media, production, research, publicity, or new product development. The two requirements most frequently obtained à la carte are creative and media services.

A *boutique* is typically a service agency used as a creative consultant, specializing in concepts, strategy development, and execution. Some advertisers employ a boutique to revitalize a tired advertising campaign or to provide services in specialized media and product categories.

A *media buying service* works with an advertiser to provide a media plan, offer counseling in the development of the advertiser's plan, or provide specialized knowledge of media and usage rates. Firms that prepare their own advertising frequently find the complexities of media purchase require the services of a professional.

À la carte services may provide the advertiser with faster response, more objectivity, and more direct communication which may lead to better results. However, the responsibility for planning and managing the advertising remains with the advertiser.

The House Agency

The *house agency* is an advertising agency established by an advertiser. This differs from an advertiser merely handling his or her own advertising since a house agency may receive recognition from media and be

---

2James W. Cagley and C. Richard Roberts, "Criteria for Advertising Agency Selection: An Objective Appraisal," *Journal of Advertising Research*, Vol. 24 (April/May, 1984), pp. 27-31.

FIGURE 5.4   How $200,000,000 Is Spent by Ralston-Purina

	VAN CAMP SEAFOOD	GROCERY PRODUCTS			CHECKERBOARD FARMS
	Tuna	Cereal Ry-Krisp	Dog Foods	Cat Foods	
FULL SERVICE AGENCIES	N.W. Ayer	D'arcy, McManus & Masius McDonald & Little N.W. Ayer Wells, Rich & Greene, Inc.	Della Femina Travisano & Partners Gardner McDonald & Little N.W. Ayer Wells, Rich & Greene, Inc.	Della Femina Travisano & Partners McDonald & Little Wells, Rich & Greene, Inc.	
MODULAR OR PARTIAL SERVICES		Advanswers	Advanswers	Advanswers Avrett, Free & Fisher	
IN-HOUSE AGENCY	Checker-board Advertising Company	Checker-board Advertising Company	Checker-board Advertising Company	Checker-board Advertising Company	Checker-board Advertising Company
AGENCIES ON PROJECTS			Foote, Cone & Belding	Foote, Cone & Belding Doyle, Dane & Bernbach	

entitled to the 15-percent agency discount, which may not be available to an individual handling his or her own advertising.

An in-house organization can perform the narrowest of specialized functions or provide marketing services greater than those of the fullest of full-service agencies. Furthermore, the house agency need not be the only source of advertising services for the sponsoring company; it may also use the services of full-service agencies as well as à la carte services.

Some companies that use independent advertising agencies may establish an in-house agency for coordinating functions. Ralston-Purina uses twelve advertising agencies, but also has a house agency called Checkerboard Advertising. Although the house agency can do creative and media services for some products, it is designed to coordinate the services of its individual advertising agencies (see Figure 5.4).

FIGURE 5.4   How $200,000,000 Is Spent by Ralston-Purina (continued)

AGRI PRODUCTS		NEW VENTURES		KEYSTONE INTERNATIONAL	RESTAURANT GROUP	INTERNATIONAL GROUP
Health Products	Chow Division	Mushrooms	St. Louis Blues		Jack-in-the-Box	
	Gardner				Wells, Rich & Greene, Inc.	
Advanswers		Vinyard & Lee & Partners	Vinyard & Lee & Partners	Heckler Bowker		
Checkerboard Advertising Company	Checkerboard Advertising Company	Checkerboard Advertising Company	Checkerboard Advertising Company	Checkerboard Advertising Company	Checkerboard Advertising Company	RPI Marketing

Source: From "Advertising Services: Full-Service Agency, Á La Carte, or In-House," Association of National Advertisers, Inc., 1979, p. 48. Copyright © 1979 by Association of National Advertisers, Inc. Reprinted by permission.

It would be reasonable to assume that a primary objective for using a house agency is saving money; however, this is not necessarily true. While most media will provide a house agency with the 15-percent discount, the amount of cost savings a house agency secures depends to some extent on the size of its budget. Also, there are significant expenses in running such a department and therefore, although the resulting costs may be lower, the savings are not necessarily large.

Although cost considerations enter into the decision, convenience and creativity appear to be of equal significance. Since the lines of communication are shorter, company managers may work more closely with the creative staff. Furthermore, despite the tendency to make generalizations about in-house talent, some house agencies have reported that their employees are as creative as those in outside advertising agencies.

A serious drawback to a house agency is the apparent loss of objectivity and specialized talent a large agency has available. Perhaps it is for these reasons that the house agency has not made serious inroads into the independent agency's growth.[3] Procter & Gamble, that employs the services of twelve independent agencies, has considered establishing a house agency, but has not yet done so.

HOW AN ADVERTISER SELECTS AN AGENCY

The selection of an advertising agency is a difficult and challenging process. Although an advertiser may have many agencies to choose from, competitive corporate accounts or actual product conflicts may preclude consideration of one or more of these agencies. Other agencies may have neither the particular philosophy nor the expertise to service the needs of a specific account. Furthermore, the size of the advertiser's account may inhibit acceptance by an agency that has established a minimum billings requirement.

Secondly, even though agencies generally have new business units designed to attract new accounts, surprisingly, many advertising agencies do not have advertising campaigns to promote themselves. They argue that they are "too busy" or such advertising "isn't effective."[4] The agencies that do advertise consider it useful (see Exhibit 5.1).

Thirdly, many successful or highly visible campaigns are never identified as the work of a specific advertising agency. Needham Harper & Steers advertising agency introduced a campaign, now a classic, using the theme of "high profile advertising."[5] One of its ads illustrated the "It's a miracle" frame from the company's famous Xerox commercial with the duplicating monks in a monastery. The headline for the ad read, "This commercial ran just 17 times."

The Selection Process

The first step in the selection process, after the initial limiting factors of conflict, expertise, philosophies have been considered, involves listing the available potential candidates. Then these agencies are screened by means of a questionnaire, which has become almost standard practice among large advertisers.

To permit an agency to answer a questionnaire intelligently, the advertiser should supply an account profile for its product. This profile serves the dual purpose of permitting the agency to respond more accurately to the questions and providing the agency with information which will allow it to make its own preliminary screening of the pro-

---

[3]"Advertising Services, . . . ," p. 7.
[4]"Why Agencies Don't Advertise," *Advertising Age* (November 19, 1979), p. 51.
[5]Philip H. Dougherty, "Advertising, Needham Division's New Head," *New York Times* (September 10, 1980).

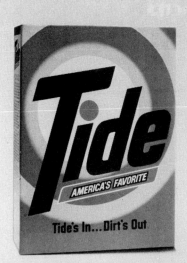

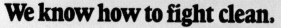

EXHIBIT 5.1
Ads Promoting Advertising Agencies

spective account and its suitability for inclusion in the agency roster. An account profile should contain such information as the product's history, competition, description, benefits, target group, proposed advertising budget, and required agency services.

The Speculative Presentation

Occasionally an advertiser may require, as part of the screening process, the preparation of a speculative presentation, particularly when a radical departure from the advertiser's current approach is contemplated. If an advertiser requires such an agency presentation he or she will, most likely, be required to subsidize its costs in agency time and talent. If not, the agency that is not chosen to represent the advertiser will be providing the client with creative ideas and talent free. The screening and presentation also may include a discussion of methods of compensation that will be helpful for the advertiser in arriving at a decision.

Once the decision is made, a letter of agreement is drawn up; when this document is approved by the advertiser, it becomes the binding contract for the advertiser-agency relationship. Letters of agreement vary from agency to agency, but generally they include the duties of the agency, the methods of payment, the procedures for billing, the limitations concerning the handling of competitive accounts, and the termination procedures, which generally require written notice ninety days before.

METHODS OF COMPENSATING
ADVERTISING AGENCIES

The compensation arrangement between an advertiser and its agency is a matter of negotiation and agreement. Some agencies may insist on only one type of arrangement; however, many have different kinds of arrangements with different clients, and sometimes different arrangements may be made with the same client on different accounts. Typically, compensation arrangements are based on commission, fee, or some combination of these. Table 5.2 identifies eight principal compensation methods used by almost 99 percent of the 4 A's clients.[6]

Media commissions, which deduct 15 percent of the media cost to pay the agency, are the largest ingredient in agency compensation, although their importance varies with the size of the agency. Large agencies with larger accounts use a great amount of space and time and tend to have more of their income in media commissions; smaller agencies tend more toward fees; however, in recent years, there has been a shift to the fee method even for large agencies. Nevertheless the traditional 15-percent media commission plan remains the most popular method of compensating advertising agencies for their services. There is a continuing movement toward arrangements that are combinations of commission and fees, or that are strictly fee.

The reasons most frequently cited for changes in compensation arrangements are more clearly defined assignments, requiring a new compensation basis better attuned to the new situation; or a desire on the part of the advertiser or the agency to bring about a more equitable price/value relationship.[7]

How Compensation Is Computed

When the agency and advertiser agree on the compensation method, they must also agree on the manner in which it is computed. There are several different methods that can be used.

Media Commission Method

The commission method of compensation evolved historically from the initial use of space salesmen who were engaged primarily in the sale of advertising space to advertisers. Since media generally allocated 15 percent of the gross space charge as a commission to the space salesman for his services, this fixed percentage of media cost ultimately became the traditional method for compensating advertising agencies. Thus, while a variety of methods may be used for agency compensation, they generally acknowledge this commission. In fact, a 15-percent commission is incorporated in the media rate cards which quote gross rates (that is, including the commission).

---

[6]"Advertising Agencies, . . . ," p. 22.

[7]"Survey shows advertisers quitting traditional commission structure," *Marketing News* (June 20, 1986), p. 13.

TABLE 5.2   Compensation Arrangements Between Advertisers and Agencies

Commission Method

1. Media commissions only
2. Media commissions plus charges for materials and services purchased for clients, but no charges for any inside services
3. Media commissions plus charges for materials and services purchased for clients, plus charges for some specified inside services

Fee Method

4. A minimum fee, against which media commissions are credited
5. An overall fee, agreed upon in advance
6. The overall cost of handling the entire account, or cost plus fee calculated after the work is done

Combination Method

7. Arrangements 1, 2, or 3 above (media commission methods) plus an overall additional fee
8. Arrangements 1, 2, or 3 above with a profit floor and a profit ceiling
   a. If profits fall below the guaranteed minimum, the client makes up the difference
   b. If profits fall between the minimum-maximum range, no adjustments are made
   c. If profits exceed the maximum, agency refunds amount agreed upon

Source: "Advertising Agencies, What They Are, What They Do, and How They Do It." Copyright © 1976 by American Association of Advertising Agencies. Reprinted by permission.

Under the media commission method an advertiser is billed by the agency at current media gross rates on all advertising placed by the agency in commissionable media. The media then bill the agency at these same rates, less 15 percent (except for outdoor advertising where the commission is 16⅔ percent) and the difference is retained by the agency. Generally a 2-percent discount is offered by media for prompt payment of bills. If the client pays his bills promptly to the agency, this 2 percent is then reduced from his net media cost.

For example, an agency may place a full-page advertisement for a client in a magazine whose gross rate for that space is $10,000. The agency will bill its client $10,000, and, when payment is due, pay the magazine $8500, retaining $1500 for its services. If the client has made prompt payment he or she is entitled to a 2-percent cash discount, so that the client pays $8330 (or $8500 less $170) for the medium plus $1500 for the agency's commission, for a total payment of $9830.

	Client's Payment	**Recipients**	
		Media	Agency
Space Cost	$10,000	$8500	$1500
Cash Discount (2% of $8500)	−170	−170	
TOTAL	$ 9830	$8330	$1500

Collateral Services Commission

The advertising agency frequently does not charge for writing copy and preparing art in connection with commissionable advertising. However, there are a number of other internal and external services the agency may perform. Collateral services performed internally, such as direct mail, point-of-purchase material, and sales promotion material may be charged as cost, or as out-of-pocket cost plus 17.65-percent commission, selected to be equivalent to the 15-percent media commission. Media rates are quoted with the agency commission included (gross card rate); for example, if the gross card rate is $10,000, the media commission is 15 percent or $1500. However, collateral services are billed at net (that is, no agency commission is included), and to equate the 15-percent commission of gross billings to a similar amount on net billings, the percentage must be raised to 17.65.

Actual Net Payment to Media	$8500
Commission Received	1500
Commission as a Percent of Net Payment to Media	$\dfrac{1500}{8500} = 17.65$

The agency charges cost plus 17.65 percent on external work such as printing, platemaking, photography, and external artwork. In addition, marketing research, public relations or publicity, new product research, trade show exhibits, and creation and preparation of package design, whether performed internally or externally, are generally billed at agency cost plus commission.

The following is an example of payment incorporating both media cost and a 17.65-percent charge for preparing the plate for an advertisement.

	Client's Payment	Recipients		
		Media	Agency	Photoengraver
Space Cost	$10,000	$8330	$1500	
Media Cash Discount	−170			
Plate Cost	+2,000			$2000
Service Charge to Agency (17.65% of $2000)	+ 353		+ 353	
		8330	1853	2000
TOTAL	$12,183		$12,183	

Fee Method

One method for establishing a fee for a client or a specific advertising campaign incorporates an estimate of direct costs, overhead, and profit. The *direct costs* are the salaries of personnel directly involved in the

TABLE 5.3   Compensation Proposal Work Sheet

Client _____		Date_____	
Direct Services	**$**	**Summary**	
Account Service		Account Service	$153,300
1 Management		Creative Service	57,500
supervisor —40%	16,000	Print Production	11,250
2 Account supervisors		Broadcast Production	13,750
1 @ 50%, 1 @ 100%	41,300	Media	38,000
6 Account executives		Research	0
6 @ 100% each	96,000	Public Relations	0
TOTAL	153,300	Total Direct Time	273,800
		Overhead 90%	246,420
Creative Service		Total Direct Cost	520,220
1 CD —15%	6,000	Profit Factor 25%	130,055
1 Group supervisor —60%	16,500	TOTAL COMPENSATION	$650,275
1 Writer/Artist			
1 @ 100%, 1 @ 75%	35,000		
TOTAL	57,500		
Print Production			
1 Production service —5%	1,250		
1 Production manager	10,000		
TOTAL	11,250		
Broadcast Production			
1 Production service —15%	3,750		
1 Production			
manager —50%	10,000		
TOTAL	13,750		
Media			
1 Media director —15%	4,000		
1 Media planner —80%	16,000		
2 Buyers —2 @ 60% each	18,000		
TOTAL	38,000		
Research	0		
Public Relations	0		

These are 1975 figures.

advertiser's service. *Overhead* not only includes rent, depreciation, and utilities, but also the salaries of other personnel, such as accountants, managers, and traffic people, not directly involved in the services of the client. Overhead costs may be estimated as a percentage of direct costs; often this is 90–100 percent. Frequently agencies use a profit target of 20–25 percent of agency income.

Table 5.3 presents a compensation proposal for a client using the fee system. While the costs are estimates, the work sheet indicates how they are determined.

THE DIFFERENT SIDES OF PAYMENT

FOR THE COMMISSION METHOD
— Results in greater agency income than would be forthcoming from direct negotiations with advertisers. This extra income permits activities over and above the immediate needs of individual advertisers, activities that are for the long-run good of advertisers and media owners.
— Provides funds necessary to develop and expand an agency's overall skills, so that its services become increasingly valuable to clients.
— Eliminates the need for bargaining and saves the time of important executives who would otherwise be continually negotiating fees.
— Has proved itself through years of practice; it works and is simple.
— Helps small advertisers either by making available to them the services of large agencies that they could not otherwise afford or by enabling small agencies to exist and serve them.
— Eliminates (a) the need for, and thus the time and expense involved in, detailed costing of agency operations and (b) arguments about the time devoted to jobs. Creative personnel dislike keeping records of time devoted to different activities or assignments; and, therefore, their reports may be unreliable.

AGAINST THE COMMISSION METHOD
— Encourages agency recommendations not always in the best interest of clients. Agencies may be influenced, consciously or unconsciously, to recommend high-rate, commissionable media rather than low-rate and non-commissionable media.
— Provides compensation not necessarily related to service rendered; neglects effectiveness of advertising as a measure of effectiveness of agency's efforts; is illogical because cost of space and time, the base for commission, may have no relationship to quality of advertising produced; rewards agency on basis of *how much* rather than *how well* money is spent.
— May bear little or no relationship to costs involved in servicing clients.
— Keeps weak agencies in existence.
— Is founded on the myth that agencies still serve media.

FOR THE FEE METHOD
— Brings compensation into line with quantity and quality of service. The more creative the agency talent, the greater its income. Good agencies get stronger and poor agencies weaker.
— Makes most sense for most industrial accounts. Since media commissions are very often inadequate to cover the costs of basic services, they serve no useful purpose.
— Provides better psychological climate for client and agency to work in.
— Leads to more careful control of personnel time.
— Is professional; fees are paid in accordance with skill provided.

AGAINST THE FEE METHOD
— Involves too much difficulty and time in arriving at adequate fee.
— If fee is on a time basis, makes for continual argument about the time necessary to complete a job, particularly in creative aspects.
— Leads to price cutting and poorer quality of advertising and thus damage to the entire advertising structure.
— Makes clients less receptive to new ideas since they feel the cost directly; if the cost is hidden in the media commission they are more receptive.

Source: Albert W. Farley and Kenneth R. Davis *The Advertising Industry* (New York: Association of National Advertisers, 1958), pp. 211–13.

Compensation Problems

Over the years questions have been raised about the equity and reasonableness of the commission method of compensation. The chief complaint has been that an agency appears to be reimbursed not for the quality of its efforts but rather on the basis of the amount of advertising time and space that is bought. This appears to lead to the unacceptable premise that the agency would encourage its clients to place more advertising in media, not because such placement is beneficial to the client, but because it will assure the agency of additional income. This suggestion is generally dismissed as untenable, since, in addition to being unethical, such an agency practice could be no less than self-defeating in the long run. Nonetheless, there is still some question in the minds of the advertising industry about the merit of a practice which appears to provide compensation for something other than the success or quality of the efforts put forth.

In addition to the question of equitable compensation, the standard media commission system has raised legal questions, particularly in relation to the apparent tendency to fix prices at 15 percent of media cost. In recent years there has been a movement toward negotiated commissions; that is, a client negotiates with an agency to reduce the 15-percent charge. Some agencies refuse to negotiate. Leo Burnett, for example, has retained both its 15-percent commission and many of its clients, such as Allstate Insurance Company who has been with the agency almost thirty years.[8]

COORDINATING ADVERTISER-AGENCY ACTIVITIES

Advertisers and their agencies operate in a close relationship, frequently designated as a partnership. However, numerous opportunities exist for dissatisfaction and friction to arise between the parties. To avoid some potential problems requires effective coordination of advertiser-agency activities.

Basic Principles of Agency-Client Relationship

Several basic principles in agency-client relations have been established by custom and trial and error.[9] Usually an agency will not handle a direct competitor without a client's consent. In turn, the client generally agrees not to engage a second agency to handle part of the advertising for the same product or service without the agency's consent. Next, an agency must secure a client's approval on all advertising expenditures. Finally, a client is to pay an agency before it has to pay the media. The agency usually agrees to give the client all media cash discounts, when the client has earned them by paying promptly.

---

[8]Leo Burnett, "A Folksy Ad Agency Goes on the Offensive," *Business Week* (August 5, 1985), p. 82.
[9]"Advertising Agencies, What They Are . . . ," p. 23.

Causes of Agency-Client Switching

Despite the reputation of instability in the advertiser-agency relationship and reports of frequent shifts between agencies and clients, there are some agencies that have maintained clients for a particularly long time. AT&T has been with J. Walter Thompson Co. since 1902; Lever Bros. with N. W. Ayer since 1908; Hammermill Paper with BBDO since 1912; and Armstrong Cork with BBDO since 1917.[10]

Nevertheless, there is a significant amount of turnover; one of the most important reasons is the ease with which switching can be accomplished. The letter of agreement generally states that a contract can be terminated by 90 days prior written notice. Termination appears to be one of the easiest decisions a marketing manager may implement and one which he most certainly turns to in times of declining sales volume or financial difficulty. Frequently a new marketing executive may decide it's time for a "clean sweep."

Evaluating Agency Performance

There is increasing awareness, particularly among large advertisers, that it is necessary to periodically evaluate an agency's performance.[11] This is due to several factors: more advertisers have multiagency relationships, they can get the traditional agency services through competitive services or can handle them themselves, and more brand and marketing executives are responsible for advertising decisions, particularly in multiproduct companies. An evaluation based on an agency's achievement of market share, quality of work, meeting of deadlines, availability of personnel, and ability to react quickly may lead to a clearer understanding of both agency operations and advertiser needs. Problem areas can be resolved before they become unmanageable, and wasteful activity can be identified and controlled. Moreover, by identifying the agency's strengths and weaknesses, there is an opportunity to capitalize on the former and "shore up" the latter.

THE FUTURE OF ADVERTISING AGENCIES

Predicting the future of advertising agencies is like all such efforts—extremely difficult. However, a number of recent changes can be noted that may suggest future directions.

Financial considerations will be of increasing importance to agencies. Many agencies have been experiencing financial problems emerging from inefficient cash flow because of the lag between the presentation of an invoice to an agency's client and the time of payment. This situation has been increasing.

[10]Darroll Swan, "Swan's Song," *Marketing & Media Decisions* (June 1980), p. 208.

[11]"Evaluating Agency Performance," (New York: Association of National Advertisers, 1979).

There are indications that the fee system of compensation will be used with increasing frequency. First, as advertising costs increase, marketers are tending to move away from the "umbrella" concept where the various regions in which they sell are provided with roughly equal amounts of advertising. They are moving toward a market-by-market approach which may cause a greater shift to the fee system. Under the commission system, some agencies are reluctant to provide individual advertising schedules for each area, since its cost may not be recovered through commissions alone. Second, the merger movement which has become fairly widespread in the agency world requires competent financial management. In addition to mergers, international expansion, computerization, personnel incentives, and profit sharing all require accurate internal cost accounting, which can be achieved more easily through the fee method than via the commission system.

There are also efforts to eliminate the restrictions against agencies handling competing accounts, but these appear to be slow in taking hold. In the past, an agency handling even one product for a client was prohibited from representing any other product that competed with even part of the client's line. Today's restrictions generally relate to directly competing products, although there may also be objections if the conflict is less direct. These prohibitions become more difficult to impose as clients diversify, and with the prevalence of mergers in both the advertising and corporate worlds, the potential for client conflict has increased extensively. R. J. Reynolds' acquisition of Nabisco and Philip Morris' acquisition of General Foods create conflicts within a number of agencies previously serviced by these companies.

To prove to potential clients that they can handle competing products, agencies have been organizing themselves like corporations with competing and fairly autonomous divisions. Interpublic, for example, is a large agency with four agency subsidiaries which tends to reduce the conflict in handling competing accounts.

The megamerger movement among advertising agencies has created even greater potential for client conflict, and some major advertisers, such as Procter & Gamble, have resigned their accounts with merged agencies. There are indications that agencies will continue to grow and expand. In part, this is in response to the needs of global marketers who are looking for agencies who can accommodate their worldwide efforts. Nevertheless, opportunities will exist for small agencies with entrepreneurial spirit to enter the business and handle the smaller client who may feel ignored. In the last analysis it seems the agencies that will survive and prosper are those which are most responsive to their client's needs.

SUMMARY

Many of today's advertisers find the services of an advertising agency desirable because of its broad and diversified background, its expertise, and the continuing structure of media compensation which includes an agency commission. Advertising agencies vary both in size and organizational structure. In addition to group and department organization, new agency forms have emerged in the development of specialized media buying services, and creative-only shops. Furthermore, there is a limited, but evident, growth in the use of house agencies.

The advertising agency performs a number of functions for the client company. Of particular importance are advertising preparation and media selection. However, the agency may be a major institution in the administration of the company's total advertising process. Accordingly, when a company uses an agency, it should select the organization with care and ensure proper and continuing coordination of all agency-advertiser relationships.

Several compensation methods may be arranged between the advertisers and their advertising agencies. The commission method, deducting a 15-percent commission from the media cost as the basic payment to the agency placing the advertising is the most frequently used technique. However, the fee method, paying the agency as a consultant for the work done, has grown in acceptance.

While it is difficult to foresee the future of the advertising agency, it is clear that successful organizations will react quickly to the changing environment and will be innovative in meeting their clients' needs.

QUESTIONS FOR DISCUSSION

1. What are the functions performed by a full-service advertising agency? Which of these do you believe to be the most important to the advertiser?

2. Under what circumstances would you recommend the use of a house agency? An agency that performs à la carte services?

3. In selecting a new advertising agency, what questions would you ask of the prospective candidates?

4. Should an agency prepare a speculative presentation? Why or why not?

5. Should an agency accept all prospective clients? Explain.

6. What techniques would you suggest for coordinating the firm and its advertising agency's activities?

7. How should you evaluate an advertising agency's performance?

8. What methods of agency compensation would you prefer as a small advertiser? as a large advertiser? Why?

9. Discuss the arguments for and against the commission and fee methods of compensation.

10. Should a firm change its advertising agency frequently? Explain.

KEY TERMS

billings
gross income
departmentalized (concentric) agency
full-service agency
à la carte services

boutique
media buying service
house agency
direct costs
overhead

AD PRACTICE

As an advertising agency you are offering a client who will spend $20,000,000 in billings the option of paying for your services by the fee or commission method. Prepare a presentation of these two methods explaining how the payments will be made in both cases.

6

The Advertising Budget

CHAPTER OBJECTIVES

— To describe the preparation of the advertising budget in terms of the people involved, the items to be included, and the factors to be considered

— To discuss the various methods used for determining the advertising budget

"Fifty percent of my advertising appropriation is wasted; the problem is I don't know which fifty percent." This is an often repeated quote in the advertising world.

Despite the development of some sophisticated techniques for this purpose, the crucial question of how much a company should spend on advertising, and how to allocate these expenditures, has not been solved. In 1986 Johnson & Johnson's McNeil Consumer Products Division introduced Medipren, a new pain-reliever whose active ingredient is ibuprofen. About half a dozen companies, including J & J, had received approval from the Food and Drug Administration to introduce new ibuprofen products. Advil and Nuprin were already available; however, they had captured only about 7 percent of the $1.7 billion nonprescription analgesic market which includes Tylenol and aspirin-based products.

To secure what is considered the necessary aggressive promotional effort, Johnson & Johnson will spend $40 million on television commercials within a few months. Consumers will be offered dollar coupons for Medipren, and doctors will be offered free samples for their patients, a tactic the company used successfully when it introduced Tylenol some twenty-five years ago.

It is difficult to forecast the results of this strategy. Johnson & Johnson is faced with many competitive products; moreover, it is concerned about the potential for cannibalizing its own Tylenol customers. To avoid the latter possibility, J & J will stress Medipren's use for body aches, rather than headaches.

Determining how much to spend on advertising is one of the most important decisions faced by a firm. Procedures for arriving at this decision range from the simple to the relatively complex.

THE ADVERTISING APPROPRIATION

In order to determine how much to spend on advertising it is necessary to analyze spending priorities based on funds available for all promotional efforts. The concept of the promotional mix, discussed in Chapter 3, implies that there are a number of strategies intertwined in a company's effort to sell a product.

Promotional funds, which usually are limited, may be allocated more efficiently in one promotional area than another. There is insufficient data currently available for such analysis. Not enough is known about the relationship between media advertising, sales promotion and personal selling, nor have techniques been developed to compare the value of a dollar invested in direct selling versus a dollar invested in television advertising. As a result, in most cases the advertising appropriations are determined as a separate form of promotional effort.

In the past, most of the advertising literature referred to a determination of the advertising *appropriation;* more recently discussion has focused on the advertising *budget.* Although the terms are used interchangeably, the advertising appropriation and the advertising budget are not synonymous. The *appropriation* refers to the total volume of funds to be set aside for advertising expenditures; the *budget* determines how these funds are to be allocated. In recent years, there has been an acknowledgement that it is not sufficient to secure a single optimum figure for the advertising appropriation, since this does not provide enough information for decision making. The necessity to estimate other expenditure decisions, such as media, copy, and geographic allocation of funds places the emphasis on budgetary analysis.

The words *plan* and *budget* are also interchanged and the term *advertising budget* is commonly used to refer to the entire advertising program submitted for approval. The *advertising plan,* however, includes a large body of information embracing sales goals, product facts, marketing information, competitive situation, creative platforms, and rough examples of copy treatment. It may also include marketing and advertising strategies, copy and media recommendations, and timing schedules.[1]

The *advertising budget* is the translation of an advertising plan into dollars and cents. It states the amount of proposed advertising expenditures and allocates available funds to various advertising activities. The major benefit of the budget is that it forces advertisers to plan and provides a control mechanism for comparing results with expectations.

Who Prepares the Budget?

The budgetary decision is a two-stage process: the first step is to determine the total appropriation figure and the second is to decide how the money will be allocated and to what areas. Generally this decision-mak-

---

[1]Richard J. Kelly, *The Advertising Budget, Preparation, Administration and Control,* Association of National Advertisers, Inc., 1967.

TABLE 6.1   Comparison of Expenses Identified by Industrial and Consumer Marketers as "White Charges"

Expenses	Percent of Respondents Indicating "White" Charges	
	100 Leading Industrial Advertisers	100 Leading Consumer Advertisers
Space and time costs in media	97	98
Direct mail to consumer	92	60
Advertising pretesting services	88	67
Readership or audience research	83	47
Storage of advertising materials	73	75
Advertising consultants	73	64
Advertising aids for sales staff	73	38
Local cooperative advertising	71	69
Cost of exhibits	71	24
Dealer-help literature	71	20
Direct mail to dealers	70	22
Industry directory listings	70	33
Advertising association dues	69	51
Subscription to periodicals	69	51
Advertising department travel and entertainment	69	46
Media costs for consumer contests	68	76
Premium handling charges	67	40
Catalogs for consumers	67	63
Catalogs for sales staff	67	27
Institutional advertising	66	75

ing process starts at the middle management level when the advertising manager or brand manager develops an initial draft. Usually the company's advertising agency participates in the process since its recommendations in terms of geographic and product breakdown are particularly useful.

Because final approval of the budget frequently takes place at a higher level in the organizational hierarchy (a study by Augustine and Foley revealed that final approval frequently rested with the president or vice-president of marketing[2]), the people involved in preparing the budget may overestimate, assuming that the final figure will contain a reduction. Often the previous year's original estimate will be used as a benchmark for the current year.

---

[2]A. J. San Augustine and W. F. Foley, "How Large Advertisers Set Budgets," *Journal of Advertising Research*, Vol. 15, No. 5 (October 1975), p. 14.

TABLE 6.1 Comparison of Expenses Identified by Industrial and Consumer Marketers as "White Charges" (continued)

	Percent of Respondents Indicating "White" Charges	
Expenses	100 Leading Industrial Advertisers	100 Leading Consumer Advertisers
Advertising in yellow pages	65	73
Catalogs for dealers	64	27
Point-of-sale materials	63	31
Mobile exhibits	61	24
Advertising department salaries	61	35
Cross-advertising enclosures	58	38
Product publicity	53	31
Cost of merchandise	48	29
Packaging charges	48	20
Sample requests generated by advertising	45	29
Advertising dept. share of overhead	45	24
Cost of contest blanks	44	31
Space in irregular publications	43	49
Contributions to industry ad funds	41	16
Cost of non self-liquidating premiums	40	29
Financial advertising	39	44
Press clipping services	38	18
Test marketing programs	38	31
Depreciation of advertising equipment	37	18
House organs for customers	35	20

From "The Advertising Budgeting Practices of Industrial Marketers" by Vincent J. Blasko & Charles H. Patti. Reprinted from *Journal of Marketing*, Vol. 48 (Fall 1984). Copyright © 1984 by American Marketing Association. Reprinted by permission.

What Items Should Be Included in the Budget?

What items are legitimately considered advertising expenditures in the advertising budget? There appears to be little question that the *white charges* of media costs, artwork, and agency fees are proper charges to advertising, and that charitable donations, industry association memberships, and salespeople's salaries are not. A whole host of items, however, fall in a gray area which some companies may classify as advertising and others as general expenses—costs of building signs, sales exhibits, and advertising portfolios for salespersons. The best way to handle this problem is to clarify company policy on this question prior to budget preparation and to treat questionable categories of expense with consistency. Table 6.1 presents a comparison of the types of expenses consumer and industrial marketers consider "white charges."

Factors to Be Considered in Determining the Budget

An individual company's decision about the amount of money to spend on advertising is a function of many variables: the funds available to the company, its sales volume, the firm's marketing mix, the extent of other promotional efforts, the stage of the life cycle of the firm's product, the advertisability of the product, the competitors' expenditures, the media that the firm considers appropriate for its campaign, and the goals of the advertising campaign. While affordability is apparently a major criterion in budgetary decisions, heavy expenditures do not guarantee success. Bacardi became the Number One sales leader in the liquor market despite the fact that it spent less than one-third of the sum spent by the heaviest liquor advertiser—VO.[3] Furthermore, there can be conflicting opinions about each decision—for example, while television may be deemed the most appropriate medium for advertising, its use may not be consistent with a firm's available funds. These conflicts result in wide variations in spending by companies in similar product categories.

SETTING THE ADVERTISING BUDGET

Generally, a firm decides how much to spend on advertising on an annual basis. Even though this is a recurring decision and a number of sophisticated techniques have been developed for its determination, many leading advertisers still "budget by ear."[4] They use their considered judgments based on experience because they believe that more sophisticated methods are too costly or time-consuming.

A number of common methods have been used over the years for setting advertising budgets. In order to provide a better understanding of these methods, as well as a means for evaluation, it is useful to examine two basic concepts that are frequently discussed in budgeting decisions: the sales generating effects of advertising and marginal analysis.

The Sales Generating Effects of Advertising

As noted earlier, advertising can be used for many and diverse objectives. However, since most companies hope that their advertising expenditures will ultimately generate sales, it is important to examine the relationship between advertising and sales, designated the sales response function.

Although there is no universal agreement as to the pattern it follows, or even its existence, the relationship between advertising and sales is frequently described as an S-shaped function. Figure 6.1 provides a graphic representation of the sales/advertising relationship. Note

FIGURE 6.1   The Sales-Advertising Relationship

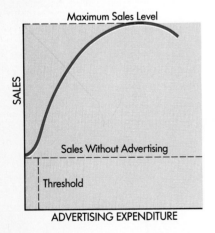

Source: From *Advertising* by Kenneth Longman. Copyright © 1971 by Harcourt Brace Jovanovich, Inc. Reprinted by permission of the publisher.

---

[3]"Liquor's Top Ten Spenders," *Marketing & Media Decisions* (October 1980), p. 73.
[4]A. J. San Augustine and W.F. Foley, "How Large Advertisers Set Budgets," p. 12.
[5]Kenneth Longman, *Advertising* (New York: Harcourt Brace Jovanovich, Inc., 1971), p. 235.

that the axes of the graph are not numbered since one campaign differs from another.[5] The graph in Figure 6.1 depicts the following:

1. Sales will occur without any advertising.
2. Below a certain threshold level, advertising expenditures will be ineffective in changing sales.
3. There is a maximum sales level and, regardless of any additional amount that may be spent on advertising, sales will not exceed this maximum. The reason for this will vary from an inability to consume more of the product to production being at its maximum to any other factor which will not allow sales of a particular product to exceed a certain level.
4. There is a diminishing return for advertising expenditures; although initially advertising may create extensive sales, it becomes less efficient as more money is spent.

There are drawbacks to using the S-curve relationship, most important of which is that it is still under discussion by researchers. Also, sales are influenced by much more than advertising. Finally, developing a model of this S-curve for a company incorporates complex mathematical and statistical problems.[6] Nevertheless, the concept of diminishing returns from advertising has been incorporated, at least intuitively, in many budgetary decisions. A review of over 100 articles on this topic suggests that advertising response is, in fact, characterized by diminishing returns.[7] This suggests the need for further research in the area to accurately determine the influence of advertising on sales.

Marginal Analysis

A logical approach to determining the advertising appropriation would be to select the point at which an additional dollar spent on advertising would bring an additional profit of one dollar—in economic terms, where marginal cost equals marginal profit. To determine that point, Figure 6.1 would have to be revised to include the firm's production, distribution, and advertising costs in order to obtain the firm's net profit before taxes.

In Figure 6.2, Panel A, the production and distribution costs are deducted from sales to obtain the gross profit curve. Advertising costs are then deducted from gross profit to obtain net profit before taxes (the shaded area in the graph). The optimum point is the place where the distance between the gross profit curve and advertising costs is greatest. To present this maximum net profit point in a more readable form, the net profit curve is reproduced in Figure 6.2, Panel B.

---

[6]J. K. Johannson, "Advertising and the S-Curve: A New Approach," *Journal of Marketing Research*, Vol. 16 (August 1979), pp. 346–54.

[7]Julian L. Simon and Johan Arndt, "The Shape of the Advertising Response Function," *Journal of Advertising Research*, Vol. 20 (August 1980), pp. 11–30.

FIGURE 6.2   Sales and Profit Curves Relating to Advertising Expenditures

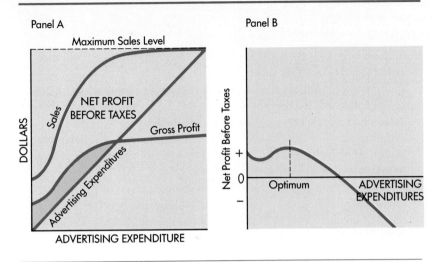

From *Advertising* by Kenneth Longman. Copyright © 1971 by Harcourt Brace Jovanovich, Inc. Reprinted by permission of the publisher.

Marginal analysis, while logical, presents a number of problems which limit its applicability. It does not take into account the lagged effect of advertising (it may take some time for the advertising to be effective), the activities of competitors offering the same or substitute products, general environmental factors, and the fact that much advertising is not designed to generate immediate sales, but to create awareness or interest. Despite the difficulties, some companies indicate they used the logical insight that marginal analysis provides, and supplement it with many other factors that relate to the effects of advertising in the marketplace.[8]

COMMON METHODS FOR SETTING THE BUDGET

The most common methods for determining the advertising budget frequently incorporate judgment and experience. These include approaches that are *arbitrarily* based on revenue, related to competitors' activity, designed as a capital investment, or designed to accomplish a specific task.

All You Can Afford

Spending all you can afford on advertising appears to be one of the "budgeting by ear" techniques. It is actually a conservative approach to promotional expenditures, since it only makes use of expendable funds.

---

[8]"Some Guidelines for Advertising Budgeting," (New York: The Conference Board, 1972), p. 20.

However, this attitude must be modified by competent marketing judgment. Firms, particularly smaller firms, use this method when funds are available and assign a percentage of profit for advertising, since profit appears to provide an affordable reservoir from which funds can be appropriated. However, as difficult as it is to determine the sales generating effect of promotion, it is even more difficult to evaluate its profit generating effect.

Arbitrary Approach

While the "all you can afford" method is arbitrary, the arbitrary approach is frequently considered a distinct method for determining the appropriation. In this method the decision maker arbitrarily selects an amount to be spent on advertising, usually on the basis of judgment or experience; affordability need not be a criterion. This technique may be used in introducing a new product.

Percentage of Sales

The percentage-of-sales method for determining the advertising budget appears to be the simplest, and, in the past, this method enjoyed widespread use. Today, although many firms use a combination of methods, they frequently report their advertising expenditures as a percent of sales.

Sales upon which the percentage figure may be based are either the past year's sales, anticipated sales for next year, or a combination of both. The percentage figure itself may be determined on the basis of historical experience—that is, in the most profitable year management spent 2 percent of sales on advertising—managerial judgment, or some established company formula. Often a company will adopt the percentage figure most prevalent in its industry, perhaps one established by the industry trade association. As an example, a company may take its last year's sales figure of $100,000, add an anticipated 10-percent increase in sales for the coming year ($110,000) and set the advertising appropriation at 2 percent of that, or $2200.

Assuming that the S-shaped advertising-to-sales ratio is valid, the percentage-of-sales method may be invalid in certain cases. The S-shaped function indicates that there is a threshold level of sales which occur without the expenditure of advertising funds. Somewhere above this threshold sales are constrained by a maximum level that cannot be exceeded regardless of any amount of advertising. Therefore, it is only between the threshold and maximum level that advertising can have any effect, while the percentage-of-sales approach assumes that advertising can continuously influence sales.

Advertising Elasticity
It has been suggested that if the concept of *advertising elasticity* (the relative change in quantity sold proportional to the relative change in

the advertising budget) is incorporated in the percentage-of-sales formulation, the validity should improve.[9]

An advertising elasticity coefficient can be established by dividing the results of changes in sales by the actual changes in advertising. For example, if there is a 1-percent change in sales as a result of a 10-percent change in advertising, the advertising elasticity coefficient is 1/10 or .10. Thus, if the company wishes to achieve a 6-percent increase in sales, it may require a 60-percent increase in advertising (6/60 = 1/10).[10]

Although advertising elasticities can vary widely from one product to another, they may tend to be stable for a mature product over time.

Advantages of Percentage of Sales
Sales related methods for determining the advertising appropriation have several advantages. First, they are related to incoming revenue and, thus, suggest that money will be available for advertising expenditures. Next, there is a consistency between this approach and the standard accounting practice of handling advertising as one of the "operating expenses" that are usually analyzed in terms of their ratio to total sales volume. When the total marketing budget is determined in the overall marketing plan this method assigns a fixed proportion of that budget to advertising. Finally, percentage of sales is simple to calculate, and it is almost second nature for management to think of costs in percentage terms. Moreover, when it is widespread throughout the industry, it results in advertising becoming proportional to market shares, and competitive warfare is made less probable.

Disadvantages of Percentage of Sales
The percentage-of-sales method is not consistent with the basic marketing principle that advertising is an important factor in stimulating demand, and, as such, precedes sales rather than being determined by sales. As Professor Dean declares, "The purpose of advertising is to increase demand for the company's products above what it would be otherwise—advertising should be viewed as the cause, not the result of sales."[11] This method also presents a static approach to advertising rather than one that responds to the particular needs of market conditions. With a fixed multiplier, advertising expenditures increase as sales increase, and the tendency is to spend the exact earmarked amount, which may or may not be profitable. On the other hand, as sales decline

[9]Donald S. Tull, James H. Barnes, and Daniel T. Seymour, "In Defense of Setting Budgets for Advertising as a Percent of Sales," *Journal of Advertising Research*, Vol. 18 (December 1978), pp. 49–51.

[10]Malcolm A. McNiven, "Plan for More Productive Advertising," *Harvard Business Review*, Vol. 80 (March-April 1980), pp. 13–136.

[11]Joel Dean, *Managerial Economics* (Englewood Cliffs, N.J.: Prentice-Hall, Inc., 1951), p. 253.

the expenditures on advertising decline, despite the possibility that it is at this point the demand may require that extra effort toward stimulation.

Future sales appear to be a more logical indicator in setting the size of the advertising effort. However, this is fraught with circular reasoning, because it is difficult to forecast sales without knowing how much is to be invested in sales-generating efforts. In order to provide a hedge against an inaccurate forecast, a firm may take its past year's sales figure and its projected sales for the current year and apply the multiplier to an average of these two years.

Nonetheless, the percentage-of-sales method is useful as a starting point in determining the advertising appropriation, since it is a simple, revenue-related mechanism and permits some comparison with the competition's efforts. The addition of an advertising elasticity coefficient may make this a more valid method.

Fixed-Sum-per-Unit Method

A variation of the percentage-of-sales method is the "fixed-sum-per-unit" appropriation technique. This method is also based on the premise that a specific amount of advertising is related to the marketing cost of each unit produced rather than total sales volume. It does not reflect price changes as does the percentage-of-sales method and it assumes that the amount of advertising effort needed to move a unit of merchandise is not closely related to increases or decreases in price. The advantage is that the manufacturer will know in advance how much the advertising cost of each unit of the product will be, which is especially useful in price determination.

The fixed-sum method works well when a firm has a number of different brands of a product, each of which may require a different amount of promotional effort—one brand may be stronger, a second weaker, and a third in its early promotional stages. In the cigarette industry, for example, the amount of dollars to be used for advertising may be determined by multiplying the sales volume forecast for each brand by a dollar amount per thousand cigarettes to arrive at an advertising allocation for each brand. For example, Fixed Sum per Unit = $1.00 per 1000 cigarettes.

Brand	Forecast	Budget Allocation
A	1,000,000,000 cigarettes	$1,000,000
B	100,000,000 cigarettes	100,000

The total inventory of advertising dollars is subject to negotiation between brand managers and marketing directors, and funds may be transferred among brands.

Build-Up Method

Build-up is not ordinarily used by itself, but rather in conjunction with others, such as those previously discussed. It tends to be a favorite of multiproduct corporations. It calls for product managers to submit preliminary budgets for each brand in their respective operating areas. These budgets are then reviewed and modified by top management. Collectively, they become the firm's total advertising budget.

The Competitive-Parity Method

An advertising appropriation geared to match an estimated expenditure of major competitors may be used by a new company to begin its advertising efforts, since this permits the company to rely, to some extent, on the industry's experience. For the established firm it adds another ingredient to the percentage-of-sales method and suggests that the competitive environment, as well as the firm's internal considerations, should determine the advertising appropriation.

The competitive-parity approach assumes the goals and objectives of all firms within the industry are similar and that their marketing strategies are alike; and that the combined thinking within the industry provides more expertise than one firm's analysis. Neither assumption may be accurate. The combined thinking may be no more valid than an individual executive's judgment.

Securing industry data, from trade associations or industry periodicals, may be helpful in setting the advertising appropriation. The experience of other firms in the industry can be evaluated. Moreover, the strategy of the firm is, to some extent, affected by the strategy within the industry. For example, a basic consideration in the total volume of advertising effort is the extent of "voice" that exists within the industry. If the "voice" is loud—that is, if all firms within the industry are advertising heavily—the advertising effort of any one firm must be disproportionately higher to be heard above the advertising din. If the industry "voice" is low, even a moderate increase in the advertising effort of one firm may permit it to stand out.

Advertising as a Capital Investment

A problem in determining the amount to spend on advertising is its *lagged effect*. Although advertising may lead to immediate sales, it may also have a holdover effect which increases brand purchase and usage in the future and creates future goodwill. This long-term effect is seen by some as characterizing advertising as a capital investment, with sales revenue generated over time. This designation may be logical for institutional advertising, which frequently is considered an investment.

Although advertising satisfies the criterion of futurity, it has some characteristics that set it apart from more traditional corporate investments. There is no certainty about the duration of benefits, since the long-term effects are difficult to predict, and since the asset is intangible, it is not treated as part of the capital budget.[12] In fact, a major restriction to considering advertising as a long-term outlay for the purchase of capital assets is the Internal Revenue Service, which treats advertising as a current expense.

While an analysis which views advertising as a capital investment is appealing, management can generally do little more than guess at the probable return from dollars invested. In an effort to solve this problem quantitative models discussed in the section on page 117, are used to isolate the cumulative effects.

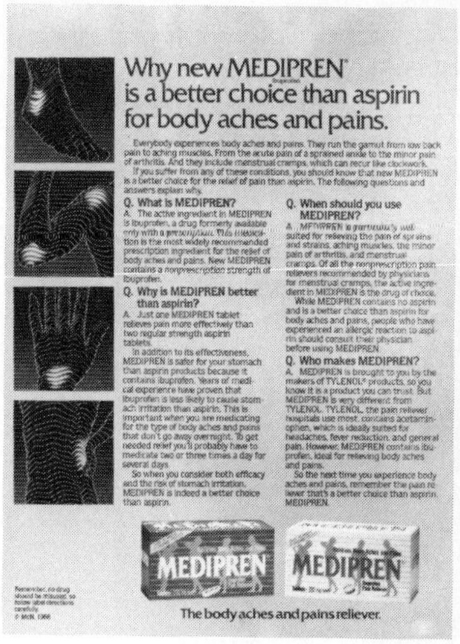

Objective-and-Task Method

All the methods discussed so far make minimal use of the basic managerial element of control. The control element involves the development of some mechanism for measuring and evaluating the results of the appropriation and for the application of the feedback information to revise efforts. Except for the consideration of advertising as a long-term capital investment (which implies that the return on the advertising investment acts as an evaluation mechanism), the methods thus far considered basically have been judgmental.

A logical, or research, way to set a budget suggests that advertising, like most other business functions, should be examined in the light of the objectives it is designed to achieve. This concept leads to the development of the *objective-and-task method,* which sets advertising objectives for the coming budget period and calculates in detail (task) the costs for achieving these objectives to determine the budget. (It should be noted that such objectives should be framed in terms of their probable contribution to profits.)[13] This plan is the most widely used by both consumer and industrial advertisers.[14]

Objectives may be long-term (to increase market share by 10 percent within the next five years) or short-term (to increase brand recognition from 20 percent to 30 percent within a six-months period). Generally the objectives are stated in quantified terms. Then the cost of advertising that is presumed necessary to achieve these objectives is

EXHIBIT 6.1
Medipren Ad Designed to Gain a Competitive Share of the Ibuprofen Market

---

[12]Joel Dean, "Does Advertising Belong in the Capital Budget?" *Journal of Marketing,* Vol. 30 (October 1966), pp. 15–21.

[13]"Some Guidelines for Advertising Budgeting," (New York: The Conference Report #560, 1972), p. 13.

[14]Vincent J. Blasko & Charles H. Patti, "The Advertising Budgeting Practices of Industrial Marketers," *Journal of Marketing,* Vol. 48 (Fall 1984), pp. 104–10.

TABLE 6.2 Steps in Objective-and-Task Method of Determining Advertising Budget

Step	Procedure
1. Determine objectives.	Analyze marketing situation and translate marketing objectives to specific (quantitative) objectives (for example, increase market share by 10 percent, increase brand recognition by 20 percent).
2. Define variables to be measured.	Specify variables (for example, market share, brand awareness) and determine their current levels, generally through research, to permit evaluation of the program.
3. Specify task and determine cost.	Decide the promotional activities required to achieve stated objective, and then estimate the costs required to perform this "task."
4. Conduct program.	Implement advertising activities.
5. Evaluate and review.	Determine extent to which initial objectives were met (has market share increased to 10 percent, or brand recognition by 20 percent?).

determined, and this sum becomes the budget for the relevant period. The basic restraint is the necessity to consider the company's financial position. Table 6.2 describes the steps in the budgeting method.

An advantage of this method is that it forces companies to think in terms of goals and their achievement. It also provides a means of evaluating the promotional costs, an incentive for measuring results, and a feedback mechanism for revising and refining budgeting efforts. It is a method that can easily be adapted or modified to fit changing conditions and does not operate on the inaccuracies involved in estimating a fixed relationship between advertising and sales or profit.

Translating advertising goals into tasks requires, among other things, the ability to make minute comparisons among the innumerable alternatives involved in media choice, theme selection, copy appeal, artwork, and timing elements. Until much more refined methods of evaluating advertising effectiveness are determined, the objective-and-task method will continue to be somewhat less than scientific. In addition, this method requires periodic implementation for the variety of objectives that the firm may have in the course of one advertising period. However, this requirement is used as a defense of the method because it calls for a company to collect data concerning the shape of its demand curves and the productiveness of various advertising campaigns. In fact, it is this research requirement that makes the objective method a rational approach.

QUANTITATIVE BUDGET MODELS

Most of the methods of budget determination discussed previously have been considered advantageous because of the relatively small cost involvement in their implementation and the limited analysis that is required. As noted earlier, however, a serious deficiency in these techniques is that they generally view the advertising budget as being determined by a given level of sales. This is contrary to what many people in marketing see as the correct relationship—advertising affects sales. While the objectve-and-task method uses the latter assumption, it is classified as a qualitative model since it still represents a static "seat-of-the-pants" method of budgeting and does not take into account various market occurrences.[15] There is increasing acceptance that many factors—the economic environment, the social environment, competitive pressures, internal changes—influence the advertising budget. This has led to the development of a number of quantitative advertising budget models that are dynamic.

An advertising budget model is used to develop a recommended course of action—the optimum amount to be spent on advertising; it is designed to avoid overspending as well as underspending. Quantitative budget models usually consist of a dependent variable (the amount to be spent on advertising) and several independent variables, based on some theoretical viewpoint about the influence of advertising.[16]

In general, the measurement of the variables in the various budget models usually necessitates some type of empirical research. For example, to determine the *decay constant* (the rate of sales loss in the absence of advertising), the organization generally must cut off all promotional effort for a product in a market to measure the results over an extended period. Such experimentation can be risky, but, if controlled properly, can provide needed information.[17]

Most of these models incorporate the concept of the *sales response function*, the effect of advertising on sales. A widely reported quantitative, carefully controlled study conducted for Anheuser-Busch in the 1960s provides some support for this sales response to advertising. However, the study revealed some interesting findings. While in some of the areas tested, a 50-percent increase in advertising was found to yield a 7-percent increase in sales, for the areas where advertising was reduced

---

[15]Edward A. Riordan and Fred W. Morgan, Jr., "A Taxonomic Evaluation of Advertising Budgeting Models," *Journal of Advertising*, Vol. 8 (Winter 1979), pp. 33–38.

[16]E. A. Riordan and Fred W. Morgan, Jr., "A Taxonomic Evaluation of Advertising Budgeting Models," pp. 33–38.

[17]Nariman K. Dhalla, "How to Set Advertising Budgets," *Journal of Advertising Research*, Vol. 17, No. 5 (October 1977), pp. 11–17.

by 25 percent there was a 14-percent rise in sales! Whether this was caused by consumers' irritation with Budweiser's excessive advertising, or whether the Budweiser sales personnel were competing inefficiently in markets where advertising created excessive demand is not clear. Furthermore, pricing was not controlled in the study. Nevertheless, it appeared as though a condition of negative returns on advertising had been created.

As a result of this study, Anheuser-Busch reduced its advertising expenditure per barrel of beer from $1.89 in 1962 to $0.80 in 1968. During this period, from 1963–68, sales of Budweiser increased from approximately 7.5 million to 14.5 million barrels and its market share increased from 8.14 percent to 12.94 percent.[18] Whether this was a special case, or would only occur under circumstances when no strong competitor existed in a market, is not quite clear. In recent years, Anheuser-Busch, faced with extensive competition from Miller Brewing Co., has increased its advertising expenditures for Budweiser extensively (up 25 percent from 1984 over 1983).[19]

Several models have been developed to assess the *cumulative effects of advertising*, the effect of advertising over an extended period of time. These have used historical company data such as sales trends, price structures, sales promotion expenditures, and advertising schedules. Other variables are generally included such as growth of population, competitive pressures, seasonal fluctuations, price changes, retail availabilities, and activities of the sales force.

Some studies have been conducted using quantitative models to determine the short-term and long-term profitability of advertising investment. Table 6.3 lists some of the studies and shows both the immediate net profit and that over a longer period of time.[20]

As can be seen from several of the minus signs in the table, when only the immediate effects are considered, the marginal advertising dollar does not always contribute to profit. In these cases, the last dollar of advertising is likely to cost more than the return it yields. However, to assess properly the economic worth of expenditures in mass media, the entire cumulative effect should be included. When this is done, as with the brands listed in the table, advertising is found to be profitable in all cases.

Computer Models

While several companies and advertising agencies have developed computer models for advertising budgeting, the details of these generally remain trade secrets. Frequently, such models are used for media allocation; however, they might be useful for managerial control as well.

---

[18]Russell L. Ackoff and James R. Emshoff, "Advertising Research at Anheuser-Busch, Inc. (1963–68)," *Sloan Management Review*, Vol. 16 (Winter 1975).

[19] "Leading 100 Hike Spending 16 Percent," *Advertising Age* (September 26, 1985), p. 24.

[20]Nariman K. Dhalla, "Assessing the Long-Term Values of Advertising," *Harvard Business Review* (January-February 1978), pp. 87–95.

TABLE 6.3 Short-Term and Long-Term Profitability of Advertising Investment

Author	Product	Marginal Net Profit Contribution per Advertising Dollar	
		Immediate	Cumulative
Palda	*Lydia Pinkham's Vegetable Compound†*	− $0.70	+ $0.22
Lambin	*Frequently Purchased Food Product*	− 0.26	+ 1.50
Simon	*Blended Whiskey*		
	Carstairs	− 0.12	+ 1.67
	Four Roses	+ 1.60	+ 3.64
	Seagram's 7 Crown	+ 2.10	+11.40
	Imperial	+ 0.14	+ 8.48
	Old Thompson	+ 0.16	+ 5.84
	Gin		
	Gilbey's	− 0.12	+ 1.26
Lambin	Gasoline (Average of 5 Brands)	− 0.81	+ 0.01

†For Lydia Pinkham's Vegetable Compound, $1.00 of advertising produced a loss of $0.70 in the immediate period (i.e., the same year). However, when the entire cumulative effect was examined, this loss turned into a profit of $0.22. The cumulative figures have not been discounted to the present cash value.

ADVISOR is a decision model developed for industrial marketers (marketers of goods and services to industrial, commercial, or government markets for consumption or resale). In this model, advertising budgeting is considered as a two-step process: first, setting a marketing budget and, then, determining advertising's role in that budget.[21] The characteristics for an existing product within an industry are collected and input to a computer program. The program feeds back budgeting guidelines that are then compared with the actual budget. If the guidelines agree with the budget, no further analysis is performed. If they disagree, reasons for the differences are sought. The model acts as a control procedure to find those product cases most in need of more detailed review.

Problems with Computer Models

Several problems exist in designing and implementing computer models. Competitors' strategies and expenditures are frequently included, and such information is difficult to come by. The cost of model implementation is a limitation and usually only large organizations can afford

[21]Cary L. Lilien, "Advisor 2: Modeling the Marketing Mix Decision for Industrial Products," *Management Science*, Vol. 25 (February 1979), pp. 191–204.

the necessary research. Moreover, the benefits of using these models are difficult to determine. In recent years, there has been an acknowledgment that one figure is not sufficient for an advertising budget; it is considered increasingly necessary to secure scientific estimates of media, copy, and geographic allocation.

One recommended technique for reducing costs is to include several companies, or even an entire industry, in such a quantitative analysis.[22] However, the companies involved would have to be convinced that the benefits outweigh the disadvantages of revealing what is usually considered top secret data.

ALLOCATING THE ADVERTISING APPROPRIATION

Allocating the appropriation is part of the budgetary process and concerns dividing up the funds available for advertising along various dimensions. The dimensions selected, such as allocation by media, product, and geographic area, frequently are based on the company's objectives and strategy. As noted earlier, some media models have been developed to aid in the allocation process. However, these usually provide intra- rather than intermedia analysis.

Allocation by product may incorporate considerations such as current and anticipated brand share, the stage of the product in its life cycle, competitive efforts, and the advertising elasticity for the particular product. In general, such considerations concern the company's objectives relevant to its specific products.

Frequently, the allocation is geographic. Some companies may use an "umbrella" system whereby various areas are bombarded with equal amounts of advertising. A more comprehensive technique would be *"bottom-up" planning* where each market is examined separately and the advertising budget varies according to the marketing objectives and needs.[23] Thus, if the potential in one area appears greater and more lucrative than another, the former would be given a larger share of the budget.

BUDGETARY CONTROL

Budgetary control, like any other management control, involves the measurement of actual performance against plans. The advertising budget represents the plan, while the systems and procedures established for measuring the actual performance against the budget constitute the company's budgetary control methods. Various techniques can be used,

---

[22]E. A. Riordan and Fred W. Morgan, Jr., "A Taxonomic Evaluation of Advertising Budgeting Models," p. 38.

[23]"More Bang for the Ad Dollar," *Dun's Review*, Vol. 112 (October 1978), pp. 106–8.

but the budgetary control process in advertising involves three phases: commitment control, expenditure control, and management control.

Commitment control begins when a purchase is initiated or a project is started. It generally incorporates details of the procedure by which purchasing groups may route orders for management's approval, releasing them to outside suppliers of advertising material.

Expenditure control takes over when invoices are received and funds are actually disbursed. Prior to such disbursement, estimates are reviewed and invoices carefully perused.

Management control embraces the review and evaluation of the entire advertising effort. It involves the establishment of standards for performance and a determination of the extent to which activities have achieved such standards. Furthermore, it permits management to vary the advertising effort in response to this feedback information.

SUMMARY

In advertising the term *budget* is used to refer to the total volume of funds set aside for advertising expenditures as well as the determination of how these funds are to be allocated to specific areas. While final approval of an advertising budget takes place at the top level in the organizational hierarchy, drafting the budget is usually the responsibility of middle management. A budget contains various expenditures including "white charges" (media costs and artwork, for example), and many "gray" areas which some companies may classify as advertising and others as general expenses (costs of building signs or sales exhibits).

There is no "one best way" to do the budgetary process; too many unknown variables may require consideration; moreover, the choice should be based on objectives of the specific company, which may vary widely from others.

A number of common methods have been devised for setting the budget. These include techniques designated as "all you can afford," arbitrary method, percentage of sales, and competitive parity. Some authorities suggest that the amount spent on advertising should be computed from the viewpoint of a capital investment.

The objective-and-task method overcomes a deficiency in these other methods by incorporating an element of control and evaluation procedures. However, there is difficulty in determining the kinds of advertising necessary to achieve the specified objectives.

More sophisticated techniques for determining the advertising budget include quantitative methods and computer models.

As part of the budgetary process the total appropriation is allocated along various dimensions, including media, product, and geographic area. Several control techniques are applied to budget design: commitment control details the procedure for routing orders for management's approval, expenditure control reviews invoices prior to payment, and management control establishes standards for performance and examines the extent to which activities have achieved such standards.

QUESTIONS FOR DISCUSSION

1. What is the difference between the advertising appropriation and the advertising budget?
2. In the preparation of the advertising budget what is meant by "white," and "gray" items? Give examples.
3. Discuss the sales generating effects of advertising in relation to determining the budget.
4. How is marginal analysis used in budget determination?
5. What method would you suggest to a small company for determining its advertising appropriation? a large company?
6. How is the percentage-of-sales method used? What are its advantages and disadvantages?
7. Under what circumstances should advertising be considered a capital investment? Explain.
8. Describe the objective-and-task method and suggest the circumstances appropriate for its use.
9. What do you believe is the future of quantitative models for budget determination?
10. What is meant by budgetary control? What methods can be used for this purpose?

KEY TERMS

budget	competitive parity
white charges	lagged effect
marginal analysis	decay constant
advertising elasticity	sales response function
"All You Can Afford"	cumulative effects of advertising
percentage of sales	"bottom-up" planning
arbitrary approach	commitment control
fixed sum per unit	expenditure control
build-up method	management control

AD PRACTICE

A soft-drink company asks you for help in preparing its advertising budget to introduce a new soft drink with an anticipated annual sales volume of one million cases at $10 per case. Select a "rule of thumb" and a research method for this presentation. Be specific in terms of presentation data.

7

Advertising Objectives

The startling commercial, "1984," that introduced Apple Computer's Macintosh, aired just once, during the 1984 Superbowl. The television spot, which evoked the theme of the famous George Orwell book, cost one million dollars to produce. It was widely criticized because it defied the conventional wisdom of advertising: it never depicted the product, 95 percent of the commercial had no apparent connection with computers, and it was not repeated on television. Nevertheless it scored high in viewer surveys and garnered the top prize at the Cannes International Advertising Film Festival. Moreover, from the company's point of view, the advertisement achieved its basic objectives of creating awareness and ultimately increasing sales.

The establishment of advertising objectives serves several purposes for a firm. When a firm's objectives for its advertising program are formalized, they can be communicated to all levels of the organization, can provide a basis for decision making, and will encourage the introduction and selection of consistent advertising alternatives. In addition, they offer the firm a standard against which the results of the advertising can be evaluated.

CHAPTER OBJECTIVES

— To discuss the functions of advertising objectives

— To explain how advertising may be designed by a firm to generate increased sales

— To describe the communication objectives that a firm may use in an advertising campaign

— To examine how positioning is used as an objective

FUNCTIONS OF ADVERTISING OBJECTIVES

The terms *objectives* and *goals*, while not synonymous, are often used interchangeably. An objective is generally stated in broad terms: to increase sales or to expand industry share. Goals are more specific; they are described frequently in terms of time and degree: to increase sales 15 percent by 1988 or to expand market share to 20 percent by 1989. In an advertising context, objectives and goals may be considered interchangeable.

Determination of advertising objectives should not be made in isolation; instead they are best derived from the firm's broader objectives. Interrelationships can be seen below:

CORPORATE OBJECTIVE

To increase profit by 10 percent

MARKETING OBJECTIVE

To increase market share by 20 percent

ADVERTISING OBJECTIVE

Communicate economy message to

70 percent of the target group

It may seem desirable for a firm to state its advertising objectives in terms of sales. In fact, the end purpose of most advertising as a promotional activity is to generate increases in sales. However, there are several reasons why using sales objectives may be unsatisfactory. As noted earlier, advertising is part of the firm's promotional mix, which, in turn, is only one element in the marketing mix; thus, advertising is not the only variable that influences a purchase. A consumer's purchase decision is affected by environmental factors, such as general economic conditions and competitive activity; company factors, such as product choice, quality, price, outlets chosen for distribution, and availability; and internal considerations such as the individual's motives, drives, attitudes, and perceptions. Setting advertising objectives in terms of sales may distort this relationship and place greater emphasis on advertising in the decision-making process than it merits.

Advertising objectives should serve as sources of advertising strategy. Sales objectives, however, do not provide sufficient guidance for an advertising program, since they rarely indicate the operational procedures that generate such sales.

Objectives should also serve the function of evaluation. Isolating advertising from all other variables is extremely difficult. Moreover, advertising has a lagged effect; its results frequently occur some time after ads appear. Thus immediate sales do not completely reflect the results of advertising, nor can the lagged effect be precisely determined.

In recent years, there has been increasing acknowledgment that the relationship between advertising and sales is not direct, but, in fact, there is a series of intermediate steps in the advertising/sales process. The development of communication theory has helped formalize this concept and has led to the practice of stating advertising objectives in terms of the intermediate stages of the process, frequently designating them as communication goals.

Nevertheless many firms continue to state their advertising objectives in terms of sales, and, in some situations it may be appropriate to do so. For example, retailers and direct mailers may find it better to state their advertising objective in terms of sales since the advertising influence is more direct and relatively easier to correlate with sales. Major manufacturers, however, whose goods and services are distributed through numerous channels and diverse efforts, may not find this method best for them.

SALES OBJECTIVES

The intention of some advertising may be to secure an immediate sale. Announcements of a price reduction or a premium offer, campaigns tied in with special events, such as "buy an Easter Bunny for the children," or advertisements that are designed to stimulate impulse sales are all sales-related campaigns. Furthermore, sales may be an appropriate goal for direct-mail and retail advertisers.

Frequently, however, to generate increases in sales, advertisers will focus on sources of business and attempt to increase the number of customers their company serves and/or increase the rate at which the product or service is used. Advertising can also be used to support other elements in the marketing mix to improve the effectiveness of the firm's total marketing strategy with the ultimate objective of increasing sales.

Increasing Number of Customers

In order to increase the number of customers it serves, a company may attempt to expand the total demand for its product. Advertising can help in this process by using campaigns whose objectives are to turn nonusers into users, attract users of competitors' products, develop loyalty to the brand among current customers, or rekindle interest among former users.

Increasing Total Demand
Advertising campaigns may attempt to increase the total demand for a product so that the individual firm's share will generate sales volume. Smoke detectors, introduced in the early 1970s, appeared in millions of homes in the eighties. Widespread advertising campaigns indicating how they could save lives apparently were successful in increasing total demand.

Advertising may also be designed to reverse a declining primary demand. The "incredible, edible egg" campaign, for example, was designed to reverse the declining demand for eggs by overcoming some of the health-related objections to the use of eggs.

EXHIBIT 7.1
Objective: Changing Nonusers to
Users

User friendly.

"In 18 years in this business, the most important thing I've
learned is what questions to ask," says Merrill Lynch Financial
Consultant Bill Scott.

"Merrill Lynch offers such a broad range of opportunities
that sorting them out can be a real challenge. My job is to work
with my clients until I truly understand each one's situation.
Then I present what Merrill Lynch has to offer in a way that is
sensible and accessible and useful to that particular client."

It's seasoned Financial Consultants like Bill Scott—the people
of Merrill Lynch—who make our vast resources so user friendly.
Come in soon and get acquainted.

More resources, better solutions.
They make Merrill Lynch people a breed apart.

 **Merrill Lynch**

Attracting Nonusers

Advertising may have as its objective the attracting of nonusers in an
effort to increase the number of customers. The airlines have frequently
attempted to turn nonfliers to fliers; lawyers, who can now advertise,
offer low-cost legal services to people who have never been able to afford attorneys. A recent coffee campaign declaring "You're going to be
decaffeinated," was directed at those who do not use such caffeine-free
products. Exhibit 7.1 shows a Merrill Lynch ad encouraging nonusers
to use the company and its services.

Maintaining Current Sources

A company can achieve sales increases by creating brand loyalty or discouraging brand switching. One method for generating increased loyalty
toward a mature product is call attention to its relationship to the past.
Scott's campaign for its Waldorf Tissue, in existence since 1900, featured

EXHIBIT 7.2
Generating Brand Loyalty

ffAs an AT&T systems technician, I know service isn't just a job, it's a way of life.

When a leading Wall Street firm caught fire, I was there before it was even out. Our team worked through the night and had the systems up before the bell rang on Wall Street.

We worked hard all night for one reason.

We can be the difference between a customer's business surviving or going up in smoke.

So we treat all our service calls as though the business were ours. Twenty-four hours a day, seven days a week, year in, year out, we're here to help. Nearly 20,000 of us, the most experienced service force in the country. Committed to the same basic idea about service. **ff**
To find out more, call 1 800 247-1212.

Whether it's telephones, information or network systems, long distance services, or computers, AT&T is the right choice.

AT&T
The right choice.

© AT&T 1985

Joseph G. Curreri
AT&T Technician

the "good old days." A commercial aimed at the Waldorf brand supporters, who were lower-middle to middle-income people, aged 25–49, with families of five or more members, declared:

When I was a kid my mother always dragged me along shopping. And I remember one thing she would always buy was Waldorf Tissue. She said it was a good value. Now my wife drags me shopping and she buys Waldorf, too ... but now it has flowers and you know what? There's no extra charge for the flowers ... Waldorf ... It's still a good value.[1]

Advertising may also attempt to create brand loyalty by reinforcing a positive purchase experience or helping to avoid a negative experience (see Exhibit 7.2).

[1]Waldorf Introductory Fact Book, *Scott Paper* (September 29, 1977), p. 7.

Much advertising is designed to create repeat purchases by advertising a product's unique or superior attributes, developing an image, or creating a "personality" for a product. Miller beer is advertised as light, Merit cigarettes as low in tar, Marlboro for the rugged "he-man," and Irish Spring soap for the "manly" man.

Rekindling Interest in a Mature Product

Many products have long lives and maintain a somewhat balanced sales pattern. Occasionally, a company may find it useful to rekindle interest in a mature product and encourage a sales spurt (see Exhibit 7.3). Nabisco Company's Ritz crackers sold for more than forty years, increasing its sales during its mature stage by 1 percent or 2 percent each year. In 1977 Nabisco doubled its advertising expenditures for this brand and designed a creative campaign featuring TV spokesperson, Andy Griffith, who emphasized that "everything tastes great when it sits on a Ritz." Sales increased over 9 percent per year.[2] For Triscuits, another mature brand which hadn't been advertised for years, Nabisco used TV commercials with Lawrence Welk to quadruple sales.

White Consolidated bought Frigidaire from General Motors Corporation in 1979. In an effort to improve sales, the company initiated a program to create awareness for Frigidaire and generate brand loyalty. The basic theme was one of longevity—specifically, "Frigidaire, here today, here tomorrow."

Rediscovering Former Users

A company may find many former users no longer wanting its product or switching to a generic product. For example, a small core of mothers (about 8 percent) had always resisted prepared baby foods; an antiprocess, natural attitude raised that group to almost 20 percent in the 1970s. Gerber's campaign, "A mother's confidence is earned with quality and concern" was designed to retrieve this segment. As a greater percentage of the food budget began to be spent on eating out, meat companies found their share declining. "Meal in a pouch" was introduced and advertised as a simple way of preparing food to encourage more home cooking and meat consumption.

Attracting Users of Competitors' Brands

Some advertising implies that the advertised product is superior to the competition—one toilet tissue has more sheets than its rivals, a paper towel is more absorbent, a drug product offers faster relief. These statements may be designed to attract users of competitive brands.

In the late 1970s, Procter & Gamble introduced its Folger brand of coffee in the Eastern market in direct competition with General Foods' leading brand, Maxwell House. P & G's advertising campaign featured Mrs. Olson who emphasized Folger's "mountaingrown" qualities, while General Foods' ads presented Cora who declared Maxwell House as the best and only coffee her store would sell. In 1980, Maxwell House was surpassed for the first time as the Number One selling brand by Folger.

---

[2]Louis J. Haugh, "Nabisco Finding New Ad Muscle Via Cell System," *Advertising Age* (June 13, 1977), p. 30.

EXHIBIT 7.3
Rekindling Interest in a Mature
Product

These results are not solely attributable to the advertising campaign; however, Procter & Gamble continued to use Mrs. Olson as its spokesperson, while General Foods replaced Cora.

Increasing the Usage Rate

A company may attempt to generate greater sales by increasing the usage rate of its products. This can be accomplished by increasing the variety of uses, the frequency of use, or reducing the time between purchases. Occasionally, a company may advertise a product to increase usage rate of companion products. This occurs in the industrial market, where parts and accessories generally accompany the purchase of capital

HEALTH INSURANCE

One of the best ways to insure good health, is to eat a well-balanced diet that includes nutritious foods like Campbell's Soup.

That's not just our opinion. The fact is university researchers found that soup plays a significant part in a nutritionally healthy diet.

That Campbell's Tomato Soup up there, for instance, is an important source of vitamin C. While Campbell's Vegetable Beef contains more than 1/3 of the day's allowance of vitamin A in just a single serving.

And not only are most Campbell's Soups a rich source of nutrition, they're also light on your stomach, and easy to digest.

So when you're picking out a good health insurance policy, remember to pick up a few cans of your favorite Campbell's Soups.

If you have any questions, talk to one of the best insurance agents around. Mom.

CAMPBELL'S SOUP IS GOOD FOOD

equipment and in the consumer goods market, where the advertising of cameras is designed to increase the sale of film and related products.

Increasing the Frequency of Use

A company may be concerned that its product is used too infrequently by consumers even though the product may have been widely adopted. Campbell's Soup is found in most American cupboards; nevertheless, it may not be used frequently enough. The company has recently begun testing campaigns designed to increase the frequency with which Campbell's soups are used (see Exhibit 7.4).[3]

Other companies try to generate increases in sales in a similar fashion. For example, a drain cleaner firm may advise the public to use its product once a week, rather than once a month. A producer of cameras may try to persuade people that pictures can tell a continuing story if they are taken more frequently.

Get first-time color every time with Q-tips Cosmetic Applicators.

The same color, applied with a used applicator (right), and with a Q-tips® Cosmetic Applicator (left).

Even the freshest, brightest makeup can turn muddy when you apply it with a used foam applicator.

But when you use disposable Q-tips® Cosmetic Applicators, today's pinks will never be overshadowed by yesterday's blues.

The secret? A soft, virtually fuzz-proof surface. And a specially contoured design that holds its shape—Just right for application and blending.

When you're done, you just toss Q-tips® Cosmetic Applicators away. And next time, count on colors just as fresh and true as the first time.

Q·tips®
Cosmetic Applicators

UNIQUE SHAPE

© 1986, Chesebrough-Pond's Inc.

EXHIBIT 7.5
Finding a New Usage

Increasing the Variety of Uses

Kleenex was introduced in the 1920s when a Kimberly-Clark executive, afflicted with hay fever, developed a tissue made of two thin layers of cellucotton bonded together. Since the company was not certain of the size of the hay-fever sufferers' market, it decided, in 1924, to sell the product as a disposable cold cream towel. The market for Kleenex, however, identified itself by 1930, when enough experiment-minded consumers had written to the company touting Kleenex as a good handkerchief. The company tested two coupon ads, one promoting Kleenex for cold cream removal, and the other as a disposable handkerchief. The handkerchief ads were much more successful, and the company altered its advertising accordingly.[4]

---

[3]Philip Dougherty, "Advertising," *The New York Times* (September 19, 1980), p. D13.
[4]"How Sniffles Market Came to Kleenex," *Advertising Age* (April 30, 1980), p. 42.

EXHIBIT 7.6
Objective: Reducing Time Between Purchases

The decision to increase the variety of uses for a product in an effort to generate sales increases may emerge for a number of reasons. The increasing competition in the household cleaning market has resulted in glass cleaners which are advertised as products to clean refrigerators, cabinets, and other kitchen appliances. The obsolescence of its baking soda caused Arm & Hammer to find many "deodorant" uses for its product.

Reducing the Time Between Purchases

More frequent use generally results in reducing the time between purchases; however, some advertising campaigns more specifically focus on this objective by declaring, "Don't wait until your toothbrush is soft before you buy a new one," or "Change the deodorant in your refrigerator before it becomes ineffective," or "Buy now, pay later." Exhibit 7.6 shows Eureka's appeal to the consumer.

Marketing Mix Objectives

When a firm wishes to introduce a new product, a product modification, or even a new package, an advertising campaign is frequently prepared to provide support. A *"teaser" campaign*, so named for its strategy to attract attention and provoke curiosity, is sometimes used prior to the new product's introduction. Ford used such a campaign prior to the introduction of its new Escort line (see Exhibit 7.7).

New prices, price changes, price discounts, rebates, and warranties all benefit from a supportive advertising campaign. Advertising also creates support for personal selling; the advertisements create familiarity with the product or the firm and ease the salesperson's first contact with potential customers.

Advertising campaigns may be used to encourage retailers to carry a product and to provide reseller support. Such campaigns, frequently designated as *pushing* through the channels of distribution, create awareness of the product among resellers, generate excitement, or feature special inducements such as discounts.

Advertisements may also *pull* products through their channels of distribution. This strategy, called "selling your customer's customer," may be used for both consumer and industrial products. A large proportion of the advertising budgets of major manufacturers is spent on advertising to consumers although they have no direct contact with them. The campaigns encourage consumers to use their products and to request they be stocked by retailers. American Steel advertises to both marketing intermediaries and consumers, extolling the benefits of cans made of steel.

COMMUNICATION OBJECTIVES

The relationship between advertising and sales rarely is direct; instead, advertising is generally viewed as a process which encourages the consumer to go through a series of steps that ultimately may result in a

EXHIBIT 7.7
A Teaser Campaign

USING A PULL STRATEGY

Alkot Industries introduced its Love Wheels line of fashion infant strollers with an unusually large $1.5 million television advertising campaign. What makes the campaign noteworthy is that juvenile equipment manufacturers rarely have advertised their baby strollers directly to consumers. Instead, they have concentrated on selling them via ads to the retail trade.

The ad campaign, with the theme "Don't get pushed around in anything less," is targeted to upscale parents and features mothers taking their babies with them to the office, the tennis courts, or out for an evening on the town.

Source: Laurie Freeman, "Alkot Targets Boomer Babies," *Advertising Age* (February 11, 1985), p. 74.

sale. This concept was expressed as early as the 1920s in the AIDA theory, which postulates that advertising should capture *A*ttention, secure *I*nterest, create *D*esire, and ultimately encourage *A*ction.

In 1961, a study on advertising objectives was prepared for the Association of National Advertisers.[5] In this widely quoted study, Colley declared, "Advertising's job, purely and simply, is to communicate, to a defined audience, information and a frame-of-mind that stimulates action."[6] The technique developed by Colley is called DAGMAR (an acronym for Designing Advertising Goals for Measured Advertising Results) and offers a method for selecting and quantifying advertising goals.

DAGMAR is based on a hierarchy-of-effects model of consumer behavior, which suggests that there is a causal or predictive relationship between changes in a person's knowledge or attitude about a product or service and changes in his or her purchase of that product or service. Furthermore, it hypothesizes that a consumer goes through a series of levels of understanding (steps) toward increased commitment to action: awareness, comprehension, conviction, and action.

Colley defines an advertising goal as a *"specific communication task* to be accomplished among a *defined audience* to a *given degree* in a *given period* of time."[7] The communication task is derived from marketing goals and may be designed to accomplish any of the steps. The goals for a hosiery firm, for example, may be as follows:

— *Marketing Goal:* Establish distribution in 1200 Grade-A retail outlets, achieve sales volume of $15 million in three years.
— *Advertising Goal:* Establish brand awareness (communication task) among 60 percent (degree) of the 10-million women who customarily wear hosiery nearly every day (defined audience) in one year (time period). Convey message of antifatigue benefits plus sheer beauty to 30 percent (degree) of the 10-million women who customarily wear hosiery nearly every day (defined audience) in one year (time period).

[5]Russell H. Colley, *Defining Advertising Goals for Measured Advertising Results* (New York: Association of National Advertisers, Inc., 1961).
[6]Colley, *Defining Advertising Goals for Measured Advertising Results*, p. 22.
[7]Colley, *Defining Advertising Goals for Measured Advertising Results*, p. 6 (not italic in original).

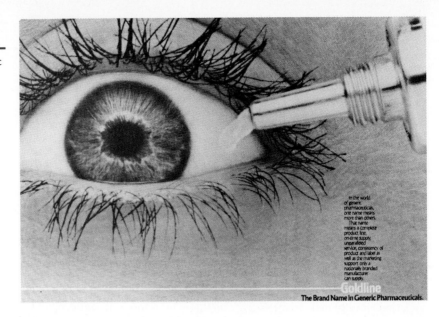

A number of hierarchy-of-effects models have been developed since DAGMAR. While the steps vary, typically they encompass awareness, interest, comprehension, conviction, and action, which may incorporate trial and repurchase.

Awareness

Most advertising campaigns have as one of their objectives the creating of awareness among prospective purchasers (see Exhibit 7.8). This is sometimes difficult for advertisers to do because there are so many competitive ads and audiences can turn off their TVs or skip the ads in magazines. When advertisements are successful firms benefit, as in the case of the "1984" ad for the Macintosh.

Interest

The product itself may be sufficient to arouse the interests of consumers who want to or are about to purchase it. Consumer behavior research has disclosed that ads for products people have recently purchased may also arouse their interest.

Rather than rely on the product itself to capture interest, advertisers frequently look for a feature that is of some importance to prospective purchasers by analyzing social and economic needs, fashion changes, and life-style changes. For example, recent emphasis on "naturalness" in today's society has resulted in ads for cereals, hair sprays, and soaps with natural ingredients.

EXHIBIT 7.9
Comprehension Goal: A Clear
Understanding of a Product's Benefits

Comprehension

Comprehension generally requires a clear examination of the features and benefits of the product (see Exhibit 7.9). It also may correct false impressions, misinformation, and other obstacles to sales. Campbell's introduced Cup of Soup for the singles' segment. To correct a mistaken impression, they advertised that Cup of Soup is not merely half a regular can of soup, but a specific serving.

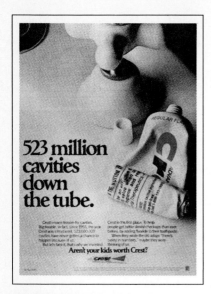

EXHIBIT 7.10
Detailing Product Superiority

EXHIBIT 7.11
Creating a Unique Position

Conviction

If the objective is conviction, advertising uses persuasion to extol the superiorities of a product, the reputation of a firm, or offer proof of a product or firm's attributes. To convince consumers of Parkay margarine's superiority, its advertisements declare "the flavor says 'butter'," and Crest ads ask, "Aren't your kids worth Crest?" (see Exhibit 7.10).

Action

An advertisement cannot compel an individual to act; however, the hierarchy-of-effects thesis assumes, everything else being equal, that if an ad follows the appropriate steps, it will ultimately lead to purchase action. Moreover, if an advertisement arouses a strong consumer motive or need, it may lead to action.

To which level of the hierarchy should the message be focused? The answer depends on a number of factors relevant to the product and its competition. These may encompass, for example, the product's stage in its life cycle, whether new attributes have been added, the consumer's attitude toward the product, and the actions of producers of competitive products.

In the early days of the handheld calculator industry, which developed in the seventies, most of the ads were directed toward the *awareness* stage, notifying consumers that such a product was available. This industry reached maturity quickly and, by the eighties, most of the ads were directed at the *comprehension, conviction,* or *action* stage. The advertising began to stress the benefits of the product, its problem-solving ability and low cost, and the reputation of the firm.

DAGMAR has made a contribution to the field of marketing. It is useful as a planning tool, as well as indicating the importance of focusing on the effects of communication activities. Critics of the DAGMAR method cite the problems of relating a communication goal to a corporate goal expressed in dollars. It is clear that all sales do not follow the simple path outlined in the DAGMAR spectrum; some purchases are made on impulse, thus skipping some of the steps. In addition, DAGMAR represents a rational approach, thereby stultifying creativity and inhibiting "great ideas."

POSITIONING AS AN OBJECTIVE

Positioning, described in Chapter 3, is considered an important objective for many advertising campaigns. The position refers to how consumers perceive the product in relation to other products. When a company uses positioning as an objective, theoretically this permits consumers to perceive the product more accurately, or, at least in a manner which the advertiser believes is more desirable (see Exhibit 7.11).

A product may be positioned to set it apart from all competitors. One way a firm can do this is by developing unique characteristics for

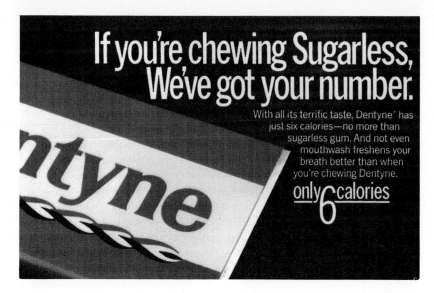

EXHIBIT 7.12
Positioning with Less

its product. Mobil One was advertised as a new synthetic oil; Cycle Dog Food was a new concept in dog feeding that concerned itself with the ages of the dog; while Hero was introduced as "the only dog food made for larger breed dogs." A second way to set a product apart is to claim something about a product that no one else has claimed before—this technique is called *preemption*. Coast deodorant soap declares it is refreshing, an unusual claim for a deodorant soap; Contac declares it is a "keeping-you-going cold medicine."

A product may be positioned to have the same attributes as others. Thus, the desirability of high fiber content and nutrition have led cereal manufacturers to advertise some of their products as similar to their competitors' in offering these benefits. A company may also use the attributes of its competitors to show how it differs. Products can be positioned as offering *more* (more cleaning shine) or, as illustrated in Exhibit 7.12, less (less calories). Chapter 10 discusses the techniques for determining appropriate positions for products.

A product can be positioned as serving the needs of a specific target group. Secret is a deodorant for women, McDonalds is a family restaurant, and Wendy's is for adults. Heinz Weight Watchers is positioned for a specific market—people on diets.

Repositioning

Advertising may be used to reposition a product; this is particularly useful when a product finds itself in a declining market or possessing an unsatisfactory image. Repositioning can indicate that the product is more current, more relevant to life styles, or possesses more salient attributes. Although diet drinks usually stress low caloric content, the emerging emphasis on the importance of calcium for older women had led Coca Cola to reposition Tab as "the one with calcium." Trident gum

UNSUCCESSFUL POSITIONING

The Marketing Intelligence Service, a company that monitors products for some of the nation's leading manufacturers, displays marketing successes and failures on the shelves of its Museum of New Products. Among the failures are products such as Singles, a baby-food product Gerber attempted to position for adults, and Nestlé's line of New Cookery products, which were all low in starches, sugar, and fats, positioned for the creative segment.

While the reasons for their failures are not clear, it appears that Singles was associated by adults with baby food and may have reminded adults that they had to eat alone. New Cookery packaging may have been too bland and its name may have suggested work, unlike the successful Lean Cuisine line which connotes taste and trimness.

Source: Sandra Salmans, "Museum Houses Shattered Dreams," *Chicago Tribune* (March 10, 1985), Sec. 15, p. 5.

was repositioned as a product that helps reduce plaque on teeth.

With the emphasis on physical fitness, several major food companies have repositioned products already naturally low in calories as diet or reduced-calorie foods. Campbell's, for example, increased its soup sales after repositioning sixteen of its low-calorie soups as "The Light Ones." Similarly, Heinz has repositioned its water-packed tuna as "great taste, great for the waist." In fact, water-packed tuna is the fastest-growing tuna category.[8]

SUMMARY

Advertising objectives are derived from the firm's corporate and marketing objectives. They crystallize the firm's advertising aims and provide a basis for decision making and evaluation. Specifically, advertising objectives help determine advertising strategy.

Advertising objectives are usually designated as sales or communication objectives. Sales objectives attempt to generate a sales increase through increasing the number of customers a company serves or increasing the rate at which its products are used. Communication objectives focus on the message and are based on the hierarchy-of-effects theory. This theory postulates changes in a person's knowledge or attitude about a product or service and changes in his or her purchase of that product or service. Thus, advertising objectives are defined in terms of a specific communication task—to encourage awareness, comprehension, interest, conviction, or action.

Positioning, defined as finding a desirable niche for a product or service, is a competitive strategy for achieving advertising objectives. A product may be positioned as having unique characteristics or having properties which are superior to those of its competitors. Products may also be positioned as fitting the needs of a specific market segment.

[8]"Fat Market for Thin Foods," *Marketing & Media Decisions* (April 1980), p. 120.

QUESTIONS FOR DISCUSSION

1. What are the problems in setting sales objectives for advertising?
2. Despite these problems, under what circumstances would you recommend such objectives? Why?
3. What specific objectives can be used to increase the number of customers for an advertiser? Give examples.
4. How can you increase the variety of uses for a product through advertising?
5. Describe some advertising campaigns whose objectives are primarily to provide support for other elements of the marketing mix.
6. What is meant by a hierarchy-of-effects model of consumer behavior?
7. Discuss the advertising goals established through the hierarchy-of-effects thesis and provide examples.
8. Why is positioning considered an important advertising objective?
9. What positioning strategies would appeal to you personally?
10. What is meant by repositioning? How is this accomplished in an advertising campaign?

KEY TERMS

objective	preemption
teaser	positioning
AIDA	hierarchy-of-effects theory
DAGMAR	

AD PRACTICE

Describe the specific advertising objectives you would use to generate sales of a new peanut butter. Using DAGMAR prepare an advertising goal for this new product. Select and describe a positioning strategy for the product.

CASE

The Advertising Agency

An agency prepared a series of print ads for a new product introduction. The agency agreement called for compensation on a commission basis. The client requested that expensive special effects be included in the ads. While the final ads met the product manager's criteria, his superiors criticized him for the very high production costs. The product manager explained he misunderstood what aspects of the advertising campaign were covered under the commission agreement.

A company requested an agency that used a fee system send a team to spend the day with him, brainstorming ideas and developing the framework for a newsletter. An account executive, public relations person, copywriter, and art director were assigned to a meeting that was a tremendous success. The client was later shocked to receive a bill

for $1800. He declared he understood the agency billed at $75 per hour, but he thought that was on a project basis, rather than per hour, per person.

Agency/client relationships are often saddled with problems. Remedies exist to cure ailing relationships, but termination sometimes is the only answer. Since starting with a new agency is a time-consuming process, many firms are reluctant to fire their agencies. Hewlett-Packard tries to solve problems by regularly evaluating the performance of some of its advertising agencies. Both client and agency perform the evaluation. Each item on the evaluation form is ranked from exceptional to unacceptable, and each entry includes additional space for comments. The agency is given a chance for rebuttal and negative evaluation results become the basis for termination of the relationship.

DISCUSSION QUESTIONS

1. Who was responsible for the misunderstanding of billing proceedings? What steps should have been taken to avoid these situations?

2. What other problems, besides payment, can cause dissension between clients and agencies?

3. What criteria should be used in an evaluation program like the one conducted by Hewlett-Packard?

Sources: Michael J. Burke, "Ad Agency Billing Policies Must Be Explained, Understood by Managers," *Marketing News* (August 15, 1986), p. 2; Debra Kent, "When to Fire Your Ad Agency and How to Avoid Needing To" *Business Marketing* (September 1985), p. 60.

CASE

Managing Advertising

The yogurt market has been growing at a rate of 14 percent annually and is expected to continue its growth in the future. The major companies who share the refrigerated-yogurt market and their advertising expenditures for 1985 are the following:

had to call it the way it is."

Dannon has boosted its advertising budget and, in an effort to cut other costs, is reducing its fleet of direct store-delivery trucks while increasing distribution through traditional warehouse channels.

have fruit on the bottom. General Mills is trying to strengthen its brand name with a campaign theme, "Let Yoplait teach you French." Yoplait's ad budget jumped 77 percent to $13.3 million in 1984 and the company spent at the same rate in 1985.

Brand	Percentage of Market Share	Sales (in millions)	Advertising Expenditures (in millions)
Dannon	25.2	$144	$ 5.7
General Mills Yoplait	14.5	83	13.3
Kraft Light & Lively and Breyer's	8.0	46	4.4
Kellogg's Whitney's	2.0	11.5	1.4
Beatrice's Mountain High	2.0	11.5	1.0

Source: From "To-Fitness Hopes For Instant Yogurt Success" by Julie Franz, *Advertising Age* (October 14, 1985). Copyright © 1985 Crain Communications, Inc. Reprinted with permission from Advertising Age. All rights reserved.

Competition in the yogurt industry is becoming increasingly intense as new companies are entering the market with powdered yogurt products that can be mixed with milk or water. To meet the growing competition Dannon has introduced Dannon Supreme, reformulated its Y.E.S. into Dannon Extra Smooth, and started selling its Dannon regular in a perforated four-pack. Ad campaigns for Dannon Supreme call the product, "Yogurt good enough to be dessert." Dannon Extra Smooth ads state, "What we created turned out to be so extra smooth and creamy, we finally

Dannon's closest competitor is General Mills' Yoplait. Yoplait beat Dannon to market with its Breakfast Yogurt, a product mixed with fruits and nuts, introduced in 1983. Dannon introduced Hearty Nuts & Raisins in mid '84. The two are also competing with flavored yogurts that

DISCUSSION QUESTIONS

1. What stage of its product life-cycle does yogurt currently occupy? How does this affect the promotional strategy for this product?

2. Evaluate the advertising expenditure strategy of the major firms in the refrigerated yogurt market. What techniques would you recommend for Dannon's advertising budget determination in the future?

3. Describe the methods you would use for selecting advertising objectives in the yogurt market.

Source: Julie Franz, "To-Fitness Hopes for Instant Yogurt Success," *Advertising Age*, pp. 7, 76.

III

Advertising Campaign and Strategy

Iɴ this part we discuss the numerous activities required for the preparation, implementation, and evaluation of an advertising campaign. The formulation of a campaign, as with most decision-making activities, involves a series of stages. These stages, however, may vary in terms of intensity of effort and need not progress in a precisely consecutive order. The stages include situation analysis, creative strategy, media strategy, and evaluation of advertising effectiveness. Finally, we examine specialized advertising campaigns and look at the preparation of a specific advertising campaign.

8

Marketing Intelligence and Segmentation Analysis

Because of a declining demand in the cereal industry Kellogg Company has been forced to closely examine the changing characteristics of the population. The most significant problem is that people under 25, the biggest cereal eaters, are decreasing as a percent of the population and will decline in absolute terms in the future. In its search for new target opportunities Kellogg has selected several demographically based market segments for targeting:

Older People: All Bran with its high fiber content

Young Adults: Most with its high nutritional content

Teenagers: Honey & Nut Corn Flakes, a sugared version of corn flakes

Children: Graham Crackos and Crunchy Loggs, both pre-sweetened

At the same time Kellogg has repositioned some of its other brands. For example, Frosted Flakes, its largest selling children's cereal, is advertised in TV scenes with adults whose faces are in shadows, declaring, "Yesterday the neighbors saw a box of Frosted Flakes on the table, and we don't even have children."

The initial step in the preparation of an advertising campaign is to gather and evaluate information necessary for both the selection of an appropriate target group and the implementation of an effective advertising program. This procedure is called *situation analysis*.

INFORMATION REQUIREMENTS FOR SITUATION ANALYSIS

It is difficult to be specific about the nature or extent of information required for situation analysis, since this may vary widely in different markets and for different products, but there are categories of information that should be analyzed. Table 8.1 outlines the information that should be gathered in developing an advertising campaign.

The modern concept of marketing emphasizes the need for more, better, and faster information so that marketing and advertising strategies can become sensitive to emerging and changing conditions. With the rapid development of computer-based technology the quantity of information available is increasing exponentially, and the problems of delineating the appropriate intelligence, isolating and preparing it in usable form, and delivering it to the responsible decision-maker are taking on equally broad proportions. Efforts to gather information involves marketing research, advertising research, and the use of Marketing Information Systems.

TABLE 8.1   Information Requirements for Situation Analysis

Market and Market Trends

Secure data on the market composition, total size, anticipated growth, technological developments, market share, market potential and seasonal fluctuations.

Competitive Situation

Compare company's product with competitors in following areas: product characteristics, pricing structure, channels of distribution, advertising and promotion activities (including expenditures, media mix, and creativity).

Problems

What are the relevant problem areas for the product or service (reaching saturation, declining demand, technological improvements, poor image, lack of brand loyalty)?

Advertising Opportunities

What are the advertising opportunities (changing life-styles, introducing new products, superiority over competitors, new benefits, solving problems)?

Target Market

Describe customers on the basis of demographic characteristics, behavioral characteristics, and usage habits.

Legal and Consumerist Issues

What are the legal, social and economic implications of advertising this product or service? What are the current pertinent consumerist issues (complaints, encouragement of nonnutritional eating habits, junk foods)?

Marketing Research and Advertising Research

Marketing research, traditionally considered the province of the intelligence-gathering function, has been defined as "the systematic gathering, recording, and analyzing of data about problems relating to the marketing of goods and services."[1] Its role is to integrate, organize, and interpret the various data flows to provide marketing intelligence which will improve the quality of managerial decision-making throughout a firm. Briefly, marketing research applies systematic research analysis to a business decision problem. It is an attempt to use the scientific tools and methods of logic to arrive at a business decision, rather than rely solely on judgment and intuition. Nevertheless, experience, judgment, and acumen are important attributes for the advertising decision-maker.

Advertising research is a specific application of marketing research to the special characteristics of advertising. In addition to traditional marketing research efforts, advertising research encompasses the numerous findings emerging in consumer behavior research, as well as pure research, which is designed to develop general theoretical approaches to the creation of advertising strategies. Advertising research can be applied to any stage of an advertising campaign, from situation analysis to the evaluation of a campaign's effectiveness.

Marketing Information Systems

In keeping with a strategic approach to marketing, the concept of marketing research is being widened to encompass a marketing information system which emphasizes the systematic and continuing flow of marketing intelligence. A *Marketing Information System* (MIS) is a formalized method of gathering and analyzing data continually in order to secure information that will help marketing managers make decisions.[2] Many firms engage in marketing research to secure such data for a specific project, but a marketing information system is continuous and ongoing.

Such systems provide information for all areas of marketing decision-making. According to Kotler, there are three distinct marketing information flows within a company[3] (see Figure 8.1):

— The marketing intelligence flow provides information from the environment to the firm, information from customers and competitors, government actions bearing on marketing, prices, and advertising effectiveness.

---

[1]Committee on Definitions of the American Marketing Association, Ralph S. Alexander, Chairman, *Marketing Definitions: A Glossary of Marketing Terms,* pp. 16–17.

[2]Committee on Definitions of the American Marketing Association, pp. 16–17.

[3]Philip Kotler, "A Design for a Firm's Marketing Nerve Center," *Readings in Marketing Information Systems: A New Era in Marketing Research,* Samuel V. Smith, Richard H. Brien, and James E. Stafford (Boston: Houghton-Mifflin Company, 1968), p. 18.

FIGURE 8.1 Three Marketing Information Flows

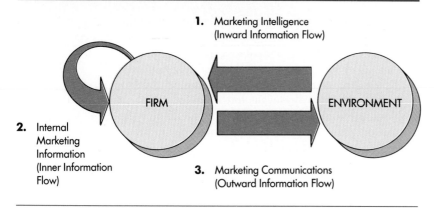

Source: from "A Design for the Firm's Marketing Nerve Center" by Philip Kotler, *Business Horizons* (June 1966), p. 67. Reprinted by permission of Indiana University.

— The internal information flow provides marketing information between relay points within the firm.

— The marketing communications flow provides information from the firm outward to the environment and consists of company information and product and company promotion.

Advertising is part of the third flow of information; however, its effective preparation and development depends on the first two.

Marketing information systems tend to be adopted by major companies; however, their use is likely to expand as more managers realize their desirability. They are particularly appropriate for advertising decisions since these decisions may have an impact on many areas in the firm. For example, the requirement that advertisers substantiate their advertising claims has led to the realization that an information flow is necessary between the advertising department and members of an organization, even in the early product-planning and development stages. Ad executives may find it useful to communicate with engineers about product development in order to ensure that there is available evidence to document product claims made in future ads.

SOURCES OF MARKETING INFORMATION

There are numerous sources of marketing intelligence that can be incorporated in a marketing information system. Information may be secured from the company's own records, from external sources, and from specialized research firms.

Primary and Secondary Data

Primary data is the term used to identify information gathered by an investigator or someone he or she has assigned to a specific need or problem. For example, if a retailer assigns someone to collect information on his or her store image, the resulting data would be primary.

Secondary data is information gathered by other individuals or organizations which are relevant to the investigator's study of a particular problem; for example, an investigator might use government or trade association studies on the number of firms in an industry. Secondary data are generally exhausted before the investigator turns to primary data, since securing secondary data is generally less expensive. In fact, much of the information concerning situation analysis is developed through secondary data.

Internal versus External Data

Another distinction that should be made is between facts from internal sources—that is, from an organization's own records—and facts from external sources, which includes all other sources of information.

Internal data includes the company's financial reports, such as its balance sheets, profit and loss statements, sales records (sales budgets and sales performance records), and production records (inventory control and factory cost data). Advertising researchers pay particular attention to advertising expenditures and sales records and find useful any breakdown of this information in terms of customers, products, geographic areas or time elements.

External data are facts from sources other than the company's own records. There is a vast resource of external data available to the researcher. The difficulty lies in locating and evaluating it in order to determine what is relevant, unbiased, and reliable. Among the major sources of secondary information are publications by the federal government. Trade associations provide information for practically every industry and various syndicated services provide data for analyzing the target market.

STEPS IN SEGMENTATION ANALYSIS

A major objective of situation analysis is to evaluate the target market. Customer information is relevant to many advertising decisions, including the creation of an ad's appeal, its execution, and the selection of media in which it will appear.

The *target group* in advertising is generally described as people who are the *best prospects* for a product or service. These best prospects, in turn, may be described on various dimensions. The most widely used techniques for isolating and examining their characteristics are market segmentation and behavioral analysis. Segmentation techniques are described in this section; behavioral analysis is discussed in the next chapter on consumer behavior.

In market segmentation the total market is divided into well-defined consumer groups who can be reached by one marketing plan. Most advertisers realize that they cannot effectively reach and serve all customers, who are too widely scattered, have different needs, are exposed to different media, and respond to different persuasive efforts. To decide which group to service, advertisers employ market segmentation analysis.

Analyzing the target market from a segmentation perspective involves several steps:[4]

1. Determine the characteristics and needs of consumers for the product or service category of the company.
2. Evaluate the differences and similarities among these consumers.
3. Determine which segments contain the best prospects.
4. Describe these segments and develop a typical profile.
5. Gather data concerning the size of the segments and location of its members, product use patterns, and other relevant information.

THE TARGET MARKET

There are various bases on which a market can be segmented. Those which have special relevance for advertising are demographic segments, psychographic segments, and product usage segments.

Demographic Segmentation

A *demographic segment* is a group of consumers classified by sex, age, geographic location, county size, education, employment, household income, race, marital status, or presence of children. A target market is frequently defined demographically as a group of housewives, teenagers, or those whose income is over $25,000. This way of segmenting consumers has provided the traditional means for advertising analysis.

While demographic segments continue to be important, they have been found insufficiently valid for discriminating between good prospects and poor prospects in all markets; thus, increasing emphasis has been placed on other variables as bases for selecting target markets.

However, the contributions that demographic classifications can make should not be overlooked. They do provide, in quantifiable terms, at least part of the explanation for differences between market segments. Moreover, changes in demographic groups may provide new opportunities in a company's search for its desirable target.

[4]Adapted from Joel R. Evans and Barry Berman, *Marketing*, 2nd ed. (New York: Macmillan Publishing Co., 1985), p. 229.

EXHIBIT 8.1
Advertising to Baby Boomers

Segmenting by Age   Some significant changes in population are important considerations for advertising strategies. The emergence of the Baby Boomers, the graying of America, and the increase in the next decade of all age groups, except for the 14–24 age group, will have a great impact on production. The forecast is for an overwhelmingly adult, largely middle-aged population. However, the long-declining birth rate has recently been reversed, suggesting young people will continue to be an important segment.

Baby Boomers   The generation of *baby boomers,* those people born between 1946 and 1964, consists of 76 million people, or nearly one-third of the U.S. population.[5] Baby boomers are competitive, ambitious,

[5]Judith Langer, "The Baby Boomers: Target Market of the 80s," *Product Marketing* (August 1985), p. 11.

EXHIBIT 8.2
40 is Fabulous

relatively affluent, and more highly educated than any previous generation of Americans. They are old enough to be wage earners and young enough to be very active. They are innovative, willing to test new products, new fads, and new ideas; they are particularly interested in new health values as well as quality in goods, services, and life styles. According to a POPAI/DuPont Drugstore survey the baby boomers comprise the largest buying segment for cosmetics and fragrances.[6]

Despite general similarities the baby boomer generation is not monolithic; boomers live diverse life styles, so portraying them only one way in advertisements can be a mistake. Advertising appeals which are particularly meaningful to these people include quality, personal growth and satisfaction, healthfulness, hi-tech modernity, and a balance of work and family/personal life (see Exhibit 8.1).

Older Groups　　The importance of the older consumer as a target group will increase. There are over 60 million Americans age 50 or older; in 1984 the number of people over 65 exceeded the number of teenagers for the first time in history.[7] This mature market will get larger, according to demographers, because of improving health care, a dwindling birth rate, and an aging of the offspring of the post-World War II baby boom.

In terms of funds available for spending, households headed by someone 45 or older control 60 percent of all discretionary income. More important these older consumers apparently have a changed outlook on life, one which suggests that they are not willing to retire to inactive lives. For example, the older consumers are good targets for the travel market; not only are they generally among the most affluent, they also have the most vacation time and see travel as important. Americans 50 years and older represent an $800 billion travel market.[8]

---

[6]Alfred Modugno, "The Baby Boomers: Who They Are, How They Shop," *Product Marketing* (August 1985), p. 10.

[7]"Misdirected Advertising Prevents Marketers from Taking Bite from 'Golden Apple' of Maturity Market," *Marketing News* (October 26, 1984), p. 19.

[8]"The Gold in the Gray," *Fortune* (October 14, 1985), p. 137.

Although the number of elderly in the population has increased in the last thirty years, the change in the frequency with which older people appear in magazine advertisements is not statistically significant.[9] Nor has there been a significant change in their portrayal, which tends to be in working situations, mostly in prestigious jobs. However, it appears that the majority of elderly models is male, which does not correlate to demographics; that is, the majority of the elderly population is female. Some older female models have been used effectively. Martha Raye is a successful spokesperson for Block Drug's Polident.

Germaine Monteil Cosmetiques ran an over-40 beauty search for a nonmodel to represent its products and selected silver-haired Tish Hooker, in her forties.[10] A company spokesperson declared that they tripled their business after featuring Ms. Hooker (see Exhibit 8.2).

Advertisers, however, are concerned that a featured product may develop an "old" stigma. In fact they note that many older women do not want to be isolated by age. Johnson & Johnson encountered problems when it introduced Affinity, a hair conditioner specifically for older hair. It found that the woman-over-40 image was so strong that the benefits of the product didn't come through. It changed its strategy to a more romantic approach which depicted a chance meeting between an older female and a male friend who complimented her looks.

The older-consumer segment is not necessarily a homogeneous market but, in fact, may be further segmented. This creates additional problems for advertisers. Moreover, advertisers do not want to alienate the young by focusing on age.

Care is also taken not to mock older people or make fun of them. An ad campaign for Country Time lemonade mix showed a somewhat deaf and befuddled grandfather repeating incorrectly what people were telling him about Country Time. General Foods withdrew the commercial after receiving a barrage of complaints and replaced it with a campaign in which the grandfather was active, vigorous, had a good memory, and touted the "good old fashioned taste" of the drink mix.[11]

Advertisers can reach older people through all media; however, a number of radio programs are now more specifically geared to this group. There are the all-news radio and the "talk" radio programs, as well as radio drama such as "CBS Radio Mystery Theater" and Mutual Network's "Radio Theater" series. Some stations are resurrecting the Big Band music of the 1950s to supplement their programs for the elderly, while a radio station in Phoenix, Arizona, KWAO, structures its programs exclusively for older adults.[12] Many magazines are also de-

[9]Anthony C. Ursic, Michael L. Ursic, and Virginia L. Ursic, "A Longitudinal Study of the Use of the Elderly in Magazine Advertising," *Journal of Consumer Research*, Vol. 12 (June 1986), pp. 131–133.

[10]Debra Kant, "Mature Advertisers Have Trouble Acting Their Age," *Advertising Age* (September 12, 1985), pp. 22, 26.

[11]Theodore J. Gage, "Ads Targeted at Mature in Need of Creative," *Advertising Age* (August 25, 1980), p. S-5.

[12]James Brown, "Radio Encore: Tuning in on the Old," *Advertising Age* (August 25, 1980), p. S-2.

TECHNIQUES FOR CREATING ADS FOR OLDER PEOPLE

1. Avoid cluttering ads or packages with too much visual information.
2. Use action in commercials if it's relevant and isn't distracting.
3. Avoid fast-speaking characters or those who don't enunciate clearly.
4. Keep the language and message simple with the focus on one or two selling points.
5. Don't insult older people. A particularly offensive commercial for Block Drug once showed an elderly couple perched in infant high chairs. The message was supposed to be that people with loose dentures need easy-to-chew foods.
6. Present the elderly as useful, competent, and coping.

Source: Bill Abrams, "Advertisers Start Recognizing Cost of Insulting Elderly," *The Wall Street Journal* (March 5, 1981), p. 27.

signed to reach the mature market, including *50 Plus, Modern Maturity,* and *Dynamic Years.*

Teenagers   Despite their decline in numbers in recent years, the teen market will continue to be important to marketers and advertisers. The population between the ages of 13–19 was reported as 25.6 million people in 1985.[13] Although the total teenage population is declining, its purchasing power is increasing. More teens work part-time and spend money on themselves. Estimates of teen spending power range from $30 billion to over $40 billion a year, and that money goes almost exclusively for discretionary purchases.

The rise in the number of working women and single-parent households has contributed to the growth in the number of teen shoppers. Recent surveys found that 49 percent of teenage girls and 26 percent of boys shop once a week or more for family groceries.[14] The current teenagers, unlike the "baby boom teen," are more likely to try new items, new methods, and new stores. Moreover, a large proportion of them are making their own brand decisions in the supermarket.

Both female and male teenagers spend most of their money on clothes, entertainment, and travel. For some products teenagers may be the most important segment. For example, *Seventeen* magazine notes that 90.5 percent of girls between 13–19 wear nail polish—and, in fact, teenage girls wear more nail polish than anyone else. Furthermore, teenagers develop strong brand loyalties which they retain through their adult years.[15]

---

[13]Doris L. Walsh, "Targeting Teens," *American Demographics* (February 1985), p. 21.

[14]Ibid., p. 23.

[15]"Teenagers: Rising in Income and Firm in Brand Loyalty," *Business Week* (April 23, 1984), p. 51.

GUIDELINES FOR ADS TO BLACK CONSUMERS

— Avoid negative images of blacks.
— Avoid long-winded copy.
— Avoid slang or street language.
— Use black models, rather than showing only the product.

— Strive for realism when depicting affluent blacks.
— Use integrated scenes, when possible, taking care that blacks are not shown as tokens or in uncommon situations.

Source: J. Robert Harris II, "Focus Groups Offer Six 'Guidelines' for Black-Oriented Ads," *Marketing News* (October 16, 1981), p. 5.

Some food firms are repositioning their products to reach the teen market. Since 1932 Frito-Lay sold its corn chips to mothers in the 24–54 age group. Today it is aiming for the teen market in television spots featuring a teen gang called "Snackers."[16]

Advertising to teenagers requires an awareness of the current influences, language, music, and habits of teenagers, as well as constant updating of trends and life-styles in the teenage culture.

Segmenting by Ethnicity   Ethnic segments are important to advertisers since these groups tend to exhibit similar values, needs, and behavioral patterns, which are useful in the development of advertising strategies. Blacks comprise the largest ethnic group in the United States; however Hispanics are the fastest growing segment.

The Black Target Market   Blacks currently represent almost 12 percent of the population. They are heavy purchasers of some products; for example, on the average they purchase 6 percent more packaged instant potatoes and eat 7 percent more rice a year than the general market. Blacks also buy 35 percent more orange juice, consume 69 percent more soft drinks, and purchase 44 percent more record albums,[17] and spend ten percent above the national average on fragrances.[18]

Some companies serve blacks as their major target market. For example, S. C. Johnson markets mainly to blacks; the company found that Enhance hair conditioner had a special appeal for blacks with dry hair, and emphasized this benefit in its advertisements.[19] According to past research, blacks are brand loyal. Some of the most popular branded

---

[16] Tom Bayer, "Frito Drops Worn Ads for Jeans and Leather," *Advertising Age* (July 1, 1985), p. 3.

[17] "Potpourri of Statistics," *Advertising Age* (May 18, 1981), p. S-11.

[18] Delores J. Brooks, "Pumping dollars into fragrance cosmetic sales," *Advertising Age* (August 28, 1986), p. 5–6.

[19] Theodore J. Gage, "RSVP: An Invitation to Buy," *Advertising Age* (May 18, 1981), p. S-8.

products used by blacks are Tide, Pine Sol, Clorox, S.O.S., Reynolds Wrap, Minute Maid, Maxwell House, Gold Medal, Crisco, Skippy, Kraft mayonnaise, Vaseline Intensive Care, Campbell baked beans, and Scott towels.[20] However, research also revealed that as prices increase, black consumers will change loyalty and become more price conscious, as will other consumers. Thus, while there is still a great deal of brand loyalty among blacks, it appears to be subject to erosion.

In preparing advertisements for blacks, several factors should be considered. Specialized appeals work well among heavy product users in the black community. Such appeals, however, require the use of realistic situations and not just the use of black models in "white" situations. Appeals may be designed to reach upscale individuals, those who are striving for upward mobility. However, some marketers believe in the cross-class approach to black-oriented advertising. This approach uses black models in a neutral setting, and the effect is designed to let consumers mentally fill in the situation from their personal reference points.[21]

Blacks are more likely to be exposed to certain types of media than to others. They tend to report higher radio-usage levels than do whites; this is particularly apparent at night and on weekends.[22] According to a BBDO study based on Nielsen Media Research ratings, the average black household viewed television 71.1 hours weekly during the 1985–86 season.

While magazines may not have heavy black readership, there are indications that the black market can be segmented and affluent blacks can be reached by special interest magazines. These include *Black Enterprise, Dollars & Sense, Black Family,* and *Black Collegian.*[23] Black readership of newspapers tends to be low, in part because newspapers do not offer black readers much relevant information. Possible changes in newspapers in the future may increase service to minorities.

The Hispanic Market Over 18 million Hispanics are living in the United States; over two thirds reside in California, Texas, and New York. More importantly for advertisers, the Hispanic market increased at a rate of over twenty percent during the last five years, making it the fastest growing ethnic segment in the country.[24]

In comparison to the United States average the Hispanic population is younger, its families are larger—averaging four members each—and its household income lower. Of Hispanics living in the United States,

EXHIBIT 8.3
Targeting Black Consumers

[20]Alphonzia Wellington, "Traditional Brand Loyalty," *Advertising Age* (May 18, 1981), p. S-2.

[21]Herbert Allen, "Product Appeal: No Class Barrier," *Advertising Age* (May 18, 1981), p. S-4.

[22]Gerald J. Glasser and Gale D. Metzger, "Radio Usage by Blacks: An Update," *Journal of Advertising Research*, Vol. 21 (April 1981), pp. 47–50.

[23]B. Drake Stelle, "Publishers See Segmentation in Black Market," *Advertising Age* (May 18, 1981), p. S-6.

[24]Ellen Lorenz, "Targeted Media Tap Minority Markets," *Product Marketing* (September 1985), p. 12.

GUIDELINES FOR ADS TO HISPANIC CONSUMERS

— Transmit the feeling that the advertiser believes in the inherent dignity of Hispanics (avoid stereotypes).
— Allow Hispanics to feel respected by using appropriate cultural values and traditions.

— Do not use a blonde blue-eyed actor.
— Do not make fun of the culture or the Hispanic tradition.
— Do not dub television commercials into Spanish in order to save production costs.

Source: Gerardo Marin, "Subjective Culture Perspectives for Culturally Sensitive Marketing to Hispanics." *Proceedings of the Division of Consumer Psychology, American Psychological Association 1985 Annual Convention. Los Angeles, Calif.,* ed., Wayne D. Hoyer (Washington, D.C.: American Psychological Association, Division 23, 1986), p. 66.

63 percent were born outside the country, and 43 percent speak no English or just enough to get by.

Although it is a subject of continuing research the Hispanic market is termed *confusing.* In part, the confusion emanates from the different subgroups who are called Hispanics but have different migration histories and cultural backgrounds. Yankelovich designates these different subgroups as Mexicans, Cubans, Puerto Ricans, and Other Hispanics.[25] Mexicans and Cubans have become assimilated and share a commitment to the United States. Puerto Ricans appear to retain a "visitor" status. Other Hispanics are the most recent immigrants and are disproportionately young and single.

With the increase in the number and affluence of the Hispanic market, advertisers such as Pepsi-Cola, Budweiser, Gillette, and Kentucky Fried Chicken are exploring this market segment for their products. Hispanics, like blacks, have been stressing product quality and tend to be more brand loyal than the rest of the nation.

Although they are all labeled Hispanic, these groups have idiomatic language and life-style differences. Differences between Hispanics appear to be especially strong in terms of their use of Spanish language media, brand loyalty, and preferences for prestige and ethnically advertised brands.[26] Nevertheless, many advertisers and their agencies feel there is only one Spanish language that is understandable to all Spanish-speaking people and believe one ad can be used effectively. In fact some researchers believe there is a blurring of differences among Hispanics of varying nationalities.[27] Others feel that using a generic Hispanic approach is undesirable and suggest that ads be "transcreated" to appeal

[25]"Spanish USA—A Study of the Hispanic Market in the United States," conducted by Yankelovich, Skelly & White, Inc., for the SIN National Spanish Television Network (June 1981).

[26]Rohit Deshpande, Wayne D. Hoyer, and Naveen Donthu, "The Intensity of Ethnic Affiliation: A Study of the Sociology of Hispanic Consumption," *Journal of Consumer Research,* Vol. 13 (September 1986), p. 219.

[27]"Understanding the People Behind the Numbers," *Advertising Age* (March 21, 1985), p. 13.

to a distinct geographic and ethnic segment of the Hispanic market. A campaign by Coors, for example, uses radio and television copy in standard Spanish, but varies the music by region. "Tex-Mex," or ranchers' music, is used in Texas, while Salsa music is used for Hispanics in Miami.[28]

According to a study of the Spanish market commissioned for SIN, Spanish language television is the leading Hispanic medium.[29] However, Caballero Spanish media represents 90 Spanish language radio stations that reach over 90 percent of the market.[30] It would be a mistake, however, for advertisers to limit purchases to Hispanic language media, since Hispanics divide their viewing time between Spanish- and English-speaking broadcasting stations.

There is agreement among advertising agencies that outdoor advertising is an effective way to reach Hispanics. Posters can be placed wherever Hispanics live and have little wasted circulation.[31] A wide range of products are advertised on outdoor boards including beer, toothpaste, soft drinks, autos, radio stations, airlines, cigarettes, and coffee.

Advertisers to the Hispanic market should try to avoid translation blunders and culture misunderstandings in preparing their advertisements. The Perdue Chickens' slogan "It takes a tough man to make a tender chicken" was translated into Spanish as "It takes a sexually excited man to make a chick sensual."[32]

EXHIBIT 8.4
Targeting the Affluent

Segmenting by Income   Traditionally consumers were divided into low-, middle-, or high-income consumers; today, however, such designations are neither precise nor predictive. The median income for a household in 1985 was approximately $25,000; however, it is possible to consider as middle income a family that earns $50,000 with both husband and wife working to meet the mortgage and college payments for two children.

Affluent Market   From an advertising perspective the emerging *affluent market*, defined as those households with incomes of at least $50,000, represents an important target group. This segment comprised nine percent of the population in 1981 and is expected to triple by 1995[33] (see Exhibit 8.4).

Although a relatively small proportion of the population, affluents account for almost two-thirds of all domestic airline trips and travelers-check purchases, and almost half of the wine consumption. Compared with other households, the affluent home spent four times as much on

---

[28]"Confusing Market . . . ," p. M-36.

[29]"Spanish USA—A Study of the Hispanic Market . . . ."

[30]Ellen Lorenz, "Targeted Media Tap Minority Markets," p. 12.

[31]Renee Blakkan, "Reaching a Growing Market Where It Lives," *Advertising Age* (March 19, 1984), p. M–10.

[32]Humberto Valencia, "Point of View: Avoiding Hispanic Market Blunders," *Journal of Advertising Research*, Vol. 23 (December 1983/January 1984), pp. 19–22.

[33]Thomas J. Stanley and George P. Mockis, "America's Affluent," *American Demographics* (March 1984), p. 28.

books, twelve times as much on stereo equipment, five times as much on major appliances, and two-and-a-half times as much on athletic equipment.[34] Many have memberships in private clubs, own homes with in-ground swimming pools, and, at least once a week or more, use their credit cards for travel and entertainment. They also entertain a great deal at home and consume many wines and liquors.

Affluents are significant prospects for various products and services. Kohler offers a Masterbath for $17,750 and General Motors Cadillac Division has introduced its $50,000 Allante.[35] However, despite their income, the affluent are highly selective in their choices of products. They tend to purchase products that exhibit an image of quality, value, American craftsmanship, class, style, tradition, and uniqueness.[36]

Like most market segments the affluents are made up of subgroups. Over ten years ago, the traditional affluent family tended to be headed by a male, in his mid-40s to early 50s, who was the sole wage earner. Today's affluent households are far more likely to be two-income families headed by individuals in their middle to late 30s.[37] These two-paycheck households are likely to make more dual-purchase decisions. They tend to place a high priority on time and, therefore, are interested in items such as microwave ovens and gourmet frozen foods. They are concerned about self-improvement and education as indicated by the success of such magazines as *Smithsonian* and *Discover*. They have been exposed to high technology and, unlike the affluent 60-year-old, are probably targets for "high tech" items in the home.

Currently, at least, they tend to have fewer children than have previous affluent generations. At the same time they are concerned with the quality of life for these children and are likely to purchase educational toys or computers.

While all kinds of media can reach the affluent, magazines are more likely to be targeted to this specialized audience. For example, a magazine called *W* informs its potential advertisers that its readers' average family income is $117,900, and one in five of its readers is a millionaire. Radio and newspapers are also considered effective media to reach the affluent. Direct mail, however, is considered particularly useful, since potential customers frequently can be identified.[38] Lincoln-Mercury has been using a direct mail program for many years with a very satisfactory response; similarly, Phaelzer Brothers, Chicago, has sold expensive meats through a direct-mail catalog.

[34]"Marketing Ranks of the Rich . . . , " *The Wall Street Journal* (March 12, 1981), p. 33.

[35]Kate Bertrand, "Glassware Ads Reflect Image of Quality," *Advertising Age* (May 9, 1985), p. 18.

[36]Laurie Freeman, "Meat Catalog Offers a Cut Above the Ordinary," *Advertising Age* (May 9, 1985), p. 38.

[37]B. G. Yovivich, "Now, It's the Baby Boomers' Turn," *Advertising Age* (April 4, 1983), p. M-11.

[38]Laurie Freeman, "Meat Catalog Offers a Cut Above the Ordinary," *Advertising Age* (May 9, 1985), p. 38.

Psychographic Segmentation

In *psychographic segmentation,* consumers are divided into different groups on the basis of psychological characteristics which were initially determined through standardized personality and interest inventories developed by psychologists. Since these psychographic traits did not closely relate to the consumption of goods and services, such information was interesting, but it was not particularly useful for describing advertising markets.[39]

To provide a more meaningful description of consumers from an advertising perspective, researchers turned to alternative techniques involving psychological considerations. These include life-style analysis and VALS.

Life-Style Analysis   Life-styles reflect the overall manner in which people live and spend their time and money. *Life-style analysis* determines the "target profile" on the basis of psychographic characteristics. The most widely used inventory for measuring life-style incorporates the use of AIO (Activities, Interests, and Opinions) rating statements. Plummer, a leader in this type of research, describes it as follows:[40]

> *AIO analysis . . . measures . . . [people's] . . . activities in terms of how they spend their time in work and leisure; their interests in terms of what they place importance on in their immediate surroundings; their opinion in terms of their stance on social issues, institutions and themselves; and finally basic facts such as their age, income, and where they live.*

While AIO inventories do not necessarily exclude demographic data, the emphasis on activities, interests, and opinions has caused many people to use the term *psychographics* synonymously with AIO analysis. Rather than use standardized personality inventories, AIO analysis asks respondents to agree or disagree with 200 to 300 statements relevant to their activities, interests, and opinions. Such statements may come from intuition, psychological research, or "hunches," and indicate, for example, what women think about the job of housekeeping or how men feel about hunting.

A study conducted for Schlitz beer revealed that heavy beer drinkers were "real macho people who lived life to the fullest."[41] This discovery led to the famous "gusto-world" commercials, in which Schlitz beer featured ultramasculine men, living exciting lives with gusto.

In applying life-style analysis to laundry detergents for Procter & Gamble, Plummer concluded that the heaviest users of detergents were

---

[39]William D. Wells and Stephen C. Cosmas, "Life Styles," in *Selected Aspects of Consumer Behavior,* pp. 300–301.

[40]Joseph T. Plummer, "Life Style Patterns," *Journal of Broadcasting* (Winter 1971–72), p. 79.

[41]James Atlas, "Beyond Demographics," *The Atlantic Monthly* (October 1984), p. 51.

EXHIBIT 8.5
Merrill Lynch's Print Ads To Three
Distinct Segments of The Women's
Market

young, middle-class women with large families—women who cared about their families but didn't want to be chained to the laundry room. He recommended that Cheer, an established, but poorly selling, Procter & Gamble brand, be repositioned as an easy-to-use, all-temperature product. Cheer went from seventh place to second among detergents in one decade.[42]

Life-style analysis can be conducted to identify the target markets for specific products or services. A financial services company, Merrill Lynch Pierce Fenner & Smith, Inc., conducted such a life-style analysis to attract certain segments of the growing women's investment market.[43] According to the company there were three important life-style segments in the women's investment market.

> The career woman *is 35 years old, career-oriented, an executive on the way up. Her concerns often focus on her growing income, how to fight inflation, and how to limit her tax liability. She can be married or single. The woman in need is usually middle class and has financial responsibility for herself and her children. She is the head of her household, divorced or widowed, and needs to know how to manage her finances. The mature woman is 45 years old or older. She is affluent, perhaps divorced but more likely widowed, and she is looking for financial guidance. Like the woman in need, she is dealing with financial responsibility for the first time in her life.*

VALS   The SRI-Values and Life-Styles (VALS) program, conceptualized by SRI International (formerly known as Stanford Research Institute), has become an important tool for psychographic life-style research. Simmons Market Research Bureau, an organization that provides research data, first introduced VALS into its data base in 1981.

VALS divides people by their values, life-styles, and demographics into three main types of consumers; the three groups are further divided into nine subgroups (see Table 8.2).

While additional data is necessary for more widespread use of the information, advertisers have incorporated into their campaigns characteristics of the target markets and media usage that emerge from VALS typologies. For example, VALS research indicated that Jell-O was a belonger brand. The "Jell-O is Fun" campaign was introduced showing women in provider roles, saying to their families, "I didn't make dessert. Instead, I made some fun."[44]

Alfa Romeo used VALS to select media for advertising its GTV and Spider automobiles.[45] The purchaser of a GTV, according to VALS research, was an achiever, generally a man making over $40,000 who liked "top-of-the-line" products and was interested in technology. Therefore, Alfa Romeo advertised the GTV in *Golf Digest, Gourmet,* and *The New*

---

[42]James Atlas, "Beyond Demographics," *The Atlantic Monthly* (October 1984), p. 51.
[43]"Merrill Lynch Campaign Targeted at Women Stresses Investment Options," *Marketing News* (November 30, 1979), p. 11.
[44]James Atlas, "Beyond Demographics," p. 56.
[45]Philip H. Dougherty, "Advertising, Marsteller Sports Car Campaigns," *The New York Times* (January 25, 1983), p. D-31.

TABLE 8.2 The VALS™ Segments

	VALS™ 1983 Population Distribution
Need-Driven	11%

Adults whose purchasing ability is severely restricted by lack of income and who buy more by need than by choice

Survivors
Those whose struggle for survival is the dominant force in their lives

Sustainers
Desire not only to survive but also to sustain and improve themselves over time

Outer-Directed	68%

The group that is primarily middle and upper-middle class; individuals who generally conduct their lives in accord with what they think others will think

Belongers
Represent the largest single group in the VALS typology; conservative and conventional

Emulators
Ambitious, upwardly mobile, status-conscious and competitive; highly visible, usually flamboyant and called Emulators because they tend to emulate the life-style of their models, the Achievers

Achievers
Those who are driven to success, fame, power, and achievement; spend much of their wealth on the material things of life

Inner-Directed	19%

A group dominated by people born after 1945—the baby boom generation; seek to satisfy their own inner priorities and pleasures rather than responding to the norm of others

I Am Me
A small group of people who are young, impulsive, individualistic, and faddy and are in a transition stage of their lives

Experiential
Those who seek direct experience, intense involvement, and a rich inner life; active in arts and crafts and are leaders in many avant-garde movements

Societally Conscious
Those activists who lead or support many social movements and seek out products that do not offend their philosophic convictions

Integrateds	2%

People who are exceptionally mature in a psychological sense; live in accord with an inner sense of what is fitting, self-fulfilling and balanced; people at this level of development are rare and SMRB does not include them in their data base

| Total | 100% |

Source: "VALS™ 1983 Population Distribution" from Values and Lifestyles (VALS™) Program, SRI International, Menlo Park, California and Simmons Market Research Bureau, Inc., 219 East 42nd Street, New York. Reprinted by permission.

Yorker. The most likely purchaser of a Spider convertible was an emulator, who was not an achiever but would like to be one. Spider was advertised in *Playboy*, *World Tennis*, and *Cuisine*.

Bank of America in California prepared a campaign aimed at achievers who tended to be competitive and individualistic. The bank's ads,

Dr Pepper's "Be a Pepper" campaign was consistently rated in consumer surveys to be among the most memorable campaigns on the air. Nonetheless, the brand's market share began to decline.

Its advertising agency, Young & Rubicam, realized that a mass appeal like "Be a Pepper" contradicted psychographic studies showing fans of Dr Pepper's unusual fruity taste to be inner-directed people. In fact the "Be a Pepper" campaign was aimed incorrectly at the outer-directed belonger.

A new campaign was initiated returning to the concept of the earlier successful slogan "the most original soft drink ever in the whole wide world." A new jingle, "hold out for the out-of-the ordinary," repositioned Dr Pepper as the choice of independent thinkers looking for an alternative to colas. Beverage analysts estimate that Dr Pepper's share of the market has increased with this new campaign.

Source: Adapted from Ronald Alsop, "Dr Pepper Is Bubbling Again After Its 'Be a Pepper' Setback," *The Wall Street Journal* (September 26, 1985), p. 33.

showing men engaged in solo sports such as water skiing and jogging, were successful in achieving its objectives.[46]

Product-Related Segmentation

In *product-related*, or product-use *segmentation* the target market is broken into groups in relation to their uses of the product or their attitudes towards its attributes. Of particular importance to advertisers is *volume segmentation*, dividing the market into groups according to the usage rate, and *benefit segmentation*, a method which looks at the product benefits sought by consumers.

Volume Segmentation An advertiser often finds it desirable to subdivide the market into heavy users, light users, and nonusers. Analysis of user categories can provide insight for advertising decisions. In evaluating a men's hair preparation, for example, it was noted that the best predictor of heavy usage was when the hair preparation was used.[47] Those who used it before work or school were heavy users; those who did not apply it at these times were light users. This suggested that the key was to encourage men and boys to integrate hair preparation into their morning grooming routine. However, nearly all the advertising for

[46]"Wizards of Marketing," *Newsweek* (July 22, 1985), p. 44.
[47] Louis Cohen, "A Rich Hypothesis Generating Process: The Key to Creative Effective Marketing Research," *Marketing Review*, Vol. 38, No. 5 (January-February 1983), pp. 13–21.

hair preparations at the time was showing dating or sports situations. These presentations were changed. Similarly, mouthwash and deodorant advertising went through this dating-scene approach but later switched to morning scenes in ads. Over time, both became everyday-use products.

Nonusers may be subdivided into future users, potential users, users of substitutes, and nonpotential users. These classifications suggest varying advertising strategies. For example, future users may become users over time—the just-married woman is a potential consumer for disposable diapers, the young boy who is just beginning to sprout whiskers is an important future target for a razor blade company. Advertising for this market need only provide information, identification, and awareness of the offerings and their individual benefits (see Exhibit 8.6). In other cases, time alone is not sufficient to develop future users, and stronger, more persuasive promotional strategies may be necessary to convert nonflyers into flyers and men who do not use hairpieces to those who do.

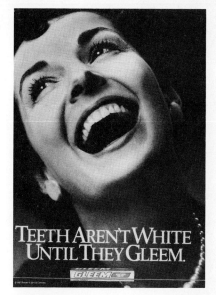

EXHIBIT 8.6
Product-Related Segmentation

There is evidence to indicate that purchase concentration in various product categories is sufficiently skewed to make it worthwhile to consider the heavy user as a distinct market segment. In an analysis of purchase concentration of eighteen product categories, for which purchasing households were arranged in order of purchase volume (light to heavy), it became apparent that one household of heavy users is equal in purchase volume to nine households of light users.[48] In some product categories over 90 percent of the purchases are made by the heavy users.

Benefit Segmentation   Benefit segmentation is based on the idea that the benefits people are seeking in consuming a product can be used as the basis for market segments. For example, some detergent users are seeking whiter-than-white laundry, others wish to remove heavy stains, and still others want their washed clothing to smell fresh.

The toothpaste market was one of the earliest to use this method. After a benefit segmentation study had been done, four major segments emerged—the worriers (particularly concerned with decay prevention), the sociables (concerned with brightness of teeth), the sensory segment (interested in the flavor and appearance of the product), and the independent segment (concerned about price).[49] Apparently the worriers made up the largest segment, and toothpastes focusing on this appeal (such as Crest and Colgate) have led the market for many years. However, the Beecham Group Ltd. has been successful in gathering a large share by stressing a different set of benefits. Several years ago they introduced MacLeans toothpaste which emphasized whitening agents (for the sociables) rather than decay prevention. In one year it garnered 15

---

[48] Dik Warren Twedt, "How Important to Marketing Strategy Is the Heavy User?" *Journal of Marketing*, Vol. 28 (January 1964), p. 71.

[49] Russel I. Haley, "Benefit-Segmentation: A Decision-Oriented Research Tool," *Journal of Marketing*, Vol. 32 (July 1968), p. 33.

EXHIBIT 8.7
Counter Segmentation

percent of the market. The sensory segment has been reached by Aim whose good taste makes "Bobby brush longer."[50]

One of the advantages of benefit segmentation is the possible elimination of potential problems, such as those which occur when a company's brands cannibalize each other by appealing to the same market segments. Ivory Snow sharply reduced Ivory Flakes' share of the market, and the Ford Falcon cut deeply into the sales of the standard-size Ford; in each case the products were competing for the same segments. Mustang, however, did comparatively little damage to Ford since the potential customers were seeking different attributes.

Occasionally, however, one particular benefit may be so important to consumers that a company may use the same characteristics for two of its competing products. This seems to be the case in Procter & Gamble's new campaign for Gleem toothpaste which emphasizes its role in plaque removal, despite the fact that P&G's Crest is targeted toward this same worrier group.

Counter Segmentation

Segmentation generally involves dividing markets into smaller clusters on the basis of some homogeneous characteristic which is relevant for marketing or advertising. The eighties have seen a revival of what is designated as *counter-segmentation* strategy—that is, combining these clusters into larger groups. This trend is said to emerge from increased manufacturing costs and reduced resources, both of which tend to raise the cost of designing and marketing products to meet specific needs. Consumer resistance to higher prices, and their presumed willingness to give up some specialized offerings as a trade-off for lower prices, is also responsible.

Examples of some of the more successful countersegmentation strategies are the offerings of nonbranded, or generic, products and the introduction of box stores, which do not rely on promotional displays, but offer savings to consumers who select their products from boxes and pack them themselves. Another example is the expansion of the markets for products, previously targeted for specific members of the family, to the entire family (see Exhibit 8.7).

---

[50] "The Big Squeeze in Toothpaste," *The New York Times* (September 21, 1980), p. F-21.

SUMMARY

The first stage in the development of an advertising campaign is called situation analysis. This essentially is a stage for gathering intelligence with particular reference to a firm's market, competition, and customers.

In order to provide the systematic and continuing flow of marketing intelligence that is required for situation analysis, an enterprising firm establishes a marketing information system. This system can be designed to provide a flow of information from the environment to the firm, an internal flow of information within the firm, and an outward flow of information from the firm to the environment.

One of the most widely used techniques for determining the desired target is market segmentation. There are a number of bases for segmenting markets. Demographic data is the traditional means of classifying consumers. For the advertiser it is important to know not only the demographic characteristics of the population and their dimensions, but also to note the changes among such demographic groupings. A number of such segments are becoming increasingly important in marketing— the elderly, teens, blacks, Hispanics, and the affluent.

Psychographics divides the market into different groups on the basis of psychological characteristics. Life-style analysis and VALS are used to determine these psychographic dimensions, and the variations in consumers' values and life-styles may be used as a basis for different segments.

Segments can also be product-related. Volume segmentation divides the market in accordance with the rate at which it uses various products. Determining heavy users, light users, and nonusers can be helpful in selecting the desired market group. Benefit segmentation, which looks at the product benefits sought by consumers, is useful both for determining the target market and developing the advertising appeal. In recent years there has been a development of counter-segmentation strategies. In some cases, the target may be considered a much larger group than typical segmentation strategies reveal, particularly where consumers may be willing to give up specialized offerings as a trade-off for lower prices.

QUESTIONS FOR DISCUSSION

1. Describe a marketing information system and explain its significance.
2. What kinds of information do you believe are most important for situation analysis?
3. What is the purpose of market segmentation?
4. Which demographic segments do you believe will be most important to the future advertiser?
5. What advertising techniques are most useful for reaching the black market? Hispanics?
6. Do you think advertisers should emphasize the youth market as they have in the past?
7. What is meant by life-style analysis? How is this applied to advertising campaigns?
8. What is the significance of segmenting the market into heavy users, light users, and nonusers?
9. Select a product for which benefit segmentation is desirable and describe the different benefit appeals that can be used in ad campaigns.
10. How would you segment the market for air travelers?

KEY TERMS

situation analysis	market segmentation
marketing research	demographic segmentation
advertising research	psychographic segmentation
Marketing Information Systems (MIS)	life-style analysis
primary data	VALS
secondary data	product-related segmentation
internal data	volume segmentation
external data	benefit segmentation
target group	counter segmentation

AD PRACTICE

Select ads targeted to baby boomers, the older consumer, teenagers, blacks, Hispanics, and the affluent. Evaluate these ads on the basis of the effectiveness of the appeal, the manner of presentation, and the choice of media.

Ads That Hit
Their Targets

Who are the people most likely to buy a certain product or service? The target market in advertising consists of those individuals who are the best prospects for what the advertiser is selling. Target groups may be defined in both demographic and behavioral terms, such as "upscale, contemporary women willing to pay $200 for an ounce of perfume," the target group for a new fragrance.

Market segmentation divides the total market into well-defined consumer groups who respond to similar efforts to persuade. Advertisements often focus on people in specific age groups.

Teenagers can be reached by ads that offer solutions to their problems, harmonize with their life-styles, and show them ways to improve their looks.

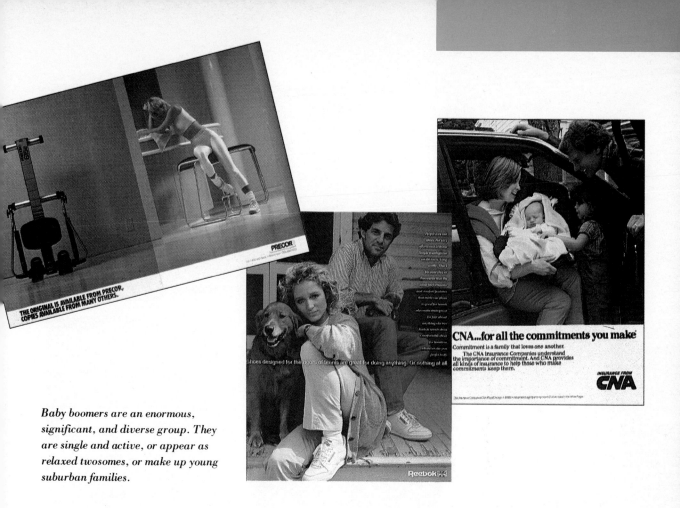

Baby boomers are an enormous, significant, and diverse group. They are single and active, or appear as relaxed twosomes, or make up young suburban families.

Older people relate to advertising messages that help them think young or acknowledge their full lives.

To reach ethnic target groups, firms
may use advertising agencies that
specialize in communicating to these
consumers. Burrell Advertising, whose
work is primarily directed toward
Black consumers, has found through
research that successful approaches in
this market include "upscale"
advertising, a focus on Black culture
and pride, and recognition of strong
family relationships.

In targeting advertising to reach consumers in Hispanic communities, emphasis on achievement and dignity are important. And advertising can only serve its communication function if it speaks its consumer's language.

The Asian American consumer is a small but growing target group.

Income is another way to select target groups.

Affluent customers are the target group for expensive products. Ads tend to reflect the group's interests and life-styles, or show the product alone—needing no words or people to make the point.

Many ads appeal to those who would be or would feel wealthy—upwardly mobile purchasers who are looking for the appearance or feel of wealth,

or who want the comforts or convenience of wealth.

All family members are important target groups. Concerned parents, working women, and working men are all the objects of various campaigns.

Values and life-styles come across loud and clear in today's advertisements.

Lives today are high-powered . . .

international . . .

interesting . . .

and forward looking!

9

The Advertising Target: Consumer Behavior Insights

When the Coca-Cola Company replaced its standard Coke with a new sweeter version in 1985, the resulting upheaval made it clear that Coca-Cola's research was unable to predict the emotional response of innumerable consumers who were upset by the change. Rather than question all Coca-Cola users, researchers had focused on the casual user segment; moreover no mention was made of the fact that the Coca-Cola Company had intended to change its formula. Despite the favorable response from the casual user segment, negative reactions among loyal Coca-Cola drinkers forced the company to reintroduce its older Coke.

In 1986 Coca-Cola Company prepared different advertising strategies for the new Coke and the older Classic Coke. For the new Coke the theme "Catch the Wave", featuring Max Headroom, reflected the company's hopes to reach the young Pepsi drinkers. For the Classic Coke the target was not as clearly delineated. Instead of focusing on a specific segment, the theme of "Red White and You" was a direct appeal to patriotism to identify Classic Coke as an integral part of American culture.

Assigning customers to market segments may not present sufficient information for the creation of an effective advertising campaign. In recent years there has been a significant increase in research providing insights into consumer behavior that has particular relevance for situation analysis and campaign development.

A clearer understanding of the consumers' actions in the marketplace has been developed through the applications of behavioral science research. In addition to the concepts drawn from the field of psychology, marketers are interested in the empirical and theoretical work of social psychology, sociology, and cultural anthropology as sources of information concerning consumer behavior.

CHAPTER OBJECTIVES

— To provide information on advertising targets from a behavioral perspective

— To discuss the environmental and individual influences that affect consumer behavior

— To describe various research techniques useful in this analysis

ASPECTS OF CONSUMER BEHAVIOR

Engel, Kollat and Blackwell, early writers in this field, define consumer behavior as "those acts of individuals directly involved in obtaining and using economic goods and services, including the decision process that precedes and determines these acts."[1] There have been major developments in the study of the field of consumer behavior in the last fifteen or twenty years. These studies are ongoing, and frequently provide conflicting results. Nonetheless, they offer important insights useful to advertisers both in designating target groups as well as an understanding of consumer behavior in the marketplace.

This discussion of the aspects of consumer behavior is based on the external environment and internal states (individual influences) that have an impact on consumer behavior. (See Figure 9.1 on page 170.)

THE EXTERNAL ENVIRONMENT

Many aspects of the consumer's external environment impact on the manner in which he or she makes decisions in the marketplace. These influences can be classified as cultural and social.

Cultural influences include those of the larger society, or those that emanate from subcultures. The previous chapter examined the influence of two major subcultural segments: Blacks and Hispanics. This chapter describes the influence of a larger societal group: American culture.

Culture

Culture is defined as the patterns of behavior that are shared by groups of people and are passed on from generation to generation as guides for recurring experiences. These patterns of behavior include:

    beliefs—a society's ideas, knowledge, lore, superstitions, myths, and legends;

    norms—the standards which specify the manner in which people should behave; and

    values—an especially important class of beliefs.

Although certain basic values are said to permeate American culture—cleanliness, youthfulness, materialism, and nationalism—values are not static; they change as the culture changes. Advertising reflects the values of a society and the changes. For example, the emphasis lately on health and nutrition has been incorporated into the ad campaigns of cereal manufacturers, while responsible drinking behavior is seen in the ads for liquor companies.

In the late 1970s there were suggestions that marketing was entering into the "Age of Me."[2] One advertiser characterized this age as in-

[1]James F. Engel, Roger D. Blackwell and David T. Kollat, *Consumer Behavior* (Hinsdale, Ill.: The Dryden Press, 1978), p. 1.

[2]Bruce Crawford, " 'Age of Me' Poses New Problems for Marketing," *Marketing News* (June 30, 1978).

GROUP INSURANCE.

Aren't you glad you use Dial. Don't you wish everybody did?

© 1987 THE DIAL CORPORATION

EXHIBIT 9.1
From Social Concern to the "Me"
Approach—and Back Again

corporating "self-interest rather than self-service" and "people caring more about satisfying themselves than society."[3] The word *me* appeared in headlines, and magazines were introduced with the word *self* in the title. Exhibit 9.1 shows the change in the campaign for Dial soap. The earlier campaign featured a social situation and a closing line "Aren't you glad you use dial, don't you wish everybody did?" This was changed to show an individual luxuriating in a Dial-lathered shower. The tag line was cut short to "Aren't you glad you use Dial?" Now the campaign has come full circle, reflecting a return to more traditional values.

Social Influences

While culture is reflected in the beliefs and values of individuals, the behavior patterns produced by these factors tend to vary depending on the social structure within which they operate. These social structures are influenced by social class and social groups, including the family.

---

[3]James U. McNeal, "Advertising in the Age of Me," *Business Horizons*, Vol. 22 (August 1979), p. 37.

FIGURE 9.1   Aspects of Consumer Behavior

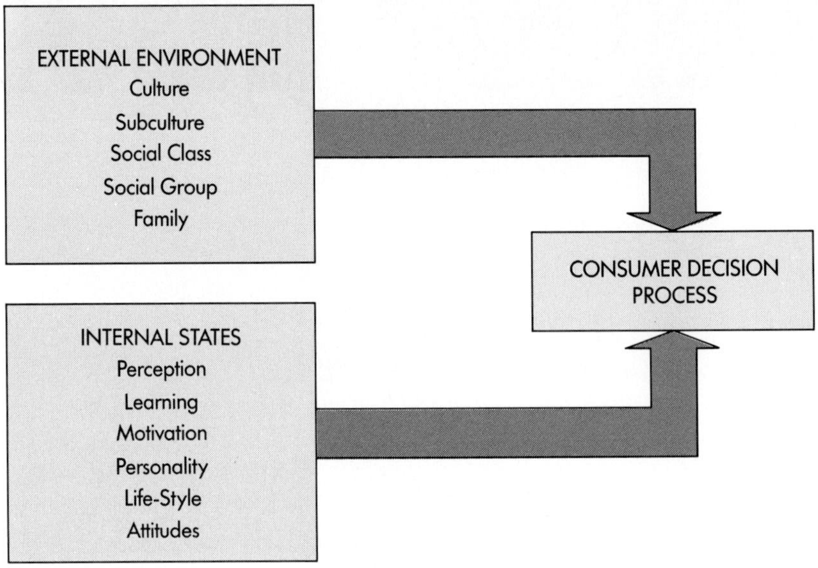

SOCIAL CLASS

Social class refers to the status systems that exist in a society. Sociologists have used a number of indicators as determinants of social-class position; these include occupation, income, and possessions. Various researchers have identified several social classes based on these criteria. Lloyd Warner, for example, recognized six classes: upper-upper class, lower-upper class, upper-middle class, lower-middle class, upper-lower class, and lower-lower class.[4] While the distinctions between the top and bottom classes may be clear, the lines for those in between appear to be blurring. Moreover, there is no certainty that those people who make up each class are necessarily similar in their behavior or consumption patterns.

A more recent view of the American status structure is presented by Richard Coleman and Lee Rainwater, who use a reputational, behavioral view of the community to divide groups into Upper Americans, Middle Americans, and Lower Americans (see Table 9.1).[5]

While there are still some continuities in the pursuit of a traditionally aristocratic life-style, Upper Americans exhibit many variations. They are now a mix of preppy, intellectual, conventional, and yuppie (young, upwardly mobile professional). Yuppies have been described as "confident, happy with their lives, interested in financial success and its

---

[4]Richard P. Coleman, "The Significance of Social Stratification in Selling," in *Marketing: A Maturing Discipline*, ed. Martin Bell, Proceedings of the American Marketing Association Winter Conference (1960), pp. 171–84.

[5]Richard P. Coleman, "The Continuing Significance of Social Class to Marketing," *Journal of Consumer Research*, Vol. 10 (December 1983), pp. 265–80.

TABLE 9.1 A View of the American Status Structure

The Coleman-Rainwater Social Standing Class Hierarchy:[b]
A Reputational, Behavioral View in the Community Study Tradition

Upper Americans

Upper-Upper (0.3%)—The "capital S society" world of inherited wealth, aristocratic names

Lower-Upper (1.2%)—The newer social elite, drawn from current professional, corporate leadership

Upper-Middle (12.5%)—The rest of college graduate managers and professionals; life style centers on private clubs, causes, and the arts

Middle Americans

Middle Class (32%)—Average pay white-collar workers and their blue-collar friends; live on the "the better side of town," try to "do the proper things"

Working Class (38%)—Average pay blue-collar workers; lead "working class life style" whatever the income, school background, and job

Lower Americans

"A lower group of people but not the lowest" (9%)—Working, not on welfare; living standard is just above poverty; behavior judged "crude," "trashy"

"Real Lower-Lower" (7%)—On welfare, visibly poverty-stricken, usually out of work (or have "the dirtiest jobs"); "bums," "common criminals"

[b]This condensation of the Coleman-Rainwater view is drawn from Chapters 8, 9, and 10 of Coleman, Richard P. and Lee P. Rainwater, with Kent A. McClelland (1978). *Social Standing in America: New Dimensions of Class*. New York: Basic Books.

Source: From "The Continuing Significance of Social Class to Marketing" by Richard P. Coleman, *Journal of Consumer Research*, vol. 10 (December 1983). Copyright © 1983 The Journal of Consumer Research, Inc. Reprinted by permission.

rewards. They view themselves as well-organized, tend to be socially liberal, but economically conservative."[6] Ford Motor Company has targeted yuppies as potential buyers of the Tempo compact; the ads show skater Dorothy Hamill driving around in the "very European" car.[7]

Middle Americans want to "do the right thing" and buy what's popular. They have a high concern for their families, homes, and children, particularly their children's education. However, they have developed a spirit of individualism lately. Seagram's V. O., promoted as a potable for the wealthy, recently began a campaign aimed at the middle class. Instead of using its theme "Break away from the ordinary" featuring drinkers in white tie and slinky ball gowns, its ads featured policemen, cowboys, and a tour manager for a band. The theme emphasized real people who did their jobs well and were being rewarded with a bottle of V.O. (see Exhibit 9.2).

[6]"Yuppies The Big Boon of the Baby Boom" *Marketing News* (June 7, 1985), p. 10.
[7]Ralph Gray, "Ford Trying to Pick up 'Yumps'," *Advertising Age* (March 19, 1984), p. 31.

Every night tour manager Brian Doyle
sees that 130 tons of lights, amplifiers,
guitars and musicians get on stage. As well
as 290 lbs. of Daryl Hall and John Oates.
So he received a 2 lb. bottle of V.O.

The reward.

EXHIBIT 9.2
Rewarding the Middle-Class American

Low-income Americans are generally separated into two subclasses: the working poor, who are low paid service workers just above the poverty line, not on welfare, and the underclass, who are primarily dependent on the welfare system. These two categories represent about one-fifth of the adult population and account for approximately one-tenth of the disposable income.

In the sixties several studies supported the use of the social class concept as a segmentation variable; by the early 1970s other studies indicated that income might be a more significant basis for selecting markets. However, a recent study provides some support for the superiority of social class as a means for segmenting some food and drink markets.[8] Nevertheless, the problems with developing accurate measurement criteria for social class criteria limit its usefulness.

SOCIAL GROUPS

A *social group* is composed of two or more individuals who share a set of norms, values, or beliefs, and whose behavior is interdependent. Several aspects of social group influence are relevant in developing advertising and advertising appeals.

Reference Groups

A reference group is particularly important to an individual, who identifies with the group's standards and beliefs and uses them as standards against which he or she defines and evaluates him- or herself. There are several kinds of reference groups:

Membership or associative groups are those to which the individual actually belongs, such as a family, a business organization, and social and religious organizations.

Ascribed groups are those to which an individual belongs by virtue of age or education. This reference group relationship involves the individual's perception of what society expects from people of his or her age, sex, or education.

Anticipatory or aspiration groups are groups to which one hopes to be accepted. Individuals may make their decisions based on their perceptions of what members of these groups might do. Pepsi-Cola has a long continuing campaign urging young people to join The Pepsi Generation.

Negative or dissociative reference groups are those to which one does not want to belong. People may avoid certain actions because they do not want to be associated with certain groups. Campaigns to discourage drinking and smoking frequently incorporate disreputable-looking models.

[8]Charles M. Schaninger, "Social Class Versus Income Revisited: An Empirical Investigation," *Journal of Marketing Research*, Vol. 28 (May 1981), pp. 192–208.

EXHIBIT 9.3
Simulating Personal Influence

Opinion Leadership

An understanding of the concept of social influence requires the recognition that not all individuals wield equal influence. One of the most extensively researched phenomena is the personal influence exerted by opinion leaders. Opinion leaders are individuals who act as channels of information, as a source of social pressure toward a particular choice, and as social support to reinforce a choice once it has been made.[9] Elihu Katz and Paul Lazarsfeld describe this *two-step flow of communication* in which information flows from mass media to mass audience through the mediation of opinion leaders.[10]

Marketers frequently attempt to simulate such personal influence through, for example, testimonial advertising by a famous person who is presented as an opinion leader. Procter & Gamble used Michael Learned who starred in the long-running television program, The Waltons, as an "authoritative but wholesome spokesperson" for its Puritan Oil (see Exhibit 9.3).

Family

The family is one of the most important social groups that influence consumer behavior, but its traditional nature is changing. The father, non-working mother, two children composition has been replaced by an average household containing 2.67 persons; one fourth of the American families are headed by a single parent, in only 23 percent of the married

[9]Charles Y. Block and Francesco M. Nicosia, "Sociology and the Study of Consumers," *Journal of Advertising Research* Vol. 3 (September 1963), p. 24.

[10]Elihu Katz and Paul Lazarsfeld, *Personal Influence* (New York: Free Press of Glencoe, 1955).

couples is the husband the sole worker, and the number of unmarried couples living together has tripled since 1980.

The number of households in the United States has increased almost three times as fast as the population during the past ten years, totaling 87.4 million in 1986. This increase is attributed to the increase in the number of one-person households (they are 25 percent of the total) and a significant increase in the number of households headed by women.

Since 1970, the number of first births to women 25 and older has more than doubled, while first births to women younger than 25 have declined.[11] This has resulted in an increasing group of mature mothers whose marketplace behavior may differ from that of younger mothers. Mature mothers tend to want products and services that reduce stress and enable them to travel. Thus portable, compact, and versatile items designed for smaller houses and requiring little or no maintenance may be desirable. While established brand names still have an appeal to mature mothers some of them are receptive to new brands that have scientific support for their claims and do not use sentimental approaches.

A study by Young & Rubicam predicted that by 1990 one-half of all households will be nontraditional—that is, men and women will be living alone.[12] The study, "Singling Out Singles," presented some insights about this burgeoning group. Singles tend to have active life-styles and are not big prime-time television watchers. Instead their viewing is skewed toward the late-fringe hours. Cable, with its typically selective, subject-delineated programming offering specifically tailored shows during the late hours, provides a growing opportunity for reaching them.

However attention should be paid to the various groups within the single market, including never marrieds, divorced, widowed, and separated. Older groups, particularly the divorced/separated/widowed segment, watch more television than the never marrieds.

The Changing Role of Women

Particular attention has been focused on the portrayal of women in current advertising, both from the perspective of social concerns and advertising effectiveness. There are numerous complaints that advertising has failed to keep up with the times, and the majority of ads continue to reflect traditional roles.[13]

There are, however, indications that marketers are responding to the multiple roles women can have. *Dual-role ads* portray women in situations that indicate their status in the workplace in conjunction with their status in the home (see Exhibit 9.4). *Role-switching ads* portray the purchase or use of products by persons of the sex opposite from the traditional stereotype. In one such ad the female declares, "It's downright upright" to invite the male to partake of a wine. *Role-blending ads* show men and women in combined activity, such as house cleaning.

[11]Judith Langer, "The New Mature Mothers," *American Demographics* (July 1985), p. 29.

[12]Gay Jervey, "Y & R Study: New Life to Singles," *Advertising Age* (October 4, 1982), p. 14.

[13]"Research Profiles Pragmatic, Unliberated Woman Segment; Suggests Marketing Appeals," *Marketing News* (May 15, 1981), Section 2, pp. i, 7.

Continued monitoring is necessary to determine how advertising should respond to the changing roles of women. It appears there may be more than one women's movement; women in traditional roles are changing too. The full-time homemaker wants to spend less time at home. There is also an apparent rise of casual cooking and cleaning and a not-so-perfect house among this group, who may no longer respond to ads that promise whiter-than-white laundry and furniture that outshines everyone else's.[14]

Advertisers are also told to avoid the new stereotype of the "working women with aspiration values," which has replaced the "housewife-mother and drudge" of the past.[15] Advertisers who use career themes to attract all women run the risk of missing those women who do not have a high desire to work. It appears a neutral advertising theme, one that is acceptable to working and non-working women, might be the most appropriate theme for capturing the largest proportion of the women's market when specific homemaker or career segments are not targeted. Another suggestion is to make the product asexual so that it appeals to the women working inside and outside the home and also to men.

EXHIBIT 9.4a,b
Dual Role and Role-Switching Ads

---

[14]Research Profiles Pragmatic, Unliberated Woman Segment; Suggests Marketing Appeals," *Marketing News* (May 15, 1981), Section 2, pp. i, 7.

[15]"Women Face New Stereotype: Day," *Advertising Age* (April 13, 1981), p. 108.

INTERNAL INFLUENCES

In addition to the external environment, the internal states of the individual influence the consumer decision process. Insights concerning these influences emerge from psychological studies in the field of human behavior and, more recently, the findings from consumer behavior research. This section examines the impact of consumer perception, motivation, and attitude on advertising strategy.

Perception

Perception is the complex process by which people select, organize, and interpret the sensory stimulations in such a way as to produce a meaningful and coherent picture of the world.[16] From a marketing perspective perception refers to the way we interpret a new product, a package, or an advertisement.

Perceptual Selectivity — Perception is selective; that is, there is a tendency for the individual to perceive only some aspects of his or her environment. For example, consumers are exposed to many ads daily; estimates vary from several hundred to several thousand. However, only a relatively small percentage of these ads are perceived by consumers.

For the advertiser who wishes to increase the chances of his or her ad being perceived, it becomes important to consider some of the factors that influence perception. These include novelty (providing a distinctive or surprising aspect in the ads), contrast, color, and size. Some of these concepts are discussed in detail in the chapters on creativity.

Perceptual Organization   Perception is a unified organized experience. This means that although consumers are presented with bits and pieces of information they tend to form them into organized patterns.

One form of perceptual organization is called *figure-and-ground differentiation.* When a scene with any detail is viewed, part of it stands out from the rest. A number of factors determine what is viewed as the figure; generally, these relate to familiarity or meaningfulness. Advertisers can design ads to ensure that the viewer focuses on the element of the ad they wish to accentuate by using special photographic techniques or defined drawings.

Frequently, when gaps exist within some presentation, people will nevertheless tend to report it as complete. This tendency is known as *closure.* It has been hypothesized, but not verified, that when an individual perceives an item that contains a gap and closes it, he or she may pay more attention to it and remember it. For example, an early advertising campaign for Salem incorporated a jingle "You can take Salem out of the country, but you can't take the country out of Salem." As the campaign progressed to encourage closure the ads included only part of the jingle, "You can take Salem out of the country but . . . ." Closure can also be shown in print (see Exhibit 9.5).

---

[16]Bernard Berelson and Gary A. Steiner, *Human Behavior: An Inventory of Scientific Findings* (New York: Harcourt Brace Jovanovich, 1964), p. 88.

Premium. Imported.

Frame of Reference   If a presentation contains ambiguous material, perceptual interpretation involves some judgment on the part of the individual. Such judgment may be made in a *frame of reference*—that is, by relating a new product to more familiar material. Advertisers frequently provide an appropriate frame of reference as a means of securing the desired interpretation. Some items, for instance, may be portrayed with an elegant background to indicate luxury (see Exhibit 9.6).

Perceived Risk   Risk is inherent in every purchase decision, because once the purchase is made, the buyer faces the consequences, good or bad. *Perceived risk* refers to the nature and amount of risk contemplated by a consumer considering a particular purchase decision. Risk may be functional—related to the product performance and financial considera-

EXHIBIT 9.6
Frame of Reference

Cobblestone roads must be built by
hand, block by block, and are
relatively rare. Their appearance in
today's ads provides the "frame of
reference" that projects an image of
customized, hand-built quality.

GIVENCHY

1987 CONTINENTAL GIVENCHY DESIGNER SERIES

GIVENCHY STYLE SUIT
AVAILABLE AT BERGDORF GOODMAN

tion—or psychosocial—involving the product's ability to enhance one's
sense of well-being or one's self-concept.

Consumers seek methods of reducing the perceived risk in their
purchase decisions, either by reducing the uncertainty of the outcome
or by reducing the penalties involved in the consequences. A number
of risk reduction methods can be incorporated into an advertising campaign.[17] Endorsements by celebrities or experts, and product testing
information, incorporating information of tests conducted by private

---

[17]Ted Roselius, "Consumer Rankings of Risk Reduction Methods," *Journal of Marketing*, Vol. 35 (January 1971), pp. 57–58.

EXHIBIT 9.7
Risk Reduction Ad

companies or by the government, are techniques to reduce uncertainty. Ads may offer money-back guarantees (see Exhibit 9.7) or they may offer free samples or suggest the availability of demonstrations. These techniques reduce penalties.

Self-Perception   Some researchers believe self-perception may be related to the perception of brands and products; that is, consumers express perceptions of themselves through the purchase of brands and products which they perceive as related to themselves or their needs.[18] While there is little research in this area, it appears that consumers are more likely to use products which have "personalities" consistent with their own. According to Plummer a brand may be characterized as modern, old-fashioned, lively, or exotic, and these characterizational aspects are purely the result of ads.[19]

American Cyanamid's Shulton Toiletries Division has tried several times to rid Breck shampoo of its pastel-girl personality. To do this, they

[18]Wayne Delozier and Rollie Tillman, "Self-Image Concepts—Can They Be Used to Design Marketing Programs?" *Southern Journal of Business*, Vol. 7 (November 1972), pp. 9–15.

[19]Joseph T. Plummer, "How Personality Makes a Difference," *Journal of Advertising Research*, Vol. 24 (December 1984/January 1985), pp. 27–31.

EXHIBIT 9.8
Changing a Product "Personality"

changed the source or spokesperson as well as the message. Rather than the former less vibrant model, Breck ads featured a model representing a newer life-style (see Exhibit 9.8).

Motivation

The terms *motives* and *needs* are frequently used interchangeably. *Needs* are internal forces that prompt behavior toward solutions. There are many human needs, and they are usually treated under two broad categories—biological and personal/social (or psychogenic). Biological needs are basic conditions that are necessary to the maintenance of life and the normal processes of healthy growth and reproduction. Psycho-

EXHIBIT 9.9
Reaching Achievers

genic needs are less objectively described as personal security, self-confidence, group status, and prestige. *Motives* are inner states that energize, activate, and/or move and direct behavior toward goals. Motives always affect behavior while needs do not necessarily have to.

Maslow's Hierarchy of Needs   The most widely popularized theory of motivation has been proposed by Maslow who presents a hierarchy of needs consisting of physiological needs at the bottom, followed by safety needs, belongingness and love needs, esteem needs, and need for self-actualization. Maslow stresses the hierarchical nature of motivation: a lower need must be satisfied before the next higher need can fully emerge. It should be noted, however, that each lower need does not have to be fully satisfied for the next higher need to emerge. The use of motives in developing advertising appeals is discussed in Chapter 10.

Social Motives   Some theorists believe that the basis for an individual's motivation stems from his or her social environment. Achievement and affiliation are two social motives that are frequently cited and incorporated in advertising strategies. In fact, achievers have been designated as an appropriate target segment for advertising campaigns (see Exhibit 9.9).

Motivation Research

Motives are frequently incorporated into the development of an advertising appeal. Motivation research attempts to determine more information concerning human behavior than is available through standard marketing research techniques. It is designed to secure data that may be unavailable, either because respondents are unwilling or reluctant to supply the information on the more overt level, or because they are incapable of proper articulation. Motivation research attempts to uncover opinions, ideas, images, and stereotypes.

The approaches discussed in this section are usually designated as *qualitative research* since they are generally exploratory in nature and conducted to understand why people behave in a certain way. The term *quantitative research* refers to activities designed to explain what is happening and the frequency of its occurrence. For example, quantitative studies reveal how many people use shampoos that are dandruff-resistant. Qualitative research attempts to determine why people use such shampoos and why they prefer one brand over the other.

Motivation research as a technique had its heydey in the 1960s. Several examples of the use of motivational research in advertising campaigns were reported in the literature of that period:[20]

— A Jell-O advertising campaign that displayed complicated Jell-O desserts conflicted with Jell-O's personality as a dessert easy to prepare. The motivation researcher advised keeping the ads simple and making them easy to look at. The result was a campaign with light copy and funny animals which perked up Jell-O sales.

— The Socony-Vacuum Oil Company contemplated putting the name Sovac on its products. When a researcher used it in a word association test, he found that the public related the name to Soviet Russia and communism. As a result the company changed its name to Socony Mobil Oil Company.

— An ad for a power shovel illustrated a huge machine that lifted an immense load of rock. The machine and its load were far more conspicuous than the operator. Motivation studies indicated that operators felt hostile toward a machine that made them look insignificant. The ad was changed so that a photograph was taken inside the cab looking over the operator's shoulder.

Although the term *motivation research* no longer tends to be used in advertising, qualitative research using similar techniques has been successfully applied to recent advertising campaigns.[21] For example:

— McDonald's research showed that people identified the fast-food franchise as not only the best place to go for a hamburger, but as a unique family experience. This resulted in the campaign "You deserve a break today."

[20]Harry W. Singer, "Examples of Helpful Motivational Studies," in Stuart Henderson Britt, ed., *Consumer Behavior and the Behavioral Sciences* (New York: John Wiley & Sons, Inc., 1968), pp. 105–7.

[21]"Healthy Research/Creative Marriage Translates Discovery, Imaginative Interpretation into Ads," *Marketing News* (May 14, 1982), Section 2, p. 13.

— State Farm's "good neighbor" ads used an insurance agent as the focus of the campaign when research determined it was the agent the policyholder was buying, not the policy or the price.

— Betty Crocker's campaign, "Bake Someone Happy," was the result of research which revealed that cake baking involves the emotional element of caring.

Depth Interviewing   Ernest Dichter, called the Father of Motivation Research, believed it was a mistake to conduct research into motives by merely asking people "Why did you do what you did?" He felt the researcher could get more information by letting the individual talk in a free-associative way. In essence he used the depth interview of clinical psychology to arrive at some of his findings.

Depth interviews are usually conducted with 50 to 200 individuals. They typically run from 30 to 45 minutes but can go longer. In addition to being relatively expensive, they require competently trained personnel to conduct the interviews and analyze the responses.

Currently, these one-on-one interviews are considered a useful advertising research technique. A recent survey of qualitative research methods used for television advertising by major advertisers and advertising agencies indicated that one-on-one interviews were used by 87 percent of the agencies and 95 percent of the advertisers surveyed.[22]

Their advantages include individual responses untainted by group pressure, more complete, detailed information, and the interviewer receiving a clearer view of the thinking process of each individual. In addition, respondents may reveal more confidential information in one-on-one interviews.[23]

Focus Group Interviews   Focus group interviews are modified depth interviews. They are conducted with a small number of representative consumers, usually from six to twelve, who are interviewed through an informal group discussion headed by a trained discussion leader. Focus groups are widely used for numerous advertising research purposes ranging from generating ideas to evaluating advertisements. In fact in a survey of large users of television advertising the most widely used research technique was the focus group.[24]

Focus groups are not used when answers to the *how* and *where* of consumer behavior is sought; they are generally considered most appropriate for the exploratory stage in the development of further research activities. For example, they are frequently used as the first step in the preparation of a large-scale survey because they are valuable in deter-

[22]Benjamin Lipstein and James Neelankavil, *Television Advertising Copy Research Practices Among Major Advertisers and Advertising Agencies, An Advertising Research Foundation Survey* (New York: The Advertising Research Foundation, 1982), p. 19.

[23]Roger B. Bengston, "A Powerful Qualitative Marketing Research Tool, One-on-One Depth Interviewing Has 7 Advantages," *Marketing News* (May 14, 1982), Section 1, p. 21.

[24]Barbara J. Coe and James MacLachlan, "How Major Advertisers Value Commercials," *Journal of Advertising Research*, Vol. 20, No. 6 (December 1980), pp. 51–54.

mining the underlying reasons for consumer behavior. This can be particularly useful in looking at the advertising of parity products, such as cigarettes, soft drinks, beer, gasoline, or banks, where the basic difference may be imagery.[25]

Focus groups, in contrast to depth interviews, depend primarily on the interactions of ideas, attitudes, emotions, and beliefs among group members. They are also more directive since the discussion leader introduces various stimuli such as products, packages, pictures, and advertisements. Discussions are recorded on tape and, occasionally, the group is observed through a two-way mirror so that additional significant reactions may be recorded.

Cigar smokers, in particular, have been subjects of earlier depth interviews and more recent focus-group interviews. Findings were similar; basically cigar smokers want to feel "big enough" to smoke a cigar. As a result of this finding Muriel Cigars portrayed a sexy, aggressive beauty, appearing at improbable times and in odd settings, such as locker rooms. The strategy behind this campaign was to satisfy the cigar smoker's need for fantasy and vicarious thrills.

Limitations to the Use of Motivation Research

Motivation research techniques were designed to be conducted by psychologists and sociologists on a one-to-one basis. In their application to advertising research, their focus has been shifted to large groups and the interviewer, although skilled in interviewing, may not be trained in psychology.

Another criticism of motivation research is that the results of such studies are difficult to replicate and, as a result, their validity and reliability are questioned. Consumers complain about the use of hidden persuaders and "brain washing" in the marketplace, while marketers question the interpretation of the studies which seemed to attribute sexual connotations to the purchase of prosaic products.

Nevertheless the idea that advertisers and marketers should look beyond traditional demographic analysis has taken hold and efforts to conduct qualitative research as well as typical quantitative research has gained acceptance. Practitioners cite as a benefit the more accurate and detailed accounts from consumers about their reasons for buying a product or selecting one brand over another. Furthermore efforts to understand the *why* of consumer behavior have resulted in the development of other types of research such as attitude research and consumer information-processing analysis.

---

[25]Philip H. Dougherty, "Advertising, Consumer Research Methods," *New York Times* (December 8, 1982), p. D19.

Attitudes

There are many definitions of *attitudes;* one early definition that has survived, with modifications, describes *attitudes* as "learned predispositions to respond to an object or class of objects in a consistently favorable or unfavorable way."[26] In a marketing context the object may be a product, brand, service, company, or even spokesperson.

Attitudes have become an important area of study in the field of advertising, in part because of the belief that they precede the individual's behavior toward a product, brand, or firm and, hence, may be useful in predicting behavior. Efforts to understand this process have generated substantial research. It should be clear, however, that such research frequently indicates that a distinction must be made between an attitude toward an object and attitude toward the act of actually purchasing and using that object. In other words, discovery that the consumer has a favorable attitude toward a product may not ensure that he or she will purchase or use it.

EXHIBIT 9.10
Changing Attitudes

Attitude Components

Three components are thought to be common to all attitudes, although their proportion varies:

1. *A cognitive component*—a person's *beliefs* about an object (a brand of mouthwash has a "minty" taste).
2. *An affective or evaluative component*—a person's *feelings* involving likes and dislikes (a "minty" taste is good or bad).
3. *An action tendency component (behavioral intention)*—a person's readiness to respond behaviorally to that object, based on the beliefs and feelings (liking a "minty" taste may predispose the individual to purchase the brand).

A knowledge of attitude components may suggest advertising strategies designed to change or bolster these attitudes. For example, to change the attitude toward Listerine, a campaign focused on the affective component, declaring that the brand had a bad taste but that was good. An ad designed to create a less favorable attitude toward sunburn and a more favorable attitude toward a sunscreen lotion incorporated both the belief component—by providing information about sun's potential harmful effects—and the affective component—by illustrating these effects (see Exhibit 9.10).

Multiattribute Models of Attitudes

Efforts to understand how attitudes influence behavior has generated substantial research into the development of structural models that would both predict and explain attitudes. These efforts have resulted in

---

[26]Gordon W. Allport, "Attitudes," in *Handbook of Social Psychology,* ed. C.A. Murchinson (Worcester, Mass.: Clark University Press, 1935), pp. 798–844.

THE AMERICAN EGG BOARD CAMPAIGN

Situation analysis revealed a steady decline in per capita consumption of eggs because of changing life-styles (people eating smaller breakfasts or none at all) and growing cholesterol fears. To reverse this declining primary demand, the American Egg Board contacted Market Facts, Inc., a research company, to perform a segmentation study on eggs prior to advertising.

Research was conducted into usage patterns among consumers who were asked to rate the following statements:

— Eggs have high quality protein.
— Eggs are among the most nutritious foods.
— Eggs are very low in calories.
— Eggs and egg dishes are very good for snacks.
— Eggs are good value for the money.
— Eggs are good for all people.

The study isolated four distinct market segments whose egg usage was closely correlated with attitudinal differences.

Egg Enthusiasts feel positive toward eggs; consume 39 percent more eggs per capita.
Breakfast Skippers like eggs but lack time.
Cholesterol Avoiders cut back on eggs because of cholesterol fears.
Egg Dislikers do not like the taste of eggs.

The advertising objective was to help reverse the decreasing per capita consumption of eggs by increasing positive awareness and attitudes of consumers. The selected target market was heavy and medium users of eggs who tend to be homemakers, 25–49 years old, having children at home 2–17 years of age. A campaign was developed using the theme "The Incredible Edible Egg", the advertising campaign was aimed at gaining a favorable attitude change by the consumer by emphasizing the benefits of eggs. A consumer research organization, *Market Facts,* monitored over 60 key attitude statements on an annual basis. The results were positive (see Exhibit 9.11).

Source: From "The American Egg Board Campaign," *Campaign Report Newsletter* (June 1980). Copyright © 1980 American Association of Advertising Agencies. Reprinted by permission.

the development of multiattribute models of attitudes, which derive from the concept that consumers form attitudes toward a product or brand on the basis of its attributes. *Attributes* are considered to be specifications or criteria that consumers use in comparing alternatives. For example, the attributes of a mouthwash may be taste, color, price, germ-killing capabilities, or an ability to make the individual "kissing sweet." In the marketing context, multiattribute models suggest that the consumer's choice of one brand or product over others on the basis of attitudes is not a case of simple like and dislike. The preferential attitude is a complex outcome of many separate judgments about the various attributes of a product.

Studies are designed to determine the salient attributes that are incorporated into an attitude toward a product or brand. Salient attributes

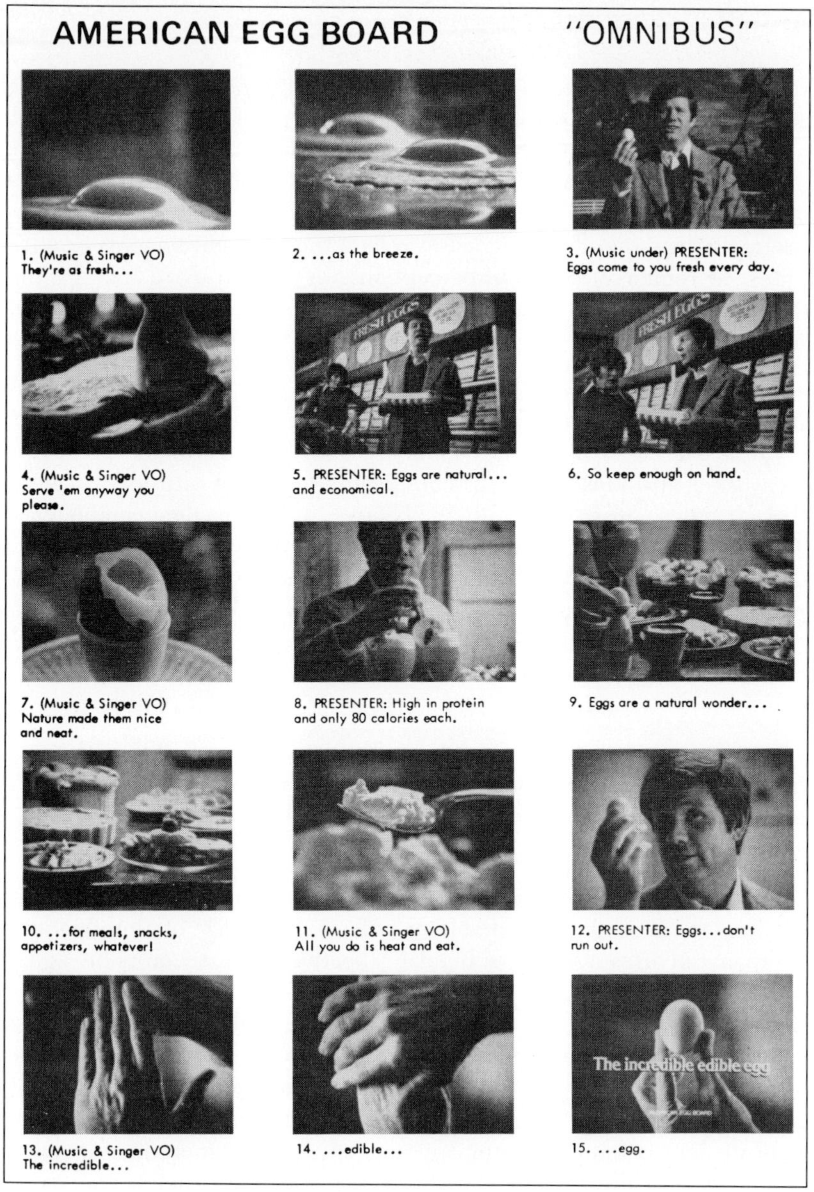

EXHIBIT 9.11
American Egg Board Campaign Ad

are those which are not only important but which will be used by consumers in making their choices. The usefulness of this approach to advertisers is the isolation of those attributes that should be stressed in promotional appeals directed at shaping brand preferences. For example, until it was ordered by the FTC to cease making this claim, Warner-Lambert's advertising for Listerine focused on a salient attribute of mouthwash—its germ-killing properties.

Attitude Research

In recent years, attitude research has taken on increasing importance in advertising. In part this is because the concept of motivation research fell into some disrepute after its initial acceptance. Attitude research can determine the most salient benefits or attributes of a particular product and consumers' perceptions about these benefits or attributes. Advertisements may then be designed to reflect these salient benefits or attributes, to reinforce favorable perceptions, or change those that are unfavorable. To gather such information attitude researchers use various scaling techniques.

Attitude Scaling Procedures

Attitude scaling is the term commonly used to refer to the process of measuring attitudes.[27] The tri-component model of attitudes suggests that attitudes consist of cognitive, affective, and behavioral components. Thus attitude scaling tends to focus on the measurement of the respondent's *beliefs* about a product's attributes (cognitive component), and the respondent's *feelings* regarding the desirability of these attributes (affective component). Some combination of beliefs and feelings typically is assumed to determine intention to buy (behavioral component).

Likert Scale   The *Likert Scale* is a technique that evaluates consumers' beliefs about a product or firm. It involves responses to a series of attitude statements. The procedure is shown in Table 9.2.

Semantic Differential   The purpose of the *semantic differential* technique is to determine a favorable or unfavorable image of a product or a company. It uses a series of bipolar adjectives on a seven-point equal-interval ordinal scale. The bipolar adjectives are concerned with three basic factors: evaluation (good-bad; beautiful-ugly); potency (strong-weak; large-small); and activity (active-passive; fast-slow). These factors are rated on a seven-point scale: extremely good, good, somewhat good, neither good nor bad, somewhat bad, bad, extremely bad. The findings indicate how a brand or company appears to consumers in relation to competitors. They indicate ways to reformulate a product as well as revise promotional emphasis.

Limitations to Attitude Research

A knowledge of attitude formation and change is useful in advertising decision-making. However, there is significant controversy concerning the extent to which attitudes can be measured and used to predict be-

---

[27]Thomas C. Kinnear and James R. Taylor, *Marketing Research, An Applied Approach* (New York: McGraw-Hill Book Company, 1979), p. 300.

TABLE 9.2 The Likert Scale

Procedure	Example
	The ABC Oil Company
1. A number of relevant statements about a subject are collected.	I. Is a leader in the oil industry II. Sincerely committed to meeting the energy needs of the country now and in the future III. Is a company worthy of the public's trust IV. Company's efforts will benefit American consumers

2. Respondents are asked to indicate the degree of agreement or disagreement with each statement. Each response is given a numerical weight.	How strongly do you agree or disagree with each of these statements about the ABC Oil Company?
	Scale: 1. Agree strongly
	       2. Agree somewhat
	       3. Disagree somewhat
	       4. Disagree strongly

3. The numerical weights of all statements are summed to get each respondent's attitude score.	Score: Respondent A; four, agrees strongly with all statements Respondent B; sixteen, disagrees strongly with all statements

havior. Similarly there is a lack of understanding about how to influence attitude change. Future research may provide improved capabilities to measure attitudes as well as techniques for applying the concepts of attitude formation and change to advertising strategies.

SUMMARY

Consumer behavior is defined as the acts of individuals in obtaining and using economic goods and services, and many of the insights evolving from this field of study are relevant to advertisers.

Studies of consumer behavior examine the major influences affecting the consumer from the viewpoint of the external environment and internal influences. Culture is a part of the external environment and it involves the beliefs or patterns of behavior for coping with recurring experience that are shared by people. Certain values are said to permeate American culture and these are reflected in ads. Subcultures are specialized segments of society, and since they tend to exhibit similar values, needs, and behavior patterns, an analysis of subcultures may be useful for advertising purposes.

Social influences also affect behavior and social patterns emerge from social class, social groups, and more specifically, the family. The consumer's values may be enhanced, diminished, or rearranged by his or her social class or the one to which he or she aspires.

Social groups help to judge the hierarchy and acceptability of values, and the consumer's reference groups may serve to mold desirables and undesirables. Furthermore, the consumer designates opinion leaders within social groups, who serve as instrumentalities in the flow of information and affect the manner in which communications are received. The changing nature of the family and the changing role of women require attention in the development of advertising strategies.

Internal influences that affect consumer behavior include perception, motivation, and attitudes. Various concepts derived from psychologists and sociologists concerning these internal states are applicable to advertising strategies.

Qualitative research techniques available for uncovering motives that may be incorporated in advertising campaigns include depth interviews and focus group interviews.

Research into attitude and attitude formation is becoming a topic of increasing importance to advertisers as well as social scientists. Attitude scaling techniques, including procedures such as the Likert scale and semantic differential are used to gather information on attitudes. Such information is useful not only for efforts to reinforce or change attitudes, but for the development and incorporation of attitude segments into a promotional campaign.

QUESTIONS FOR DISCUSSION

1. Do you believe American values are changing? How would you incorporate your beliefs into advertising campaigns?
2. How are reference groups important to advertising?
3. Explain opinion leadership and give examples of its use in advertising.
4. Why is the changing nature of the family important in preparing advertising campaigns?
5. How can advertisers address the changing role of women?
6. Explain several perceptual concepts that are relevant to advertising and describe how these may be incorporated in an advertising campaign.
7. How are focus groups used in the preparation of an advertising campaign?
8. What are some of the deficiencies of motivation research?
9. Discuss the three attitude components and their use in advertising strategies.
10. Describe an attitude scaling procedure you would use to prepare an advertising campaign for the business air traveler.

KEY TERMS

internal influences	figure-and-ground differentiation
culture	closure
beliefs	frame of reference
values	perceived risk
norm	needs and motives
social class	qualitative research
social group	quantitative research
reference group	depth interview
membership groups	focus group
ascribed groups	attitudes
anticipatory groups	behavioral intention
negative groups	attributes
dual-role ads	attitude scaling
role-switching ads	semantic differential
role-blending ads	likert scale
perception	

AD PRACTICE

In terms of current life-styles select ads representing changing roles. Choose a number of ads you believe provide an inaccurate portrayal of current roles. Provide recommendations for appropriate changes.

CASE

Situation Analysis

The big surge in the beauty business was fueled by baby-boom girls who started wearing makeup as teenagers and continued to be heavy users as they moved into the work force. Although the number of working women is expected to continue rising until 1995 this will be offset be a significant demographic change. The population of teenagers, traditionally the heaviest and most experimental makeup users, is declining. By 1990 there will be 15 percent fewer 18–24-year-olds than there are now. With more women working there are fewer left at home to answer the door when a sales representative from Avon Products or Mary Kay Cosmetics calls. The sales of some of the major cosmetic companies are also declining. Avon, Max Factor, and Revlon have suffered large profit declines and loss of market share.

Although a recent survey has indicated that the baby boomers comprise the largest buying segment for cosmetics, they are not a cohesive group; they include both males and females who have a wide variety of interests and life-styles. While Revlon has segmented its fragrance market with some success, (Charlie, Jovan, Scoundrel) it has not provided such segmentation in its cosmetics offerings.

Door-to-door sales of cosmetics have remained at 11 percent of total retail sales, the percentage of cosmetics sold in drug and department stores has decreased from 72 percent to 66 percent, and cosmetic sales in mass merchandisers and food stores has increased from 17 to 23 percent.

Companies who have done well in sales and earnings include Maybelline and Noxell's Cover Girl, typically sold in drugstores or mass merchandisers. For many years companies such as Revlon advertised their cosmetics in situations representing romance, fantasies, and dreams. Maybelline on the other hand has emphasized low price.

DISCUSSION QUESTIONS

1. What kinds of segments do you think cosmetics makers should target in their advertising?
2. Describe some research methods available for determining these segments.
3. How can behavioral research be used to determine the characteristics of the appropriate target groups for cosmetic advertisers?

Sources: "How Cosmetics Makers Are Touching Up Their Strategies," *Business Week* (September 23, 1985), pp. 66, 68, 73, and Alfred Modugno, "The Baby Boomers: Who They Are, How They Shop," *Product Marketing* (August 1985), pp. 8.

CASE

Target Market Analysis

J. D. Power & Associates, an independent market research firm concentrates on the automotive industry. Its 1985 survey of consumer satisfaction rated Mercedes-Benz and Subaru at the top of the list, with American Motors and Peugeot at the bottom. Imports dominated the higher rankings, with Ford's Lincoln the only domestic nameplate to make it into the top ten. Buyers of larger, older-design American cars, such as the Chevrolet Caprice, were most satisfied with their purchases, despite the generally low rank of domestic manufacturers, and buyers of small sporty cars were least satisfied. The survey underscored that younger car buyers tended to be more demanding than older ones; and the buyers of traditional American cars were generally older than those who prefered sporty ones.

The company also did an attitudinal survey which found that car buyers fell into six basic categories: *autophiles*, who knew a lot about cars and liked to work on them; *sensible-centrists*, who prized practicality; *comfort-seekers*, who tended to favor options and luxury; *auto-cynics*, who viewed cars as appliances; *necessity-drivers* who wished there were another way to get around; and *auto-phobes*, who cared most about safety (see Table below).

Autophiles comprise the greatest percentage of car buyers.

According to the survey the groups varied demographically. The sensible-centrists had the lowest family income at $34,000 a year, while the comfort-seekers had the highest, $52,100.

DISCUSSION QUESTIONS

1. Based on these data what suggestions would you make to automobile manufacturers in terms of their target market?
2. What is the significance of the car buyer categories?
3. Using the attitudinal segments, suggest an appropriate appeal for each group.

Car Buyer Categories

Category	Percentage	Description	Make
Autophiles	24	Know a lot about cars and enjoy working on them	Dodge, Pontiac
Sensible-centrists	20	Prize practicality	Volvo, A.M.C.
Comfort-seekers	17	Favor options and luxury models	Jaguar, Mercedes, Lincoln
Auto-cynics	14	View cars as appliances	Porsche
Necessity-drivers	13	Prefer an alternative way of traveling	A.M.C.
Auto-phobes	12	Care most about safety	Oldsmobile, Mercury

Car buyers fall into six basic categories, according to a survey done by J. D. Power & Associates in early 1985. Above are the categories, along with the percentage and types of cars they buy.

Source: "Car Buyer Categories" from "A Noted Voice on Car Buying" by John Holush, *The New York Times* (January 21, 1986). Copyright © 1987 by The New York Times Company. Reprinted by permission.

10

Creative Strategy: The Appeal

In the 1960s and early 1970s the award-winning "I can't believe I ate the whole thing" advertising campaign made Alka-Seltzer famous. Each ad featured a humorous situation, such as a newlywed preparing marshmallow meatballs, and indicated that Alka-Seltzer would provide the necessary relief.

In the 1980s, however, faced with declining sales, and research which suggested that overindulgence was not consistent with current lifestyles, Miles Laboratories changed Alka-Seltzer's appeal to one for stress found among executives with the campaign "For the symptoms of stress that go with success." This campaign attracted yuppies to Alka-Seltzer's consumer group, and to retain its past customers, a subsequent campaign brought Alka-Seltzer "to the rescue" of those with blazing stomachs caused by heartburn. Furthermore Miles Laboratories decided to provide additional support for its product with the introduction of lemon-lime Alka-Seltzers and ads that focus on taste appeal.

Although creativity is part of every stage of an advertising campaign, the term *creative* here refers to the way the messages are to be communicated and the manner in which they are to be presented. Creative strategy is closely related to media strategy, and although many creative decisions are made prior to media choice, some are made on the basis of the medium in which the message is to appear.

Creativity is critical in today's markets. New products proliferate, substitutes appear rapidly, and with the inflationary spiral, competition for the consumer's dollar grows keener. To gain and maintain market share a company cannot merely engage in conventional marketing practices; it must distinguish its offerings from those of competitors.

THE CREATIVE PROCESS

Creativity is generally defined in aesthetic terms: the ability to produce new, useful ideas; originality; imagination; or the capacity for joining two or more elements to form a new unity or purpose. However, each definition leaves out the utilitarian or productive function of creativity which applies to advertising.

An individual creates in an environment which affects the extent and manner of his or her creativity. What emerges is not only an expression of the inner state of the creator; it is also designed to meet externally defined needs and goals. Creativity in advertising is an example of a combination of both aesthetics and problem-solving.

The Creative Individual

In past years a number of studies have tried to isolate the distinguishing characteristics of highly creative and original people. Although the studies are not directly comparable or additive, there are some generalizations that seem to be emerging:[1]

1. Creativity is not simply a matter of intelligence. A high IQ is necessary for creativity in some fields like nuclear physics, not necessary in others like graphic arts, and is never sufficient. Highly intelligent subjects are found in low-creativity groups in virtually every study.
2. Highly creative people show a preference for, and interest in, complexity and novelty; they have intrinsic interest in situations that require some resolution, rather than those that are cut-and-dried.
3. Highly creative people are more likely than others to view authority as conventional rather than absolute; to make fewer black-and-white distinctions; to have a less dogmatic and more relativistic view of life; to show more independence of judgment and less conventionality and conformity, both intellectual and social; to be more willing to entertain, and sometimes express, their own "irrational" impulses; to place a greater value on humor and, in fact, to have a better sense of humor; in short, to be somewhat freer and less rigidly controlled.
4. In general, highly creative work is produced relatively early in the artistic, scientific, or scholarly career—typically from a person in his or her thirties.
5. The highly creative person has more ability to associate research data into problem-solving advertising communications.[2]

---

[1]Bernard Berelson and Gary A. Steiner, *Human Behavior: An Inventory of Scientific Findings* (New York: Harcourt, Brace & World, Inc., 1964), pp. 227–34.

[2]Leonard N. Reid and Herbert J. Rotfeld, "Toward an Associative Model of Advertising Creativity," *Journal of Advertising*, Vol. 5 (Fall 1976), p. 29.

6. The highly creative person suffers less from functional fixedness and is more flexible. This characteristic has led to the development of creative tests composed of questions intended to measure flexibility, such as "How many uses can you find for a bicycle tire?"[3]

7. Creative people may have a particular cognitive style. *Cognitive style* refers to recurrent patterns in the way a person approaches problems or processes information. Some patterns of thinking promote creativity—for example, the problem-solving approach to tasks.[4] Creative people are more reluctant to judge whatever they encounter, while less creative people seem prone to evaluate quickly and turn to other matters. Creative people have a tendency to think in terms of opposites or contraries and unite them in inventive ways.

CREATIVITY IN ADVERTISING

Creativity in advertising does not exist in a vacuum. Productive originality and imagination are useful in all areas, even those that relate to such typically managerial tasks as the planning and organization of advertising departments, and the establishment of controls. In a recent survey of top managers in large corporations the lack of innovative thinking in promotion was identified as a major concern. Specifically, there appeared to be general unwillingness to take necessary risks, as well as an inability to define new methods for promoting products to customers in the face of major increases in the cost of media advertising and personal selling.[5]

The creative process is not a scientific process; rather it evolves from insight or inspiration. Nonetheless creativity in advertising must not only produce unique and interesting results, it must also produce useful solutions to real problems. Baker likens the concept of creativity to a pyramid divided into three parts. Advertising creativity frequently takes off from a base of a systematic accumulation of facts and analysis. The second phase represents processing, or analysis, and the third part—the idea—is the culmination of creative efforts.[6] We now focus on the idea, which is considered the heart of the creative process.

---

[3]*Psychology Today: An Introduction,* 3rd edition, CRM Books (New York: Random House, 1975), p. 137.

[4]D. N. Perkins, *The Mind's Best Work* (Cambridge, Mass.: Harvard University Press, 1981), p. 270.

[5]Frederick E. Webster, Jr., "Top Management's Concern About Marketing Issues for the 1980s," *Journal of Marketing,* Vol. 45 (Summer, 1981), pp. 9–16.

[6]Steven Baker, *Systematic Approach to Advertising Creativity* (New York: McGraw-Hill, Inc., 1979), p. 2.

EXHIBIT 10.1
Creativity in Action

Ads from the Volkswagen Lemon campaign, considered the most creative of all advertising campaigns by members of the advertising community.

Generating the Idea

Ideas, according to William Bernbach of Doyle Dane Bernbach advertising agency, may emerge from that "intangible, indefinable intuition that reaches out toward what is new."[7] This approach has led to one of the most creative campaigns of all time—Volkswagen's Lemon ads, shown in Exhibit 10.1. But how does an idea for an ad campaign originate?

Brainstorming

In 1939 a technique called *brainstorming* was introduced by Osborn in the advertising agency Batten, Barton, Durstine, and Osborn. It was subsequently widely used in a large number of major corporations and

---

[7]William Bernbach, "Advertising's Greatest Tool," in *Speaking of Advertising*, eds. John S. Wright and Daniel S. Warner (New York: McGraw-Hill Book Co., Inc., 1963), p. 315.

CREATIVITY

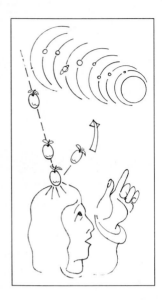

The essence of the creative act, at least for me, is the ability to find a correspondence between things that an average person would find disparate and completely unrelated. Isaac Newton was sitting contentedly under an apple tree reading when an apple fell on his head. Apples have been falling from apple trees for eons, but Newton was able to deduce from this interruption the gravitational force that glues all the planets and stars together and keeps them in their positioned orbits. We've all felt the force of the wind. What if, one man conjectured, what if the wind blew the other way—backward? When Mr. H. C. Booth put a suction motor, already in existence, in a cloth bag, he created the vacuum cleaner.

In the sixteenth and seventeenth centuries, a few European artists used a device called a *camera lucida*. Through a lens a portion of a scene could be projected onto a back wall, even onto a canvas. We know that the Italian painter Caneletto used this camera to paint his detailed views of Venice.

Leonardo da Vinci wrote that he assiduously studied the cracks and stains on old walls, because he saw in them landscapes, battle scenes, and the basis for many of his drawings and paintings. One of the old Chinese painters, whom I would have enjoyed watching, put ink in his mouth and spurted a fine spray, through a crack in a tooth, onto his rice paper, and the fall of the spray gave him the initial concept of his painting.

The creative person must also be able to take advantage of what chance may offer. At a dinner in his honor, near the end of Pasteur's notable career, a colleague, burning with envy, said to the distinguished scientist, "Louis, isn't it interesting how many of your discoveries have happened only by chance." Pasteur thought a while and he answered, "That's true, but have you ever thought of the persons to whom such chance happens?" Was it not Beethoven who was inspired to write a sonata by the chance notes his playful cat struck running across the composer's piano? And wasn't the chance observation of the bacteriologist, Alexander Fleming, destroying many harmful bacteria in the jars in his laboratory that changed the whole course of the treatment of infectious diseases?

There always comes a time when some particular thing is needed. For example, a swifter mode of transportation to supplant the horse carriage; a better braking system on railroad cars; engines that can give more power to an airplane and, by the same token, more speed than the gasoline engine. These problems have always been solved by creative individuals. In one classic example, mathematicians in the seventeenth century needed a mathematical method to determine rates of change. How fast was the apple falling an instant before it landed on Newton's head? How could the rate of fall, and the changes in that rate, be predicted at any instant? Sir Isaac Newton, and the German philosopher and mathematician, Gottfried Leibnitz, working apart from one another, devised a calculus to provide solutions to this problem.

Source: "Creativity" by Romare Bearden, artist. Reprinted by permission of the author.

in various governmental and military agencies. The process of brainstorming, in which people work on a problem as a group, encompasses four basic rules:[8]

[8]David Krech, Richard S. Crutchfield, and Egerton L. Ballachey, *Individual in Society* (New York: McGraw-Hill Book Company, Inc., 1962), p. 488.

1. No ideas are criticized.
2. "Freewheeling" is encouraged. The more farfetched and wild an idea, the better.
3. Quantity of production is stressed. The larger the number of ideas, the greater the probability of getting a winner.
4. "Hitchhiking" is encouraged. Participants are urged to improve the ideas of others and to combine the ideas to form new and more complex ones.

Today firms still use brainstorming as a method of developing creative ideas. How effective the group-think process is for developing creativity is subject to some question. "Individual think" may result in more creativity, since the more diverse the approaches to a problem, the greater the expected number of different ideas for its solution. Nonetheless, brainstorming does provide the benefit of interaction, a means by which one individual's undeveloped idea may be expanded through the creative capabilities of another participant.

Focus Group Interviews

Focus group interviews involve a group of people as well, but in a more structured setting. Such groups have been used for generating ideas and for analyzing a target market. A focus group may consist of six to twelve members of a target market, who are brought together, with a moderator, for a discussion. As in brainstorming, the process is interactive; however, unlike brainstorming, the moderator exercises some control over the discussion.

The effectiveness of the group depends on the characteristics of the members as well as the skills of the individual selected as moderator. Recent research indicates that larger groups (with eight members) generate more ideas than smaller groups (those with four members).[9]

Attribute Listing

The technique of attribute listing for generating ideas does not need to be done by groups. It involves listing the major attributes of an existing object and then imagining ways to modify each attribute. Osborn suggested that useful ideas could be stimulated by asking questions about an object and its attributes, such as: can it be put to other uses, adapted, modified, magnified, minified, substituted, rearranged, or reverse combined?[10]

Steps in Advertising Creativity

There is an increased awareness that advertising creativity should be the responsibility of all members of the advertising community—media buyers as well as members of the typical "creative" groups. This section of

---

[9]Edward F. Fern, "The Use of Focus Groups for Idea Generation: The Effects of Group Size, Acquaintanceship, and Moderator on Response Quantity and Quality," *Journal of Advertising Research*, Vol. 19 (February, 1982), pp. 1–13.

[10]Alex Osborn, *Applied Imagination*, 3rd ed. (New York: Charles Scribner and Sons, 1963), pp. 286–87.

CREATIVITY

For years the word *creativity* has produced an odd schizophrenia in our business, seeming to sort out those who were in favor of it from those who wanted to sell things.

David Ogilvy in his "Confessions of an Advertising Man" confessed, among other things, that he would not permit his creative department to use the word *creative* in describing themselves.

A major competitor has sought to bridge the gap by announcing: "It isn't creative unless it sells."

Our own Jeremy Bullmore, in a previous issue of this publication, has said, "I define creativity . . . as an ability to communicate to the people most likely to be interested in your brand or your service . . . most quickly and persuasively, most accurately and economically . . . advertising must work. It is not an end in itself."

I think that in those last two sentences Jeremy has put his finger on the root cause of the persistent schizophrenia that afflicts advertising whenever it gets onto the subject of its own creativity. "Advertising must work. It is not an end in itself."

Art is an end in itself. It has no obligations except to itself—to be beautiful, or wonderful, or awe-inspiring, even terrifying. Its only purpose is to be what it is.

Advertising, on the other hand, is a craft. While it may be wonderful or beautiful, its basic purpose is to sell, to persuade, in short, to work. In that respect it is like other crafts. A silver pitcher, no matter how beautiful, is designed to pour something. The American Indian blankets we now treasure in our craft museums because of their intrinsic beauty were originally designed to keep an American Indian warm.

Now all of this may seem to obvious to need repeating; however, Burt Manning reports that whenever he addresses one of our creative departments and points out that effectiveness is our basic criteria of success, someone will almost inevitably respond: "Oh, then you don't want to be creative."

Schizophrenia, it seems, still lives—and not too far from home.

The answer, of course, is that the whole purpose of advertising creativity is to produce sales effectiveness—just as the purpose of a silver pitcher, no matter how beautiful, is to pour something. Neither is an end in itself.

There is a very real danger in this assumption of some inherent opposition between creativity and sales effectiveness. If you assume that "creativity" is our sole goal, you may indeed produce advertising that attracts attention, the admiration of your peers, a quantity of golden statuary, and no sales. On the other hand, if you assume that a goal of sales effectiveness is an invitation to the use of stale ideas and dull or strident executions, you will probably wind up with neither sales nor statuary.

Helen Lansdowne Resor was frequently described as the greatest copywriter of her generation. It was said of her that she was "tortured by the commonplace." That is still a useful affliction for a creative department.

Effective advertising can only be maintained, again in Jeremy's words, by "original solutions to commonplace problems."

In the real world in which we operate, there is no room for the either/or implied in the debate between creativity and sales effectiveness. You cannot have one without the other.

Source: "Creativity" by Don Johnston, CEO, J. Walter Thompson Co. Reprinted by permission of the author.

CREATIVE ADVERTISING PERSONNEL

David Ogilvy surveyed his creative directors and presented the following description of the creative person in advertising:

1. Skilled in the art of brain-picking
2. Possesses a sense of humor
3. Not boring
4. Ambitious
5. Passionate student of advertising, its history, what works, what doesn't work
6. Hard worker
7. Well-furnished mind
8. Able to recognize differences between ordinary and extraordinary advertising
9. Knows all there is to be known about the product

Source: Carl Hixon, "A Conversation with the 'Scottish Blade' DAVID OGILVY," *Advertising Age* (September 14, 1981), p. 64.

the text, however, discusses the areas traditionally defined as *creative strategy in advertising*. Typically the term is used to refer to two basic steps in the preparation of the advertising campaign:

1. What is to be said—the selling message, the theme, the consumer proposition, the "positioning statement," or the *appeal*.
2. How it is to be said—the method of *execution*.

This second step involves a number of creative decisions including the selection of the execution device (the use of humor, sex, or celebrity presentations), the development of a brand name or trademark, the preparation of the copy, the artwork and layout, and the determination of the methods of preparing ads for their reproduction in media.

A good creative strategy is an outgrowth of advertising objectives that have been determined by the firm, frequently with the aid and advice of its advertising agency. As discussed in Chapter 8, advertising objectives are derived from marketing and corporate objectives. Furthermore creative decisions of *what to say* and *how to say it* are interrelated with a determination of *where to say it*—that is, the choice of media. (Media strategy will be discussed in the next section.) Table 10.1 on page 202 gives some examples of advertising objectives translated into creative strategies.

CREATING THE ADVERTISING APPEAL

The selling message in the advertisement is frequently called the appeal. Several methods may be used to determine the appeal.

TABLE 10.1   The Translation of Advertising Objectives into Creative Strategies

Example	Advertising Objective[1]		Creative Strategy	
	Task	Target Group	Appeal	Execution
American Tourister Luggage	Increase sale of luggage by attracting new users and/or encouraging brand switching	Travelers, prospective travelers	Emphasize attribute of strength	Humor
French's Mustard	Increase demand for one brand of a relatively homogeneous product class	Housewives, parents	Emphasize attribute of superior taste	Slice-of-life storytelling
Federal Express	Communicate dependability of service	Senders of small packages	Solves problem of late delivery	Humor

[1]Objectives, as described in Chapter 7, typically include the degree to which the task is to be accomplished and the time period.

Benefit/Attribute Approach

Consumers do not buy a product; they buy its taste, texture, nutritional value, or ability to clean and brighten;[11] in other words, consumers buy a product's benefits or attributes. That is why advertising frequently looks at a product's salient attributes in developing its appeal because they are the ones most likely considered in a purchase decision. For example, safety is obviously important to consumers. However, where items such as appliances are considered, safety may not be deemed *salient*, since consumers rarely consider this factor in their choices of appliances—perhaps because they assume all appliances are safe. On the other hand, while safety in flying is most likely *salient*, airline advertisers rarely mention this for fear of distressing potential flyers. With the tampering of Tylenol, safety replaced "fast relief" as the most salient attribute for over-the-counter analgesics.

---

[11]G. David Hughes, *Attitude Measurement for Marketing Strategists* (Glenview, Ill.: Scott, Foresman and Co., 1971), p. 87.

Selecting the Salient Benefit/Attribute

The decisions about which attributes are salient may vary depending on the advertiser. Exhibit 10.2 shows the differences in benefits/attributes as perceived by three wine producers.

An advertiser may decide which benefits to feature by using product inspection, a unique selling proposition, preemption of an idea, examination of competitors' ads, or consumer research.

EXHIBIT 10.2
Salient Attributes as Seen by Wine Advertisers

Inspection The product itself may be closely inspected by both the client company and the advertising agency to determine if there are any outstanding "talking" points. Judgment determines if these ideas are good and can be profitably expanded upon in ads. For example, General Foods believed that the fiber in its product was as important to consumers as the taste. It introduced a product called Fruit & Fiber with ads that emphasized the fiber content.

The value of judgment in selecting positive benefits cannot be overemphasized. DuPont, for example, promoted its Corfam synthetic leather by noting that it "breathed" and had a "memory" which kept it in its original form. The latter characteristic, which meant that the material kept its shape, turned out to be a significant problem. It refused to conform to the wearer's foot and never was "broken in." The product had to be withdrawn from the market. United Airlines advertised a "take me along" campaign which declared that wives could go along on a husband's business trip. This was criticized not only by husbands, who were not anxious to take their wives along, but by wives, who felt they were placed in secondary roles.

Unique Selling Proposition In the 1940s, Rosser Reeves conceptualized the *unique selling proposition,* an advertising approach which stressed an unusual product benefit. A successful and classic example is "At sixty miles an hour the only noise you hear in the Rolls-Royce is the ticking of a clock."

To some researchers, developing a unique selling proposition is considered the most powerful of the possible creative strategies (see Exhibit 10.3).[12] It is described as consisting of three parts:

1. Each advertisement must make a proposition to the consumer ("Buy this product and you will get this specific benefit").
2. The proposition must be one that the competition either cannot, or does not, offer. It must be unique to the product or the claim.

[12]Don E. Schultz and Sharon D. Ainser, "Toward the Advances in Advertising Developments of a Hierarchy of Creative Strategy, Research and Management," *Proceedings of the Annual Conference of the American Academy of Advertising,* 1978, ed. Steven E. Permut (American Academy of Advertising, 1978), pp. 128–31.

EXHIBIT 10.3
Unique Selling Proposition

3. The proposition must be strong enough to pull over new consumers to your product.

Creating a unique difference for a company's product is frequently the goal in new product development. When such a difference emerges it becomes fairly simple to develop a creative strategy around that difference. In introducing its Pampers to a public accustomed to cloth diapers, Procter & Gamble featured its disposability. If this strategy is to be successful, however, the feature must be perceived by consumers as important. A male deodorant product, Mennen with E, which contained vitamin E, failed despite its advertised uniqueness. Apparently very few men saw the need for vitamin E in their deodorants.

EXHIBIT 10.4
Preempting an Idea

Preemption of an Idea Even if the product does not possess a unique difference, it may be advertised as though it does. This approach, called the *preemption of an idea*, suggests that a company's product is the only one that has a specific feature. "Fly the Friendly Skies of United" or "when it rains, it pours," slogans used by United Airlines and Morton salt respectively, are examples of such preemptions (see Exhibit 10.4).

A preemptive claim may emerge through research. The F&M Schaefer Brewing Co. conducted a research study which showed that beer drinkers were divided into three consumption categories: light drinkers, who drink approximately three glasses of beer per week; medium beer drinkers, who drink 4 to 11 glasses per week; and heavy beer drinkers, who drink 12 or more glasses per week.[13] The research also showed that heavy beer drinkers thought that the second glass of beer did not have the same good taste and pleasure that the first glass provided, but they rated Schaefer, as compared to other beer brands, as having a far better consistency of flavor from one glass to the next.

Based on this research, an advertising appeal directed to the heavy beer drinker was developed by emphasizing Schaefer's apparent uniqueness—the quality of flavor consistency. The theme for the campaign was "Schaefer is the one beer to have when you're having more than one." Although the company has changed its theme many times in recent years, it is considering reintroducing that theme.

Competitor's Ads   Attributes featured by competitive products may be considered sufficiently important to incorporate into an advertising campaign. For a number of years Procter & Gamble's appeal for Crest toothpaste focused on its long-lasting protection. When other toothpastes, such as Beecham's Aquafresh, which became the third-largest-selling brand, were introduced offering not only protection, but good taste, they took market share away from Crest.[14]

Initially, Crest's approach was to denigrate the "fancy stripe gels" of the newer toothpaste, and reinforce the protection aspect. In one commercial a busy, competent housewife declares, in a phlegmatic manner, "Toothpastes don't excite me. Good check-ups. That excites me." However, the good taste and gel characteristics of its competitors finally caused Crest to introduce a new "great cavity-fighting" weapon—New Tartar Control Crest Gel (see Exhibit 10.5).

Consumer Research   When attributes are not clearly designated or benefits are not apparent, researchers ask consumers what it is that they want from a product, generally in focus group interviews. Shampoo manufacturers, for example, have discovered that consumers want shampoos that create high suds levels, are not harmful to the hair despite excessive use, and leave hair fluffy and clean. One shampoo manufacturer advertised that its product offered consumers "bouncing and behaving" hair.

Surveys, sometimes called "needs/wants" surveys, may also be conducted to reveal salient benefits and attributes. When Kodak was developing its new disc camera it was aware that the public did not seem to have a particular need for this product. Prior to its introduction Kodak conducted an extensive one-thousand-person consumer test to determine whether consumers would perceive any product benefits and whether they would want these benefits. The survey revealed a number of features consumers considered appealing. Of these, three were found to be most important—the automatic flash, the rapid flash recycling, and the automatic film advance—and these three were emphasized in the advertising.[15]

---

[13]"Case Study Agenda," The F&M Schaefer Brewing Co., New York, 1975.

[14]Nancy Giges, "Crest Counters Stripes," *Advertising Age* (August 25, 1980), p. 1.

[15]"Case Histories: How Pepperidge Farm, Kodak and New York Air Met Existing Consumer Needs—Or Created Them," *Advertising Age* (August 30, 1982), p. 54.

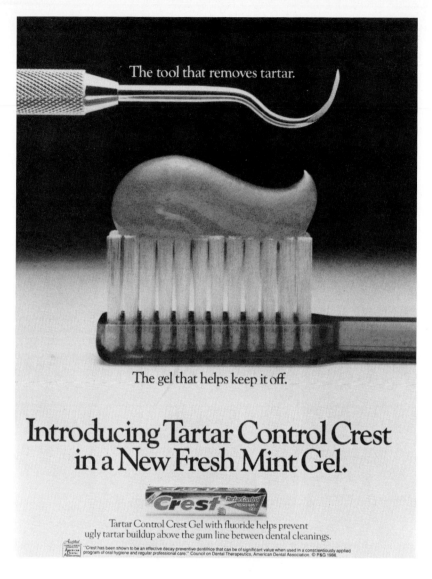

The tool that removes tartar.

The gel that helps keep it off.

Introducing Tartar Control Crest in a New Fresh Mint Gel.

Tartar Control Crest Gel with fluoride helps prevent ugly tartar buildup above the gum line between dental cleanings.

"Crest has been shown to be an effective decay-preventive dentifrice that can be of significant value when used in a conscientiously applied program of oral hygiene and regular professional care." Council on Dental Therapeutics, American Dental Association. © P&G 1986.

EXHIBIT 10.5
Featuring the Same Benefit as the Competitor

Problem Detection Strategy

To some advertisers, the emphasis on benefits and attributes tends to create similarity in advertising. Consumers who are questioned mention similar attributes, possibly because they "play back" benefits that they already know or those that they learn in advertising. To overcome these problems a strategy called *problem detection* is used to determine the basic appeal. Although it is sometimes difficult to distinguish between what may be considered an important attribute or a solution to the problem, problem detection permits wide latitude in researching appeals (see Exhibit 10.6).

EXHIBIT 10.6
Solving a Problem

Raise your hand if you're Sure.

For that confident, dry, secure feeling, raise your hand and reach for Sure.

© 1987 Procter & Gamble

Problem Detection Research

A typical problem detection approach starts with the development by the copy researcher of a long list of possible problems—as many as 100.[16] The next step is to interview a number of prospects (perhaps 150) and ask each consumer to rank each problem.

1. Is problem important?
2. Does problem occur frequently?
3. Has solution to problem been preempted by some existing product?

---

[16]*Advertising Age* (March 17, 1975), p. 46.

The problem score is then computed by combining the importance, frequency, and preemptibility ratings into a single number. The higher the score, the greater the opportunity to offer a solution to the problem

The following examples indicate situations where it appears that problem detection was superior to benefit-attribute research in developing appeals.[17]

— Dog food manufacturers found that, according to their consumer research, the three most wanted attributes were balanced diet, good nutrition, and vitamins. However, these were benefits for the dog rather than the purchaser. Problem detection research revealed dog food smelled bad, costs too much, didn't come in different sizes, and didn't meet the needs of different dogs. To overcome these problems, one company introduced a good-smelling stew, another mixed chunks with dried food to create an inexpensive product, a number of companies came out with different sizes, and General Foods introduced Cycle to meet the needs of different dogs.

— Viva found that consumers identified absorbency as the number-one attribute of paper toweling, but durability as a problem. Its advertising campaign emphasizes the durability of its product.

— H&R Block found people hated to pay income tax and had many problems with it, so it introduced a campaign in which it periodically specified one or another of "seventeen problems." For example, an ad would detail one of the problems and offer a solution to it.

— Dry Look was introduced when problem detection disclosed that many men felt that hair grooms made them feel like a "spitball."

— Burger King found that not all consumers wanted a hamburger with lettuce, pickles, and ketchup; some consumers preferred it plain. Burger King solved this problem in a campaign that declared "Have it your way!"

Consumer surveys may also be used to reveal problems. Dancer Fitzgerald Sample advertising agency has developed a consumer appeals study whereby surveys are conducted to provide information for various types of appeals.[18] Table 10.2 is an example of the kinds of appeals relevant to a nonfat powdered milk as revealed in a survey.

There are no clear-cut rules to determine when problem analysis is superior to benefit analysis for the appeal. An exploratory study was conducted to find out if benefit analysis or problem analysis was more effective in predicting consumer choice behavior. The study, which related to consumer savings level, revealed that salient problem-analysis was more effective than salient benefit-analysis in predicting savings

---

[17]*Advertising Age* (March 17, 1975), pp. 43–46.
[18]Edward M. Tauber, "Point of View: How to Get Advertising Strategy from Research," *Journal of Advertising Research* (October 1980), pp. 70–71.

TABLE 10.2   A Survey of Users and Nonusers of Nonfat Powdered Milk

Creative Approach	Appeal
Product Benefits and Attributes	
Unique Selling Proposition	Ingredient to make yogurt
Preemption of an Idea	Health orientation
Salient Benefits and Attributes	Economy, lack of fat, taste superiority, solvability
Problem Solving	
Consumer Problems Solved	High cost of fresh milk Fat consumption is too high Recipes require milk Fresh milk may not be on hand when wanted
Competitor's Problems Solved	Poor taste Poor dissolvability
Correct Misconceptions About Category or Brand	Poor taste Not real milk Contains additives

Source: Edward M. Tauber, "Poinnt of View: How to Get Advertising Strategy from Research," *Journal of Advertising Research* (October, 1980), pp. 70–71.

level.[19] While the study had some limitations, it did suggest that problem analysis may be a useful approach to developing an effective advertising appeal.

Consulting Lists of Instinctive Tendencies

The method of developing appeals has its basis in psychological research, which indicates that people are motivated by psychological and physiological drives. Advertisements for food are designed to offer satisfaction for the physiological drive of hunger and advertising for other products attempts to satisfy the psychological needs of love and affection. Sex has always been an important motivating factor in advertising, and today its use is increasing both overtly and covertly.

Basic Human Appeals

Psychological and physiological drives can be expressed as numerous basic appeals. According to Burton, they may include the following:[20] fear of pain, death, poverty, criticism, loss of possessions, beauty, popularity, or loved ones; desire for money, power, prestige, material possessions, physical comfort, rest, leisure, peace of mind, elimination of work, easier tasks, a new experience, beauty, popularity, family togeth-

[19]Richard H. Evans, "Benefit Analysis or Problem Analysis?" *Journal of Advertising*, Vol. 9, No. 1 (Winter 1980), pp. 27–31.
[20]Philip Ward Burton, *Advertising Copywriting*, pp. 16–17.

WOMAN: Joey called this morning.

MAN: And why are you crying?

WOMAN: 'Cause Joey said, "I called, just 'cause I love you, Mom."

SINGERS: Reach out, reach out and...

EXHIBIT 10.7
Love and Affection

"Reach Out and Touch Someone" minidramas were the best-recalled television spots among viewers in a survey.

erness, good health, longevity, youthfulness, patriotism, travel, entertainment, and sensory appeals (see Exhibit 10.7).

Fear as an Appeal

Fear is frequently cited as a strong motivating force and, as a result, some advertisers consider fear to be a potent advertising strategy. It is hypothesized that fear serves as a drive, and increased amounts of induced fear lead to an increased potential for attitudinal or behavioral changes.

Insurance companies and personal-care products manufacturers have used fear appeals over the years. Early life-insurance ads featured a weeping child being led to an orphanage, declaring "Her daddy didn't leave enough life insurance." More recent ads for Mony have focused on the father who died before he could save for his son's education, and the parents who died leaving children whom the sister was now required to take care of.

Some studies have indicated a negative relationship between fear arousal and persuasion.[21] Other studies have suggested that fear can lead to withdrawal of attention, dislike of the source, and interference with attention to and comprehension of the message. Still others have indicated that the fear appeal may work better with some target segments than others. Fear appeals are apparently effective with those groups of individuals whose anxiety about a product or service is low and for those who would not normally search for information about the product. For

---

[21]Irving L. Janis and Seymour Feshback, "Effects of Fear-Arousing Communications," *Journal of Abnormal and Social Psychology*, 48 (January 1953), pp. 78–92.

example, the fear appeal in insurance advertisements was more effective for those who had not been concerned with insurance nor actively considering its purchase.[22]

The Positive Versus the Negative Appeal

Advertising appeals that arouse emotional tension can be used to achieve a desired attitudinal change. Some people respond better to a negative appeal while others respond better to a positive approach. Simply put, the negative appeal dramatizes the situation to be avoided through the uses of a product, while the positive appeal tries to dramatize the situations to be gained through the use of a product.

Over the years there has been a great deal of controversy about the desirability of using the negative appeal in advertising. Critics maintain that it has made the American public overly conscious and unnecessarily concerned about such innocuous considerations as body offenses. Nevertheless, this approach has been used and continues to be used successfully. For some products, such as soaps and mouthwashes, the "hard sell" negative appeal of the past has been replaced by a somewhat subtler, softer approach. The halitosis which Listerine had eliminated is now avoided by using Scope "once in the morning and your breath is fresher for hours"; the elimination of body odor by Lifebuoy is now avoided by Coast deodorant soap, which is "refreshing."

There may be some opportunities for the successful use of negative appeals where the target market is composed of individuals of low anxiety. A test of the effectiveness of two types of insurance copy revealed that the low-anxiety groups who were exposed to negative copy experienced a more favorable attitude shift than those who were shown positive copy. It also reinforced the finding that high-anxiety groups responded more favorably to positive copy than to negative copy.[23] It is difficult to say when the negative approach will work best. In general, when a product solves a problem, the negative side may be presented effectively in advertising. However, the advertising may be more successful when correcting, curing, or relieving is more desirable than just preventing or avoiding the problem.

Which Creative Appeal Is Best?

Creative strategies are frequently judged by advertising professionals; awards are provided for those selected as outstanding. Although some of these awards attempt to determine effectiveness (the American Marketing Association's "Effie" award is based on how well the advertising achieved its objectives), frequently the criteria are subjective and the most original, not the most effective, ads may win.

---

[22]Michael L. Ray and Wendell L. Wilkie, "Fear: The Potential of an Appeal Neglected by Marketing," *Journal of Marketing,* Vol. 34 (January 1970), pp. 54–62.

[23]J. J. Wheatley and Sadaomi Oshikawa, "The Relationship Between Anxiety and Positive and Negative Advertising Appeals," *Journal of Marketing Research,* Vol. 7 (February 1970), pp. 85–89.

Despite efforts to provide objective measurement of creative appeals, researchers have concluded that the creative function remains resistant to attempts at quantification, but they noted that other forms of analysis suggest its significance.[24]

Consumers buy utilities and psychological satisfactions. Obviously all of a product's utilities and satisfactions cannot be presented in a single advertisement, and if they were, the consumer could not possibly grasp them all with that one advertisement. Advertising may present more than one benefit at one time, but the total number should be limited and the benefits presented should harmonize with each other and attempt to provide a single impression. The advertiser should also be aware that the effectiveness of the appeal varies with the manner of execution; the creative strategy must extend to the copy, artwork, and typography.

Generalizations about the forms of appeals and their relative effectiveness are dangerous. Research may help uncover some potent appeals, but only when they are presented as part of an advertising campaign can their true value be assessed. Moreover, the fact that an appeal was successful in one period of time does not preclude it from failing in another. Rapidly changing conditions and life-styles in our society suggest that feedback is necessary to assure that an appeal merits continuing use.

SUMMARY

Creativity can be defined in many ways and finds its expression in many areas. The need for creativity in advertising is evident, particularly since creativity involves not only originality and inspiration but also problem-solving techniques.

While it is difficult to isolate the precise characteristics of the creative individual, some generalizations have emerged. These include interest in the complex and novel, more relativistic view of life, more independence of judgment, and greater flexibility.

Creativity can be involved in almost every area of advertising; however, the term is most frequently used in relation to the creative strategy—what is said—the selling message, and its methods of execution—how it is said (discussed in detail in the next chapters).

There are a number of methods for determining the basic theme or appeal. These include determining the salient product benefits or attributes, finding solutions to problems, and consulting a list of instinctive tendencies. It is difficult to decide which is the best technique or specific appeal. Rapidly changing conditions and life-styles in our society suggest that continuing research may be necessary to uncover potent appeals.

---

[24]Alan D. Fletcher and Sherilyn K. Zeigler, "Creative Strategy and Magazine Ad Readership," *Journal of Advertising Research*, Vol. 18 (February 1978), pp. 29–36.

QUESTIONS FOR DISCUSSION

1. Do you consider yourself to be creative? Why or why not?
2. Is there a difference between creativity in art and creativity in advertising? Explain.
3. What techniques are useful for generating ideas?
4. Select a magazine that is several years old and compare the ads for a particular product with current magazine ads. Have the basic appeals changed? How?
5. Find ads for a product that represent both the benefit/attribute and problem-solving approaches. Which do you think are more effective? Discuss.
6. Describe several research methods that may be used for determining appeals.
7. What is meant by the unique selling proposition? a preemption of an idea?
8. What are some of the basic motives that can be used effectively as advertising appeals?
9. Can fear be used as an effective appeal? Discuss.
10. Under what circumstances would you use a negative appeal? a positive appeal?

KEY TERMS

creativity	inspection
brainstorming	unique selling proposition
creative strategy	preemption of an idea
appeal	problem detection

AD PRACTICE

Select a product or service category (for example, analgesics, cereals, computers, airlines). Review both print and broadcast advertisements to determine the appeals used by various competitors in the category. Are the appeals consistent or are there wide variations? What reasons can you offer for these findings?

11

Creative Strategy: The Execution

Bill Cosby, John Houseman, Joan Collins, Kirk Douglas—who would you like to buy your toothpaste from? A recent study revealed that only 19 percent of the 1000 consumers surveyed believed that celebrities increase interest in products. About half said celebrities do commercials only for the money; others believed that entertainers didn't actually use the products they endorsed. Moreover, celebrities lose favor fairly rapidly; only half of the ten most convincing Hollywood celebrities picked in a 1982 survey turned up on the 1985 list. Bill Cosby remained number one on the list, partly because he varied his style depending on the product he was endorsing. John Houseman, however, who slipped from the list, used the identical approach—stern and professorial—for Smith Barney, Puritan cooking oil, Plymouth cars, and McDonald's.

Celebrity ads may still be successful if the product match is right and the star is believable. Dinah Shore is a good spokesperson for Holly Farms chicken because she is known as a good cook. Comedienne Martha Raye, who wears dentures and goes by the nickname "the big mouth," is considered perfect for Polident.

Significantly less advertising research focuses on selecting the method of execution than on choosing the appeal. Nevertheless, the manner of execution is as important to an advertising campaign as the appeal of the ad.

CHAPTER OBJECTIVES

— To examine the types of execution most frequently found in today's advertising

— To suggest the circumstances when these various techniques may be used

Figure 11.1   "Missing Person" 60-Second Radio Commercial

ANNCR: Here's Stiller and Meara for Lanier Dictating Equipment.

Stiller: May I come in?

Meara: Who are you?

Stiller: I'm your husband.

Meara: Oh yeah, George. The guy who works late every night. I'm married to a missing person.

Stiller: I finally got caught up.

Meara: Say hi to your son, Ronny.

Stiller: How's my little cub scout?

Meara: He's in law school. He grew up.

Stiller: (chuckle) Still wearing that funny little hat, huh?

Meara: Listen, if you don't start coming home earlier, I'm gonna put us all up for adoption.

Stiller: I can't help it. I work as fast as I can.

Meara: We need Lanier.

Stiller: Who's Lanier? A marriage counselor?

Meara: Lanier is dictating equipment.

Stiller: I've never used dictating equipment.

Meara: Dictating is six times faster than writing. With Lanier's Action Line you'd be home at 5 instead of 10. And with a Pocket Secretary Portable, you could bring work home.

Stiller: I think Lanier can bring us back together.

Meara: Oh, terrific! Now you'll be more to Ronnie than just that strange little man in our wedding picture. I'm so happy.

Stiller: I'm happy, too, Donna.

Meara: Donna? Who's Donna?

Stiller: I don't know. I made it up.

Meara: Oh, George.

Stiller: Elaine? Phyllis? Give me a hint.

ANNCR: Get more done with Lanier Business Products. In the yellow pages under Dictating Machines.

Source: "Missing Person," 60 Second Radio Commercial, *Advertising Campaign Report Newsletter* (Dec. 1980). Copyright © 1980 American Association of Advertising Agencies. Reprinted by permission.

THE CREATIVE EXECUTION

Successful campaigns are those which achieve their objectives. Thus, once the appeal is selected it must be executed in a manner that is most consistent with the advertiser's objectives. Moreover, both the appeal and execution vary to conform with changing advertising objectives and target markets.

When Lanier Business Products Company introduced its "Pocket Secretary," its creative strategy focused on increasing awareness and preference for Lanier and securing leads for salespeople. The target group consisted of business and professional people who had never tried dictating equipment. The humorous ads emphasized the productivity that could be achieved with a machine that was small and portable (see Figure 11.1).

Subsequently the company felt its original objectives—awareness and brand preference—had been achieved. A new campaign was prepared designed to reinforce Lanier's leader position and image and maintain sales force enthusiasm. The target group was the same—business and professional people. This time, however, the ads featured Arnold Palmer who was selected as spokesperson to build leadership image (see Exhibit 11.1).

THE PRESENTATION OF MATERIAL

An important component in the success of an advertising campaign is the manner in which the basic appeal is presented. This section discusses those execution techniques most widely used in today's advertising, including straight sell, mood creation, demonstration, storytelling, humor, sex, and personalities.

Straight Sell Approach

A simple presentation of a product and its benefits may be used when the product has characteristics that are important to the purchaser's choice decision (see Exhibit 11.2).

Emotional or Mood Creation Approach

Video Storyboards, a company that rates commercials through surveys, questioned 15,000 people about the most outstanding commercials they had seen recently.[1] Only a handful of respondents pinpointed a product benefit or attribute as the reason for their choices. *Outstanding* was almost always related to the creative presentation. *Happy, warm, entertaining,* and *fun to watch* were the words often used to describe outstanding commercials. Highest recall scores were achieved by ads such as the Mean Joe Greene commercials for Coca-Cola.

Mood creation or an emotional approach does not only mean sympathetic characters and touching vignettes; moods can also be created by invoking various images. Chanel No. 5's "Share the Fantasy" commercial, shown in Exhibit 11.3, attracted significant favorable attention. It was described as *surrealistic, thought-provoking, classy,* "very close to pornography," and "a weird strange commercial that doesn't make sense"—but, all in all, it was described as unique.

Support for the use of mood creation or emotional advertising has increased in recent years. Mood creation ads are particularly useful for products or services that lack distinctive characteristics. Robert Fizdale, president-chief creative officer of Leo Burnett Co., noted big, enduring ideas are those which appeal to emotions; furthermore, "feelings are energies that sell products."[2] Plummer declared that all great selling

Exhibit 11.1
Using a Spokesperson

Exhibit 11.2.
Simple Execution: Present Product

---

[1]David Badehra, "Coke, McDonald's Lead Outstanding TV Commercials, *Advertising Age* (May 26, 1980), p. 37.

[2]"Big-Idea Advertising Generic, Says Fizdale," *Advertising Age* (September 2, 1985), p. 60.

Exhibit 11.3
Creating a Mood

ideas established a vital emotional bond with their prospects.[3] Avis tapped the inherent sympathy for the underdog; Miller Lite assured its consumers that the boys wouldn't think they were sissies for drinking a light beer; and American Express promised that even achievers wouldn't go unnoticed when traveling.

With the increase in advertising clutter, advertisers have turned to mood creation ads in hope that these will stand out among their competitors, will persuade viewers to stay tuned a little longer to the message, and will minimize the tendency to "zap" out commercials.[4]

Demonstration

While television is especially suited to demonstration, the technique can be used successfully in print media as well. Demonstrations are useful in ads designed to prove a product's superiority, particularly when it can be depicted easily. Duracell shows its batteries last longer than others when placed in toys. When the Gillette Company introduced its new shampoo, Silkience, the basic appeal was a problem-solving one: "Beats the grease without beating the ends." Using computer graphics the ads demonstrated how Silkience was a self-adjusting shampoo. The campaign won an award for advertising effectiveness.

The before-and-after demonstration has been used for many years. The 1930s ads for a body-building service showed the "97-pound weakling" transformed to a muscleman. Currently, the before-and-after technique is particularly relevant for presenting appeals that emerge through problem-solving. The *before* element indicates the undesirable situation (the problem) and the *after* element indicates the change or solution (see Exhibit 11.4). A shampoo ad shows various individuals declaring "I was flat, till I went fluffy." One caution in using the before-and-after technique is to ensure that it is believable.

Slice of Life

The basic theme or appeal can be developed through a series of stories or vignettes. Eastman Kodak has, for years, used the slice of life technique, shown in Exhibit 11.5, and has advertised its product as the story teller.

Some ads incorporate a kind of story-telling technique; a slice of life focuses on a situation that may occur to the average individual in his or her everyday experiences. Procter & Gamble has used this approach for many years and for many of its products. Frequently, a strong central character dramatizes the situations, such as Rosie depicting the benefits

---

[3]"Emotions Important for Successful Advertising," *Marketing News* (April 12, 1985), p. 18.

[4]"The TV Commercial Tries on Some Disguises," *The New York Times* (September 1, 1985), p. F7.

Exhibit 11.4
Before and After

of Bounty paper towels. The classic early ads for Alka-Seltzer used slice of life—the newlyweds' first home-cooked meal—and more recently, Cheer moved from Number Seven to Number Two as the all-purpose detergent in a slice-of-life commercial featuring the boy, home from college, doing his own laundry.[5]

A successful slice-of-life series of commercials for Aim carried a repetitive theme. More than fifty TV commercials used the same repertory cast featuring a dominant, young mother to carry the message to relatives, friends, plumbers, and handymen that "Bobby brushes longer with Aim because he likes the taste."

---

[5]Harry McMahan and Mack Kile, "'Slice' Sells with Drama," *Advertising Age* (September 14, 1981), p. 68.

Exhibit 11.5
Telling a Story

In 1986 the International Advertising Film Festival awarded the Grand Prix, its highest honor, to a John Hancock Financial Services advertising campaign featuring real-life situations.[6] Television spots showed a young couple signing for their first mortgage, a man talking to his younger brother, whose idea of a good investment is buying a new car, and a retiring football player planning for his future.

Humor

In the 1970s advertisers tended to avoid humor; the 1980s, however, has brought about a resurgence of humorous ads for a number of reasons. Stronger competition has led to the use of techniques that may create greater attention and remain in the mind longer. McCollum

---

[6]Claire Wilson, "Enlightening strikes twice," *Advertising Age* (July 7, 1986), p. 3.

Exhibit 11.6
Dry Humor by "Just Plain Folks"

Spielman & Co. found, in a survey to measure advertising effectiveness, that humorous commercials substantially outscored ads featuring celebrities and real people.[7] The rising cost of television has influenced many advertisers to use radio. Humorous ads, which may have to be heard several times before they register, can be repeated relatively inexpensively in this medium.

Humor may be used for products with low interest. Samsonite designed a campaign to revitalize its sale of luggage, considered a relatively low-interest item. The commercials portrayed children using luggage as playground material and subjecting it to excessive abuse, as well as the Pittsburgh Steelers using luggage for football practice purposes.

In order to distinguish itself from typical automobile advertising American Motors uses humor for its Izuzu commercials. The car, according to a spokesperson, "gets 94 miles per gallon city, 112 highway . . . Its top speed is 300 miles per hour . . . They're selling them for $9 . . . And if you come in tomorrow, you'll get a free house. You have my word on it." A printed disclaimer accompanies each promise.

An award-winning campaign, featuring the dry humor of two people representing themselves as owners of Bartles & Jaymes Wine Cooler Co., was considered responsible for a significant increase in sales of a relatively new product (see Exhibit 11.6).

Most advertisers agree that humor enhances audience attention, at least in the first few exposures to the message. It may, however, inhibit comprehension and, thus, reduce overall message reception. Furthermore, humorous ads may "wear out" quickly. The fundamental question that is yet to be answered is: "Is a humorous message more influential than a serious version of the same appeal?"[8]

---

[7]John Koten, "After Serious '70s, Advertisers are Going for Laughs Again, *The Wall Street Journal* (February 23, 1984), p. 31.

[8]Isadore Barmash, "Advertising Humor: Tarnished Attribute," *The New York Times* (August 12, 1980), p. D14.

Using Humor in Advertisements

Guidelines are only suggestions; they are based on past experiences and are designed to prevent the repetition of past mistakes. Rigid adherence to them, however, may stultify creativity and limit the development of successful presentations. The following serve as indications of the ways humor should be used in advertising.

1. Humor should not belittle the consumer. Alka-Seltzer's humorous ads were faulted for this tendency; however, Federal Express' ads were considered very successful (see Table 10.1 in Chapter 10).
2. Humor should have built-in, word-of-mouth possibilities (repeatability), such as Wendy's "Where's the Beef?"
3. Humor should have an element of human interest. Chivas Regal presented a series of successful ads, indicating the problems caused by an extensive demand for a product that may not always be available.
4. Excessively funny "gags" tend to have short life spans.
5. Ethnic humor may backfire.
6. Humor may overpower the ad, rather than make it memorable; therefore, be restrained in the use of humor.
7. It is generally inadvisable to use humor to launch new products, despite the success of Bartles & Jaymes.[9]
8. For products which have high emotional appeal and status value, such as cosmetics and fragrances, humor is inappropriate and trivializing.[10]
9. Service companies such as banks, insurance companies, and real estate firms find it difficult to use humor since money, property, and life and death are not laughing matters.[11] Prudential Insurance Company abandoned the use of humor when it found that the serious approach scored much higher with viewers. Nevertheless, some creative people believe humor can be used for a very serious subject if it can be employed with sensitivity, avoiding stereotypes and not evoking prejudices.[12]

Sexual Approach

There is clearly widespread use of sex in the execution of advertising appeals; however, the nature and extent of its effectiveness is not clear. Explicit sex is rarely used in advertisements; implicit sex occurs in various forms, including nudity, the use of the *double entendre*, and sexual

---

[9]"Humor is Best Utilized with Established Products," *Marketing News* (October 1, 1982), p. 6.

[10]"Humor is Best Utilized with Established Products," p. 6.

[11]John Koten, "After Serious 70s Advertisers are Going for Laughs Again," *The Wall Street Journal* (February 23, 1984), p. 32.

[12]Ed Fitch, "Insurer Finds Laughter is Best Medicine," *Advertising Age*, (January 31, 1985), p. 36.

situations. The manner in which the sexual aspects are depicted may vary with the communication objectives and the message.

Nudity

Using nudity in advertising is clearly designed to attract attention and awareness, but it is less successful in brand recall.[13] These conclusions, results of research done in 1969, were supported by a later study. In the 1978 research, significantly more brand names were recalled for those advertisements containing a mountain or forest scene than those with a nude model.[14] This study provided additional support for the proposition that when the objective is men's brand recall, a nude woman should not be used in advertisements. Furthermore, in examining how consumers perceived the use of a nude female model in advertisements, the researchers found that the ads containing the nude model were perceived as the least appealing, while the associated product and producing company were perceived as, respectively, possessing the lowest quality and being the least reputable.[15]

Ads for jeans featuring partly nude models have lead to criticisms, particularly when they also used children.

Double Entendre

The use of *double entendre* (double meaning) usually has sexual overtones, but it is more likely designed to create interest and awareness than to motivate someone sexually. One of the earliest examples of the use of double entendre was a Clairol ad that asked "Does she or doesn't she?" The ad was successful in attracting attention and recall; whether this was because of the sexual implications in the message has not been determined. In fact, *Life Magazine*, at first, rejected this ad, but later accepted it when its secretaries interpreted the message as "Does she or doesn't she—color her hair."

In a campaign for Campari, an imported Italian aperitif, the advertising objective was to position the product as a mixed drink, rather than as an aperitif. A problem with the product appeared to be its unique bittersweet taste which Europeans tended to like, but Americans didn't. In order to attract consumers to something new and to accept an unusual taste experience, a basic theme was developed, "Campari . . . the first time is never the best." A double entendre was employed in the creative execution by featuring various female and male celebrities talking about their "first times."

In recent years, there has been controversy surrounding the use of sexual situations. Depending on its presentation, it can be seen as "too cute," locker-room humor, or sexist. An ad for Revlon's first fragrance, Intimate, which NBC refused to air as too sexually suggestive was shown

---

[13]Major Steadman, "How Sexy Illustrations Affect Brand Recall," *Journal of Advertising Research*, Vol. 9 (February, 1969), pp. 15–18.

[14]M. Wayne Alexander and Ben Judd, Jr., "Do Nudes in Ads Enhance Brand Recall?," *Journal of Advertising Research*, Vol. 18 (February, 1978), pp. 47–50.

[15]M. Wayne Alexander and Ben Judd, Jr., "Do Nudes in Ads Enhance Brand Recall?," *Journal of Advertising Research*, Vol. 18 (February 1978), pp. 47–50.

on television by ABC and CBS networks. The camera zooms in on a man's hand as he moves a piece of ice very slowly from a woman's chin along her neck to the top of her low-cut dress. Then he removes his hand. In the "cool" version, shown by the two networks, the ad ends with the woman pulling the man's hand back to her neck. In the "hot" version, shown by several affiliate stations, she moves his hand lower, to the top of her dress.[16]

For some advertisers the numerous competitive products and their similarities suggest the need for advertising executions with significant impact. Calvin Klein has used a sensual approach in its executional designs for various products (see Exhibit 11.7).

THE USE OF PERSONALITIES

The technique of using a personality as a spokesperson for a product derives from communication theory and research about the importance of a message's source. A personality may create recognition by providing a familiar face for an unfamiliar brand, enhance the credibility and memorability of a message, or even create a "symbolic personality" for a company or its product.

Numerous advertising campaigns use personalities, generally celebrities from the motion picture industry, the sports world, and the theater; however, personalities can also be "average individuals." The choice varies with the product advertised and/or the marketing and advertising strategy devised.

Celebrities as Personalities

Celebrities are those people who are widely known. When such people appear in advertisements, they do so as presenters or spokespersons.

Presenters
The individual who is a presenter of a product usually offers his or her own opinions and experience, frequently in the form of testimonials or endorsements. A presenter may provide a *testimonial* about the excellence of the product based on the individual's own personal experience. A testimonial by Arnold Palmer for a golf club would be considered an *expert* testimonial; however, when Lanier Corporation selected Arnold Palmer to promote its Vest-Pocket Secretary, he provided a *nonexpert* testimonial.

Endorsements, like testimonials, may either be expert or nonexpert, but unlike testimonials, they do not indicate that the celebrities have actually used the products or services they endorse. For example, Joe Namath endorsed a brand of pantyhose and racing car drivers have endorsed toy racing cars. If a presenter indicates that he or she uses a

---

[16]Ann Hagedorn, "TV Networks Find Revlon's Sensual Ad Too Hot to Handle," *The Wall Street Journal* (April 27, 1987), p. 28.

Exhibit 11.7
**Using a Sexual Situation in
Advertising**

product, this must be so. Moreover, it is the responsibility of the advertiser to periodically determine whether or not the presenter continues to use the product if the advertising campaign continues.

Spokespersons

A spokesperson does not endorse the product; rather, the personality speaks for the company. Individuals selected as spokespersons are usually high in status and have widespread acceptance, because they are frequently used for corporate or image advertising campaigns. Actor Cliff Robertson, who made headlines in the late 70s for his help in breaking a Hollywood scandal, is the spokesperson for AT&T. He was chosen by *Advertising Age* as outstanding spokesperson of 1985.[17] When Walter Cronkite retired from his full-time reporting, many companies attempted to secure him as their spokesperson—at this writing, he has not accepted any of these offers.

Selecting a Celebrity

In selecting a celebrity as the personality of an ad campaign, a number of criteria are used:

1. *Compatibility of the Individual with the Product.* A product that is designed to project an image may find that image can be enhanced by a particular type of celebrity. Coty introduced a new brand of perfume named Sophia (for Sophia Loren) which was positioned for the older, more sophisticated woman. Revlon signed a contract with Joan Collins to act as its spokesperson for its fragrance Scoundrel, a name which apparently reflected the role she played in the television series *Dynasty*. When her contract expired Susan Lucci, who has been called everything from a vamp to a witch for her performance on ABC's soap opera *All My Children*, was named spokeswoman for Scoundrel Perfume and Scoundrel Musk. Male celebrities, particularly those who represent a "macho" character, offer the appropriate image for men's toiletries.

2. *Acceptance of the Individual by the Target Audience.* A number of characteristics are presumed to make personalities acceptable to the public; these include the attributes of popularity, credibility, and sincerity. Bill Cosby has been considered an outstanding celebrity spokesperson since he projects both credibility and sincerity. When Firestone had adverse publicity because its tires were often recalled, it employed James Stewart to provide an aura of respectability in its advertising. Before his death, John Wayne, as a spokesperson for a western bank, was said to have created an image of stability and security, which apparently was successful in attracting depositors.

Popular sports figures are frequently used as celebrity spokespeople, but this may vary with the perceptions of the target audience about the sport itself. As a general rule of thumb, football reaches a variety of age and income groups, baseball is considered a middle-income game, golf and tennis are sports for upper-income people, and basketball is popular among those 18 to 35. Some sports figures, however, are accepted by consumers in any situation; Reggie Jackson, for example, has had a candy bar named for him.

A company may use a celebrity to reposition itself in terms of its target market. With the sharp decline in the consumption of coffee among the younger age groups General Foods selected Justine Bateman, Mariel Hemmingway, and Bronson Pinchot as spokespersons for

[17]Jennifer Pendleton, "Robertson Believe-Ability, Star Presenter Oozes Honesty," *Advertising Age* (July 8, 1985), p. 5.

JOVAN EVENING EDITION.
A totally new kind of musk.

For a woman who wants
a man to know
she's sophisticated, subtle
and yet, sexy.
Jovan Musk Evening Edition.

Exhibit 11.8
Using a Male Celebrity to Create an
Image

its Maxwell House Coffee. These ads helped increase the brand recall rating among consumers significantly.[18]

Many advertisers choose celebrities on the basis of Performer Q ratings compiled by Marketing Evaluations. This organization measures how well-liked celebrities are; however, they do not predict selling potential. When Alan Alda rated Number One in Performer Q ratings, Atari signed him to a multimillion-dollar contract. However, Mr. Alda did not make Video Storyboard Tests' (a television testing service) list of the most convincing celebrity endorsers.[19]

[18]Julie Franz, "Youthful Stars Play it to Max for GF Coffee," *Advertising Age* (October 27, 1986), p. 88.

[19]Ronald Alsop, "Jaded TV Viewers Tune Out Glut of Celebrity Commercials" (February 7, 1985), p. 33.

Noncelebrities as Personalities

It is not always necessary to use a celebrity. While celebrities have greater popularity, at least initially, the characteristics of sincerity and credibility are sometimes more likely to emerge from an "average individual" such as Mrs. Olson for Folger's coffee, Mr. Whipple for Charmin, and the lonely Maytag repair man. Using a noncelebrity is seen as consistent with the common-man technique, designed to have consumers see the personalities as similar to themselves. Particularly successful campaigns have used company presidents, such as Tom Carvel (ice cream) and Frank Perdue (chickens), who accentuate their idiosyncracies to make themselves more human and believable. Frank Perdue, for example, happily emphasizes his resemblance to his most lucrative product, the chicken. Tom Carvel has a raspy speaking voice, which makes his narrations all the more memorable.

Using noncelebrities in ad campaigns offers both advantages and disadvantages. While it is clear that celebrities usually give more professional performances, amateurs in ads may, in fact, provide new expressions, interesting innuendos, and crisper presentations.

Nonetheless, consumers may distrust real people, believing that those who appear in ads have been coached to say what they do and, in fact, are professional actors. Furthermore, if such spokespersons are too stilted or unattractive, they may call more attention to themselves than to the product. Finally, when average consumers are told before endorsing a product that they will receive payment or will appear on television as compensation, viewers of the ad must be informed. Such disclosure is not required when celebrities are endorsers.

How Long Should a Personality Be Used?

Among the most successful ads are those in which a personality has been used for a long period of time. Timex featured John Cameron Swayze for over 22 years, while Madge the Manicurist advertised Palmolive dishwashing liquid for over 17 years, and actor Jesse White has been waiting to fix a Maytag washer for almost two decades.

When an advertiser contracts with an individual to promote a product, the advertiser cannot anticipate every occurrence. Athletes may be injured and traded; motion picture stars, as well as non-celebrities, may become involved in controversial situations. In such circumstances, the advertiser must decide whether the celebrity has lost his or her appeal. Both Goodyear Tire and Cutty Sark were quick to discontinue John Z. DeLorean shortly after he was accused of illegal activities.

Occasionally, a company has no choice but to withdraw its ads using celebrities. Such a situation arose when a J. B. Williams Lectric Shave commercial featured quarterback Michael Kruczek in a Pittsburgh Steelers uniform and Mr. Kruczek was traded to the Washington Redskins.

WHICH EXECUTION STRATEGY IS BEST?

Currently there is no consensus as to the *best* strategy for the execution of an ad. A number of factors may influence the choice of execution techniques; in some situations the choice may appear obvious. For example, in terms of the appeal, the benefit/attribute approach suggests the straight sell, the problem-solving approach suggests demonstration, and the use of instinctive tendencies indicates techniques such as mood creation, story-telling, or the use of humor, sex, or personalities. Similarly, in terms of the target group, mood creation, story-telling, humor, sex and personalities apparently are desirable for consumers, while the straight sell or demonstration seems most useful for the industry or the trade.

Despite such apparent relationships advertisers do not always follow these assumptions; in fact, successful advertising campaigns have deviated from them. An outstanding campaign of the 1980s is the use of a Charlie Chaplin character for "telling the story" of IBM computers in small business offices (see Exhibit 11.9.). When IBM introduced its Personal System/2 in 1987, they replaced Chaplin with several characters from the television series, M*A*S*H. While Charlie Chaplin was considered the symbol for everyman's personal computer, the larger cast of characters was used to indicate the new, wider-ranging line of mainframes, printers, and copiers.

Problems in Execution Strategy

A "dilemma of creative advertising" is that people involved in executing advertising are "deprived of the natural rewards that sincere individuals want."[20] Advertising people sell their executions to clients and are not able to oserve what specific phrases or artwork elicit responses from customers. These primary rewards to creators are replaced by the secondary rewards of praise from colleagues, superiors, and clients, as well as creative awards.

Another problem is the attempt to harmonize two potentially conflicting trends—the pressure toward more creative execution and the growing need to ensure the effectiveness of advertising. The creative person feels the need to be distinctive, inventive, and unique. The client wishes to be assured that this distinctive, expensive advertisement will achieve corporate goals. One method for obtaining such assurances is through research, and both clients and agencies are relying increasingly on research techniques. However, to the creative advertising in-

---

[20]Alfred Politz, "The Dilemma of Creative Advertising," *Journal of Marketing*, Vol. 5 (October, 1960), p. 6.

Exhibit 11.9
Softening a Starchy Image

dividual such research appears to establish rigid rules, stifle inspiration, and reduce advertising to its lowest common denominator.

In an effort to reconcile these two pressures, some advertising agencies turn to research as a tool for gathering information that is diagnostic and predictive. They undertake research designed to give the creator something to be creative about and attempt to secure information that will channel his or her thinking toward those kinds of executions susceptible to persuasion. David Ogilvy, creative head of Ogilvy and Mather advertising agency, emphasizes the need for more research in the area of creative execution. Advertising can achieve better results if more efforts are made to determine which execution techniques are most likely to work.[21]

There are a number of other considerations affecting creative execution decisions. These include product or service requirements (Is long explanatory copy necessary?), cost (Is the creative concept too expensive?), and media selection (Is musical accompaniment desirable? Are visual demonstrations necessary?). Many of these considerations are discussed in detail in subsequent chapters.

SUMMARY

Execution is the second step in the creative process. The manner in which a selling message is executed is of major significance in an advertising campaign. In this chapter, a number of techniques for presenting the selling message were discussed, including straight selling, mood creation, demonstration, story telling, using humor, incorporating sex, and using personalities.

The straight-sell is useful for presenting the salient benefits or attributes of a product translated into the target's frame of reference. Mood creation is a technique that is frequently used for products or services lacking significant characteristics that distinguish them from the competition. Demonstrations tend to be used for products or services possessing attributes or benefits that may be lacking in competitive items and can be clearly depicted.

Story-telling/slice-of-life ads present the product's benefits or use in real-life situations. Humor is designed to enhance audience attention; however, humorous ads may "wear out" rapidly. The use of sex in advertising has increased. Like humor, sexy ads may enhance the attention-getting value of the ads; however, the use of sex may tend to detract from the perception of the message and arouse consumer objections.

Personalities are used in advertising to create images, to break through the advertising clutter, and to improve recognition by providing familiar faces for unfamiliar brands. Celebrities and noncelebrities may be used as personalities in advertising.

There is little empirical evidence concerning which execution strategy is best; however, future research may provide more data for efficient decisions. Execution strategy relates to much more than the techniques used for presenting the advertising message.

---

[21]David Ogilvy and Joel Raphaelson, "Research on Advertising Techniques That Work—And Don't Work," *Harvard Business Review* (July/August, 1982), pp. 14–18.

QUESTIONS FOR DISCUSSION

1. Which step do you believe is most important in creative strategy: what to say or how to say it? Why?
2. Select ads for one product that show both the straight sell and mood approach. Which do you believe is more effective? Why?
3. Under what circumstances would demonstration be an effective execution technique?
4. Describe the slice-of-life execution technique.
5. What are some of the guidelines concerning the use of humor?
6. Under what circumstances would you consider the sexual approach appropriate in an advertising campaign?
7. What are some of the criteria for selecting a celebrity as a personality for an ad?
8. Under what circumstances would you consider it desirable to use a noncelebrity as an ad personality?
9. What is the difference between a presenter and a spokesperson?
10. What are some of the factors that influence the manner of execution? Explain.

AD PRACTICE

Select ads that illustrate each of the execution strategies discussed in this chapter. For each ad state whether you believe the execution strategy was desirable or suggest alternatives. Give reasons for your beliefs and recommendations.

12

Creative Symbols: Names and Trademarks

CHAPTER OBJECTIVES

— To describe the kinds of names used in advertising

— To examine the functions of names

— To discuss brand name and trademark strategy in terms of the name's role, the selection process, the procedures for protecting the name, and the reasons for changing a name

Procter & Gamble made the decision to change its corporate symbol after years of battling rumors about its meaning. The symbol, or logo, shows "the man in the moon" and thirteen stars. Rumors of the company's connection to Satanism and devil worship emanated from the contention that, when a mirror is held up to the design, the curls in the man's beard appear as "666"—the sign of the anti-Christ. Also, P & G executives were said to have appeared on the Phil Donahue and Merv Griffin talk shows and stated that the company supports Satanism. Consumers were told to boycott P & G products.

After years of trying to ignore the rumors, the company hired two investigative agencies to trace their sources, resulting in libel suits against a number of people for spreading false and malicious rumors. These were settled out of court after the defendants stated publicly that the rumors were not true. P & G also made it clear that no one from the firm had appeared on the talk shows.

Nonetheless, Procter & Gamble, concerned about its corporate image and the effect of the rumors upon sales of its products, decided to remove the "man in the moon" from its packages. The logo remains, however, on the company's letterheads and on its corporate headquarters in Cincinnati.

Although Procter & Gamble's problem was based on the imaginations of just a few people, the company knew its image was at stake—and it took its situation very seriously. An effective symbol for identifying a firm and its products is a thing to be protected. The development and dissemination of a name or trademark that serves as a company's symbol, can be a major creative effort in the design of the advertising campaign. In addition to the creative aspects, these activities require careful administration and control.

TRADE NAMES, BRAND NAMES, AND TRADEMARKS

Names in business serve both as identification and communication devices. Various terms are used to categorize names including trade name, brand name, and trademark. Although these terms are used interchangeably, there are significant differences.

A *trade name* is the name under which a company conducts its business. General Motors Corporation, the Coca-Cola Company, the Borden Company, Procter & Gamble Company, and General Foods Corporation identify organizations in the business world.

A *brand name* is the name by which the manufacturer identifies the goods and services sold by the company and distinguishes them from competitors' products. A brand name can usually be vocalized and may be the same as the trade name—the Coca-Cola Company sells Coca-Cola soft drinks and the Borden Company sells Borden's milk. In fact, Borden's condensed milk is one of the earliest branded products of a specific manufacturer. The brand name need not be the same as the manufacturer's name; for instance, General Motors calls its products Cadillac, Chevrolet, Buick, and Oldsmobile, and with the increasing proliferation of automobile models, it has added many additional brand names to its product lines.

Much that we touch, see, use, eat, drink and wear is likely to bear a trademark. A *trademark* is a broader term than *brand name* or *trade name;* it is defined by the United States Department of Commerce as "a distinguishing word, emblem, symbol or device, or any combination of these used to indicate or identify a manufacturer or distributor of a particular product." Each year almost 450,000 marks are kept actively registered in the United States. In addition, probably thousands that are not registered are protected under common law and thousands more are registered in some 50 states.[1]

The major difference between a brand name and a trademark lies in the legal connotations. The Lanham Act, passed in 1946 is the federal statute that applies to trademark law. Many states have their own trademark statutes. Unlike an unprotected name, a trademark may be used only by the legally designated owner, or with his or her permission, for a particular line of business. An unprotected brand name may ultimately serve as identification for an entire product line, rather than the product of one particular seller. Aspirin, which was once the trademark of the Bayer Company, now is used to designate an analgesic product sold by many different pharmaceutical firms.

There are four types of marks which are entitled to such legal protection. *Trademarks* are used to identify goods; *service marks* identify and distinguish services; *collective marks* are used by members of cooperative collective organizations, such as the Shriners' emblem; and *certification marks* indicate that goods or services have been certified by a given entity such as Underwriters' Laboratory or Good Housekeeping.

---

[1]Dorothy Fey, "Trademarks: What's in a Name?," *The Practical Lawyer*, Vol. 24, No. 8 (December 1978), pp. 75–81.

A *logotype*, or logo, is the presentation of the company brand name or trademark in a distinctive form or style. It usually appears in all the company's advertisements and communications; it tends to offer recognition as well as continuity. The Procter & Gamble symbol is an example of a logotype.

FUNCTIONS OF NAMES

It is possible to sell a product without a name. This is the case with the so-called generic brands as well as with agricultural products sold to consumers in supermarkets. From a firm's point of view, however, a name provides an opportunity to carve out its own share of the market. Many initial advertising campaigns are to promote, or at least secure recognition for, names; subsequent campaigns may be designed to develop continued acceptance of a firm's product (or brand loyalty) or encourage competitors' customers to switch to the company's brand.

For consumers names facilitate the purchasing process. A name not only identifies the maker of a product, it may connote the reputation of the firm and communicate a mental image of the company or its products. The name enables a consumer to pinpoint the firm responsible for the product and its quality and also offers an opportunity for the consumer to veto the defective product in the marketplace.

A strong brand franchise, through extensive promotion of a name, can create a valuable asset. In recent years a number of major companies acquired already recognizable brand names, those that had become household names. This strategy is considered desirable because of the extensive cost and potential risk of introducing and developing a new brand.[2] Recent acquisitions include R. J. Reynolds' takeover of Nabisco Brands with its well-known Oreo Cookies and Philip Morris' acquisition of General Foods with its Maxwell House Coffee and Bird's Eye Foods.

Occasionally a firm will engage in a strong effort to advertise the name of a product ingredient to encourage manufacturers to use this ingredient in the products they produce and consumers to look for or request it in the products they purchase. G.D. Searle & Co. spent extensive funds on television commercials directed at consumers featuring its NutraSweet brand sweetener. Searle also funded cooperative advertising conducted by firms such as soft drink manufacturers who used NutraSweet as a sweetener in their products.

Names Designating Ownership

A name may be used to indicate who owns the brand, particularly when the source is reputable and offers assurances of quality. *National brands* are owned by manufacturers and may be promoted nationally, regionally, or even locally, such as General Electric toasters, Kraft American

---

[2]John Crudele, "Brand Names: Growing Lure," *The New York Times* (August 19, 1985), p. D4.

cheese, and Jell-O gelatin dessert. *Private brands* are owned by whole-salers and retailers; they too may be distributed nationally, regionally, or locally; Ann Page (A&P) and Craftsman (Sears, Roebuck and Company) are examples of private brands.

Generic is a term that is used to indicate a product class (automobile) rather than a particular manufacturer's brand (Cadillac). In recent years there has been an acknowledgement that, in some product categories, consumers are willing to trade off some of the assurances provided by the national brand or private label for lower prices. *Generic brands* refer to those products without national brands or private labels which now are sold as *generic* at lower prices.

Generics recorded their highest growth rate in 1982; however their market share has declined since then.[3] Nonetheless generics are apparently becoming a permanent feature of the grocery industry. This suggests that marketers should formulate both offensive and defensive strategies for their national brand franchises against the threat posed by generics. Some suggested strategies include:[4]

— Maintain and strengthen the quality advantage that consumers perceive in the nationally advertised brands.
— Introduce "fighting brands" that do not carry the name of the manufacturer.
— Improve packaging to reinforce the product's quality image and provide additional consumer benefits.
— Use advertising to demonstrate the superiority of the manufacturer's brand over the generic version. For example, Procter & Gamble's campaign for its dishwashing products demonstrates they can wash many more dishes than the cheaper brands.

Brand Extension Strategies

As a company adds new products to its line there are decisions about the names under which they are to be introduced and promoted. Firms use a number of strategies, each representing the particular perceptions of what is most desirable in terms of needs and resources.

Family Brand
If the same brand name is used for several of a company's products, it is called a *family brand*. It may be the name of the company (Heinz) or one of its divisions or subsidiaries (Kraft), or even a name that was developed for one of its product lines.

Using a family brand has several advantages. It is a simple task to

[3]"No-Frills Products: An Idea Whose Time Has Gone," *Business Week* (June 17, 1985), p. 64.
[4]Brian F. Harris & Roger A. Strang, "Marketing Strategies in the Age of Generics," *Journal of Marketing*, Vol. 49 (Fall 1985), pp. 70–81.

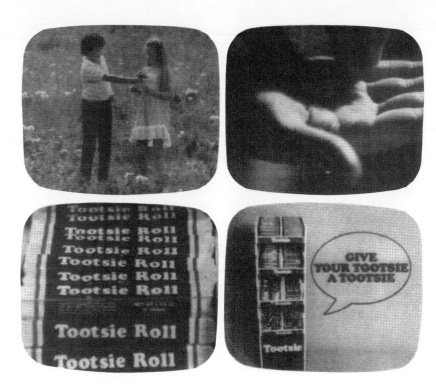

EXHIBIT 12.1
Using a Family Brand

Tootsie Roll Industries uses the company name for a number of its products—Tootsie Rolls, Tootsie Pops, and Tootsie Pop Drops.

name a new product and transfer company good-will. It facilitates institutional advertising and makes it easier to incorporate a product in the company's advertising campaign (see Exhibit 12.1). Introducing a brand under a family name can help it achieve more rapid acceptance, because consumers are more willing to try it and do not have to be "educated" as much. It may generate greater display space and distribution strength by offering distributors a variety of products under one name.

Family brands have been used successfully even in agricultural markets. United Fruit was one of the earliest companies to brand fruits, and its Chiquita banana carved out a large share of the banana market. It was many years before a competitor used the same strategy. When Dole, whose brand name appeared on its canned pineapple products, extended the Dole name to fresh bananas, the company became Number One in banana sales.[5]

It may not always be possible to use a family brand, particularly when the perceptions created by the new product are inconsistent with the company's image. Consider consumer response to the introduction of a Campbell's bug spray. Moreover, a company brand makes it difficult for a firm to pursue several markets simultaneously. It is for this reason that General Motors designates some of its cars as Chevrolet and others as Cadillac.

---

[5]Philip H. Dougherty, "Advertising, Dole Finds Labeling Profitable," *The New York Times* (March 19, 1981), p. D14.

Individual Brand

Some companies consider individual brands more desirable; they expand market share and offer alternatives to dissatisfied customers who might switch to competitors' products. For example, the consumer who is dissatisfied with Procter & Gamble's Tide detergent or Crest toothpaste may turn to other products—Cheer and Gleem—but both are made by P&G as well.

Using individual brand names gives a company flexibility. Individual brand names allow the company to trade in different markets. When Campbell's introduced a very expensive line of boxed candy, it disassociated itself from the product by designating it as Godiva.

Use of individual names may require extensive advertising campaigns promoting both the product name and the company name in order to compete effectively. Lever Brothers' individual brand names apparently have suffered from insufficient advertising support in recent years and some of its most famous brands—Lifebuoy toilet soap and Lux liquid soap—have only tiny market shares now.[6] When a product name differs from a company name the latter may require a separate advertising campaign. GTE (General Telephone and Electronics) successfully increased consumer awareness form 15 percent to 53 percent through advertising its corporate name, although the electronics company does not have any product called GTE.[7]

A Company Name Combined with an Individual Brand Name

To achieve the advantages of family branding plus the distinctiveness of individual brands, some companies combine the two. Kellogg uses this approach by advertising its cereals as Kellogg's Special K, Kellogg's Corn Flakes, and Kellogg's Sugar Pops; but other companies have different philosophies. Procter & Gamble lets its brands stand alone (see Exhibit 12.2); on the other hand, California Packing Corporation felt it had too many products to attempt to establish brand names for each. Consequently all brands are now carried under the housemark Del Monte. A company name may not be included when the association is meaningless—for example, the Gillette name is not used in its advertising of Paper-Mate.

Using Names for Push/Pull Strategies

For a manufacturer a name is a means of identification as well as a communication device. It serves as one of the cues that help present and maintain a company's image. To some extent a brand permits a manufacturer to carve out a market for a product by making it a specialty good, one which consumers will go out of their way to buy. By promoting the name in extensive advertising the manufacturer has opportuni-

---

[6]"New and Improved? Trying to Halt Years of Decline, Lever Brothers Co. Is Charting Course for Comeback," *The Wall Street Journal* (February 5, 1981), p. 14.

[7]Philip H. Dougherty, "Advertising, Corporate Name Building," *New York Times* (February 14, 1981), p. D6.

ties both to *pull* the item through the channel of distribution and to *push* wholesalers and retailers to carry the merchandise. Murine ear drops were recently introduced by the makers of Murine eye drops with an extensive consumer advertising campaign.

BRAND NAME AND TRADEMARK STRATEGY

A brand name and trademark strategy requires a planning process, including the determination of objectives and the development of orderly procedures for execution. The major steps in this process are evaluating the role of the name, selecting the name, and identifying methods for its protection. These issues have special relevance, not only at the initiation of an advertising campaign, but during its evolution.

The Role of the Name

The name of a product depends on the objectives of the firm and its compatibility with the firm's future products. A name may be used to position a product, introduce a new characteristic, indicate a product benefit or use, or create a personality for the product.

A name plays an important role in *positioning strategy*. It may be used to specify the niche or space which the product occupies, as the name Mr. Clean does. It may be used to develop a new niche for a product category that seems excessively competitive. Tylenol is said to have been successful in using a coined or fanciful name to indicate that its product did not belong to the group of analgesics that contain aspirin. A name may indicate that the product is to be used by a specific target group—for example, Weight Watchers TV dinners, Virginia Slims cigarettes, First Lady Scotch, or Children's Tylenol. The name may suggest that the product occupies what is now a popular "space." Campbell's took several of its regular soup products and incorporated them under the name The Light Ones to position them as low in calories.

A firm that has designed a *new product attribute* may use the name as emphasis—Ziploc storage bags, No-Cal beverages. The relatively small Minnetonka Company, competing in a soap market dominated by giant firms, successfully introduced its liquid soap under the name Softsoap. Squibb Corporation's Life Saver division, in competition with William Wrigley, Jr. Company, introduced its new gum with a "unique flavor delay system" as Replay.

A *product benefit*, while not new, may be considered important enough to feature in a name; for example, there is Renuzit cleaning product, Hefty plastic bags, Bag-A-Bug, Ty-D-Bol cleaner, Twice-as-Fresh room deodorant, Eveready batteries, and 20-Mule-Team power bathroom cleaner.

A name may indicate *how a product is used*, such as Spray N' Wash, One-a-Day vitamins, Hamburger Helper, Touch-Tone telephone, Airwick Stick-Up.

From 1879...

...to 1979

EXHIBIT 12.2
Eliminating the Company Name

With its proliferation of soap products, Procter & Gamble's Ivory kept its brand name—but lost its family identification.

EXHIBIT 12.3
Creating a Personality

A name may be used to create or reinforce a *product personality.* Ralph Lauren selected the name Polo for his line of men's toiletries and accessories. While probably 99 percent of his customers never play a game of polo, the name establishes a feeling of money, elegance, and adventure (see Exhibit 12.3).

In developing a name, consideration should be given to its compatability with present brands as well as its applicability in extension decisions. If a name is to be used for brand extensions generally, then describing a particular form of a product would be undesirable (Liquid Plumber Crystals). Furthermore a name that specifies a particular use would limit alternative uses (compare, for example, Windex versus Glass Plus).[8]

Occasionally the brand name can be extended to the same product category to provide a product variation. L'Eggs introduced its lighter weight pantyhose as Summer L'Eggs. Or a brand name may be extended to completely new product categories—Dial deodorant and Gerber infant wear.[9] Even when a name is compatible with other product introductions, the problem of cannibalizing an old product by using a similar name for the new one should be considered. This appears to have happened to Alka-Seltzer Plus, which ate into the market for Alka-Seltzer,[10] and to Maxim, which cannibalized some of the market for Maxwell House.

Name Selection Process

A name serves as both an identification and communication device, and while it is only one of a number of cues that perform this function for an organization, its selection should be planned and orderly. The selection process, which occasionally involves research, should include a review of sources of names and evaluation procedures.

Choosing a valid mark requires the selection of one that can be federally registered for protection; this eliminates marks that are deceptive, immoral, disparaging, confusing, or generic. Figure 12.1 depicts the hierarchy developed by the courts for determining eligibility for registration; in descending order of protection these categories are fanciful, arbitrary, suggestive, descriptive, and generic, which are never protectable.[11]

Sources of Names

There are almost unlimited sources for product names. The field narrows significantly, however, when considerations are given to legal protection. Over the years guidelines have been established to protect a firm from competitors adopting the same or similar names.

The whole *company name* (the trade name) may be used as the brand name—Pet milk, Hotpoint appliances, Electrolux vacuum cleaners—or its parts can be combined to form a trademark—Nabisco (National Biscuit Company), Alcoa (Aluminum Company of America). The company initials may also be used—AT&T (American Telephone and

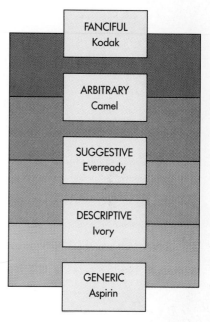

FIGURE 12.1   The Relative Protectability of Trademarks

HIGHLY PROTECTABLE

FANCIFUL
Kodak

ARBITRARY
Camel

SUGGESTIVE
Everready

DESCRIPTIVE
Ivory

GENERIC
Aspirin

UNPROTECTABLE

---

[8]Theodore Karger, "Analyze Existing Product's Values When Researching Brand Extensions," *Marketing News* (January 23, 1981), p. 1.

[9]Kathryn Feakens, "What's in a Name?," *Marketing Review*, Vol. 36, No. 1 (September-October 1980), p. 28.

[10]"Homework," *Marketing & Media Decisions* (February 1981), p. 176.

[11]Carol A. Melton, "Generic Term or Trademark?: Confusing Legal Standards and Inadequate Protection," *The American University Law Review*, Vol. 29 (1979), pp. 109–33.

Telegraph). The Number One product in food sales is called by its company name—Campbell's soup.

Family names are generally not protected because others with similar surnames are entitled to use them. In the past, however, the name of a company's founder was often used to identify its product—Hershey chocolate, Gerber baby foods, Wrigley gum, Whitman candy, and Gillette razors. Throughout the years the public has associated them with their products (the legal term is *secondary meaning*) and as a result they are considered protectible trademarks. Currently, while the use of a surname may be unprotected, an individual's full name, like Elizabeth Arden or Fanny Farmer, can be registered as a trademark.

Words that are primarily *geographical names* cannot be trademarked at this time. However, some geographical trademarks are valid since they have been used for years and have acquired secondary meaning. These include Elgin watches and Kalamazoo stoves.

The most prolific source for brand names and trademarks is the *dictionary*. This appears to be in contradiction to the requirements for protection of a trademark, because a dictionary word which generally describes a product cannot be used as a trademark. For example, the word *ivory* cannot be used as a trademark for a product made of ivory. A word must be selected that is arbitrary, suggestive, or used in a fanciful manner. Arrow shirts, Bicycle playing cards, Camel cigarettes, and Toastmaster electric appliances use dictionary words in arbitrary ways. Tame hair shampoo, Gripper snap fasteners, Ripple Ribbed shoe soles, Talon zippers, and Ivory soap are suggestive and fanciful, permitting the consumer to use his or her imagination to get an impression from words that are not truly descriptive of products.

The advantage of using dictionary words for brand names is that the words are already understood and accepted and may create a pleasant association. The hazards involve the potential difficulty in securing legal protection for a word in the dictionary.

To eliminate the difficulties of using words in the dictionary some firms *coin* their own, permitting these words to become distinctive, suggestive, outstanding, and, in some cases, memorable. Meaningless words have been developed with some success. Kodak was coined by George Eastman, who liked the fact that the name began and ended with an infrequently used consonant and could, therefore, remain distinctive even when translated into foreign languages. Kleenex tissues, Dacron polyester fiber, Orlon acrylic fiber, and Plexiglas acrylic plastic are all coined words that are almost too successful—they are in danger of being declared generic. Some names, like Coke, Bud, and Luckies, may be coined by the public and eventually adopted by the firm.

Trade Characters

Distinctive people, cartoon characters, animals, or puppets may be used as trademarks; the term generally applied is *trade character*. Many companies have adopted trade characters as their identifications, to provide continuity and additional associations, as well as to increase recognition.

One creative authority designated the trade character as a VI/P (visual image personality) and noted that its use could be extremely rewarding.[12] The Pillsbury Dough Boy puppet, over twenty-years-old, is valued as a more than $20,000,000 property. The puppet has not only appeared in media ads; it is also used in point-of-sale material and premiums, and even has its own section in many supermarkets for Pillsbury Brown-and-Serve products (see Exhibit 12.4). Other trade characters have had long lives as well. Tony the Tiger has lasted 23 years; after over 30 years, Kellogg's Snap, Crackle, and Pop are still going strong, while Morris the cat continues to be finicky after 10 years.

The Green Giant was initially used to promote a particular variety of peas, but his use was expanded to include the entire product line of the Green Giant Company, which is now a unit of Pillsbury (see Exhibit 12.5). While the basic character remains the same, several changes were made to make him less frightening and more acceptable. The word *jolly* was added because it was considered alliterative. When the character began to appear on television his "ho, ho, ho" was developed.

Some trade characters, such as the Campbell's twins and Buster Brown, have been discontinued; however they tend to retain their identification capabilities for consumers. Recognizing that such characters can provide easily recalled and identified symbols, numerous companies in recent years have resurrected their trade characters. Although NBC had replaced its peacock with an N in 1976, the earlier-used symbol appeared to provide greater identification. As a result, in 1980 the peacock was resurrected and incorporated with the N into a new logo.

EXHIBIT 12.4
A Trade Character That's a VI/P

Licensing

Some firms license successful marks in order to eliminate the problems of developing their own. Fruit of the Loom, Roy Rogers, and even Coca-Cola are available for use under certain considerations and license fees (see Exhibit 12.6). The disadvantages of using this method are the continuing costs incurred through licensing and the lack of exclusive use.

For the firm that develops a successful trademark, however, the potential for generating future income from licensing may be significant. Sunkist has derived a great deal of outside income from licensing its trademark to numerous soft drinks and has benefitted from the licensee's advertising.

Developing a successful trade character also provides licensing capabilities. Usually the character has been well established in the public mind through a comic strip, movie, or television. One of the first trade characters to be licensed was Walt Disney's Mickey Mouse. Since then characters, such as Snoopy, the Muppets, and the company of Star Wars have been licensed. Similarly, the Pink Panther, first introduced in a 1964 film, is used by some 60 companies domestically and 175 overseas, who pay anywhere from $5000 to $40,000 for the license itself plus at least 6 percent of the revenues they derive from the sales of Panther

EXHIBIT 12.5
The Life of a Trade Character

---

[12]Harry Wayne McMahan, "Do Your Ads Have VI/P?," *Advertising Age* (July 14, 1980), p. 50.

EXHIBIT 12.6
Licensing a Trademark

products. According to some users, the Pink Panther has an image associated with affluence, and he portrays the Rolls-Royce of characters.

Some licensed properties have a relatively short life. Smurfberry cereals came and went with the short-lived popularity of Smurfs, but Pebbles cereals and Flintstone vitamins have endured for a long time. Cabbage Patch Kids, licensed to 150 companies selling 1000 products globally, continues to attract licensees.[13]

---

[13]James P. Forkan, "Cabbage Patch Proves Fertile," *Advertising Age* (August 19, 1985), p. 63.

DESIRABLE AND UNDESIRABLE CHARACTERISTICS OF A NAME

While it is difficult to predict the success of any name, a review of products that have attained the most widespread use indicates the following desirable characteristics:

1. A name should be easy to spell, to master, to read, to write, to recognize, and to remember. Crest, Tide, Cheer, and Crisco utilize these factors.

2. A name should have attention value such as Head & Shoulders shampoo, Aim toothpaste, Pampers disposable diapers, Stopette deodorant, Mustang automobile, and Yes cleansing tissues.

3. A name should connote quality such as Star-Kist and Chicken of the Sea tuna and Halo shampoo.

4. A name should be pleasant sounding, such as Evening in Paris perfume and Glad plastic bags.

5. A name should translate easily into a foreign language, if international distribution is the intention.

Generally speaking, commonplace names are considered undesirable. However, no one can argue with the success of General Foods, General Motors, General Electric, and General Mills. Negative connotations are also to be avoided, despite the questionable success of Dr. Sweat Root Beer and Le Gout seasoning. Confusing similarity is subject to legal restrictions and is of limited effectiveness. For example, Pepsico Inc. was successful in preventing the registration of the mark Teamonade for a powdered concentrated flavor because of the potential conflict with its Teem soft drink and syrup. Although Pretty Kitty cat food was not declared in conflict with Kitty cat food, the confusion created by this similarity may be undesirable from a marketing standpoint.

Name Research

Researching a name can include all aspects of the name selection process, from discovering the initial source to determining its acceptability by consumers. If a company wanted its advertising agency to develop a fairly short name without intrinsic meaning but suggesting advanced technology, a group of copywriters and art directors might develop an impressive list of futuristic, technical-sounding syllables, prefixes, and suffixes. A computer would print out all of the possible combinations that could result and a number of these could then be selected for consumer testing.

There are companies that specialize in naming products as well as making sure they are protected. For example, NameLab Inc. works from morphemes—the core semantic unit within a word. They used the *Tra-* in *transport* for Softra, the name for a software distributor, Compaq (*pak* meaning a small object) for a small disk, and Acura (conveying precision) for Honda's new luxury car.[14]

---

[14]Jeffrey A. Trachtenberg, "Name that Brand," *Forbes* (April 8, 1985), p. 130.

Recent attention has focused on the research involving *semiotics*, theories of signs and symbolism. Studies in consumer behavior acknowledge that individuals make inferences about products, services, and organizations through available cues. Trademarks represent signs or symbols that function in this way. Future research may discover how consumers learn to favor some trademarks and how they learn to distinguish among trademarks that include common terms such as "general" and "united."[15] The answers should help managers to create appropriate brand identities and maintain their distinctiveness.

Protecting a Name

On many corporate balance sheets a trademark is technically valued at one dollar, but since it often represents substantial investments in promotion it can be worth a great deal more; and the good will in a trademark may have extensive market value.

Protecting a trademark requires organization, planning, and proper procedures. A trademark committee should be established within an organization with the responsibility of overseeing and coordinating the development of the trademark. Necessary to interpret all of the relevant aspects, it is useful. To avoid conflicts it is necessary to continually supervise the trademark's use in advertising, particularly in two broad areas: preventing the term from becoming generic and responding to all attempts at infringement.[16]

Preventing "Genericide"

A major objective of a company in the development of a trademark for its brand is to publicize and promote the brand widely, in the hope that consumers will request the product by the company's brand name. If these efforts are extremely successful, then the company faces the hazard of having its brand name declared generic. When a name is declared generic, it is said to refer to the entire product class rather than to a specific manufacturer's brand and, thus, any company can use the name.

A number of well-known trademarks have been declared generic and are available for use by any company who wishes to adopt them; these include aspirin, milk of magnesia, celluloid, kerosene, shredded wheat, yo yo, corn flakes, linoleum, cellophane, and escalator. Some of these names originally were used on new products which were patented for a specific period of time. Insufficient protection was maintained for the trademark so that when the patent expired, and others were legally free to make the product, the only name which was associated with that good also became available to competitors. To prevent the loss of trade-

---

[15]Sidney J. Levy and Dennis W. Rook, "Brands, Trademarks, and the Law," *Review of Marketing, 1981*, eds., Ben M. Enis and Kenneth J. Roering, (Chicago: American Marketing Association, 1981), pp. 185–94.

[16]Dorothy Cohen, "Trademark Strategy," *Journal of Marketing*, Vol. 50 (January 1986).

mark rights, adequate protection must be provided under the key principle that "a trademark always must be identified as such on labels, in advertising, and wherever else it may appear." This may be accomplished in a number of ways.[17]

1. Use the generic name of the product in association with the trademark. Product names which are in danger of being declared generic make frequent use of this method: Q-Tips cotton swabs, Kleenex facial tissues, Vasoline petroleum jelly, and Sanka brand coffee.

2. Provide notice that the brand name is a trademark. Although registration is not a prerequisite for protection, it is helpful, because then the trademark symbol (the letter *R* enclosed in a circle) can be displayed. It is important to specify that a product is the trademark of a particular company. The advertising for Orlon usually carries a footnote that reads, "DuPont trademark for its acrylic fiber."

3. Some form of special typographical treatment should be used to present the mark. The trademark may be capitalized or presented in quotation marks, in hand lettering, in italics, in bold face, underscored, set larger than body copy, in a different type face, or in a different color than the balance of the text.

4. The trademark should be used in the correct grammatical form. A trademark is not to be used as a noun, in the plural, as a verb, or in the possessive. Advertisers should not encourage people to *Sanforize* or *Clorox* their clothes or to prepare *Jell-O*.

5. Continual policing is necessary to ensure proper trademark usage.

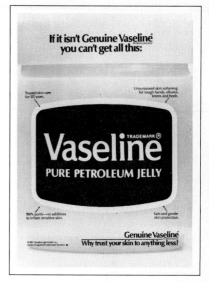

EXHIBIT 12.7
Preventing Genericide

Infringement

The owner of a patent can exclude anyone from making, using, or selling a patented invention, and a copyright proprietor can prevent anyone else from copying his or her work. A trademark owner, on the other hand, has only the limited right to stop the use of an identical or similar mark under circumstances where confusion, mistake, or deception are likely to occur.[18]

The owner of a mark has not removed it from the English language. For example, although Ivory is a trademark for a soap product, anyone is free to use *ivory* in its dictionary context as a color or elephant tusk. A company may even use Ivory as a trademark provided that the goods or services are not closely related to the soap. The enforcement of trademark rights is in the interests of the consumer, and, in fact, infringement of a trademark or deception by trademarks are usually considered in terms of the public—would the public be confused, mistaken, or deceived?

---

[17]Sidney A. Diamond, "Protect Your Trademark by Proper Usage," *Journal of Marketing*, Vol. 26 (July 1962), pp. 17–22.

[18]Sidney A. Diamond, "The Trademark: It Protects and Identifies," *Advertising Age* (January 7, 1980), pp. 59–60, 64, 66.

PERCEPTION OR MOTIVATION

A recent trademark infringement case appeared to have set new standards for determining whether a trademark is generic. In 1971, Ralph Anspach, a professor of economics, created and attempted to market a game emphasizing the values of the competitive enterprise system under the name Bust the Trust. The marketing attempt failed. Two years later Professor Anspach established a company to produce and sell the same game under a new name, Anti-Monopoly. Within three years, Anti-Monopoly Inc. sold approximately 419,000 games, earning the company close to one million dollars. General Mills instituted suit claiming the game's name infringed on the Monopoly trademark of its Parker Brothers' Division.

A lower court found that a survey by Anti-Monopoly showed consumers were motivated to buy Monopoly because they like the game—not because it was a Parker Brothers' product. Since the term *Monopoly* identified a specific product category—or a genus—it was declared generic. The Supreme Court let this decision stand.

In the past the traditional standard for determining genericness was based on consumers' *perceptions* of the mark as only a *type* of product or as a source. If it indicated source, it was a trademark; if it indicated a type of product, it was a generic term. When the court decided that consumers were motivated to buy the product Monopoly because they liked the *game* and not because it was a Parker Brothers' product, they used a motivation test.

If the motivation test for generics were left standing, a great many trademarks would be endangered. For example, in a survey, 89 percent of those interviewed recognized Tide as a brand name; thus, under the perception test, Tide would be considered a very strong trademark because it was clearly perceived as denoting a *source* to the public. In a survey based on the purchaser motivation test, more than two-thirds of those interviewed gave product-related reasons for purchasing Tide; thus, Tide could be considered as its own product class or genus and be subject to cancellation as a trademark because it was generic.

The motivation approach was criticized as threatening to undermine the clarity and stability of federal trademark law. In late 1984 Congress passed the Trademark Clarification Act (P.L. 98–610) which reiterated the traditional trademark protection legal test and declared, "The primary significance of the registered mark to the relevant public, rather than purchaser motivation, shall be the test for determining whether the registered mark has become the common descriptive name of goods or services." The legislation, however, did not overturn the Monopoly decision; moreover it did not offer specific criteria for determining genericness.

Changing a Name

A corporation may spend extensive funds to establish its image with the public. Since most people are not in close contact with the firm, this image is created through continued association of the firm's name and the activities in which it engages. A change in the name may hinder marketing communication efforts and require rebuilding of the association.[19]

A decision to change a name must be approached with care. There are, in fact, relatively few product name changes. However, many firms find it desirable to change their corporate names for one reason or another and, in one year alone, over 400 American companies adopted new names. A name change may be considered desirable when a company abandons its original objectives and the name becomes too restrictive. When Noxema Chemical expanded to other industries it developed a less restrictive name, Noxell.[20]

To indicate its diversification, and yet retain its original identification, a company may merely drop the part of the name that is obsolete. Monsanto Chemicals became Monsanto; Canada Dry Ginger Ale became Canada Corp.; and Allied Chemicals became Allied Corporation. The organization may also use initials; thus RCA was formerly Radio Corporation of America. Allegheny Airlines wanted to eliminate its regional image and secure greater recognition as a national airline. To do so the company changed its name to USAir.

Although a completely new name provides no carryover effect, it does permit a firm to use effective promotional efforts in order to reestablish a desirable association. When American Can Company was redirected out of manufacturing and into financial services and specialty retailing, they introduced their new name, Primerica, in an ad campaign declaring: "John Wayne was Marion Morrison. When he broke into movies he changed his name—Marion just didn't seem to fit him anymore." When Consolidated Foods found its name was recognized by only 2 percent of consumers, the company changed its name to Sara Lee Corporation. The name was taken from Consolidated's first brand name, Kitchens of Sara Lee, which had a 98-percent recognition among American consumers and was the only American-based Consolidated brand to be known internationally. According to the company, however, the name change was not designed to benefit consumers, but rather to end confusion among interested investors.[21]

Modernizing a Trade Character

A trade character that has been used for many years may tend to present an old-fashioned image. Rather than retire the character, the company may periodically modernize the symbol to provide continuity. Morton Salt, for example, has modernized the dress and hairdo of its Umbrella Girl five times since 1914 and General Mills continues to update Betty Crocker (see Exhibit 12.8).

1936

1986
EXHIBIT 12.8
Modernizing a Trade Character

---

[19]Laurence P. Feldman, "Of Alphabets, Acronyms and Corporate Identity," *Journal of Marketing*, Vol. 33 (October 1967), pp. 72–75.

[20]Walter P. Margulies, "Beware Pitfalls in a Name Change," *Advertising Age* (March 2, 1981), p. 48.

[21]"Sara Lee Aims Name at Investors," *Advertising Age*, (April 8, 1985), p. 83.

In modernizing the trade character the company occasionally changes what may be considered an undesirable symbolic representation. William Underwood Company's deviled ham, for example, has been using the red devil since 1867. In 1959, however, the devil was transformed from a foreboding figure into a smiling, impish Satan.[22]

SUMMARY

A name plays an important role in a firm's communication process. It not only provides identification for a product, it serves as an aid in new product introduction and helps maintain control over sales in outlets.

A brand name and trademark strategy requires an evaluation of the role of the name, a name selection process, and the institution of procedures for protecting the name. A name may play an important part in an advertising campaign and be used to position a product, introduce a new characteristic, indicate a product benefit or use, or create a personality for the product. In addition it may provide an umbrella for new product introductions.

The name selection process requires a knowledge of sources and a consideration of desirable and undesirable characteristics of names. Occasionally firms use research to develop outstanding names.

A name can be an important asset for a company and as such should be carefully protected, frequently by having it designated as a trademark. Such protection requires both an understanding of the legal guidelines as well as continuing supervision of the trademark, particularly as it appears in advertisements.

A firm may change its name for numerous reasons; some of these have special relevance to the advertising campaign. The name change may be designed to indicate its diversification, to eliminate a limited geographic image, or to attain greater recognition and a stronger awareness level.

---

[22]"Play It Again, Sam," *Dun's Review* (March 1980), p. 11.

QUESTIONS FOR DISCUSSION

1. Describe the brand extension strategies that may be used by a firm. Which technique would you consider most effective in preparing an advertising campaign for a firm's new product?
2. Describe the various roles that a product name may perform in advertising.
3. Select some ads in which the name plays a role in achieving a firm's positioning objective. Discuss.
4. Which of the various sources of names do you consider most important?
5. When would you use a trade character in an advertising campaign? Explain.
6. In selecting a name, which desirable and/or undesirable characteristics do you feel merit the most attention?
7. When can trademark infringement actions be initiated?
8. What is the significance for an advertising campaign of a name being declared generic? What methods can be used to prevent this from happening?
9. Under what circumstances may a firm decide to change its name?
10. Should trade characters be modernized? Explain.

KEY TERMS

trade name

brand name

trademark

service mark

collective mark

certification mark

logotype

national brand

private brand

generic brands

family brands

individual brand

trade character

semiotics

Lanham Act

AD PRACTICE

Briefly describe a new product you intend to introduce into the market. Select a name for this product and explain how you arrived at this name and how you will protect it.

13

Copy Strategy

According to J. Walter Thompson USA, one way to find good copywriters is to advertise. The agency ran a one-time-only ad in a newspaper with the headline, "Write If You Want Work." The ad, which drew more than 1400 responses, contained an eight-question test with tasks such as "write a Dialogue in a Dark Alley," or "describe, in not more than 100 words, the plot of the last episode of 'Dynasty'." The agency hired nine respondents for its copywriting training program.

There is now a growing understanding that although a compelling idea is at the heart of a truly creative ad, ideas, copy, and art, work as a unit rather than as separate elements. This understanding has resulted in closer cooperation between the copywriter and the art director and greater contact with the client. Creative groups in a major agency, consisting of artists, copywriters, and TV producers headed by an associate creative director, generally create copy lines together. Frequently the copywriter and art director work together in the development of the advertising. The extent to which each influences the final ads may be determined by the agreed solution—for example, if it appears that a solution to the ad is best presented graphically, the artist will have the greatest input; if the solution seems to be verbal, the copywriter may take the primary initiative.

COPYWRITING

Copy has a variety of meanings in advertising. In this text *copy* refers to all reading matter in print advertising and all written and spoken words in broadcast advertising.

Although successful advertisements have used no illustration, it is rare for them to contain no copy. At a minimum the advertisement must provide information about the name of the product or the name of the company that produces it. While it is conceivable that a visual representation of the product would be sufficient identification, such circumstances are rare.

The simplest copy consists of an idea of interest to the reader and an idea of interest to the advertiser.[1] For example: Keep cool. Use Fedder's air conditioning. An IBM ad also provides an example of simple copy that is effective. It states, "The three most important letters in typing. IBM."

BBDO, an advertising agency that has won many awards for advertising creativity, describes the copywriting process.[2]

1. Know your prime prospect—identify whom you are talking to.
2. Know your prime prospect's problem—pinpoint the problem he or she would like solved.
3. Know your product—dig to find out how your product can offer the prime prospect a solution to his or her problems.
4. Break the boredom barrier—the ultimate challenge to the creative individual is to break through the mental defense system which blocks out most of the advertising messages that bombard them every day.

Life Cereal is an example of a successful BBDO campaign. Life's prime prospect is a concerned mother who would like her children to eat cereal. The problem is the reluctance of her children to try cereal, believing it does not "taste good." Solution: "Let Mikey try it!"

THE STRUCTURE OF COPY IN PRINT MEDIA

Copy in print advertisements may be presented in a structure containing the following elements: headline, subheadline, body copy, close, logo, or tag line (see Exhibit 13.1). All print ads do not embody all six elements. Some advertisements eliminate features; other combine two or more elements in the presentation.

---

[1] Otto Kleppner, *Advertising Procedure*, 4th ed. (Englewood Cliffs, N.J.: Prentice-Hall, Inc., 1960), p. 54.

[2] From "Who Do You Think You're Talking To?" Copyright © 1969 Batten, Barton, Durstine & Osborn, Inc. Reprinted by permission.

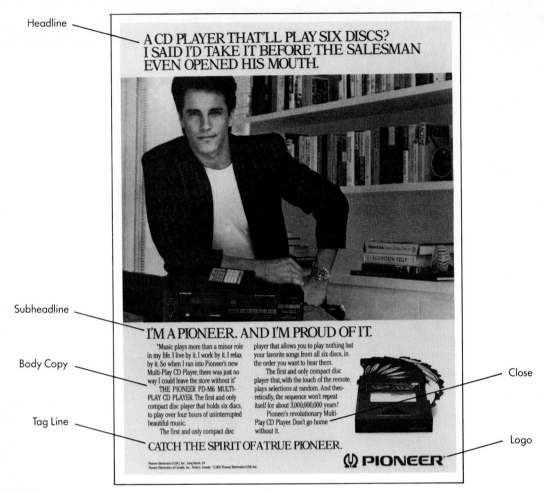

Headline

Subheadline

Body Copy

Tag Line

Close

Logo

EXHIBIT 13.1
Standard Structure of Copy

Headlines

The headline is the most important part of the advertisement. As one advertising agency noted to its creative personnel, "Research shows that 90 percent of the people who see your ad *read only the headline.* It follows that when you have written the headline, you have spent 90 cents of your client's dollar."[3]

The essential purpose of a headline is to secure attention, and with the rising "voice level" which much advertising is subjected to, a copywriter may not use a headline so that the ad will be different. Exhibit 13.2, with no headline and practically no copy, won the Magazine Publishers Association Award for the year's best magazine ad.

Most advertisements do have headlines, however, even though they may not incorporate all the other elements. Because legal restrictions

---

[3]"Rules for Creative Strategy" at J. Walter Thompson Company.

EXHIBIT 13.2
An Ad Without a Headline

offer little opportunity to elaborate on the benefits of some products, such as cigarettes, and other products are considered well-known, only a headline or logo may be necessary to remind those in the target audience of the product's benefits.

Headlines may be classified as follows:

— *By content.* The dominant quality is what it says, or its objective: it may identify, provide advice, promise benefits, solve problems, present news and information, contain familiar sayings, or offer contrasts.
— *By form.* The dominant quality is the manner in which it is said: it may be a question, a command, designed to provoke curiosity, or offer the "big boost."

Frequently headlines fall into one or more of these classifications, but for clarification each will be considered separately.

Content Headlines

Exhibit 13.3 is an example of an *identification headline*, which is designed to identify the product or the company that sells the product. This type of headline may use the company name, the product name, the slogan, or logo. It may simply say "Clinique" or may expand by stating, "My Brand is Fruit of the Loom." Although the identification headline places the name of the product or company in the most attention-getting position, it is essentially a weak headline. It assumes the consumer knows about or is anxious to learn more about the product.

An *advice, benefit, or problem-solving headline* is more powerful, since it promises consumers a realization of hopes or offers a solution to problems. Consumers are advised to rent, not buy, videocassette re-

EXHIBIT 13.3
An Identification Headline

© 1982 Clinique Laboratories, Inc.

corders (VCRs), promised that Honda will give them the benefit of gas mileage, or offered a mascara that solves a problem under water.

This type of headline is designed to reveal the way in which a product meets a specific need. Unlike the identification headline, which stresses the self-interest of the seller, the advice, promise, and benefit headline stresses the self-interest of the reader.

Usually a *news headline* dispenses with gimmicks and uses a straightforward news-story approach. Its effectiveness derives from the fact that consumers want to keep abreast of what is current and are attracted to what is new. The news that is featured can relate to the product, its package, its prices, its uses, or the company that produces

EXHIBIT 13.4
News Headline

it. The news headline can merely state the fact of newness or may tell an entire story. "Only Zenith Lets You Make a Telephone Call Through Your Television Set."

The news headline may emphasize the currency of the appeal. While the word *new* may be featured, words like *finally, at last,* and *announcing,* may also be used, particularly since the Federal Trade Commission permits the word *new* to be applied to a product only for a period of six months after its introduction (see Exhibit 13.4).

The *familiar saying* headline provides a new twist on a familiar phrase, a play on words, an unusual use of a common expression or a frequently recognized sequence of words. According to a content analy-

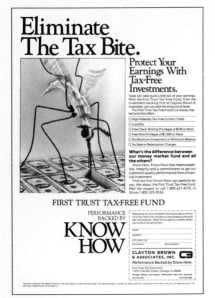

EXHIBIT 13.5
A Command Headline

This command headline provides orders that are acceptable to the reader.

sis of 81 award-winning consumer newspaper and magazine advertisements, the largest proportion of these ads were judged to hold in common the use of familiar sayings.[4] For example, a boot advertisement stated "Most boots have a hard time coping with the realities of life." Similarly, a motorcycle advertiser declared, "If we've told you once, we've told you ten times," referring to the success the motorcycle had experienced in ten consecutive championships at the Daytona 200 race.

In a *contrast* headline opposite words, phrases, or concepts are used, as for example, before/after, and up/down. This technique was also frequently present in award-winning headlines. For example, a ski-lodge restaurant advertised, "After a day of down-hill skiing, getting a fine meal shouldn't be an uphill battle." A knife advertisement declared "In every lie about the Boker knife there's a certain amount of truth."

Form Headlines

The *question headline* is designed to gain attention by arousing interest and encouraging the consumer to look for an answer. The question should not be too restrictive—that is, it should be of interest to a large group. The answer should appear in some part of the copy; frequently it is provided in the subheadline and other times it appears in the text. "Can sensitive skin be made less sensitive . . . Yes. Introducing Soothing Care for Sensitive Skin. . . . It's more than hypo-allergenic."

Exhibit 13.5 gives an example of a *command headline*. This type of headline is seen infrequently since it is difficult to build a buyer benefit into a command. In order to use this headline effectively it should not attempt to convert consumers, but rather tell them to do what they already want to do.

The *curiosity headline* (also called the "gimmicky" or provocative headline) is used to arouse a consumer's curiosity, to encourage the consumer to find the answer to a riddle, or to decipher something. It is designed to have the reader see the ad as a game that is to be played and to induce him or her to read the text for further information. The headline may be a single word, an incomplete sentence, or a blind statement that makes no sense by itself but offers a challenge to the reader. Like the question headline, an explanation must be offered, but it generally appears in the text of the copy rather than the subheadline. "The Shadow Knows . . . [Taster's Choice] . . . looks, smells and tastes like ground roast" and "How to capture a gorilla . . . uses a Kiron camera."

The *boast headline* features sweeping, extravagant claims for a product or an advertiser. "Listerine Stops Bad Breath 4 Times Better Than Any Tooth Paste." The boast must be believable and significant or it will be rejected and ignored. Moreover, it must be truthful: first to insure that the purchaser will not be disappointed, and also, and perhaps more important, to prevent complaints from competitors and regulatory agencies.

---

[4]Richard F. Beltramini and Vincent J. Blasko, "An Analysis of Award-Winning Advertising Headlines," *Journal of Advertising Research*, Vol. 26 (April/May 1986), pp. 48–52.

Principles in Writing Headlines

Headlines gain attention and arouse interest. Sometimes, but not often, the headline alone delivers the complete selling message. Headline reading is always greater than text reading, but the good headline should encourage, rather than discourage, reading of the text.

Some creative people feel the main point of the advertisement should appear in the headline. This point should reflect the self-interest of the buyer, not the interest of the advertiser.

The headline and the body text should be complementary to present a unified advertisement and the information in the headline should be pertinent to the copy. The same headline was used with some success by Phoenix Mutual Company for 35 years, except "retire at $150 a month" was upgraded periodically.

There is no clearcut determination of the ideal length of a headline. The limitations to length are the attention span of the reader and the amount of space allocated for the advertisement; but headline content is considered more important than the number of words. It's been said, "It is not the length or the position of the headlines that is important—it is their *graspability*." A generous range for the number of words is considered three to fourteen words. Although there have been successful one-word headlines, as well as headlines which practically restated all of a product's selling points, Percy and Rossiter believe the shorter headline is more effective and indicate it should be from five to eight words.[5] This length is consistent with psycholinguistic theory that suggests shorter sentences are easier to remember and understand.

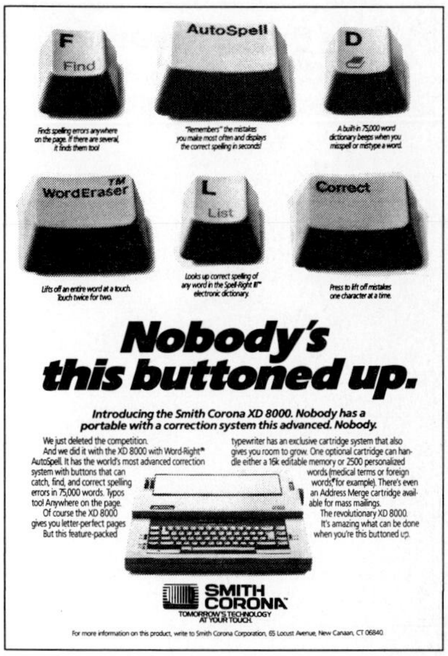

EXHIBIT 13.6
The Subheadline Explains the Headline

In this ad, the headline and subheadline can be easily transposed.

Subheadline

The headline may be expanded by a subheadline which is subordinated to the main headline but is usually in larger type than the body text. This subheadline may explain, develop, qualify, or amplify the headline; it may present the product as the solution to the problem identified in the headline (see Exhibit 13.6).

Body Copy

Once the headline has attracted attention, the rest of the text should stimulate interest and desire, communicate information and/or secure action. Good body copy follows the pattern of a well-planned presentation and can be categorized into six types: straight-line copy, narrative copy, mood-building copy, dialogue or monologue copy, picture-and-caption copy, and gimmick copy.

---

[5]Larry Percy and John R. Rossier, "10 Ways to More Effective Ads Via Visual Imagery, Psycholinguistics," *Marketing News* (February 19, 1982), p. 10.

EXHIBIT 13.7
Straight-Line Copy

Straight-Line or Factual Copy

Factual copy offers straightforward, no-nonsense sales talk. This *reason why* copy is used most effectively where the advertised item is purchased in response to rational motives or where the product has a specific competitive advantage (see Exhibit 13.7). The copy tells how the product is made, what it does, and why the consumer will benefit from it. It makes claims, offers benefits, and supports these claims and benefits by providing evidence. The evidence may be the results of performance tests, laboratory tests, guarantees or testimonials, or any other proof that will support the rational appeal of the copy.

Emotional Appeal or Mood-Building Copy

Emotional appeal copy, emphasizes human interest and stresses consumer satisfactions rather than product advantages. Since human motivation tends to be underlaid with strong emotional stimuli, much consumer advertising depends rather heavily on emotional copy. Typical buying motives with an emotional basis are the desire for food and drink, the desire for romance, the desire to be socially acceptable, the desire for travel. According to reports Mr. Revson used to say, "I'll only approve an ad if it convinces my customer that by wearing Revlon she'll get dragged into bed that night."[6]

Frequently copy will begin with the emotional approach and continue with factual material. This combination makes use of both techniques. The emotional approach is designed to stimulate interest; once the reader's interest is attained the product benefits are presented.

Rather than use strong emotional stimuli, some advertising copy is designed to create a mood—to incorporate what has been designated as the *soft sell*. This approach is frequently used with products that have few distinctive attributes—such as fragrances. According to McCollum/Spielman, a communication research organization, the soft sell attempts to reach the consumer via analogy, imagery, emotion, humor, involvement with a mood, identification with people, life style, or human interest or a combination of these elements[7] (see Exhibit 13.8).

Narrative Copy

Narrative copy tells a story. The product plays a role in the life of someone with whom the reader can identify. The elements of narrative copy, shown in Exhibit 13.9, are predicament, discovery of a solution, happy ending, and transition and direct suggestion to the reader. This type of copy is frequently used for television commercials since it fits fairly well with the character of the medium. In narrative copy things happen—a sequence of events occurs which may lead logically into a sales message. Narrative copy is also used in print advertising and it's particularly successful where a specific problem appears to exist.

---

[6]Leonard J. Reiss, "For Bright Ad Copy, What Outranks How," *Advertising Age* (July 28, 1980), p. 48.

[7]Eric Pace, "Advertising Soft Sell: A 'Secret' Document," *The New York Times* (September 14, 1981), p. D12.

EXHIBIT 13.8
The Soft Sell

Dialogue or Monologue Copy

Dialogue or monologue copy usually features an individual talking about a product. This technique can sometimes add to the credibility of the narrative message, which is frequently in the form of a testimonial. As noted in Chapter 10 it can be presented by celebrities, "real" consumers, or "average" persons.

Picture-and-Caption Copy

Captions are small units of type used in connection with illustrations or other parts of an ad. When such captions are the principal means of telling a copy story, the ad is said to be a picture-and-caption ad. This

Predicament

Discovery
of Solution

Happy Ending

Transition
to Reader

EXHIBIT 13.9
Narrative Copy

technique requires the availability of space and is best used for large ads. Furthermore, it is more effective with some products than with others. Ads for food, for example, do well, particularly if various types of foods are used. Ads for autos do not lend themselves easily to the picture-and-caption method since the various components of the auto tend to be less interesting than one overall view.

Gimmick Copy
Unusual copy techniques are considered gimmick copy. The gimmick may be in the way in which the copy is presented—upside down, sideways, or as a poem—or the way in which the information is presented. The obvious objective is to attract attention, but sometimes the gimmicky aspect tends to limit the selling ability.

Creative Print Production Process

Creativity in advertising involves originality and imagination; it also requires attention to process, procedure, and detail. The creative process entails the way messages are communicated and the manner in which they are presented. Working in tandem with the creative process is the production process. Before a print ad is approved, it is visualized, drawn as a thumbnail sketch or a rough, discussed, altered, and often made into a comprehensive. Following client approval, the ad is produced—composed into a reproducible format, photographed, made into printing plates, and printed. The elements—illustration, headline, and copy in most cases—have been designed and written to work together in presenting an attractive and effective selling message.

CLIENT: Olympus Camera
AGENCY: Kameny Communications

Advertisements often begin with a thumbnail sketch. Thumbnails are small, usually measuring only a few inches square, and have very little detail. Their purpose is to show alternative visualizations of an ad, including basic elements and different arrangements of these elements.

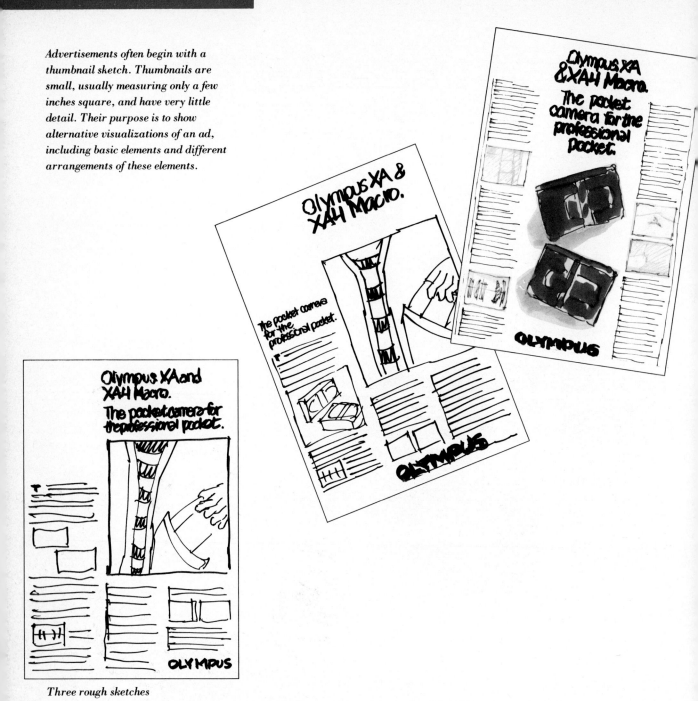

Three rough sketches

Some designers do not begin with thumbnails but instead proceed directly to a rough. A rough is still sketchy but usually the same size as the future ad and more detailed. Often roughs are presented for approval because they can be done rather quickly and are still able to show color, type of illustration, and spacing and positioning of elements and type. In a rough, illustrations are sketched in, headlines are lettered hastily, and copy is designated by using blocks of horizontal lines.

The rough may be further refined as a comprehensive, or "comp." This is usually prepared on cardboard or heavy paper and still more details are drawn or simulated. Copies of photos or illustrations are put into place, headlines are exacted, and typeface and color can be shown. The body copy is finalized, and the ad is approved.

Alternate comprehensive

Olympus XA and XA4 Macro.

The pocket camera for the professional pocket.

Original comprehensive

Olympus XA & XA4 Macro.

The pocket camera for the professional pocket.

OLYMPUS

The last step inside the agency in getting an ad ready to be printed is the mechanical. All of the elements are put together on the mechanical, which is an exact representation of the layout. The art is sized and a print is placed in position. The final copy is set in galleys, which are proofs of the typesetting. The galleys are corrected and printed on non-glare paper ("repro") from which a clear reproduction can be made. The repro is cut and pasted carefully into position. Type is photographed in this way from the mechanical, while art is shot separately. The film elements are combined, or "stripped" together, to form an actual-size piece of film from which printing plates can be made.

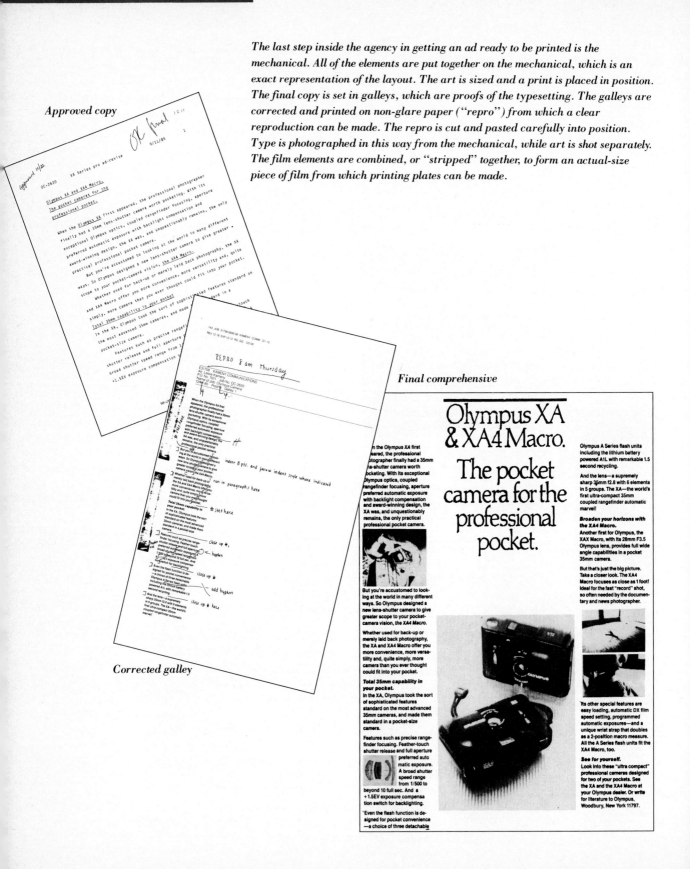

Approved copy

Corrected galley

Final comprehensive

Olympus XA & XA4 Macro.

The pocket camera for the professional pocket.

When the *Olympus XA* first appeared, the professional photographer finally had a 35mm lens-shutter camera worth pocketing. With its exceptional Olympus optics, coupled rangefinder focusing, aperture-preferred automatic exposure with backlight compensation and award-winning design, the XA was, and unquestionably remains, the only practical professional pocket camera.

But you're accustomed to looking at the world in many different ways. So Olympus designed a new lens-shutter camera to give greater scope to your pocket-camera vision, *the XA4 Macro.*

Whether used for back-up or merely laid back photography, the XA and XA4 Macro offer you more convenience, more versatility and, quite simply, more camera than you ever thought could fit into your pocket.

Total 35mm capability in your pocket.
In the XA, Olympus took the sort of sophisticated features standard on the most advanced 35mm cameras, and made them standard in a pocket-size camera.

Features such as precise rangefinder focusing. Feather-touch shutter release and full aperture-preferred automatic exposure. A broad shutter speed range from 1/500 to beyond 10 full seconds. And a +1.5EV exposure compensation switch for backlighting.

Even the flash function is designed for pocket convenience

—a choice of three detachable Olympus A Series flash units including the lithium battery powered A1L with remarkable 1.5 second recycling.

And the lens—a supremely sharp 35mm f2.8 with 6 elements in 5 groups. The XA—the world's first ultra-compact 35mm coupled rangefinder automatic marvel!

Broaden your horizons with the XA4 Macro.
Another first for Olympus, the XA4 Macro, with its 28mm f3.5 Olympus lens, provides full wide angle capabilities in a pocket 35mm camera.

But that's just the big picture. Take a closer look. The XA4 Macro focuses as close as 1 foot! Ideal for the fast "record" shot, so often needed by the documentary and news photographer.

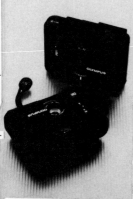

Its other special features are easy loading, automatic DX film speed setting, programmed automatic exposures—and a unique wrist strap that doubles as a 2-position macro measure. All the A Series flash units fit the XA4 Macro, too.

See for yourself.
Look into these "ultra compact" professional cameras designed for two of your pockets. See the XA and the XA4 Macro at your Olympus dealer. Or write for literature to Olympus, Woodbury, New York 11797. They'll sure take a load off your shoulders.

OLYMPUS

In the four-color process, four separate printing plates are made. Filters called subtractive primary process filters are placed over the camera lens to photograph the transparency. Each filter enables the camera to register the intensity of either yellow, cyan (blue), magenta (red), or black. The result is four color-separated negatives, which will make four printing plates. The type, often black, appears only on the negative or negatives of its color or colors. Progressive proofs, called so because they progressively display color mixtures, are printings of each plate separately and in combination.

Yellow proof

Cyan proof

Magenta proof

Olympus XA & XA4 Macro.
The pocket camera for the professional pocket.

When the Olympus XA first appeared, the professional photographer finally had a 35mm lens-shutter camera worth pocketing. With its exceptional Olympus optics, coupled rangefinder focusing, aperture-preferred automatic exposure with backlight compensation and award-winning design, the XA was, and unquestionably remains, the only practical professional pocket camera.

But you're accustomed to looking at the world in many different ways. So Olympus designed a new lens-shutter camera to give greater scope to your pocket-camera vision, the XA4 Macro.

Whether used for back-up or merely laid back photography, the XA and XA4 Macro offer you more convenience, more versatility and, quite simply, more camera than you ever thought could fit into your pocket.

Total 35mm capability in your pocket.
In the XA, Olympus took the sort of sophisticated features standard on the most advanced 35mm cameras, and made them standard in a pocket-size camera.

Features such as precise rangefinder focusing. Feather-touch shutter release and full aperture-preferred automatic exposure. A broad shutter speed range from 1/500 to beyond 10 full seconds. And a +1.5EV exposure compensation switch for backlighting.

Even the flash function is designed for pocket convenience

—a choice of three detachable Olympus A Series flash units including the lithium battery powered A1L with remarkable 1.5 second recycling.

And the lens—a supremely sharp 35mm f2.8 with 6 elements in 5 groups. The XA—the world's first ultra-compact 35mm coupled rangefinder automatic marvel!

Broaden your horizons with the XA4 Macro.
Another first for Olympus, the XA4 Macro, with its 28mm f3.5 Olympus lens, provides full wide angle capabilities in a pocket 35mm camera.

But that's just the big picture. Take a closer look. The XA4 Macro focuses as close as 1 foot! Ideal for the fast "record" shot, so often needed by the documentary and news photographer.

Its other special features are easy loading, automatic DX film speed setting, programmed automatic exposures—and a unique wrist strap that doubles as a 2-position macro measure. All the A Series flash units fit the XA4 Macro, too.

See for yourself.
Look into these "ultra compact" professional cameras designed for two of your pockets. See the XA and the XA4 Macro at your Olympus dealer. Or write for literature to Olympus, Woodbury, New York 11797. They'll sure take a load off your shoulders.

OLYMPUS

Black proof

Yellow, magenta, and cyan proof

There are newer technological developments in color separation, such as the electron scanning camera that is able to separate the colors from a transparency or reflective illustration in one pass rather than four. Also, sometimes color separation is checked with the use of simpler, composite proofs, although progressives are still considered the most accurate way to proof four-color work.

For the final product, each color is printed over the others in perfect registration, and a full-color (four-color) advertisement is produced.

Olympus XA & XA4 Macro.

The pocket camera for the professional pocket.

When the *Olympus XA* first appeared, the professional photographer finally had a 35mm lens-shutter camera worth pocketing. With its exceptional Olympus optics, coupled rangefinder focusing, aperture-preferred automatic exposure with backlight compensation and award-winning design, the XA was, and unquestionably remains, the only practical professional pocket camera.

But you're accustomed to looking at the world in many different ways. So Olympus designed a new lens-shutter camera to give greater scope to your pocket-camera vision, *the XA4 Macro.*

Whether used for back-up or merely laid back photography, the XA and XA4 Macro offer you more convenience, more versatility and, quite simply, more camera than you ever thought could fit into your pocket.

Total 35mm capability in your pocket.
In the XA, Olympus took the sort of sophisticated features standard on the most advanced 35mm cameras, and made them standard in a pocket-size camera.

Features such as precise range-finder focusing. Feather- touch shutter release and full aperture-

preferred automatic exposure. A broad shutter speed range from 1/500 to beyond 10 full seconds. And a +1.5EV exposure compensation switch for backlighting.

Even the flash function is designed for pocket convenience

—a choice of three detachable Olympus A Series flash units - including the lithium battery powered A1L with remarkable 1.5 second recycling.

And the lens—a supremely sharp 35mm f2.8 with 6 elements in 5 groups. The XA—the world's first ultra-compact 35mm coupled rangefinder automatic marvel!

Broaden your horizons with the XA4 Macro.
Another first for Olympus, the XA4 Macro, with its 28mm f3.5 Olympus lens, provides full wide angle capabilities in a pocket 35mm camera.

But that's just the big picture. Take a closer look. The XA4 Macro focuses as close as 1 foot! Ideal for the fast "record" shot, so often needed by the documentary and news photographer.

Its other special features are easy loading, automatic DX film speed setting, programmed automatic exposures—and a unique wrist strap that doubles as a 2-position macro measure. All the A Series flash units fit the XA4 Macro, too.

See for yourself.
Look into these "ultra compact" professional cameras designed for two of *your* pockets. See the XA and the XA4 Macro at your Olympus dealer. Or write for literature to Olympus, Woodbury, New York 11797. They'll sure take a load off your shoulders.

OLYMPUS®

Elements in Body Copy

Regardless of the approach used, the body copy may consist of a lead-in paragraph, an interior paragraph, and a close.

The lead-in develops the thought presented in the headline and subheadline. It should immediately transfer reading interest to product interest.

Headline: The mark of a good razor is no mark at all.

Lead-in Paragraph: Techmatic shaves you close but it's also lighter
     on your skin. It's shaped to go easily over hard-to-shave places.

The lead-in paragraph may begin to present the claims and benefits by appealing to the reader's self-interest.

Interior paragraphs develop the message and expand on it. They also provide proof to wary consumers of the claims and benefits that have been promised. The most common types of proof are the following:[8]

Construction evidence	Product's rank in the market
Product feature	Guarantee
Performance	Testimonial
Tests the advertisers ran	Endorsement
Tests the consumer can run	Trial offer
Tests by research firms	Demonstration offer
Case history	Sample

The type of proof used varies with a product's benefits, attributes, usage, price, and its target market. Many companies use trial offers for relatively inexpensive, frequently used products; others use personalities in their ads for testimonials and endorsements.

Close

To be successful copy should invite action. This is similar to the element of closing in personal selling. Since not all advertising is designed to create an immediate sale, the close of the advertisement may take several forms, from a subtle suggestion to a definite command.

Indirect action copy may close with an implied suggestion or a soft suggestion. Coca-Cola Company has used the implied suggestion in advertising with "The pause that refreshes." This became more of a soft suggestion with the "Things go Better with Coke" campaign, then a somewhat stronger suggestion that "It's the real thing!" to a stronger statement "Coke Is It!"

Direct action close usually requires an immediate response of some kind, whether it is purchase or merely further inquiry. The close for this kind of copy should make this action easy. Mail-order advertising can provide coupons or prepaid business reply cards or envelopes. If pur-

---

[8]C.A. Kirkpatrick, *Advertising Mass Communication in Marketing*, p. 178.

EXHIBIT 13.10
The Signature or Logo

Life would be empty without Kodak professional film.

chase is desired, all the pertinent information necessary for action should be included.

Signature

An important element in copy is the signature, logotype, or logo. The copywriter is responsible for including in the ad the whole signature, the use of the corporate name in its agreed-upon form (usually the company trademark), the address, and any other legal formalities that a given business or industry may require.

A well-designed logo should be legible, distinctive, appropriate and handsome. It should be usable in many sizes so that it can appear in all kinds of advertisements as well as on business cards. It should provide quick identification of the company or the product (see Exhibit 13.10).

Slogans and Tag Lines

Slogans are a series of words, phrases, or sentences that are designed to be repeated. The primary functions of slogans are to provide quick and easy identification of the advertisers, to create deep and lasting impressions, and to develop a method of ensuring continuity.

Many slogans created in the past have lasted for years and identify the advertiser quickly, even when the slogan is no longer widely used: A diamond is forever (De Beers Consolidated Mines); When you care enough to send the very best (Hallmark); 99 and 44/100% pure (Ivory soap).

If the objective of the campaign is to provide coordination for several elements of the firm, a *tag line* may be prepared that offers direction for the rest of the campaign. Currently, the term *slogan* is used interchangeably with *tag line*. However, although a tag line performs the functions of a slogan, it provides the additional benefit of incorporating a positioning or repositioning statement. A company's tag line may position it as possessing desirable competitive characteristics, such as the success suggested by Thank you Paine Webber; or superior attributes, such as faster relief: Ex-Lax—the Overnight Wonder; or desirable benefits, as in Campbell's—Soup Is Good Food.

Slogans and tag lines are designed to be repeated over and over again. Before a firm invests in frequent presentations of the same message, care should be taken to ensure that they serve the company's objectives, which may go beyond ease of identification and recognition.

A number of techniques can be used to enhance the success of the tag lines.

1. Include visual images. Slogans are particularly effective for both identification and recognition when they are accompanied by visual representations.
   "Good to the Last Drop"   Maxwell House Coffee
   "You're in Good Hands with Allstate"
   "When It Rains, It Pours"   Morton Salt
2. If possible, include the name of the company in the tag line. For clearer identification it is useful to incorporate the firm's name or product in the tag line. For example:
   "We're American Airlines—Doing What We Do Best"
   "You're Going to Like Us—TWA"
   "The American Express Card—Don't leave home without it"
3. Use rhymes, alliteration, jingles. To encourage memorability, many tag lines are alliterative.
   "A sandwich is a sandwich, but a Manwich is a meal"
   "Fill your cup to the rim with the rich taste of Brim"

MESSAGE STRATEGY

Creative copywriting suggests uniqueness, originality, and many other innovative characteristics. Good copy, however, is dependent on specific objectives and is required to attract attention, communicate clearly, persuade effectively, and encourage memorability. Guidelines for designing messages to achieve these goals emerge from examining past successes, principles of persuasion, and research. While any or all of these principles need not be observed by the creative copywriter, it is important to know what they are before they can be rejected.

The Informative Message

The current economic climate creates a demand for more information in advertising copy, and the concern is echoed by the regulatory agencies who now determine the acceptability of advertising copy not only by what it says but by what it fails to say. This trend toward full disclosure and affirmative statements in advertising suggests that reliable and verifiable facts will be required in consumer advertising, and the policy of overlooking exaggeration as acceptable commercial "puffery" may be considerably revised.

Generally, people with no experience with a product prefer simplified ads. However, according to Anderson and Jolson, as a consumer acquires even a limited amount of experience with a product, his or her responsiveness to technical content rises at an accelerating rate.[9] They recommend that for widely used products, such as cameras, it may be better to provide too much technical language than too little.

One-Sided Versus Two-Sided Messages

Most advertisements contain *one-sided messages*—that is, their information focuses on the benefits of the product or service that is offered. Research has indicated that a *two-sided message*—one which offers information both on the position advocated by the advertiser and an opposing viewpoint—may be an effective persuasive technique under some circumstances.

The one-sided message may be more persuasive in influencing the attitudes of those familiar with the issue and less educated groups. If the audience does not know there are two sides and is unlikely to find out, a one-sided message would obviously be more effective.

The two-sided message may be more desirable when (1) the audience, regardless of its initial position, will be exposed to later counterpropaganda, and (2) the audience is opposed to the position advocated by the communicator.[10]

In medicine, the individual can be given weakened dosages of the biological attack and, by overcoming this, develop an immunity to future attacks. So also in the case of persuasion, the individual can be presented with negative information that is subsequently weakened in the ad. The initial exposure to negative information, identified as an inoculation effect, results in resistance to counterinformation from other sources. The advertisers of Wonder Bread used this approach in an effort to inoculate consumers who might reject white bread as lacking proper nutritional content. Their campaign featured the statement "Wonder Bread does not contain as much nutrients as whole wheat, but for these important ones it does," followed by a listing of nutrient content.

[9]Ralph E. Anderson and Marvin A. Jolson, "Technical Wording in Advertising: Implications for Market Segmentation," *Journal of Marketing*, Vol. 44 (Winter 1980), pp. 57–66.

[10]David Krech, Richard S. Crutchfield and Norman Livson, *Elements of Psychology*, 3rd ed. (New York: Alfred A. Knopf, 1974), p. 770.

The two-sided message may be seen as more credible. Some of the most outstanding and memorable campaigns presented two-sided messages. Avis was Number 2 and therefore "tried harder." Volkswagen could be considered a "lemon" since it did not change its style, and, therefore, it concentrated on superior performance. A recent campaign by General Motors Corporation's Buick division used an approach in print ads which suggested that car buyers "consider Buick, not because it's perfect, but because it's so good at the things that really count."

While two-sided messages may be appropriate for some situations, an excessively negative presentation is usually undesirable. Criticism was directed at an ad that was headlined "Some people are hesitant to use an ad agency." The body copy began: "They fear that the cost will be too high, that the advertiser will change their image, or, quite simply, that agencies cannot be trusted."

Good Grammar

When Wendy's fast-food franchises felt they needed a campaign that would help them achieve awareness, they featured the phrase "Ain't no reason to go anyplace else." Although initially this effort achieved its objective of creating awareness, it was criticized by the company and its many franchisees, as well as by some consumers.[11] To change the tone of the campaign, and reposition itself as a quality fast-food firm, Wendy's changed its theme to "You're Wendy's Kind of People," people who want "something better."

Good copy incorporates grammatically correct phrases and sentences in the message. While there are occasional deviations from this principle, generally this is done with a specific objective in mind.

Use Concrete Words and phrases Concrete words easily define objects, persons, places, or things that can be seen, smelled, or tasted, and stimulate high imagery. In a test print ad for a hypothetical new imported beer, using concrete copy such as "Bavaria's No. 1 selling beer for the last 10 years," "winner of 5 out of 5 taste tests in the U.S. against all major American beers and leading imports," and "affordably priced at $1.79 per six-pack of 12 oz. bottles" generated twice the favorable attitude toward the new brand as when abstract copy such as "Bavaria's finest beer," "great taste," and "affordably priced" was used.[12]

Use Simple, Common and Familiar Words Some research tests have shown that high-frequency words tend to be less associated with negative feelings than low-frequency words. "Never let them see you sweat" is used effectively in ads for Dry Idea antiperspirant.

[11]Richard Kreisman, "Wendy's Finds 'Something Better' for Ads," *Advertising Age* (May 10, 1982), p. 14.
[12]Larry Percy and John R. Rossier, "10 Ways to More Effective Ads Via Visual Imagery, Psycholinguistics," *Marketing News* (February 19, 1982), p. 10.

Avoid Negative Words and Sentences Words such as *no, never,* and *less than* have been found to increase the time necessary to understand a sentence. Such negatives, however, may be useful when trying to make consumers think the opposite of what they normally would—such as "Orange juice is not just for breakfast anymore,"[13] or "Danskins are not just for dancing."

Mnemonic Devices

One way to make copy memorable is to incorporate mnemonic devices. Mnemonics is a method of remembering items by imposing a structure of organization on the material to be remembered.

Key Word System The key word system is a mnemonic device wherein certain key words are associated with the items to be remembered. The key words may be incorporated into vivid images in a story, and they frequently are alliterative. Alka-Seltzer's "Plop, plop, fizz, fizz" and Purina Cat Chow's Ms. Patsy Garrett and her chow-chow-chow dance are parts of successful long-remembered advertising campaigns. Alliteration is not necessary for achieving key-word association, as for example, Federal Express' "Absolutely Positively" and Raisin Grape Nut's "Crunchychewynuttysweet" taste.

Method of Loci With this mnemonic device people or objects to be remembered are imagined in specific spots in familiar locations. It requires that one walk, in one's imagination, through a familiar environment and put items to be remembered in conspicuous places. This method works because it takes advantage of the organization already present in a person's memory. Marlboro's "Come to Where the Flavor Is" is a long-continuing campaign that provides a method of loci for the cigarette smoker who sees himself as a strong silent cowboy (see Exhibit 13.11).

Imagery Many of the popular mnemonic devices rely on visual imagery. It has been noted that people do learn verbal materials better when they are connected with some visual image—"The Maiden Form Woman—You Never Know Where She'll Turn Up."

Copy Check List

Many methods have been devised for testing copy effectiveness; they will be discussed in Chapter 23. Before putting copy to any rigid test, however, one simple method of evaluation is to check the copy against a prepared list of copy attributes. While this is by no means a precise evaluation mechanism, it is a simple method of examining copy to de-

---

[13]Larry Percy and John R. Rossier, *Marketing News*, p. 10.

Come to where the flavor is.

SURGEON GENERAL'S WARNING: Quitting Smoking Now Greatly Reduces Serious Risks to Your Health.

16 mg "tar," 1.0 mg nicotine av. per cigarette, FTC Report Feb '85

EXHIBIT 13.11
Method of Loci

Marlboro, with equally memorable print and television advertising, was rated in a survey of advertising people as the second most outstanding advertising campaign (bowing only to Volkswagen).

termine whether it is consistent with tried and tested rules and may uncover some of the more obvious and glaring deficiencies. The following list is not comprehensive but suggests some of the checks to which copy should be subject:

1. Is the copy sincere and believable?
2. Does it get the audience involved?
3. Is it keyed to the self-interest of the prospect?
4. Does it use the language of the prospect?
5. Is it written smoothly and coherently?

6. Does it provide the necessary information?
7. Is it interesting and persuasive?
8. Does it invite action?
9. Will it pass the inspection of the regulatory agencies?
10. Does it make the reader want the product advertised?

SUMMARY

One of the most important creative functions is the writing of copy. Copy is not written in isolation; rather it is prepared in conjunction with other creative people in both the advertising agency and the client company. Information concerning the company, the target market, the product, and the media is necessary before the copywriter can begin the task.

A typical structure for print copy includes a number of elements: headline, subheadline, body copy, logo, and tag line. However, all of these need not be incorporated in every ad. Most important is the headline since it is the part of the copy read by most consumers. Headlines can be classified by content or form; the choice is dependent on the objectives of the ad.

In writing the body copy, a number of approaches can be used. These are designated as straight line, narrative, mood building, dialogue or monologue, picture and caption, or gimmick. The body copy frequently includes a lead paragraph, interior paragraph, and a close.

Most ads must have some form of signature to identify the advertiser. This is called a logo and serves as an identifying symbol. Many ads today use tag lines or phrases that are repeated, provide quick and easy identification, offer memorability, and help position the product or service.

While creative copy is usually innovative, there are a number of guidelines for effective message strategy that should be observed. These include providing information, using good grammar, and using mnemonic devices as an aid to memorability.

A simple device for evaluating copy is a copy checklist. This is a list of questions that relate to some of the desirable features of good copy.

QUESTIONS FOR DISCUSSION

1. What is the basic structure of print copy? Select an ad that follows this structure and explain the elements.
2. Select two ads that have no headlines and two that feature only headlines. Discuss and evaluate advertisers' objectives in these presentations.
3. Select ads with headlines that fall into several of the categories mentioned in the text and discuss their effectiveness.
4. Select several ads that make use of the various types of body copy. Would you use these techniques for the product advertised? Discuss.
5. What are the elements of narrative copy?
6. Why are tag lines used in advertising? Select an ad containing a tag line you consider effective and explain why.
7. Under what circumstances would you present a two-sided message in an advertisement?
8. Is it necessary to observe good grammatical construction in ads? Explain.
9. What is meant by mnemonic devices? How are these used?
10. Using the copy checklist analyze copy in several ads and discuss any obvious deficiencies that emerge.

KEY TERMS

copy	logotype or logo
headline	tag line
subheadline	soft sell
body copy	captions
close	

AD PRACTICE

Select a new product or service (you can dream up one or look through publications such as *Advertising Age* or *Fortune* for forthcoming introductions). Following the steps for the structure of print copy, prepare a print advertisement for this new product. What guidelines in message strategy have you incorporated in your ad?

14

Artwork and Layout

CHAPTER OBJECTIVES

— To describe advertising layout in terms of its functions, the steps in the layout process, the requisites of an effective layout, and the formats that may be used

— To examine the techniques used to illustrate an ad and discuss the benefits and disadvantages of each

— To describe the artistic devices available for depicting an illustration in the ad

The Arrow Company professes to own the white dress-shirt market and, recently, decided it wanted to be able to say the same about the "fancies," the colored shirts the retailers tend to feature in in-store displays.

Because Arrow has had so much success with the classic model for its shirts, created in 1905 by illustrator J. C. Leyendecker, it decided to employ Leroy Neiman, an artist who frequently paints men in active situations, to illustrate its new campaign. Neiman's Arrow Man is featured in several print ads and in television spots in which live actors are transformed into Neiman paintings.

Creative strategy, like the one used by Arrow, requires artists as well as copywriters. Although the message is considered the province of the copywriter and the artwork the responsibility of the art director, these two creative people usually work as a team to develop the artwork and layout for advertisements. Art refers to the entire visual presentation of the advertisement, including the copy as well as the type of illustration. It also encompasses the layout, which provides the architectural design for the elements in the ad.

LAYOUT

In the initial stages of an ad's development either the copywriter or the art director forms a mental image of the ad. The copywriter may use rough sketches to develop the theme and to convey ideas to the artist; the artist will visualize the thought sketch and provide a pictorial representation of it.

Visualization is often confused with the terms *illustration* and *layout*. *Visualization* precedes both the illustration and layout and is the process of forming a mental image, picture, or representation of an object or idea. The *layout* is the physical arrangement of the elements in an advertisement so that this mental idea may be effectively presented. The picture portion of the layout is generally referred to as the *illustration*.

Much of the creativity in advertising evolves from the process of visualization and the countless ways in which mental images can be made to represent ideas. Impending danger is vividly and graphically presented by an onrushing train over an old trestle, a child retrieving a ball in a street crowded with traffic, a pedestrian walking down a dark empty street, or a flashing red light. Effective advertising requires that these images be consistent with an advertiser's messsage, which is concerned with the need or desire the product fulfills (see Exhibit 14.1).

It is the job of the layout artist to combine all the elements in the idea into a single, effective communication. This requires adding to the idea a headline, illustration, body text, logotype, and occasionally a subheadline, picture caption, trademark, coupon, or seal of approval.

Functions of Layout

A layout shows how an ad is to look and, therefore, must contain all the necessary elements. The layout provides a working blending of the creative abilities of all personnel involved in the preparation of the advertisement. It permits all interested parties, particularly the client, to see the advertisement before final steps are taken to put it in print. The layout also serves as a gauge to determine if all the materials that will go into the advertisement will fit into a given space. Finally, it provides a blueprint to meet the mechanical requirements of engravers, typographers, and others, as well as giving specifications for estimating costs.

Steps in the Layout Process

Various types of layout may be prepared. To some extent they represent stages in the layout process—a logical progression from the visualization to the completed arrangement.

EXHIBIT 14.1
Rough Layouts of Visualizations

Thumbnail

Frequently layout starts with *thumbnail sketches,* simple drawings that contain an ad's basic elements. These small sketches are generally drawn in the experimental stage to show the different ways of arranging the elements. Not every designer uses a thumbnail sketch, however; some skip this step altogether and begin with the rough.

Rough

The *rough,* or visual, evolves from the acceptable thumbnail and, although it is still somewhat sketchy, it begins to present more detail. The purpose of the rough is to convey the idea to agency personnel. It is the same size as the future advertisement, but the illustrations are roughed in, the headlines are lettered hastily, and the copy blocks are represented by horizontal parallel lines. Despite the hasty sketching and lack of detail, tonal values are clearly apparent, as is the spacing of the elements. The rough is good for analysis and criticism and a number of roughs may be completed before the final one is accepted.

Many agencies feel that roughs are fresher and have more spontaneity than the comprehensives which are the next step; therefore, they use roughs exclusively to show to clients. (See the essay following p. 262 for an example.) The philosophy behind this is that the client is required to judge the idea, not its execution. Roughs are also less expensive.

The Comprehensive

A *comprehensive* usually appears on heavy paper or cardboard and provides further refinement of the rough. The artwork is shown in approximately its final form or, when a photograph is used, the photograph or a carefully prepared pastel representing it, will be pasted into position. Headlines are carefully traced or reproduced by other means. Typed matter is shown by ruled lines, and careful lettering is shown in its exact hue and value to indicate tone and color.

Comprehensives are expensive. They are frequently prepared by a free-lance artist or art studio and used to help the client judge the effect of the finished advertisement. Payment for the artwork is subject to negotiation when an agency is hired. Generally advertising agencies absorb the cost of finished layouts in commissions they receive from media, but the client may be billed for the additional expense of a comprehensive layout. When a comprehensive is not prepared, the finished layout, which is more carefully executed than the rough, may be submitted to the client for approval.

Pasteup or Mechanical

The *pasteup*, or *mechanical*, is actually a step beyond layout, but is so closely allied that it is frequently considered as part of the process. To determine the size for the pasteup, the designer can refer to a publication rate card or to Standard Rate and Data Service which offers such information for various media.

The pasteup contains all the elements of a layout. Often the type is photographed in place but the art elements are photographed separately. Then all parts are "stripped in" and made into a final film—from which plates are made.

Elements of an Effective Layout

Fundamentally a good layout should attract attention and interest and should provide some control over the manner in which the advertisement is read. The message to be communicated may be sincere, relevant, and important to the consumer, but because of the competitive "noise" in the communication channel, the opportunity to be heard may

EXHIBIT 14.2
The Optical Center

EXHIBIT 14.3
Informal Balance

depend on the effectiveness of the layout. In addition to attracting attention, the most important requisites for an effective layout are balance, proportion, movement, utility, clarity, and emphasis.

Balance

Balance is a fundamental law in nature and its application to layout design formulates one of the basic principles of this process. *Balance* is a matter of weight distribution; in layout it is keyed to the *optical center* of an advertisement, the point which the reader's eye designates as the center of an area. In an advertisement a vertical line which divides the area into right and left halves contains the center; however the optical center is between one-tenth and one-third the distance above the mathematical horizontal center line (see Exhibit 14.2).

In order to provide good artistic composition, the elements in the layout must be in equilibrium. Equilibrium can be achieved through balance, and this process may be likened to the balancing of a seesaw. The optical center of the advertisement serves as the fulcrum or balancing point, and the elements may be balanced on both sides of this fulcrum through considerations of their size and tonal quality.

The simplest way to ensure formal balance between the elements to the right and left of the vertical line is to have all masses in the left duplicated on the right in size, weight, and distance from the center, as shown in the ad for Grand Marnier in Exhibit 14.4. Formal balance imparts feelings of dignity, solidity, refinement, and reserve. It has been used for institutional advertising and suggests conservatism on the part of the advertiser. Its major deficiency is that it may present a static and somewhat unexciting appearance; however, formal balance presents material in an easy-to-follow order and works well for many ads.

To understand informal balance, think of children of unequal weight balanced on a seesaw; to ensure equilibrium it is necessary to place the smaller child far from the center and the larger child closer to the fulcrum. In informal balance the elements are balanced, but not evenly, because of different sizes and color contrast. This type of a symetric balance requires care so that the various elements do not create a lopsided or topheavy appearance. A knowledge of a sense of the composition can help create the feeling of symmetry in what is essentially asymmetric balance.

Informal balance presents a fresh, untraditional approach. It creates excitement, a sense of originality, forcefulness, and, to some extent, the element of surprise. Whereas formal balance may depend on the high interest value of the illustration to attract the reader, informal balance may attract attention through the design of the layout. The Dannon ad in Exhibit 14.3 illustrates informal balance.

Proportion

Proportion helps develop order and creates a pleasing impression. It is related to balance but is concerned primarily with the division of the space and the emphasis to be accorded each element. Proportion, to the

EXHIBIT 14.4
Formal Balance

advertising designer, is the relationship between the size of one element in the ad to another, the amount of space between elements, as well as the width of the total ad to its depth. Proportion also involves the tone of the ad: the amount of light area in relation to dark area and the amount of color and noncolor.[1]

As a general rule unequal dimensions and distances make the most lively design in advertising. The designer also places the elements on the page so that each element is given space and position in proportion

---

[1]Roy Paul Nelson, *The Design of Advertising*, 4th ed., (Dubuque, IA: Wm. C. Brown Co., 1981), p. 118.

EXHIBIT 14.5
Proportion

to its importance in the total advertisement and does not look like it stands alone (see Exhibit 14.5).

Movement

If an advertisement is to appear dynamic rather than static, it must contain some movement. *Movement* (also called *sequence*) provides the directional flow for the advertisement, gives it its follow-through, and provides coherence. It guides the reader's eye from one element to another and makes sure he or she does not miss anything.

Motion in layout is generally from left to right and from top to bottom—the direction established through the reading habits of speakers of Western language. The directional impetus should not disturb the natural visual flow but should favor the elements to be stressed, while care should be taken not to direct the reader's eye out of the advertise-

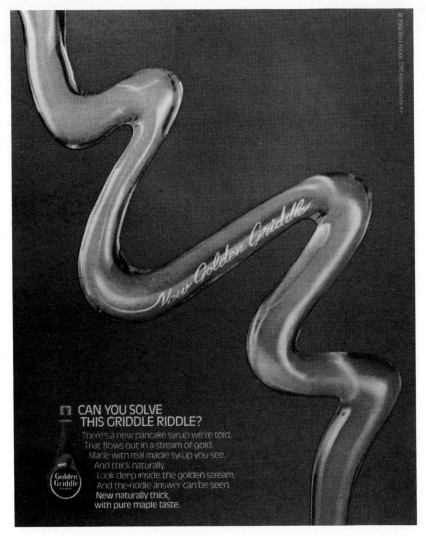

EXHIBIT 14.6
An Example of Structural Motion

ment. This can be done by the following:

— *Gaze motion* directs the reader's attention by directing the looks of the people or animals in an ad. If a subject is gazing at a unit in the layout, the natural tendency is for the reader to follow the direction of that gaze; if someone is looking directly out of the advertisement, the reader may stop to see who's staring.

— *Structural motion* incorporates the lines of direction and patterns of movement by mechanical means. An obvious way is to use an arrow or a pointed finger. The arrangement of the elements, shapes, and lines in Exhibit 14.6 shows how this subtle means can achieve structural motion. Sequence can also be achieved by building the layout in accordance with certain letters of the alphabet, *(S, J, C, V, Z,* and *O)*.

EXHIBIT 14.7
The Use of White Space

Unity

Another important design principle is the unification of the layout. Although an advertisement is made up of many elements, all of these should be welded into a compact composition. Unity is achieved when the elements tie into one another by using the same basic shapes, sizes, textures, colors, and mood. In addition, the type should have the same character as the art.

A *border* surrounding an ad provides a method of achieving unity. Sets of borders may occur within an ad, and, when they are similar in thickness and tone, they provide a sense of unity.

Effective use of white space can help to establish unity, as shown in Exhibit 14.7. *White space* is defined as that part of the advertising space which is not occupied by any other elements; in this definition, white space is not always white in color. White space may be used to feature an important element by setting it off, or to imply luxury and prestige by preventing a crowded appearance. It may be used to direct and control the reader's attention by tying elements together. If white space is used incorrectly, it may cause separation of the elements and create difficulty in viewing the advertisement as a whole.

Clarity and Simplicity

The good art director does not permit a layout to become too complicated or tricky. An advertisement should retain its clarity and be easy to read and easy to understand. The reader tends to see the total image of an advertisement; thus it should not appear fussy, contrived, or confusing. Color contrasts, including tones of gray, should be strong enough to be easily deciphered, and the various units should be clear and easy to understand. Type size and design should be selected for ease of reading, and lines of type should be a comfortable reading length. Too many units in an advertisement are distracting; therefore, any elements that can be eliminated without destroying the message should be. One way in which clarity can be achieved is by combining the logo, trademark, tag line, and company name into one compact group.

Emphasis

Although varying degrees of emphasis may be given to different elements, one unit should dominate. It is the designer's responsibility to determine how much emphasis is necessary, as well as how it is to be achieved. The important element may be placed in the optical center or removed from the clutter of other elements. Emphasis may also be achieved by contrasts in size, shape, and color, or the use of white space.

Layout Formats

There is a wide range of potential layout formats or styles that are consistently used and there are a limitless variety that can be developed by creative personnel. Usually a designer will try several different formats before deciding which one to use.

Conventional (or Picture Window) Format

In the *conventional,* or picture window, *format,* the picture occupies most of the layout and is usually placed at the top of the page with the copy underneath (see Exhibit 14.8). It can also be placed on the bottom or in the center and then the copy appears above or below. Since there is very little space for copy, it must be clever and tightly written.

EXHIBIT 14.8
The Picture Window Format

This type of layout is the most frequently used in advertising since it offers a simple, but clear, method of presenting an ad's elements. In fact, readership studies indicate that the highest scoring ads usually use a single dominant illustration that occupies between 60 and 70 percent of the advertisement's total area.[2]

Mondrian (or Grid) Format

The *Mondrian format* (derived from the painting style of the Dutch artist Piet Mondrian) uses rectangular elements of pleasing proportions. It consists of a fitted set of vertical and horizontal rectangles, occasionally with a square element inserted. These rectangles are all different sizes,

---

[2]J. Douglas Johnson, *Advertising Today* (Chicago: Science Research Associates, 1978), pp. 91–92.

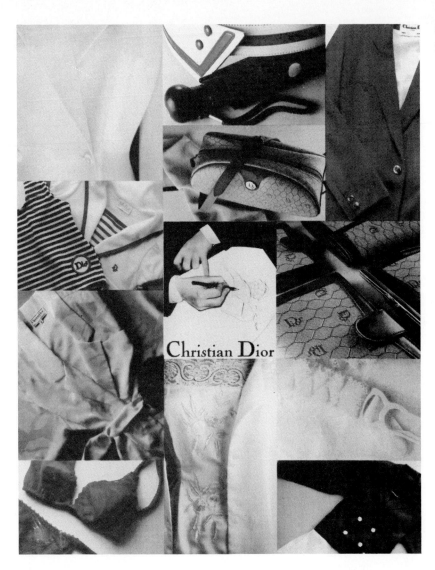

Christian Dior

EXHIBIT 14.9
A Mondrian Layout

and the lines separating them can be of varying widths.

The mondrian layout such as the one shown in Exhibit 14.9 offers a means of introducing a more visually interesting element in an advertisement and of suggesting that the product or service is exciting rather than dull. However, this layout may also tend to distract the viewer from organized perusal of the copy text.

Copy-Heavy Format

The copy-heavy format usually uses no pictures or illustrations. It is used by firms to provide to the target market a long and detailed message, particularly when the information is considered important.

Copy in this format is broken into easy-to-read segments and subheadlines may be used to help the reader; a border may sometimes be used to give the layout distinction.

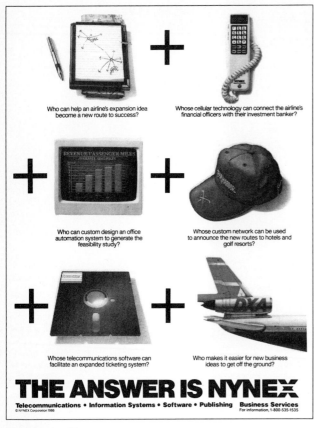

EXHIBIT 14.10
Other Formats

Pictured above are examples of a rebus layout and a poster layout.

Other Formats

There are many other techniques including the *poster layout,* where the emphasis is almost all visual; *cartoon layout,* which incorporates some type of cartoon; the *comic strip* layout, which follows the format of comics; and the *rebus layout,* which uses a number of pictures to suggest words. All of these techniques may be used to attract more attention than may be secured through the conventional picture-window format, and tend to be used more frequently by national advertisers than retail advertisers (see Exhibit 14.10).

THE ILLUSTRATION

With the advent of television, we have come to depend more and more on a visual image. How something looks can affect how we react. A good illustration should stimulate and arouse sufficient interest so that the prospect will read the copy in the advertisement. An illustration should provide the proper setting for the product and be relevant to the copy. A picture of a pretty girl may be eye-catching, but it may not be successful in selling bricks, machinery, or chewing tobacco.

Methods of Illustration

Even if the form of an ad is conventional, the illustration used may not be. Whether an illustration shows only a product or magnifies a detail depends on a product's characteristics, its advertising objective, the target audience, and the medium to be used.

The Product Alone
The product alone is the simplest form of illustration and one which depends upon the product itself to capture the interest of the reader. It is a useful technique when:

1. appearance is an important sales factor,
2. it is to be ordered and you wish to describe it as clearly as possible, and
3. it is new and different and you wish to show the public its detailed features.

Product in a Setting
Placing a product in a setting or background aids the visual communication process. A plain, cane-seated chair, next to a table topped with a wine bottle and an expensive-looking menu, can look elegant; the same chair on the back porch of a home has a down-to-earth association. For this method of illustration to be effective, the background should be simple and in keeping with the potential image of the product. All background details should be correct and consistent with each other.

A backdrop brings out the favorable highlights of a product, suggests its benefits, and creates a desired atmosphere. It is particularly well suited for expensive or prestigious products.

Product in Use
To provide vitality, a product may be pictured in use. Consumers then see not only the object but how it will help them. Soap ads showing models with their faces and hands enveloped in foam have received favorable attention. Notice, in Exhibit 14.11, how the eyes are directed naturally to the advertised item and the product is the major feature of interest.

Result of a Product's Use
To a consumer, the product itself may not be as important as the satisfactions derived from its use. Ads for ocean liners feature the fun that will be had aboard, rather than the tonnage of the ship. Cosmetics illustrations that show the finished results are more effective than those demonstrating the application.

Dramatization of a Headline
The headline and the illustration are the major attention-getting factors in the layout. Dramatizing the headline may solidify this effort and help to clearly define the appeal in the advertisement. Sometimes the head-

EXHIBIT 14.11
A Product in Use

line tells a story that can be dramatized easily. "Halfway down this 90-foot spar I reached the end of my rope!" The illustration showed a contestant in a high-rigger's race climbing down a spar tree and using a rope to stop his fall. Neither the headline nor the illustration showed any relationship to the product, a blended whiskey, but they both managed to attract the reader's attention and gain interest.

Occasionally a headline may be dramatized in a humorous fashion as shown in Exhibit 14.12. This ad, part of the campaign for the Health Education Council, helped establish Saatchi & Saatchi Advertising Agency's creative reputation.

EXHIBIT 14.12
Dramatization of a Headline

Dramatization of a Situation

An illustration may be a visual presentation of the story told in the copy. Since the copy generally contains several situations suited for dramatization, the major problem is to find the incident that will illustrate most effectively. Generally the illustration will reveal the happy ending to a predicament. With pain-relief advertising, however, it appears that people with aches apparently like to look at others in pain. When one major advertiser tried to run advertisements showing the way people felt after taking their pills readership dropped to about one-third what it would have been if the ad showed a contorted face.

Comparison

A comparison illustration relates the product to a concept that is established and acceptable in the eyes of the consumer. It is important that the attempted comparison does not appear farfetched and that the advertiser's product does not suffer or appear unsatisfactory from this comparison.

The comparison is generally made to something familiar—such as ice and diamonds. One illustration effectively compared pieces of a sterling silver flatware set with a fine violin; ordinary tableware used in a similar advertisement would have created an aura of unbelievability.

Contrast

Comparison attempts to show how a product is similar to another concept; contrast emphasizes the differences. A modern appliance may be contrasted with an old-fashioned model, or the opportunities for a man with a college education contrasted with those for a high-school dropout. Contrast provides emphasis and illuminates the advantages of the advertised product.

Before-and-after advertising makes use of contrast. A situation is presented before the product is used and then a revised situation is presented after product use. Although this type of illustration may be effective in revealing a product benefit, there is a tendency to overdramatize the changes. The less dramatic, but more acceptable, before-and-after illustration keeps all details in the before-and-after picture exactly the same, except those that picture the changes brought about by the product.

Magnification of a Detail

With so many competitive products on the market, the product differences may not provide major impact. Magnification techniques are used to emphasize specific advantages—a steam iron may be magnified to reveal the water window, a cigarette may be enlarged to show the charcoal granules in its filter. Sometimes arrows, darts, a magnifying glass, or a pointing object is used to emphasize the detail. The relationship between the emphasized part and the rest of the product should also be shown.

Symbolic Illustrations

Symbolic illustrations portray abstract qualities or traits. Abstractions such as dependability, quality, prosperity, respectability, and speed are difficult to communicate; their symbolic representations are used to provide comprehension.

Occasionally an abstraction may be converted into a physical reality, such as "A Man You Can Lean On," which is illustrated by depicting a leaning man. Here the symbol is correlated with an idea in an easily understood manner.

Which Method of Illustration Works Best?

A number of research firms have measured the attention that advertisements have received over the years. Although these measurements are not correlated with sales, there are indications that some types of illustrations are more effective in attracting attention than others. Generally the higher scoring ads are those with the standard layout using a single illustration that occupies more than half of the ad's total area. Illustrations showing the product in use as well as the result of having used it score better than average. Injecting a story (dramatization of a situation) into the illustration increases chances of attracting attention. Before-and-after advertising also does well.[3]

PHOTOGRAPHY AND ARTWORK

An illustration must be viewed not only creatively and visually but also technically. It is important to determine the medium and technique which best fits the creative and productive needs. Advertising artists generally use comparatively few mediums. The selection of the medium is based on artistic suitability, mechanical fitness, time, and expense.

The advertiser should keep in mind that the reader expects from an advertising illustration such qualities as interest, truth, drama, and the clear presentation or the vivid enhancement of the sales idea. These requirements do not suggest the superiority of either handwork or photography but depend on the particular needs of the communication. If the message requires the personal interpretation of the artist, then drawing or painting are recommended. If the requirements include microscopic detail, authentic realism in form and color, or instantaneous action, the camera can capture these in a split second.

Photography

The trend toward realism has hit advertising; the largest proportion of all advertisements feature photography, a medium whose strength is accuracy, realism, and a capacity for minute detail. Research has indicated that everything else being equal, photographic illustrations receive higher readership.

The desire for realism is even more obvious in the selection of models for photographs. Pictures of aloof beauties have good attention-getting value but are often disappointing in their impact. Short men, older

[3]David Ogilvy and Joel Raphaelson, "Research on Advertising Techniques That Work—And Don't Work," p. 15.

women, and models wearing glasses are used with increasing frequency, as are people with broken noses, crooked mouths, and even bald heads. A great many men and women who appear in today's advertisements are not professional models.

Photos may be secured from a stock-photo service which maintains a file of photographs of almost every conceivable subject. These range from photographs of historical landmarks to posed scenes of housewives in the supermarket. Catalogs of photos are available from large photo services. Reproduction rights to these photos may be given to the advertiser for a fee.

The stock photo, however, is not useful for every occasion. Moreover, the advertiser runs the risk that the same pieces of photography might be used by another advertiser because no exclusive rights to stock photos are granted.[4]

Photographers are often commissioned to take photos; this is relatively expensive but common to advertising—budget permitting. Some photographers charge high fees for their services; moreover, if any individuals appear in the ad they must be compensated.

Drawn or Painted Illustration

Many types of artwork are available for advertising, in the form of single black-and-white line drawings, oil or acrylic paintings, wash drawings, pastels, scratchboard drawings, grease-crayon drawings, or dry-brush drawings. Illustrators have greater freedom of expression than photographers. They can create their own scenes and models.

Line Drawings
Line is the most direct means of artistic expression and has the virtues of simplicity and sharp handling of detail. Line drawings, commonly made with pen and black ink, are easier and less expensive to reproduce than those in tone. However, there is no continuous blending of color from light to dark as in photographs; instead the drawing is made of solid blacks and pure whites. The type of line drawing selected depends upon the paper stock on which it will be printed. A good, smooth paper will reproduce fine lines close together with a sharp distinctive clarity. If newsprint is to be used, it is wise to draw broad lines and to leave plenty of white space.

EXHIBIT 14.13
An Example of a Line Drawing with Water-color Wash

---

[4]Richard M. Schlemmer, *Handbook of Advertising Art Production*, 2nd ed. (Englewood Cliffs, N.J.: Prentice-Hall Inc., 1976), p. 147.

Wash Drawing and Oil

Wash drawings provide the ability to emphasize important portions of a picture. The color or shading on the drawing is "washed" on with a brush to give the desired tonal values. Most wash drawings are water-color renderings which have been executed in a single color. The color values are reduced by the addition of water. Properly executed wash drawings are ideal for the rendering of fashion ads, particularly where there is a need for emphasis on fashion detail.

Oil permits a wide range of effects, in both black and white and in color. Its strengths lie in power, solidity, and range; in fact the tonal range of oil gives it one illustrative advantage over its principal competitor, the color photograph. However, oil presents special problems in reproduction. Brush marks or lumps of paint may catch the light unequally. Moreover, it is almost impossible to make a thoroughly satisfactory plate for a black and white printing of an oil painting in full color. Currently acrylic painting is replacing oil.

Scratchboard

Scratchboard is an art technique which may be utilized to duplicate the effect of wood engravings. A board coated with a thick, white clay surface is covered with black poster paint or drawing ink, and white lines are scratched into the black areas with a sharp scratch knife. The result is a series of crisp and precise white lines on a black surface. Because it is time consuming and expensive, it tends to be used for special effects.

SUMMARY

Although art and layout are the creative elements in advertising, they are guided, but not limited, by a number of principles. Layout is the architectural design for the elements of the advertisement. Visualization is the formation of the mental image which is translated into the illustration (the picture portion of the advertisement) and the layout. Layout performs a number of functions, among which are the provision of a blueprint to meet all mechanical requirements and the blending of all creative abilities in the preparation of the advertisement.

The layout process generally includes the preparation of a thumbnail sketch, a rough, a comprehensive, and a mechanical. A good layout should attract attention and have balance, movement, proportion, unity, clarity, simplicity, and emphasis.

A number of methods may be used to present an illustration, and the method selected depends on the specific advertisement and its objectives. Artwork for these illustrations may be done in pencil, crayon, charcoal, or paint, or through photography, engraving, or etching.

QUESTIONS FOR DISCUSSION

1. What is meant by visualization? How would you visualize impending danger? happiness? apprehension?
2. What are the functions of layout? Which of these are most important?
3. What are the major requisites of a good layout? Must all of these appear in one layout in order for it to be effective?
4. Select some ads that represent formal balance and informal balance. Do you consider these layouts appropriate for the products they present? Why?
5. Select a number of ads which you believe use proportion effectively. Explain how they achieve their effects.
6. How is emphasis created in layout?
7. Briefly define *gaze motion* and *structural motion*. Why are these devices useful in layout?
8. Select a number of ads that represent different methods of illustration. Which do you consider most effective? Why?
9. What kinds of illustrations are best for a product that is in the introductory stage of its life cycle? The competitive stage? Explain.
10. Why is photography used in advertisements? What are the advantages and disadvantages of this illustrative technique?

KEY TERMS

layout	movement (or sequence)
visualization	gaze motion
illustration	structural motion
thumbnail sketch	unity
rough	white space
pasteup (or mechanical)	clarity
balance	emphasis
optical center	picture window format
proportion	Mondrian format

Prepare a rough layout for an advertising campaign designed to attract students to your university. Explain the concepts of layout illustration and indicate the artwork you intend to use.

15

Creative Print Production

Printing, as we know it today, has developed from years of experiment. As early as the fifth century, jade, ivory, and metal seals, and carved blocks of wood were inked and stamped on paper in China and Japan. In the Western world, wood blocks were first used for printing pictures; later, a block was made for each page of a book carrying both words and pictures. With the invention of movable type between the years 1440 and 1450 by Johann Gutenberg, type-printed books began to appear. Probably the earliest type-printed book is the famous Gutenberg Bible printed between 1453 and 1456.

In 1846, Richard Hoe of New York patented the first rotary press, in which the type was placed on revolving cylinders. This development and the combination of presses into great multiple units made the rapid production of newspapers possible. Nevertheless it took 500 years to develop Gutenberg's press into its modern complex counterpart. In fact most of the technical developments since Gutenberg's time have been to facilitate the speed with which printing can be accomplished.

After the copy and artwork have been selected and the total layout approved, they must be converted into materials for reproducing the advertisement in media. The process by which this material is prepared for reproduction in media such as newspapers, magazines, and direct mail is called print production. Reproduction of advertisements for print media requires decisions in three major areas: determining the process to be used for printing the ads, choosing the type and typesetting method for reproducing the copy, and selecting the technique for reproducing the illustration.

THE PRINTING PROCESSES

The reproduction of advertisements for print media requires both technical and creative decisions. The techniques of mechanical reproduction have improved considerably throughout the years and newer and more efficient methods are continually developed. Although many of these processes are considered mechanical in nature, their proper representation requires the capabilities of skilled artisans. Moreover, there is a tendency to overlook an important requisite for effective reproduction—the creative aspect. Creativity in advertising encompasses more than bright, witty copy and unusual visual representations; it includes close attention to the total advertisement, which covers the mechanical assembly of details.

Today most advertising is prepared through the following printing processes: letterpress, lithography and gravure, which use printing presses, and silk screen printing, which does not.

Letterpress

Letterpress, or *relief* printing, is similar to rubber stamping—the letters are raised and backward. The stamp is pressed into the ink and then transfers the image to the paper. In the early letterpress process each letter was cast from a mold. The paper was fed into the press by hand and the inked type was brought into contact with it by the pressure of a hand-operated platen or flat plate—thus the term *letterpress*.

There are three types of modern letterpress equipment: platen, flatbed cylinder, and rotary press (see Figure 15.1). The *platen* press obtains an impression by bringing two flat surfaces together. In the clamshell type, the platen rocks against a form placed in vertical position against the press bed and held securely by a clamp. The *flatbed* (or cylinder) press prints by means of a cylinder which rolls against the form. The paper, which is held to the cylinder by grippers, is carried between the press and the form. The bed moves back and forth on its track, and, as the cylinder turns, the form advances with it. The *rotary press* is particularly effective for high-speed work and for long runs. In the rotary press, printing is done from curved plates wrapped around the plate cylinders. The printed material is carried on a revolving cylinder, while another revolving cylinder impresses the paper on the plate. Inking is accomplished by a roller which is in continuous contact with the plate cylinder.

Lithography

In *lithography*,, or *planographic printing*,. the ink is transferred from a flat surface to the paper. This technique employs the principle that water and grease do not mix. The non-image area of the plate is given a coating of gum or arabic that retains water; the design area is treated to accept oil-based substances. Water is applied and, because of the incompatibility of water and grease, the design area refuses the water although the rest of the surface accepts it. When the ink is passed over the printed surface, the design area accepts it, since it is oil based, but the watered area does not.

FIGURE 15.1   Types of Letterpress

PLATEN PRESS

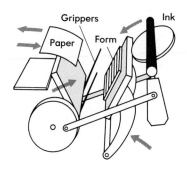

DRUM CYLINDER

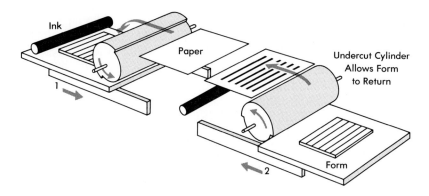

WEB-FED
ROTARY PERFECTING

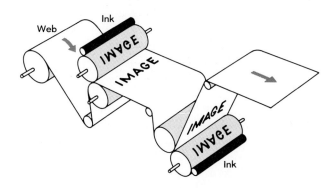

Source: From *Handbook of Advertising Art Production,* 3/e by Richard M. Schlemmer, pp. 44, 58, 72 & 127. Copyright © 1984 by Richard M. Schlemmer. Reprinted by permission of Prentice-Hall, Inc., Englewood Cliffs, New Jersey.

**FIGURE 15.2   Offset Lithographic
Press**

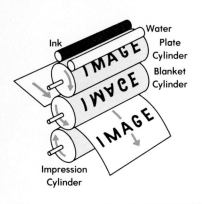

Source: From *Handbook of Advertising Art Production*, 3/e by Richard M. Schlemmer, pp. 44, 58, 72 & 127. Copyright © 1984 by Richard M. Schlemmer. Reprinted by permission of Prentice-Hall, Inc., Englewood Cliffs, New Jersey.

In *direct lithography* the impression is transferred directly to the paper. In *offset lithography*, illustrated in Figure 15.2, an additional cylinder, known as a *blanket cylinder*, receives the image from the plate before transferring it to the paper. The rubber blanket, unlike the metal plate, permits printing on less expensive paper and enables finer details to be printed on the irregular surface of rough or uncoated paper stock.

Offset lithography is currently used for the majority of printed advertisements. Offset is less expensive than letterpress for short runs and is especially adaptable for large-sized work because there is little preparation required in offset lithography, which results in savings in both time and money. Moreover, it will print on almost any surface and is especially suitable for printing on metal.

Gravure

The gravure process uses *intaglio* printing; *intaglio* means *cut in* or *incised*. In this method of printing the design is cut or etched into the plate. The plate is covered with ink, filling all the wells. The surface of the plate is wiped clean by a doctor blade (a flexible steel scraper) which removes all the surplus ink. The plate is brought in contact with paper and the ink-filled wells produce the printed results. Shades in color are reproduced in accordance with size and depth of the wells. The deep wells contain the most ink and produce a strong color; the shallow wells, with less ink, produce a lighter color. Soft effects and deep shadows can be produced in a single impression by varying the depth of wells (see Figure 15.3).

Rotogravure is a combination of the rotary and web-fed press and photogravure. *Roto* is an intaglio process printed from paper rolls at a high speed. The most common example of roto is the illustrated Sunday supplement. Rotogravure is an excellent medium for the reproduction of the color photography and produces deep rich effects. However, it is a time-consuming process and does not reproduce detailed copy text matter as clearly as by other means.

Gravure plates are expensive, but *newsprint*, the paper used for gravure, is comparatively inexpensive. The use of gravure for short press-runs is neither practical nor economical because of high plate costs, but it is good for long runs.

Silk Screen

The silk screen printing process, shown in Figure 15.4, is one of the oldest methods of reproduction, although graphic arts purists claim it is not real printing. However, it has been used successfully by advertisers for poster displays and packaging.

Silk screening, known as *serigraphy*, uses the stencil principle and requires no printing plates. The screen, which is a woven mesh made traditionally of silk (although today nylon, polyester, and wire cloth can be used effectively) is stretched on a wooden frame. The stencil design is applied either by painting directly on the screen, from a prepared stencil film which has been cut and attached to the screen, or by coating the screen with a photosensitive emulsion and developing the image photographically. The stencil blocks out the nonprinting areas. Ink is

FIGURE 15.3   The Gravure Press

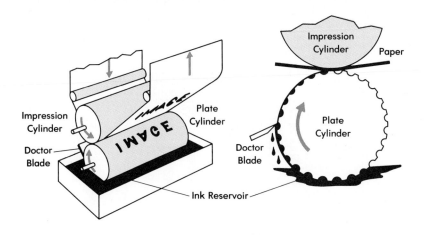

Source: From *Handbook of Advertising Art Production,* 3/e by Richard M. Schlemmer, pp. 44, 58, 72 & 127. Copyright © 1984 by Richard M. Schlemmer. Reprinted by permission of Prentice-Hall, Inc., Englewood Cliffs, New Jersey.

forced through the mesh of the screen with a squeegee. The printing ink penetrates through portions of the screen not covered by the stencil and reproduces the image on the printing surface.

The prime advantage of silk screen printing is its economy for extremely short runs. Since it is essentially a hand process, it is possible to go into the silk-screen printing business with less capital outlay than for any other area of the graphic arts. The extended use of silk screen printing to all kinds of surfaces has brought it into more widespread acceptance and resulted in automated means of production, so that fully automatic presses for silk-screen printing are now available.

TYPOGRAPHY

In order to reproduce the message of a print ad, type must be set. Because the advertiser should be able to evaluate its readability and appropriateness, a knowledge of *typography,* the art of specifying and setting type, becomes important and useful.

Categories of Type

Several terms are used to classify type: among them are *typeface, type group,* and *type family.* There are many thousands of kinds of type available and designers are continually creating new ones—a designer's interpretation of a basic form of type is called a *typeface.*

Typeface Groups
The various kinds of typefaces prepared by designers are usually placed in groups based on the similarities of their design. Major type design

RE 15.4   Silk Screen Process

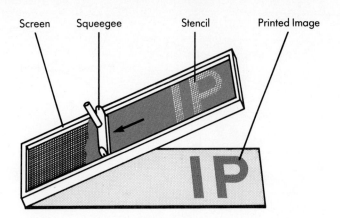

Source: Adapted from William P. Spence and David G. Vequist, *Graphic Reproduction*, (Peoria, Ill.: Chas. A. Bennett Co., Inc. 1980), p. 28.

groups, illustrated in Figure 15.5, are the Roman old style, Modern Roman, Gothic san serif, and the contemporary Gothic with square serifs.

1. *Roman old style* has wedged-shaped *serifs* (cross lines at the end of the strokes) which are bent and rounded off at the stem. *Garamond* (a designer's name for this typeface) is an example of old-style type.

2. *Modern Roman* has distinct, thin, straight clean-cut serifs, and contrasting light and heavy strokes, as characterized by *Bodoni*, the display face in this text.

3. *Gothic sans serif*, as the name implies, is without serifs and is easily identified. The strokes of each letter are even and uniform, giving it a modern feel and tone. The absence of serifs and the uniform weight of all strokes makes the block-letter group less easy to read than Roman faces. It is wise to set *sans serif* typefaces in shorter paragraphs. *Futura* is an example of Gothic type.

4. *Contemporary Gothic*, similar to Gothic, contains uniform strokes in its letters. Unlike Gothic it has serifs which are square in shape. This typeface is also called *slab serif*. *Girder* is an example of this slab serif type and the name reflects the buildinglike quality of the letters.

5. *Miscellaneous*. There are a number of other basic typefaces which do not fall clearly into any of the above groups. These general classifications include *Text, Old Fashioned, oversized serifs, Cursive unjoined script,* and *Brush.* These kinds of type are not used too

FIGURE 15.5   Illustrating Type Groups

These four general classifications are listed below in a typical sample face:

1 ROMAN OLD STYLE
wedge serifs

2 MODERN ROMAN
fine hair lines

3 GOTHIC no serifs

4 CONTEMPORARY GOTHIC

Several other general classifications are used to identify various categories. Some of these are:

5 𝕿𝕰𝕏𝕿 imitates medieval writing

6 OLD FASHIONED oversize serifs

7 *Script Modern Handwriting*

8 *CURSIVE unjoined script*

9 *BRUSH*

frequently in advertising. Although they add some freshness and excitement, they are generally less easy to read than other typefaces.

Type Family
A type family uses a basic typeface (such as Garamond, Futura, Bodoni, or Girder) but offers different sizes as well as variations of this one design—such as *regular, italic, light, bold, book, light condensed, book condensed,* etc. Thus, even if only one kind of type is selected there are many different kinds of presentations that can be used (see Figure 15.6).

FIGURE 15.6   Variations in a Type Family

Typeface: Garamond
Type group: Old style roman
Type family: See variations below

Regular

Type font refers to the complete assortment of capital and lower case letters and figures of a single size typeface, as shown. New techniques may result in the development of new fonts, including not only old-style figures, but foreign characters and special superior figures. Type font refers to the complete assortment of capital and lower case letters and figures of a single size typeface, as shown. New techniques may result in

Light

Type font refers to the complete assortment of capital and lower case letters and figures of a single size typeface, as shown. New techniques may result in the development of new fonts, including not only old-style figures, but foreign characters and special superior figures. Type font refers to the complete assortment of capital and lower case letters and figures of a single size typeface, as shown. New techniques may result in

Book

Type font refers to the complete assortment of capital and lower case letters and figures of a single size typeface, as shown. New techniques may result in the development of new fonts, including not only old-style figures, but foreign characters and special superior figures. Type font refers to the complete assortment of capital and lower case letters and figures of a single size typeface, as shown. New techniques may result in

**Light
Condensed**

Type font refers to the complete assortment of capital and lower case letters and figures of a single size typeface, as shown. New techniques may result in the development of new fonts, including not only old-style figures, but foreign characters and special superior figures. Type font refers to the complete assortment of capital and lower case letters and figures of a single size typeface, as shown. New techniques may

**Book
Condensed**

Type font refers to the complete assortment of capital and lower case letters and figures of a single size typeface, as shown. New techniques may result in the development of new fonts, including not only old-style figures, but foreign characters and special superior figures. Type font refers to the complete assortment of capital and lower case letters and figures of a single size typeface, as

FIGURE 15.7   A Complete Font

abcdefghijklmnopqrstuvwxyz
ABCDEFGHIJKLMNOPQRSTUVWXYZ
1234567890&1234567890$$¢£%
AÇ ÐELØ ÆŒßaçđeløäẽôèfi
(:;,.!?·-""''/#*)[†‡§(())1234567890]

abcdefghijklmnopqrstuvwxyz
ABCDEFGHIJKLMNOPQRSTUVWXYZ1234567890
ABCDEFGHIJKLMNOPQRSTUVWXYZ1234567890

Type Font

Type font refers to the complete assortment of capital and lower-case letters and figures of a single size typeface, as shown in Figure 15.7. New techniques may result in the development of new fonts, including not only old-style figures, but foreign characters and special superior figures.

Type Measurement

The Point

The *point* is the unit of measurement for indicating the size of type in depth. The term refers to the vertical measurement of the letter, which includes not only the body of the letter, but its ascender and descender. *Ascenders* are found in the letters *b, d, f, h, k,* and *l. Descenders* are found in the letters *g, j, p, q,* and *y.* There are 72 points to an inch, and a type size of 72 points is quite large and usually reserved for headlines (see Figure 15.8). Body, or text, type is generally from six to fourteen points; headline, or display type, is larger—generally from eighteen to ninety-six points.

FIGURE 15.8   Sizes of Type

ABCDEFGHIJKLMNOPQRSTUVWXYZabcdefghijklmnopqrstuvwxyz $1234567890$1234567890
6 POINT

ABCDEFGHIJKLMNOPQRSTUVWXYZabcdefghijklmnopqrstuvwxyz $123
8 POINT

ABCDEFGHIJKLMNOPQRSTUabcdefghijklmnopqrstu $456
10 POINT

AVWXYZABCDEFGHIavwxyzbcdefghijklm $567
12 POINT

AJKLMNOPQRSTUVWanopqrstuvw $890
14 POINT

AXYZABCDEFGaxyzabcdef $123
18 POINT

AHIJKLMaghijklm $123
24 POINT

ANOPQRanopqr45
30 POINT

ASTUVastuv 67
36 POINT

AWXawxy9
48 POINT

AYazab 0
60 POINT

AZacd 1
72 POINT

The Pica

The pica is the unit of measurement that indicates the width of the line in which the type is to be placed. There are 6 picas to an inch and in fitting copy picas are used to calculate how many characters will fit the width of a line. The length of a line of text in this book is 26 picas.

A standard unit of measurement is the *pica-em*, frequently called an *em*. This derives from the letter *M* which is closest to a square in design; a 12-point *M* is 12 points wide. Since 12 points measure ⅙ of an inch—the equivalent of one pica—hence the *pica-em*. The *em* is particularly useful as a spacing element for paragraphs, indentations, and dashes.

Criteria for Selecting Type

All the principles of good layout are applicable to the type in advertisements. There should be balance, unity, movement, clarity, and simplicity, as illustrated by Exhibit 15.1. In addition, since type performs a number of functions for an advertisement, it should offer a pleasing appearance, encourage reading, provide emphasis, and project a sense of continuity.

Harmony

Avoid too many styles of type in one advertisement. Usually one or two styles is enough, but if they are to be combined, they should complement each other. Color contrasts may be achieved by using a heavier weight for the headline and by putting the slogan or tag line in *italics*.

Readability

The most important attribute of type is its readability, which is a function of many factors: a type's design, the size of an individual letter, the length of a line, and the spacing between lines. Lines that are too long are difficult to read; lines that are too short present a choppy appearance. The number of characters that appear in a line depends on the size of the type, but, generally, 35 to 55 characters to a line provide excellent reading quality. Lines set in all capital letters are harder to read than those using capital and lower-case letters.

Leading Requirements

Spacing between lines of type is called *leading*. Figure 15.9 shows the traditional practice of using thin strips of metal between the lines of type to produce white space. *Solid* is the term applied when no leading is used. When type is set solid, the only white space appearing between the lines is that provided by the shoulders of the pieces of type from which the letters are printed.

Leading, like type, is measured in points and expressed in relationship to type size. For example, 12-point type with two-point leading is indicated as 12 on 14 or 12/14. If no leading is used the specification would be 12/12.

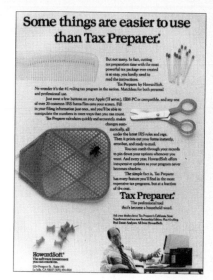

EXHIBIT 15.1
An Example of Simplicity, Clarity, Readability, and Harmony in Type

FIGURE 15.9 Inserting Line Spacing

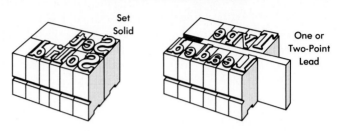

HOW LINE SPACING IS INSERTED

Source: From *Handbook of Advertising Art Production*, 3/e by Richard M. Schlemmer, pp. 44, 58, 72 & 127. Copyright © 1984 by Richard M. Schlemmer. Reprinted by permission of Prentice-Hall, Inc., Englewood Cliffs, New Jersey.

Emphasis

Type can provide emphasis as well as a sense of excitement to an ad. Its creative use can support the message the copy is required to deliver. (See Exhibit 15.2).

Continuity

Type can supply an element of continuity in a campaign. Bloomingdale's department store, for example, has exclusive rights to a typeface and the same type style appears in most of the store's graphic material to establish continuity and ease of recognition (see Exhibit 15.3).

**EXHIBIT 15.2
Using Type Creatively**

EXHIBIT 15.3
Continuity in Type Style

HOW NOT TO USE TYPOGRAPHY

CRITIC'S CORNER
Jojoba jumble

Some old print principles are violated with this ad, and it's a shame because the subject is beauty. The Indian legend, the long-haired model, the headband, the earrings. But beauty does not prevail here.

The reader's eye is sorely challenged. Starting off, the model's face is both facing right (the reader's right) and placed far to the right, leading the eye off the page—away from the beginning of headline and copy. (The legend box appears left behind, as well.) The headline type is hard to read, particularly since there is no space between words of varying typefaces. Then there is the shampoo bottle running up through the head and subhead (a lost subhead that ties in the aforementioned legend—notice the word legend right there on top of the bottle in question), and the fact that there are too many bottles anyway, counting the repeat in the ever-present coupon.

The ad cries for the serenity of the upper left portion, the wasted part. There's just too much clutter in the bottom third of the page—alas, where the sell is.

Source: "Critic's Corner," *Advertising Age* (August 16, 1982), p. N-42. Copyright © 1982 by Crain Communications, Inc. Reprinted with permission from Advertising Age.

TYPESETTING

From the invention of movable type in the fifteenth century down to the middle of the twentieth century, all printers' type for continuous reading was cast in metal. All typographic design was conditioned by the constraints of metal technology. Now, with the development of film setting, the constraints and limitations of metal technology no longer apply; the attractiveness of the presentation as well as the speed and cost of producing the ad control the typesetting choices.

In the past the basic method of producing type was known as *hot composition*, since molten metal was employed. Relatively few of the "hot metal" techniques remain in use. Some of the concepts of this technology have been applied to the newer typesetting techniques.

Cold Type

Cold type is so named because there is no molten metal involved in its production; its output is a result of photography, and the image is produced directly on film or paper. *Cold type composition*, as a term, is frequently confused with *photocomposition;* the first is the broad heading encompassing several techniques and the second refers to a form of cold type composition.

Several cold type techniques are used to produce large size letters, such as those used in headlines. These include *hand lettering, hand setting of letters printed on sheets*, and *photolettering.*[1] The first two, as the names indicate, are produced by hand. Photolettering is done by machine into which negatives of complete alphabets are placed. A light shines through the desired letter to record it on sensitized paper.

Hand lettering can produce exceptionally beautiful, as well as aesthetically pleasing, results. Hand setting of letters on printed sheets may require competence and is a tedious technique. However it offers special capabilities to smaller firms.

Strike-On Composition

Strike-on setting is a cold-type technique. It covers all instruments which, on the depression of keys, produce an immediate image on paper, such as the IBM "golf ball" electric typewriters.

IBM Selectric composers are, in effect, electric typewriters that can set camera-ready copy up to 72 spaces wide in type sizes from 6 to 12 points on magnetic tape for higher-speed composition. The quality of this copy may not equal that of the hot-metal machine system; however, it offers designers and publishers the opportunity to see their own copy.

Strike-on is less aesthetically pleasing than other techniques, but it is a rapid and efficient means of typesetting. It is relatively inexpensive and is frequently used in direct-mail advertising.

Computer Typography

Photocomposition was developed in the 1930s; however, advancement in computer technology accelerated its application and use. A computerized photocomposition system involves the use of keyboard entry devices, computers, and output devices.

The typesetting process starts at the video display terminal (VDT) where an operator punches a keyboard.[2] A cathode-ray tube (which looks like a television screen) is above the keyboard and shows what is being typed as well as recording corrections. The material can be stored and called up later for editing. Type material may also be stored digitally

---

[1]Roy P. Nelson, *The Design of Advertising*, 4th ed. (Dubuque, Iowa: W. C. Brown Co., 1981), pp. 155–156.

[2]Roy P. Nelson, *The Design of Advertising*, p. 159.

in a computer that uses a laser beam to expose the material on film or paper.

The output device involves a phototypesetter, whose basic function is to expose the character being set to photosensitive film or paper. As noted this can be done by cathode-ray tube or by laser exposure. Currently, there are four basic categories of phototypesetters based on computer technology that relate to how the characters are stored, and how they are generated[3] (see Figure 15.10).

1. *Photo/Optic.* Electromechanical methods are used in photo optics. Characters are stored photographically in a negative form in film strips or other devices. A light source is flashed and the image of the character is projected through a lens to film or paper. The entire character is exposed as a unit.

2. *Photo/Scan.* Storage of the characters is photographic. They are scanned through cathode ray tubes and generated piecemeal (at high speeds, much like a television picture). The completed character is built up from dots or lines, depending on the generating mechanism.

3. *Digital/CRT/Scan.* Master characters are stored digitally. They are generated similarly to photo/scan devices by electronic scanning. Each font is a digitalized record of the original character (there are no photographic masters in the machines). This direct approach permits extremely high operating speed.

4. *Digital/Laser.* This technique also uses digital storage for the characters; however, it uses a laser beam which exposes the material on film or paper with considerable reliability. No cathode ray tubes are necessary and extremely high speeds are possible.

Cold type techniques offer high speed capabilities in almost unlimited variations. There are many new developments and these should offer increasing benefits which require future evaluation.

PHOTOPLATEMAKING

Photoplatemaking is the process used to convert the original art material, drawings or photographs, into printing plates or other image carriers required by the print media carrying the ads. (Information concerning a specific medium's requirements is available in SRDS *Print Media Production Data Directory*.) For offset and gravure printing films are sent to the publications to produce their own plates or cylinders. For letterpress the advertiser is required to furnish *photoengravings*, combinations of photography and chemical engraving.

---

[3]Edward M. Gottschall, *Graphic Communications 80s*, p. 143

FIGURE 15.10 Computer Techniques for Storing and Generating Type

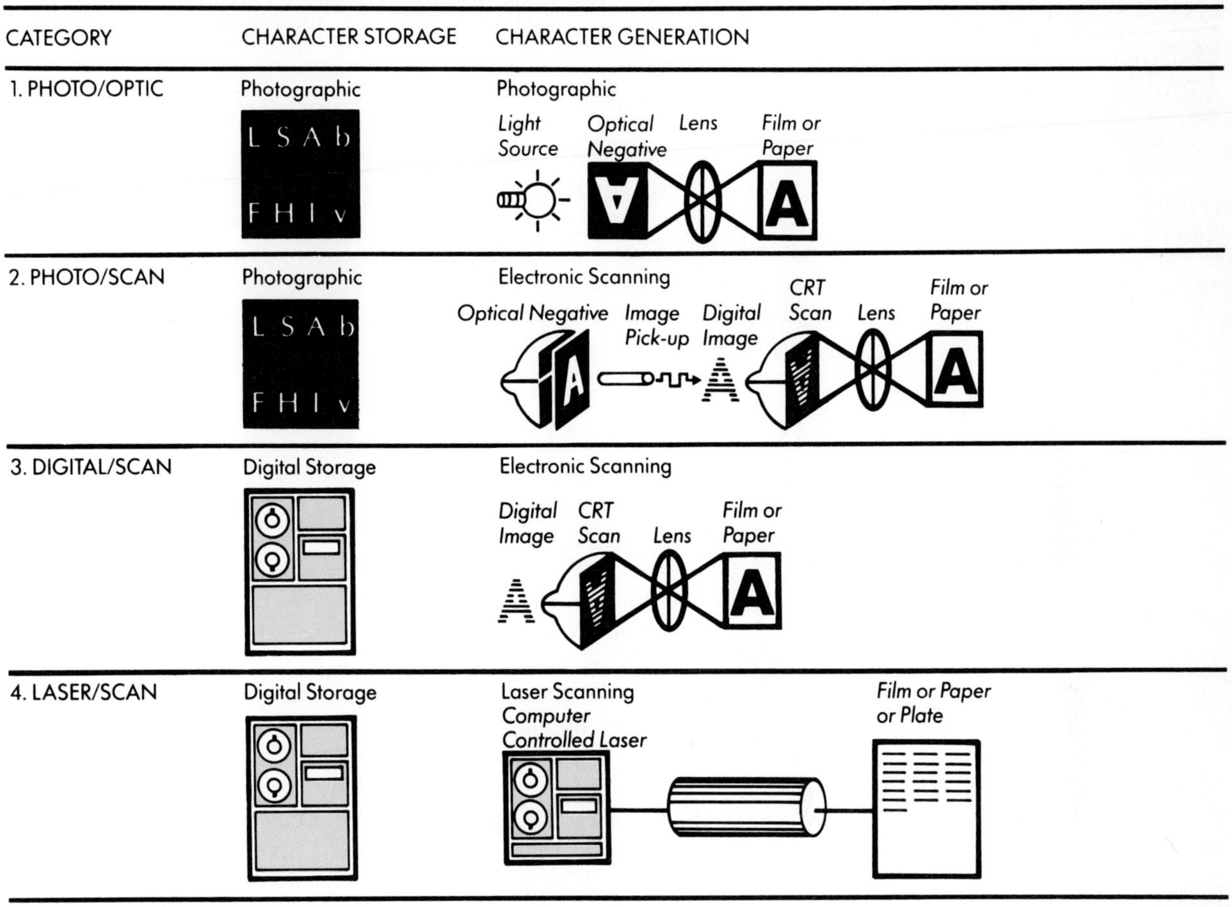
CATEGORY
CHARACTER STORAGE
CHARACTER GENERATION
1. PHOTO/OPTIC
Photographic
L S A b
F H I v
Photographic
Light Source
Optical Negative
Lens
Film or Paper
2. PHOTO/SCAN
Photographic
L S A b
F H I v
Electronic Scanning
Optical Negative
Image Pick-up
Digital Image
CRT Scan
Lens
Film or Paper
3. DIGITAL/SCAN
Digital Storage
Electronic Scanning
Digital Image
CRT Scan
Lens
Film or Paper
4. LASER/SCAN
Digital Storage
Laser Scanning
Computer Controlled Laser
Film or Paper or Plate

Source: From *Graphic Communication '80s* by Edward M. Gottschall. Copyright © 1981. p. 143. Reprinted by permission of Prentice-Hall, Inc., Englewood Cliffs, New Jersey.

Kinds of Plates

The plates that are prepared for reproducing advertisements include line, halftone, and combination plates.

Line Plates

In preparing a line plate a photograph of the art is taken with a high-contrast film. The negative is placed against a sensitized plate and exposed to a strong light. Since the tonal values of the negative are in reverse, the strong light passes through the design areas to the plate.

When the line plate is prepared for letterpress printing, an emulsion is used to form a protective acid-resistant covering over the printing

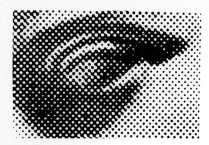

EXHIBIT 15.4
A Dot Pattern

areas of the plate. When the plate is dipped in an acid bath, the nondesign area is washed away, leaving a printing image in relief on the surface of the plate. This is the process of photoengraving. When the illustration is prepared for offset lithography a different kind of plate is used and it does not have to be etched.

Line plates reproduce drawings that are of only two tones. They are reproduced from copy made up entirely of solid blacks and whites and contain no tonal values that are present in photography. Pen-and-ink drawings, newspaper clippings, type proofs, typewritten copy, charcoal, and crayon drawings are accepted copy for reproduction in line engraving.

Line color plates may be printed in any number of colors, but a plate must be produced for each color. Art copy is prepared in black-and-white with overlays indicating the color areas and the color scheme.

Halftone Plates

A halftone plate is used to print continuous tones such as those found in photographs, wash drawings, and paintings. The process is the same as for line plates, except for the photographic process used when making the negatives.

A halftone reproduces the tone pattern shades, from white through black, of a continuous tone image. These tones are achieved by breaking up the tone values of a picture into dots of various sizes, as shown in Exhibit 15.4.

The dots are created by photographing the copy through a halftone screen, a frame containing two sheets of clear glass, put together so that the parallel lines etched on their surfaces form squares. This screen is placed between the lens and negative of the camera and light from the photographed object passes through the squares in the screen and spreads on its way to the negative. The dot pattern on the negative is determined by the light reflected from the photograph. The dark solid areas show up as large dots and the highlights as widely scattered small dots. The size and density of these dots ultimately determine the amount of ink that will be transferred onto the paper. The eye mixes the individual dots that appear on the printing surface to produce the effect of varying tones of gray.

The choice of the screen depends on the requirements of the publication, the amount of detail required, and the smoothness of the paper. A fine screen will give a rough paper a smudged appearance. The higher the screen number the more dots to the square inch and the greater the fidelity and detail in the resulting reproduction.

Ben Day Process

To apply the tonal look to a line plate, the *Ben Day process* may be used. In 1881, Benjamin Day designed a mechanical process for producing interesting and effective tones and shades while using line engraving. In the original method, the shading pattern was applied directly to

FIGURE 15.11   Combination Plates

the letterpress plate. Selection was made from patterns which were combined to offer endless variety of tints and patterns.

Ben Day may be applied to the negative instead of the plate, or to the original artwork. It results in a print that lacks the blending of tone that appears in the halftone, but it offers greater uniformity of pattern. It is less expensive than halftone engraving.

Today *Ben Day* has become a generic term used to denote a screen tint of a color produced by reducing an area to a uniform pattern of tiny dots. Although shading is available in a wide variety of patterns, unless otherwise specified, the term *Ben Day* implies a dot pattern.

Combination Plates

Occasionally the engraver wishes to combine the clarity of line with the tonality of halftone in one engraving. To achieve this he combines a line negative and a halftone negative etched on copper or zinc to make one printing plate. A combination plate can also be made of several line and several halftone negatives which are stripped together to make a composite or combined unit.

Figure 15.11 indicates the following combinations:

Mortise   A mortise is a place in an engraving where part of the halftone plate has been cut out to insert type or other illustrative line material.

Surprint   Line work may be superimposed on the halftone area, thus appearing as a solid color on top of the halftone background.

Dropout   Line work may be removed or "dropped out" of the half-tone, thus appearing as white (or the paper color) against the halftone background.

Duplicate Plates

While the cost of preparing a print ad tends to be significantly lower than, for example, the cost of preparing a television commercial, it may still involve a significant outlay. One method of reducing this cost is to provide duplicate material. Frequently an advertisement may run in several publications simultaneously so that duplicates must be sent to the various publications. Occasionally, in order to produce more copies, a number of impressions may be printed simultaneously on one press. Advertisers may also wish to send duplicating material to their dealers to use in cooperative advertising efforts. There are a number of methods for producing duplicate materials, and selection depends on the publication's requirements.

Four Color Process

Although stark realism and news illustrations appear more believable in black-and-white pictures, the use of color may bring returns in readership that compensate for the increased costs. Color is usually a prime requisite for food and cosmetics advertising.

Color serves many purposes besides attracting the reader. Additional functions include:

1. emphasizing some special part of the message or product;
2. representing objects or scenes with greater fidelity;
3. creating prestige for the product or advertiser;
4. fastening visual impressions in memory;
5. suggesting abstract qualities appropriate to the selling appeal;
6. stimulating a mood or feeling; or
7. indicating an attribute such as odor or taste.

The trend toward the increased use of color in advertising is accelerating. Audiences of media and potential purchases have vastly expanded, and a slight percentage of difference in the reaction to an advertisement may make the additional expenditure for color reproduction worthwhile. Moreover, items that were produced only in black, such as typewriters and telephones, now appear in a variety of colors. Kitchen appliances and bathroom fixtures are produced in many different hues and shades, while color is also becoming a fashion item of increasing importance.

The color selection process requires careful consideration. Some are *cool*, such as blues and greens, and others are *warm*, such as reds and orange. Dark colors suggest security; light colors suggest a sense of airiness. Odors may be connoted through colors—pale delicate colors seem to offer the scent of flowers.

Color Reproduction

Four-color process printing, although containing perhaps all colors of the rainbow, is usually reproduced by printing in yellow, red, and blue inks. A black plate is used to give more detail to the illustration. These plates are halftone plates, and each is made through a filter which enables the camera to register the intensity of the color being photographed.

Color separation is the division of a continuous tone multicolor original into several basic parts. Color filters are used in the photographic process.[4] Each filter separates one color in the original and allows it to be imposed on a negative. Red, blue, and yellow are primary colors. Subtractive *primaries* are complementary light colors—cyan (blue), magenta, yellow—because each is minus a primary light color. A subtractive primary color filter absorbs its complemented color. A magenta filter absorbs green, a cyan filter absorbs red, and a yellow filter absorbs blue.

To secure continuous tone-color images, such as in a color photograph, four separations are prepared through color filters: for yellow, cyan, magenta, and black. After color corrections are made, the separation negatives are used to make printing plates. Each color has a separate plate.

The engraver returns a complete set of color proofs and a set of progressives. *Progressives* usually consist of seven proofs: (1) a proof of the yellow plate; (2) a proof of the red plate; (3) a proof of the yellow and red plates printed together; (4) a proof of the blue plate; (5) a proof of the yellow, red and blue plates; (6) a proof of the black plate; and (7) a proof of the yellow, red, blue, and black plates printed together. (See essay following p. 262 for an example of progressive proofing.)

Each color is printed over the printed image of the other in perfect register. This overprinting of halftone dots, which relies on a blending of colors, reproduces a multicolor, continuous-tone copy.

---

[4]William P. Spence and David G. Vequist, *Graphic reproduction*, pp. 432–463.

Holograms

There are indications that *holograms*, which are three-dimensional photographic images, will appear in future advertising. Holograms have been used with significant effect on magazine covers and on credit cards; however, they are considered too expensive for advertising.

Graphic designers have been working with a new high-quality film developed by Polaroid which provides brighter and clearer holograms and may be massed produced economically.[5] With lowered costs holograms may be used to create more interest in packages, point-of-purchase displays, and direct-mail advertising.

Scheduling Print Production

Production decisions are the responsibility of the advertiser and/or the agency. Many individuals may be involved in the decision process which requires appropriate planning. A useful planning device is a time schedule.

A time schedule is prepared by working backwards from the *closing date*, the date when all the material must arrive at the media for publication. An estimate of the time needed for the plates or duplicating material permits a determination of when the material must be sent to the photoplatemaker so that it can be prepared and shipped to the publication on time. An estimate can then be made as to how much time is required for the selection and approval of the type and artwork and the preparation of the layout and copy.

SUMMARY

A number of creative and technical decisions are required for reproducing print ads. The printing process through which the ad is prepared must be selected. The methods that may be used include letterpress— relief printing from a raised surface, lithography—planographic printing from a flat surface, and gravure—intaglio printing from an incised (or etched) surface. In addition silk screen, which is essentially a hand technique requiring no printing plates, can be used.

The type most appropriate for the reading matter in the ad must be chosen. Type may be selected from numerous designers whose typefaces fall into groups classified as Roman old style, Modern Roman, Gothic, Contemporary Gothic, as well as numerous miscellaneous categories. For the selection of typeface there is a type family that offers different sizes and variations of this one design designated as regular, light, and bold. In selecting type consideration should be given to both its appearance and the functions to be performed.

---

[5]David Stipp, William M. Bulkeley and Sandra Ward, "Holograms," *Wall Street Journal* (January 28, 1986), p. 33.

The method for setting type must also be determined. The earlier used hot-metal techniques are rarely applied today. Most typesetting is done through cold type, including hand lettering, strike-on techniques, and computer typography methods.

Techniques for reproducing the illustrations in a print ad must also be selected. *Photoplatemaking* is the term used for the process of converting artwork and photography into printing plates. The kinds of plates that may be selected include line, halftone, or combination plates. The four-color process is widely used today since it offers many benefits in both the presentation of the ad and the manner in which it is perceived.

QUESTIONS FOR DISCUSSION

1. Select several print ads in which type is featured and discuss them from the following perspectives:
   — Do you consider the type used appropriate for the ad? Why?
   — Does the type selected detract from the ad? Why?
2. Select several four-color ads and discuss whether color contributes to the appearance and the viewer's perception of each ad.
3. What are the basic methods of printing? What are the major differences among these printing processes?
4. What kind of typeface is used in this book? What size type?
5. What is meant by *cold type*? Briefly describe a typesetting method using this technique.
6. How may the advertising message affect the kind of type selected for the advertisement?
7. What is the difference between a line plate and a halftone?
8. Briefly define *type font*, *point*, and *pica*.
9. What are the advantages of using color in advertising?
10. What colors are used in the four-color process? What are the progressive steps used for printing a four-color ad?

KEY TERMS

letterpress (relief printing)

platen

flatbed cylinder

rotary press

lithography (planographic printing)

direct lithography

offset lithography

blanket cylinder

gravure

intaglio

rotogravure

newsprint

silk screen (serigraphy)

typography

typeface

serif

type font

point

pica

pica - em

leading

hot composition

cold type

strike-on setting

photoplatemaking

photo engraving

halftone

mortise

surprint

dropout

Ben Day process

four-color process

color separation

primary colors

subtractive primaries

progressives

hologram

closing date

AD PRACTICE

Prepare the copy and a rough illustration for advertising a product used by hobbyists, (golfing, fishing, boating, for example) and select the magazine you wish it to appear in. Determine the size of the type that you would use in the headline, the company logo, and the body copy.

Check with SRDS *Print Media Production Data Directory* to determine the production requirements of the magazine you selected. Describe the method used for reproducing the illustration in this print ad.

16

Creative Broadcast Production

 W hat do Domino's Pizza, Nike, and Kentucky Fried Chicken have in common? They have all discovered claymation, an animation style featuring manipulated clay figures. In an effort to create excitement and generate interest in a somewhat dull, generic product a commercial using these figures was produced for the California Raisin Advisory Board in Fresno, California. Will Vinton Productions, which prepared the spot, presents a conga line of clay raisins—finger snapping their way past other potential snacks to the song "I Heard It Through the Grapevine." The Advisory Board received many letters from appreciative viewers who both praised the commercial and declared they intended to purchase raisins.

 Many innovative techniques are used in the production of broadcast advertisements. While print production facilities developed slowly, techniques for designing electronic messages have emerged rapidly. With the creation of new technologies it is clear that the coming decade will offer advertising prospects a diversity of audio and video experiences.

CHAPTER OBJECTIVES

— To explain the basic formats used in television and radio commercials

— To discuss the guidelines for writing copy for television and radio commercials

— To discuss the methods by which television and radio commercials are produced

317

EXHIBIT 16.1
Creativity in Commercials

CREATIVE STRATEGY FOR TELEVISION

Television offers the greatest potential for creative capability of all media. Commercials appearing on television do more than sell; they are occasionally considered good entertainment. "TV's greatest commercials", aired on NBC-TV, ranked number one in the Nielsen prime-time audience report for the week.[1]

Types of Television Commercials

All of the creative executions described in Chapter 11 can be used for television. Particularly effective are the approaches that incorporate mood creation and demonstration, since these can take advantage of the sight and sound capabilities of the medium. Moreover, television offers the presentation of song-and-dance as well as special effects commercials, such as the raisin ad described at the beginning of this chapter (see Exhibit 16.1).

Song-and-Dance Productions
Soft-drink advertisers are primary users of elaborate and extravagant musical commericals, due, in part, to what is considered the memorability problems in advertising soft drinks. Soft drinks usually provide no major benefits and solve no inherent problems for customers. Research has shown that since consumers don't watch a problem being solved by

---

[1]"For the Record," *Advertising Age* (June 7, 1982), p. 79.

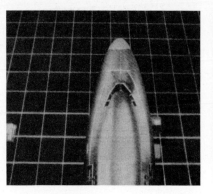

EXHIBIT 16.2
Special Effects Commercial

a soft-drink commercial (such as a malfunctioning muffler being replaced), they tend to forget it almost immediately. Thus Coke, Pepsi, and Dr. Pepper have tried to overcome this memory lapse by regularly producing lavish and expensive commercials.

The most successful of these are the faceoffs on the Busby Berkely extravaganzas of the thirties, with their extensive choreography and numerous chorus girls. These extravaganzas now feature a more youthful group of dancers and singers and are designed to create a mood, rather than extol a product's benefits. Music not only functions as the mood setter but gives the viewer cues about what is coming. The music must mesh with the visual in timing, pauses, anticipation, intensity, and, of course, action.

Even the music videos appearing on television have been adapted to commercials. Pepsi made effective use of Michael Jackson ads and used Lionel Richie in musical extravaganzas featuring some 3000 extras in 1985.[2]

Special Effects Commercials

Creative as well as emerging high-tech capabilities offer almost unlimited opportunities for a variety of special effects commercials. A commercial prepared by Marsteller for Flying Tiger, considered by the agency as "one of the best commercials we've ever produced,"[3] used a combination of film/tape techniques. These included a slit-scan over a motion graphics grid; still photography of a Flying Tiger's truck; and live-action photography of miniature packages with a computer controlled camera (see Exhibit 16.2). Although these new wave commercials are likely to attract attention, they may tend to be perceived as impersonal and remote from the viewer, since they generally do not present benefits or solve problems.

---

[2]Jennifer Pendleton, "Pepsi: Richie Spot Truly a Winner," *Advertising Age* (February 25, 1985), p. 3.

[3]Hooper White, "Flying Tiger Ad by Marsteller Flies in Face of Convention," *Advertising Age* (December 20, 1982), p. 32.

EXHIBIT 16.3
Procter & Gamble's Animated Fable

In a move away from its traditional slice-of-life ad execution, Procter & Gamble is using an animated fable. The ad shows black and white outlines of people washing with soap. The line drawings are enhanced with splashes of color and, at the end of the spot, the animated characters have decided that there's nothing better than to "experience Ivory for a real feeling of clean."

Nevertheless, special effects may be seen as a way of distinguishing a commercial from the competition. Traditionally Procter & Gamble has used slice-of-life commercials to communicate its products' benefits. Now, however, the company is faced with increasing competition from other firms, and there is a feeling among Procter & Gamble's managers that all P&G advertising is beginning to look alike. In an effort to respond to changing consumers "who may be motivated by entirely different graphic values and by new interpretations in sights and sounds," a number of Procter & Gamble ads are being designed to create moods or images[4] (see Exhibit 16.3).

WRITING COPY FOR TELEVISION

Many of the principles discussed in preparing copy for print media apply equally well to the preparation of copy for television. However, writing copy for television involves some considerations that do not occur in print media; nor can television copywriting be considered radio copy with pictures added. Good television copy blends well with visual images.

The main appeal of a television commercial is visual. The words support and supplement the picture. A television copywriter must cre-

---

[4]Nancy Giges and Jennifer Alter, "New Look Takes Hold at No. 1," *Advertising Age* (May 16, 1983).

ate a mood, convey a selling message, and invite action in a time space of 60 seconds, 30 seconds, or sometimes even 10 seconds.

Guidelines for Writing Television Copy

Writing copy for television is a creative exercise—and, as such, offers many opportunities for innovation and originality. Nonetheless several guidelines for effective television copy have emerged through research.[5]

1. Commercials that start with a key idea stand a better chance of holding attention and persuading the viewer.
2. Copy should be limited to one message.
3. The greater part of the message should emanate from the video portion of the commercial.
4. The message should not be presented in many short scenes or with many changes of situation.
5. *Supers* (words on the screen) add to a commercial's power to change brand preference, but the words must reinforce the main point.
6. Commercials should show the package or mention the brand name in the presentation. Ending the presentation with the brand name is also effective.
7. Using everyday, conversational language and familiar, comfortable settings will help the viewer to grasp the message.

Writing copy for a personality includes the following suggestions:

1. Try to get the feel of the personality's style. Discover how he or she feels about the product.
2. Ask the star for suggestions. Listen to his or her speech pattern and see if some of the phrases used will work well in a commercial pitch. Don't put him or her in a forced or contrived position.

The Use of a Storyboard
A *storyboard* is a device used to translate a script into a more detailed presentation. It is the equivalent of a layout used for print media, and not only serves as a guideline for the final production of the commercial, but is used to secure approval from the various personnel in both the agency and the client organization.

After the copy has been reviewed and approved, the copywriter works with the art director who puts the action on the storyboard—a preprinted drawing board with a series of double panels. As shown in Exhibit 16.4, the upper panel, usually shaped like a small television screen, is used by the artist to rough in a succession of scenes that will

---

[5]Some of these research findings are reported in David Ogilvy and Joel Raphaelson, "Research on Advertising Techniques That Work — And Don't Work," in *Ideas for Action*, edited by Timothy B. Blodgett, *Harvard Business Review*, (July-August, 1982), p. 15.

1. WOMAN: Sitting all day made my legs feel like lead.

2. Then I discovered ...

3. (MUSIC UNDER) CHORUS SINGS: Sheer Energy.

4. WOMAN: The pantyhose with all-day massage.

5. The massage started as I slipped 'em on.

6. Then Sheer Energy springy yarn stimulated and refreshed my legs more and more.

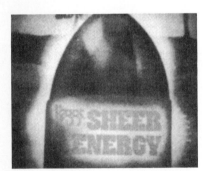

7. CHORUS SINGS: Sheer Energy.

8. WOMAN: Give your legs an all-day massage,

EXHIBIT 16.4
Storyboard—Narrative-Style Commercial

appear. The lower panel carries the accompanying audio. The individual who is to present the dialogue is defined in type beneath each scene; if this person is the announcer, it is called a "voice-over" (ANNCR. VO). The storyboard may also present a brief description of sound effects (SFX) that accompany the audio.

The frames representing the action in the storyboard may be very roughly drawn in the initial presentations. When it is shown to the client, it may be prepared in the form of a comprehensive. When the storyboard receives final approval and goes to production, it frequently is accompanied by a shooting script, which provides precise instructions for those who will ultimately film or tape the commercial.

Timing

Currently the 30-second time period is most widely used; therefore, in television commercial development, the best approach is to combine the creative processes and arrive at the visual and soundtrack components at the same time. However, when the writing of the copy comes first, two tools are of major importance—the tape recorder and the stop watch. According to Hooper White, TV advertising production consultant, "There is nothing more discouraging to an advertiser than to accept a good idea and then find out it can't be done in the 30 seconds allowed."[6]

A copywriter cannot rely on the announcer to speed up the reading; rather the copy must be fit to the commercial's time frame. In preparing the copy fewer words should be used than for radio, with a *maximum* of around 65 per 30-second commercial. The number of scenes should be carefully planned so that they each last an average of 5 or 6 seconds and not less than 3. Less than 2 words per second has proved to be an effective average audio pace if the video is a demonstration; if a verbal superimposition is used on screen, identical words should be used in the audio portion.

Commercial Length

There are wide variations in commercial length. The 8½-second commercial is actually a 10-second commercial whose sound track is only 8½ seconds. This length has been used successfully by such advertisers as Anheuser-Busch. The relatively few words are frequently paraphrased from longer commercials and help capture the essence of the full-scale advertising campaign.

There are indications that a 15-second commercial, which has limited use at this writing, may become a standard time period in the future.[7] Advertisers may find it more economical to purchase a 30-second

---

[6]Hooper White, "Long and the Short of It," *Advertising Age* (March 22, 1982), p. M-39.

[7]Robert Parcher, "15-Second TV Commercials Appear to Work Quite Well," *Marketing News* (January 3, 1986), p. 1; Sally Bedell Smith, "15-Second Commercials Are Blossoming on TV, *The New York Times* (August 24, 1985), p. 46; and Lynn G. Reiling, "Mixed Spot Lengths Increase the Effect of the Longer," *Marketing News* (April 26, 1985), p. 6.

Creative Broadcast Production

spot and use it for two commercials. Also, recent legislation has removed some of the restrictions formerly placed by broadcasters on the use of 15-second commercials.

However, the trend toward single 15-second spots may generate some potential problems. Viewers may not like the proliferation of shorter commercials and will not listen to their messages. Although informational ads seem to do well in this time frame, it is difficult to present some messages in 15 seconds, particularly those that are designed to present newness or have an emotional appeal. The 15-second commercial has been found to be 20 to 30 percent less effective than the 30-second spot. The appeal to advertisers, however, is the significantly lower price which tends to make the 15-second version cost-efficient.

The availability of alternate viewing channels will permit the presentation of commercials much longer than those previously shown on commercial television. For example, an 8½-*minute* commercial was used by Pillsbury Co. in a Modern Satellite Network show to tie in with its annual bakeoff.

Time Compression

In recent years, attention has been focused on sound compression systems that can speed up the contents of a commercial without causing high-pitched "chipmunk or Donald Duck side effects." The technique was initially developed for the educational market.[8] Research results indicated that information presented in a compressed-time fashion was not only understood, it also apparently was well remembered.

Time compression may be applied to commercials by deleting sections of the audio wave by computer, so that additional time can be provided for a local tag line or to squeeze in more content.

Use of the technique, however, has been limited. Rather than exploit time compression, some advertisers feel they can accomplish the same effect by careful editing. Furthermore, time compression may present ethical problems, for example, in making the presenter in testimonial commercials appear more enthusiastic or in demonstrating a product as working faster and more efficiently than it does.[9] It may also face legal constraints; for example, there may need to be a disclosure in an ad that the sound is "time compressed."

PRODUCING THE TELEVISION COMMERCIAL

Television commercials are rarely produced by an advertiser or its agency; instead they are prepared by independent producing houses who bid on a commercial production. Currently a system known as *cost plus/fixed fee* is popular. The costs of production are totaled and the

---

[8]James P. Forkan, "New Compression System Trims Seconds Off Ads," *Advertising Age* (November 19, 1979), p. 58.

[9]"Recession Calls for Imaginative Solution." *Advertising Age* (August 25, 1980), p. 70.

fixed fee (or profit mark-up) is added and applied to the total cost by the production company.[10] To facilitate the bidding system and provide for uniform input, the Association of Independent Commercial Producers has prepared a form that identifies costs. A summary page of this form is presented in Figure 16.1.

The Preproduction Meeting

A preproduction meeting is held prior to the shooting of the commercial to iron out potential problems. The storyboard is reviewed, responsibilities assigned, and the cast may be selected. The basic production techniques may also be determined at this point.

Sometimes commercials originate, not on a storyboard, but with a music track for which a storyboard is drawn.[11] The theme line (or the tag line) is presented to a composer who, in conjunction with the creative director, may find ways to surround these words with music. In fact the music track becomes the focal point of the commercial, such as in musical campaigns "I Love New York" and "You Deserve a Break Today." A storyboard is drawn and timed to the track. In the preproduction meeting, many decisions concerning how the ad will appear are based on the mood and rhythm of the track.

The Television Producer

The television commercial is prepared within the large advertising agencies by a television producer who is responsible for its creative, legal, and financial functions. Although his or her contributions in the creative field may not be clearly defined, they sometimes work together with the art director to prepare the storyboard. Basically, the producer functions as an "awareness factor" — he or she should be aware of vogues, innovations, and new supply houses.

The producer works very closely with the legal department and is responsible for the clearance of any potential legal problems. This requires foreseeing any possible lawsuits about photographing pictures, faces, or buildings and awareness of the union contracts with acting personnel, determining that specified salary minimums and fees for residuals are met.

Financially, it is the producer's responsibility to determine the cost of the commercial production, to ask for competitive bids if independent producing companies are to prepare it, and, finally, to recommend the company that is to be awarded the contract. The agency producer also decides whether to tape or film the commercial; the choice is dictated by the message concept.

---

[10]Hooper White, "How a Simple Form Helps Hold Down Cost of Production," *Advertising Age* (July 7, 1980), p. 50.

[11]Hooper White, "Striking a High Note: Music in TV Production," *Advertising Age* (November 12, 1979), p. 67.

FIGURE 16.1 Film Production Cost Summary

Film Production Cost Summary

	Bid Date	Actualization Date

Production Co.:	Agency:	Agency job #
Address:	Client:	Product:
Telephone No.: Job #		
Production Contact:	Agency prod:	Tel:
Director:	Agency art dir:	Tel:
Cameraman:	Agency writer:	Tel:
Set Designer:	Agency Bus. Mgr.:	Tel:
Editor:	Commercial title: No.: Length:	
No. pre-prod. days pre-light/rehearse	1.	
No. build/strike days Hours:	2.	
No. Studio shoot days Hours:	3.	
No. Location days Hours:	4.	
Location sites:	5.	
	6.	

SUMMARY OF ESTIMATED PRODUCTION COSTS	ESTIMATED	ACTUAL		
1. Pre-production and wrap costs Totals A & C				
2. Shooting crew labor Total B				
3. Location and travel expenses Total D				
4. Props, wardrobe, animals Total E				
5. Studio & Set Construction Costs Totals F, G, and H				
6. Equipment costs Total I				
7. Film stock develop and print: No. feet mm Total J				
8. Miscellaneous Total K				
9. Sub-Total: A to K				
10. Director/creative fees (Not Included In Direct Cost) Total L				
11. Insurance				
12. Sub-Total: Direct Costs				
13. Production Fee				
14. Talent costs and expenses Totals M and N				
15. Editorial and finishing per:				
16.				
17. Grand Total (Including Director's Fee)				
18. Contingency				

Comments:

COPYRIGHT AICP 1980

Source: "Film Production Cost Summary," *Advertising Age* (July 7, 1980). Copyright © 1980 Crain Communications, Inc. Reprinted with permission from Advertising Age.

CURTAILING PRODUCTION COSTS

Television commercial production costs have risen almost 100 percent in the last five years. These spiraling costs are attributed to a number of factors. The increase in television clutter and the effort to provide "zap proof" commercials have led to the rise of state-of-the art special effects, exotic location shoots, and requests for blockbuster commercials by advertisers who are impressed with the Macintosh "1984" or British Airways' "Flying Manhattan."

To achieve feature-film quality, agencies sometimes produce 75 versions of a television spot and reject 74 of them. Television spots now take longer to shoot; the former ten-hour shoot now requires 13 hours. Camera crews are insisting on using only the newest and most expensive camera and lighting equipment. Three little words — *in the rain* — can add $15,000 to production costs.

Several suggestions have been offered to decrease production costs. One suggestion is to train brand and advertising managers on the client side to evaluate and control cost. Another is to streamline the process for approving production expenditures. Particularly useful would be a log detailing the total hours needed for filming, as well as days of production. Finally, it is suggested that music, video animation, and special effects be kept to a minimum and used only when necessary. The ultimate decision, in terms of acceptability, however, should not be cost, but *fair value* for the expenditures which are related to objectives.

Sources: "Complex Productions Proving Costly to Advertisers," *Marketing News* (December 6, 1985), p. 7; Judann Dagnoli, "Spots' Production Costs Soar to New Pique," *Advertising Age* (January 27, 1986), p. 92; and Philip H. Dougherty, "Advertising, High Cost of Making TV Spots," *The New York Times* (January 20, 1986), p. D9.

Costs

The costs of commercials vary widely. The average cost of a 30-second commercial at the end of 1985 was $130,000, ranging to over one million dollars. The sum involves not only the filming or taping costs, but the studio and set costs, talent costs, customer costs, and, frequently, the music costs.

Acting personnel can be extremely expensive; some personalities have been given contracts for $1,000,000.[12] Generally, professional actors and actresses belong to performers' unions such as the Screen Actors Guild, the American Federation of Television and Radio Artists, and the Screen Extras Guild. They are not only compensated for their time in making the commercials, but also for their appearance each time the spots are run. These payments are called *residuals*, and the amount paid depends on the union scale and the number of cities involved in the schedule.

When amateurs are involved—the average housewife or the man at the auto center—payment for services is usually in the form of a negotiated *talent buy*, usually a one-time package.

---

[12] Sherilyn K. Zeigler and J. Douglas Johnson, *Creative Strategy and Tactics in Advertising: A Managerial Approach to Copywriting and Production* (Columbus, Ohio: Grid Publishing Co., 1981), p. 220.

Methods of Production

Several techniques may be used to produce commercials. The method selected depends on considerations such as cost, time limitations, and the need for special effects. Commercials may be produced live, on tape, or on film.

Live Television Production

Live commercial production is infrequently used; it is usually limited to local broadcasts where the local announcer is well-known and adds credibility to the message. Such live presentations offer lower cost for the one-time commercial and usually require less time than other production methods.

These advantages, however, are clearly offset by the problems that may occur when anything is produced live—from unexpected fluffs to deliberate misstatements. Moreover, live productions do not permit the use of various techniques that can improve a presentation.

Tape Production

Videotape, or tape, production puts direct electronic impulses on electromagnetic tape during the recording process and projects those impulses through the television system on the air. Since the original information on the tape itself is transmitted, such videotape pictures appear to have a live image quality.

Tape provides for immediate playback; it enables the production crew to see the scene on a TV monitor as they are shooting so that they can correct any mistakes immediately. Because of this ability, tape is less expensive than film, where the results of the shooting may not be seen until the following day, requiring an expensive reshooting schedule should errors appear.

At one time, the special effects that could be achieved on tape were limited. Today techniques have been developed that permit such effects at relatively low cost. Furthermore, tape requires less time than film.

Film Production

Film can be used for the production of any commercial since it permits a wide variety of sets, many types of optical tricks, and careful editing. Generally the most creative commercials, those that present unusual situations, use film, because it is the medium that best handles distant locations and unusual positions.

Many producers choose to shoot scenes more than one time in case some part of the scene is unsatisfactory. This eliminates the need to reschedule and reshoot the entire commercial, but it means using more film. The finest quality film (35mm), used for most national commercials, is expensive. Today many local advertisers and some national advertisers use the less costly 16mm film. In a normal day's shooting the film camera may expose 2000 to 3000 feet of 35mm film, although only 45 feet will be used in the final 30-second commercial. For a 16mm film

800 to 1200 feet will be taken, although only 18 feet will be used in the 30-second commercial.[13]

Film can be effectively used for *slow motion, stop motion, reverse motion,* and for various kinds of trick photography. A commercial prepared for Northwest Orient Airlines used a locked-down camera (a camera that cannot be jarred or moved) to shoot the servicing of a Northwest Orient 747, frame-by-frame, over a period of eight days and nights. In the Purina Cat "Chow-Chow-Chow" ads, the cat's cha-cha footwork effect was achieved by running the film forward and backward *(reverse motion).*

Special Production Techniques

Several techniques are available to enhance the presentation of the message on television. Advancements in computer technology should provide new and unusual capabilities for commercial delivery and design. Interest in this area has been generated by the increase in commercial clutter resulting from the use of shorter commercials, and the elimination of restrictions on the amount of broadcasting time that can be spent on non-program material. The widespread adoption of video cassette recorders with the attendant ability to use the fast-forward button on commercials has also encouraged advertisers to use unusual or unique techniques in an effort to overcome the effects of "zapping." In fact a recent survey revealed that creative executions such as Coke's Max Headroom ad were able to cause some viewers to stop zapping and watch the commercial.[14]

Opticals
Opticals refer to the techniques used for smooth transition in scene changes. These are usually inserted during the final editing stage after the rough cut is reviewed. Some of the most commonly used opticals are the following:

> *Cutting or Taking:* a quick switch from one scene to another
> *Dissolve:* a gradual disappearance of one camera's shot and gradual appearance of the other camera's shot.
> *Wipe:* using a new picture to literally wipe the old one off the screen—horizontally (from left to right), vertically (up or down), or diagonally (wipe across in a circular fashion).

Matte Shot
A *matte shot* limits viewing to highlight a product or package. A *cut out,* or matted form, is placed in front of the camera lens, and viewers see the scene as if through a telescope, a keyhole, or a porthole.

---

[13]Otto Kleppner, *Advertising Procedure,* 7th ed. (Englewood Cliffs, N.J.: Prentice-Hall, Inc., 1979), p. 413.

[14]Craig Reiss, "Fast-Forward Ads Deliver," *Advertising Age* (October 27, 1986), p. 3.

Animation

Mention the technique of animation, and someone immediately thinks of the cartoon technique popularized by Walt Disney, which calls for a specific type of talent as well as tedious and costly artwork involving hundreds of separate drawings. There are other types of graphic expression, however, that allow us to enjoy, for example, the antics of a king-fish named Charlie. These techniques are *stop motion,* in which stationary objects are photographed one frame at a time with a slight change in position between each exposure so that the resultant film creates the feeling of motion, and *photo animation,* which uses still photographs of objects in the same manner.

Currently, Dolphin's Computer and Electronic Design System is used to create video art. It is particularly useful for animation since it is less expensive and takes less time to produce. Dolphin's special computer uses a single negative with black-and-white artwork to produce sequential movement.

Rotoscoping

Rotoscoping is a technique that allows an editor to add drawings to previously shot, live-action film footage. A particularly effective commercial for Schick, shown in Exhibit 16.5, was shot without the beard and Zander's Animation Parlour created the whiskers. First the film was projected onto white paper and 750,000 whiskers were drawn by black pen frame-by-frame. Then the paper was photographed, and the hand-drawn film combined with the live-action film was run through an optical printing machine, thus producing the white-whiskered effect.

Claymation

Claymation is a highly polished version of a technique that made the television character, Gumby, famous two decades ago. This stop-motion animation technique developed by Will Vinton Productions uses clay figures that are manipulated and filmed at the rate of 24 gradual changes for each second of film.[15] Vinton first films live actors; then, once the clay figures are ready, animators run the film over and over, trying to imitate the actors' movements and expressions. It often takes several months of tedium to film a 30-second spot. Despite the time and expense involved in preparing claymation commercials, a number of companies using this technique consider it effective and successful. Sales for Domino's Pizza increased in some regions by 5 percent to 15 percent after commercials featuring a goofy, red clay creature—called a Noid—appeared. California Advisory Board's "I Heard It Through the Grapevine" featuring clay raisins has become a classic, and *Advertising Age* selected it as the best television commercial of the fourth quarter of 1986.

Animation is said to have accomplished a great deal for advertising. It has developed brand franchises, brought charm and humanity to television commercials, and has cut through visual clutter.[16] It serves to

---

[15]"You've Come A Long Way Gumby," *Business Week* (December 8, 1986), p. 74.

[16]Al Samuelson, "Animation in Advertising: An Uncertain Future," *Advertising Age* (October 25, 1982), pp. M4–5.

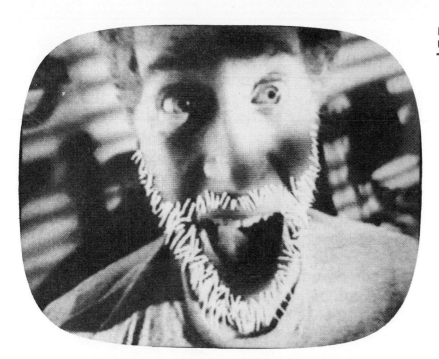

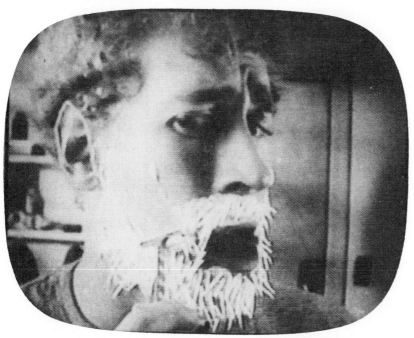

EXHIBIT 16.5
Using Rotoscoping

EXHIBIT 16.6
Example of a Photoboard

Real chips off the old block

CLIENT: HERSHEY FOODS
PRODUCT: "CHOCOLATE CHIPS"
AGENCY: OGILVY & MATHER
COMMERCIAL NO.: HUCC-6243

MUSIC UNDER THROUGHOUT:
Chocolate. Rich, mouthwatering

Hershey's Chocolate.

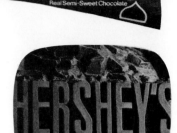

America's favorite chocolate for generations.

That's the chocolate you get

every time you bake a batch of cookies

with Hershey's Chocolate Chips.

Every chip is pure Hershey's

So every cookie

is pure pleasure.

Hershey's Chocolate Chips.

They're real chips off the old block.

personalize products and may provide opportunities for fantasy that do not exist in live-action production.

This technique, however, is generally most effective for impulse purchases. For more serious purchase decisions, it should be combined with live action presenting "reason-why" copy, which relates to the use of the product and its benefits.

Production Procedures

How does a commercial get produced? First, the producer shoots the scenes, making sure there is more than one take for each one. The next day the *dailies* are screened and an editor puts them together in a *rough cut*. The *voice over* of the announcer is included in this rough cut as is any music that is required. This becomes an *interlock* or a preliminary version of the commercial, which is presented for approval.

After the client has approved the interlock, the video, audio, and special effects are combined to form an *answer print*, which is the final print used for review and approval before duplicating. When the answer print is corrected for color and timing, it results in the final *release print*, which is released for network origination and sent to stations for their use.

Once the television commercial has been produced, both the agency and client may wish to keep records for reference and comparison. They prepare *photoboards*, such as those in Exhibit 16.6, which are essentially photographed versions of the commercials.

CREATIVE STRATEGY FOR RADIO

Radio commercials also have several options for effective presentation, but they are limited, to some extent, because their messages are received aurally. The creative strategies to overcome this and other constraints, developed in the past years, have renewed advertisers' interests in radio as a successful medium. In fact, with the emergence of the 15-second television commercial, it has been suggested that radio can now play an important role in providing reinforcement for television messages that provide minimal information.

Types of Radio Commercials

The sales message for radio can be developed in a variety of formats. A critical fact to remember is that realism is important. Messages that sound artificial or overly rehearsed are boring—and easily ignored. Furthermore, special effects are useful in creating impact. A number of basic formats may be used for the radio commercial.[17]

---

[17]Philip Ward Burton, *Advertising Copywriting*, pp. 198–201.

TURNING TO RADIO

The Bulova Watch Company, which used both spot television and magazines for advertising in 1984, turned to radio in late 1985 as a way to reach the always-busy and on-the-move 18-to-44 age group who do not appear to have time for television. In each of the 60-second radio spots the principal talent reads the lines in "rush-rush" fashion, accompanied by special music from the Bottger-Martin music house, which used a synthesizer to get the sound of a great many strings.

Source: Philip H. Dougherty, "Advertising Bulova Watch Decides to Use only Radio Ads," *The New York Times* (October 30, 1985), p. D23.

The Straight Commercial

The straight sell is devoted to the merits of the product and merely reveals the product advantages and competitive benefits. Sound effects may be used to gain and hold the attention of listeners.

The Dialogue Commercial

The writer develops the message by presenting a series of conversations between the announcer and other interested parties, such as users, dealers, or experts. Dialogue commercials often make use of testimonials.

The Dramatized Commercial

The dramatized commercial is similar to the narrative copy approach in which a problem is dramatized and the product is introduced as its solution. A series of believable events invested with dramatic unity and interest may be presented leading up to the message, and the close may be the straight product sell.

Humor has been interspersed in both the dialogue and the dramatized commercial with some success. Dick Orkin and Bert Berdes, specialists in humor, have won numerous awards for their radio commercials. One, in particular, a radio commercial for the College of Automation, a Chicago data processing school, resulted in as many as 130 calls a day for an institution that had previously been virtually unknown.[18] Jerry Stiller and Anne Meara are also well known for their humorous radio commercials, and are credited, at least in part, for the early success of Blue Nun wines.

The Musical Commercial

The vast majority of today's radio commercials include some kind of music or sound effects. If original scores are not required, libraries of "stock" music and sound effects are available.

Musicals are effective if well done. If the entire commercial is sung or even if it is interspersed with jingles which deliver the sales message,

---

[18]Ed Zotti, "Message Sticks Better with Wacky Fillip," *Advertising Age* (June 7, 1982), p. M-20.

some cautionary warnings are necessary — the music should be easy to commit to memory and the words should be understandable. According to Dick Orkin, drama, humor and music are the best ways to make a radio commercial memorable.[19]

The Integrated Commercial

In an integrated commercial, the commercial is presented live by the personality of the radio show, who delivers the message from a fact sheet rather than from a script. The *fact sheet* contains the major points of information about the product, the company, the basic appeals to be stressed, and certain suggested phrases to be used; but the actual presentation is left to the discretion of the personality.

This type of radio fare is rarely used by national advertisers, but may be used in local areas, particularly where there is a popular local personality, such as a disc jockey or master of ceremonies. The benefits of using this technique include its relatively low expense, the greater interest that may be generated by variations in presentation, as well as the credibility of the announcer, particularly if he or she is a well-liked personality.

One of the major disadvantages is the loss of control. The announcer can say what he or she wants and even "knock" the product. In addition, the live commercial places limitations on the use of music and sound effects.

Writing Radio Copy

In writing copy for radio, a number of factors peculiar to this broadcast medium should be kept in mind. The radio audience usually listens with divided attention. Someone at home listens while doing household tasks, the motorist listens while driving, and the student listens while talking to friends. Unlike television, which can communicate a message visually as well as aurally, radio relies on audio alone. The ear cannot receive a signal as quickly as the eye, nor assimilate as much information as the eye, which is a better path to the brain. This means that radio copy must be clear, precise, and understandable. Since the message is transitory (that is, it disappears at the end of the transmission), repetition is helpful in assuring that some portion of it may be retained by the listeners.

Generally, radio copy follows a less rigid grammatical pattern than print copy. It makes use of fragmentary sentences and phrases. Short, easy-to-pronounce words are best. Care should be taken, however, to avoid tongue twisters, difficult combinations of sounds, or sibilant hissing effects. Alliteration, which is fine in print, may be destructive in radio announcing. A good rule in writing radio copy is to read it aloud so that any of these pitfalls may be avoided. Particular attention should

---

[19]Kevin Higgins, "Humor Takes the 'Ho-Hum' out of Radio Ads," *Marketing News* (June 7, 1985), p. 23.

be paid to determining whether the brand is identified clearly and often and whether the benefit is repeated a number of times.

Radio can reinforce television commercials, particularly when the same audio is used. A successful radio spot for Diet 7-Up featured Don Rickles and Lynda Carter repeating their video statements.

Evoking Images Through Radio

Although radio copy is limited to sound, pictures can be created by stimulating a listener to imagine scenes. One technique, *scene setting*, uses familiar sounds such as a fire engine siren, an airplane engine's motor, or coffee percolating. *Word painting* uses words and descriptive dramatic language to paint pictures of the product and to create mental images of its benefits. Stan Freberg, a creative consultant in advertising, prepared a radio demonstration several years ago that conjured up the picture of Lake Michigan being drained and filled with a 700-foot mountain of whipped cream. A crowd of 25,000 cheered the air drop of a 10-ton maraschino cherry! The commercial concluded with a defiant statement, "Now try that on television."[20]

When Western Union introduced Mailgram in 1970 it was uncertain about the most effective positioning strategy. Two approaches were possible: A "new high-speed service for important messages" (fast delivery of mail) or "the impact of a telegram at a fraction of the cost" (low-cost telegram). Market tests showed the telegram positioning was more effective since Mailgram was a product or service that was used only when needed; radio was considered a desirable medium. To support the "impact of a telegram" approach, emphasis was placed on sound effects. In one of the award-winning commercials, an announcer declared, "Words are like music arrangements. Some have more impact than others. For example, compare this arrangement (a small piano version of Beethoven's Fifth). . . with the impact of this one. . . (a full orchestral presentation)." Another commercial featured a Shakespearean actor, with an echo chamber as support, to convey the extra impact of simple words and phrases, such as "Hello" or "Please pay me what you owe me," in a Mailgram message.[21]

Timing Radio Copy

Given the time limitations of preparing a commercial for radio, word count becomes important. Since many radio and television commercials are 30 seconds in length, it is useful to think in terms of seventy-five to ninety words for this time span.[22] An 80-word commercial is for easy listening, with pauses and background music; a 90-word version is for a great many facts and a staccato approach.

It is better to have fewer words that can be read with clarity and sincerity than to try to get a long message in a commercial. Key words

[20]Philip H. Dogherty, "Advertising, Celebrity Radio's Success," *The New York Times* (June 26, 1980), p. D13.

[21]*Monday Memo Broadcasting* (July 31, 1978), p. 18.

[22]Cort Sutton, *Advertising Your Way to Success* (Englewood Cliffs, N.J.: Prentice-Hall, Inc., 1981), p. 85.

and names should be repeated fairly often to make sure the listener has heard them, but not often enough to make the copy boring. The number of words will vary depending upon the additional audio effects used.

Checks for Radio Copy
Research designed to develop guides for writing effective radio copy has isolated eight checks to apply in evaluation. There are four positive elements to attain:

1. meaningful content,
2. stimulation of product-relevant associations such as benefits and pleasures,
3. identification by listeners with the situation presented in the message,
4. good fit with the listener's expectations and with the ideas and images the listener already has about the product;

and four negative ones:

1. offense or alienation of the listener,
2. suspicion and disbelief ("phoniness"),
3. confusion that distracts the listener from the message,
4. boredom and dullness.

Radio Commercial Production

Producing a radio commercial is usually quicker, simpler, and less expensive than the preparation of a television commercial. There are no production costs in a live commercial and, in fact, no "static" production. It is flexible and variable, and the message can be easily changed to meet changing conditions. The live commercial has the advantage of vitality and personal appeal. It may have special appeal if delivery is made by a personality who has an established reputation.

The taped commercial results in a more carefully structured advertisement which can be repeated over and over again. This may be an advantage, since it eliminates human error and results in a more precise, mistake-proof delivery. The commercial can be varied for listener interest.

The taped commercial has the disadvantage of creating a "canned" effect and intruding inappropriately on the mood of a program. It also tends to wear out. Often the combination of a live and taped commercial is used, with the live announcer introducing and closing a taped commercial message.

Radio is primarily a local medium, and many radio stations produce commercials for their local clients. However, it is also used in regional or national campaigns by advertisers in different markets. In this case prerecording the radio commercial is usually done by recording studios commissioned by advertisers or their agencies.

In preparing a taped commercial, dialogue and narration are generally taped separately. If music is to be used, the narration and dialogue tapes are mixed with the music. This becomes the *master tape* of the commercial from which as many duplicates as necessary can be made.

SUMMARY

Many creative techniques have been developed for disseminating advertising messages through broadcasting, and new methods are continually evolving. The formats that are used in television commercials include dramatization or slice-of-life, demonstration, song-and-dance productions, and the use of personalities. In writing copy for television, it is best to limit the presentation to one message, much of which should emanate from the video portion of the commercial. Particular attention should be paid to timing; frequently it is useful to use a tape recorder and stop watch to judge the time frame. A storyboard is used to translate a television script to a more detailed presentation which may be used to secure approval and as a guideline for final production of the commercial.

A number of factors must be considered in producing a television commercial—particularly cost. Typically television commercials are produced on tape or film—the choice depends on the objectives of the ad as well as the particular concepts that are to be reproduced. Animation permits variations in presentation formats.

Radio commercials are usually less expensive and less time-consuming to produce. The formats most frequently used in radio are straight commercial, dialogue commercial, dramatized commercial, integrated commercial, and musical.

In preparing copy for radio, particular attention should be paid to clear, precise, and understandable presentations. Although radio copy is limited to sound, pictures can be created through the techniques of scene setting and word painting.

Radio commercials may be produced live or on tape. Many of them contain music or sound effects and may be prepared either by a local radio station or a recording studio.

QUESTIONS FOR DISCUSSION

1. What is a storyboard? How is it used?
2. Select several television commercials you consider to be outstanding and for each describe the creative approach used for the presentation of the message. Could another technique have been used with equal effectiveness? Why or why not?
3. Select several radio commercials which use image-evoking techniques. What are they and how are they used?
4. What are some of the principles for writing television copy?
5. What are the basic timing considerations in a TV commercial? What is meant by *time compression*?
6. What items must be considered in estimating the cost of a commercial?
7. Compare the advantages and disadvantages of tape versus film production.
8. What advertising functions can be performed by animation?
9. What are some of the principles of writing copy for radio?
10. Describe the basic formats that are used in a radio commercial.

KEY TERMS

supers	rotoscoping
storyboard	claymation
cost plus/fixed fee	dailies
time compression	rough cut
residuals	voice over
talent buy	interlock
opticals	answer print
cutting or taking	release print
dissolve	fact sheet
wipe	scene setting
matte shot	word painting
stop motion	master tape
photo animation	

AD PRACTICE

Based on the product you dreamed up in Chapter 13, prepare a storyboard for a television commercial. You may use rough drawings for the video section or paste in elements from drawings or other ads.

CASE

Creative Strategy

A new approach has been introduced to television commercials—the miniseries. Jordache has resorted to teenage soap opera to make its jeans commercials more provocative. Their ads feature teenagers talking frankly about their physical appearance, their parents, and their love life. Some of the scenes imitate popular teen movies.

A Miller Lite campaign consisted of a series of six ads entitled, "The Case of the Missing Case." The first commercial showed how a case of beer vanished from a black-tie party; later ads dropped clues about the beer burglar's identity and announced a sweepstakes promotion offering prizes to people who solved the case. Finally, the culprit was unmasked in an ad shown simultaneously on all three networks.

Pacific Bell, a local telephone company in California, conducted a twelve part serialized campaign scheduled to run for one year and featuring "Garland and Me." The ads are labeled on the television screen by number and title and present flashbacks of Lawrence Bishop and Garland Parks growing up on the farm during the depression. An ad called "The Dance" shows Garland and Lawrence as teenagers at a barn dance and establishes their rivalry for the affections of Mary Ellen Thompkins. In the next ad Garland steals a kiss from Mary Ellen while the three are on a picnic. In the following ad Lawrence gets revenge by spiking Garland's soda pop with castor oil.

DISCUSSION QUESTIONS

1. What are the basic formats used in television commercials?
2. Why have these companies turned to the miniseries approach?
3. What problems may the miniseries approach encounter?

Source: Ronald Alsop, "Tune in Next Month to Learn How These Commercials End," *The Wall Street Journal* (November 13, 1986), p. 35.

CASE

Artwork and Layout

As a result of the rising costs of television advertising and the increasing clutter of ads, advertisers are trying to develop new concepts in print ads. Rather than using a great many words to explain the product's features, strong visuals are used in print advertising to create a product image.

One example of the new graphic look is a series of ads for International Business Machines Corp. typewriters. Each ad pictures one huge letter or character found on a keyboard to point out a particular feature of the typewriters; for example, "A is for asynchronous module." Similarly, an ad for the Electo-Motive division of General Motors Corp., uses an image of the Frankenstein monster to warn railroad companies of the consequences of buying cheaper imported parts.

A number of ads also break with stereotypes that have been considered standard fare for certain product categories. For example, ads for William Grant & Sons' Frangelico Liqueur does not feature a man and a woman in a romantic setting with a bottle on the table between them. Instead, there are swirls of amber-colored liquid that fill up the entire page. One headline reads: "Close your eyes . . . Imagine yourself away . . . far away." An ad for To Boot, A New York-based men's shoe store, shows a blurred photo of the lower half of a business-man, with a man's shoe the only clear element.

DISCUSSION QUESTIONS

1. What methods may be used to illustrate products in ads?
2. Which of these methods is described above?
3. What suggestions would you make for preparing an effective layout for the ads described above?

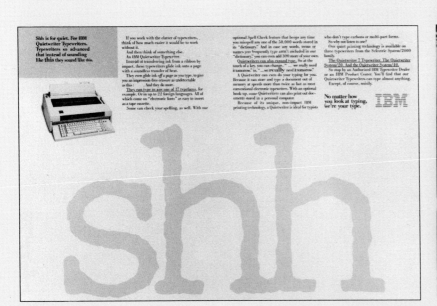

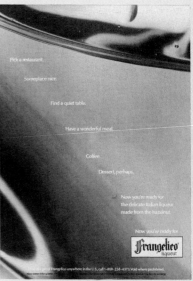

Source: Aimee Stern, "Resurgence in Print Advertising," *Dun's Business Month* (January 1986), pp. 46–49.

17

Media Strategy: The Media Plan

In 1977, Tostitos, a newly introduced product, became successful by advertising on daytime television to female heads-of-households. Its ads featured Mr. Escandon talking to mothers about Tostitos as good food.

Several years later, research showed that the Tostitos buyer had changed from the female head-of-the-household to the 18–34-year-old, upwardly mobile, entertainment-oriented young adult who watched TV primarily in the evening. Accordingly new commercials showed Mr. Escandon talking to the characters of popular television series the target buyer watched as a child—"Leave It to Beaver," "Dragnet," and "Mr. Ed." The commercials appeared during "St. Elsewhere," "Night Court," "Cheers," "Saturday Night Live," and some cable programming. This campaign resulted in double sales increases.

One of the most important decisions in advertising management involves the selection of the channel to carry the message. This process requires a comprehensive knowledge of the various media opportunities as well as the development of a plan for their effective integration.

PREPARING A MEDIA PLAN

The major advertising media in terms of advertising expenditures are newspapers, magazines, television, radio, out-of-home, and direct mail. The terms *medium* and *vehicle* are sometimes used interchangeably. Generally, however, a *medium* is a channel or system of communication such as newspapers or radio. A *vehicle* is a specific carrier within the channel. For example, *The New York Times* is a specific vehicle within the newspaper channel.

The proliferation of the types of media available, the variation in the ways messages can be communicated, and the increase in competitive distractions have all led to the growing importance of media strategy. It is important for a firm to make the most efficient use of its advertising budget, which involves careful analysis and planning. A firm must, therefore, prepare a *media plan*, a program emerging from the firm's overall marketing strategy and its advertising requirements, and providing a means for determining media objectives (including the target market) and a framework for designing media strategy (the selection of the media and a determination of how they are to be used by the advertisers). The plan frequently incorporates a media schedule which designates the vehicles to be used. The media carrying the heaviest advertising volume are listed in Table 17.1.

Analyzing the Situation

Situation analysis is the first stage in preparing a media campaign, and involves similar considerations to those examined in the development of the total advertising campaign, such as market trends, competitive activity, advertising opportunities and problems, and legal issues. A number of factors, however, have specific relevance for media choice.

Defining the Target Market
The target market for a firm's message must be the primary consideration in media choice. The target market may be defined as purchasers of the product, prospective purchasers, product users, best prospects, or more generally as, for example, women age 18 to 39. The description of the target market enables the media planner to match the media to the market. Media-market matching is the process of selecting the media whose audience contains a relatively high concentration of target market members.

Company Considerations
The nature of the firm's product, its distribution system, as well as the constraints placed by the company's advertising budget are all factors that influence media choice. Products may be refused time or space in specific media because of health risks or their personal nature. For example, cigarettes have not been advertised over broadcast media since 1971. Some products may require a medium where their appeal can be demonstrated visually.

TABLE 17.1   Advertising Volume in the United States in 1984 and 1985

Medium	1984 Millions of dollars	1984 Percent of total	1985 Millions of dollars	1985 Percent of total	Percent change
Newspapers					
National	3,081	3.5	3,352	3.5	+8.8
Local	20,441	23.3	21,818	23.0	+6.7
Total	23,522	26.8	25,170	26.5	+7.0
Magazines					
Weeklies	2,224	2.5	2,297	2.4	+3.3
Women's	1,209	1.4	1,294	1.4	+7.0
Monthlies	1,499	1.7	1,564	1.6	+4.3
Total	4,932	5.6	5,155	5.4	+4.5
Farm Publications	181	0.2	186	0.2	+3.0
Television					
Network	8,526	9.7	8,285	8.8	−2.8
Spot	5,488	6.2	6,004	6.3	+9.4
Cable (National)	492	0.6	637	0.7	+29.5
Local	5,084	5.8	5,714	6.0	+12.4
Cable (Local)	80	0.1	130	0.1	+62.5
Total	19,670	22.4	20,770	21.9	+5.6
Radio					
Network	320	0.4	365	0.4	+14.0
Spot	1,197	1.3	1,335	1.4	+11.4
Local	4,300	4.9	4,790	5.1	+11.4
Total	5,817	6.6	6,490	6.9	+11.6
Direct Mail	13,800	15.7	15,500	16.4	+12.3
Business Papers	2,270	2.6	2,375	2.5	+4.6
Outdoor					
National	562	0.6	610	0.6	+8.3
Local	310	0.4	335	0.4	+8.3
Total	872	1.0	945	1.0	+8.3
Miscellaneous					
National	8,841	10.1	9,551	10.1	+8.0
Local	7,915	9.0	8,608	9.1	+8.8
Total	16,756	19.1	18,159	19.2	+8.4
Total					
National	49,690	56.6	53,355	56.3	+7.4
Local	38,130	43.4	41,395	43.7	+8.6
Grand Total	87,820	100.0	94,750	100.0	+7.9

The McCann-Erickson U.S. advertising volume reports represent all expenditures by U.S. advertisers—national, local, private individuals etc. The expenditures, by medium, include all commissions as well as the art, mechanical and production expenses which are part of advertisers' budgets for each medium. *Source: Prepared for Advertising Age by Robert J. Coen, McCann-Erickson Inc.*

Source: from "Ad Spending Fails to Equal Predictions" by Robert J. Coen, *Advertising Age* (May 11, 1986). Prepared for Advertising Age by Robert J. Coen, McCann-Erickson, Inc. Reprinted by permission.

   The location of a firm's distribution system may dictate the geographic areas where the advertising should appear. Consumers frequently complain of seeing advertisements for products that are not available locally. The kinds and number of media selected are limited by the advertising budget established by the firm. Some media, such as television, require a fairly large investment of promotional dollars. Advertising in national consumer magazines is also expensive, while local radio and newspaper advertising is relatively inexpensive (see Exhibit 17.1).

Creative Requirements

Creative and media decisions are closely interrelated. The intimacy provided by the medium, the availability of color, the ease with which it may be used, and whether it adds to the prestige of the product are all considerations of the media selection process.

   The message and the manner in which it is presented influence media choice. If the copy contains words that are difficult to pronounce and understand, radio is a poor choice. If, however, short staccato phrases and catchy jingles are desired, radio becomes an acceptable medium. Long copy with difficult, technical wording favors print media; a message supported by demonstration will require television. Technical capabilities in both print and electronic media, such as quality of paper and quality of sound, vary from one medium to another, making some more suitable for certain types of copy format.

Media Characteristics

Rapidly changing conditions may suggest a medium that can easily adapt to unanticipated circumstances. Because of the early closing period for media such as magazines and television, copy must be submitted some time in advance of its presentation. An advertiser who wants to capitalize on current events may not be able to offer his or her message in these media. The advertiser may have to turn, instead, to newspapers or direct mail, which are more flexible.

   A limiting factor that is most obvious to the firm's media buyer is the extent of media availabilities. Both newspapers and magazines tend to place maximum limits on the size of their issues. In electronic media this problem is more acute. It is said that the most difficult advertising to place is spot radio and spot television (*spot* refers to a specific geographic area), because the premium time slots are generally not available to the advertiser who would like to have advertising appear simultaneously in several areas throughout the country.

Sources of Media Information

One of the prime requisites of a competent media planner is familiarity with the many media choices and various sources of information available. Media information is available from sources within the medium itself as well as from external groups.

EXHIBIT 17.1
Advertising on a Limited Budget

Oak Tree Farm Dairy Inc. introduced its new gourmet ice cream to the New York area through a relatively inexpensive campaign costing $75,000. Media used included radio, posters (pictured here) in all Long Island railroad trains, since commuters represent 30 percent of the market for this product, and freestanding inserts offering a discount in Sunday newspapers.

Media-Connected Sources
Each medium will supply an advertiser with a rate card, which is essentially a price list for the space or time offered for sale. Other information, such as closing dates, mechanical requirements, circulation figures, and nonacceptable advertising, also appear on the card. Various media prepare reports offering information about the kinds of markets they cover, the demographic profile of their audiences, and the kinds of products the audience purchases. Some media provide marketing data such as market indexes, which may be used to determine the potential demand for a prospective advertiser. Media representatives are also available to answer questions.

Standard Rate and Data Service
The most widely used service by national advertisers is the Standard Rate and Data Service (SRDS). The SRDS publishes directories of detailed information for most of the major media compiled from their rate cards. Separate sections classify rates and data for newspapers, consumer magazines and farm publications, business publications, community publications, spot radio, spot television, network radio and television, direct-mail list rates, and Canadian media. There are also separate publications for newspaper circulation analysis and print media production data.

Audit Bureau of Circulations
In the early days of advertising, each medium determined its own circulation figures. There were many inconsistencies in reporting and a tendency for media to overstate their circulation and to include in the circulation count those newspapers and magazines that were distributed free of charge. To provide a more impartial judgment, an organization was created supported by newspaper publishers, magazine publishers, advertisers, and advertising agencies. The Audit Bureau of Circulations (ABC) provides advertisers with an impartial check of circulation statements of member publications.

Business Publications Audit and Traffic Audit Bureau
Because of their lack of paid circulation, business publications do not qualify for membership in the ABC. The Business Publications Audit verifies circulation for their publications. It audits controlled circulation, which routes business publications to a selected list (such as key executives) on a free distribution basis. To measure the circulation for outdoor advertising, a Traffic Audit Bureau has been established. The TAB, however, computes the data rather than just verifying it.

Media Associations and Independent Research Associations
Various media associations publish material about the nature and merits of advertising in the media they represent. Information is obtainable from such organizations as Magazine Advertising Bureau, Bureau of Advertising of the American Newspaper Publishers Association, Radio Advertising Bureau, Television Bureau of Advertisers, The Institute of

Outdoor Advertising, and the Direct Marketing Association (formerly the Direct-Mail Marketing Association).

Independent research organizations, such as A. C. Nielsen rating services, are widely used for information on audiences of broadcast media, as are Arbitron ratings. Starch INRA Hooper provides information concerning magazine advertising and Simmons Market Research Bureau offers data on audience composition for both print and broadcast media in its *Study of Media & Markets.*

Data on Competitors' Media Expenditures

A knowledge of competitors' media expenditures is useful for decision making by advertisers.[1] Only large national advertisers' expenditures are reported, and since this information is gathered by sources outside the advertising firm, some data may be missing.

Information on media expenditures is available through several organizations. Media Records reports newspaper expenditures by large national advertisers in about 60 markets in the United States. It provides, by product classifications, both the number of dollars and the advertising linage purchased by each advertiser for each of the newspapers listed.

A report of advertising expenditures in six media—magazines, newspaper supplements, network television, spot television, network radio, and outdoor—is provided by Leading National Advertisers Company. Its reports show expenditures by brand as well as company and permit an advertiser to compare a brand's expenditures.

Leading National Advertisers Magazine Analysis Service compiles expenditure data in consumer magazines about national advertisers for the Publisher's Information Bureau. The data is provided by category of product and shows expenditures for each month as well as cumulative data.

Broadcast Advertiser Reports (BAR) provide information on network and spot television and network radio expenditures. *Barcume* is a special section that reports expenditures by company, individual brand, and expenditures for each month as well as a cumulative compilation of year-to-date.

STEPS IN THE MEDIA PLAN

A media planner who has carefully analyzed the situation, particularly in reference to those factors relevant to media choice, and who has gathered sufficient preplanning media information is now ready to prepare the media plan. A number of steps are required in the formulation of an efficient plan.[2]

---

[1]Jack Z. Sissors and Jim Surmanek, *Advertising Media Planning,* 2nd ed. (Chicago, Ill.: Crain Books, 1982), pp. 86–96.

[2]This is adopted in part from Herbert Zeltner's "How to Write and Recognize a Good Media Plan," *Advertising Age* (September 26, 1977), pp. 31, 59.

Objectives

As with all planning the proper media plan starts with a clear, concise statement of objectives, incorporating a statement about the target which has been chosen.

— *Statement of Target.* The target is designated as the heavy user, the early adopter, the opinion leader, the competitors' users, and so forth.

— *Customer/Target Profile.* This section provides a complete description of the target.

— *Scope of Effort.* Objectives include the scope of the effort; that is, its reach, frequency, and continuity. Where possible these are designated in quantifiable terms. For example:

Reach	60 percent of heavy users, or 55 percent of the target audience defined as females ages 18–49.
Frequency	a minimum of three impressions monthly for households of $20,000 or over.
Continuity	a continuous advertising campaign is to be presented for a 3-month period.

Strategy

A discussion of strategy includes a summary explanation of the choice of media in the recommended amounts and forms. It explains why the media is best in the light of the objectives. For example, the media reaches the specific target most efficiently, there can be repeated impressions, it is relatively economical, it provides for the best demonstrations, it offers the greatest impact on resellers.

Budget

The heart of the media plan is a table that sets up the various media used and the cost of each. This part may be prepared in summary form, with an appendix exhibit presenting the details. It may summarize prime-time network TV usage, fringe time, local TV, the top 25 markets in women's magazines, or run-of-press (r.o.p.) newspapers (the newspaper may place the ad wherever they wish), and so on, and it states the dollar amount and the percent of total budget spent on each medium. For example:

	Dollars	Percent
Local TV	$ 51,000	41
Top 25 markets women's magazines	62,000	50
R.O.P. newspapers	11,000	9
Total	$124,000	100

Rationale for the Recommendations

The plan is a logical outgrowth of the overall advertising marketing effort of the firm, based on current, complete, and accurate facts and figures. It explains how target profiles are matched with appropriate media, using demographics, lifestyle segmentation factors, and other information.

Discussion of Alternatives

The discussion of alternative media placement is generally presented in two sections: an individual medium analysis of all primary media recommendations and a comparative analysis of alternative recommendations. The primary recommendations include such information as the type of medium, the name of the vehicle, demographic characteristics of the market, the circulation, the cost of insertions, dates for insertions, and sizes of insertions. Reasons for favoring the primary recommendations over the alternative media are usually documented in the plan.

Competitive Activity

Competitors' potential activities and recommendations for possible changes relevant to their activities are also part of the media plan. For example it may be desirable to use a head-on competitive approach or shorter bursts of activity during competitors' lulls.

Supporting Documentation

Tables, charts, and comments are used to clarify each point in the recommendation. A helpful technique for presenting information is the media flowchart, which frequently details the media schedule, an important component of the plan (see Figure 17.1).

MEDIA SCHEDULING

A major component in the media plan is a schedule detailing the timing of the advertisements. The schedule reflects the total audience coverage, the frequency with which the members of the audience view the advertising message, and the continuity or the period of time over which an opportunity for exposure is available. All of these factors are interrelated in the development of the media schedule, but there are no clear-cut guidelines about which is to be emphasized. For example, questions to which there are no definitive answers include: Is it better to have one person see the message twice or two people see the message once? Should the advertiser use up funds in a concentrated burst of advertising over a thirteen-week period, or should the advertiser spread out expenditures over a fifty-two-week period? The answers to these and other

FIGURE 17.1   A Media Flowchart

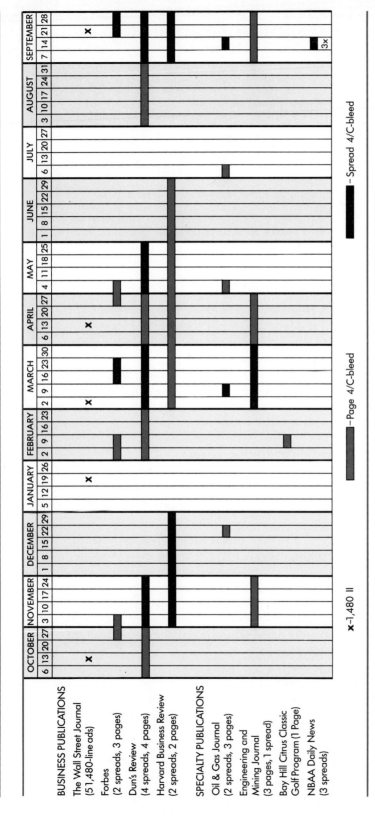

Source: From *Advertising Media Planning*, 2nd Edition by Jack Z. Scissors and Jim Surmanek, p. 236. Copyright © 1982 by Jack Z. Scissors and Jim Surmanek. Reprinted by permission of National Textbook Co., Lincolnwood, IL.

questions depend upon many factors including the purpose of the advertising, the competitor's strategy, the kind of product advertised, and its attributes. However, a number of concepts have been developed for media scheduling which are useful in arriving at a decision.

Media Weight Theories

A media schedule may contain only one medium or a relatively large number of media. Media weight theories concern the number of media selected and the emphasis placed on each of these in the schedule.[3]

The Wave Theory

The advertiser purchases time and space in various media for a relatively short time and moves in and out of these media in "waves." The advertiser hopes that the impact of the advertising will carry over from the periods of heavy concentration to those of no advertising. The wave theory sacrifices continuity and builds up coverage and/or frequency.

The Media Dominance Theory

The theory of media dominance suggests that the advertiser buy an unusually large amount of space in one medium for a short period of time. After building up coverage and frequency in that medium, the advertiser shifts expenditures to another medium, again for a short period of time. Thus, although exposure time is limited, the advertiser benefits from dominance in one particular medium, as well as a maintenance of continuity over a variety of media.

The Media Concentration Theory

Media concentration offers media dominance and continuity within one medium only. It suggests that the advertiser develops strength by concentrating in one medium rather than expending funds over a variety of media.

Timing Strategies

In addition to deciding on which media to concentrate, scheduling requires a determination of the extent of advertising that should occur in various time periods. Timing strategies should be coordinated with consumer purchasing patterns and may even help extend them.

Continuous

Continuous advertising reaches consumers during the purchase cycle as well as during nonpurchase times. It is useful for reminder purposes. Media discounts are available to continuous advertisers, and some media provide the best positions to advertisers who buy advertising over a long

---

[3]Lyndon O. Brown, Richard S. Lessler, and William M. Weilbacher, *Advertising Media*, p. 122.

period of time. A continuous ad campaign is good for products such as electric light bulbs or groceries, whose purchase cycles are not erratic.

Flighting

In a flighting schedule, heavy advertising occurs in certain time periods with little or no advertising in others. Flighting allows a series of ads or commercials to appear as a unified campaign. An ad's infrequent appearance may also tend to attract more attention than a continuous ad. Flighting may be a more popular strategy as media costs increase. For new product introduction, or for a seasonal product, flighting is a useful schedule device. Much "new use" advertising can be effective with this schedule, such as a new recipe, or a new use for hand cream as first aid.

Some advertisers try to tie their products to special events, particularly sports. Gillette Company has been connected with baseball's World Series since 1939, when the company purchased the radio broadcast rights of the total series for $100,000 (an amount that would not buy 30 seconds of television advertising for that event today).

Pulsing

Pulsing is similar to flighting except that it is scheduled at regular intervals, not necessarily in seasonal patterns. Pulsing may also be used with a somewhat continuous advertising campaign, to support a special promotion or to encourage a change in purchase cycles. Pulsing is particularly useful for a product that has a heavier concentration of sales at intermittent periods. Beer companies, such as Anheuser-Busch and Miller, use pulsing.[4]

Some authorities believe pulsing is the safest of the three strategies since it incorporates both continuity and flighting when needed; advertisers use all three strategies to reach different objectives.

QUANTITATIVE CRITERIA FOR MEDIA CHOICE

To evaluate media choice, quantitative criteria such as cost per thousand, reach and frequency, and gross rating points are used. This chapter explains these concepts and subsequent chapters describe how these factors are applied in evaluating specific media.

Cost per Thousand

A commonly used measurement to determine media efficiencies is the cost per thousand people (or households) delivered by a medium. It is used to compare media of varying audience size and cost, as well as to compare different vehicles within the same medium.

---

[4]Russell L. Ackoff and James R. Enhoff, "Advertising Research at Anheuser-Busch, Inc.," *Sloan Management Review* (Winter, 1975), pp. 10–11.

TABLE 17.2   Cost per Thousand in Various Media, 1986

| | Cost-per-Thousand | |
	Men	Women
Outdoor (posters)	$ 1.70	$ 2.15
TV (prime time— 30 seconds)	16.20	12.40
Magazine (page, 4/c)	7.30	4.60
Radio (30 seconds)	4.10	3.30
Newspaper (600 line, b&w)	7.00	6.75

$$\text{Cost per Thousand (CPM)} = \frac{\text{Dollars spent on ad in medium} \times 1000}{\text{Number of people (circulation)}}$$

Thus,

$$\text{CPM} = \frac{\$50,000 \times 1000}{12,000,000 \text{ persons}} = \$4.17$$

This translates into the statement that "it costs $4.17 to send an ad in this medium to one thousand people." Similar computations can be made for other media and the costs compared. Table 17.2 presents the average cost per thousand for men and women in major media for 1986.

The cost per thousand varies by media and specific vehicles. For example, prime time network television may have a high cost per thousand, but daytime network and spot television may have a lower CPM than magazines. The cost per thousand households is usually less expensive than the CPM for a specific target segment, such as men 18 to 39. Moreover, except in outdoor advertising, it is generally more expensive to reach men on a cost per thousand basis than women (see Table 17.2). Typically, for all media, both the cost per unit of advertising and the cost per thousand in each medium tend to rise each year.

Reach and Frequency

Reach is a term used to refer to the number of different people (or households) who are exposed at least once to a particular vehicle or an entire schedule. Sometimes the terms *nonduplicated audience* or *cumulative audience* are used to indicate reach. *Frequency* refers to the average number of times an individual or household is exposed to a vehicle or entire schedule within a specified period of time.

Gross impressions are the total number of households or people delivered by a particular media schedule without regard to any possible duplication that may occur.

Reach × Frequency = Number of Gross Impressions

Gross impressions do not indicate that the ad has been seen; they indicate that the opportunity *exists* for people to view an ad. The gross impression count includes single and duplicated viewing. Accordingly, a campaign that provides for 4000 gross impressions can achieve this in various ways:

Reach	×	Frequency	=	Number of Gross Impressions
4000 people	×	1 time	=	4000 gross impressions
2000 people	×	2 times	=	4000 gross impressions
1000 people	×	4 times	=	4000 gross impressions

Generally advertisers would like to maximize their number of gross impressions. An obvious limiting factor is the available budget; although exposures in some media are less expensive than others, there is a point at which increasing the exposures in the least expensive media becomes too costly for the firm. Moreover, as a learning factor, increasing the number of exposures is not the only important element. In an effort to secure retention of a message, the advertiser must also consider the number of times an individual is exposed to this stimulus. Given the same number of exposures, it is possible that more people will receive the advertising message less frequently, or fewer people will receive the message more frequently.

Reach and frequency are useful for providing quantitative information about an advertiser's media schedule. A media plan can specify that it is designed to reach 1000 members of a particular target audience with an average frequency of 3 times. It should be clear that *reach* does not mean actual contact, but only that the target member has the potential to be exposed to a message on the media used. Nor does *average frequency* mean that each individual has the opportunity to see this message 3 times. Some may see it once, some twice, and some four times.

How Much Frequency?

There is no cut-and-dried conclusion about which is more desirable— greater reach or greater frequency. The optimum frequency rate depends on a number of factors that include the purpose of the advertisement, the extent of previous promotion used, the stage of the product in its life cycle, and the severity of competition in the medium as well as in the total market for the product.

The concept of repetition is receiving widespread attention in the field of advertising. Ongoing studies are being conducted about the amount of repetition that is necessary for a media plan, particularly since such decisions have a significant effect on the advertising budget.

The conclusions proposed by Ebbinghaus in 1885 in his theories of learning seem to be supported today: longer and more complex messages need to be repeated more often to be remembered. Researchers have found that the greater the interference from competing messages, the greater the amount of repetition necessary to produce retention. Therefore, similarity of messages—that is, ads for various brands of the same product appearing together—may not be remembered. One ad for toothpaste placed among ads for different products is more likely to be remembered than an ad for toothpaste surrounded by two other toothpaste ads.

Current advertising practices denote a movement away from the "numbers game," which concentrates on reaching the greatest number of people, and suggests that efforts be directed toward achieving exposure among prospective purchasers. The theories discussed earlier on the effects of repetition in advertising indicate there is value to repeated exposures within this group of potential customers. However, there are also indications that, beyond a certain level, repetition may be unnecessary or ineffective (see Exhibit 17.2).

Computer Reach/Frequency Models

A variety of computer models have been developed to aid in calculating reach and frequency distribution of media vehicles. In these formula models a number of alternative campaigns are selected that incorporate the media that will deliver the selected target characteristics and the proposed budget. When preparing a magazine schedule, for example, the models are designed to provide such information as:

1. What is the size of the total audience for the product?
2. What are the most efficient magazines for reaching that audience—based on each vehicle's cost and ability to reach the best prospects?
3. To what extent is there duplication among the magazines selected?

4. How many people have the potential to see the ad?

5. How many times will they see it?

6. Are they potential purchasers of the product?

The use of formula models as an aid in the reach/frequency decision to select among alternative media schedules is widespread. A survey conducted among media directors at the top 200 advertising agencies in the United States revealed that the majority of the respondents' agencies (85.9 percent) use computerized models to estimate reach and frequency distributions.[5] The most popular reach/frequency models are those provided through syndicated media organizations such as Telmar and Interactive Market Systems (IMS) and proprietary models that are developed in-house. Use of models to evaluate schedules for magazines and network and spot television is most common; such models are rarely used for outdoor and combined media-type schedules.

While the media directors noted some satisfaction with the models, they also indicated the problems which arise. These include lack of knowledge about the accuracy of these techniques and an overemphasis on numbers. Moreover they felt that reach/frequency models were a tool to be used for directional purposes only to compare alternatives. A recent empirical test of a proprietary television media model revealed that the model produced poor estimates of reach and frequency and the exposure distribution of network television schedules.[6] This suggests that greater attention should be paid to evaluating the performance of the various models and the strengths and limitations of each model be clearly specified.

Gross Rating Points

The concept of reach and frequency is used, not only in print media, but also in broadcasting. In broadcasting, however, the term *reach* is generally used to designate a percentage of the target audience, rather than a number of people. The percentage of people reached and the frequency are combined to arrive at gross rating points. Thus,

(Percent) Reach × Frequency = Gross Rating Points

One gross rating point means that 1 percent of the audience has been reached one time.

Ratings are determined by services that provide estimates of audience-viewing for broadcast media. A program may achieve a 20 percent rating, meaning 20 percent of the total audience that could receive the program actually were watching at the time.

---

[5] John D. Leckenby and Marsha M. Boyd, "How Media Directors View Reach/Frequency Model Evaluation Standards," *Journal of Advertising Research* (October/November, 1984), pp. 43–52.

[6] Marshall D. Rice and John D. Leckenby, "An Empirical Test of a Proprietary Media Model," *Journal of Advertising Research* (August/September 1986), pp. 17–21.

If a company decides that it would be useful to have an advertising schedule that includes 60 gross rating points in a particular period, it might place 3 ads at different time periods during a program with a rating of 20 percent. It could also use a program with a rating of 30 percent and place 2 advertisements at different times. Either way the total gross rating points for the advertiser's schedule would be 60.

Gross rating points can exceed 100 percent, since they are a combination of reach and frequency. Thus a schedule including programs rated at 20 percent with 6 ads at different time periods would provide 120 GRPs. Reach, however, cannot exceed 100 percent of the target audience.

Cost per Rating Point

Gross rating points are useful in determining media budgets or analyzing media expenditures for broadcasting. Advertising agencies and the networks frequently provide advertisers with an estimate of the cost per rating point. This is based on an evaluation of the cost of the commercial time and the percentage rating of the audience.

$$\text{Cost per rating point} = \frac{\text{commercial time cost}}{\text{percentage of audience}}$$

Assuming it cost $40,000 to place a 30-second commercial on a program that has a rating of 20 percent,

$$\$2000 = \frac{\$40,000}{20 \text{ percent}}$$

Thus one rating point, or reaching one percent of the audience one time on this program, will cost $2000.

Another use of this concept is to determine advertising weight by evaluating the total number of gross rating points achieved by a budget.

$$\text{Gross Rating Points} = \frac{\text{Budget}}{\text{Cost per rating point}}$$

$$1000 \text{ GRPs} = \frac{\$2,000,000}{\$2000}$$

Thus a budget of $2,000,000 spent on commercials which provide an average cost per rating point of $2000 will offer 1000 gross rating points.

Determining the Number of Rating Points

The number of gross rating points selected for a campaign is usually based on the necessity to achieve a particular objective. While there is interest in determining the most efficient number of GRPs in a campaign, there is relatively little empirical data available. Foote, Cone & Belding advertising agency conducted studies of 14 new products it

MCDONALD'S TELEVISION MEDIA PLAN—AN EXAMPLE

In 1979 McDonald's was faced with Wendy's success in the fast-food market. The objective of McDonald's 1979 television media plan was to provide strong competition to combat this success.

Continuity: McDonald's media plan included continuous programming to children every weekend of the year, incorporating 140 GRPs per week.

Pulsing: To reach adults, 18 to 34, McDonald's used a pulsing schedule incorporating at least 75 GRPs per week, rising intermittently to 100 or 120 GRPs.

Flighting: The daytime television audience was to be reached in only two flights—June and October/November.

Roadblocking: Roadblocking is a term used to indicate the ads are to appear on all three major networks simultaneously. It usually involves extensive reach as well as significant frequency. The roadblocking tactic incorporated the delivery of 600 GRPs in a three-day period the second week in January. This tactic translated into a 30-second spot every 30 minutes on the three major networks during prime time. It was designed to reach 85 percent of the adults, 18 to 34 years old, an average of seven times (85 percent $\times$ 7 = 595 GRPs).

Source: "McDonald's 1979 Media Plan," *Advertising Age* (February 19, 1979), p. 89.

helped introduce in the 1970s.[7] Based on an objective of high awareness its analysis disclosed the following results:

1. Television campaigns involving 2500 GRPs in the introductory period had a 70-percent likelihood of high awareness.
2. Those containing between 1000 and 2500 GRPs had a likelihood of 33-percent high awareness.
3. Below 1000 GRPs the likelihood of high awareness was nil.

Currently studies requiring computer analysis as well as an understanding of the effects of repetition in learning, are being conducted to evaluate effective reach and frequency. *Effective reach* is based on a predetermined level of frequency which is considered desirable to achieve the advertising schedule's objectives.

QUALITATIVE CRITERIA FOR MEDIA CHOICE

While information concerning the size and characteristics of a medium's audience, as well as the cost of reaching this group, is significant in media deicision making, such quantitative data should not be used in isolation. There are a number of qualitative characteristics of various

---

[7]"ARF Hears Andrews' Defense of Copy Testing," *Advertising Age* (March 24, 1980), pp. 6, 86.

360   *Media Strategy: The Media Plan*

FIGURE 17.2   Which Media Do It Best?

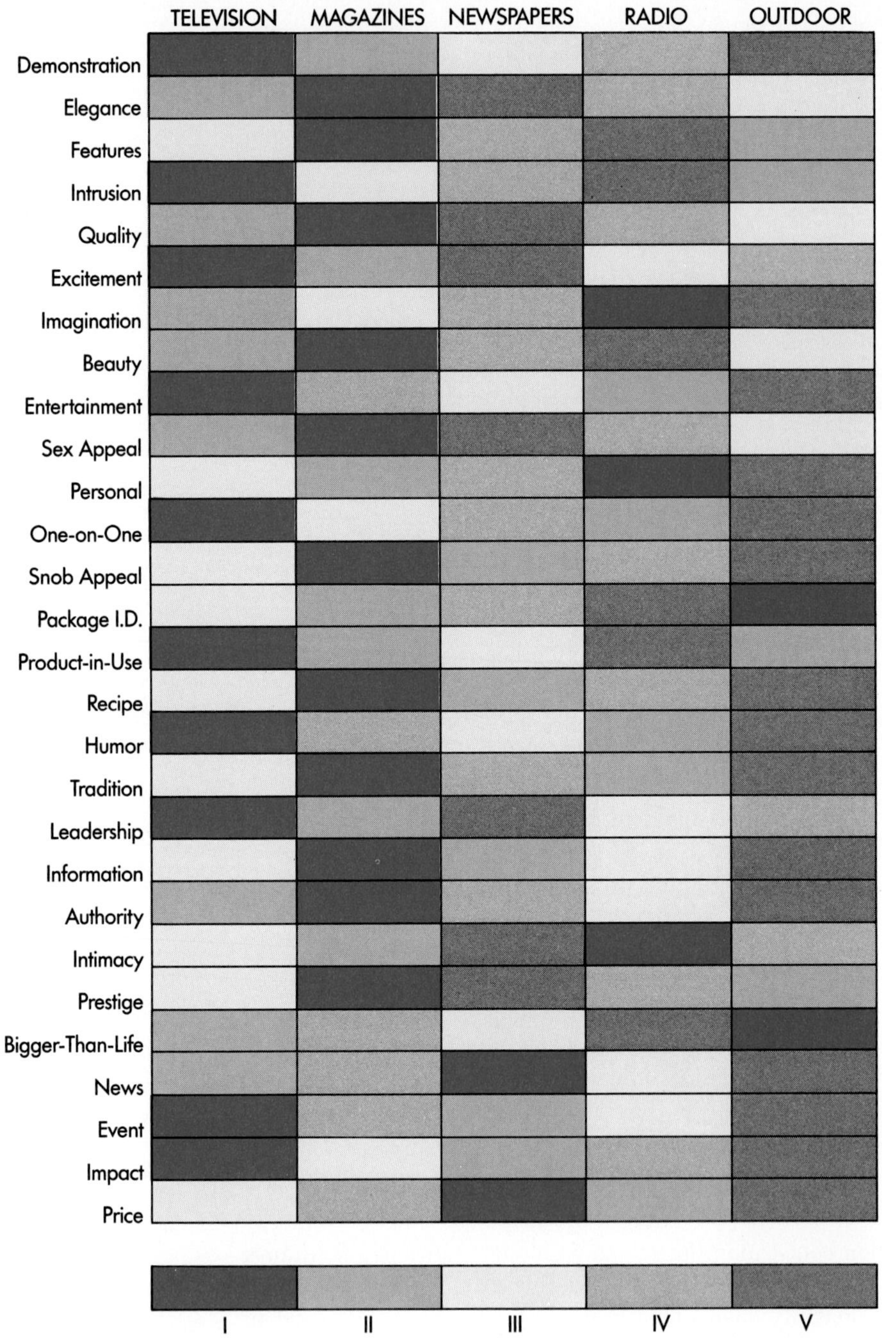

Darkest areas indicate the medium is best for providing the specific qualitative characteristic.
Source: from "100 Leading Media Companies," *Advertising Age* (June 27, 1983), p. M-74. Reprinted by permission of DDB Needham.

media that may affect the extent, manner, and effectiveness of message reception (see Figure 17.2).

Qualitative criteria can be those of authority, prestige, mood, impact, believability, expertness, image, atmosphere, excitement, leadership, emotional stimulation, sensory stimulation, or ability to stimulate the imagination. While some media can be readily characterized—for example, television is "very strong" on excitement, while newspapers are "poor"—it is difficult to measure these qualities and to relate them to message effectiveness.

Nevertheless in a national survey of media directors who were requested to check the factors used in media evaluation and indicate their degree of importance, qualitative criteria were considered relatively important.[8] Despite this assessment relatively little empirical research has been conducted concerning the qualitative characteristics of media. Future research may reveal evidence of qualitative criteria that influence the manner in which the message is received and can be used to distinguish among alternative media and vehicle opportunities.

THE MEDIA BUYING FUNCTION

The media planner should be familiar with the cost, circulation, publication schedule, mechanical requirements, closing dates, and special services offered by the various media. Most of this information is available in Standard Rate and Data Service. Additional information, such as availabilities, restrictions, and special offerings may be secured through the medium itself.

The media planner must know the consumer profile (the characteristics of the readers) of each medium and determine its relationship to the brand's target audience, particularly from the points of view of age, sex, income, and family size. In addition, the planner should have information concerning the attitudes toward the brand and toward competitors' brands.

Media planners are given the budget and the media objectives. They then prepare a number of alternatives, each of which has varying reach and frequency levels against the target audience.

In purchasing broadcast time, for example, media planners turn the plans over to buyers, who go to the networks and tell them how much the client has to spend, who the target audience is, the kind of programming desired or not desired, the most favored time periods, how many GRPs are needed for each week, and how many weeks are needed.

Agencies will then prepare their own estimates of the audience delivered by the various shows and negotiate with the networks. If the network does not deliver on its CPM, because its audience falls short of

---

[8]John D. Leckenby and Shizue Kishi, "A National Survey Reveals . . . How Media Directors View Reach/Frequency Estimation," *Journal of Advertising Research* (June-July 1982), pp. 64–69.

estimates, it often gives the advertisers "bonus units"—additional commercial slots without charge.[9]

Several services are available to aid in media planning and to purchase time and space. The media buying function may be performed within the advertiser's own organization or advertising agency or through a specialized media buying service.

Media Representatives

The salespeople for media are known as *media representatives*. A medium may have its own salespeople selling time or space or may use the services of independent sales agents who represent a group of noncompetitive newspapers, magazines, or television stations. The services of the media representative are of value to the advertiser or agency who maintains a media buyer as well as those who cannot afford such specialists.

Media Buyers

Large advertising agencies organize media selection departments with media buyers who are responsible for space purchases, time purchases, and other specialized areas. These media buyers must acquire large amounts of information about audiences and the various types of media. Their task is to determine what publications, broadcast stations, or other devices can best carry the advertiser's message to the right audience. Media buyers interview media representatives, negotiate for time and space, and issue contracts on behalf of their clients.

Media Buying Services

Media buying agencies have developed relatively recently. They are defined as middlemen or space buyers. Their function, as seen by some of these organizations, is to provide service to, rather than replace, the media department within an agency. The media buying companies offer a specialized service in time buying, particularly in the area of spot broadcasting, with its innumerable combinations of offerings, enormous variety of spot lengths, and its requirement of a knowledge of extensive data on demographics.

Another reason media buying services are particularly useful in broadcasting is that the cost of advertising time is frequently negotiable in this medium. Some buying services purchase special bargains that deviate from established advertising rates. They can then sell this time to the advertiser at a lower cost than the station would charge and still turn a profit.

---

[9]Philip H. Dougherty, "Advertising, Things You Won't See in the Ads," *The New York Times* (December 4, 1981), p. D.16.

Computer Applications

The computer has changed the role of the media planner in recent years, and there are indications that additional changes will take place in the near future. From 1970 to about 1983 media planners and buyers used time-sharing terminals to gather information out of mainframe computers owned by the time-sharing services. A. C. Nielsen, for example, permits agency users to access its general data bases offering information on national and local television viewing, through the services of such secondary suppliers as Interactive Market Systems. Personal computers have been used for media analysis since 1983. However, due to their limited power and memory they basically served as time-sharing terminals. More recently software packages have been developed for micro-computers. Media Management Plus, for example, provides a package that enables the media planner to use a personal computer screen which constantly updates figures showing the share of the budget spent, percent of the budget spent to reach the primary demographic group, and the cost per ratings point and CPM for specific time periods on broadcast media. Simmons Market Research Bureau, which has long made its Study of Media and Markets available through time-sharing services like Telmar and IMS, will now offer most of the same information on a hard disk drive for access through a personal computer. This new service is called Choices.

For media planners the computer offers the capability of using more magazines in developing a schedule, as well as more mathematically precise schedules and doing all this in a shorter time period. To some observers, however, the increased use of computers in media analysis may lead to the problem of GIGO, or garbage in, garbage out—that is, the excessive use of meaningless information, and an extensive emphasis on "numbers crunching." Moreover, the computer does not consider qualitative criteria; for example, it may select a magazine for its high efficiency, but the advertiser may not want to use the magazine because of its editorial environment, image, or lack of pass-along circulation.[10]

It is obvious that the computer will be increasingly applied to media planning. However, it cannot be the sole decision-maker, since this requires judgment and creativity as well as analytical ability.

SUMMARY

Major media decisions in advertising are those that relate to media selection and media scheduling. A number of sources are available to the advertiser for media information; these include ABC, SRDS, and the media themselves. Purchases for time and space may be made by the advertiser, the agency, or a specialized buying service.

The choice of media is determined by examining such factors as the firm's marketing requirements, advertising requirements, and produc-

---

[10]This section was adapted from Rich Zahradnik, "Media's Micro Age," *Marketing & Media Decisions* (April 1986), pp. 34–50.

tive requirements, as well as evaluating the different characteristics of specific media.

There are a number of steps involved in the development of a media plan. These include a statement of objectives, a determination of strategy, a budgetary breakdown, a discussion of rationale for recommendations as well as alternative suggestions, an analysis of competitive activity, and the presentation of supporting documentation. Scheduling is an important component in the media plan, and a variety of timing strategies may be used.

A number of quantitative criteria are available for evaluating the media plan. These include cost per thousand, reach, frequency, gross impressions, and gross rating points. Qualitative criteria are also valuable in this analysis. Recent developments in media computer models have helped to improve the decision-making process.

QUESTIONS FOR DISCUSSION

1. What is the significance of Standard Rate and Data Service?
2. What broad marketing factors should be considered in selecting media for advertising?
3. Discuss the influence of creative requirements on media choice.
4. Describe the various steps in preparing a media plan.
5. Describe three media timing strategies. Which do you believe are most effective? Why?
6. What is the meaning of CPM? How is it computed?
7. What is the significance of gross impressions? How are they computed?
8. What is meant by *reach? Frequency?*
9. How do you define one gross rating point? Compute the number of gross rating points in a television schedule that places two advertisements a week for ten weeks on a program that has an average rating of 20 percent.
10. What information should the media planner gather?

KEY TERMS

medium	continuous advertising
vehicle	flighting
media plan	pulsing
spot	reach
media availabilities	frequency
rate card	gross impressions
media flowchart	nonduplicated audience
the wave theory	cumulative audience
the media dominance theory	roadblocking
the media concentration theory	

Gillette recently introduced a "revolutionary" shaving product, called Brush Plus. The product combines a shaving brush and cream in one package. Initially the consumer buys a kit that includes the brush, which is placed on top of a plastic cylinder, and a plastic cartridge of shaving cream that is screwed into the brush component. A flick of the cartridge's dial delivers cream through the top of the brush cylinder, moistening the brush. According to the product manager for Brush Plus, the product is designed to offer the quality that men associate with a brush shave, while making it more convenient.

1. Prepare a media schedule for this product.
2. Which media would you particularly recommend? Why?

Source: Kate Bertrand, "Convenient and Portable Packaging Pays," *Advertising Age,* *Thursday* (February 20, 1986), p. 16.

18

Print Media: Newspapers and Magazines

With such headlines as "Psychic Says Your Grandparents May Be From Another Planet: Here's How You Can Tell," it's little wonder why 4.5 million people buy the *National Enquirer*. Unfortunately for the *Enquirer*, few of those readers are corporate advertising executives and the paper's advertising revenues have been relatively small. Recently, however, there have been efforts to change the paper's image to increase advertising revenues; the *Enquirer* now runs, along with its celebrity and gossip news, recipes and how-to articles on caring for pets, coping with cancer, and getting along with a spouse.

U.S. News and World Report, the magazine that used to promote itself as "no fluff, no sports, no entertainment, no nonsense," is redesigning its dull image. Although research showed strong reader loyalty to the magazine, its circulation lags far behind *Time* and *Newsweek*. The magazine has redesigned its interior and exterior, adding more color photography, charts, and maps, and added new editors and writers with a livelier writing style. This redesign is an effort to attract new advertisers as well as readers.

The term print media is generally used to refer to newspapers and magazines. Advertisers serve as an important source of revenue for print media which, in turn, offer numerous and varied capabilities for presenting the advertiser's message. How advertisers make their choices among the multiplicity of newspapers and magazines available is the subject of this chapter.

KINDS OF NEWSPAPERS

In 1986 there were 1675 daily newspapers in the United States with paid circulation over 64 million.[1] In addition to those published daily there are also weekly newspapers, Sunday newspapers, and Sunday supplements. (On the average Sunday newspapers account for approximately 30 percent of a newspaper's total advertising revenue.)

A newspaper supplement is one that is distributed either as part of a newspaper's weekend or Sunday edition. One type of supplement is a *syndicated Sunday magazine*, distributed by several Sunday newspapers. It is separately produced, has a central editorial policy, and carries advertising on a national and regional basis. Examples of syndicated groups are *Parade* and *Family Weekly* with circulations of over 12,000,000. Another type is the *local Sunday supplement* which is distributed by its parent paper only and whose advertising is sold alone or in concert with other local Sunday magazines. The editorial content of such supplements is local in nature and the advertising may be either local, regional, or national.

Although relatively few in number, national newspapers have been in existence for many years. *The Wall Street Journal*, for example, recently celebrated its one hundredth birthday. It has the largest daily circulation of any newspaper and its success appears to be based on a very specialized target audience: business. According to the paper's associate publisher, it is easy to picture the reader of *The Wall Street Journal*, because the paper provides a "cohesive, almost self-defining national audience."[2]

The New York Times has had a national edition since 1980 and *USA Today* was introduced in 1982. Although these publications are both national, they are aimed at different audiences. *The New York Times'* national edition is designed to reach the highly upscale, predominantly professional/managerial audience, while *USA Today* is more interested in the mobile audience, the "many millions of people who have moved in recent years," as, for example, from the Frostbelt to the Sunbelt.[3]

Unlike traditional newspapers, which rely on a foundation of local retail advertising, national newspapers are specifically designed for the national advertiser. For example, *USA Today* is positioning itself similarly to magazines; it offers excellent four-color capability and describes its potential readership as close to *Time* and *Newsweek* audiences. *USA Today* has become the third largest newspaper and is considered "one of the most extraordinary concepts and successes in U.S. press history."[4] Recently, Simmons Market Research Bureau (SMRB) reported that *USA*

[1]"A.M. Dailies Keep Continued Rise in News Circulation," *Marketing News* (March 28, 1986), p. 4.

[2]"*Wall Street Journal* Shows It Can Be Done," *Advertising Age* (July 19, 1982), p. M–16.

[3]B. G. Yovovich, "Tomorrow Arrives for *Today*," *Advertising Age* (July 19, 1982), p. M–8.

[4]"Significant Marketing Achievements Listed for National News Daily," *Marketing News* (March 28, 1986), p. 16.

**TABLE 18.1   Leading Print Properties
Top 10 Newspapers by Daily Circulation**

Rank	Newspaper	Daily Circulation
1	*Wall Street Journal*	1,952,283
2	*New York Daily News*	1,270,926
3	*USA Today*	1,179,052
4	*Los Angeles Times*	1,086,383
5	*New York Times*	1,001,694
6	*New York Post*	731,668
7	*Washington Post*	748,019
8	*Chicago Tribune*	744,969
9	*Detroit News*	680,800
10	*Detroit Free Press*	656,477

Today has the most readers (not circulation) of any daily newspaper in the United States.

Classification of Advertising in Newspapers

Newspapers vary in size. A standard *broadsheet* newspaper, such as *The Wall Street Journal*, contains 6 columns and is approximately 21 inches deep and 13 inches wide. A *tabloid*, such as *The New York Daily News*, is 5 columns and is approximately 14 inches deep and 10-13/16 inches wide.

Advertising space is distinguished from space devoted to the editorial content of a newspaper and is identified by its use: display, classified, special, and inserts. These four categories are then divided as follows:

— Display Advertising
    National or general advertising
    Local or retail advertising
— Classified Advertising
    Regular classified advertising
    Classified display advertising
— Special Advertising
    Reading notices
    Public notices
    Legal notices, political and government reports
    Financial reports

— Inserts

Advertisements that are inserted or freestanding in
newspapers and not placed in conjunction with editorial
matter.

Display Advertising

Display advertising accounts for the largest portion of a newspaper's advertising revenue. A display ad requires extensive preparation, including the planning of the advertising campaign, the creative preparation
of the ad (which includes headlines, illustrations, and copy), and the
development of periodical promotional efforts.

National display (or *general*) *advertising*, such as that for RC Cola
in Exhibit 18.1, involves consumer advertising by manufacturers and
producers and requires extensive budgets and careful selection of media. National advertising is purchased through special representative
companies with offices and salespeople in key business centers. The
rates are generally higher than local advertising rates; originally this was
because of the presumed extra costs involved in servicing national advertisers. Today the differential exists to support the local advertiser,
who makes use of the bulk of the advertising space. This dual rate system is a topic of continuing controversy among advertisers. Some newspapers have adjusted their rates to accommodate national advertisers
who complain that the practice is discriminatory, and to encourage national brand manufacturers to advertise more frequently in this medium.

Retail display advertising (or *local*) *advertising* generally serves the
stores and local service establishments; local display ads account for 80
percent of display advertising. Exhibit 18.2 shows a particularly clever
ad campaign for Filene's Department Store.

Classified Advertising

Classified ads may be considered professional or transient, depending
upon their source. They are generally designated as want ads, arranged
according to subject matter for the convenience of the reader.

Classified ads account for approximately 30 percent of all newspaper
advertising revenue. There are generally no headlines, no illustrations,
and a single size of type throughout the advertisement. However, there
is a more elaborate kind of classified, called the *classified display*, since
it employs a number of display elements, such as moderately larger type
for headings, some white space, and occasionally simple illustrations.

Special Advertising

There are various kinds of special advertising, usually designated as notices. They may provide financial, political or legal information. *Reading
notices* are advertising matter made up to look like editorial matter and
are charged at higher rates than display advertising. To prevent the
reading notice from being confused with a news story the word *advertisement* must appear at the top of the notice.

Advertising Inserts

Most Sunday newspapers carry advertising inserts. "Freestanding" inserts in newspapers can be in the form of small cards, envelope order

EXHIBIT 18.1
A National Display Advertisement

This ad was considered among the
"best of press" by *Advertising Age*. It
used newspaper space extremely well
by running two pages back-to-back,
so that the reader was prompted to
look for the reason for the ad. It also
aided promotion by carrying a
coupon.

EXHIBIT 18.2
Retail Display Advertising

Filene's Basement of Boston used this teaser campaign in newspapers when it opened branches in the New York area. The first ad appeared on August 9, 1982 in The *New York Times,* but the store did not identify itself until the second ad was placed the following day.

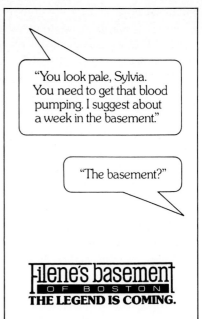

forms, or brochures printed on high-quality gloss paper stock. They may be printed by the advertisers through insert publishers and then delivered to the newspaper to be inserted into a specific edition either by machine or by the newscarriers. These freestanding ads generally contain coupons and are delivered with the newspaper. Inserts have a high readership and have been considered one of the most cost-effective advertising vehicles available. They are used by advertisers in package goods, household products, and over-the-counter drug categories such as General Foods, Procter & Gamble, and Colgate-Palmolive.

In 1985 some 180 billion coupons were distributed and inserts carried 60 percent of them. More recently, price wars and increases in production and distribution costs have created problems for insert publishers; moreover prices for inserts tend to be lower than newspaper run-of-press advertising, causing newspapers to refuse inserts they consider competitive. Insert publishers are responding to these problems by adding new advertisers such as appliance companies and financial service companies like credit card marketers.[5]

WHY ADVERTISERS USE NEWSPAPERS

For many years newspapers have remained the largest advertising medium in terms of total advertising volume. Although television and magazines have been replacing newspapers in national advertising volume,

---

[5]Paul Edwards, "Insert publishers retool as profitability sags," *Advertising Age* (November 17, 1986), p. S-21.

when local and national expenditures are combined, newspapers continue to remain the major advertising medium. In fact the printed matter in the average newspaper contains approximately two-thirds advertising matter and one-third editorial matter. Furthermore, most of the newspapers' income (approximately three-quarters) is derived from advertising revenue.

The medium is essentially local, running advertisements for local stores and services, many on a continuing basis; but it also appeals to national advertisers. The heaviest users are cigarette companies, automobile companies, airlines, and food companies. The medium's strengths derive from the manner in which the consumer accepts and utilizes this communication device.

Newspapers Are Read for Their Ads

A newspaper is read differently from a magazine or book. Instead of leisurely reading (except for Sunday), a consumer will devote many free moments scattered throughout the day to newspaper reading. Also, a newspaper is read by the entire family. The paper is edited for persons of all ages and provides items of interest to all readers. Moreover, reader interest in the advertisements is almost as high as it is in the news items. Newspaper readers do not object to long copy.

Newspapers have catalog value for consumers who are gathering information about products they wish to buy. In many cases the information in the newspaper causes the item or brand to be presold. Consumers usually search newspapers either on the day before or on the same day as they shop; often they cut the ads out of newspapers and take them along as references.

Newspapers Are Timely

The timeliness of newspapers offers several advantages. The daily publication schedule permits an advertiser to tie in advertising to current events. An urgent or topical advertising message can be developed to meet immediate emergencies. Changing conditions may force a withdrawal of advertising, and this can be accomplished more easily in newspapers than in practically any other advertising medium. Information about special promotional events can appear the day before or even the morning of a special sale.

Newspapers Provide Frequent Exposure and Are Flexible

Newspapers also provide a high degree of geographic flexibility. Advertisers can place sales messages in the markets where they believe the messages will do the most good and avoid the markets that may be wasteful. The availability of newspapers in different sections of the country permits advertisers to open new markets one by one or several at a time, as conditions dictate.

As an audience becomes more fragmented it becomes difficult to reach everyone in the typically national medium. The local quality of newspapers permits them to be directed at specific target markets, particularly among localized ethnic groups (see Exhibit 18.3).

40% of the Miami market doesn't understand your language.

40% of the people in Miami speak Spanish.

And the Spanish-speaking people of Greater Miami are also the Spanish-reading people of South Florida. This 40% of the total Miami market represents more than $4 billion in buying power.

Intelligent, informed, affluent and acquisitive people who believe in Diario Las Américas, because it has been their daily newspaper for more than a quarter of a century. They know it. They trust it. And they buy what Diario Las Américas sells.

To find out more about Diario Las Américas and one of the most dynamic markets in America today, send the coupon below for our free brochure.

Diario Las Américas

The Spanish-language Daily Newspaper
Founded July 4, 1953
2900 N.W. 39th Street
Miami, Florida 33142-5193
(305) 633-3341

¡SI! I WANT TO KNOW MORE ABOUT THE $4-BILLION GREATER MIAMI LATIN MARKET.

NAME
TITLE
COMPANY
ADDRESS
CITY/STATE/ZIP   AA-7

Newspapers offer flexibility to all sizes of advertising appropriations. Local advertisers can use the medium infrequently at a fairly low cost, while national advertisers may use newspapers often to tell consumers where they can buy products locally.

Newspapers Are Good for Cooperative Programs

Newspapers offer excellent opportunities for expending cooperative advertising funds. They look favorably upon cooperative advertising since it makes more consistent advertisers out of retailers, and the quality of the advertising provided by the manufacturer is generally better than that supplied by a retailer's advertising department. In addition, dealer "tie-ins" to advertising run nationally by the manufacturer can be formatted easily in newspapers.

How Advertisers Buy Newspaper Space

Large newspapers such as *The Chicago Tribune* sell space directly to advertisers; smaller newspapers, however, find the services of newspaper representatives very useful for selling space. Some even advertise to attract customers.

There are two types of newspaper representative companies. Some larger newspaper groups, such as Gannett Newspapers and Newhouse Newspapers, have their own reps. The second type is the independent rep who acts on behalf of various sizes of newspapers.

Basic considerations in purchasing newspaper space relate to the size of the area required for the advertisement, the cost, and the newspaper's circulation.

Measuring Newspaper Space

For many years rates for newspaper space were quoted by the *agate line,* a unit of space one column wide and $1/14$ inch deep. With the advent of photocomposition and the increasing prices of newsprint, newspapers turned to a variety of formats for ads. With the proliferation of formats advertisers no longer knew how their ads would look in each newspaper and how to price a schedule for several newspapers.

To resolve this problem the American Newspaper Publishers Association developed a *Standard Advertising Unit System* (see Figure 18.1). Under this system there are 56 ad sizes which are fixed in width and depth and measured in standard column inches. Since tabloids are generally shorter than broadsheet newspapers (only 14 inches compared with the standard 21 inches) 33 of the sizes are designed to fit the tabloid format. Currently 95 percent of all newspapers use the SAUs.

Newspapers participating in the SAU™ system offer rates in terms of standard column inches. A *column inch* covers an area one column (or $2 1/16$ inches) wide and one inch deep. An ad 1 column wide by 1 inch deep (the smallest available) is described as 1×1 and is billed as 1 column inch of space. An ad 2 columns wide by 3 inches deep is described as 2×3 and is billed as 6 column inches. A horizontal half-page is described as 6×10.5 and billed as 63 column inches.

Cost of Newspaper Advertising

Although newspapers represent a relatively low cost medium, rates may vary widely depending on the paper selected, the frequency of insertions, and the positions chosen. Information concerning the cost of advertising in specific newspapers is available from the individual newspaper's rate card and the *Standard Rate and Data Service.*

Flat Rate   When the rate per line is fixed, regardless of the frequency of insertions or the amount of advertising space used, it is designated as a *flat rate.*

Sliding Scale Rate   If a newspaper offers a discount structure, it is said to provide a *sliding scale* rate. The *open* rate is the charge for the minimum amount of space for an advertisement that appears one time. *The New York Times,* for example, charges $272.69 per column inch for an ad appearing once in its daily paper (see Exhibit 18.4). A 2×3 ad appearing once in the *Times* would cost:

6 column inches $\times$ $272.69 = $1636.14

Bulk discounts offer a descending rate for increasing the number of column inches used, usually on an annual basis. *The New York Times,* for example, charges $253.02 per column inch for 12,600 column inches yearly.

Combination Rates   Combination rates are available for advertising appearing in the morning and evening editions of the same newspaper, for combining a weekday with a Saturday or Sunday newspaper, or for advertising with a specified group of newspapers. At one time some of

FIGURE 18.1   The Expanded Standard Advertising Unit System

The Expanded [SAU]® Standard Advertising Unit System
(Effective July 1, 1984)

Depth in Inches	1 COL. 2-1/16"	2 COL. 4-1/4"	3 COL. 6-7/16"	4 COL. 8-5/8"	5 COL. 10-13/16"	6 COL. 13"
FD*	1xFD*	2xFD*	3xFD*	4xFD*	5xFD*	6xFD*
18"	1x18	2x18	3x18	4x18	5x18	6x18
15.75"	1x15.75	2x15.75	3x15.75	4x15.75	5x15.75	
14"	1x14	2x14	3x14	4x14 N	5x14	6x14
13"	1x13	2x13	3x13	4x13	5x13	
10.5"	1x10.5	2x10.5	3x10.5	4x10.5	5x10.5	6x10.5
7"	1x7	2x7	3x7	4x7	5x7	6x7
5.25"	1x5.25	2x5.25	3x5.25	4x5.25		
3.5"	1x3.5	2x3.5				
3"	1x3	2x3				
2"	1x2	2x2				
1.5"	1x1.5					
1"						

(top ruler marked 13")

1 Column 2-1/16" 2 Columns 4-1/4" 3 Columns 6-7/16" 4 Columns 8-5/8" 5 Columns 10-13/16" 6 Columns 13"	**Double Truck 26³/₄"** (There are four suggested double truck sizes:) 13xFD* 13x18 13x14 13x10.5	***FD (Full Depth)** can be 21" or deeper. Depths for each broadsheet newspaper are indicated in the Standard Rate and Data Service. All broadsheet newspapers can accept 21" ads, and may float them if their depth is greater than 21".	**Tabloids:** Size 5 x 14 is a full page tabloid for long cut-off papers. Mid cut-off papers can handle this size with minimal reduction. The 5 size, measuring 9⅞ x 14, represents the full page size for tabloids such as the New York Daily News and News-day, and other short cut-off newspapers. The five 13 inch deep sizes are for tabloids printed on 55 inch wide presses such as the Philadelphia News. See individual SRDS listings for tabloid sections of broadsheet newspapers.

SAU° is a registered trademark of the

American Newspaper Publishers Association.

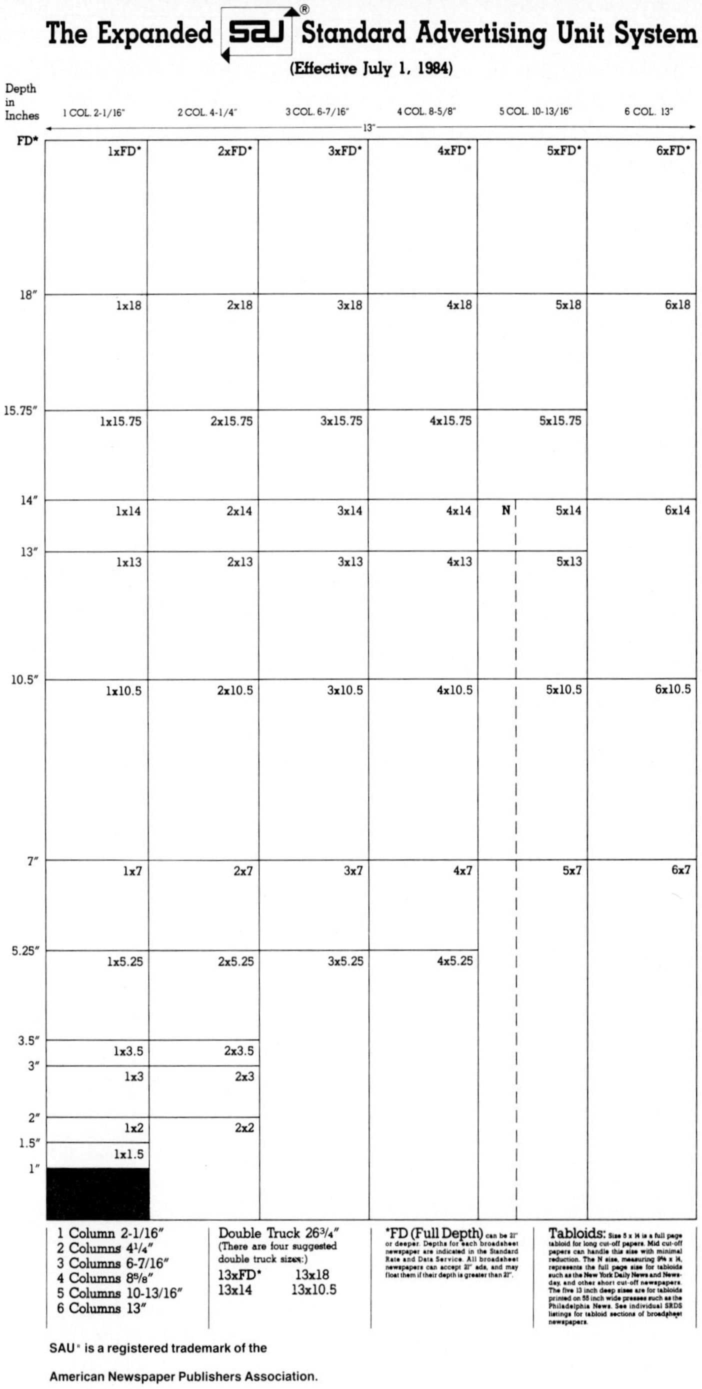

Source: "The Expanded SAU® Standard Advertising Unit System." Reprinted with the permission of the American Newspaper Publishers Association, Reston, Virginia.
SAU® is a registered trademark of the American Newspaper Publishers Association, Reston, Virginia.

these combination rates were forced; that is, advertisers were forced to use a combination of newspapers. More recently, the courts have ruled against this and now combination choices are optional. Some newspapers have zone editions for which they offer special rates.

Position Charges   An advertiser may place an advertisement R. O. P. (run of press). This means that the newspaper editor can place the advertisement where he or she considers best. The advertiser may request a preferred position.

The newspaper generally charges a higher rate for certain preferred sections or preferred pages. *Newsday*, a major New York state newspaper, charges 25-percent extra for an ad appearing on the comic page.

Higher rates are also charged for preferred placement on the page. *Full position*, which refers to top of the column and alongside reading matter, may be quoted at a premium of 25 percent. *Next to* and *below reading matter* are sometimes charged at 15 percent over the regular rate. The most preferred position—the *island position*—is rarely offered. It is placed top of the column and surrounded on all three sides by reading matter. *Buried position* (surrounded by ads) is least desirable, and, of course, something the advertiser wants to avoid.

Color   Many newspapers offer color at an extra charge. Closing dates for color advertisements are in advance of the normal closing time set for black-and-white advertisements. A number of newspapers have purchased digital color scanning equipment. These machines allow precise separation of color artwork for ads and give newspapers the ability to compensate for the shortcomings inherent in printing color on newsprint.[6]

Split-Runs   A great many newspapers offer split-runs to advertisers who wish to test their advertisements. The split-run provides the advertiser with the opportunity to run two advertisements in separate runs of the same issue of a newspaper to test which advertisement has greater pulling power. Usually there is a minimum requirement for advertising linage for the split-run and an extra charge.

Newspaper Circulation

As noted in Chapter 17, the Audit Bureau of Circulations (ABC) was established in 1914 to provide an independent audit of the circulation of newspapers. These circulation figures are available from the newspaper rate card and the *Standard Rate and Data Service*. ABC figures relate only to the number of copies of a newspaper that are sold; however, there is generally more than one reader per copy. Newspapers also provide advertisers with quotes on "readership."

---

[6]William F. Gloede, "Technology Transforms Production and Package," *Advertising Age, Thursday* (January 23, 1986), p. 20.

The New York Times
(Manhattan Borough)
229 W. 43rd St., New York, NY 10036.
Phone 212-556-1234, TWX710-581-6599, Phone. (after hours & holidays) 710-581-49, 27..

ABC Coupon Distribution Verification Service

Media Code 1 133 6000 2.00   Mid 017018-000
MORNING, SATURDAY MORN. AND SUNDAY.
Member: INAME; NAB, Inc.; ABC Coupon Distribution Verification Service; ACB, Inc.
1. PERSONNEL
   Publisher—Arthur Ochs Sulzberger.
   V.P./Advertising Director—Erich Linker.
   Nat'l Advertising Director—John Guerin.
   Int'l Advertising Director—Basil Bicknell.
2. REPRESENTATIVES and/or BRANCH OFFICES
   Boston 02109—2 Faneuil Hall Marketplace. Phone 617-227-7820.
   Chicago 60601—233 N. Michigan Ave. Phone 312-565-0969.
   Dallas 75247—1341 W. Mockingbird Lane. Phone 214-637-0485.
   Detroit 48226—211 W. Fort St. Phone 313-962-8484.
   Houston 77027—50 Briar Hollow. Phone 713-871-0305.
   Los Angeles 90017—900 Wilshire Blvd. Phone 213-628-3143.
   Miami 33132—100 N. Biscayne Blvd. Phone 305-379-1601.
   Philadelphia 19107—Avenue of the Arts Bldg., Phone 215-735-4904.
   San Francisco 94111—1750 Montgomery St., Phone 415-421-9700.
   London-EC4A 3JB, London Bureau Ltd., Suite 408, 76 Shoe Lane, Phone (011-44-1) 353-2174/3472.
   Paris, 3, Rue Scribe 75009.
   Toronto-M5E 1E6, 1 Yong St., Phone 416-828-2090.
3. COMMISSION AND CASH DISCOUNT
   15% to recognized agencies only; 15th following month. No cash discount.
4. POLICY-ALL CLASSIFICATIONS
   Minimum five days notice given of any rate revision
   Alcoholic beverage and cigarette advertising accepted.
      ADVERTISING RATES
      Effective January 1, 1987.
      Received January 22, 1987.
5. BLACK/WHITE RATES

	Daily	Sunday
SAU open, per inch	295.87	355.81
Inches charged full depth: col. 21; pg. 126.		
Within 1 year:	Daily	Sunday
126"	286.40	345.24
252"	285.30	344.14
630"	284.50	343.07
1,260"	282.61	341.99
2,520"	281.53	340.10
3,780"	280.18	339.30
5,040"	278.84	337.12
7,560"	274.78	332.81
9,450"	272.63	330.12
12,600"	270.73	328.22

Ads repeated on Saturday within 3 weeks, 170.27.
      ANNUAL BLANKET CONTRACT
Full run general contract advertisers may apply magazine linage, color and monotone, to fulfillment of their black and white contracts. The rate for such linage is same as though amount of space used were equivalent to the specified in black and white space contract.

continued

539

EXHIBIT 18.4
Standard Rate and Data Schedule

In evaluating newspaper circulation, an advertiser should take note of the qualitative characteristics of the newspaper audience as well as the quantitative values. For example, the advertiser should consider the socioeconomic characteristics of the readers, their buying habits, and the kinds of merchandise they purchase.

Cost/Circulation Comparisons   In selecting a newspaper, the advertiser should be concerned about both circulation and cost. For newspapers that still use the agate line rate an artificial rate called the *milline rate* enables advertisers to compare the cost effectiveness on the basis of both cost-per-agate-line and circulation. In theory the milline rate represents the cost to an advertiser of sending one agate line of advertising in a specific newspaper to a million people:

$$\text{Milline Rate} = \frac{\text{Cost of 1 Agate Line} \times 1{,}000{,}000}{\text{Circulation}}.$$

For example, if a newspaper with a circulation of 500,000 has an agate line rate of $10, then

$$\text{Milline Rate} = \frac{\$10 \times 1{,}000{,}000}{500{,}000} = \$20$$

This translates into, "It costs $20 to send one agate line of advertising in this newspaper to 1,000,000 people."

For newspapers that use the column-inch rate, the *cost per thousand* may be used to provide cost/circulation comparisons. For example, Newspaper A may have a column-inch cost of $200 and a circulation of 500,000. Newspaper B's column-inch cost is $150 and its circulation is 300,000.

$$\text{Cost per thousand (CPM)} = \frac{\text{Cost of 1 column Inch} \times 1000}{\text{Circulation}}$$

$$\text{Newspaper A CPM} = \frac{\$200 \times 1000}{500{,}000} = \$.40$$

$$\text{Newspaper B CPM} = \frac{\$150 \times 1000}{300{,}000} = \$.50$$

Thus, although Newspaper A charged more for the column inch, everything else being equal, it is more cost efficient than Newspaper B, since it costs 10 cents less to send 1 column inch of advertising to 1000 people in Newspaper A.

The advertiser must consider that some of the total circulation is waste circulation, and to increase the efficiency of the comparative figures, the advertiser may include only the circulation in his or her retail trading area in computing the cost per thousand.

Additional Considerations in Buying Newspaper Space

In addition to cost and circulation, a firm purchasing newspaper space should consider a number of other factors. It should evaluate the comparative benefits of morning versus evening versus Sunday papers, particularly as they exist within its market area. The advertiser should examine the editorial content of each newspaper and its image and consider how these factors may affect the advertising messages.

One of the major advantages of the newspaper as a medium is the merchandising services it offers, which may be free or part of a "package." Merchandising aids to the smaller advertiser include the creation of promotional pieces, the planning and budgeting of the advertising, the actual creation of the copy, and the rough layout for an advertisement. For the national advertiser, the newspaper may conduct trade surveys, provide route lists of manufacturers and distributors to salespeople, or offer to talk to meetings of the trade.

Newspaper Limitations

A number of factors limit the growth of newspapers as an advertising medium. Perhaps the most important is the fact that newspaper readership has been on a gradual decline. In 1973 nearly 75 percent of the adult population read a daily newspaper on an average day. In 1985 the percentage of readers fell to 64.2 percent.[7]

1. *Limited Reproductive Techniques.* Because of the frequency of newspaper publication and the vast amount of newsprint necessary, the application of fine reproductive techniques to newspaper advertising is somewhat prohibitive. The coarse paper tends to create a less impressive effect than that achieved by the smooth paper used in magazine advertising.

   R. O. P. color varies from newspaper to newspaper. These variations may result in the advertiser's message being more effective in one market than another, even though the markets have the same value.

2. *Little Socioeconomic Flexibility.* Although newspapers provide geographic selectivity, they do not offer selectivity in terms of all socioeconomic groups. The decline in the number of newspapers and the consolidation of newspapers, even in major market areas, have intensified this limitation and resulted in most newspapers reaching broad heterogeneous groupings, which may be incompatible with the market segmentation policies of advertisers.

3. *Short Life.* Most newspapers last only one day (although *The New York Times*, Sunday edition, is said to have an average life of three to four days). Unlike a magazine, a newspaper is not likely to be reread or put aside for later examination; thus the opportunity for exposure to the advertising message is limited to one reading. On the other hand, the newspaper message, unlike that transmitted via electronic media, can be torn out or set aside for future reference.

---

[7]Debbie Solomon, "Trends in Newspaper Readership," *Marketing and Media Decisions*, April 1986, p. 104.

4. *Increasing Costs.* The cost of buying national advertising in newspapers is high, particularly since many advertisers' publishers charge more to national advertisers than to local ones. Even if the national advertiser provides the local retailer with co-op funds to purchase the ads, the retailer may be charged for a national ad.

5. *Small Pass-Along Audience.* Although many members of the same family may read the same newspaper, the pass-along rate outside the home is very small.

6. *Too Many Ads.* The volume of advertising appearing in newspapers detracts from the capabilities of any one advertisement achieving extensive awareness. The positioning of the advertisement may also minimize its capabilities for exposure, particularly when it is surrounded by other advertising.

MAGAZINE CLASSIFICATIONS

Magazines are classified under three general headings: consumer magazines, business magazines, and farm magazines. They may also be classified according to frequency of production, which may vary.

Consumer Magazines

Consumer magazines may be divided into general and special interest publications. In general magazines, the editorial content covers subjects that might be of interest to anybody, such as *Reader's Digest*. Special interest magazines cater to specific audience segments, such as consumers interested in art and antiques, boating and yachting, mechanics and science, photography, or homemaking. They have proliferated in recent years; moreover, the special interest magazines of today deal with an increasingly narrow editorial specialty which closely circumscribes their audiences. For example, rather than a magazine which focuses on sports we have *American Soccer, Backpacker, Bow and Arrow, Coaching, Women's Athletics,* and *Senior Golfer.*

Business Publications

A business publication is one dealing with management, manufacturing, sales, operation of industries or businesses, or some specific industry, occupation, or profession. It is published to interest and assist persons actively engaged in the field it covers.

Farm Publications

Farm publications include such classifications as dairy and dairy breeds, farm education and vocations, farm organizations and cooperatives, and livestock. Some farm publications such as *Successful Farming, Progressive Farmer,* and *Farm Journal* have circulations in the millions. Although the farmer may be reached through general magazines, he or she can be approached more effectively through these magazines which are slanted to a particular interest.

Why Advertisers Use Magazines

Advertising has been the major source of magazine revenue for many years, and it is becoming an increasingly important financial resource. To insure a continuing flow of advertisers, traditional magazines are undergoing changes while magazines with newer formats designed to attract audiences desired by advertisers are entering the market (see Exhibit 18.5). Major advertisers in magazines are cigarette, automobile, cosmetic, and food companies. Cigarette companies became the top advertisers after they were prohibited from advertising on radio and TV.

Audience Selectivity

The most important benefit of magazines for advertisers is audience selectivity. Except for direct mail, magazines are the most selective of all media in terms of being able to pick out particular target groups. As indicated earlier, there are a vast number of special interest magazines available to the advertiser who wishes a specialized target market. A relatively new magazine, *Modern Maturity*, has become one of the largest in terms of circulation by targeting the mature market.

Editorial Content

People buy magazines to read, encouraging their exposure to advertisements. Moreover, advertisements can be related to the editorial matter of a magazine, whose audience probably has a common interest. A magazine audience is characterized by slow, leisurely reading, permitting longer exposure to advertising. Lifestyle magazines have been attracting particular interest, and publications such as *Country Living*, *Home*, *Success!*, and *Mature Outlook* have increased their circulation considerably since 1985.[8]

Mechanical Reproductive Quality

Magazines have a high mechanical reproductive quality. The kind of paper stock used for magazines permits fine photographic reproductions and the efficient use of color. Moreover, magazines have expanded their services and offer a wide variety of new and interesting advertising presentations (see Exhibit 18.6).

Media and Message Life

The life of magazines is perhaps longest of all media. People have saved the earliest issues of *National Geographic*, and it is not uncommon to see very old copies of *Reader's Digest* in waiting rooms.

A magazine's life is increased by passing it along to others, and the exposure of a message to any one member of an audience may be increased through repeated perusals of the magazine. According to an *Au-*

EXHIBIT 18.5
Using Posters to Advertise to Advertising Agencies

Ladies Home Journal used New York for its new ad campaign for the "new and improved" *Journal*. Kingsize posters appeared on buses traveling the avenues of midtown New York, where they presumably were spotted by agency executives. The ads transferred the *Journal* logo to those products it wanted to recruit for its advertising pages.

---

[8]Belinda Hulin-Salkin, "Seeds of optimism sown on rocky ground," *Advertising Age* (November 10, 1986), p. S-1.

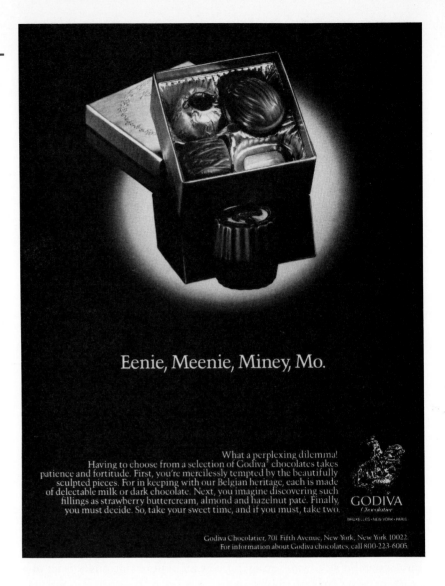

dit and Surveys report conducted for the Magazine Publishers Association, the average magazine page generates an average of 1.7 readers' exposures per reader. Furthermore, the second exposure significantly increases familiarity with the brand and its claims.[9]

Audience Characteristics and Prestige

Magazine-reading families are said to be above the mean average for the nation in purchasing power, income, and education. A full-color advertisement in a big-circulation magazine gains value from its very appearance in the medium, derived in part from the prestigious characteristics of the magazine's audience.

---

[9]*MPX—A Study of Magazine Page Exposure*, Magazine Publishers Association, Inc., 1982, New York, New York.

Additional Services for Magazines

As a service to advertisers who want to copy test their products, many magazines offer split-runs. If advertisers wish to test copy, they can place two different advertisements in identical halves of the magazine circulation and include in these advertisements some kind of response mechanism, such as a coupon, which will show which copy drew the greatest proportion of responses.

Although magazines do provide some merchandising support, it is generally not free of charge. Moreover, magazines are not close to the mass of retail outlets for advertised goods and cannot offer close cooperation between the manufacturer and the dealer as in newspapers and radio stations. Merchandising cooperation from some magazines includes planning and participation in sales meetings and trade conventions; aid in designing sales brochures, contests, and dealer incentive campaigns; and preparation of display material.

Buying Advertising Space in Magazines

The firm buying advertising space in magazines uses a number of criteria. These include quantitative criteria, such as costs and circulation, as well as qualitative criteria, such as the editorial policy of the publication, its image, the manner in which an ad is presented, the services offered, and the innovative techniques that may be used.

Magazine Advertising Size

The standard advertising unit for magazines is one page; however there are numerous space designations available to magazine advertisers. In addition to the typical half-page or two-page spread, a number of other space sizes have been introduced that offer both economy and the capability of attracting the reader's interest. Figure 18.2 presents some of these ad sizes and their designations.

The issue of size has generated much controversy over the years. It is generally accepted that two full-page ads, side by side, have only one-third more impact than a single ad. This suggests that an advertiser might do better to double the number of times an audience sees a single ad than to double its size. A recent survey, while supporting this thesis, suggests that there may be circumstances under which a two-page spread will generate much greater interest than a single ad. These results were found in banking or financial image advertising—areas considered to be of low interest. A two-page spread in *Fortune* was "noted" (a Starch term indicating the percentage of people who note the ad) 90 percent more than a single page.[10] While more research in this area is needed, it appears that an advertiser should give consideration to the relationship between the size of the ad and its effectiveness in a media plan.

---

[10]Philip H. Dougherty, "Advertising," *The New York Times* (November 24, 1981), p. D-25.

382 Print Media: Newspapers and Magazines

FIGURE 18.2 Magazine Ad Sizes

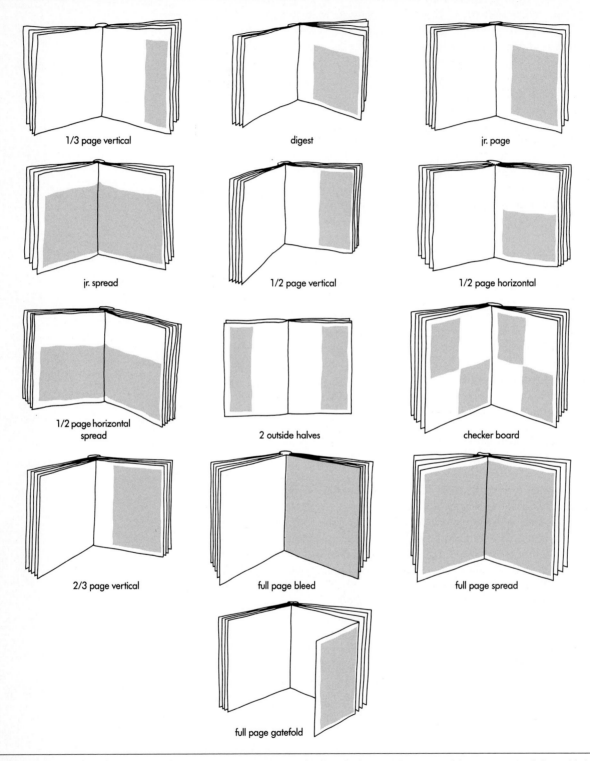

TABLE 18.2   Four-Color Page Rates for Selected Magazines

	Page Rate	Circulation
Time	$114,955	4,696,320
Reader's Digest	104,600	17,884,817
Fortune	42,900	733,224
New Yorker	20,765	506,103
Modern Maturity	120,000	11,818,316

Source: from SRDS Consumer Magazines and Agri-Media Rates & Data (February 27, 1986). Reprinted by permission of Standard Rate and Data Service, Inc.

Cost of Magazine Advertising

Magazines base their rates on the cost per page, which is generally computed on their circulation. Page rates vary widely depending not only on circulation but also on other factors, such as quality, selectivity of the audience, and the costs of publishing the particular magazine. Table 18.2 indicates the space cost and circulation for several widely used magazines.

Discount Structure
There is a built-in discount in the rate schedule related to the size of the advertisement; for example, a one-page advertisement in a magazine costs less than two half-pages, and a half-page advertisement costs less than two quarter pages. Magazines also offer frequency discounts for placing more than one page of advertising during a 52-week period, and volume or bulk discounts based on the total dollar volume expended by a corporation in that magazine during the contract year.

Purchasing Magazine Groups
Various publishing organizations offer special discounts that can be earned by buying advertising space in a group of magazines. For example, the Ziff-Davis Magazine network offers a combination including *Boating, Cycle, Popular Photo, Skiing,* and *Car & Driver.* The Conde Nast package of women's magazines includes *Vogue, Glamour, Mademoiselle, Bride's,* and *Self.* Publishers offer many combinations and discount structures; information is available from the sales offices of the publishers.

Position Policies
Which position in a magazine is best? For Harley Procter (son of one of the founders of Procter & Gamble), the favorite position in a magazine was the page facing the inside back cover. Mr. Procter was known to say, "How often when you come into a home, do you see the back cover is ripped off? Then the first thing you notice is the Ivory ad."[11]

---

[11]Nancy F. Millman, "The Saga of P&G's Ivory Soap; Keeping a Brand Afloat 100 Years," *Advertising Age* (April 30, 1980), p. 51.

Magazines generally do not charge a premium for any special page position within the covers. The advantages of one page over another in a magazine are related to the advertiser's expereinces and policies rather than to any technical or audience preference factor. For example, advertisers of food products want their ads to appear near a cooking column or household hints. They do not want their ads to run near drug products or a medical column.

Franchised Positions   Certain advertisers stake out claims to positions (called *franchised positions*) by virtue of their long-standing use of a magazine and a particular position. For example, the "Campbell Soup page" is the right-hand page following editorial material in the magazines in which Campbell's Soup advertises.

Cover Positions   Many magazines require premiums for cover positions, particularly the fourth cover. (Second, third, and fourth covers are the inside of the front cover, the inside of the back cover, and the back cover, respectively.) A number of advertisers consider the back cover in major magazines an important position and are willing to pay a premium to advertise there.

Color and Bleed Rates

Magazines offer the printing of four-color advertisements at rates that range from 20 percent to 40 percent over the one-page rate. *Bleeds,* where the color extends beyond the normal margins of the advertising space on a page, are available usually at the basic rates plus an additional 15 percent. Paying an additional charge for bleeds may be worth it. A recent survey by Starch Advertising Readership Service revealed that bleed ads are better read than non-bleed ads.[12]

Closing Dates

Most magazines accept space reservations which guarantee that advertising space will be available in desired issues. While space reservations can be made almost any time in advance of an issue, the final date for contracting to appear is called the *closing date*. The closing date may vary by publications—for monthly magazines it is generally 60 to 90 days in advance of issue; for weekly publications it is usually 3 to 7 weeks prior to issue. *Fortune* has a 6-week closing date and *Reader's Digest* usually requires 8 weeks.

New Magazine Advertising Techniques

In order to compete effectively with broadcast media, particularly television, magazines have developed new advertising techniques designed to offer the flexibility and demonstration capabilities of other media. Costs to advertisers are usually available from the medium. Listed below are nine of the techniques developed recently.

---

[12]"Starch Says Bleed Worth It," *Advertising Age* (March 30, 1981), p. 82.

For over 50 years Transamerica has stood for innovation. Today, Transamerica Insurance Companies stand as leaders in their fields. And more than ever, the Power of the Pyramid is working for you.

EXHIBIT 18.7
A Magazine Pop-Up

A three-dimensional ad for Transamerica Corp., an insurance company, attracted a great deal of attention when it appeared in the United States edition of *Time*.

1. *Gatefolds and Dutch Doors.* Gatefolds—double and triple pages that fold out to reveal one advertisement—and *dutch doors*—pages that partially cover each other to add interest and excitement to the advertisement—appear frequently in many magazines.
2. *Catalog, Guide, and Recipe Booklets.* In 1957 General Mills placed a Bisquick cookbook detachable insert in *Coronet*. Since then food advertisers, as well as automobile, wine, garden supply, and gift-wrapping firms, have placed booklets in their magazine advertising.
3. *Reply Redeemable Coupons.* As an extension of standard coupons that must be clipped from advertisements and sent to advertisers, detachable business reply cards and coupons that are redeemed at dealers now appear in magazine advertising.
4. *Perfumed Advertisements.* Perfumed ink has been used primarily in sales promotion and trade paper advertising. "Scratch and sniff" strips, embodying the new 3-M microencapsulation technique, are used for men's cologne, for women's perfume, and for a mint-scented soap.
5. *Actual Product Samples.* Sample packages of Scott Towel, Curtiss Candy, Vanity Fair lanolin facial tissue, and Glidden's Spread Satin latex paint, appear as part of magazine advertising.
6. *Pop-Ups and Novelties.* Pop-ups of animal stars in the Wrigley zoo and three-dimensional prefab buildings for a building company or an insurance company present the advertiser's product in a novel way (see Exhibit 18.7).
7. *Advertorials.* Advertorials are sections in magazines with a basic theme where ads are placed next to complementary editorial matter. Readers are drawn in by the editorial content, which directly relates to the product or service being advertised. For example, in 1986 the *New Yorker* offered a special advertising section which presented numerous products and services tied to the America's Cup yacht race. While advertorials tend to add to advertising revenue, they are controversial since they may be read

TABLE 18.3   Top Ten Magazines by Circulation

Rank	Magazine	Circulation
1	*TV Guide*	16,800,441
2	*Reader's Digest*	16,609,847
3	*Modern Maturity*	13,597,330*
4	*National Geographic*	10,764,998
5	*Better Homes and Gardens*	8,091,751
6	*Family Circle*	6,261,519
7	*Woman's Day*	5,743,842
8	*Good Housekeeping*	5,221,575
9	*McCall's*	5,186,393
10	*Ladies' Home Journal*	5,020,551

*Audit Bureau of Circulations' reports for the first half of 1986.

as editorial rather than advertising, or give the impression that advertisers are influencing the editorial content of the magazine.

8. *Single sponsor issues.* Some magazines have begun to offer advertisers the opportunity to be the only sponsor of all of the ads to appear in a specific issue. Merrill Lynch paid approximately 2 million dollars to tell its story in 37 advertising pages in an early 1987 issue of *Fortune* magazine. For Merrill Lynch this was seen as a method of breaking through the communication clutter and establishing a strong presence in the investment market. For *Fortune*, this assured the magazine it would secure sufficiently large advertising funds; however, it may have generated unfavorable attitudes from other potential advertisers.

Magazine Circulation

In selecting among the various alternatives, initially advertisers must consider circulation as well as page rates. In the past each magazine attempted to increase its circulation in order to present an advertiser with a vast number of potential exposures. Today there is increasing awareness that it is not necessarily the total number of exposures that is significant; rather, it is the number of prospective purchasers reached. Accordingly, some general-interest magazines with large circulation figures are attempting to weed out members of the audience who will not serve the needs of their advertisers. Nonetheless, a count of circulation remains important in selecting media (see Table 18.3).

Primary Versus Secondary Circulation

The primary circulation figures are available from the Audit Bureau of Circulations which validates the sales figures of every magazine. Secondary circulation includes the readership (the number of people who read each copy) and the pass-along circulation (the number of people who receive the copy from the original recipient). Secondary circulation is important to an advertiser who is concerned not only with the number of copies sold, but the number of people exposed to his message. Obviously it is difficult to audit this secondary circulation figure, and, in many cases, the advertiser must rely on the estimates of the media.

Guaranteed Versus Delivered Circulation

A magazine's rate structure is based on its circulation. A *guaranteed circulation figure* assures an advertiser that a specific number of copies of an issue will be sold. Since some of these copies may be sold on newsstands, the medium has no control over, and cannot always predict, the actual number of copies that are delivered to consumers. If this *delivered circulation* is below the guaranteed amount, the medium may offer an advertiser a rebate. Generally the magazine places the guaranteed circulation figure slightly below the actual circulation count.

Regional Issues

To lower the cost of advertising in magazines, and to cut down on the waste circulation inherent in a national audience, some magazines offer regional issues. For example, a one-page black-and-white ad in *Modern Maturity's* New England edition costs $11,605 compared to $108,800 for a similar ad in the regular publication. Regional issues are useful to introduce products area by area, bolster weak market areas, support regional promotions, and match seasonal or geographic differences in product appeal.

Comparing Cost and Circulation

In computing the cost of magazine advertising, an advertiser combines the circulation and cost of the magazine to form a basic comparison rate, just as an advertiser in newspapers does. However, in magazines, the cost per thousand (CPM) is computed by multiplying *the page rate* by 1000 and dividing by the circulation figure.

$$\text{Cost per thousand (CPM)} = \frac{1 \text{ page rate} \times 1000}{\text{Circulation}}$$

Accordingly:

$$\text{Cost per thousand for } \textit{Reader's Digest, } \text{February 1986} = \frac{\$104,600 \times 1000}{17,884,817} = \$5.85 [13]$$

---

[13] That is, it costs $5.85 to reach 1000 people through one page of advertising in the *Reader's Digest*.

TABLE 18.4   Comparing Cost and Circulation on the Basis of a Specific Target Audience

	Audience and Cost per Thousand: Men 18 +	
Magazine	*Audience (000)*	*4/c CPM*
Sports Illustrated	12,923	$6.92
Newsweek	10,388	8.33
U.S. News & World Report	6,394	8.65
Time	13,283	9.04

Source: 1986 SMRB and 1987 SRDS Consumer Magazine.
Latest Announced 1 × 4/c rate

To make the CPM more meaningful it is usually computed on the basis of a specific target audience rather than on total circulation. *Audience* in magazine readership usually includes both primary readers and pass-along readers (see Table 18.4)

Audience Characteristics

Advertisers are interested not only in the number of people who read magazines, but in their characteristics as well. When Stroh Brewery Company decided to launch its Signature premium beer, it decided to spend the major share of its $10 million budget in magazines rather than on television, since it felt its target group watched relatively little television and read relatively more magazines.[14] Therefore, Stroh advertised in *Sports Illustrated, Time, Runner,* and *Skiing.*

Information concerning the demographic and psychographic characteristics of a magazine's audience is available through the publication. While the techniques may vary, generally there are two basic methods for measuring magazine audience: *through the book* and *recent reading.* There is a continuing controversy over which method is the most effective. At this writing the two major sources of magazine audience data are Mediamark Research Inc. (MRI) which uses the recent reading method, and SMRB which uses a combination of the methods.

Through the Book   In this method almost complete magazine issues are shown to respondents who are asked if they have read the magazine. Those who report that they have looked at an issue are counted as members of the audience. This method is sometimes modified so that only a "stripped" or skeletonized part of an issue is presented.

Recent Reading   This method counts the number of people who can recall reading a certain magazine within a given time frame when they are shown, instead of specific issue material, just the magazine logo.

Several syndicated services provide magazine audience information. Table 18.5 lists the major services and indicates the items shown to respondents as an aid in recalling the magazine.

---

[14]Raymond Searagin, "Stroh Signature Signs Off TV for Launch" (March 17, 1986), p. 92

TABLE 18.5 Evolution of Magazine Audience Measures

	Service	Number of Magazines	Aid to Recall
1930–40	Developed by *Life* to show total audience	1	whole issue
1960–70	BRI (Norton Garfinkle)	80	list of magazines
1963	Nielsen Magazine Service	24	skeleton issues
1966	Politz	12	whole issues
1963–78	W.R. Simmons	74	skeleton issues
1970	Starch experiment	60	cover/table-of-contents
1972	TGI (Target Group Index) set up by Timothy Joyce for J. Walter Thompson	100	list of magazines
1978	W.R. Simmons — additional titles in second interview — results not published	80+	12-item skeleton
1978	TGI and Simmons merged into SMRB		
1979	MRI introduced by Timothy Joyce and partners	140	logos only
1979	Starch Primary Readership	19	cover/table-of-contents
1979–80	SMRB — two-tier system	44 100	12-item skeleton logos only
1981	MRI-recent reading Starch proposal SMRB — two-tier system	140 120 44 100	logos only cover/table-of-contents 12-item skeleton logos only

Source: From "Frank, Tim and Jay Make It a Free-For-All," *Marketing & Media Decisions*, April 1981. Copyright © 1981 Decisions Publications Inc. Reprinted by permission.

LIMITATIONS OF MAGAZINES

Cost
A major factor limiting the use of magazines is cost. At a rate of $104,600 for one four-color advertisement in one issue of *Reader's Digest* in 1986 (a rate that increases every year), the number of advertisers who can afford such expenses becomes severely limited. Despite the fact that the cost per thousand is relatively low ($5.85) few advertisers can afford the large initial outlay. In order to meet the needs of the less affluent advertiser, many magazines are offering regional issues at significantly reduced rates.

Waiting Time
Generally there is a long time lapse between an insertion order and the delivery, to the reader, of the finished advertisement. Some magazines require a two-month advance for their closing dates. This extensive wait-

ing time causes many, often unforeseeable, difficulties for the advertiser. A number of advertisers have prepared advertisements and contracted for their appearances in magazines only to be faced by strikes or even major product changes by the time a magazine is issued. Moreover, rapidly changing conditions may make a message ineffective. Advertisers have, on occasion, used well-known figures to endorse their products, only to find that, by the time the advertisement appears, the endorser has lost some favor with the public. In general, advertisers in magazines have to predict the conditions that will exist at the time their advertisements will actually be circulated.

Reach Builds Slowly

Reach builds slowly in some magazines. Active people who are always on the go may ignore a number of issues and read only the current one. Occasionally they will scan a number of issues at one time to catch up on their reading.

SUMMARY

Newspaper advertising categories include display, classified, special, and inserts. Advertisers may buy space directly from newspapers or through their representatives. Currently most newspapers use a Standard Advertising Unit System as their space measurement. Rates for newspaper space are quoted in column inches, areas one column wide and one inch deep. The individual newspaper may have a flat rate—that is a fixed rate—or a sliding scale rate, which provides discounts for increasing the number of column inches used.

Data on newspaper circulation is available through the rate card or Standard Rate and Data Service. The cost per thousand, (CPM), that is, the cost of sending one column inch of newspaper advertising to 1000 people, is used to compare cost and circulation of newspapers.

Magazines provide advertisers with audience selectivity which permits focusing on a particular target group. They also offer excellent photo reproductive capabilities and prestigious impact.

Magazine classifications include consumer magazines and business and farm publications. Advertising is sold in terms of pages or fractions thereof, and advertisers are offered discounts for bulk purchases. To attract advertisers magazines offer a number of innovative concepts, including gatefolds, perfumed ads, product samples, and pop-ups.

To provide lower costs, magazines offer regional issues to an advertiser. Cost per thousand is also used to compare circulation and cost, but, in magazines, the cost is stated in terms of page rate. Several organizations offer information on the characteristics of magazine audiences useful for advertisers. Two basic methods for measuring magazine audiences are "through the book"—whereby almost complete issues are shown to respondents as aids to recalling the magazine—and "recent reading"—in which only the magazine logo is shown to the respondent.

The primary limitations to magazines as advertising media are their high cost, particularly for national issues, and the long lead time required in presenting the ad for future publication.

QUESTIONS FOR DISCUSSION

1. What kinds of advertisements appear in newspapers? Select representative examples from newspapers.
2. What are Standard Advertising Units and why are they used?
3. What is meant by *flat rate? Sliding scale? Milline Rate? CPM?*
4. Select a page in a newspaper and indicate various positions available for ads.
5. What are the limitations to the use of newspapers for advertising?
6. Should a major goal of magazines be to increase total circulation? Explain.
7. What positions are available for magazine ads? Which do you consider most desirable? Why?
8. Select some ads in magazines that offer interesting or innovative advertising techniques. Discuss their effectiveness.
9. What is meant by these circulation terms—*primary, secondary, guaranteed* or *delivered circulation?*
10. Discuss the strengths and limitations of magazines.

KEY TERMS

supplement

broadsheet

display advertising

classified advertising

classified display

Standard Advertising Unit
   System

column inch

flat rate

sliding scale rate

bulk discounts

full position

island position

buried position

split-run

milline rate

franchised position

closing date

gatefolds

dutch doors

guaranteed circulation figure

through the book

recent reading

AD PRACTICE

You want to advertise a new line of designer sheets and towels, but you can't decide if you should place your ad in a newspaper or in a magazine. For each decide on the specific type of ad you would use in terms of size, position, use of color and bleed, and special technical design.

    Using Standard Rate and Data Service determine the costs and requirements for placing this ad. Determine the circulation and compute the cost per thousand for both a newspaper and a magazine.

19

Broadcast Media: Television and Radio

Television as an advertising medium has the ability to reach members of a vast audience simultaneously, but the cost is high. The final segment of M*A*S*H aired on television in 1983 and achieved a program rating of 60.3 percent, the highest rating to date. It was estimated that 100 million people viewed this broadcast. The 1986 Superbowl was only the sixth highest-rated show in television history—however it cost $550,000 for a 30-second message.

Radio cannot reach similarly large audiences for any one program; however 99 percent of all American households have an average of 5.5 radio receivers. Ninety-five percent of all cars are radio equipped. Together with the many Walkmans™ and headphones used on portable radios, these devices deliver messages to people while they are driving, walking, working, studying, playing, and eating.

This chapter discusses the nature of broadcast media and its use by advertisers. It also examines the technological advancements that affect the future of broadcasting.

TELEVISION BROADCASTING

Television was authorized commercially by the Federal Communications Commission as of July 1, 1941, but it was relegated to the sidelines during World War II. By 1986 the majority of households had more than two sets and the daily time a home was tuned to television was over seven hours. The U.S. viewer has an increasing number of channel choices. According to the Federal Communications Commission there are 1493 television stations (1167 commercial and 326 public) on the air. Over two-thirds of the households can receive nine or more television stations. When cable channels are also included with television, the number of viewing choices is even greater: 84 percent can receive nine or more channels and 19 percent can receive over 30 channels.[1]

Television broadcasting stations fall into two categories: very high frequency (VHF) and ultra high frequency (UHF). In an effort to equalize coverage for all television stations the Federal Communications Commission assigns different wattage to different frequency bands. Thus channels 2 through 6 (100,000 watts) and channels 7 through 13 (316,000 watts) are very high-frequency channels, while 14 through 83 (5,000,000 watts) are ultra-high frequency channels. Despite the attempts by the FCC to extend coverage and, therefore, competition, the UHF stations have not developed as rapidly as the VHF stations.

Advantages and Disadvantages of Television as an Advertising Medium

In the past the high cost of network television has limited users of this medium to large national consumer-product companies such as Procter & Gamble and General Motors. In recent years there has been a significant growth in the use of this medium by others. Companies in the field of office equipment, telephone equipment, computers, stationery, and related wares have greatly increased their television budgets. Television is now considered an effective medium for business-to-business advertising, since it reaches everyone who may have an influence in the decision-making process.

Locally, the highest television expenditures are made by retailers including restaurants, drive-ins, food stores, banks, department stores, furniture stores, and movies. Television generates excitement and high impact, which permits these institutions to stand out from their local competitors. In the past few years department store retailers across the country have begun to advertise on a regular basis. Other retailers consider television a means of competing with the increasing trend toward off-price and discounting among retailers.

Currently television offers the advertiser a number of benefits. Some of the most important are the following:

---

[1]"Television, 1986 Nielsen Report," A. C. Nielsen Company, 1986, p. 2.

EXHIBIT 19.1
A Creative Television Commercial

The original "Heartbeat" commercial covered at least 30 locations across the country. There were 51 scenes (almost one per second) in the final 60-second version.

Large Audience Size   Television offers the advertiser the opportunity to reach the largest audience with one advertising message. Over 98 percent of the homes in the United States have television sets.

Low Cost Per Exposure   Since television has such an extensive circulation the cost per exposure for each advertising message is relatively low.

Creative Capabilities   Television provides an outlet for all creative elements in talent. It offers the use of sight, sound, motion, color, demonstrations, and so on. An outstanding campaign for General Motors Chevrolet division synergizes all these elements in its "Heartbeat" commercials (see Exhibit 19.1).

Unaccompanied Message   The advertising message on television appears by itself; there are no competitive advertisements or even editorial matter to distract the viewer from the message. Moreover, there are no limitations on the size of the advertisement. Each message is seen full-screen, center stage.

Personal Appeal   Unlike newspapers and magazines, television can accommodate a group of viewers because one exposure reaches many people, watching the same TV set. Moreover, television is considered a personal medium. Viewers watch in the privacy of their homes and identify with the realistic actors in commercials.

Market Segmentation   Audience selectivity may be achieved on television in a variety of ways. The day of the week, the time of the day, and the programming material all permit the advertiser to select a specific market segment.

Encourages Dealer Support   Television advertising by national advertisers elicits dealer enthusiasm and support. Television is a highly visible medium and offers "talk" value; salespeople and dealers are more readily motivated by television support than support from any other medium.

Limitations of Television

Despite its creative capabilities and the excitement it generates, there are a number of factors limiting the use of television as an advertising medium.

High Cost   Television is expensive and requires a large initial outlay. This eliminates it as a potential medium for the small advertiser and puts a strain on the budget of the large advertiser. A small budget devoted to television would result in a thin and ineffective effort.

Short Message Life   As with other electronic media, the message on television is fleeting and brief. The physical representation of the message evaporates after viewing and can only be retained through repetition.

Time Limitations   In television the advertiser buys *time* (in print media the advertiser is purchasing space). This time purchase leads to a number of problems. First, the total time available for television viewing is limited to a twenty-four-hour day. Next, the public has specific viewing habits—few people watch during the early morning hours or in the middle of the night. For the national advertiser, other time problems occur because of the use of daylight saving time only in designated areas, and because of the different time zones. These problems can be, and have been, solved through the use of tape for recording and through different scheduling for different time zones.

Ignored Message   Television advertising does not have editorial matter appearing next to it to attract a viewer. If a message itself does not interest a viewer, there is nothing else to keep that viewer from "tuning it out" by turning away from the television set, leaving the room, or just ignoring the message completely. Currently one of the most serious problems facing broadcasters is the ability to "zap" commercials; that is use remote controls or fast-forwards on VCRs to tune out advertising messages.

Accurate Assessment of Audience Size   The size of an audience is difficult to compute and is subject to error in measurement. The development of new communication techniques will affect the size and composition of an audience and result in greater segmentation and more fragmentation of an audience for an advertiser.

Changing Media Environment   The new electronic media are growing rapidly both in kinds and capabilities. While traditional broadcasting facilities will no doubt continue to be available, it is clear that future advertisers must consider these alternatives in developing a media plan.

Commercial Television Broadcasting Facilities

Advertisers who wish to use television have a choice among several broadcasting facilities for the delivery of their messages. These communication channels are called network, spot, and local.

Network Advertising

An advertiser may select one of the three major national television networks: Columbia Broadcasting System, National Broadcasting Company, and American Broadcasting Company. The Federal Communications Commission defines a network as an interconnected service delivering 15 or more hours of programming per week to at least 25 stations in ten or more states. The new Fox Broadcasting Company, which launched its flagship program, "The Late Show Starring Joan Rivers," in late 1986 is striving for network status. Networks are made up of owned and operated stations (O&Os) and affiliates. The broadcasting companies are now permitted to own twelve stations, but they may have many independent stations throughout the United States as affiliates. CBS, for example, has over 200 affiliates, while the new Fox organization is carried by nearly 100 stations.[2]

Network telecasting involves tying together stations by means of either microwave relays or coaxial cables. With microwave relays, relay stations are spaced from 25 to 50 miles apart and beam the sound and video messages from one station to the next. Coaxial cable is a special type of underground cable (used by the telephone company) that is capable of carrying both audio and video messages.

The majority of an advertiser's television expenditures are for network advertising. Using network facilities permits an advertiser to have national coverage and the best prime time opportunities, since the affiliates generally allocate a large portion of their prime time (the best time periods) to the networks. Network broadcasting also offers an advertiser the advantage of greater prestige, usually first-rate talent, and wide and simultaneous coverage through a single telecast. The total cost is also generally lower than the same stations would charge if they were purchased on a spot basis.

Network advertising has its disadvantages. It may result in reaching members of the audience who are not in the geographic area serviced by the advertiser, and it is generally expensive. Although all affiliates need not be purchased, networks prefer to sell to those who buy more of the stations on their rosters. For a hesitant purchaser there are usu-

---

[2]Peter W. Barnes, "Fox Launches TV Network Tonight Amid Wary Reception by Advertisers," *The Wall Street Journal* (October 9, 1986), p. 12.

ally limited availabilities, as the best programs and time periods are bought out fairly early in the season.

Spot Advertising

Spot advertising refers to geographic spots and to television time purchased on a market-to-market basis rather than through a network. Spot telecasts originate in the studio of the station from which they are telecast. Stations that are affiliated with networks sell the major part of their advertising time through spot purchases.

The advantages of spot advertising are that it offers advertisers greater flexibility, it permits them to purchase only those markets in which their items are sold, it permits the introduction of a new product in one area at a time, and it enables advertisers to place greater efforts in some markets than in others. Spot purchasing may be more difficult than network purchasing, since it generally requires contacts with a great number of stations rather than just one network. In addition, a large portion of prime time is allocated to the network and, thus, may not be available to spot purchasers.

Local Advertising

Local advertising, also called *local spot,* is primarily advertising by retailers. It may be advertising placed by a retailer and paid for through cooperative advertising funds supplied by the manufacturer. In recent years manufacturers of nationally branded merchandise have begun to look to local advertising as a potentially effective medium.

How Advertisers Buy Television Time

In addition to selecting the facilities for transmitting their messages, advertisers must decide on the amount of time to be allocated for message delivery. To secure time periods for their messages, advertisers may sponsor a program, be a participant, or use spot announcements.

Sponsorship

When advertisers sponsor programs, they undertake the total financial responsibility for the content as well as for the advertising. For sponsors such as Hallmark and Xerox, the advertising becomes more prestigious—the product can be included in the program content and benefit from repeated impressions. However, because of the rising costs in television advertising over the years the extent of sponsorship has declined considerably.

Participation

Participation is a method of dividing up the cost of advertising time among various partners so that each one purchases a number of minutes of a particular show. This method provides continuity and repetition for the messages but minimizes the extent of influence exerted by an individual. Participations can be purchased on both network and spot.

Spot Announcements

Spot announcements are not the same as spot advertising. The former refers to individual messages interspersed in television programs, while the latter relates to the geographic area where the message originates. Both national and local spot television offer an advertiser spot announcements of varying lengths of time. This permits advertisers to spread their money over a wide variety of time slots and markets. However, the extent of an advertiser's influence on the program content is severely curtailed by the purchase of spots. Moreover, spot announcements are run in clusters in a program and their impact may be diminished.

Syndication

A *syndicated television program* is one that airs in more than one market, and, unlike network, is not transmitted by telephone lines to the stations carrying it.[3] A syndicated program may be sold directly to an individual station by its producer or a representative—the syndicator. The station then sells commercial time to advertisers who must purchase the program on a market-by-market basis. The top-rated syndicated shows are currently "Wheel of Fortune," asking advertisers for $95,000 per 30-second spot, and "Jeopardy," priced at $53,000 per 30-second spot.[4]

In the *barter* system a syndicator goes to a station with a program such as "Donahue" or "Sha Na Na" and trades (barters) it for a time period. Thus the station receives free programming. The syndicator retains up to one-half of the commercial minutes in the program and may sell these to national advertisers. The station retains the other half which is usually sold to local advertisers.

Syndication needs a smaller investment than does network television and offers advertisers programs that are more compatible with their messages and more effective in reaching the right target audience. Generally, however, syndicated programs do not receive as high ratings as network programs and contain an excessive amount of commercial clutter.

How Much Station Time Is Available for Advertising?

For a number of years the National Association of Broadcasters (a trade association of radio and television broadcasting stations) promulgated a code specifying the amount of time that could be used for advertising on television:

1. *Maximum Commercial Time*
   9 ½ minutes of commercials per hour of prime time
   16 minutes of commercials per hour all other times

[3]Jeffrey A. Manoff, "Syndication's Many Facets," *Advertising Age* (March 8, 1982), pp. M-10–14.

[4]Marcy Gray Rubin, "Drop in network ad rates cramps barter's style," *Advertising Age* (September 22, 1986), p. 5–2.

2. *Interruption Standards*
   Maximum four interruptions for commercials per hour
   Number of consecutive announcements per interruption; maximum
   is five

3. *Multiproduct (piggybacked) Ads*
   Advertisements for more than one product cannot appear in a
   commercial lasting less than 60 seconds

In 1982 the Justice Department filed an antitrust suit against these provisions. A district court ruled that the multiple-product (piggybacking) standard which prohibits advertisements of more than one product in a commercial lasting less than 60 seconds was *per se* illegal. Subsequently the NAB signed a consent decree which prohibited them from establishing time and interruption standards for broadcasters.

Individual broadcasters, however, may set standards for their advertisers.

While they have tended to retain the time standards as is, there has been a significant increase in the use of 15-second commercials (two 15-second ads in one 30-second spot) as a result of the removal of the piggyback ad restrictions.

CRITERIA FOR PURCHASING ADVERTISING ON TELEVISION

The criteria for selecting advertising time on television are similar to those for selecting space for advertising in print media. The nature of broadcasting as a communication medium, however, requires additional considerations such as the selection of the appropriate time periods and programs.

Selecting the Time Period

An advertiser purchases a period of time in which to place a message. The cost of this time varies widely, depending on the time of day and the program that is appearing.

Television time periods are divided into *dayparts*, specific segments of a broadcast day. A typical breakdown of time segments into dayparts is as follows:

Early morning	Sign on to 10:00 A.M.
Daytime	10:00 A.M. – 4:30 P.M.
Early Fringe (just before prime time)	4:30 P.M. – 8:00 P.M.
Prime time	8:00 P.M. – 11:00 P.M.
Late fringe (just after prime time)	11:00 P.M. – 1:00 A.M.

Prime time provides the advertiser with the greatest viewing audience and is therefore the most expensive. The individual station may designate its own prime time, continuous period of not less than three consecutive hours between 6:00 P.M. and midnight; the most popular is usually 8–11 P.M. The various dayparts, however, draw different demographic groups and selecting the right daypart allows an advertiser to target his or her message to the appropriate market segment.

Selecting the Program

Advertisers on television are not only concerned with the time period but also with the program that appears during that time. In the early days of television many advertisers owned their own programs, which they sponsored and identified with their name, such as "The Bell Telephone Hour" and "Armstrong Circle Theater." However, when costs of production began rising, networks took over production or bought shows from independent producing houses called *package houses*. Currently networks may pay over a million dollars per half-hour program. "Hill Street Blues" costs NBC $1.5 million per episode.[5]

Because of the high production costs both affiliates and independents tend not to produce their own programs, except for local news and sports. For those stations affiliated with a network, the network shows are available during prime time. Otherwise these stations generally depend on syndicated programs.

The prime considerations for an advertiser in selecting programs are frequently costs and program ratings. Obviously the higher the ratings the larger the audience. However, rather than total audience size an advertiser may choose a program where the audience composition includes, for example, a great proportion of women aged 20 to 49 or single men aged 18 to 25. An advertiser also looks at program content, particularly if it is excessively violent. A number of organizations conduct surveys designed to determine the extent to which various advertisers support such programming. As a result some advertisers have refused to advertise on programs that are designated as violent.

Cost of Television Advertising

Television advertising costs are primarily based on time periods and programs. To facilitate their purchase broadcasters have established rate structures.

Network Rates
Network rates are quoted on rate cards that list the various affiliated stations and their rates for one-half hour of their time. An advertiser who wants network broadcasting can select more than one of these affiliates. Usually a local affiliate receives 20 to 30 percent of the time charge for a network broadcast, while 70 to 80 percent of the time charge goes to the network for the program and for the costs involved in getting the program to the affiliate.

---

[5]Drew Fetherton, "Are Prime-Time Soaps Washed Up?," *Newsday* (December 22, 1985), Part II, p. 3.

As noted earlier relatively few advertisers sponsor a program. Most network purchases are made for spot announcements for advertising; the 30-second segment predominates. The price the network charges for these spots is based not only on costs but on the popularity of the show determined by its ratings. Figure 19.1 lists the estimated prices in 1986/ 1987 for a 30-second commercial on prime-time programs.

The network rate structure has become extremely complicated and is subject to many pressures. For example as a time interval that has not been sold approaches, the broadcaster is willing to offer potential advertisers many discounts that do not appear on the rate card. Also many of the network rates currently are established on the basis of individual bargaining and negotiation.

Cost of Spot Television Advertising

Although SRDS provides more information about spot broadcasters than it does about network, some stations do not list their rates. Like the network these spot broadcasters' rates are subject to negotiation and, to some extent, predicated on the potential size of the audience. Typically spot television is purchased on the following two bases.

Spot Announcement Rate   Spot announcements are bought for varying rates depending on the times and programs. Currently the vast majority of spot announcements are 30-second ones; however 60-second, 15-second, 10-second, and 8-second spots are also available.

A 30-second spot on KGTV, an ABC Television Network affiliate in San Diego, costs $800 on "Good Morning America," aired Monday through Friday from 7 to 9 A.M.; the spot costs $6,000 on "Moonlighting," aired Tuesdays at 9 P.M. Lower rates are available for run-of-the-station (ROS) packages, which allow the broadcaster to choose the time period in which a message will appear.

Preemptible Rate   Most spots are sold at a *preemptible rate*, which means the spot is subject to cancellation by another advertiser paying a higher rate. If an advertiser does not want his spot preempted, he may buy it at a higher rate. For example, the difference between a 30-second fixed (nonpreemptible announcement) and one which may be preempted with no notice by the station may be as high as 25 percent.

Measuring Television Circulation

Circulation in television is not audited by independent auditing agencies as is circulation in print media; nor is an advertiser usually offered a guaranteed circulation figure. However, for purchases of prime time spots in the upfront market (in advance of the new season which begins in the fourth quarter of the year and runs through the first three quarters of the next year) the three major networks offer guarantees for program ratings. If actual ratings fall short of the guarantee, the networks provide "make goods" to the advertiser. Make goods are frequently in the form of other time slots provided for these commercials without compensation.

FIGURE 19.1   Networks' 30-second Price List, 1986—87 Season

		7:00	7:30	8:00	8:30	9:00	9:30	10:00	10:30
MONDAY	ABC			MacGyver $96,000		NFL Monday Night Football $135,000-$175,000			
	CBS			Kate & Allie $122,00	My Sister Sam $110,00	Newhart $151,000	Designing Women $150,000	Cagney & Lacey $120,000	
	NBC			ALF $90,000	Amazing Stories $117,000	NBC Monday Night at the Movies $145,000			
TUESDAY	ABC			Who's the Boss? $215,000	Growing Pains $205,000	Moonlighting $215,000		Jack and Mike $125,000	
	CBS			The Wizard $59,000		CBS Tuesday Night Movies $91,000			
	NBC			Matlock $115,000		Crime Story $82,000		1986 $59,000	
WEDNESDAY	ABC			Perfect Strangers $116,000	Head of Class $106,000	Dynasty $185,000		Hotel $130,000	
	CBS			Together We Stand $80,000	Better Days $78,000	Magnum P.I. $86,000		The Equalizer $99,000	
	NBC			Highway to Heaven $128,000		Gimme a Break $108,000	You Again? $101,000	St. Elsewhere $125,000	
THURSDAY	ABC			Our World $30,000		The Colbys $63,000		20/20 $105,000	
	CBS			Simon & Simon $78,000		Knots Landing $132,000		Kay O'Brien $102,000	
	NBC			Cosby Show $380,000	Family Ties $300,000	Cheers $230,000	Night Court $206,000	Hill Street Blues $148,000	
FRIDAY	ABC			Webster $78,000	Mr. Belvedere $77,000	Sledge Hammer $59,000	Sidekicks $61,000	Starman $64,000	
	CBS			Scarecrow and Mrs. King $86,000		Dallas $145,000		Falcon Crest $103,000	
	NBC			The A-Team $82,000		Miami Vice $195,000		L.A. Law $139,000	
SATURDAY	ABC			Life With Lucy $74,000	Ellen Burstyn $75,000	Heart of the City $74,000		Spencer: For Hire $82,000	
	CBS			Downtown $79,000		The New Mike Hammer $90,000		Twilight Zone $108,000	
	NBC			Facts of Life $107,000	227 $120,000	Golden Girls $175,000	Amen $131,000	Hunter $114,000	
SUNDAY	ABC		Disney Sunday Movie $105,000			ABC Sunday Night Movie $131,000			
	CBS		60 Minutes $161,000	Murder, She Wrote $156,000		CBS Sunday Night Movies $118,000			
	NBC		Our House $71,000	Easy Street $101,000	Valerie $132,000	NBC Sunday Night at the Movies $134,000			

1986 network television unit costs reflect the average advertisers will pay during October and November, one of the highest priced periods of the broadcast year. Eastern Time.

Source: "Networks' 30-Second Price List, 1986-87 Season," *Advertising Age* (September 29, 1986). Copyright © 1986 Crain Communications, Inc. Reprinted with permission from Advertising Age. All Rights Reserved.

Various broadcast rating services have been developed that provide an advertiser with audience estimates for both radio and television. Several different terms are used in describing the size of the audience.

Coverage

Coverage refers to the total number of homes that can be reached by a signal. Over 87 million American households (over 98 percent of the total) owned at least one television set by 1986. Accordingly, network broadcasting has a potential coverage of over 87 million households. Coverage is not equivalent to circulation in print media where households receiving a newspaper or magazine are included in the circulation count. In broadcasting, the ability to receive a signal does not insure that the television set will be turned on or tuned to a particular station.

Sets-in-Use

Sets-in-use [Nielsen calls this *TV households using TV* (HUT)] refers to the number of television households that are using television at any one time period. This is usually stated as a percentage of coverage.

Assume the total coverage of a particular broadcast area where signals can be received by several broadcasting stations is equivalent to 10,000 television households. If at eight o'clock in the evening 6000 of these sets are turned on, then the sets-in-use for that time period is 60 percent.

8:00 P.M.

Coverage	10,000 households
Number of Sets in Use	6000
Percentage of Sets in Use	$\dfrac{6000}{10,000} = 60$ percent

Program Rating

The term *program rating* indicates the size of the audience as a percentage of all television households that can receive the TV signal and are *tuned in* to a specific broadcasting station during a specific time period. A rating can be based on households or individuals in a particular area. Thus if a broadcast area has a coverage of 10,000 households, and 2000 of these households' TV sets are tuned in to a program presented by one of the broadcast stations in that area (the audience), the program rating for that particular program is 20 percent.

8:00 P.M.

Coverage	10,000 households
Households tuned to WXYZ	2000
Program Rating (WXYZ)	$\dfrac{2000}{10,000} = 20$ percent

Share of Audience

Share of audience refers to a percentage of the total audience *viewing television* in a specific time period tuned to a particular station. To arrive

RATINGS OR SHARE?

A recent conflict over who was rated Number One during a "sweeps period" (one of the four times a year when local programs are rated by the ratings services) was resolved with Rex Reed and Bill Harris' "At the Movies" claiming No. 1 in rating points, and Gene Siskel and Roger Ebert's "And the Movies" attaining No. 1 in share points. For the advertiser it is important to understand the distinction.

Ratings refer to a percentage of television sets tuned in to a particular show in a particular time slot. These ratings achieved through a sample can be applied to the total number of television sets that can receive the signal in the area to determine the audience size. "The Cosby Show," for example, consistently achieved over 30 percent ratings in late 1986, and this number-one rated show had an audience size of over 26 million households (30 percent × 87 million households).

Share refers to the relative popularity of a program in a particular time period, and is based on the number of television sets that can receive the signal and are turned on. Thus if 60 percent of the sets were turned on at that time period and the ratings were 30 percent, "The Cosby Show" had a one half share (50 percent) of the audience viewing television. Share, however, does not reveal audience size; nor does a high share necessarily mean a large audience. For example, a program appearing at two A.M. with a rating of one percent (a relatively small audience) may be the only program being viewed at that time period (one percent of the sets were in use). Since share is determined by program rating over sets in use, this low-rated show's share in that time period would be 100 percent.

Source: "Blam! Zap! Pow! . . ." *Chicago Tribune*, December 9, 1986.

at the share of the audience, the program rating for the specific broadcast station is divided by the sets-in-use in the entire area.

$$\text{Share of audience} = \frac{\text{program rating for WXYZ}}{\text{percent sets-in-use for entire area}}$$

In our previous example, the program rating was 20 percent and the sets-in-use was 60 percent. Therefore the share of the audience the program achieved for that particular time period was 33⅓ percent.

$$\text{Share of audience (WXYZ)} = \frac{.20}{.60} = .3333$$

Broadcast Rating Services

Several different broadcast rating services are available to advertisers who want to determine the size of the audience viewing certain programs. Ratings are determined by asking a sample of households to par-

EXHIBIT 19.2
The Nielsen Electronic Recorder

The Audimeter has a built-in electronic memory that records when the TV goes on and off.

ticipate in a survey through one or several of the following methods: electronic recorders, diaries, coincidental telephone calls, or personal interviewing.

Electronic Recorders

The most widely used network ratings are supplied by A. C. Nielsen Company which offers television advertisers information about the size of an audience and its composition. To secure information on national television ratings Nielsen uses *Audimeters*—mechanical devices attached to television sets in 1700 households (see Exhibit 19.2.) Audimeters primarily record the times sets are turned on and off and to which stations they are tuned. Meters connect these households to a Nielsen computer that delivers viewing statistics. The Nielsen Television Index provides national network audiences derived from the Audimeter (see Figure 19.2 on page 406).

Another major rating service, Arbitron Rating Company, does not measure the three television networks. It does, however, use an electronic meter for audience measurement in a number of the largest markets, including New York, Chicago, Los Angeles, and San Francisco. Data are fed to a computer which provides instantaneous reports ("overnights").

Electronic recorders eliminate interviewer bias and provide a complete and accurate record of tuning. They have been criticized, however, because they show only if sets have been turned on, not if someone is watching.

Diaries

Nielsen uses diaries to supplement its audimeter information in about 2700 households. The National Audience Composition (NAC) provides estimates of audience categories based on household demographics such as age and income. Arbitron compiles television reports for more than 200 markets, primarily through the use of diaries in which product consumption as well as individual viewing and audience characteristics are tabulated (see Exhibit 19.3).

The diary method provides a record of an individual's viewing rather than merely set operation; it is adaptable to any size area; it can cover all broadcast hours; and it can provide a wide variety of information very economically.

It is, however, difficult to secure respondents who are willing to record information; moreover, some of the diary entries may be made on the basis of hearsay or the estimate of the diary keeper. As with any written questionnaire, the transcribing of information from the point of inception to the final report is subject to human and mechanical error. Also, there may be a possible difference in viewing habits between those who keep a diary and those who do not.

EXHIBIT 19.3
Arbitron Ratings Television Diary

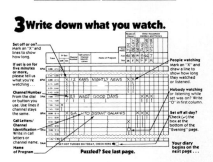

Source: "Arbitron Ratings Television Diary." Copyright © 1986 Arbitron Ratings Co. Reprinted by permission.

FIGURE 19.2   Nielsen National TV Audience Estimates

EVE. FRI.   SEPT. 19, 1986

WEEK 1

TIME	7:00	7:15	7:30	7:45	8:00	8:15	8:30	8:45	9:00	9:15	9:30	9:45	10:00	10:15	10:30	10:45	11:00
ABC TV																	
TOTAL AUDIENCE (Households (000) & %)					15,470 / 17.7 (Sidekicks Special (R)(SD))				16,870 / 19.3 (Starman (SD))				14,420 / 16.5 (Funny (R))			
AVERAGE AUDIENCE (Households (000) & %)					11,800 / 13.5	13.1*		13.8*	12,590 / 14.4	14.1*		14.7*	10,310 / 11.8	12.1*		11.4*	
SHARE OF AUDIENCE %					25	25*		25*	25	25*		26*	22	22*		22	
AVG. AUD. BY 1/4 HR. %					12.5	13.7	13.9	13.8	13.8	14.4	14.8	14.7	11.9	12.2	11.2	11.7	
CBS TV																	
TOTAL AUDIENCE (Households (000) & %)					15,910 / 18.2 (Scarecrow & Mrs. King (SUS-SD))				16,170 / 18.5 (CBS Friday Night Movies — Many Happy Returns (SD))							
AVERAGE AUDIENCE (Households (000) & %)					11,890 / 13.6	12.9*		14.2*	8,910 / 10.2	10.3*		9.9*		9.8*		10.6*	
SHARE OF AUDIENCE %					25	25*		25*	18	18*		17*		18*		20*	
AVG AUD BY 1/4 HR. %					12.5	13.3	14.1	14.3	10.6	10.0	9.9	10.0	9.9	9.7	10.6	10.6	
NBC TV																	
TOTAL AUDIENCE (Households (000) & %)					13,110 / 15.0 (A Team (R)(SD))				18,440 / 21.1 (Miami Vice (R))				18,790 / 21.5 (Crime Story Fri Preview)			
AVERAGE AUDIENCE (Households (000) & %)					9,440 / 10.8	10.3*		11.4*	14,420 / 16.5	15.8*		17.3*	14,860 / 17.0	17.1*		16.9*	
SHARE OF AUDIENCE %					20	20*		20*	29	28*		30*	32	31*		32*	
AVG AUD BY 1/4 HR. %					10.0	10.6	11.3	11.4	15.2	16.4	17.4	17.2	17.1	17.2	17.0	16.7	

Source: from "Nielsen National TV Ratings" (September 2, 1986). Reprinted by permission of A.C. Nielsen Company.

Coincidental Telephone Methods

Various companies provide coincidental telephone-call service, usually to offer an immediate reaction to a broadcast. The findings are shown as home ratings; that is, findings are identified as the percentage of television households watching a particular program during an average minute.

The advantage of a coincidental telephone interview is that it can be conducted at the same time a program is broadcast, providing more accurate data, since it eliminates the problem of memory and recall. However, it also places a restriction on the amount of data obtained, because the questions must usually be brief, and the resulting estimates are not as comprehensive as those provided by the diary method. Nevertheless, telephone interviewing is a quick and economical way of securing immediate data.

Personal Interviewing

Personal interviewing is expensive, time consuming, and subject to more interviewer and interviewee biases than other techniques. It can, however, provide the most comprehensive information. Most organizations use personal interviewing for special types of television audience research rather than for broad and comprehensive coverage of audience measurement.

People Meters

Dissatisfaction with current audience measurement devices have led the broadcasting industry to experiment with people meters as replacements for both electronic recorders and diaries. A *people meter* is a hand-held device slightly larger than a TV channel selector. It has eight buttons for family members and two more for visitors. Anytime a person selects a program the appropriate button must be pushed. The meter is equipped with sonar to eliminate the problem of people entering or leaving the television room without checking in or out on the meter. In 1987 Nielsen announced it was replacing its diary with people meters.

Cost Per Thousand

To make cost and circulation comparisons, the following formula is used in television:

Cost Per Thousand (CPM)
$$= \frac{\text{Cost of time period (typically 30 seconds)} \times 1000}{\text{audience (or program rating} \times \text{coverage)}}$$

In 1986 a 30-second spot in a relatively high-rated show (such as "The Cosby Show") sold for over $270,000. To compute the cost per thousand per household:

Coverage: approximately 86,000,000 households
Cost: $270,000
Program Rating: 30 percent

$$CPM = \frac{\$270,000 \times 1000}{.30 \times 86,000,000 \text{ households}}$$

$$CPM = \frac{\$270,000,000}{25,000,000 \text{ households (audience)}}$$

$$CPM = \$10.80$$

The basic rate for an undifferentiated audience was approximately $10.80 per thousand. However, companies that look for a particular target market pay more per thousand. For example, cosmetic companies may pay as much as $14.00 per thousand to reach women, ages 18–49. In making cost per thousand comparisons care should be taken to insure that the same audience is compared in all cases.

Gross Rating Points

When placing multiple ads on television, it is difficult to determine the exact composition of the audience, and to evaluate the precise number of times each person has been exposed to the message. Thus these two measurements are combined into one—designated as gross rating points.

Gross rating points refers to the total number of rating points delivered by an advertiser's television schedule. To determine gross rating points, reach is multiplied by average frequency. One gross rating point indicates that one percent of the audience (reach) has the opportunity to be exposed to a message one time (frequency).

Gross rating points are usually computed on a four-week basis with 240 GRPs as a standard for measurement. Thus 12 spots over a four-week period in programs with average ratings of 20 percent achieves 240 GRPs (see Table 19.1).

It is assumed that the above 240 GRPs will provide a reach of 77 percent of the audience with an average frequency of 3.1 times based on estimates using a typical frequency distribution. Recently average ratings have declined so that currently it is difficult to receive 240 GRPs with only 12 commercials. Moreover as the television audience becomes more fragmented the frequency distribution is likely to change.

Cost Per Rating Point

Many television advertising schedules are determined on the basis of *cost per rating point*. This simply means that the total cost of advertising time is computed to determine the budget, and this amount is divided by the number of rating points achieved in the schedule.

TABLE 19.1 240 GRPs in Network TV Schedules for Four Weeks

TV Network	Time	Program	Cost	Frequency × (# of spots)	Reach = (Program Rating, Est.)	GRPs
NBC	Sat. 9 P.M.	Golden Girls	$175,000	3	22%	66
NBC	Sun. 8 P.M.	Easy Street	101,000	3	20	60
NBC	Tues. 8 P.M.	Matlock	115,000	3	20	60
NBC	Wed. 8 P.M.	Highway to Heaven	128,000	3	18	54
					Total	240

In the illustration in Table 19.1, the cost per rating point may be computed as follows:

3 spots @ $175,000 = $ 525,000
3 spots @ 101,000 = 303,000
3 spots @ 115,000 = 345,000
3 spots @ 128,000 = 384,000
Budget $1,557,000

$$\text{Cost Per GRP} = \frac{\text{Budget}}{\text{Number of GRPs}} = \frac{\$1,557,000}{240} = \$6,487.50$$

Buying Time on Spot Television

Advertisers rarely buy one advertisement on spot television; generally the purchase is for a *flight*—a series of ads. The media plan may specify the target to be reached and the time period—women 18–34 to be reached prime time over a five-week period—and may also set a budget—$500,000 to be spent in ten markets.[6]

The television stations and their representatives will then submit a listing of "avails"—what's available in shows and commercial time. The advertiser must then compute what these markets and their stations normally sell for on a cost-per-rating-point basis. The advertiser can then determine how many points he or she will be able to afford for $500,000. The actual purchase of time periods is based on negotiation.

To determine the efficiency of the media purchase an advertiser uses *post analysis* (called "posting out"). An optimum purchase achieves 100 percent of what is bought; that is, if 100 weekly rating points were purchased at $1000 per point for the ten markets, the post analysis would reveal that the $500,000 purchased the desired number of rating points (500).

---

[6]"How Spot TV Prices Are Set," *Marketing & Media Decisions* (Fall 1982, Special), pp. 106–12.

There is usually an allowance for a 10-percent deviation. A successful purchase means that the advertiser achieved 90 or 110 percent of what he or she bought.

For advertisers who use spot broadcasting, advertising agencies provide information on the number of gross rating points in the schedule and the average cost per rating point. These are typically computed on the basis of average cost per rating point in various markets.

CHANGES IN TELEVISION BROADCASTING

While the future of television cannot be predicted it is certain to be affected by the growing number of alternative viewing opportunities. Some of these are cable television, subscription television, public broadcasting, interactive television, video cassettes and video discs, and teletext and videotex.

Broadcasting refers to the transmission of a television program to a large number of households. Both network and local television stations are categorized as broadcasters even though the latter reaches substantially fewer households than the former.

Narrowcasting is used to refer to specialized programs which reach specialized audiences. Cable companies reaching a limited number of households within a community and transmitting over many more channels are considered to be narrowcasting. The distinction does not necessarily refer to the size of the audience. A narrowcast may be transmitted to many communities across the country by a network of cable companies and command a larger audience than that of a local broadcast channel. In narrowcasting, however, no attempt is made to try to appeal to everyone or even a majority of a community.[7]

Cable Television

Cable television is the oldest of the "new" methods of transmission and is the most highly developed. Originally called *community antenna television* it was introduced to provide good video reception for people who could not otherwise receive signals well.

The theory of CATV's function has changed over the years. Now it is not only designed to improve reception but also to provide a greater number of alternative offerings to the viewing public, particularly to the community target group. At the end of 1986 it was estimated that cable TV reached 40 million households, or 46.7 percent of all households having TV sets.[8]

---

[7]Philip A. Harding, "The New Technologies: Some Implications for Consumer Policy," in *Consumerism and Beyond: Research Perspectives on the Future Social Environment,* Paul N. Bloom, ed. (Cambridge, Mass.: Marketing Science Institute, 1982), pp. 82–84.

[8]Christopher Colletti, "Narrowcasters gird for program war with Big 3," *Advertising Age* (December 1, 1986), p. S–8.

Cable is still not permitted to show current network programs such as "Dallas," except on the network channels on which they are shown normally. Cable systems must also continue to black out local sporting events if the local broadcast station is also obliged to do so.

The number of channels on cable television varies from fewer than a dozen on the oldest systems to as many as 54 under the newer ones. Until recently the FCC required that cable systems carry all the stations within a 35-mile radius (and within a 50-mile radius in smaller markets). For these stations cable systems served only as carriers, running each station's programming complete with its advertising. A 1985 Supreme Court decision eliminated this "must carry" rule. While its effect is still uncertain some observers feel the decision may result in the demise of some local television broadcasters who will not be able to survive without cable aid.

Cable offers a number of services. The most popular are the pay networks such as Home Box Office (HBO) and Showtime which feature commercial-free, first-run movies and other entertainment at a separate monthly cost to subscribers.

Advertising on Cable

Advertising expenditures for cable were estimated at $948 million for 1986.[9] To provide advertisers with maximum exposure and penetration, cable systems have formed *interconnects* which combine various subscriber bases and create larger demographic groupings. There are also national networks such as WTBS, MTV, ESPN, CNN, and the USA Network.

Most of the advertising currently on cable is in the form of spots sold to national advertisers on programming in networks. Rates are available in Standard Rate and Data Service and from the networks. Top cable advertisers include Procter & Gamble, Philip Morris, and Anheuser Busch (see Table 19.2).

Cable offers the opportunity to create innovative advertisements. However, because of the relatively small audiences on cable, advertisers limit the time and money they spend on such messages. In many cases commercials prepared for television are presented on cable, even though they may not be effective. Advertisers curtail production costs by producing multiple versions of a commercial, some for broadcast and others for cable use. Chevrolet, for example, developed a 90-second hard rock music spot with visual collages to run on MTV, Music Television as well as on USA's "Night Flight." It also developed 30-second and 60-second versions to appear on late-night broadcast television.[10] There is, however, a growing awareness that cable commercials should be different from the typical presentations on television, and that adver-

TABLE 19.2 Top 10 Cable Advertisers

1.	Procter & Gamble Co.	$30,487,371
2.	Philip Morris Cos.	21,061,420
3.	Anheuser-Busch Cos.	15,345,131
4.	General Mills	12,144,905
5.	Time Inc.	11,006,706
6.	Mars Inc.	8,163,657
7.	RJR/Nabisco	7,530,852
8.	Thompson Medical Co.	7,060,414
9.	Ford Motor Co.	6,159,088
10.	Kellogg Co.	4,554,186

Source: from "Cable Tests Hot-Wired to Consumer Preferences" by Judann Dagnoli, *Advertising Age* (December 1, 1986). Copyright © 1986 by Crain Communications, Inc. Reprinted with permission from Advertising Age. All Rights Reserved.

[9]Wayne Walley, "Profit picture sends operators a clear signal," *Advertising Age* (December 1, 1986), p. S–1.

[10]Ronald B. Kaatz, "Cable Advertiser's Handbook, 2nd ed. (Lincolnwood, Illinois: Crain Books, an Imprint of National Textbook Company, 1985), pp. 129–47.

tisers have an opportunity to develop creative techniques specifically suitable to this medium.

A particularly effective advertisement for cable is the *informercial,* which offers a lengthy message including typical message information and provides the means for securing more information, a sample, or the product or service itself. Informercials can be as long as ten minutes and have the advantage of demonstrating products more carefully. A disadvantage is that they tend to "wear out" quicker than conventional commercials because of their length.

In anticipation that cable may become more widely used by advertisers several firms have begun to measure the audience in cable television. A. C. Nielsen established the Home Video Index from which it hopes to gather viewing data from 1200 metered sets. A Nielsen service, Local Cable Index, will monitor local cable viewing. Arbitron has been conducting yearly reports consisting of random telephone calls that determine the viewers for each national cable network on one hundred geographically dispersed systems. However, it appears that advertising on cable will not be more widely used until there is much more audience data available to advertisers.

Home-Shopping Services

Several cable television channels are offering home-shopping services. Most home-shopping channels rely on impulse buying; goods are presented in 24 hour, game-show environments, and viewers are given a few minutes to call in orders by telephone. The approach has generally been successful and recently large retailers such as Sears, Roebuck and Co. and J. C. Penney Co. have begun to use cable channels to sell their stores' merchandise in the home.[11] These services are also available through UHF broadcast stations through Homeshopping Network, a successful sales organization that is rapidly expanding its facilities.

Advantages and Disadvantages of Cable Advertising

Cable is particularly useful for reaching a narrowly defined market, with little waste coverage. It can be tailored to consumers concentrated in small geographic areas. It offers significant opportunities for advertisers who wish to cater to a "singles" market, a fast-growing segment whose lifestyle and viewing habits coincide with specifically tailored late-hour shows. Moreover, their higher discretionary income and their propensity to live in urban areas make this group more apt to subscribe to cable.

Cable is also useful for experimentation or to improve coverage without diverting funds from other media schedules. It can offer publicity and promotion of noncable efforts for the advertiser.

The major disadvantage of cable is its lack of audience information. While efforts are made to design appropriate measurement services,

---

[11]Jonathan Dahl, "Sears to Sell Merchandise on Cable TV Through New Firm Called QVC Network," *The Wall Street Journal* (November 17, 1986), p. 7.

these have not yet been developed. The highly concentrated audiences tend to provide only spotty coverage for a national advertiser. Multiple cable offerings cause frustration both in the creation of advertising and the purchase of advertising time.

Subscription TV

Subscription TV (pay TV) in the home was authorized by the Federal Communications Commission in 1969. Subscription TV does not require cable tie-in. Programs are broadcast over the air with electronically scrambled signals and subscribers are supplied with devices that unscramble these signals. Arbitron found that the chief reason people subscribe to pay TV is to get movies not shown on television. Sports programming is apparently less important than might be expected.

The growth of subscription television has been inhibited by cable and the development of videocassettes. Satellite transmission is expected to increase the number of subscribers who receive direct transmissions and bypass the traditional TV stations.

Videocassettes and Videodiscs

Services such as videocassettes and videodiscs place control of content and schedule in the hands of the consumer. *Videocassettes* permit a consumer to view a prerecorded program or to record a program for later playback. Some prerecorded videocassettes are being used for advertising purposes. The Coca-Cola Co. placed soft-drink commercials at the beginning of the European cassette version of "Ghostbusters" produced by Columbia Pictures, a Coke subsidiary. More recently Pepsi Cola placed a 30-second commercial for Diet Pepsi in a videocassette for the film "Top Gun." Video Information Network in Seattle is distributing tapes that contain only commercials to 1000 video stores in the Northeast and Southern California. Each tape is 15 to 20 minutes long and advertises a single product such as Caribbean cruises or food processors. While the cassettes have to be checked out just like a movie, there is no rental charge.[12]

Videodiscs are similar to phonograph records. They are put into a player attached to a television set and play both picture and sound. The major advantage of discs over cassettes is their low cost. Advertisers may find videodiscs an attractive medium for implementing phsychographic marketing strategies or to reach more specialized marketing groups. For example, marketers of baby products may produce programming aimed at new mothers.

A problem with the use of these techniques by advertisers is the possibility that the consumer will erase any ads that appear. Producers of cassettes and discs admit the potential exists, but declare it is not yet a serious problem. They also note that, in order for these ads to be erased, the viewer must be exposed to them at least once.

---

[12]Ronald Alsop, "Advertisers get Reprimanded for Saying 'Free' Too Freely," *The Wall Street Journal* (March 26, 1987), p. 39.

Teletext

Teletext is a non-cable subscriber service provided by local television stations, which allows viewers to switch from standard television programming to pages of information on the TV screen. Teletext systems deliver news, video games, learning programming, sports, travel, food, advice about health, and many other services. Teletext has some potential as an advertising medium for advertisements that complement the information the viewer has called up on the screen. Currently usage is limited, but with applications of personal computer technology it should be more widely adopted in the future.

Videotex

Unlike teletext which is a one-way interface information system, videotex is an interactive television system linking a television set and a telephone to a central computer bank. Through videotex consumers are able to perform a variety of tasks, including retrieving news and information, paying bills, banking, buying and selling stocks, and shopping.

Videotex offers many marketing and advertising options, including the dissemination of electronic brochures and catalogues (at a relatively low cost), image building or sponsorship advertising to a specific market segment, direct electronic mail, interactive surveys and research, and the capability of the home computer's printer to print redeemable coupons. There has been a rapid evolution in the adoption of videotex in recent years and there are indications that this will be a growing medium in the future.

The Future of Television

Television broadcasting's future does not appear as bright as its past. There are complaints about television's influence on lifestyle, encouragement of violence, and advertisements of controversial products such as alcohol and pep pills.

Critics cite advertising clutter as destroying television's effectiveness as an advertising medium, while the elimination of restrictions on the 15-second commercial portends even greater clutter. "Zapping" commercials through the use of remote controls and fast-forwards on VCRs limit the size of the audience and confound ratings measurements. Sponsorship has given way to scatter plans and commercial time is purchased for shorter intervals. The rapid growth of new technologies and methods of transmitting messages is resulting in an increase in competition to attract advertisers as well as a fragmentation of the audience for their messages.

To accomodate advertisers reaching smaller audience segments traditional broadcasters, rather than emphasize large numbers of viewers, will have to introduce innovative concepts. They will have to develop techniques for measuring audiences with more precision and help advertisers design "zap-proof" advertisements.

RADIO BROADCASTING

Radio became an advertising medium about 1920. Radio broadcast stations are controlled by the Federal Communications Commission on the basis of its licensing power. To license stations the Commission assigns their wavelengths, prescribes their broadcasting power, and sets the standards for operation. Until recently, the Commission was instructed to consider public interest, convenience, and necessity (PICON) in granting these licenses which were given for a period of three years and could be renewed.

In the 1980s the FCC lifted the public service requirement and the 19-minute ceiling on commercial messages per hour. It no longer requires stations to document their efforts to ascertain community need; it assumes that competition will require stations to provide public service efforts and to limit their advertising time.

Radio stations are assigned four classes of channels:

1. *Class I* is a clear channel assigned 50,000 watts, a wattage which provides almost exclusive use of the frequency. Clear channels serve a wide area free from interference.
2. *Class II* covers hybrid stations that are on clear channels during the day and must go off at sunset. A ceiling of electrical particles called the *Kennelly Heaviside layer* bounces the signal back to earth more strongly at nighttime. Hybrid stations go off the air at night so they don't interfere with the Class I stations.
3. *Class III* incorporates stations on regional channels with ranges of 5000 watts. This type of channel may cover several markets, but it is limited by interference and may share its frequency with another distant station.
4. *Class IV* includes local stations or community stations that receive a range of up to 250 watts.

Advertisers on these radio stations can use network, spot, or local broadcasting facilities. Hence radio advertising is designated as network, spot, and local advertising.

Network Advertising

Network advertising on radio is growing. For an advertiser, the network affiliation of a particular radio broadcasting company may be important, because it provides the opportunity of discount rates through the network and offers certain specialized network services.

The original radio networks were ABC, NBC, Mutual, and CBS. These have been split into many different networks, usually on a demographic basis. In addition there has been a growth of numerous additional networks, including RKO, Black National Radio Network, and Sheridan Black. This breakdown into demographic networks has encouraged advertisers to look more closely at the networks for such targets as

**You've seen a cow calf.
But did you ever see a cow laugh?**

In April 1984, five little
Laughing Cows in red net bags
went on the radio. What a gig!
In less than 13 weeks sales of
these celebrity cheeses increased dramatically.

When the Minis took their
act on the road, they were an
instant hit. In one year sales
nearly doubled in LA and in

San Francisco. In Boston,
Philly and Miami, Mini sales
set new records.

With a modest budget
Fromageries Bel President
Frank Schnieders saw his cow
jump over the moon.

Asked if he ever expected
success like this, Frank said
"No." But the fact is. . .

"I SAW IT ON THE RADIO."

To find out how radio can produce sales results for you, contact:
Radio Advertising Bureau, 304 Park Avenue South, New York, NY 10010

**EXHIBIT 19.4
Encouraging Radio Network
Advertising**

ethnic groups and youthful audiences. Despite its growth, network advertising remains a relatively small part of radio advertising. In 1985
network radio accounted for only 5 percent to 7 percent of all radio
advertising expenditures.[13] The Radio Advertising Bureau is attempting
to attract more advertisers to network (see Exhibit 19.4).

Spot Advertising

Spot advertising is an important marketing vehicle for radio users, because it provides the benefits of flexibility and audience segmentation
which are radio's major attributes. Spot advertising initially derived
from spot announcements, but today these two are distinct. Spot advertising is currently a geographic concept and provides an advertiser with
the capabilities of choosing spots or markets in which advertising will
appear. By selecting the time and stations independently, an advertiser
has the advantages of eliminating waste circulation, tailoring advertising
to fit the specific broadcast station's time availabilities, content characteristics, and audience appeal, and the facilities for engaging in test marketing.

Local Advertising

Local radio refers to time purchased on a local radio station by a local
advertiser. Local is similar in concept to spot; the major difference is
the location of the advertiser. The largest proportion of radio advertising
funds are spent in local advertising.

How Advertisers Buy Radio Time

Radio advertisers may purchase programs, participations, spot announcements, or package plans. In purchasing *programs*, advertisers
buy time and many sponsor their own programs, subject to the approval
of the broadcasting station. Frequently broadcasters offer program suggestions and submit talent costs on request.

Participations are available to advertisers who are unwilling to absorb the entire cost of the time and program, but are willing to share
these costs with other advertisers. The cost of the time and talent is
divided among all participants and each receives an equivalent amount
of advertising time. Broadcasters generally offer lists of qualified participating programs and state the rates for each of these.

Spot announcements are one-minute, 30-second, 20-second, and 10-
second commercial messages that occur at various times during the day.
Two 30-second spots cost more than one 1-minute spot, and there are
frequency and dollar volume discounts available. The announcement
rates may also vary according to the time during which they are scheduled.

---

[13]J. Fred MacDonald, "New Luster Reflects Another 'Golden Era'," *Advertising Age*
(April 14, 1986) p. S-1.

FIGURE 19.3   Radio's 1986 Top 25 Spot Advertisers

			Millions Of $
1.	$50.420	Anheuser-Busch	
2.	$35.153	General Motors	
3.	$28.724	Miller Brewing	
4.	$22.342	PepsiCo.	
5.	$21.928	Sears, Roebuck	
6.	$21.708	Delta Air Lines	
7.	$21.071	Chrysler	
8.	$19.962	Southland	
9.	$18.670	Van Munching & Co.	
10.	$18.178	Pillsbury	
11.	$18.146	Texas Air	
12.	$17.914	Pabst Brewing	
13.	$17.610	Ford	
14.	$16.608	Coca-Cola	
15.	$16.377	People Express	
16.	$14.407	American Airlines	
17.	$12.110	Beatrice	
18.	$11.684	Hormel	
19.	$11.376	Bell South	
20.	$11.249	TWA	
21.	$11.115	United Airlines	
22.	$10.382	Nissan	
23.	$10.317	Southwestern Bell	
24.	$9.598	Mobil Oil	
25.	$9.318	Martlett Importers	

Source: from "Radio Facts," 1987-1988. Reprinted by permission of Radio Advertising Bureau.

Radio stations offer *package plans*, which provide special rates for various arrangements of 1-minute, 30-second, 20-second, and 10-second spots. They provide discounts for announcements that are staggered throughout time periods and various days. TAP (Total Audience Plan) is the designation for package plans offering a flat rate for a specific number of time slots distributed over the various dayparts.

Radio is used by both national and local advertisers. When Filene's Basement of Boston opened three outlets in Long Island, New York, it made heavy use of local radio. AT&T spent over $24,000,000 advertising on network radio in 1985, and the company and its former subsidiaries spent over $45,000,000 in spot radio advertising the same year (see Figure 19.3).

With the advent of television, radio turned to audience segmentation, offering a wide range of markets and programs to choose from. It became a much more localized medium providing a variety of musical offerings such as underground rock, pop, country and western, middle of the road, rhythm and blues, gospel, and classical. In addition, it developed ethnic appeal programming, beamed toward the blacks or foreign-language groups; all-talk shows; two-way phone talk, and news.

Since programming has segmented the audience and provided something of local interest, more and more local advertisers are using radio. Radio is considered a particularly effective method for reaching the growing Hispanic population.

In recent years there is a resurgence of interest in radio by package-goods producers and mass advertisers. Companies such as Cheseborough Pond, General Foods, General Motors, and Chanel have become strong radio advertisers, and their entry has supported the growth of networks. Some of the state networks exist in highly agricultural states and provide news services for the farmer and an advertising medium for agribusiness.

Advantages and Disadvantages of Radio Advertising

Its changing nature in recent years has benefitted radio as an advertising medium, particularly for local advertisers. Yet its increasing mobility and its potential for expanding listening time suggests that radio may have the potential for again becoming a vehicle of some significance to national advertisers.

Immediacy of Information
Of all media, radio presents the greatest opportunities for immediacy of information. Through the midafternoon the greatest percentage of the interested audience turns to the radio as a source of news.[14] Its mobility increases this potential for immediacy, particularly during the summer when outdoor activities increase.

Large Reach
Radio provides the potential for reaching almost the entire American public. Over 96 percent of the people 12 years of age and over report listening to the radio at least once a week.[15]

Possibility of Extra Coverage
Although radio advertising is usually purchased because it reaches a given market very well, radio signals may be carried far from the originating market into other geographical areas. As noted earlier, radio signals travel further at night, and, for the national advertiser who is trying

[14]*Radio Facts*, 1986-1987, Radio Advertising Bureau, New York, N. Y.
[15]*Ibid.*, p. 16.

to build brand awareness in many different markets, this added feature
may be perceived as a bonus when buying radio locally.

Flexibility

Radio offers flexibility in terms of geographic selectivity and special audience interests. There are over 8500 commercial radio stations in the
United States, presenting an advertiser with a large number of alternatives. Moreover, radio offers a simple means of reaching special markets:
there are stations offering foreign-language programming and others
highlighting Black issues. In addition, radio reaches farmers and the
farm market.

Low Cost

Compared to television, radio is a relatively low-cost medium, and,
compared to other media, radio has a fairly low cost-per-thousand-listen-
ers. Advertisers may be surprised at the low rates offered by some local
radio stations and discover that what they consider to be a prohibitive
communication device is, in fact, inexpensive, in terms of investment
cost as well as cost per thousand.

Adaptability

Radio is an adaptable medium; changes can be made fairly easily and
quickly in programs, commercials, radio copy, and even timing. Advertising can be adapted to local needs and local interests, and even national advertising can be given a local flavor.

Radio Is a Good Supporting Medium

Because of its low cost and ability to contact specific target segments,
radio is often used as a supporting medium to round out a media plan.
For example, when the plan is predominantly print, radio can bring
sound to the campaign at a relatively low cost.

Radio is becoming increasingly effective for retailers who use this
medium for announcing special events, special departments, and sales.
Regional advertisers reach their special markets through spot advertising, and, in recent years, national advertisers have found radio an effective way to localize national advertising.

Disadvantages of Radio

Radio stations are finding it difficult to stay on top of intensely competitive markets. Several characteristics tend to limit radio's growth as an
advertising medium.

Lacks Prestige

Radio no longer has the prestige it once had, nor is its prestigious image
likely to return. This is mainly because of the development of more
sophisticated broadcasting techniques.

Aural Transmission Only

Radio transmission offers an aural message only and is therefore limited in its communications capabilities. The eye is said to be a stronger path to the brain than the ear, and many products and ideas require some kind of visual communication to reinforce reception. However, a radio advertiser can make allowances and adjustments for the communication deficiency of radio by painting word pictures and scenes, and by frequent repetition to reinforce the message transmission. The radio jingle is another device that has been used with some success to overcome the lack of visual communication.

Too Many Stations

The growth and diversity of radio stations has made it increasingly difficult to incorporate radio in a media campaign. The local character of a large number of radio stations creates an audience that is considered too fragmented to meet the needs of some national advertisers who find the necessity of catering to the special interests of these varying groups too demanding.

Short Message Life

A radio message is fleeting and perishable. A commercial message lasts only a moment, and once that moment is gone, the message as it existed cannot be recaptured for future reference. Moreover, there is no editorial matter to draw a listener's attention to a commercial message, unlike magazines and newspapers where the advertisement may be placed next to attention-getting editorial material. This characteristic of radio (and television) is viewed by some as a potential advantage, since, at the moment the message is delivered, it has the stage all to itself.

Shared Audience Attention

Radio listening usually accompanies some other activity. This means that the audience's attention is shared by the medium and some other effort, and the message may, therefore, lose some of its impact. On the other hand, since the audience can do other things while listening, this tends to increase the listening time and, with it, the opportunities for greater reach and frequency.

CRITERIA FOR PURCHASING ADVERTISING TIME ON RADIO

In purchasing radio time advertisers examine a number of criteria. While costs, program, and size and composition of the listening audience are of major significance, several criteria that are more qualitative in nature are also important.

Cost of Radio Time

Rates are scheduled in dayparts, the most important of which (prime time) is driving time. Typically dayparts may be designated as follows:

Morning drive	5:30 A.M. – 10:00 A.M.
Daytime	10:00 A.M. – 3:00 P.M.
Afternoon or evening drive	3:00 P.M. – 7:00 P.M.
Nighttime	7:00 P.M. – 12:00 P.M.
All night	12:00 A.M. – 5:30 A.M.

Each station establishes its own classes and varies its rates accordingly. Information concerning dayparts is available in station rate cards and Standard Rate and Data Service. For example, SRDS data for KWIZ indicates that a 60-second spot announcement in drive time (AA) would cost $110. For nighttime (B) this announcement would cost $29. The rate card also designates frequency discounts and the cost of package plans.

Radio stations also offer lower rates to advertisers who buy run-of-the-station (ROS) or best-time-available (BTA) ads. These concepts are similar to run-of-the-paper offerings in newspapers since advertisers leave the scheduling of the spots up to the media.

Network Radio Rates

Rates for network radio are also available in SRDS and rate cards. These rates, however, are flexible, and bargaining can occur so that the actual price is usually negotiated.

Programming

Radio stations usually list their programming descriptions on their rate cards. They may describe the audience they intend to reach (for example, programming for young adults 18–45) as well as the material presented (music, news).

Standard broadcast classifications for radio programming include album-oriented rock, country, Black, Spanish, and classical. Although the largest number of stations offer adult contemporary, those stations that offer top seller recordings geared to the young audience (contemporary hit radio) have the largest listening audience (see Table 19.3). Radio stations provide programming descriptions to facilitate an advertiser's selection process, and research firms offer data to enable an advertiser to relate his or her potential customers and their listening habits to the programming schedule of the broadcaster.

TABLE 19.3 Hit Radio Still Tops the Charts

Format	Number of Stations	1984	1985	Percentage Change
Contemporary hit radio	340	16.87%	17.74%	− 15.7%
Adult contemp./oldies	525	13.62	15.91	+ 1.6
Country	474	11.79	11.19	− 2.7
Album-oriented rock	220	10.76	10.71	+31.9
Easy listening	179	11.02	10.05	−11.9
News/talk	120	8.61	8.77	− 1.0
Black/urban	219	10.12	8.53	+14.1
Middle of the road/variety	244	7.31	7.02	− 6.6
Nostalgia/big band	157	4.13	4.02	− 7.0
Spanish	76	2.56	2.31	+15.2
Religion/gospel	213	1.76	2.00	−11.5
Classical	37	1.20	1.37	− 4.4
Others	70	0.24	0.38	+47.4

Percentage of listening based on one-quarter hour average in 173 Arbitron markets (2974 stations)

Source: From *American Radio*, Spring 1986 Edition. Copyright © 1986 Duncan's American Radio, Inc. Reprinted by permission.

Radio Circulation

Information concerning the size and composition of an audience is important in purchasing advertising time. *Primary coverage* refers to the areas where a radio signal can be heard clearly, and *secondary coverage* includes those areas where a signal is not as clear. For an advertiser a radio station's coverage is significant but not as important as its actual circulation.

Circulation refers to the audience who listens to the program and, thus, has an opportunity to hear a message. This concept is similar to the circulation of print media, because it assumes the physical capability of being exposed to the message but does not guarantee that anyone heard it.

Radio circulation is not measured by an independent auditing service, but instead is determined by rating services who offer this information to subscribers. Many organizations have provided audience data for radio including Nielsen, who dropped its radio division in the mid-sixties, The Source, and Pulse. Currently, however, the major company in the field is Arbitron.

Arbitron uses a seven-day personally kept diary of radio listening which is delivered and returned by mail. It is difficult to obtain a perfect record of radio listening behavior due to the proliferation of radio stations, and the popularity of portable radios and car radios which make measurement difficult (see Figure 19.4).[16]

---

[16]Jack McGuire, "Numbers Game Needs Players," *Advertising Age* (September 15, 1980), p. S-24.

Arbitron basically measures numbers, but efforts to provide qualitative data emerge from other research services, such as Simmons Market Research Bureau and RAM. Simmons, for example, has been providing profiles of the listeners—what they eat, drink, and wear, and where, when, and how they travel—in addition to other life-style patterns. National radio networks sponsor annual surveys (called RADAR surveys) to measure radio audiences nationwide.

Evaluating Radio's Audience

In evaluating radio's audience an advertiser can use a number of concepts that provide the ability to make comparisons among alternative radio schedules. Arbitron provides radio audience estimates on the basis of average quarter-hour ratings and cumes.

Average Quarter-Hour Rating (AQH Rating)

Ratings are based on the size of an audience as a percent of a station's coverage. Thus if a radio station has a coverage of 1000 persons, and the *audience size* for a program in a particular time period is 50 persons, the AQH rating is 5 percent (50/1000).

Gross Rating Points

In the previous example, 5 percent of the audience was reached with a message. Assuming 10 spots were used, the total gross rating points can be determined by the following:

$$\text{Reach} \times \text{Frequency} = \text{Gross Rating Points}$$
$$5 \times 10 = 50 \text{ GRPs}$$

These 50 GRPs do not precisely define the reach or average frequency, since some members of this audience may hear the message once, some twice, and so on.

Cumes

Also called *unduplicated audience, cumes* refers to the number of *different* persons listening during a specified time period, a distinction that gross rating points do not provide. In the previous example, although there were 50 GRPs, these can be more precisely determined by an evaluation of cumes.

Thus the total of 10 spots may have reached 200 different people, or an "accumulated" audience equal to 20 percent of the total 1000 people available for this radio station. The 50 GRPs can now be more precisely defined as

Percent Reach (Cumes)		Frequency		GRPs
20	×	2½	=	50

That is, 20 percent of the audience had an opportunity to hear the ad an average of 2½ times each.

FIGURE 19.4 An Arbitron Ratings Radio Diary

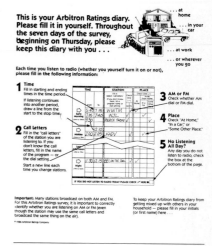

TABLE 19.4   Spot Radio Cost Per Point*

Market Survey Area	U.S. Pop 12+ %	Women				Men			
		18+ $	18–34 $	18–49 $	25–54 $	18+ $	18–34 $	18–49 $	25–54 $
Top 5	20	980	633	843	1,013	1,004	574	905	1,054
Top 10	28	1,624	1,072	1,368	1,656	1,588	1,029	1,582	1,720
Top 25	42	2,575	1,754	2,260	2,591	2,545	1,641	2,475	2,785
Top 50	54	3,739	2,501	3,177	3,715	3,831	2,299	3,465	3,984
Top 75	61	4,465	2,981	3,799	4,375	4,578	2,714	3,996	4,827
Top 100	65	4,956	3,325	4,209	4,841	5,249	3,132	4,525	5,543

*Costs are based on a 50 Reach and an 8 Frequency over a 4-week period, Mon.-Sun. 6am-12Mid., in each Market Survey Area.

Source: From "Grey, 1986 Media Modules," p. 63. Reprinted by permission of Grey Advertising, Inc.

Cost Per Rating Point

The budget for radio advertisers may be evaluated on the basis of cost per rating point, as follows:

$$\frac{\text{Budget}}{\text{Total Rating Points}} = \text{Cost Per Rating Point.}$$

For example, if we assume that the 50 gross rating points in the schedule discussed before cost the advertiser $50,000, the cost per rating point is $1000.

For users of spot radio, comparisons can be made about the average cost per rating point in various markets, using demographic breakdowns. (See Table 19.4)

Additional Considerations in Buying Radio Time

Advertisers examine a number of factors in the purchase of radio time. Initially they evaluate the advantages radio might offer over other media in terms of cost, type of audience, presentation of advertising, frequency with which the audience can be contacted, type of programming offered, ability to tie-in point-of-purchase advertising, and so on.

Once the advertisers have decided upon radio, other criteria should be evaluated in the purchase of time on specific radio broadcasting vehicles. First, advertisers must examine the market and evaluate the socioeconomic characteristics of the population in terms of broadcast coverage. To gain a clearer understanding of the audience, the advertisers should examine program content, because the kind of programming by the radio station determines the audience.

Other considerations in selecting a radio station include services and facilities of the station, merchandising services offered by the station, rating service information and coverage data provided, image of the particular station, frequency with which customers can be reached, and availability of time for program sponsorship, participations, and spot announcements, as well as specific package plans.

SUMMARY

Advertising on television is called network, spot, or local. Firms may sponsor an entire program, be a participant, or purchase spot announcements during TV programs. Syndicated programs are also available to advertisers at a smaller investment than network television.

Television time periods are divided into dayparts, specific segments of a broadcast day that are available at different rates; the most expensive is prime time. Purchasing network advertising is complicated, since the rate structure is subject to many pressures and tends to be negotiable. Spot advertising can be bought in the form of spot announcements and package plans.

Circulation in television is measured by rating services using electronic recorders, diaries, coincidental telephone calls, and personal interviews. Information is provided in terms of program ratings, the percentage of television households tuned in to a broadcasting station, and share of the audience, the percentage of the total audience in a specific time period tuned to a specific station.

Cost-per-thousand households or individuals is used to make cost and circulation comparisons. Gross rating points are determined by multiplying reach by frequency. Cost per rating point may be used to evaluate a television program by dividing the total budget allocated for the advertising by the number of gross rating points.

Commercial television is faced with significant competition from new technologies including cable, subscription television, public television, videocassettes and videodiscs, interactive systems, and teletext.

Radio advertisers can use network, spot, or local broadcasting facilities. While there are many radio networks, advertisers spend only a small amount of their advertising funds on network. Most radio advertising is of a local nature. Radio advertisers purchase programs, participations, spot announcements, or package plans. Information on radio costs is available through Standard Rate and Data Service and radio rate cards. Rates are scheduled in daypart classes. Radio stations offer a variety of different program formats, including contemporary hit radio, country, and news/talk.

Rating services provide audience data. The major company in the field is Arbitron. Like television, radio costs can be evaluated in terms of program rating, gross rating points, and cost per rating point.

QUESTIONS FOR DISCUSSION

1. What is meant by *sponsorship, participations, spot announcements,* and *syndication?*
2. As a sponsor of a program would you be as satisfied with a 20-percent share of the audience as you would be with a 20-percent program rating? Explain.
3. What are the various methods by which television circulation can be measured? Which technique do you consider best?
4. What is meant by *cost of one rating point?* How is cost per rating point computed?
5. What is the difference between broadcasting and narrowcasting? Briefly describe the alternative electronic media.
6. How and why has the nature of radio programming changed over the years?
7. What kinds of services provide information on radio circulation?
8. What is meant by the terms *average quarter hour, gross impressions,* and *cumes?*
9. What are the strengths of radio? The limitations?
10. What do you see as the future program content in radio? How will this affect advertising in this medium?

KEY TERMS

spot advertising	gross rating points
local advertising	cost per rating point
participation	post analysis
spot announcements	flight
syndication	narrowcasting
barter	broadcasting
package houses	interconnects
preemptible rate	infomercial
make goods	video cassettes
coverage	video discs
sets-in-use	teletext
program rating	primary coverage
share of the audience	secondary coverage
audimeter	circulation
viewing log	AQH rating
people meter	cumes

AD PRACTICE

Prepare a network television advertising schedule for the producer of a new dry cereal, listing the programs that should be used for spot announcements. Estimates of cost for a thirty-second commercial can be taken from Figure 19.1 on page 402. Look in your local newspaper for program ratings. Determine the cost per thousand and the share of the audience (assume that 60 percent of the audience have their sets turned on) for the spots selected. Compute the gross rating points for the entire schedule and the cost per rating point.

20

Direct-Mail and Out-of-Home Advertising

In the late 1800s Aaron Montgomery Ward mailed his first catalog, a one-page edition offering goods, furniture, and even a 14-karat gold ring for two dollars. Since then direct mail has become a major advertising medium accounting for over 15 percent of the total advertising volume. Out-of-home advertising has an even longer history; in fact, it is the oldest advertising medium. It currently accounts, however, for a little more than 1 percent of total advertising revenues. Nevertheless out-of-home advertising can be used creatively and effectively. For example, a Spokane pest-control firm used an outdoor advertising campaign to combat the notion that termites were not a problem. The first sign declared "There is no termite problem in Spokane." Later, several chunks of the sign were removed in a pattern that suggested the wood had been eaten away. The "termite" problem continued until there was nothing left except the pest control firm's name, address, and the word *Burp!* from an obviously contented and somewhat bloated termite.

In both direct mail and out-of-home advertising, messages are transmitted through what may be considered as print media. However, there are significant differences between these media and newspapers and magazines.

DIRECT-MAIL ADVERTISING

Direct-mail advertising refers to all forms of promotional messages sent through the post office and through private delivery firms to a specific individual or organization. Since the delivery is made through a mass medium—the post office—direct-mail is categorized as an advertising medium. The term *direct-mail advertising* is frequently used interchangeably with *mail-order selling, direct marketing,* and *direct response advertising.*

Mail-Order Selling

Mail-order selling is not an advertising medium but a method of distributing products that uses the mail. To sell via mail-order promotional efforts, including sales letters soliciting orders or print or television messages asking readers to order products by writing to the company, can be used. Thus the promotion used for mail-order selling can occur in all media including direct-mail.

Direct Marketing

Direct marketing is also a method of product distribution, but the term includes all techniques of consumer buying through nonstore means. Direct marketing is the offering of goods and services directly to potential customers through nontraditional channels of distribution, such as vending machines, door-to-door selling, and mail order.

Direct Response Advertising

Direct response advertising is the name given to an advertising technique eliciting an immediate order, inquiry, or visit to a store. This technique may be used in various media; however, the major segment of direct response advertising emanates from direct-mail. To indicate this relationship, the Direct-Mail Marketing Association, a trade association for direct mailers, changed its name to the Direct Marketing Association. Other media that are used for direct response advertising include television, radio, newspapers and magazines as well as supplementary forms such as yellow pages (see Figure 20.1).

Kinds of Direct-Mail Advertising

One of the major advantages of direct-mail advertising is the opportunity to create all varieties of direct mailers. Limitations are primarily those that relate to size (based on post office restrictions) and cost of the advertising.

1. Letters—the most widely used of all direct mailers because they are the most adaptable, most personal, and most flexible.
2. Booklets—used when the message is lengthy and when information is desired. Instruction books, price lists, directories, sales books, and house organs are examples (see Exhibit 20.1).

FIGURE 20.1   Direct Response Billings by Nine Categories

MEDIA	TOP 25 AGENCIES BILLINGS 1986	$ AS % OF TOP 500'S	TOP 100 AGENCIES BILLINGS 1986	$ AS % OF TOP 500'S	TOP 500'S BILLINGS 1986
Yellow Pages	$259.7	52.8	$423.4	86.2	$491.4
Direct mail	229.5	18.3	598.9	47.9	1,251.1
Catalogs	0.0	0.0	37.8	31.1	121.4
Direct response TV	99.8	37.3	236.9	88.6	267.4
Direct response radio	7.2	21.1	16.5	48.5	34.0
Direct response newspaper	25.8	23.7	79.6	73.1	108.9
Direct response magazine	30.8	16.1	160.2	83.8	191.1
Telemarketing	0.0	0.0	31.5	62.6	50.3
Free-standing inserts	2.4	3.4	20.9	29.9	69.8
Total direct response	655.2	25.3	1,605.7	62.1	2,585.4

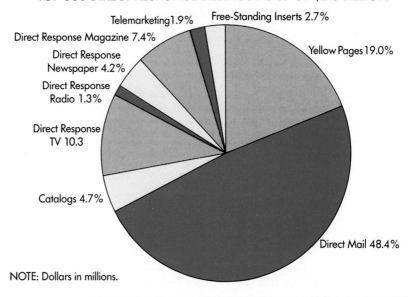

TOP 500 DIRECT RESPONSE BILLINGS AS % OF $2.6 BILLION

- Telemarketing 1.9%
- Free-Standing Inserts 2.7%
- Direct Response Magazine 7.4%
- Direct Response Newspaper 4.2%
- Direct Response Radio 1.3%
- Direct Response TV 10.3
- Catalogs 4.7%
- Yellow Pages 19.0%
- Direct Mail 48.4%

NOTE: Dollars in millions.

3. Catalogs—a form of booklet, having widespread usage in direct mail. Sears prints and distributes more than 300,000,000 annually. In the past catalogs were considered a means of reaching less affluent consumers; in recent years, they have been used to reach segmented markets such as the specialty catalogs for the "upscale busy woman."

4. Brochures—considered the "glamour" mailers; they make use of creative capabilities in illustration, color, materials, size, and bindings. Brochures are designed to reflect the richness and stature of the company or product and imply value and prestige.

5. Broadsides—large folders that are used when "smash or bigness" is necessary. Broadsides offer the psychology of excessive size and use

large pictorial displays and bold copy. A well-designed broadside can ultimately be used as a counter card by a retail establishment.

6. Circulars—an inexpensive form of direct mail that can be used to get across a strong message in a brief period. They are generally flat pieces of varying sizes offering big headlines and telling their story quickly and briefly.

7. Mailing Cards—usually the least expensive of all forms of direct mail. They can be used for brief announcements, to introduce "teaser" campaigns, for notices, invitations, or short direct messages.

8. Statement Stuffers—the most universally used form of retail direct mail. They range from simple black-and-white imprinted sheets to elaborate full-color folders. Often they have a coupon to use in ordering products by mail, but they are primarily designed to build store traffic.

EXHIBIT 20.1
Direct Mail Booklet

Kimberly-Clark reaches a very identifiable market segment with a booklet mailing to new parents.

Reproduced with permission of Kimberly-Clark Corporation and Lionel Kalish, artist.

The Advantages of Direct Mail

Practically every business engages in some form of direct-mail advertising, even if they only put their names on their stationery; however, direct-mail is rarely the major advertising medium for a company. In most cases it provides support that is beneficial in specific circumstances. Firms traditionally making heavy use of direct-mail include catalog companies, publishing houses, fund-raising groups, and books and record clubs. Recently there has been an increase in direct-mail usage by financial service organizations and retailers.

Direct mail as an advertising medium has several advantages. The following descriptions highlight its distinguishing features.

Selective
Direct mail is the most selective of all media. It permits an advertiser to pinpoint a particular target and provides assurances that the target will be reached. Waste circulation is held to a minimum with direct mail.

Controllable
It is an advertising medium that is controlled exclusively by an advertiser, except when the advertiser must observe the postal regulations. He or she does not have to contact a vehicle for the timing, placement, or acceptance of advertisements; the advertiser also controls circulation because he or she creates the audience. The sales campaign is hidden from competitors when only direct mail is used.

Flexible
The medium is flexible, adjustable, and adaptable. An advertiser can begin a campaign at a moment's notice and discontinue it in the same time period. No advertising budget is too small for initiating a program; an advertisement can be sent when, where, and to whom an advertiser

wants and, except for the constraints applied by postal regulations, in any shape the advertiser wants.

Personal
Direct mailings may be addressed to buyers with specialized appeals and delivered directly to them. There are few distractions competing with an advertisement at the time it is received.

Creative
Because of the few limitations on space, style, and format, direct-mail advertising can use ingenuity, novelty, and a variety of materials and processes. Three-dimensional presentations are increasing; a recent successful mailing featured a miniature gift box that literally popped out of the envelope.[1]

Secures Action
Direct mail provides the means to secure the most important steps in the advertising process—action. It can provide business reply cards, order blanks, and other ways for the advertiser to know that the reader has taken action.

Measures Performance
It is easy to measure performance through direct-mail advertising. It is an excellent medium for research through the use of questionnaires, reply cards, coupons, and so on.

The Disadvantages of Direct Mail

Media directors predict that direct mail will grow more rapidly than other media in the future.[2] However, there are a number of disadvantages that tend to limit the use of direct mail as an advertising medium.

Negative Image
The most serious limitation to direct-mail advertising, at least in the past, has been the consumers' presumed dislike for such material. People refer to direct mail negatively as "junk mail" and discard much of it without reading the information it offers. However, in recent years, as more prestigious corporations have turned to direct mail, its image as a respectable advertising medium has improved.

High Cost
While its image appears to be improving the cost of this relatively inexpensive medium is rising. In addition to postal rates, which appear to be increasing, a direct mailer spends large sums producing the mailing

---

[1]"Gimmicks grab addressee's attention," *Advertising Age* (October 27, 1986), p. S–13.
[2]Lori Kessler, "Media directors predict soft market will continue in 1987," *Advertising Age* (November 17, 1986), p. S–4.

material. There are wide variations in production costs depending on the kind of material used, and while folders and leaflets are fairly inexpensive, a catalog of 1500 pages represents a large investment.

Also the direct mailer may have to buy a list of names which will add to the cost. The average mailing list may rent from a commercial broker for about $35 per thousand, but lists requiring extensive research may cost as much as a dollar per name.

Lack of Editorial Matter

A major limitation of direct mail as an advertising medium is that it provides no articles, stories, or other material to attract a reader's attention. Moreover, the piece itself must persuade consumers to read it; otherwise they may discard it without paying attention to the message.

Distribution Delays

Most media have scheduled delivery times, so that an advertiser has some assurances that the message will be received at a certain time period. This is not true for direct mail. If the material is sent third class the Post Office makes no delivery commitments for it at all. Delays may occur even if it is sent first class! This means that the advertising may be received too late for a scheduled "sale" or other special offering.

The Direct-Mail Campaign

Direct-mail advertising, similar to other advertising campaigns, should begin with a statement of objectives. Direct mail can be used to announce a new product, distribute coupons and samples, introduce sales people and gain entry for the salesforce, and secure direct orders.

Circulation

In direct-mail advertising an advertiser builds his or her own circulation via a mailing list. Ideally the mailing list contains a complete roster of people the advertiser wishes to influence, an up-to-date and accurate compilation of names and addresses, with no duplications. Mailing lists are usually classified as *internal* or *external*.

Internal Mailing Lists

The ideal mailing list is not readily available to an advertiser, but there are several sources that an advertiser can turn to. The best source for a potential mailing list is a firm's own customers; such information can be secured through charge accounts, order slips, salespeople, and correspondence. Responses to a company's advertising may indicate a number of important potential customers.

External Mailing Lists

External mailing lists may be purchased, rented, exchanged, or compiled by an advertiser from various sources. Specialized lists can be purchased for doctors, owners of a certain type of automobile, mothers of new-born babies, college students in a specific area, and so on.

Lists may be rented from list brokers whose price generally includes addressing the material of the mail-order advertiser. Information concerning the costs of lists is becoming increasingly important and *SRDS* "Direct Mail List Rates and Data" which was issued twice a year is currently published on a bi-monthly basis. This publication contains the names of companies that offer lists.

Rentals for external lists are usually on a one-time basis and cost from $30 to $50 per 1000 names. Frequently they are sold through brokers who receive approximately 20 percent of the transaction.

Mailing lists should be continually maintained: adding new names, eliminating duplications, correcting errors, and using the post-office list-checking service that is available at some post offices for a fee.

Copy for Direct-Mail

Since one of the basic advantages of direct mail as an advertising medium is its "personal" quality, this characteristic should be built into the mailing. A personal salutation (Dear Mr. Jones) can be used; some mention of the addressee's name or city in the body of the copy has been known to increase its pulling power.

It is best to present one basic idea and offer it simply and logically. Since much direct mail is designed for mail-order selling, the action element becomes extremely important; it can tell a reader what to do, how to do it, give the reader an impulse for action through samples, free trial, or demonstrations, or supply a card, or a card and an envelope. Guidelines for direct mail copy are presented in Chapter 12.

Evaluating the Campaign Results

A significant advantage of direct mail is its ability to precisely measure achievement in terms of response or other goals. Moreover, direct mail is frequently used as a mechanism for mail-order sales. To evaluate the extent to which the direct-mail campaign generates action, concepts of *cost per inquiry* and *cost per sale* are used.

$$\text{Cost per Inquiry} = \frac{\text{Total cost of mailing (including mailing list, production, and postage costs)}}{\text{Number of Inquiries}}$$

$$\text{Cost per Sale} = \frac{\text{Total cost of mailing}}{\text{Number of sales}}$$

These data are useful for comparing campaigns and evaluating specific campaigns. For example, American Telecom Inc. successfully positioned itself as a phone equipment manufacturer in the telecommunications equipment field with a direct-mail campaign in which chocolate telephones were mailed to 279 potential customers.[3] When the sales

---

[3]"Sweet Sell Garners 100% Response for Phone Equipment Manufacturer," *Marketing News* (April 1, 1983), p. 3.

manager called on these dealers they all acknowledged awareness of the chocolate telephone and every one of them expressed interest in handling the line (see Exhibit 20.2). The total mailing cost of $14,000 for only 279 mailings was relatively high. However the 100-percent response rate offered a relatively low cost of approximately $50 per major

sales opportunity $\left(\dfrac{\$14,000}{279} = \$50.18\right)$.

EXHIBIT 20.2
Successful Direct-Mail Campaign

Changes in Direct-Mail Advertising

From an advertiser's viewpoint the ability of direct mail to select a target market and control the dissemination of a message makes it an efficient medium. A unique aspect of direct-mail advertising is its ability to build an extensive and detailed data base. This requires recording every order as well as detailed information concerning customers. Computers offer an excellent capability for storing and retrieving all kinds of detailed information about direct-mail customers, including data about merchandising class, product class, dollar amount, method of ordering, method of payment, and recency of order. Moreover, customer information concerning demographic factors, lifestyles, beliefs, feelings, expectations, and motivations may be recorded and retrieved.

The extent to which this data base may be cultivated is limited by the criticisms of gathering, recording, and providing such detailed information about consumers. In addition to the question of sensitivity of information these kinds of data are likely to lead to increased complaints about invasion of privacy.

In response to current criticisms the Direct Marketing Association offers a Mail Preference Service which permits an individual to request that his or her name be removed (or added to) any of twenty-four categories of lists. An individual may write to every organization suspected of renting his or her name to direct mailers. Many companies, such as American Express and J. C. Penney Co., include with their bills the option to remove one's name from rentable lists. Certain information about people is considered inviolable; for instance, a person's precise income or intimate medical and/or sexual problems. In anticipation of future criticisms it will be necessary for the direct-mail industry to provide clearer definitions of "sensitive" information and to offer guidelines for policing excessive dissemination of such data.

OUT-OF-HOME ADVERTISING

Out-of-home advertising is a term used to describe the various media that deliver messages outside of the home. The most widely used forms of these media are outdoor and transit advertising. Out-of-home advertising can be as small as a card in a subway train or as large as the 11,600-square-foot sign painted on Northwest's hangar in St. Paul's In-

ternational Airport (see Exhibit 20.3). Northwest's sign exceeds the former recordholder for out-of-home advertising—the Winston cigarette spectacular in New York City.

OUTDOOR ADVERTISING

Outdoor advertising refers to all advertisements displayed out of the home with the exception of those appearing on transportatioin facilities and vehicles. Although it is the oldest form of advertising, its volume represents only a little more than 1 percent of the total advertising expenditures in major media. However, with 10–20 percent of the roads carrying 80–90 percent of the traffic, there are extensive opportunities for outdoor advertising to reach a wide portion of the total population. Moreover, outdoor advertising has the potential for a high frequency; an individual may be exposed to an advertisement several times during the course of one time period.

Kinds of Outdoor Advertising

Many of the complaints about outdoor advertising are directed at the advertising messages *(bills)* on numerous wooden boards (hence the term *billboards*) marring the landscape and creating traffic hazards. Instead of using the objectionable term *billboard*, the outdoor advertising industry classifies outdoor advertisements as *poster panels*, *painted bulletins*, and *electrical spectaculars*.

Poster Panels
A poster panel is generally 12-feet high and 25-feet long. Originally it took 24 sheets of paper to cover a panel; thus a poster was called a 24-sheet poster. Today presses are larger and a poster may be printed in only 10 sections.

24-Sheet Posters
The printed copy area measures 19′6″ by 8′8″. The area between the design and the frame is covered with white blanking paper.

30-Sheet Posters
The printed copy area measures 21′7″ by 9′7″. It provides about 25% more design space than the 24-Sheet Poster.

Bleed Posters
The printed copy area measures 22′8″ by 10′5″. It provides 40% more design space than the 24-Sheet Poster.

Even though posters can be as large as 36 sheets, in recent years the 30-sheet poster has become the most popular size. There has, however, been a rapid growth in the use of an 8-sheet poster, sometimes called a *junior panel*. It is usually an unlighted sign of horizontal configuration with a copy size 5 feet high by 11 feet wide.

EXHIBIT 20.4
Poster Panels

Painted Bulletins

The structure on which outdoor ads appear is called a plant or bulletin. In posters these messages are printed on sheets of paper which are pasted to the bulletin; in *painted bulletins* the messages are painted directly on the face of the bulletin. Messages for these painted bulletins

EXHIBIT 20.5
Award-Winning Painted Bulletin

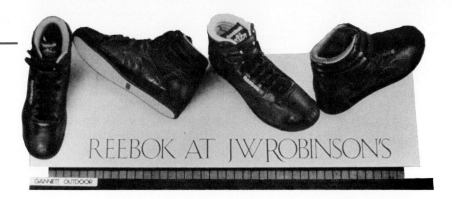

EXHIBIT 20.6
Outdoor Gets New Dimension

may be hand painted in sections in a plant's paint shop and then assembled on the site.

Painted bulletins vary in size and form. They are frequently larger than posters and since they are not mass produced but custom built, they can be made in any size and shape (see Exhibit 20.5). Painted bulletins are usually illuminated and repainted several times a year to maintain a fresh look.

Spectaculars

Spectaculars are large electrical signs of all shapes and colors that are used in areas of extensive traffic. They are found in the downtown areas of big cities and have achieved their greatest use and fame in the Times Square district of New York City.

Spectaculars have no standardization and, in fact, attempt to live up to their name by their unique use of excessive size, movement, brilliance, and illustration. Because of the complicated nature of the installation, they do not change frequently, and maintenance becomes an important component in their cost.

Technological Improvements

Several technological developments have been introduced that permit variations in and attract attention to outdoor advertising. Various effects

EXHIBIT 20.7
Nike's Promotional Effort

such as cutout letters or three-dimensional effects are used to dramatize the messages. Plastic-faced, back-lighted units, moving messages, unusual treatment of light and color are other techniques used in outdoor advertising. "Tri-Vision" or "Multi-Vision" uses vertical triangles that turn at intervals, showing three different messages on the same panel. Solar signs use raised reflective discs that flicker in both natural and artificial light and move with the wind to create the illusion of animation. Inflatables are sometimes used to create a three-dimensional effect; for example, a car may suddenly lunge out of a bulletin (see Exhibit 20.6).

Who Uses Outdoor Advertising

National companies use outdoor advertising for several reasons. Hotels, such as Holiday Inn and Ramada Inn, make use of outdoor both for directional purposes—to indicate where their hotels are located—and for corporate image-building. Automobile manufacturers, such as Chevrolet, believe outdoor is useful to reach motorists; this large-scale advertising permits the automobile to be seen full-size. Other national advertisers use the medium to supplement their schedules. Nike, for example, found their athletic shoes were being bought more by older women than by athletes. It included an extensive outdoor advertising campaign in promotional efforts to reassociate its shoes with athletes and attract young adults and teenagers[4] (see Exhibit 20.7). In an effort to get retailers involved in its new product launch, Hanes used outdoor ads to introduce Isotoner pantyhose.[5]

Local advertisers use outdoor advertising to encourage people to trade at specific places of business. Local hotels, restaurants, shopping centers, and even hospitals make use of outdoor (see Exhibit 20.8).

[4]"Billboard Put Nike Back in the Running," *Marketing News* (June 7, 1985), p. 7.

[5]Richard Edel, "Advertisers jump on the bandwagon," *Advertising Age* (May 12, 1986), p. S–4.

EXHIBIT 20.8
Local Outdoor Advertising

Advantages and Disadvantages of Outdoor Advertising

Outdoor advertising offers several advantages to a firm that advertises. The following are some of the most important reasons to use this medium in an advertising campaign:

1. *Never Stops Working.* With proper positioning and illumination, outdoor advertising can operate 24 hours a day, 365 days a year.
2. *Low Cost.* When computations are made on a cost-per-thousand basis, it is a fairly low-cost medium. The availability of stock posters helps cut the production costs.
3. *Proximity to Point of Purchase.* An advertiser can place a message as close to the point of purchase as possible, permitting reinforcement of a customer's purchase intent and reminding a retailer, clerk, and salesperson of the item. This capability is particularly important for products, such as distilled liquors, which cannot display promotional material in stores in some states.
4. *Flexible.* Outdoor advertising can be used not only for national advertisers but also for local markets and even specific neighborhoods. Moreover, a local advertiser can identify with the local market and relate a message to specific needs.
5. *Permits Innovation.* New techniques and innnovations have permitted outdoor advertising to become a bold, colorful, and exciting medium.
6. *Reaches People "On-the-Go".* Outdoor advertising is unique—it takes advantage of a population on the move, delivering its message while people travel to and from work, go shopping, or visit friends.

There are a number of limitations to the use of outdoor advertising by firms. The following are the most important reasons:

1. *Limited Selectivity.* To some extent outdoor advertising is limited to mass markets. Except for geographic selectivity, its audience is comprised of all groups and classes, some of whom may not be the target for the message. However, with the dramatic increase in the number of working women, out-of-home is considered a viable medium by various package goods and food advertisers, such as Procter & Gamble, Nestle, and Campbell.[6]
2. *No Editorial Matter.* There is no editorial matter to attract a reader, and, in fact, trees, sky, buildings, people, and scenery act as strong detractors.
3. *Subject to Criticism.* Outdoor advertising, despite its increased acceptance, still suffers from extensive criticism and hostile legislation.

---

[6]Richard Edel, "Segmentation attracts new product categories," *Advertising Age* (May 12, 1986), p. S–1.

4. *Brief Message.* The message must be brief and simple, requiring an outdoor advertiser to provide supplementary information through other media.
5. *Cannot Secure Complete Attention.* An outdoor message is read while a motorist is driving or while a consumer is walking, not the best ways to concentrate on the communication.

How Advertisers Buy Outdoor Advertising

The outdoor advertising industry is made up of numerous small local organizations and several large regional and national companies. These firms own the structures (frequently called "plants") on which the advertising messages are placed. An organization may have only a few structures in one town or thousands of structures throughout many states. Its responsibility is to find suitable locations, put up outdoor plants, contract with advertisers for rentals of the posters, affix the poster panels or paint the displays, and make sure the lights are kept working and the torn sheets are replaced.

Circulation

The term *circulation* does not mean in outdoor advertising what it means in other media. In outdoor advertising the vehicle does not circulate among people; rather the people circulate around the medium. Moreover customers of outdoor advertising do not have to take any action to be exposed to its messages.

Showings and Gross Rating Points

Earlier circulation of outdoor advertising was computed in *showings*. A plant owner divided a market into poster zones made up of approximately equal sections of the main traffic arteries used for commerce and industry. The basic unit of sale, a number 100 showing, meant the number of posters required to provide daily effective circulation approximately equal to the population of a specific market. Generally, a #100 showing included two panels per zone, a #50 showing, one panel per zone, and so on.

Currently circulation is counted in gross rating points. Posters are sold in gross-rating-point packages that will deliver exposure opportunities equal to a certain percentage of the population each day for a month. In other words a 50-GRP showing will generate gross impressions equal to approximately half the total population each day. Similar to the concept of gross rating points in other media, one GRP is equal to 1 percent of the population served.

The number of nonilluminated and illuminated poster panels in a showing is called a *market allotment*. Each allotment varies by market size according to the number of panels needed to achieve comparable GRP coverage. For example, in the rate card for Gannett Outdoor (a sales organization for outdoor advertising companies), 11 nonilluminated and 11 illuminated panels were necessary to achieve 25 daily GRPs in

Phoenix, Arizona. In Northern California Metro area, however, 16 non-illuminated and 60 illuminated panels were necessary for the same 25 daily GRP coverage.

Cost of Outdoor Advertising

The cost of outdoor advertising includes the space cost (rental of the plant) and the costs of production (preparing the sheets, painting the bulletin, or erecting the spectacular). The rate structure for poster panels, painted bulletins, and spectaculars varies.

Rates for Poster Panels
Posters are sold in daily GRP packages on a monthly basis, and the rates are quoted by market. The greater the population in a market, generally the greater the number of panels necessary for coverage, and, therefore, the higher the price per market. For example a monthly rate for 25 daily GRPs in Phoenix (22 panels) is $7360, while the monthly rate for 25 daily GRPs in Northern California Metro (76 panels) is $24,100. Discounts are available for posters purchased for a year or more.

Rate for Bulletins
Bulletins are generaly bought on an individual basis, because the location and the amount of traffic determine the size of the bulletin and, therefore, its cost. Because of the costs involved in the creation of painted displays, they are generally purchased by advertisers for periods of one, two, or three years.

Bulletins may be purchased individually or in groups. They may be bought in fixed locations or on a rotating schedule. In a *rotary plan* advertisers display several painted bulletins in the same market and change their locations every 30, 60, or 90 days according to a schedule determined by the plant manager.

Rates for Spectaculars
Spectaculars are also purchased on an individual basis. The costs of construction are usually quite high, and fees range from $5000 to $50,000 per month. The locations carry a three- to five-year lease and presently have a five-year waiting list.[7]

Organizations for Outdoor Advertising

In an attempt to improve the image and control undesirable activities, a number of organizations have developed that serve the outdoor industry. Members are asked to observe a code of practices adopted by the outdoor advertisers.

---

[7]Raymon Goydon, "Ginza on the Hudson," *Forbes* (July 2, 1984), pp. 100–101.

1. *OAAA*   The Outdoor Advertising Association of America, Inc., is the trade association of the standardized outdoor medium. The Association recommends standards for the construction, illumination, and placement of outdoor advertising panels and for acceptability of copy.

2. *IOA*   The Institute of Outdoor Advertising serves as the research, marketing, and promotional arm of the OAAA.

3. *Sales Organizations*   Many individual plants are represented by sales organizations that maintain sales offices in major cities. In 1985, an affiliation of 29 outdoor companies, with coverage of 85 percent of the United States, formed the Outdoor Network USA to ease the process of purchasing outdoor advertising through regional companies.[8]

4. *Traffic Audit Bureau*   The Traffic Audit Bureau (TAB) is a corporation sponsored jointly by advertisers, agencies, and the outdoor industry to count traffic and audit the circulation of outdoor panels. The TAB, which is similar to the ABC in print media, determines the circulation by counting the traffic that passes a poster, either with mechanical counters or through tabulators who record the passers-by.

5. *AMMO*   In an effort to provide information about audience characteristics the Institute of Outdoor Advertising offers a service called AMMO—an acronym for Audience Measurement by Market for Outdoor. It provides audience data related to market characteristics including geographic region, TAB audited circulation, population size, and sex-age-income composition, as well as reach and frequency information.

TRANSIT ADVERTISING

Transit advertising is frequently considered part of outdoor advertising, although, in fact, transit is a medium in its own right. Although sales have tripled in the last decade transit advertising represents little more than .02 percent of the total advertising expenditures in major media.[9] *Transit advertising* refers to advertising messages appearing in or on transportation vehicles. It is, however, underutilized, since there are estimates that the average rail commuter is held captive for about 44 hours each month and the average one-way bus journey takes 30 minutes.

Kinds of Transit Advertising

Transit advertising may be exterior or interior. *Exterior transit advertising* consists of outside display units placed on the sides, front, and rear of vehicles. On buses they may be super king-size posters, king-size

---

[8]"Outdoor Network strives to post increasing sales," *Advertising Age* (May 12, 1986), p. S–2.

[9]"Mass Transit Making Strides," *Advertising Age* (December 20, 1984), p. 22.

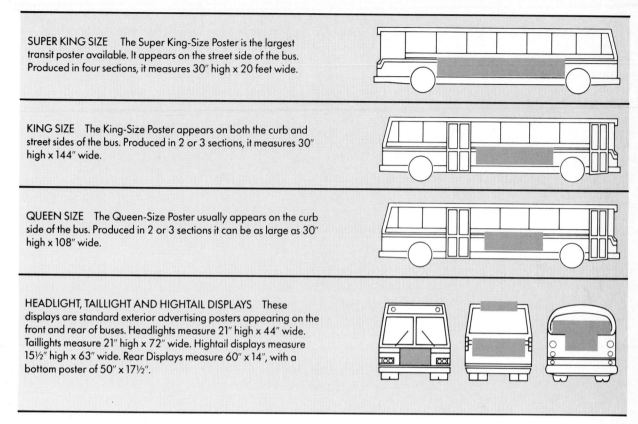

SUPER KING SIZE   The Super King-Size Poster is the largest transit poster available. It appears on the street side of the bus. Produced in four sections, it measures 30″ high x 20 feet wide.

KING SIZE   The King-Size Poster appears on both the curb and street sides of the bus. Produced in 2 or 3 sections, it measures 30″ high x 144″ wide.

QUEEN SIZE   The Queen-Size Poster usually appears on the curb side of the bus. Produced in 2 or 3 sections it can be as large as 30″ high x 108″ wide.

HEADLIGHT, TAILLIGHT AND HIGHTAIL DISPLAYS   These displays are standard exterior advertising posters appearing on the front and rear of buses. Headlights measure 21″ high x 44″ wide. Taillights measure 21″ high x 72″ wide. Hightail displays measure 15½″ high x 63″ wide. Rear Displays measure 60″ x 14″, with a bottom poster of 50″ x 17½″.

EXHIBIT 20.9
Exterior Transit Advertising

posters, queen-size posters, or headlight, taillight, and hightail displays (see Exhibit 20.9). Posters in bus shelters and on taxi tops are also forms of transit advertising.

The majority of *interior transit advertising* occurs on interior bus cards and interior rail cards (see Exhibit 20.10). Interior car cards are also used on subways.

Transit advertising also appears in railroad stations and airports in the form of one, two, or three sheet poster panels and dioramas (back-lighted displays featuring products and advertising messages).

Advantages and Disadvantages of Transit Advertising

Transit advertising dates back to before the Civil War and has contributed to the success of such well-known products as Campbell's Soup, Wrigley's chewing gum, Vick's Vapo-Rub, and Ivory Soap. Currently transit advertising is used extensively by alcoholic beverage companies, soft-drink companies, and manufacturers and distributors of food and drugs on a national basis, and by financial institutions, retail stores, automotive dealers, and restaurants on a local basis.

To most advertisers, transit advertising is not a major medium but merely a supplementary medium that is used to back up their other

INTERIOR BUS CARDS   Inside the bus these cards are mounted in frames. They measure approximately 11″ high x 28″, 42″ or 56″ wide, or 22″ high x 21″ wide.

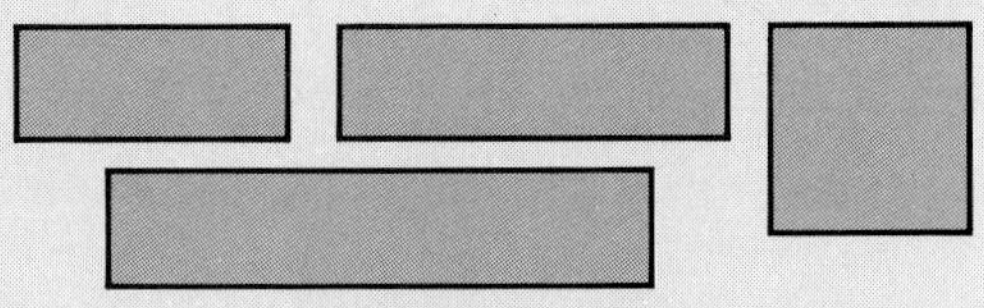

INTERIOR RAIL CARDS   Interior Rail Car cards produced in one section only are available in two sizes with areas of 21″ wide x 22″ high or 21″ wide x 33″ high.

EXHIBIT 20.10
Interior Car Cards

advertising. However, there are several reasons why they include this medium in their advertising campaigns.

1. *Low Cost.* The dollar outlay required for transit advertising is generally less than that required for any other medium.
2. *Large Audiences.* Mass audiences are reached by transit advertising. More than 70,000 vehicles carry transit advertising to a large population continually on the move. Moreover, important target groups (for example, working women) are exposed to transit advertising.
3. *Repetition of Exposures.* The length of the average transit ride has been computed to be 22 minutes. This means that a reader is not only forced to read the message but may read it more than once.
4. *Flexibility.* Transit advertising offers geographic flexibility, as well as an opportunity to reach the users of public transportation, private transportation, and pedestrians. Moreover, it offers point-of-purchase reinforcement; other media are usually viewed in the home, but transit advertising reaches the shopper on the way to buy.
5. *Lengthy Messages.* Unlike outdoor advertising, which is restricted by the limited time of exposure, transit advertising can present fairly long copy. Type that is legible from a distance is important; Gothic type that is bold and emphatic is considered good. The layout itself is simple; however, extensive use can be made of color and of attention-getting devices. (Because of the curve on car cards, the optical center, unlike that in magazine advertising, is in the lower two-thirds of the card.)

Transit advertising is a relatively unimportant medium, and it is likely to remain that way. A number of limitations that may be difficult to overcome exist in transit advertising.

1. *Limited Target Market.* Transit advertising misses some important segments of the population. Rural dwellers, suburbanites who use automobiles, and many professional and business leaders do not use mass transportation vehicles.
2. *Lacks Prestige.* Most advertisers use this medium to supplement other advertising. It has not yet attained the status and stature of a major advertising medium.

How to Buy Transit Advertising

Transit advertising is sold in *showings* or on a unit basis. Rates for showings are quoted on a monthly basis, and discounts are granted for 3-month, 6-month, and 12-month contracts. Cards or posters used in transit advertising are provided by an advertiser at the advertiser's expense.

On a national basis transit advertising costs average 70 cents per thousand, according to research conducted for the Transit Advertising Association. Inside transit advertising costs are lower.

Cost depends on the length of the showing, the number of displays used, and the size of the space used for the advertisement. In Portland, Oregon, for example, a #100 showing consisting of 140 king-size posters cost $15,400 per month. In New York City a #100 showing consisting of 970 king-size posters cost $145,500 per month.[10]

In recent years transit advertising has attempted to provide valid circulation data. Since there are two basic types of media in transit advertising, circulation is reported in two terms: riders and exposures.

Riders   Circulation is computed on the basis of the average number of monthly riders reported yearly. Included in the circulation count of inside transit audiences (which is measured by the fare box) are paying passengers, paid and nonpaid transfers, free passengers, and school tickets.

Exposures   *Exposures* refer to the total number of individuals (pedestrians and people in buildings or vehicles) exposed to outside transit advertising. Special research techniques are used to measure exposure in a sample of markets. The eye camera is a technique that records people facing exterior advertising. Only persons with two eyes facing the advertisements are counted in the compilation. Diary keeping is also used to measure exposures in a sample of markets.

In an effort to provide relevant data to advertisers transit advertising companies such as Winston Network are developing computerized data systems. Through a system known as M.A.P.P.I.N.G. (Marketing Analysis of Predictable Patterns by Intra-Neighborhood Geo-demographics), Winston gathers information on audience location and socioeconomic characteristics as well as reach and frequency evaluations.

---

[10]"Rates & Data Bus Posters and Cards, Effective 1/1/86," Winston Network, 275 Madison Avenue, New York, New York 10016.

Changes in Out-of-Home Media

It appears that the demand for out-of-home media will expand in the eighties. The relatively low cost per thousand is appealing to advertisers. The new technologies provide capabilities for creativity in the medium. Moreover, out-of-home offers good opportunities for reaching specific local markets, particularly in urban ethnic areas, as well as the ability to reach working women and infrequent television viewers.

In addition to the changes in traditional outdoor and transit capabilities, a number of new forms of out-of-home advertising are emerging. There are advertising displays in shopping malls, bus shelters, on trash cans, and on airplanes. Moreover, the vast outdoors provides almost unlimited opportunities for sending advertising messages.

SUMMARY

Direct mail is a major advertising medium in which numerous varieties of direct mailers can be used. It is the most selective of all media and is controlled exclusively by the advertiser. However, it tends to have a somewhat negative image and may require a high investment per contact.

In direct-mail campaigns an advertiser builds circulation through the development of a mailing list. Costs of the campaign include the production and postage costs as well as the cost of the list. A major advantage of direct mail is its ability to evaluate results through a determination of the cost per inquiry or the cost per sale.

Out-of-home advertising includes outdoor and transit advertising. Outdoor advertisements are classified as poster panels, painted bulletins, and electrical spectaculars. Outdoor ads provide national and local advertisers several advantages including relatively low cost, proximity to point of purchase, and continuing exposure. Its disadvantages include its limited selectivity, brief messages, and the criticism which such advertising has faced. Circulation for outdoor advertising is quoted in gross rating points. Posters are sold in GRP packages, usually at a monthly rate. Bulletins and spectaculars are usually purchased on a unit basis.

Transit advertising refers to messages that appear in or on transportation vehicles, and are designated as *exterior* or *interior* transit advertising. These ads are low cost, reach large captive audiences, and can be relatively lengthy. However transit advertising lacks prestige and its target market is limited to those who use mass transportation.

Transit advertising is sold in showings or on a unit basis. Rates are generally quoted for monthly showings by the transit advertising company. Efforts are made to evaluate audience characteristics and estimate reach and frequency.

QUESTIONS FOR DISCUSSION

1. What are the differences between direct-mail advertising, mail-order selling, and direct response advertising?
2. Discuss the kinds of direct mailers that can be used in an advertising campaign.
3. What is the significance of a mailing list? How is it developed?
4. What criteria would you suggest for establishing a good mailing list?
5. What is meant by *cost per inquiry? cost per sale?* How is each one computed?
6. Explain the differences among poster panels, painted bulletins, and spectaculars.
7. How does the rate structure for poster panels differ from that of painted bulletins?
8. What are the strengths and limitations of outdoor advertising?
9. Do you see transit advertising as a growth medium? Explain.
10. Describe some out-of-home media you consider viable in the future.

KEY TERMS

direct mail advertising
broadsides
internal mailing lists
external mailing lists
out-of-home advertising
billboards
poster panels
painted bulletins

electrical spectaculars
circulation (for outdoor advertising)
showing
market allotment
rotary plan
transit advertising
exposures

AD PRACTICE

The proprietor of a newly-opened bookstore asks you to prepare a direct-mail advertising campaign. Provide details for this campaign, including the kind of mailer you would use, how you would secure a mailing list, and how you would evaluate the results of the campaign.

21

Sales Promotion and Supplementary Media

In 1985 Procter & Gamble placed 500 one-third carat diamonds worth $600 each in boxes and bottles of Spic & Span. Sales increased significantly! In 1986 P&G enclosed diamonds, emeralds, sapphires, and garnets worth $70 million inside containers of Spic & Span. However, this time some supermarkets refused to endorse this promotional event, fearing that overzealous customers would rip through packages and wreak havoc, as happened in the earlier promotion.

Although this example shows what can happen if a promotion is *too* "successful," the addition of sales promotion devices and supplementary media to an advertising campaign provide useful support. These marketing activities used to encourage consumer and trade support require careful planning and implementation.

SALES PROMOTION

The AMA defines *sales promotion* as marketing activities other than personal selling, advertising, and publicity, that stimulate consumer purchasing and dealer effectiveness. These stimulants are used to encourage trade to accept and carry the merchandise, the salesforce to increase their solicitations and push the product, and the consumer to purchase and repurchase the product. Although sales promotion is not media advertising, in some cases they are interrelated; there are advertisements that offer premiums or cents-off coupons, and those that promote sweepstakes and contests. Furthermore, sales contests and demonstrations, both sales promotional devices, do make use of salespeople.

Characteristics

A number of characteristics distinguish sales promotion as a marketing tool. First, its activities are rarely conducted independently of other promotional efforts; they are intended as supplementary. Second, sales promotion has an element of immediacy to it—a cents-off coupon is designed to encourage a purchase; a point-of-purchase display motivates impulse buying.

A third characteristic of sales promotion is that its rates are not fixed, nor are media commissions available for its performance. Therefore, manufacturers often conduct these activities within their own organizational structures rather than use advertising agencies, because of the lack of standardization of sales promotion efforts, their intermittent use, and their varying rates. When an agency is used, it frequently charges an advertiser a fee for planning and producing sales promotion devices. In recent years a number of agencies specializing in sales promotion have been formed to provide expertise in this area.

Categories

Sales promotions are classified according to their goals as *trade stimulants*, activities designed to *push* merchandise through channels of distribution, or *consumer stimulants*, activities used to *pull* merchandise through manufacturers' outlets.

Some sales promotion activities may accomplish push and pull tactics simultaneously; for example, some coupons stimulate consumer purchases and encourage retailers to stock merchandise in anticipation of sales. A few can be used for either push or pull tactics; for example, contests may involve either consumers or retailers and wholesalers' salesforces.

TRADE STIMULANTS

Sales promotion may be used to encourage dealers and distributors to carry a manufacturer's merchandise and to stimulate these institutions and their salesforces to do better jobs in handling and selling these products. Trade stimulants take the form of trade deals, trade shows, advertising allowances, and cooperative salesforce incentives.

Trade Deals

Buying allowances are discounts offered as temporary price reductions when new products are introduced. *Free goods trade deals* offer a certain amount of a product to wholesalers or retailers at no cost if they purchase a stated amount of the product. For example, a retailer who purchases six cases of a new product will receive two cases free.

Trade Shows

Many industries and professions combine trade, industrial, or professional exhibits with their national or regional meetings. Conference participants can examine products and make comparisons with competing products, while exhibitors can enlarge their dealer contacts and distribute literature and samples.

Companies exhibiting at trade shows have various selling goals[1]: identification of prospects; gaining access to key decision makers in current or potential customer companies; disseminating facts about vendor products, services, and personnel; actually selling products; and servicing current accounts' problems through contacts made. There are also a number of nonselling functions that can be performed by trade shows. These include maintaining a company image with competitors, customers, the industry, and the press; gathering intelligence on competitors' products, prices, and other important marketing variables; and maintaining and enhancing corporate morale.

Unlike most other promotional tools, trade shows meet a broad range of different objectives simultaneously. An evaluation should be conducted after the trade show by examining the results in comparison to preset objectives. Sales effectiveness can be determined by computing the sales achieved at the trade show, and handing out discount coupons to identify sales that may occur after the show. Nonsales goals, such as image building objectives, can be calculated on the basis of exhibit and booth attendance figures, amount of literature distributed, and publicity coverage.[2]

Cooperative Advertising Allowances

Wholesalers and retailers are encouraged to advertise and display merchandise through contractual relationships with manufacturers called *cooperative advertising*. The contracts specify the kinds of advertising that are considered acceptable, the media in which the advertisements may be run, the length of time for the contract, and the percentage of a

[1]Thomas V. Bonoma, "Get More Out of Your Trade Shows," *Harvard Business Review* (January/February, 1983), pp. 75–83.
[2]*Trade Shows in Black and White: A guide for marketers*, (New Cannan, Connecticut: Trade Show Bureau, 1986), p. 21.

dealer's cost for advertising that a manufacturer will pay. Most arrangements for sharing advertising charges call for a 50-50 split, although other arrangements are possible. Manufacturers usually set limits on the amounts they will spend, frequently a percentage of the amount spent by the dealer in purchasing the manufacturer's product. Although dealers may prepare their own ads if they want, some manufacturers offer standardized advertisements.

Cooperative advertising can benefit manufacturers. Dealers are more likely to advertise with financial assistance. Also, the combined efforts of manufacturers and retailers will often exceed manufacturers' efforts alone without such programs.

However, not all dealers will take advantage of these programs, since they require that dealers add funds for advertising. Smaller dealers, who may not be able to commit many dollars, will resent larger retailers who seem to be securing a price discount through these funds. Policing of funds is a difficult task; it requires extensive bookkeeping and may entail legal problems since the Robinson-Patman Act requires that manufacturers offer all retailers promotional allowances on proportionately equal terms.

Direct Stimulation of Channel Members' Salesforces

A number of methods are used to encourage the saleforces of wholesalers and retailers to promote a specific manufacturer's product. These techniques are designed to encourage greater sales of a manufacturer's product as compared with his or her competitor's.

Contests
Contests may be used to encourage an outlet's salesforce to sell more of a manufacturer's merchandise. To be effective such channel-of-distribution contests must provide a chance of winning for everyone eligible to enter. Usually, to win a prize, a participant must show a certain percentage increase over a specified sales quota. While a contest can help generate increased sales, it may be a short-run effect, resulting from shifting future sales. At its conclusion, sales may revert to below the previous precontest levels, while those who did not win prizes may be antagonized.

Push Money
Push money (also called *premium money, PM,* or *spiff*) is a special incentive to sell a specific manufacturer's product. Even if consumers enter a store with a particular appliance brand name in mind, frequently a salesperson can encourage them to switch. The PM is designed to back a manufacturer's advertising campaign or counteract the effects of competitors' advertising. PMs, in existence for a long time, are periodically evaluated to determine their legality and desirability. Currently, this practice is not illegal if the manufacturer notifies the retail outlet and the retailer agrees to permit its salespeople to secure this special compensation.

CONSUMER STIMULANTS

Sales promotion devices distributed to consumers are designed to pull items through marketing channels. These stimulants to encourage consumer purchases include offering potential customers free samples, other items with a purchase (premiums), price reductions (coupons or refunds) or gifts (contests or trading stamps).

Although the basic objective of all these sales promotion devices is to increase sales, their primary impacts may differ. For example, contests and sweepstakes increase brand awareness; samples attract new customers; and coupons most often increase sales to present customers.

Most consumer stimulants are disseminated by manufacturers who want to motivate consumers to ask for and purchase their products and encourage retailers and wholesalers to stock their merchandise in anticipation of such requests. Distribution outlets also offer consumer stimulants in the form of trading stamps, contests or sweepstakes, and "double" or "triple" coupon redemptions—all designed to increase store traffic.

Samples

In sales promotion the term *sampling* designates a method of offering a customer a free trial of a product. Samples, unlike other consumer stimulants, are actually based on the merits of the merchandise. For effective sampling, an item should be an accurate representation of a product; the product iteself should be one that is frequently used, is low cost, and offers repeat sales. Sampling can induce a consumer to try a new or improved product; secure part of the competitor's share of the market by demonstrating a brand's superiority; and gain retail distribution for a product.

There are a number of methods by which samples may be distributed. They can be delivered through the mail or door to door. In-store sampling is less expensive but does not receive the same aggressive promotion. Moreover, retailers are not likely to devote much display space to such nonprofit producers, nor will they carefully police the area to prevent pilferage. A sample may also be attached or inserted in another package, usually one in which there is a natural product association.

The basic advantage of sampling is that it attracts new customers who are persuaded to purchase on the merits of the product. Thus sampling is more likely to generate brand loyalty than other promotional activities whose relationships to product attributes are tenuous.

A sampling campaign cannot stand alone as the major part of an advertising effort. It must be subordinate to the advertising campaign and conducted in conjunction with advertising in mass media. The major disadvantage of sampling is the cost. To limit this expense, firms such as Welcome Wagon now specialize in the delivery of samples from various organizations in comprehensive packages. Samples may generate unfavorable publicity from unexpected hazards. When Lever Bros. introduced Sunlight dishwashing liquid in a mail sampling campaign some

Sure mom,
McDonald's sounds great.

THIS PUB'S
Chancery
FOR YOU

MILWAUKEE • RACINE • WAUKESHA • WAUWATOSA

Advertising Award Winners

Ads and agencies in this section have been recognized as outstanding for 1986 and 1987 by various professional organizations, including Crain Communications' Advertising Age, the Institute of Outdoor Advertising, and the Clio Awards, the industry's Oscars.

A wonderful local ad appealed to Wisconsin newspaper readers in the image of this baby face, asking them to take a chance on Chancery Restaurants. Agency Frankenberry, Laughlin, and Constable, Milwaukee, reported that it gave away 2000 posters of the ad.

Say Natural.

If you love
your husband,
give him a pat.

The natural goodness of butter enhances
the flavor of everything it touches. And, it has no
more calories than margarine. So when you
cook for the people you love, do something special.
Give them all a pat. And cook with butter.

REAL BUTTER

If you love
someone,
give him a pat.

Butter brings out every delicious detail
of everything you make. And, it has no more
calories than margarine. So when you
cook for the one you love, do something special.
Give him a pat. And cook with butter.

REAL BUTTER

Be picky. We are.

LEVI'S STREETLIGHTS. THE HOTTEST JEANS ON TWO LEGS. Levi's

*According to Advertising Age, the agency of the year for 1986 was Foote, Cone &
Belding, which directed the California Raisin Board's charming and funny
claymation raisin campaign (see pp. 318, 514). The agency also won four Clio
Awards, three for the dancing raisins. Other highlighted ads were those for the
California Milk Advisory Board, Sunkist, and an impressive outdoor ad for
Levi's—a 30-by-66-foot painted wallscape set up in downtown Detroit.*

As Thin As a Giraffe.

So thin. And yet, so rich. That's the Noblia watch series. Bracelets crafted with hundreds of gentle links. Creating a deep, beaded quality. A luxuriously soft feel. Yet, each timepiece is impeccably thin. Because each one is designed with a new ultra-thin quartz movement. For accuracy to within seconds a year. Watch shown priced at $395.

NOBLIA CITIZEN

A Unique Breed of Watch.

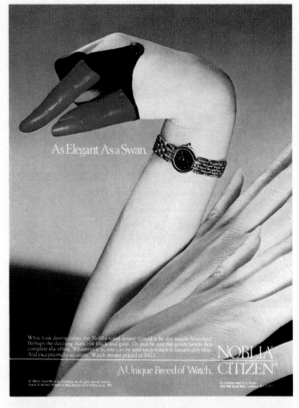

As Elegant As a Swan.

What trait distinguishes the Noblia watch series? Could it be the supple bracelets? Perhaps the dazzling dials—in black and gold. Or maybe just the gentle bends that complete the effect. Whatever it is, you can be sure each watch is remarkably thin. And exceptionally accurate. Watch shown priced at $425.

NOBLIA CITIZEN

A Unique Breed of Watch.

Classy products, a creative concept, and beautiful photography made the "Hanimal" ads for Citizen watches breath-takers. The agency is SSC&B, New York.

A clever magazine piece from Ketchum Communications, San Francisco, was part of a primary demand campaign for the National Potato Board.

The North Carolina Travel and Tourism campaign won its creators, McKinney & Silver, Raleigh, a top award from the Magazine Publisher's Association.

How Far Must We Go Before You Think Of Us As A Vegetable?

We can't figure it out.

We're nutritious, and we're low in calories. We're even a plant. But still, most people don't think of potatoes as a vegetable.

So we thought—maybe it's because we're not green. After all, vegetables are green, right? There's spinach, broccoli, lettuce, cucumbers, even green beans and green peppers. So maybe if we paint our

self green you'll start thinking of us as a vegetable. Then again, carrots are orange, squash is yellow and cauliflower is white. And you consider those vegetables, don't you?

There must be something special about potatoes. But then, that's what we've been saying all along. **Potatoes. America's Favorite Vegetable.**

In North Carolina, some of our greatest works of art never hang in a museum.

Dove-In-The-Window Star of Bethlehem. Wild Goose Chase. Wedding Ring.

High in the North Carolina mountains, quilts are made to be purely practical. Yet their ageless patterns make them purely beautiful. Quilts, however, are just one expression of our highland artistry.

Some people can put their penknife to a block of sugar maple and magically reveal the form of a wild turkey or a good hunting dog.

Others make sturdy pots with glazes as guardedly secret as prized family recipes.

And still others display their art in jars of jam and jelly, or in jugs of amber apple cider found at roadside stands.

Wherever you travel, from our mountains to our shore, you'll be certain to find art that exhibits itself proudly.

So if you're the kind of person who appreciates finer things, you really don't have to visit the museums.

Come to North Carolina, and visit us instead.

North Carolina

For our new travel package, write North Carolina Travel, Dept. 321, Raleigh, N.C. 27699. Or call 1-800-VISIT NC. Operator 321.

If you are what you eat, a visit to North Carolina could make you a very interesting person, indeed.

Grits Soufflé. Squash Pie. Wild Persimmon Pudding. Chow Chow. Corn Dodgers.

Across the gently rolling midlands of North Carolina, what we eat is hardly the same old blue plate special.

To family reunions and church dinners across the state, we bring dishes like our Green Tomato Pie and Pig Pickin' Cake, which puzzle the uninitiated and thoroughly delight the old timers.

But you don't have to call North Carolina home just to sample our great home cooking. Because we also cook like this away from home.

Which means you'll find these interesting dishes in small cafes and old inns, when you travel from our Blue Ridge mountains to our shore.

So come. Because a visit to North Carolina is more than food for the appetite.

It's also food for the soul.

North Carolina

For our new travel package, write North Carolina Travel, Dept. 321, Raleigh, N.C. 27699. Or call 1-800-VISIT NC. Operator 321.

Bud Light's Spuds MacKenzie, the "original party animal," has been a hit with younger drinking-age beer consumers, gaining what Advertising Age called near cult popularity. Spuds' agency is DDB Needham, Chicago.

"The Liar," smarmy auto salesman "Joe Isuzu," pitched outrageous claims, while superimposed subtitles cleared up the mess and added real facts about the Isuzu cars.

Liar: Here in my factory, I equip these I-Marks with millions of standard features. Like a breakfast nook. Twin satellite dishes. And for the kids—a frozen yogurt machine.

Super: He's lying.

Liar: And if you miss 8 or 9 payments, that's okay. I trust you.

Super: Your bank may feel otherwise.

The campaign has been enormously popular, almost a joke by advertising on itself—but one that has been successful so far. Della Femina, Travisano & Partners, Los Angeles, created the campaign.

He's lying.

Your bank may feel otherwise.

ED: (WINNY) Hello.

FERNANDO: Wilbur says you ate all the Tostitos Brand Tortilla Chips.

Frito-Lay's Tostitos TV campaign cut actual footage from popular 1950s and 1960s shows—Leave It to Beaver, Dragnet, and Mister Ed—with new footage of spokesman Fernando Escandon filmed on carefully reconstructed sets, with camera and lighting identical to those used in the original. In the original Mr. Ed program, the loquacious horse was defending himself against charges that he pillaged a vegetable garden. Tracy-Locke, Dallas, handled the campaign.

ED: Me? (HICCUP)

FERNANDO: There are hoofprints all over the kitchen.

ED: I was hungry.

FERNANDO: Tostitos are for sharing. Now what do we do?

ED: Run down to the market.

ANNCR: Share America's best tasting tortilla chips.

This Is Our Competition.

A dog's first meal comes from a highly developed nutritional source.

Which leaves man with a pretty tough act to follow.

Ideally, a dog food should continue to provide such perfectly tailored nutrition. That's why 10 years ago, Cycle Dry Dog Food was born. It was specifically developed by Gaines to suit every stage of a dog's life.

But when nature is the standard by which you judge yourself, there's always room for improvement. So in addition to containing no added sugar, today Cycle has no artificial color. And even lower sodium.

Together, we think these changes bring Cycle even closer to our goal of providing a lifetime of the best possible nutrition.

And that much closer to our competition.

Gaines CYCLE. A friend for life.

After 15 years of building the most successful sports car in history, Professor Porsche declared "We have reached the end."

But that was only the beginning.

In the Spring of 1948, the first Porsche 356 emerged, without fanfare, from a converted sawmill in Gmünd, Austria.

And changed forever the world's perceptions and expectations of a sports car.

Eighteen years of refinement and improvement followed. And during that time—on race tracks and rally circuits, highways and winding back roads—the 356's lightweight, aerodynamic body, air-cooled rear engine and fully independent suspension offered a driving experience unmatched by any other sports car of its day.

So when, in 1963, Professor Ferry Porsche announced that the 356 had reached its design and engineering limits, the potential for alienating a legion of Porsche fanatics was high.

But it never materialized.

Because the car that succeeded the 356, the 911, was—in the eyes of objective observer and fanatic alike—a significant improvement. While retaining the basic philosophical underpinnings that had made the first Porsche such a classic.

Once again, Professor Porsche and his staff had risen to the challenge of taking a proven idea and proving it could be better.

There was never any question, of course, that the 911's shape should evolve from the best features of the earlier design. Or that its engine should continue to be air-cooled and mounted over the rear drive wheels for superior traction, handling and reliability.

Nor was there any question that the 911 should remain, at its heart, a product of our racing heritage—with performance as its reason for being.

Today—24 years, 7 engine displacements, innumerable engineering improvements and countless racing victories later—the 911 is better than it's ever been.

And there's no end in sight.

PORSCHE

Without an oil-bathed ignition, we couldn't run this three-wheeler. Or this ad.

We realize that the chances of finding anyone riding a three-wheeler 30 feet below the surface of the Pacific Ocean are slim.

But the fact that this Yamaha could operate in this environment says that we do things just a little differently.

We don't test our machines in the warmth and comfort of a test lab, because, chances are, you won't ride our machines in a test lab.

So we get off the beaten track.

To places you wouldn't go, like the bottom of the Pacific Ocean. And to places you would go, like the Deep South.

Not to a hotel or a campground, but into the bayou. Where you'll find some of the thickest mud in the world. The most torturous sand in the world and, most of all, swamps.

Miles and miles of swamps. So much water that you can't ride more than a minute or two without being up to your axles (or worse) in brown H_2O. Not to mention snakes or gators.

Not the kind of place you want to break down. So it didn't take long for our engineers to invent a way to keep our three-wheelers from falling prey to the most common

killer of machines ridden in the wet. Water in the ignition system.

The cure: Oil-bathed ignition.

A theory based on the fact that oil and water don't mix. So it follows that if you put a barrier of oil between the ignition and the water, the water will stay out and the ignition will stay dry.

So much so that Three-

Wheeling magazine recently heralded Yamaha's three-wheelers as the most waterproof in the industry has to offer.

Out of our rather unorthodox testing facilities have come a whole family of machines. Each one improved year after year.

This year's Tri-Z250, for example, now has a six-speed

transmission for faster acceleration and even more top speed than last year's model.

And to handle that extra speed, we've also added lower profile tires that slide easier in the corners.

On the other hand, our YTM225DR, and our kids three-wheeler, the Tri-Zinger 60, have only minor changes. The 225 does

have a new paint scheme that matches the machine's reputation as the "Cadillac" of three-wheelers. But for the most part we left these two proven machines well enough alone.

That's another thing the swamps can teach you. If it works, don't fix it.

YAMAHA
We make the difference.

Tri-Z250

YTM225DR

Tri-Zinger

PA PA OOM MAU MAU

THE REAL STUFF

Chiat/Day was another of Advertising Age's top three agencies for 1986. Clients Gaines Foods came on strong with emotional appeal, Porsche relied on clear, informative copy, Yamaha threw the reader a surprise, and California Coolers turned a fast phrase.

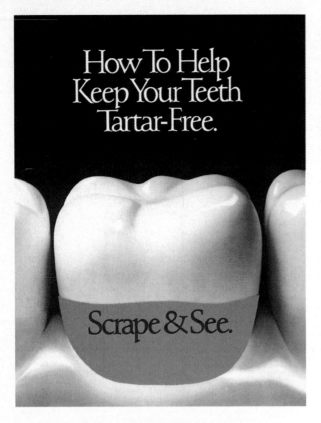

How To Help
Keep Your Teeth
Tartar-Free.

Scrape & See.

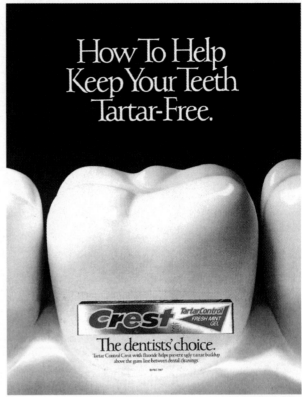

How To Help
Keep Your Teeth
Tartar-Free.

Crest Tartar Control FRESH MINT GEL

The dentists' choice.

Tartar Control Crest with fluoride helps prevent ugly tartar buildup above the gum line between dental cleanings.

THE CAR FOR PEOPLE WHOSE MEANS HAVE CHANGED BUT WHOSE VALUES HAVEN'T.

Back when you had precious little in the way of means at all, you may have been one of those pioneering souls who bought a Volvo.

It was the perfect family car. Spartan? Perhaps. But also very sensible. A Sherman tank with room for six. And a growing reputation for durability and safety.

Both of us have come a long way since then.

You, for example, may have reached that point in life where you view a car not as a necessity so much as a reward.

And we have reached a point where we can create a car like the Volvo 760 Turbo.

A car that surrounds you with every comfort a person of means could want in a car. A turbo-charged phenomenon capable of embarrassing cars much more famous for performance.

Admittedly, the Volvo 760 Turbo is an indulgence.

But underneath you'll discover it's still a Volvo. A totally sensible car with an enviable reputation for durability and safety.

A car that lets you indulge your senses.

Without taking leave of your sense.

VOLVO
A car you can believe in.

PARACHUTE NOT INCLUDED.

SFX: M.J. FOX DROPS BOOK ON TABLE.
M.J. FOX: Hmmm.

SFX: SNAPS FINGERS. CLAPS HANDS.
COPIER MACHINE MAKES PHOTOCOPY
OF PEPSI CAN.

SFX: PICKS UP PHOTOCOPY.

SFX: CAN OPENING SOUND.

SFX: FIZZING NOISE.

SFX: SQUEAK OF MOISTURE ON CAN.
SOUND OF PHOTOCOPY BEING ROLLED
INTO A CAN.
M.J. FOX: Whistles.

SFX: DRINKING SOUNDS.
M.J. FOX: Ahhh.

STUDENT: Ssssh!
SFX: CAN CRUSHING. CAN BANGING IN
METAL GARBAGE CAN. M.J. FOX: Ssssh!
VO AND SUPER: PEPSI. THE CHOICE OF A
NEW GENERATION.

According to agency D'Arcy Masius Benton & Bowles, 40 million special inserts for Procter & Gamble's Crest were printed on heavy paper stock. The reader was tempted to scratch away the gold color for a peek at the difference the product could make. The panel at the right is the completely scratched-off ad. Eight impressions were made in the printing process, including three applications of latex "tartar."

Past and present were engagingly compared in this ad for Volvo that spoke to a middle-age, upper middle class target group. Scali, McCabe, Sloves, New York, is the agency.

Nike's "Parachute Not Included" piece ran in one place only—the program for the NCAA basketball championship tournament. It was created by Wieden & Kennedy, Portland.

Michael J. Fox was the star performer in a TV spot called "Copier," in which he drank a refreshing Pepsi from a copy of a can! BBDO, New York, won acclaim from the Clio Awards as well as Advertising Age; judges liked the performer's style and the piece's creativity.

HISS AND HERS.
WOODLAND PARK ZOO

"Hiss and Hers" is a good example of imaginative advertising recently appearing in out-of-home media. Livingston & Company, Seattle, is responsible for this almost-too-lively painted board with extensions that promotes a local zoo.

Budweiser won a creative award from the Institute of Outdoor Advertising for their "Surfer" display. D'Arcy Masius Benton & Bowles, St. Louis, did the work for Anheuser-Busch.

KODAK
POURS ON
THE COLOR.

GANNETT OUTDOOR

MIRÓ MIRÓ ON THE WALL.

MINNEAPOLIS INSTITUTE OF ARTS

*A seemingly three-dimensional woman mops up butter dripping from a brilliant
graphic corn-on-the-cob in Kodak's outdoor poster board. Agency: Rumrill-Hoyt,
Rochester, New York.*

*The Institute of Outdoor Advertising also recognized a brilliant outdoor
display, "Miro, Miro," for the Minneapolis Institute of Arts. The agency is Ruhr/
Paragon, Minneapolis.*

LIFE INSURANCE, SIMPLIFIED.

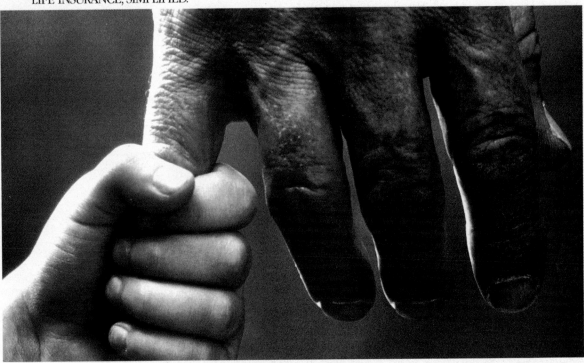

It's very simple. You want to protect those who depend on you.

Well, no one makes that easier to do than Amex Life Assurance Company,

an American Express company.

We've written more than $30 billion worth of insurance. Our policies are straightforward — and a lot more

affordable than you might think.

For more information, or an application, just call us at 1-800-231-1133. Simple.

AMEX *Life Assurance Company*

An American Express company

As many of you know, the Bartles & Jaymes Premium Wine Cooler is not only perfect as a refreshment, . . . but with meals as well.

Ed says it even goes with these big doughnuts they like to eat here.

Hal Riney & Partners won acclaim as a 1986 top agency from both the Clio Awards and Advertising Age. Its campaigns included those for American Express Insurance, Bartles & Jaymes wine coolers (represented by a very dry-humored duo), Gallo wines, and Henry Weinhard's Private Reserve beer.

I personally would not have thought Bartles & Jaymes and doughnuts would go together, much less doughnuts and fish.

So please continue to enjoy Bartles & Jaymes with all kinds of food, and we thank you once more for your support.

We wanted to introduce you to all of our Sonoma and Napa County Growers. But only the good-looking ones showed up.

We can't imagine why the others were so shy.

After all, a lot of the growers have been our friends for nearly fifty years.

But in any event, we simply wanted to illustrate a few things.

First, that Gallo's wine grapes aren't grown just anywhere, but in such prized growing regions as California's Sonoma and Napa Counties.

Second, that Gallo has more growers in these areas than anyone else.

And third, Gallo growers have more experience than any group of winegrowers in America. For example, Sattimo Dal Porto (that's Sattimo leaning on the rear tire) has been raising premium wine grapes for over seventy years.

So if you've ever wondered how Gallo can make such extraordinary wines at such reasonable cost, you now have some of the answers.

Superior wine grapes.

The finest growing regions.

And the best, and the most, wine grape growers in the business.

That is, if—in addition to those fellows pictured above—you count the 117 who didn't show up.

Today's Gallo.

(NO AUDIO)

And there came a moment when all the elements came together…

…Design, engineering, and technology. Unleashing a new breed of compact car.

The Dodge Shadow. A superbly equipped two door or four door performance sedan.

With a 5/50 protection plan. An affordable price.

And an insatiable appetite for the

sheer thrill of driving.

The new Dodge Shadow is going to cast a giant shadow across America.

(NO AUDIO)

An eerie commercial for Chrysler Corporation called "Junkyard Dog" featured a powerful voiceover by veteran actor/director John Huston and some high-tech special effects. An astounded hound watched in wonder as an ancient Dodge Dart transformed itself into a 1987 Dodge Shadow. BBDO, New York, took the honors.

EXHIBIT 21.1
Demonstrating a Computer

80 people, apparently thinking they were getting samples of lemon juice, ingested the product and became ill, none seriously, however.

Demonstrations

Products such as washing machines, vacuum cleaners, kitchen appliances, and cosmetics are demonstrated to potential consumers either in stores or at home. These demonstrations are used in situations similar to those used for effective sampling, but where sampling is too expensive or cumbersome. Retail demonstrations are generally organized by manufacturers in an effort to show how their products work. In an award-winning program, Apple Computer offered potential buyers the opportunity to take Macintosh Computers home and try them (see Exhibit 21.1).

Premiums

A *premium* is an incentive designed to produce an immediate and obvious increase in sales. It is usually an item of merchandise that may be offered free or at a relatively low cost as a bonus to purchasers. The purpose of a premium campaign is to switch users to an advertiser's product, to encourage more extensive use or the purchase of larger sizes of a product, or to encourage repeat purchases or long-term customer loyalty through the savings of stamps or coupons for redemption of premiums in catalogs.

Premiums may be distributed in a number of ways. They may be enclosed in packages or attached to packages and thus be included with products when purchases are made, such as Spic & Span's diamonds. Premiums can also be redeemed through the mail, usually by showing evidence of purchase, such as box tops.

A "free" premium, by law, must be offered at no extra cost, and the

EXHIBIT 21.2
An Example of a Self-Liquidating Premium

Marlboro offers a self-liquidator designed to build ties to the Old West, including a sheepskin coat for $225.

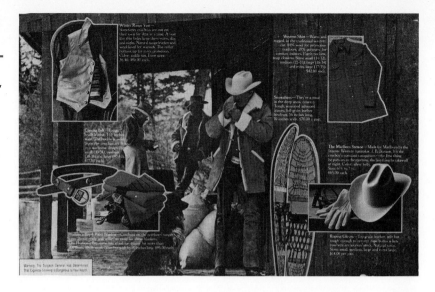

price of the product it accompanies cannot be raised. However, other premiums, called *self-liquidators,* require that a proportion of the cost be paid for by consumers. Although at one time fifty cents to a dollar was considered the most acceptable price for self-liquidators, today advertisers successfully offer premiums for much larger costs. Marlboro uses country stores where self-liquidating premiums in the form of "Marlboro Country" clothes are priced up to several hundred dollars (see Exhibit 21.2).

Coupons

Of all consumer stimulants, coupons are the most widely used. Approximately 202.6 billion coupons were distributed in 1986, and 95 percent of all companies participating in an annual survey reported using them.[3] *Coupons* are certificates for discounts on specific merchandise that customers present to retailers. Retailers sort them, by issuer, and submit them (usually through a clearing house) to the issuers who reimburse the retailers for their face value plus a dealer handling charge.

Coupons are distributed door-to-door, through the mail, on packages, through media, and in stores through coupon-dispensing machines. In recent years "free-standing inserts"—individual ads that are inserted in, but not attached to, newspapers—have become widespread (see Exhibit 21.3).

Coupons are used for numerous purposes: to encourage consumers to try new products, to generate repeat purchases after an initial trial,

---

[3]Nancy Zeldis, "Targeted Coupons Hit Non-Users," *Advertising Age* (April 27, 1987), p. S-26.

or to increase the use of established products. They can introduce new and larger sizes or obtain consumer trial of improved products or variations. It has been estimated that, in one year, for every pound of coffee sold in the United States, four coupons were distributed.[4]

Coupons are an effective promotional tool which may cross all income groups (upper as well as lower), particularly when the economy is in a decline. In fact their acceptance seems to correlate more closely with recession and inflation than with social class.

Despite their widespread distribution many coupons are never redeemed. In fact, the redemption rate is approximately 6 percent. Coupons do little to build an image for a product and can, in fact, be detrimental. In general, coupons are not successful for products that do not have established brand names.

Another problem with couponing is the high rate of fraudulent redemptions. In an effort to decrease misredemptions various controls have been instituted, including coupon investigations, supervision of newspapers which print coupon inserts, and coupon fraud investigations by the Post Office. Even "sting" operations are used; the most successful to date was launched when coupon ads for a fake detergent called "Breen" were placed in several New York and New Jersey newspapers. Over 220 storekeepers and operators who misredeemed these coupons were convicted of fraud.

EXHIBIT 21.3
Coupon in Free-Standing Insert

Refunds

Refunds refer to sums of money offered to consumers who provide to manufacturers proof that they purchased particular products. They are a useful way to induce consumers to try products or switch brands (see Exhibit 21.4). As a result of inflationary pressures that cause consumers to look for ways to save, refunds are being used as a promotional tool more and more; however, they can generate ill will among consumers who receive them after months of waiting or who never receive them.

In recent years refunds, in the form of *rebates*, have been offered for the purchase of expensive products such as automobiles and appliances. Rebates are considered temporary reductions that do not affect prices, unlike discounts that suggest items are less expensive and that create difficulties in instituting subsequent price increases.

Since they have to be relatively high to interest customers in expensive items, rebates tends to be costly for manufacturers. Moreover, they create some problems for dealers and customers. Rebates generate from manufacturers, but frequently they require the cooperation of dealers who must absorb the cost of the refunds. Thus, in some cases, automobile dealers who normally would offer consumers a significant discount find it necessary to raise their prices in order to cover their costs of a manufacturer's rebate.

EXHIBIT 21.4
A Full-Refund Offer

---

[4]Louis J. Haugh, "Promotion Trends, Facts of Redeeming Value," *Advertising Age* (March 14, 1983), p. M-32.

EXHIBIT 21.5
Contest

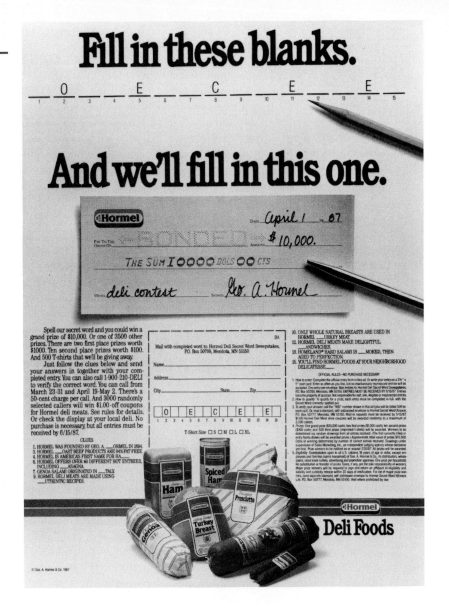

Contests, Sweepstakes, and Games of Chance

Contests, sweepstakes, and games of chance are designated as "strong" sales promotion devices designed to create a high level of consumer involvement in the advertising of products, while at the same time encouraging action at the retail level (see Exhibit 21.5). Contests and sweepstakes are generally used by mass marketers such as Procter & Gamble, General Food Corporation, and Quaker Oats. Recently, they have been introduced into the financial community, airline industry, veterinary medicine, agricultural insecticides, lingerie, and heavy equipment fields. These techniques are defined as follows:

Sweepstakes are sales promotion devices in which prize winners are selected by chance, generally by some type of random drawing. Sweepstakes merely require participants to submit their names to be included.

Games are sweepstakes with more involved entry systems. For example, entrants may be required to save up game cards that match each other or that can be put together to complete a game diagram.

In *contests* prize winners are selected on the basis of skills. Contests may be of many types: limerick contests, sentence completion, jingle completion, letter writing, or naming products or trade characters. Moreover, contests may require entrants to purchase products.

Successful contest and sweepstake promotion entails the following: it should be simple and not offer confusing prizes; it should combine excitement, suspense, and action resulting in minimum frustration (no long period of waiting should be required); it should be capable of being rerun; it should be of low cost to the advertiser; and it should appeal to both sexes.

Although contests and sweepstakes have a high readership and tend to cut through advertising clutter, they are considered more effective in generating consumer interest than in increasing product sales. Contests may attract professional contestants who have no interest in the products or the companies but purchase one time only; and there are always losers who feel that the judging was not fair. As a result of some of the criticism directed against these "games of chance," the Federal Trade Commission promulgated a rule prohibiting misrepresenting participants' chances of winning.[5]

Trading Stamps

The first documented use of trading stamps in the United States was in the 1890s when Schuster's Department Store of Milwaukee instituted a plan called the Blue Trading Stamp System. Later the Sperry and Hutchinson Company started the first independent-issuer stamp plan in 1896. Over the years the industry has flourished and foundered and flourished again. A saturation level was reached in 1962, and since then the share of market held by stamp-giving stores has decreased.

There are some indications of a resurgence in the use of trading stamps, for example, by retail gasoline stations concerned with price wars brought on by the increase in oil supplies. However, it is not anticipated that trading stamp activities will reach their earlier high level. The Trading Stamp Institute of America (TSIA) recently announced its new name—The Sales & Incentive Association—using the same initials, but indicating that the scope of its new activities will go beyond trading stamps.[6]

[5]"Legal Developments in Marketing," *Journal of Marketing* (April 1970), p. 87.
[6]Lori Kesler, "The Creative Game: A Science and an Art," *Advertising Age* (May 3, 1982), pp. M20–M21.

SUPPLEMENTARY MEDIA

Supplementary media are those vehicles other than the mass media that disseminate messages for promotional purposes. These vehicles are not considered traditional advertising media, since they do not reach mass audiences; moreover, in some cases they more closely resemble sales promotion activities. However, since they represent channels for the delivery of promotional messages paid for by sponsors they are designated as supplementary advertising media. There are almost an unlimited number of vehicles that can be used to carry advertising messages. These range from "Beetleboards" on the sides of Volkswagens, to milk cartons, to the recommendation to place ads on stamps to defray postal expenses of the United States Post Office. This section describes the most widely used of these supplementary media: specialty advertising, motion picture advertising, directory advertising, and point-of-purchase advertising.

Specialty Advertising

Specialties are useful items containing promotional messages (names, trademarks, slogans and/or statements) that are given away free to a target audience. Unlike premiums, which is a form of sales promotion, specialties contain a message and do not require the recipient to make a purchase. The use of these items is referred to as *specialty advertising*.

Specialty advertising is not a major medium, but a supplemental promotional effort that can enhance publicizing product information, improving public relations, enlivening the impact of direct mail, promoting branch openings, introducing sales representatives, or merely saying thank you. There are over 10,000 different specialty advertising items in the following categories that are commonly offered through the industry:[7] calendars, writing instruments, business gifts, and other imprinted specialties (for example, coffee mugs, keychains, and T-shirts).

Specialty advertising offers a number of benefits to advertisers. In essence it is a direct medium under the control of advertisers who preselect their audiences. It is readily identifiable with specific advertisers since it usually carries their names, slogans, trademarks, and occasionally, messages. Specialties may last a long time and provide frequent exposures at favorable locations, such as the home or point of purchase.

There are two notable drawbacks to specialty advertising. It is a high-cost-per-contact medium and, therefore, cannot be used to reach mass audiences. Because of space limitations the size and extent of the message delivered is limited; frequently specialty advertising carries no more than an advertiser's name and address.

---

[7]Dr. Dan S. Bagley, III, "Specialty Advertising, A New Look," Prepared by Specialty Advertising Association International and Specialty Advertising Association Southwest (1978), pp. 1-2.

Motion Picture Advertising

Motion picture advertising is occasionally designated as a supplementary medium that reaches the trade and consumers. Similar to television, motion picture advertising offers an advertiser the combination of sound, sight, movement, and the possibility of undivided attention. The problem, unlike commercials on television, is in securing acceptable distribution. There are two types of distribution for advertising through films—theatrical and nontheatrical.

Nontheatrical distribution requires that advertisers build audiences for their films by securing the cooperation of schools, churches, clubs, or lodges. Theatrical advertising is seen most frequently in small-town theaters, where advertising for national advertisers or local businesses will appear on screen between films. It may also be seen in larger cities at drive-in theaters. It is used by practically any kind of local advertiser and by national advertisers of such items as automobiles, jewelry, and watches.

The advantages of such theater screen advertising are that it provides a captive audience, offers the local flavor, and furnishes repetition.

Product Placement in Motion Pictures

A method that is attracting increasing attention is the use of specific products in the movie scene itself (see Exhibit 21.6). Interest in this activity increased significantly after Reese's chocolate pieces appeared in "E.T." Although the use of merchandise in movies is fairly random, such activities have become more organized in recent years. Product placement firms, such as Associated Film Promotions of Century City, California, provide services for a number of companies at a fee.[8] These firms secure product placement in motion pictures and ensure that the presentations are satisfactory. They may also act as watchdogs to prevent a company's products from appearing in undesirable positions. Anheuser-Busch for example turned down a request for its products to appear in "E.T." because beer was used to intoxicate a child, as well as an extraterrestrial.

Directory Advertising

Directories are a form of advertising most frequently used in the industrial field. General industrial directories, such as *Thomas Register of American Manufacturers*, are referred to by all types of industries. These directories list the names of manufacturers, their locations, and a description of the products or services offered. They also carry advertisements.

Service directories are becoming more widely available today. For example, the *International Directory of Marketing Research Houses and*

---

[8]Janet Maslin, "Plugging Products in Movies as an Applied Art," *The New York Times* (November 15, 1982), p. C11.

EXHIBIT 21.6
Advertising in Movies

Services presents information on firms conducting research services. Such directories also accept advertising designed to help the firm stand out from its competitors.

Telephone book advertising, more familiarly known as the yellow pages, is the most widely known directory in the consumer field. In fact, it is promoted through a successful advertising campaign of its own, and its slogan—"Let Your Fingers Do the Walking"—has consistently achieved high scores on recall tests.

Yellow page directories list every business in an area that has a telephone number. Advertisers can buy display space or listings in many different local classified telephone directories through national representatives. This type of promotion offers a 24-hour availability and a long

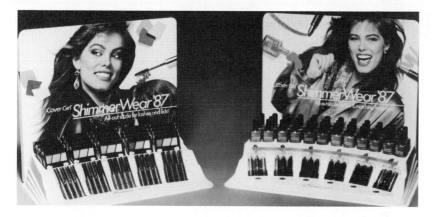

EXHIBIT 21.7
Point-of-Purchase Advertising

Noxell's 1986 Fall Eyes display won a
1986 POPAI award. The retailer had
a choice of placing the right amount
of product in the store, and the
consumer could view the full fall line
from Noxell.

life expectancy. According to a study commissioned by the National Yellow Pages Service Association (the medium's bureau) and conducted by Statistical Research Inc., 17.8 percent of all adults use yellow pages on a typical day, and 47.7 percent of those referrals result in a purchase within 48 hours.[9]

With the 1984 breakup of AT&T, there has been increasing competition among the seven regional "Baby Bell" companies in the publication of yellow page directories. In addition to standard yellow page listings, targeted directories for senior citizens, and competitive directories far from their regional homebases have appeared. Southwestern Bell, for instance, the largest yellow pages publisher, launched directories to compete directly with Nynex's Manhattan book. It is difficult for these firms to maintain an official identity since neither the walking fingers insignia nor the name "yellow pages" are proprietary. Competitive directories have turned to advertising to attract customers.

Point-of-Purchase Advertising

The term *point-of-purchase advertising* is preferred to the earlier used expression *point of sale*, because the former emphasizes the concept of consumer orientation. The trade association for the industry calls itself the Point-of-Purchase Advertising Institute (POPAI). The materials used in such activities are also designated as dealer's help and dealer's display (see Exhibit 21.7).

Point of purchase is advertising material located at, on, or in the retail store. Despite its location, the vast majority of such materials are produced and paid for by manufacturers. The advertising may be exterior, such as service station banners or window displays, or interior, such as counter displays, floor displays, wall displays, banners, or mobiles. It may be permanently installed (barometers and clocks that carry the product or manufacturer's name) or temporary (counter cards, cutouts, or streamers) (see Exhibit 21.8).

---

[9]Rebecca Fannin, "Run Don't Walk," *Marketing and Media Decisions*, May 1986, p. 70

EXHIBIT 21.8
Exterior and Interior P. O. P.
Advertising

Just prior to purchase is an important time for firms to contact and influence a store's customers. For manufacturers, this advertising also helps to increase goodwill; for retailers, it provides the means and incentive to stock merchandise in better locations. For consumers, point-of-purchase advertising provides information about what is new, what is available, and occasionally how it may be used.

There are estimates that less than one-half of all point-of-purchase materials received free by retailers are ultimately used. One of the problems is that such materials must be capable of attracting two publics—

first, the retailers, and then, ultimate consumers. Retailers have a limited amount of display space available and, therefore, are reluctant to use too much of the material.

Like cooperative advertising point-of-purchase promotional materials must be offered by manufacturers to all retailers who are eligible or it may be viewed as discriminatory. Moreover there are difficulties in measuring its effectiveness. Although retail display may be effective as a reminder medium, its ability to influence impulse purchases is still open to question.

PLANNING AND COORDINATING SUPPLEMENTAL ACTIVITIES

The development of an effective sales promotion and supplementary media campaign requires that management clearly define the role of these activities in achieving its marketing objectives. Since these supplemental methods are usually conducted in conjunction with other promotional activities, their relationship to the elements must be determined in defining the objectives and planning the campaign. Complaints of recent promotional activities, for example, have included criticism that the sales promotion and advertising, rather than support each other, appear to be in conflict.

Defining Objectives

There may be many objectives for promotional activities. For example an objective for a minor brand might be to build the long-term market share, while for a new brand the objective might be to gain suitable distribution. Moreover, there are a variety of constraints on the manager's selection of a promotion. For example the manufacturer may wish to retain control over the promotion. Another constraint on the selection of a promotion may be the total financial liability of the promotion. Table 21.1 offers suggestions concerning the type of promotion that can be used to meet the objectives of a promotion and remain within its constraints.[10]

To achieve a particular goal it may be necessary to employ a combination of techniques. For example, a campaign by Mobil Chemical Company to attract new users for its Hefty trash bags included, in addition to advertising, sales promotion in the form of sweepstakes, premiums, and dealer allowances as well as point-of-purchase advertising.

Before implementing a program, it may be useful to conduct pretests of samples or specialties in a small target area, particularly if these can be done quickly and inexpensively. Implementing a program requires gaining the cooperation of distribution outlets as well as media.

---

[10]John W. Keon and Judy Bayer, "An Expert Approach to Sales Promotion Management," *Journal of Advertising Research* (June/July 1986), p. 24.

TABLE 21.1   Given Specific Management Objectives and Constraints, What Types of Promotion Should Be Run?

Management Objective	Promotion*	Coupon*
Product Movement	(1) Cents-off label (2) Free goods	
Defensive Strategy	(1) Rebates (2) Coupons	(1) On-pack (2) In-store
Long-Term Profit	(1) Coupons (2) Cents-off label	(1) Free-standing inserts (2) Direct mail
Build Market Share	(1) Coupons (2) Free goods	(1) Direct mail (2) In-store
Gain Distribution	(1) Free goods (2) Coupons	(1) Free-standing inserts (2) In-store
Brand Awareness	(1) Sweepstakes (2) Coupons	(1) Magazine (2) Free-standing inserts
Management Constraints		
Maximize Control	(1) Coupons (2) Cents-off label	(1) Direct mail (2) On-pack
Minimize cost	(1) Rebates (2) Sweepstakes	

*First and second choice for general promotion and first and second choice for coupon is provided when a coupon choice is desirable.

Source: from "An Expert Approach to Sales Promotion Management," by John W. Keon & Judy Bayer, *Journal of Advertising Research*, (June/July, 1986), Vol. 26, No. 3, p. 25. Reprinted by permission of Advertising Research Foundation.

Merchandising the Advertising

An important factor in a successful promotional campaign is securing the support and enthusiasm of the institutions involved in distributing the merchandise to consumers. When manufacturers try to influence distributors, dealers, and salespeople by explaining the consumer advertising effort, they are said to be *merchandising the advertising*.

Manufacturers can merchandise consumer advertising to dealers by word of mouth, through exhibits and trade shows, printed materials, motion pictures, or slide films. They can provide information concerning the media to be used, their schedules, the campaign theme and the reasons for its selection, comparisons of competitive advertising, and so on. They can provide merchandising materials such as banners, display pieces, press releases, stickers, and streamers that reflect the consumer campaign. In merchandising the advertising, manufacturers use their salespeople, sales managers, advertising agency representatives, and media representatives. They place advertisements in trade papers and house organs to help sell the program.

Coordinating and Evaluating Promotional Activities

A combined promotional effort using diverse activities requires coordination to eliminate conflict and ensure mutual support. Coordination

COORDINATING A SALES PROMOTION CAMPAIGN

Gillette Company develops many successful promotions to coincide with sporting events such as the World Series, Olympics, and baseball's All-Star game. The firm uses an overall strategy to make its advertising and incentives work in concert. Gillette's promotions typically start with retail trade allowances on best-selling brands, supported by a sweepstakes to attract consumer attention. Gillette's Super Bowl promotion offered a 1986 Ford Thunderbird and $25,000 cash as the grand prize, for example. Next, free-standing newspaper inserts are used to encourage customer traffic in stores. Point-of-purchase advertising in the form of store displays tie in the advertising message and usually contain entry coupons. The entry coupons may include a rebate offer to stimulate in-store buying. Gillette generates added excitement by offering prizes for a competition that relates to the event itself, such as picking the most valuable player in the World Series.

Source: Richard Edel, "Manufacturers Create Package of Ads, Incentives, Promotions," *Advertising Age,* Thursday (February 6, 1986), pp. 22–24.

begins in the planning stage, when objectives are determined and continues throughout the implementation of the plan.

Evaluation of the supplementary efforts is necessary for determining effectiveness and providing feedback for future promotional decisions. Such activities can be conducted by a firm—such as monitoring sales—or through research services available from several firms specializing in the design and evaluation of these supplementary techniques.

SUMMARY

Sales promotion is an element in the promotional mix. Its specific purpose is to offer extra value or incentive for the product to the sales force, resellers, or ultimate consumers. Sales promotion to the trade stimulates dealers to do a better job of handling and pushing manufacturers' products. Such trade stimulants as trade deals or trade shows encourage retailers to carry manufacturers' merchandise. Incentives to salespeople to sell manufacturers' products may be offered through contests or push money. Cooperative advertising funds encourage retailers to supplement manufacturers' promotional efforts. However, manufacturers must eliminate any question of discrimination from these offerings.

Consumer stimulants have a variety of forms. Samples are designed to influence consumers to try new products and, if satisfactory, may create brand loyalty. Premiums may influence users to switch to an advertiser's product and may provide an immediate increase in sales. Coupons and rebates may encourage consumers to try new products, generate repeat purchases, or increase the use of established products.

Contests and sweepstakes serve to create a high level of consumer involvement in the advertising of a product and encourage action at the retail level. Trading stamps were heavily adopted by supermarkets as a means of differentiating themselves and creating store loyalty, but their effectiveness has diminished in recent years.

Supplementary media refers to vehicles other than the mass media that are used for the dissemination of messages. These include specialty advertising, motion picture advertising, and directory advertising. In addition point-of-purchase advertising disseminated by manufacturers offers their outlets the opportunity to display the merchandise attractively and to stimulate impulse purchases. A major problem in point-of-purchase advertising is influencing retailers to select a specific manufacturer's promotional material from the many displays offered.

An effective sales promotion and supplementary media campaign requires careful planning and implementation. The activities chosen should be consistent with the objectives of this campaign as well as those of other promotional efforts.

QUESTIONS FOR DISCUSSION

1. Distinguish between sales promotion and advertising, sales promotion and personal selling. How does sales promotion aid these other efforts?

2. Which of the various promotions to the trade do you believe would most likely encourage a reseller to stock a new product? To actively sell a product? Explain.

3. Describe the conditions under which an advertiser would use samples or demonstrations.

4. What is meant by a *self-liquidating premium?* What problems may result from its use?

5. Why are so many coupons distributed? What reasons can you offer for their relatively low redemption rate?

6. What are the hazards of using refunds? How effective do you believe automobile rebates will be in the future?

7. What are the characteristics of an effective contest or sweepstakes promotion?

8. Under what circumstances are specialties useful in a promotional campaign?

9. Describe a point-of-purchase display that recently stimulated an impulse purchase on your part and offer reasons for its success.

10. Describe the requirements you view as most important in the planning and implementation of a supplementary promotional campaign.

KEY TERMS

sales promotion	coupons
trade stimulants	refunds
consumer stimulants	sweepstakes
buying allowances	games
free goods trade deals	contests
cooperative advertising	supplementary media
push money (spiff)	specialty advertising
sampling	point-of-purchase advertising
premium	merchandising the advertising
self-liquidators	

AD PRACTICE

From a Sunday newspaper gather all the free-standing inserts that contain coupons. Classify the coupons by products or service offered. Evaluate them in terms of their attractiveness and appeal. How many of them would you redeem?

CASE

The Media Plan

When the Hyundai car was introduced in 1986 a $25 million campaign was used to promote it. Advertising appeared on television in thirty-one spot markets seventeen days before the product went on sale. All of the 30-second commercials were aimed at building up the parent company, the Hyundai Motor Company of Seoul, South Korea, as a maker of ships and locomotives and as the maker of the best-selling imported car in Canada. The theme line "We make cars that make sense" was used in teaser spots that hid the car. Seventy percent of the commercials appeared during prime time, while the remaining were divided equally between early and late fringe times.

This was followed by a magazine advertising schedule in *People*, *Newsweek*, *Psychology Today*, *Omni*, *Life*, *Gentlemen's Quarterly*, and *Cosmopolitan*, as well as in *Car and Driver*, *Motor Trend*, *Road and Track*, and *Autoweek*. The three-page ads started off with just eight words in big black type against a stark white background: "Introducing something most car companies don't make anymore." *Sense* was the single word headline on page 2, and the copy that followed on the second and third pages led up to the car's photograph and statements about its price ($4995) and features.

DISCUSSION QUESTIONS

1. What factors concerning the product and its market led to the choice of this media plan?
2. What media scheduling theories are incorporated in this plan?
3. In terms of the magazine schedule was Hyundai interesting in maximizing its reach or frequency? Explain.

Source: Philip H. Dougherty, "Advertising, Hyundai's $25 Million Campaign," *The New York Times* (January 23, 1986), p. D24.

CASE

Television Ratings

New developments in digital computer technology improve color, sound, and picture reception of audio tapes and videocassette recorders. Digital television sets can provide nine different pictures within a screen at one time, permitting the viewer to watch multiple programs simultaneously.

According to a study released by J. Walter Thompson Co., some 58 million Americans practice "flipping," and the trend is increasing, especially among younger audiences. Flipping, jumping from channel to channel instead of staying with a single program, is now the typical viewing pattern of 34 percent of all television watchers, and the figure climbs to 51 percent for viewers aged 18 to 24. Flipping is compared to "zapping" (electronically avoiding commercials) and "zipping" (fast-forwarding past commercials while watching programming recorded on a VCR). Flipping, the

Digital television and remote controls are becoming increasingly common. Flipping, zapping, and zipping are all made easier by using one or both of these products, and advertisers are aware that commercials are being seen less and less.

survey shows, exceeds zapping and zipping and raises critical questions for advertisers, their agencies, and ratings services.

DISCUSSION QUESTIONS

1. What methods are currently used to provide ratings for television programs?

2. What problems with these rating methods are created by flippers, zippers, and zappers?

3. What rating techniques would you suggest to resolve these issues?

Source: "New Report on Changing TV Viewing Habits," *Marketing Review* (December 1986), p. 15.

22

Advertising Research

Perception Research, based in Englewood Cliffs, New Jersey, uses beams of infrared light, computers, and cameras to track the movement of people's eyes as they peruse magazines. According to the company, ads placed in the second quarter of *Time* or *Playboy* work as well as those in the first quarter, while ads in *Forbes* and *Business Week* work best in the first quarter. Food marketers, according to this research, are wrong when they run mouth-watering photographs of cakes and cookies, since the readers' eyes linger on the luscious illustrations and overlook the product name. Automobile ads catch readers' attention surprisingly well in women's magazines and, contrary to popular belief, people are not naturally more inclined to read ads on right-hand pages or in the front of magazines.

Studies to identify the factors that contribute to successful advertising campaigns indicate that successful ads are based upon market research findings; they are based on careful media planning; and they are likely to use messages that are perceived to be creative and unique.

OBJECTIVES OF ADVERTISING RESEARCH

Advertising research, the application of marketing research to the special characteristics of advertising, can improve the basis for decision making in any of the stages in the advertising campaign. In the initial stages it may be used to analyze a situation and a target market by gathering quantitative and qualitative data. In subsequent stages, research may identify which of two headlines is superior in a specific advertisement or the suitability and economy of various media as vehicles for carrying an advertisement.

A major portion of the advertising research effort focuses on creative strategy research and evaluation of advertising effectiveness. It is sometimes difficult to distinguish between these two basic efforts. Creative strategy research is generally conducted prior to the development and implementation of an advertising campaign to generate ideas for the creative approach and execution. Advertising effectiveness research can be conducted either before or after advertising appears in the media. The testing, which can be conducted by the advertising company or its advertising agency, evaluates techniques used in an individual advertisement or an entire campaign (see Table 22.1). The American Marketing Association issues an annual directory of research firms who provide testing aids through syndicated services or specially designed research for assessing advertising's performance.

CREATIVE STRATEGY RESEARCH

Creative strategy research is conducted to elicit information prior to the development of the creative aspects of an advertising campaign. Much of this research is designed to gather insights into the product or service's market and target group such as those discussed in Section One on situation analysis. Specifically, these efforts can include motivation, attitude, and psychographic research as discussed in Chapters 8 and 9. Bank of America's ad based on psychographic research appears in Exhibit 22.1.

Usually the data secured through these research techniques are sufficient for advertising development. However, sometimes there are two or three ideas that appear strong. *Concept testing*, based on consumer motives, attitudes, and perceptions can help identify the most appropriate creative strategy.

A *concept* is an early approximation of some future potential reality.[1] A company can test its idea before it commits money and personnel to producing it. Concept testing was used as early as 1946 when a group of designers, developing a new electric iron for Proctor Silex, each argued that his idea was superior. The company decided to show the prototypes to a group of consumers and see which one they preferred.

---

[1]Sid Hecker, "A Brain-Hemisphere Orientation Toward Concept Testing," *Journal of Advertising Research*, Vol. 21, No. 4 (August 1981), pp. 55–60.

TABLE 22.1 Advertising Research by Agencies and Advertisers

	Total		Agencies		Advertisers	
Total Respondents	*Number* 112	*Percent* 100.0	*Number* 39	*Percent* 100.0	*Number* 73	*Percent* 100.0
Undertake preliminary, background, or strategic research in preparation for advertising campaigns	104	92.9	39	100.0	65	89.0
Evaluate copy ideas, storyboards, other formats prior to rough commercial	85	75.9	34	87.2	51	69.9
Evaluate rough commercial execution of other formats prior to finished commercial	102	91.1	38	97.4	64	87.7
Evaluate finished commercials	105	93.8	35	89.7	70	95.9
Evaluation of television campaigns	98	87.5	37	94.9	61	83.6
Test competitive commercials	73	65.2	27	69.2	46	63.0
Test commercials for wearout	29	25.9	9	23.1	20	27.4

Source: from "Television Advertising Copy Research: A Creative Review of the State of the Art" by Benjamin Lipstein & James P. Neelankavil, *Journal of Advertising Research* (April/May, 1984), Vol. 24, No. 2, p. 21. Reprinted by permission of Advertising Research Foundation.

Concept tests can be used in developing advertising strategy particularly in terms of appeals or the positioning approach. Such tests are usually conducted with target groups of potential product users who are given written factual statements accompanied by rough visuals of advertisements. For example, Ralston Purina had developed a cat food which contained 25 percent real fish—more real fish than in any other cat food—and came in a bag. Four advertising concepts were developed; each communicated the product's key benefits (real fish/convenience) in a different way. Consumers were shown four ads, identical except for the body copy (see Exhibit 22.2). The respondents gave the highest rating to Concept 2—"For the first time, real fish without a can."

There are some drawbacks to concept testing. While it is a useful technique for advertising decisions, problems exist in the way the concept is initially presented to consumers. Although the test can generate comparative data, the ultimate selection may still be weak. Moreover, concept testing techniques lack rigorous research validation.

EVALUATING ADVERTISING

The greatest expenditures of time and effort in advertising research can focus on two areas—effectiveness of the advertisement (*copy testing*) and effectiveness of the advertising campaign. Increased product sales can be attributed to conditions other than advertising, so sales cannot be used as the sole basis for evaluating ads. As a result evaluation frequently focuses on communication effectiveness. The rest of this chapter examines this rationale. The specific techniques used for these assessments are described in the next chapter.

EXHIBIT 22.1
Applying Psychographic Research to
Rugged Individualists

EXHIBIT 22.2
Concept Testing

Sales Effectiveness of Advertising

Although a logical approach to evaluating advertising suggests testing in terms of purchasing effectiveness, this is not easily accomplished nor is it always desirable. Advertising is not always designed to achieve immediate sales; frequently its goals may be long range. Where the effects are immediate, they may not be observable in sales. Advertising may be used to secure leads for salespeople, as an alternative to more expensive distribution costs, or to induce retailers to stock and display merchandise. Assuming the goal of advertising is to increase immediate sales, problems exist in terms of developing adequate and valid measuring devices.

Isolating advertising from all other variables that cause a sale is extremely difficult, and although it is the subject of much current research, it is yet to be successfully demonstrated. Furthermore, even if a causal relationship between an advertisement and a sale were demonstrable, there still would remain the question of which specifics within the advertisement caused the sale—the headline, the illustration, the size, or the color.

Nevertheless several evaluation techniques focus on sales, particularly those that relate to the cumulative effects of an advertising campaign. These are discussed in the next chapter.

Communication Effectiveness

To some people the purpose of advertising is not to generate sales, but to create awareness and favorable attitudes that will ultimately change predispositions to companies and their products. Most techniques designed to measure this kind of effectiveness are based on theories about the ways in which consumers process information. They determine whether the communication was received and what its impact was on the consumer. As with sales tests, problems occur in isolating advertising's effect on, for example, awareness and attitude, since changes in these aspects of consumer behavior may also be a result of much more than the advertising message.

Several theories postulating "how advertising works" have been developed and others are emerging.[2] This section examines hierarchy-of-effects theories, high involvement/low involvement concepts, information processing, and psychophysiological research.

Hierarchy of Effects Theories
Various hypotheses about the effect of advertising, based on the hierarchy-of-effects theories as described in Chapter 7, suggest that consumers go through a series of steps of increasing commitment to action. The AIDA and DAGMAR approaches discussed earlier provide examples of

---

[2]Edward Tauber, "Editorial," *Journal of Advertising Research*, Vol. 22, No. 6 (December 1982/January 1983), p. 7.

TABLE 22.2   A Model for Measurement of Advertising Effectiveness

Related Behavioral Dimensions	Movement Toward Purchase	Some Types of Promotion or Advertising Relevant to Various Steps	Some Research Approaches Related to Steps of Greatest Applicability
	PURCHASE ↑	Point-of-purchase; retail store ads; deals; "last-chance" offers; price appeals; testimonials	Market or sales tests; split-run tests; intention to purchase; projective techniques
Conative—the realm of motives. Ads stimulate or direct desires.	CONVICTION ↑ PREFERENCE ↑		
Affective—the realm of emotions. Ads change attitudes and feelings.	↑ LIKING ↑	Competitive ads; argumentative copy; "image" ads; status, glamor appeals	Rank order of preference for brands; rating scales; image measurements, including check lists and semantic differentials; projective techniques
Cognitive—the realm of thoughts. Ads provide information and facts.	KNOWLEDGE ↑ AWARENESS	Announcements; descriptive copy; classified ads; slogans; jingles; sky writing; teaser campaigns	Information questions; playback analyses; brand awareness surveys; aided recall

Source: from "A Model for Predictive Measurements of Advertising Effectiveness" by Robert J. Lavidge & Gary A. Steiner, *Journal of Marketing*, XXV (Oct. 1961). Copyright © 1961 American Marketing Association. Reprinted by permission.

these steps. Evaluative measures can determine whether advertising is an effective influence on consumers in achieving these steps.

Lavidge and Steiner's classic model of the movement toward purchase includes the following steps[3]: (1) awareness, (2) knowledge, (3) liking, (4) preference, (5) conviction, and (6) purchase. It suggests that different advertising and promotional techniques may be used to accomplish each one of these levels and provides recommendations for specific kinds of measurements to determine whether these various levels have been reached (see Table 22.2).

High Involvement/Low Involvement Concepts

Some researchers indicate that while the hierarchy-of-effects thesis may provide a valid measurement of advertising effectiveness in certain situations, this may not be true under other conditions. For example, variations in responses to advertising may occur in high involvement versus low involvement situations. Though the term *involvement* has not been precisely defined, it is generally considered to suggest importance. The classical hierarchy of effects where consumers go through the various stages from awareness to purchase is relevant for high-involvement products, services, or situations where cognitive considerations prevail, such as the purchase of cars, appliances, and insurance.

---

[3]Robert J. Lavidge and Gary A. Steiner, "A Model for Predictive Measurements of Advertising Effectiveness," *Journal of Marketing*, Vol. 25 (October 1961), p. 61.

If there is low involvement these steps may not take place; a product may be purchased on the basis of habit, such as milk; on the basis of convenience, such as paper tissues; or on the basis of personal taste, such as candy and beer. For these purchases the affective dimension (a person's feelings) may be most influential.

Accordingly, for high-involvement products research may focus on their salient attributes and on convincing consumers of their superiority. For low-involvement products research may be required to design advertisements that radiate warmth, touch people's emotions, or help create impressions of the intangible aspects of the product.

A widespread measurement technique to determine whether a message has been received is the recall test, which requires consumers to repeat messages. While there is no clear relationship between recall and persuasion, if an audience actively receives a message, the response pattern is assumed to progress through a sequence of steps such as awareness, knowledge, liking, preference, conviction, and purchase. Under low-commitment theory, however, the result may be a simple and collapsed hierarchy-of-effects purchase sequence—from awareness to purchase.[4]

Television is seen by many people as a low-involvement medium where consumer responses to television advertising take the form of passive learning while they are in a low-drive relaxed state.[5] Under such circumstances, however, there may be limited cognitive defenses to advertising. The resulting effect may be that television advertising is quite persuasive even when it is not recalled.

Thus to evaluate the effectiveness of advertising under high- and low-commitment conditions a different measurement variable may be required. Two basic measurement techniques used are *recall* (Do you remember seeing an ad?) or *recognition* (Do you recognize this ad as one you have seen before?).

High-involvement decisions about such items as automobiles and clothing require a recall response. For example, recall of the message may be necessary to assure that consumers are aware of what dealer or store to visit.[6] Low-involvement decisions may require a recognition response, since recognition typically occurs at the point of purchase. Currently, however, there tends to be a reliance on recognition measures for print media and recall measures for broadcast media, regardless of high or low commitment considerations.

Information Processing

Advertising research examines the consumer as a processor of information; that is, the consumer is characterized as interacting with his or her

---

[4]Thomas S. Robertson, "Low-Commitment Consumer Behavior," *Journal of Advertising Research*, Vol. 16 (April 1976), p. 22.

[5]H. E. Krugman, "The Impact of Television Advertising: Learning Without Involvement," *Public Opinion Quarterly*, Vol. 29 (Fall 1965), pp. 349–356.

[6]John R. Rossiter, "Predicting Starch Stores," *Journal of Advertising Research*, Vol. 21, No. 5 (October 1981), p. 64.

TABLE 22.3 The Communication/Persuasion Matrix, Indicating the Divisions on the Input (Communication) Side and on the Output (Persuasion) Side

OUTPUT	INPUT				
Steps in Being Persuaded	Communication Variables				
EXPOSURE	*SOURCE*	*MESSAGE*	CHANNEL	RECEIVER	DESTINATION
— simple exposure	— credibility	— appeal			
— attention to communication	— likability	— style			
	— power	— organization			
EMOTIONAL RESPONSE	— quantity	— quantity			
— arousal	— demographics				
— effect					
ENCODING					
— attention to content					
— perception					
— learning					
— remembering					
ACCEPTANCE					
OVERT BEHAVIOR					
CONSOLIDATION					

Source: "The Communication Persuasion Matrix" by Wm. J. McGuire from *Evaluating Advertising: A Bibliography of the Communication Process* by Benjamin Lipstein & Wm. J. McGuire, Editors, 1978. Reprinted by permission of Advertising Research Foundation.

choice environment, seeking and taking information from various sources, processing this information and then making a selection among alternatives.[7]

This information processing theory of advertising research has been adapted in a communication-persuasion matrix (see Table 22.3). In this matrix the *communication process* is seen as composed of a series of interrelated variables—source, message, channel, receiver, and destination. The *persuasion process*, similar to the hierarchy-of-effects approach, includes the following steps:[8] exposure, emotional response, encoding, acceptance (persuasion), and behavior (purchase).

Evaluating advertising under this communication/persuasion matrix requires an analysis of the interrelationships among the communication and persuasion variables. Thus studies may be designed to determine the effect of celebrities (source) on acceptance (persuasion); or the influence of humor or fear (message) on emotional responses.

McGuire and Lipstein have provided a bibliography which identifies

---

[7]James Bettman, *An Information Processing Theory of Consumer Choice* (Reading, Mass.: Addison-Wesley Publishing Co., 1979), p. 1.

[8]William J. McGuire, "The Communication Persuasion Matrix," in *Evaluating Advertising: A Bibliography of the Communication Process*, Benjamin Lipstein and William J. McGuire (eds.), (New York: Advertising Research Foundation, 1978), p. xxvii.

sources of information for numerous studies conducted in these areas.[9] Almost 1000 items are concerned with measuring persuasion, 657 relate to measuring comprehension, and 328 measure recall.[10]

Psychophysiological Research

A variety of measurement techniques for assessing advertising effects are based on the measurement of autonomic responses. These emerge from psychophysiological studies which indicate that physiological (bodily) reactions reflect psychological (emotional) states. Psychophysiological research focuses on the autonomic nervous system (ANS) which exerts control over such bodily functions as glandular secretions and internal organ functioning.[11]

Most of the psychophysiological measurements in evaluating advertising effectiveness examine autonomic responses—primarily the extent of "arousal" caused by the ad. These measurements are based on assumptions that messages may result in "pleasurable arousal," such as sexual, or "unpleasurable" arousal," such as anxiety, fear, or stress. Autonomic measures may also provide data on a message's attention-getting capability.

Most psychophysiological tests focus on autonomic responses primarily by measuring the extent of "arousal." This is determined by examining the speed, frequency, and amplitude of the response to advertisements.

Pupilometrics

Pupilometrics is based on the relationship between pupil dilation and the interest value of visual stimuli. Many studies have been conducted to evaluate packages, graphic designs, or advertising materials by measuring, through pupil responses, the degree of interest exhibited by consumers.

The popularity of pupilometrics in advertising research has declined in recent years. A primary reason is the uncertainty of what is being measured, since large pupils can either indicate a very positive attitude or a mental effort because the ad is difficult to understand, while small pupils may indicate loathing or boredom. Moreover, retests in the field have produced different results.

However, pupillary responses appear to accompany a number of other psychological processes, including arousal, attention, problem solving, learning, and memory; and the amount of "mental energy" demanded during these psychological processes may determine pupil

---

[9]Benjamin Lipstein and William McGuire (eds.), *Evaluating Advertising: A Bibliography of the Communication Process* (New York: Advertising Research Foundation, 1978).

[10]Benjamin Lipstein and James Neelankavil, *Television Advertising Copy Research Practices . . .* , p. 9.

[11]Paul J. Watson and Robert J. Gatchel, "Autonomic Measures of Advertising," *Journal of Advertising Research*, Vol. 19, No. 3 (June 1979), pp. 15–26.

EXHIBIT 22.3
Eye-Movement Recorder

size.[12] Pupilometrics, therefore, may be useful in evaluating advertising even if it does not directly measure consumer likes and dislikes.

The Galvanometer

The galvanometer, like pupil dilation, measures the amplitude of the response to an advertisement. The galvanometer, a device that looks something like a lie detector, has been used to measure changes in bodily responses, such as changes in respiration, heartbeat, and perspiration, as the viewer looks at advertisements. The BSR (basal skin resistance), a type of galvanometer that measures the change in sweat gland activity, is used in advertising testing.

The use of this device is limited to advertisements and products about which people may have strong feelings. Moreover, a strong reaction does not connote a favorable advertising response. It may be useful in revealing any discrepancy between verbal responses and physical reactions which may then provide a more valid interpretation of the test data.

Eye-Tracking

Eye-movement recorders allow researchers to determine what creative elements consumers see or read when exposed to ads, billboards, product package designs, and other advertising material. The route a person's eye takes is superimposed over the tested material to determine the path taken and the areas that attract and hold attention. This technique is widely used as new eye-movement recorders have been developed. Telcom Research, for example, uses a Telcommeter eye-tracking device which is the size of a slide projector and easily portable (see Exhibit 22.3). The development of computers has permitted the recording of each eye movement and the analysis of this data from videotape, thereby making the eyetrack movement recorder economically feasible for advertising purposes.

Eye-tracking tests are objective measurements of the areas of interest in an advertisement and may help improve the design. Such tests

---

[12]Paul J. Watson and Robert J. Gatachel, "Autonomic Measures of Advertising," *Journal of Advertising Research*, Vol. 19 (June 1979), pp. 15–28.

can reveal the reason for poor communication and can identify the ad elements that aren't working. For example, in testing commercials for RCA Colortrak TV sets and Lincoln-Mercury cars, Telcom found that respondents were focusing on the celebrity presenters (actresses Linda Day George and Catherine Deneuve, respectively) instead of on the products. According to Telcom, a spokesperson who is too attractive will be a "visual vampire" draining attention away from the product rather than toward it. Frank Sinatra was designated as a "visual vampire" in commercials for Chrysler cars.[13]

Eye tracking is generally considered more useful for print ads, because in TV commercials there is so much movement on-screen that the viewer's eye movements don't fall into an identifiable pattern.

According to researchers, eye-movement studies have disproved the notion that the more time people spend looking at an ad, the better they remember it, as well as the belief that bigger type automatically attracts more attention.[14]

Eye tracking is particularly beneficial when it is used to develop a large body of knowledge about how the same ads are viewed by different people. As a result ads can be designed to appeal to particular target audiences. Such tests, however, are conducted under artificial conditions which may influence the route the eye takes. Also they are expensive and they do not indicate the viewer's thoughts.

Tachistoscope

The tachistoscope is a device that measures physical perception under varying conditions of speed, exposure, and illumination. It is a slide projector with an attachment for the recording of the speed of the response. This device has been used as a fast method for pretesting advertising in a laboratory situation. It has been found that high readership scores correlate with the speed of recognition of the elements under analysis. However, it can provide little more than a measure of physical perception.

Voice-Pitch Analysis

Larynx-produced voice pitch is one of the many autonomic responses which express an emotional reaction. This is based on the rationale that when emotions are "felt" in the mind the autonomic nervous system is stimulated causing a tightening of the vocal cords, which results in an increase in the pitch of the sound emanating from these vocal cords. Measurements of these changes can indicate whether the response was favorable or unfavorable. In addition, studies conducted by universities and government agencies have documented that there is an empirically defined range of changes in voice pitch which indicate the veracity of the response.[15]

---

[13]Adapted from Bernice Whalen, "Telcommeter Now Can Pretest TV Ads, Eye Tracking Technology to Replace Day-After-Recall by '84," *Marketing News* (November 27, 1981), Section 1, p. 18.

[14]"Determining How Ads Are Seen," *Dun's Business Month* (February 1982), pp. 85–6.

[15]Ronald G. Nelson and David Schwartz, "Voice-Pitch Analysis," *Journal of Advertising Research*, Vol. 19, No. 5 (October 1979), pp. 55–62.

EXHIBIT 22.4
Advertising Appeal Selected Through
VOPAN

In voice-pitch analysis an initial conversation with a respondent can determine normal voice-pitch baseline levels through a computer which isolates the pitch of the sound from the voice cord. The computer is then used to analyze vocal responses to yes/no attitudinal questions to determine if statistically significant increases in voice pitch over baseline levels occurred.[16] This is said to indicate emotional commitment behind the response.

Voice-pitch analysis (VOPAN) was used with a panel of teenagers to determine their responses to ads for Levi Strauss's 501 jeans. The agency found that the teenagers' voice-pitch response was more favorable for advertisements stressing such qualities as the jeans' button-fly feature and their "shrink to fit" ability. The ads were re-edited, and those that did not do well were dropped. Exhibit 22.4 shows a Levi ad that tested well.

The benefit of voice-pitch analysis over some other autonomic measures is that this form of physiological analysis determines whether the emotional response is favorable or unfavorable. However, it is not considered adequate as a sole testing technique and should be used in connection with, rather than in place of, other methods of measurement.

Response Latency

Response latency, like voice-pitch analysis, is generally used in conjunction with other measurement techniques. *Response latency* is defined as the amount of time a respondent spends in deliberation before answering a question.[17] Several researchers found that response latency is an indicator of a subject's certainty in a given response, and declared it may be useful in measuring preferences.[18]

---

[16]Nancy J. Nighswonger and Claude R. Martin, Jr., "On Using Voice Analysis in Marketing Research," *Journal of Marketing Research*, Vol. 18 (August 1981), pp. 35–5.

[17]James MacLachlan, J. Czepiel, and P. LaBarbera, "Implementation of Response Latency Measures," *Journal of Marketing Research*, Vol. 16 (November 1979), pp. 573–7.

[18]David A. Aaker, Richard P. Bagozzi, James M. Carman, and James M. MacLachlan, "On Using Response Latency to Measure Preference," *Journal of Marketing Research*, Vol. 17 (May 1980), pp. 237–244.

Response latency can be easily incorporated in voice-pitch analysis. Data used for voice analysis are recorded on tape; therefore the latent response of the subjects can be obtained with a voice-pitch measurement. Combining voice and response latency analysis can provide two simultaneous measures of the same phenomenon. However, neither voice-pitch analysis nor response latency have met the rigorous testing requirements of validity and reliability.

Brain Hemisphere Analysis

Recently attention has focused on measuring brain waves as a means of assessing advertising effects. Based on emerging concepts in brain hemisphere research, indications are that there are differences between the manner in which information is processed in the right and the left hemispheres of the brain. The left hemisphere of the brain is primarily responsible for traditional cognitive activities relying upon verbal information, symbolic representation, sequential analysis, and the ability to be conscious and report what is going on. The right hemisphere is more concerned with pictorial, geometric, nonverbal information—without the individual being able to report verbally about it.[19]

Brain hemisphere research is related to the high-involvement/low-involvement theses discussed earlier. Krugman has proposed that even when *attention*, in the sense it is normally referred to in advertising research, is not present, it is still possible for an individual to receive and store information.[20] Moreover this process is particularly efficient with pictorial material, such as television, and that information is stored in a fashion different from the way we normally store verbal and similar information.

If this hypothesis is confirmed, that even with very low levels of attention some information can still be received, the view of how advertising works will change. It is possible that a considerable amount of the advertising material to which an individual is exposed and which we normally conclude has no effect, may still be extremely important in forming habits, behavior, and attitudes.

A number of studies have been conducted in brain hemisphere research. The findings include the following:[21]

1. The brain reflects stimuli which are arousing, alerting, and interesting.
2. The hemispheres respond differentially—the left for verbal, sequential-processing, and cognitive, and the right for spatial, parallel-processing, and emotional stimuli.
3. Recent data indicate that the right hemisphere appears directly to mediate positive affect, and the left negative affect.
4. These relationships are routinely measurable by means of standard Brain Wave Analysis techniques.

---

[19]Fleming Hansen, "Hemispheral Lateralization: Implications for Consumer Behavior Research," prepared for a project sponsored by the Danish Social Research Council, p. 4.
[20]H. E. Krugman, "The Impact of Television Advertising . . ."
[21]Sidney Weinstein, "A Review of Brain Hemisphere Research," *Journal of Advertising Research,* Vol. 22, No. 3 (June/July 1982), pp. 59–63.

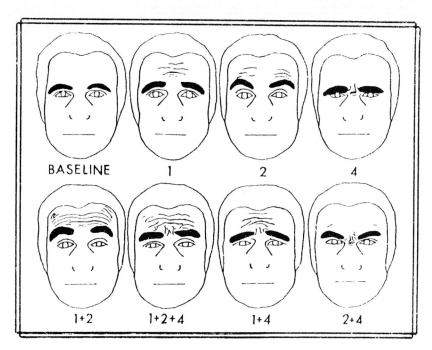

BASELINE   1   2   4

1+2   1+2+4   1+4   2+4

EXHIBIT 22.5
Evaluating Through Facial Analysis

Example of FACS application, developed by P. Ekman and W. V. Friesen. Baseline is normal expression. Numbers 1, 2, and 4 are called Single Action Units, which represent actual muscle movements (50 have been identified). Singly or in combination, the eyebrow configurations represent emotions. Thus, 1 + 4, combined with appropriate eye region and lower face action, can be interpreted as a sadness response. FACS can also measure happiness, surprise, anger, disgust, and fear.

Brain wave analysis requires a laboratory setting. In evaluating an advertisement through these techniques subjects are exposed to advertisements, and Beta waves from both sides of their brain are tracked to determine which elements in the advertising are thought-provoking and which stimulate emotional responses. Currently there is limited use of brain wave analysis in testing advertisements. However, recommendations for their future use are that they may be able to provide information that is not available through other techniques.

Facial Action

New methods are being developed to examine nonverbal responses to advertising. One such technique, facial analysis, employs a Facial Action Coding System (FACS) which identifies various emotions based on their corresponding muscle movements.[22] Using such facial analysis in copy testing may provide information about emotional responses (happiness, sadness, surprise, anger, disgust, and fear) to advertising appeals (see Exhibit 22.5).

Measuring such emotional responses may give information about attitude change and information processing that is not available in other consumer-decision models. However, there is still a great deal of study required to determine the extent to which such emotional responses can be related to an ad's effectiveness.

---

[22]"Facial Analysis Tests Responses to TV Commercials," *Marketing News* (August 22, 1980), p. 7.

Strengths and Limitations of Physiological Procedures

Since physiological procedures do not rely on verbal reporting, to some extent they are objective and free from response bias. When used in conjunction with verbal response, they can point out areas of discrepancy and suggest further evaluation.

The expense of equipment, laboratory, and trained personnel is high, especially since few respondents can be accommodated in any one time period. Also, although these methods eliminate response bias, they do create an artificial exposure condition that may bias objective reactions. Furthermore, it is difficult to interpret the results of these tests, and the relationship between objective responses and intent to purchase are not quite clear.

In general it is suggested that if autonomic measures are to be used in advertising, as many of these psychophysiological techniques as possible should be used in decision making.

COMPUTER RESEARCH APPLICATIONS

Technological developments in the computer field have had a major impact on advertising research. Currently, however, most computer applications relate to collecting, storing, transmitting, retrieving, and analyzing data. Computers have significantly increased the ease and speed with which data can be analyzed.

Numerous software packages provide aids in tabulating and analyzing advertising research data. For example, advertisers can secure demographic profiles of each mail-carrier route within every Zip code area in the United States. Other customized reports are available as are data bases and cross-tabulation techniques that can be used on personal computers.

Interactive viewing systems can be used to ask respondents questions. Data on eye tracking can be retrieved from consumers' television sets. Techniques are available for keeping electronic purchase diaries, as well as recognizing which person in the room is watching television. Computers can provide instant analysis of audience research data, help in developing information networks, record the extent of response latency, and transmit consumer purchase data collected by scanners in stores.

Computer models are available that simulate test marketing. Using DEFENDER, a computer model developed by Management Decision Systems, a company can determine what effect a competitor will have on its market and how best to ward off the threat. DEFENDER can tell a company how changes in advertising, pricing, or promotion will alter preferences for its products over new entries. When G. D. Searle's natural-fiber laxative, Metamucil, was faced with a new competitor, DEFENDER advised that the best way to protect market share would be to launch and advertise a less expensive line of Metamucil—which was done with great success.[23]

---

[23]"Wizards of Marketing," *Newsweek* (July 22, 1985), p. 43.

Currently, however, computers are essentially aids to information-processing. With the development of artificial intelligence (computers that "think" and imitate an expert's problem-solving ability) the computer of the future may aid in the development of innovative advertising research and evaluation capabilities.

SUMMARY

A major function of advertising research is to improve the basis for advertising decision-making. Research strategies described in Chapters 8 and 9 provide information for creative strategies. Concept testing is a research technique that is useful in selecting the basic appeal or positioning approach. Not all campaigns require such testing; however, it offers an alternative source for data on which to base advertising decisions.

Most advertising research efforts focus on evaluating advertising effectiveness. Such activities can examine the effectiveness of the advertisements—most frequently called *copy testing*—or the affect of the advertising campaign.

Efforts to evaluate the sales effectiveness of advertising are not accomplished easily—advertising as a variable is not easily isolated nor are its effects always traceable. In addition, advertising objectives are not always related to immediate sales.

More frequently efforts are made to measure the communications effectiveness of advertising. Such evaluation activities are usually based on a number of theoretical constructs of "how advertising works." These concepts are based on theories such as hierarchy of effects, high-involvement/low-involvement, information processing, and psychophysiological concepts. Computer technology has provided advertising researchers with increased ability to collect, store, transmit, retrieve, and analyze data.

QUESTIONS FOR DISCUSSION

1. What is the purpose of creative strategy research? How does this differ from evaluating advertising effectiveness?
2. What is meant by concept testing? How is the information from this test used for advertising purposes?
3. Why is it difficult to measure the sales effectiveness of advertising?
4. How are the hierarchy-of-effects theories related to evaluating communication effectiveness of ads?
5. What is meant by the *low-involvement/high-involvement hypothesis*?
6. Why is psychophysiological research used in evaluating advertising? What are these techniques designed to measure?
7. What is meant by eye-tracking? What are its benefits?
8. Define *voice-pitch analysis* and *response latency*. What are their deficiencies as research techniques?
9. How is brain hemisphere analysis related to advertising research?
10. How is the computer applied to advertising research?

KEY TERMS

creative strategy research	eye-tracking
concept	tachistoscope
involvement	voice-pitch analysis (VOPAN)
recall	response latency
recognition	brain hemisphere analysis
pupilometrics	facial action
galvanometer	

AD PRACTICE

Prepare a series of three rough ads for the prevention of drunk driving that are similar except for the basic appeal. Using concept testing survey a number of your friends and relatives to determine which concept is most effective.

23

Techniques for Evaluating Advertising Effectiveness

When Pillsbury Company was ready to market its new Crusty French Loaf it chose, as a spokesperson, a character resembling Inspector Clouseau, the detective portrayed by the late Peter Sellers in the humorous Pink Panther movie series. Since the product-introduction time was close, the company decided to prepare and test a finished commercial rather than a rough one. The consumer test revealed that people tended to remember the Clouseau character, not the product. Therefore the commercial was revised to build in greater exposure to the brand name. The revised version effectively communicated the company's message.

The advertising community generally agrees on the desirability of evaluating advertising. There is less of a consensus, however, concerning when such evaluation should occur, or the techniques which should be applied. Evaluating the effectiveness of advertising can be conducted prior to the appearance of the ad, during its presentation, and after it has been disseminated. Many different methods are available for these purposes.

CHAPTER OBJECTIVES

— To examine various techniques for evaluating the effectiveness of an advertisement

— To discuss methods for evaluating an advertising campaign

EVALUATING THE ADVERTISEMENT—COPY TESTING

Copy testing is a term applied to the evaluation of an individual advertisement. It is estimated that there are thousands of different ways to test copy. A prerequisite to making a decision among alternatives is to set advertising objectives. A copy test should be designed to assess an advertisement's potential for achieving its stated objectives.

Most copy testing techniques are designed to evaluate the communication effectiveness of an advertisement by measuring consumers' responses. The selection of the specific responses to be measured relates to the various theories of "how advertising works" discussed in the previous chapter and ranges from "awareness" to "purchase."

When to Test?

Testing of advertising can take place at various stages in the development and implementation of an advertising campaign; it can be conducted prior to the insertion of ads in media (which is *pretesting*), *during* their appearance, or after they have appeared (which is *posttesting*).

Advertisements may be pretested at any stage in the creative process, from the preparation of the rough copy to the creation of the finished layout. Pretesting may suggest some means of improving the creative effort and eliminating weaknesses. Importantly it may limit costly errors on the part of an advertiser.

Testing advertisements during a campaign can be used to determine which of two advertisements is superior; however such tests tend to eliminate the "confounding" aspects caused by media variations.

Posttesting may occur early in a campaign—to evaluate the advertisements—or after a campaign has continued for some time—to measure both attitude and sales effect of advertising. Posttesting offers the capability of testing under more natural conditions; however, it involves considering more variables than testing in the other two ways. An advertiser must also consider the choice of media and the effects of competitive advertising. Moreover, mistakes at this time are more difficult and more costly to rectify. Posttesting of copy includes readership and recall tests as well as scanner testing.

The Testing Environment

Depending upon the way that respondents are exposed to the advertisements, testing conditions can be designated as *artificial, forced,* or *natural*. An *artificial environment* is generally used for pretesting, since ads do not appear as they normally would—in the media. The conditions for testing may range from very artificial—tests conducted in laboratories—to those designed to approximate natural conditions. Copy can be pretested in shopping malls or in testing sites developed by research organizations, in theaters, or in the home.

The term *forced* indicates that the respondents' cooperation was secured through some form of inducement such as free samples or prizes.

TABLE 23.1   Copy Testing an Ad

Type of Test	When Test Conducted (in Relation to Commitment to Media Schedule)	Testing Environment (Advertising Exposure)	Primary Response(s) Measured
Laboratory	Pretest	Artificial	Autonomic Responses (Emotional "Arousal")
Consumer Jury	Pretest	Artificial or Natural	Awareness, Liking, Preferences, Comprehension, Believability
Theater	Pretest	Forced	Persuasion (Brand Preference Shift, Attitude Shift)
On-Air	Pretest During	Natural	Recall
Inquiry	During	Natural	Awareness, Interest
Split-Run	During	Natural	Awareness, Interest, Purchase
Recognition & Recall	Posttest	Natural	Recognition, Recall
Scanner	Pretest During Posttest	Natural	Purchase

Efforts are made to simulate natural environments in forced situations. Forced exposure techniques are designed to provide a measure of an advertisement's "persuasiveness" as well as diagnostic information such as comprehension, likes/dislikes, and believability.

The most desirable conditions occur when testing is conducted in a *natural* environment. In testing commercials, for example, they appear on air with normal, prime-time programming. Respondents have no prior knowledge that they may be interviewed when they are exposed to a commercial in their homes. By contrast, other commercial testing systems invite consumers beforehand to view a program. Natural exposure systems most frequently test overall memorability; however, they also can provide information about which copy points registered most strongly with respondents and offer diagnostic information about comprehension and believability. Table 23.1 lists the types of copy tests, when they are conducted, the testing environment, and the primary response measured.

Pretests

The largest variety of copy tests occur in the pretesting category. The psychophysiological tests described in the previous chapter, for example, are conducted before the ads appear. Several other widely used pretests are described here.

Consumer Jury Tests

The philosophy behind the consumer jury test is one that is fundamental in all advertising: Consumer prospects are superior to professional advertising experts in selecting the advertising most likely to influence them. Indeed, the entire concept of evaluating advertising effectiveness is predicated on the fact that the professional is not always certain of what may be most effective.

Consumer jury tests examine the reactions and opinions of consumers to proposed advertisements. They may attempt to determine which advertisement performs best under stated conditions, to learn reactions to specific elements in an advertisement, to see which message is more clearly understood or believed, or to discover how a message is perceived.

Jurors may be members of continuing panels or they may be selected for one study only. The basic requirement is that a juror be a person who is an actual or prospective consumer of the product advertised.

Tests are designed to secure conscious or unconscious preferences. Theoretically, an unconscious choice is more accurate, because consumers become critics instead of respondents if they know they are evaluating a product.

Consumer Jury Tests in Print Media

Several types of consumer jury pretests can be performed for print media. They include order of merit, the paired comparison, and folio tests in artificial situations; and "tip-in" tests in a more natural environment.

In the *order-of-merit* method, two or more possible forms of an advertisement can be shown to potential customers, with instructions to rank them according to quality. When the responses are tabulated, the combined ranking presents the form with the highest merit rating. This, however, may provide little assurance that the advertisement is outstanding; it may merely suggest that this choice was the "best of the worst." Measurements may also be made of interest, believability, and attention-getting capabilities of the advertisement. However, the responses suffer from what is designated as the "halo effect." The respondents tend to rate one or two preferred advertisements as high in all characteristics.

In the *paired comparison* method of testing, each advertisement is compared with every other advertisement in the group. This method is relatively easier for it permits a more discriminating choice than order-of-merit. On the other hand, it is a tedious method, and respondents may attempt to provide consistent evaluations rather than reveal their true feelings.

In *folio* tests, a consumer is asked to look through a portfolio containing from five to ten advertisements, including the advertisement to be tested. The consumer is then questioned on what he or she remembers or found interesting. This method may serve to point up problems in copy or message, and, to some extent, measures the attention-getting power of the proposed advertisement.

To provide a more natural setting, advertisements may be "tipped" (inserted) into advance copies of current magazines in which they were not scheduled to appear. These magazines are placed with consumers in their homes or in shopping malls. The respondents are contacted the following day through telephone or personal interviews and are asked to recall or play back the ads. The questioning may include diagnostic evaluation, such as comprehension or believability, during the interview.

The basic benefit of the *tip-in* test is that it provides a normal setting for the ad that is being tested. However, respondents may offer biased responses in order to provide satisfaction to the interviewer.

Consumer Jury Tests for Television Commercials

Commercials may be tested either in their finished forms or as unfinished roughs. The term *rough* is a misnomer of sorts, since the image it brings to mind is of a hastily done sketch. Actually some roughs may be done very carefully and completely. The advantage is that they are relatively inexpensive, costing perhaps 80 percent to 90 percent less than a commercial produced in finished form. (The finished commercial is the taped or filmed ad that appears on television.) There are three types of roughs:

1. *Animatics* are photographs of a series of drawings (see Exhibit 23.1).
2. *Photomatics* are photographs of a series of still pictures.
2. *Liveamatics* are live-action commercials on videotape, frequently without sound.

Any of the roughs may be used in pretesting television commercials.

In-home projector tests show television programs to people in their homes. Included in the commercials on the programs are specific ones to be tested for audience reaction. *Trailer tests* eliminate the problems of securing permission to enter people's homes and bringing equipment for viewing purposes. Shoppers are shown commercials and interviewed in trailers located in shopping centers or in supermarket parking lots. The tests measure commercials' abilities to attract attention and provide diagnostic information for improving them.

Consumer Jury Tests for Radio Commercials

Most radio commercial testing services invite their respondents to an interviewing-type center. However, the respondents are not always directly questioned about radio commercials. Some services disguise interest in the test commercial by splicing it into a radio program format

EXHIBIT 23.1
Testing a Chee-tos Commercial Using
Animatics

or just by playing the test commercial while the respondent is waiting for the interviewer. Questions about the test commercial are casually interspersed with other questions so that the respondent does not know he or she is being questioned about a particular brand, product, or commercial.

Radio commercials are pretested in forced exposure situations. Respondents are invited to participate in *simulated driving tests* during which commercials are played on the "car radio." The respondents are recontacted at a later time to secure recall and playback material as well as diagnostic information. While these tests may give measures of recall and playback, they are limited to particular research samples. Moreover the target groups used do not tend to be diverse or large.

Strengths and Weaknesses of Consumer Jury Tests

Consumer jury methods can obviously isolate good communications from poor ones. They have caught omissions and misunderstandings, checked the comprehension of specific phrases, prevented mistakes, and checked the appropriateness of an illustration. Consumer jury tests are used to establish norms for communication ability, believability, and other criteria, which then are correlated with measures of success such as readership and attitude change.

Although these tests are not infallible, some are fairly easy and quick to administer and relatively inexpensive. Sample size is frequently small; however, judgments tend to converge in a fairly stable pattern after fifty or sixty interviews.

The basic disadvantage of these methods is that they are subjective tests, usually conducted in artificial or forced situations. Most of them are designed to disclose consumers' opinions and their understanding and acceptance of messages, not whether the messages will induce attitude change and ultimate purchase.

Theater Tests

The theater test is one of the earliest methods of pretesting commercials and was developed by the Schwerin Research Corporation which operated test theaters in a number of American cities. It is used to measure comprehension or to evaluate a variety of presentation elements in test commercials, such as the credibility of the presenter or the comprehension of visual devices used in the copy. Its primary purpose, however, is to measure persuasion in the form of brand preference or attitude shifts.

A theater test occurs in a forced viewing situation—that is, the conditions are not completely artificial, since the respondent does not know he or she is being asked to rate commercials, nor are they "natural" since the respondent is not viewing the commercial in an "on-the-air" context.

The audiences, selected at random from telephone directories, receive free tickets in the mail to a "Network Television Preview Theater," presumably to view pilots for proposed television series. Prior to the viewing each respondent is given a sheet on which nine or ten different products are listed and is asked to check the "one brand you truly want." Then a drawing is held for, say, a year's supply of that product. After the pilot programs are run, interspersed with several commercials, another drawing is held. The extent of shift in product choice after viewing the commercials is presumed to be related to the effectiveness of the commercials.

Over the years norms have been developed for product categories so that commercials can be scored. For example, commercials for products in the women's beauty field have averaged scores of about +5, indicating that 5 percent more women in the audience will choose the sponsor's product after seeing a commercial than did so before. Therefore, if a commercial for a beauty product scores +8, it is very effective; if it scores +2 it is not.

ASI, a commercial theater testing agency that offers services to measure shifts in brand preference, also provides information about specific elements in a presentation. Its theater seats are equipped with dials which audience members are instructed to turn clockwise to indicate interest and counterclockwise for lack of interest. The dials are hooked into an electronic device that records the reaction of the entire audience second-by-second throughout the viewing. This permits an advertiser to receive a detailed breakdown of reactions to the beginning, middle, and end sequences of an advertisement.

ASI also includes a system known as BSR, a galvanometer that picks up the sweat gland responses from wires attached to the second and fourth finger of the viewer. The measurement of the unconscious physiological change is compared to the conscious measure of interest (the dial readings) to determine if there are unconscious ideas affecting interest.

Generally theater testing is designed to determine future sales effectiveness of advertisements based on their identified "attitude shifts." The usefulness of this "shopping list" approach is obviously limited, since viewing is in a forced situation and the shift is rarely significant. Frequently it is found that commercials that are "straight from the shoulder, hard-sell commercials" outperform all others in a theater situation. This merely indicates that in a narrow environment such a commercial is more likely to stand out. Moreover, this method does not test effectiveness after commercials have been seen several times, which is more like a real situation. Nevertheless, manufacturers tend to use theaters to check their agencies' offerings.

Theater tests are one of the few testing techniques that offer a measure of "persuasion" in terms of brand-preference shift. While the validity of this measure is questioned, for advertisers it offers a means of evaluating which seems to have a closer relationship to intent to purchase than the traditional awareness and/or recall techniques.

On-Air Testing

Testing recall, based on the presumption that there is a relationship between recall and persuasion, is measured in both pretesting and posttesting situations. If the test is conducted prior to committing the commercial to a media schedule, it is a pretest; after media commitment it is a posttest. Most pretests of recall are designated as "on-air" tests, which present commercials in a natural situation, surrounded by programs and other commercial clutter. People are contacted afterwards to determine what they remember about the commercials. The tests measure *recall* by recording the number of people who can prove they remember a commercial and relating that number to a percentage of the people who watched the program.

Day-After Recall
The most widely used on-air testing procedure is designated as day-after recall. In DAR people are contacted by telephone and asked if they watched a specific television show the previous day. If they saw the show, respondents are asked if they remember seeing a commercial for a product in the product class of interest. If they do not, aid is provided in the form of the test brand name, and respondents are asked if they remember a commercial for this brand. Those who recall the ad in either fashion are asked questions about specific copy points. The percent who recall the tested commercial is usually compared against norms that have been previously established.

The benefits of on-air testing are that viewing occurs in a natural setting and the results relate to finished commercials. The tests provide an accurate measure of recall; moreover, everything else being equal, it appears that a commercial that is recalled is more likely to affect a final buying decision than one that is not.

The basic disadvantage is that such tests tend to measure *only* recall, and high recall does not mean that people will necessarily purchase the product. As discussed earlier, under low involvement conditions, recognition may be a better measure of advertising impact than recall. In addition, day-after recall testing may penalize "feeling" ads and favor "thinking" ads, because a testing method that requires verbalization— such as day-after recall—favors thinking or left-brain advertising.[1]

Recall Versus Persuasion   The widespread use of day-after recall to test television commercials has led to a "recall versus persuasion" controversy. Persuasion, resulting in attitude changes or sales, is considered by some advertisers as a more appropriate determination of advertising effectiveness than recall which indicates ability to remember. Recall tests assume a relationship between recall and persuasion, even though such a relationship may not exist. For example, respondents may recall an ad but may have negative feelings about it. Or they may not recall the ad—if, for example, there is a psychological benefit presented—but it may sell. Recall testing tends to be used more widely than persuasion, since tests of recall are relatively standardized.

Persuasion is measured in many ways, under a variety of circumstances.[2] In fact *persuasion* is defined in a number of ways—mostly in terms of its relationship to subsequent shopping and buying behavior. Measurements to determine these effects are usually designated as "attitude shifts" or "brand preference shifts" and are used in such techniques as theater tests, described earlier.

Efforts have been made to design a system that measures both day-after recall and brand-preference change simultaneously.[3] A sample audience is prerecruited to watch a prime-time program on UHF or an independent station. As part of the invitation to view the program, people are questioned about their brand preferences for a number of different product categories. The respondents provide brand names on an unaided basis. For their cooperation, respondents are given the opportunity to participate in a drawing for three cash awards.

The day following airing of the test commercial, respondents are contacted by telephone and questioned, again on an unaided basis, about their brand preferences for several product categories. Next, they are asked on an aided basis about recall of commercials that appeared within the program. Proven recall and brand-preference change data are based upon samples of 200 program viewers of either sex or 250 if both are included. Currently there is no rigorous evaluation of this technique.

---

[1]Herbert A. Zielske, "Does Day-After Recall Penalize 'Feeling Ads?'—in TV Versus Magazines," *Journal of Advertising Research*, Vol. 22, No. 1 (February/March 1982), pp. 19–22.

[2]Lawrence D. Gibson, "Not Recall," *Journal of Advertising Research*, Vol. 23, No. 1 (February/March 1983), pp. 39–46.

[3]Harold L. Ross, Jr., "Recall Versus Persuasion: An Answer . . . Based on a Large Longitudinal Study," *Journal of Advertising Research* (February/March 1982), p. 16.

Copy Tests During a Campaign

Copy tests performed while an advertising campaign is in progress include several types. The "on air" tests described in the previous section can offer evaluative information during a campaign; other popular evaluative techniques are called inquiries and split run.

Inquiries

One of the oldest and most logical forms of testing advertising is to keep count of the number of responses the ad generates. *Inquiries,* or responses by consumers to coupons, hidden offers, or free gifts, are intended to either aid in the selling process or to test the effectiveness of an advertising message. The number of inquiries received indicates only a small portion of the total number of people an advertiser wants to influence, but it may provide information about the impact of the advertising on all prospective buyers. This form of testing is inexpensive, simple to run, and provides quick results. Moreover, it is conducted under fairly natural conditions, placing ads in the media in which they will ultimately run.

The weakness of the inquiry test lies in the difficulty to correlate inquiries and reader interest. There appears to be some doubt about the correlation between motives leading to requests and motives leading to the purchase of the product advertised.

An inquiry test during an advertising campaign may measure the effectiveness of a single advertisement or the relative effectiveness of two or more advertisements. Several factors external to the firm and its advertisements affect the number of inquiries received. There are seasonal differences—the number of inquiries is generally highest in February and March and lowest in June and July. There are media differences caused by the differences in size and characteristics of an audience and positioning of the advertisements. Responses can be encouraged by the use of various techniques.

Using a *coupon*, which is usually dominant in an advertisement and offers ease of clipping, is desirable if an advertiser wants a large number of replies and information about the respondent characteristics. The coupon generates the largest number of respondents but usually the poorest qualitatively.

The *hidden offer* which appears in the copy of the ad minimizes responses from children and "coupon clippers." It suggests that the sender has read the copy and has an interest in the product.

A "free gift" can induce more requests, but may have no relationship to the pulling power of an advertisement. Although the number of requests may be increased by *sweetening the offer,* care should be exercised in selecting the item. It is best for the offer to be related but incidental to the advertisement, such as a recipe book for a food product, or a designer's booklet for floor patterns.

Where two or more advertisements are being tested, it is important to provide keys for the response so that an advertiser can identify which inquiry came from which advertisement. These identifying keys may be in the form of variations in the addresses on the coupons of the several advertisements; for example, one response may be sent to Box 170 and the other to Box 173.

Split Runs

Many variables may influence test results when comparing two advertisements. If they were placed in two different media, displayed at two different times, and shown to two different audiences, there will be difficulty drawing conclusions about which is more effective. To eliminate some of this confusion and to provide a way to eliminate many of the variables that may cause distortion, the technique of split runs is used. *Split runs* permit two different advertisements to appear in the same medium at the same time.

Numerous publications offer such capabilities, some at no extra cost. However, similar to the problem with inquiries, split-run advertisements may provide a comparison of one advertisement's performance over another, not a measure of an advertisement's relative effectiveness. The validity of such a measurement may be increased, however, by using one advertisement in the split run whose performance has already been demonstrated.

Split Runs in Print Media

Many print media offer an alternate-copy split. One advertisement appears in every other copy of the run, while the other advertisement appears in the alternate copies. Split-run techniques are best used to test one element in an advertisement—for example, the headline, different illustrations, or some changes in copy. When this method is used under controlled conditions, such as assuring the same position in the same issue with the same editorial content and reaching the same type of viewers, a difference in returns may suggest strong evidence of the amount of reader interest generated.

Split Runs in Broadcast Media

Split runs in broadcasting may be used to pretest advertisements as well as to test them during a campaign. For example, subscribers to cable television may become members of a consumer panel, each week filling out and mailing to the testing service diaries of that week's package-goods purchases. Half the panel is hooked into one cable and half to another; both halves have similar demographic backgrounds. Using this split cable, advertisers can substitute spots during the time they have bought from the network.

An analysis of the substitution of commercials and the purchase reports kept in the diaries provide clients with a method for determining the effectiveness of various advertisements in a natural setting.

TABLE 23.2   Starch Readership Summary Report

House Beautiful   October 1986   [2A]
Total of 52 1/2-Page or Larger Ads   Women Readers

Page	Size & Color	Advertiser	Rank By Assoc.	Percentages			Readership Indexes		
				Noted	Associated	Read Most	Noted	Associated	Read Most
		Home Furniture							
		Serta Perfect Sleeper							
55	1P4	Mattress/Du Pont Teflon	38	41	31	2	77	76	22
62	1P4B	Ethan Allen Furniture	6	65	57	31 —	123	139	344 —
139	1P4	Keller Furniture	34	44	34	9	83	83	100
177	1P4	Harden Furniture	19	53	48	17 —	100	117	189 —
		Household Fabrics/Finishes							
12	1P4B	Louver Drape Vertical Blinds	16	63	49	9	119	120	100
18	1P4B	Cowtan & Tout Fabrics & Wallcoverings	16	60	49	**	113	120	**
33	1P4B	Raintree Designs Victoria Morland Fabrics & Wallcoverings	3	68	60	29 —	128	146	322 —
36	1S4B	Schumacher Fabrics & Wallcoverings	6	72	57	11	136	139	122
39	1P4B	Utica Pipeline Towel & Rug Collection/Du Pont Antron	10	63	53	12 —	119	129	133 —
41	1P4B	Brunschwig & Fils Fabrics	6	59	57	**	111	139	**
116	1P4B	Slumber Rest P.M. Personal Monitoring System Blanket/ Du Pont Bi-nell	40	40	29	3	75	71	33
179	1P4	Fieldcrest Royal Velvet Towels & Sheets	10	61	53	14 —	115	129	156 —
181	1P4B	Sears Floor-Length Draperies	14	57	51	14	108	124	156
		Liquor & Whiskey							
2	1P4B	Kahlua Liqueur	19	53	48	9	100	117	100
		Major Appliances							
17	1P4	Whirlpool Appliances	33	42	36	2	79	88	22
130	1P4B	General Electric Spotscrubber Washing Machine	37	46	33	8	87	80	89
135	1P4	Kitchenaid Superba Dishwasher	29	47	39	2	89	95	22
		Misc. Household Furnishings							
3C	1P4B	Levolor Blinds	25	52	42	13 —	98	102	144 —
47	V2/3P4	Goebel M. I. Hummel Figurine	16	62	49	14	117	120	156
148	1P4B	Kirsh Cirmosa I Traverse Rods	29	50	39	8	94	95	89
153	1P4B	Lenox Bone China Nativity Sculptures/The Holy Family	1	71	64	11	134	156	122

[—] Fewer than 50 Words
[**] Not Applicable

POSTTESTS

Research into the effectiveness of an advertisement after it has been run in a media schedule is called *posttesting*. Recognition and recall, the most frequently used techniques for posttesting advertisements, may be used to check the effectiveness of current advertisements and to provide guidelines for future advertising situations. Scanner services are also used in posttests to measure sales.

Recognition Tests in Print Media

Currently there appear to be no syndicated services that provide recognition tests for broadcast media. In fact, recognition tests are designated as "readership" tests. The most widely used recognition test technique in print media is available through Starch INRA Hooper.

Starch Readership Service

The basic premise of the Starch Readership Service is that whatever else an advertisement is designed to accomplish, its initial goal is to be read. The principle behind this method is one of recognition—that of identifying something as having been seen before.

Daniel Starch and Staff, now called Starch INRA Hooper, has been in existence since 1932 and, in a typical year, studies 1000 different issues of numerous publications. The studies are conducted through personal interviews, using a quota sample of 100 readers per sex for each issue. Interviews generally begin shortly after publication of the magazine; for monthly magazines they may begin two weeks after the on-sale date and continue for three weeks thereafter.

Interviewers present a coded copy of a magazine to each eligible reader, a person who meets the demographic characteristics requirement and who has glanced through or read some part of the magazine prior to the interview. The respondent is asked to go through the magazine page-by-page with the interviewer. Different starting points may be used to equalize the fatigue element.

For each ad the respondent is asked, "Did you see or read any part of this advertisement?" If the answer is yes, a prescribed question procedure is followed to determine the observation of and reading of each component part of the advertisement—the headline, illustrations, signature, and copy.

A summary readership report presents information of advertisements in an issue of a magazine according to product categories (see Table 23.2). The information provided includes the following:

1. *Rank in Issue* The rank data show the relative standing for each ad 1/2 page or larger, based on the number of readers who "associated" the ad.

2. *Percentages* In order to produce scores for the advertisement respondents are classified as follows:

— "Noted"—The percent of readers who remember having previously seen the advertisement in the issue being studied.

— "Associated"—The percent of readers who not only noted the advertisement but also saw or read some part of it that clearly indicates the brand or advertiser.

— "Read Most"—The percent of readers who read half of the written material in the advertisement.

3. *Readership Index* The readership index compares each ad's performance against the issue's median, which is assigned an index of 100. Thus if a "noted" readership index for an ad is 150, this indicates that the ad is 50 percent above the average in that issue (in terms of being noted). An "associated" readership index of 75 would indicate that the ad was 25 percent below the issue average (in terms of being associated). According to Table 23.2 the ad for Lenox Nativity Sculptures which ranked first, was noted by 71 percent of the readers (34 percent above average), associated by 64 percent (56 percent above average), and read most by 11 percent (22 percent above average).

Advertisers are also provided with copies of ads which contain yellow stickers detailing the Starch scores for the illustration, headline, copy, and signature (see Exhibit 23.2).

Evaluation of Recognition Studies

In offering their research capabilities, Starch INRA Hooper point out some potential problems in evaluating the information they provide. It is important to remember that advertisements for different things get different readership no matter how they are written (autos versus laxatives). Also, different media get different readership (a chess player reads a chess magazine more passionately than he or she reads *Life*). People bring to each advertisement their own set of views or prejudices. Because of these limitations, Starch INRA Hooper states that the best use of readership data can be made by averaging the figures for several insertions (rather than using the figures for single advertisements), and by looking for recurring factors in order to establish trends and principles.

Obviously, the most important benefit offered by this service is the information that the advertising is being read. Whether the data are accurate depends upon the extent of error that occurs through the interviewing and recording procedures. The noted scores, the most widely used Starch data, may be affected by factors other than the content of advertisements: for example, the number of advertisements in the issue and their tendency to generate respondent fatigue or boredom, the degree of reader interest generated by each issue's editorial content, the time spent reading each issue, and the exposure to the same and similar advertisements in other media. There may also be an element of bias in the interviewer's recording of the data. Insufficient evidence that the reader had previously read the magazine may be ignored, and there may be variations in the care with which the interviewer questions the respondent. Even if these scores are valid the recognition method does

EXHIBIT 23.2
Starch Readership Scores for Ad in
House Beautiful

not measure advertising effect, but only what has been noted, read, or examined.

Nonetheless, these methods are useful since they test the advertising under natural conditions of exposure. Moreover, recognition is designed to measure specific behavior, not just opinions or attitudes. It offers an objective statement of advertising reading; and reading behavior is an evidence of interest. Recognition tests are available through syndicated services, and to some extent, this tends to provide lower costs. For the advertiser it also gives an opportunity to compare performance with competitors. As noted earlier, recognition may be the most desirable technique for evaluating television advertising for low-involvement products.

Recall Methods

To some extent all measures of recall offer a recognition factor, but recall goes beyond recognition and suggests there were some memorable impressions left by an advertisement. Recall tests, like recognition tests, involve surveys with persons previously exposed to advertisements under natural conditions, but they are more objective measures of actual retention. Recall methods can be unaided or aided; aided recall is most frequently used.

As discussed earlier, recall as a measurement device is most widely used for pretesting television commercials "on air." There are, however, opportunities to posttest recall after advertisements have appeared in media schedules for both magazines and television.

Unaided Recall   Unaided recall is a measure of memory relying on no extra cues. Nonetheless, it is necessary to give some direction to interview responses, such as "What advertisements have you noticed recently?" or "What do you particularly remember seeing in this issue?" These questions are difficult to answer, and, when more direction is provided, the procedure turns into aided recall. The unaided recall technique is rarely used as the only measure and frequently is continued into the aided-recall process.

Aided Recall   The chief purpose of aided recall research is to measure total effective communication. A respondent is given some form of "aid" to jog his or her memory, in the form of a roster of ads or by referring to brand or corporate names. The interviewer then engages in a probing recall process to encourage the interviewee to remember specific features.

Evaluation of Recall Methods

Although the recognition method provides more quantitative data, the recall method secures more qualitative data from the respondents. While some forgetting does occur causing recall to diminish with time, recall measures are reasonably stable over the length of time required for a test. Moreover, recall of advertisements has been shown to be independent of their positions within a magazine. One simple way to report and compare idea impact is by coding and counting the number of specific points mentioned by the respondents.

There are a number of problems connected with the use of recall measures. One limitation, similar to that of recognition methods, is lack of correlation between the recall of a message and the extent to which that factor influences behavior. Also, the value of the information received through recall is a function of an interviewer's skill. Recall data are also sensitive to sample design, to the length of the interview, to the likelihood of the respondent being a prospect of an advertiser, and to the position of an advertisement in the interviewing sequence.

The information obtained through recall may not emerge from a respondent's view of the recent advertising, but from his or her knowledge of the product and the previous advertising. Some information is difficult to articulate, although it has been suggested that rating scales to measure emotional appeal be added to clarify emotional reactions to advertisements. Studies in the area of selective perception and selective retention suggest that the recall of an advertisement is not solely the function of the advertisement's ability to attract attention, but depends greatly on the predispositions of people exposed. Moreover, as discussed earlier, recall may be a more effective measure in high-involvement situations than under low-involvement conditions.

Scanners

The development and proliferation of electronic scanner technologies in supermarkets have led to scanning research services, provided by Burke Marketing Services, Information Resources, Inc., and A. C. Nielsen Company. Scanners, however, are more of a return to the trial-and-error approach of evaluating advertising and away from information-processing research and hierarchy-of-effects theories. Scanners do not show *why* something works; they merely indicate *when* it does by providing purchase data.

Both Burke and IRI approach shoppers in participating grocery stores and drugstores to be members of testing panels. A. C. Nielsen not only uses this technique but also uses a random sample from local telephone books to select panelists. While the only requirement of panel membership is that the panelist have a television set that is hooked up to the local cable television station, A. C. Nielsen also directs ads to homes that are not wired for cable. With this system consumer product companies can test a representative sample of the entire market, not just the cable television segment. Burke's Viewscan and IRI's BehaviorScan panelists receive incentives for regular participation (such as monthly prizes). A. C. Nielsen's Testsight Service offers similar incentives.

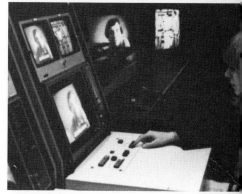

EXHIBIT 23.3
Scanner Testing by BehaviorScan

Panelists receive ID cards resembling credit cards. Their only obligation is to show the card to checkers as they pay for groceries, so their purchases can be identified and entered into the store's computer.[4] In addition, panelists' coupons are electronically recorded in their purchasing records. If they shop in a store that does not participate in the scanning system, panelists are asked to record those purchases in diaries, using Universal Product Code numbers.

Cable television cut-in equipment may be used to test alternative advertising approaches. Two different commercials may be transmitted simultaneously to test groups and control groups; a scanner provides data indicating which advertisement produced the higher level of consumer sales. Scanners can also be used to test the effect of inserts and special newspaper ads in relatively small markets.

---

[4]Julie Liesse Erickson, "Picking Panel Members to Pass Judgment," *Advertising Age, Thursday* (February 13, 1986), pp. 12, 16.

Evaluation of Scanner Techniques

Since scanner technology is in the development stage and new applications are in the process of emerging, a precise assessment of these techniques for evaluating advertising must await future developments.

Currently, scanner testing methods appear to offer a number of advantages. The data they provide are an accurate assessment of actual sales. Moreover, the information relates not only to the number of people purchasing a given product, but also to the number of units purchased and the amount spent. The data are real—consumers are actually purchasing—and the feedback is immediate.[5]

The primary disadvantage of current scanner techniques is that they basically measure *only* behavior—in terms of purchases—and provide no diagnostic or procedural information concerning creative strategies or attitudes. In addition, scanners currently are not useful in providing information about delay or cumulative effects of advertising.

EVALUATING COPY-TESTING TECHNIQUES

Copy testing performs an important function in providing advertisers with information that may aid in reducing risks that are inherent in decision making. Nevertheless there are numerous criticisms about these methods.

What Responses Should Be Measured?

Much of the criticism focuses on the response measured in copy testing. Although extensive efforts are devoted to measure "awareness" in copy testing, a recent study on advertising effectiveness noted, "As a measure awareness is weak and subject to distortions and fallibilities of consumer memory."[6]

Researchers have noted a distortion from using awareness as a response measure in what has been designated as "spurious awareness."[7] This effect is evident when respondents declare they have tasted Olivetti tomato sauce and smoked Smith-Corona cigars when these products do not even exist. Spurious awareness occurs because consumers really do think they have heard of products that carry familiar names, such as Kodak tissues. It also emerges because respondents want to please the researchers.

According to Oxtoby Smith, a research firm, spurious awareness occurs in testing advertising for line-extension products that have familiar names—such as Coca-Cola's introduction of its Diet Coke line. Although a researcher can attempt to correct for the exaggerated number of people who say they have seen the ads, sometimes it is difficult to determine the extent.

[5]Theodore J. Gage, "IRI Develops New Systems for More Exposure," *Advertising Age* (February 21, 1983), p. M-29.

[6]Philip H. Dougherty, "Advertising, Studies Discussed by A. R. F.," *The New York Times* (March 9, 1983).

[7]Philip Greer and Myron Kandel, "The Greer/Kandel Report, Have You Been Checked for 'Spurious Awareness'?" *New York Law Journal* (March 24, 1983), p. 3.

TABLE 23.3   PACT Principles

A good copy testing system:

— provides measurements which are relevant to the objectives of the advertising.

— is one which requires agreement about how the results will be used *in advance* of each specific test.

— provides *multiple* measurements—because single measurements are generally inadequate to assess the performance of an advertisement.

— is based on a model of human response to communication—the *reception of* a stimulus, the *comprehension of* the stimulus and the *response to* the stimulus.

— allows for consideration of whether the advertising stimulus should be exposed more than once.

— recognizes that the more finished a piece of copy is, the more soundly it can be evaluated and requires, as a minimum, that alternative executions be tested in the same degree of finish.

— provides controls to avoid the biasing effects of exposure context.

— is one that takes into account basic considerations of sample definition.

— is one that can demonstrate reliability and validity.

Source: "PACT Principles" (January 1982). Reprinted by permission of American Association of Advertising Agencies.

As discussed earlier, much copy testing is designed to measure recall, while many advertisers feel that the response measure should be persuasion. Currently, however, there is little consensus concerning what techniques are efficient for measuring persuasion.

What Is the Ideal Copy Test?

An effective copy test should determine whether an ad has a high level of attention impact, communicates a clear message about a product's assets, persuades consumers that the advertised brand is more desirable than prevailing alternatives, and is free of any negatives that might antagonize prospects over time.[8] In addition this must be done quickly and economically. Currently no single copy-testing system offers this.

Whether it is possible to have this "ideal" remains to be seen. In an expression of concern for the criticisms in copy-testing procedures, a number of marketing researchers from major advertising agencies have developed a series of principles they consider appropriate for a valid copy-testing system. These principles were enunciated in a public statement, Positioning Advertising Copy Testing, or PACT (see Table 23.3).

The controversy over testing techniques is one of long standing. As noted, efforts are made to address criticisms through improvement of copy-testing methods. However, most of these activities are based on currently accepted concepts of how advertising works, such as those described in the previous chapter. Future research efforts devoted to the

---

[8]Calvin L. Hodok, "On-Air Recall from Theater Tests," *Journal of Advertising Research*, Vol. 16, No. 6 (December 1976), pp. 25–34.

development and evaluation of theories of how advertising works may offer additional measurements for determining *if* advertising is working.

EVALUATING AN ADVERTISING CAMPAIGN

Most of the efforts discussed previously related to copy testing—or evaluating the effects of individual advertisements. In some cases it is considered desirable to provide a test for an advertising campaign. Such tests are usually designated as *market tests* since they involve testing an advertising campaign in one or various markets. These are frequently pretests and may be designed to secure information about other marketing variables besides advertising.

Efforts to measure the cumulative effects of an advertising campaign may be conducted during the campaign as well as after it has been completed. Usually such tests involve the use of *tracking studies*.

Market Tests

In high-risk situations it may be useful to market-test an entire advertising campaign approach. These market tests may be full scale or limited. Full-scale tests usually are designed to secure information about variables other than creative aspects. Most market tests for advertising purposes only are of the limited variety called mini-market tests (See Exhibit 23.4). Services for such purposes are not syndicated but are designed according to the testing requirements of a particular firm.

Matched Market Pairs
One of the most frequently used limited market tests is called *matched market pairs*. The chosen sites are matched to control markets with respect to relative size, brand development, consumer buying power, and so on. Objectives for the test are established (for example, comparing two advertising campaigns), and data from the test and control markets are collected before, during, and after the test period. The data gathered may relate to advertising's effect on sales, attitudes, or other required information and may be provided through scanning services.

Controlled Test Markets
In this technique one small test area may be selected for testing one or more variables under controlled conditions. An effort is made to select a market considered "typical" of the nation in the use of most products. The determination of a "typical" market or "Little America" is one that has been the subject of interest to test marketers for many years. Whether such a market exists is questionable; moreover the target group the advertiser wishes to reach may be an "atypical" segment. Cleveland, Ohio; Portland, Oregon; Kansas City, Missouri; Buffalo, New York; and Charlotte, North Carolina, are considered preferred test markets.

The objective is to test an advertising campaign primarily in terms of its ability to generate sales. Store audits are conducted before, during, and after the test periods. Research companies such as A. C. Niel-

EXHIBIT 23.4
Research Firms Design Mini-Market Tests

sen and Audits & Surveys take the responsibility for distribution and shelf-stocking of the product tested as well as for sales measurement.

Since there are no controls the testing is considered "unnatural" and limited in scope; therefore, it is not projectable to future strategies. However, it is the less expensive way to learn if advertising is successful under "ideal" conditions.

Simulated Test Marketing

In simulated test marketing consumers are exposed to a commercial for a new product and then provided with a simulated shopping experience in a laboratory store. This is followed up by telephone interviews with those who bought the product to measure their reactions and repeat-purchase intentions. Responses are fed into a computer, and computer models such as ASSESSOR are used to integrate information including estimates of distribution, advertising spending, and consumer behavior and attitudes.

Simulated test marketing offers a relatively fast, low cost, and confidential means of screening advertising options. However, it does not approximate "real world" conditions, so the data are often limited in application.

Tracking Studies

Tracking studies are designed to monitor the effects of advertising over time. While sales may be the most desired effect, as noted earlier, advertising and sales are not easily correlated. The hierarchy-of-effects theory indicates that advertising effects generally flow from awareness through knowledge, liking, preference, conviction, and purchase. Tracking can help determine advertising effectiveness during these phases as well as determine belief and attitude shifts.

Tracking studies, usually designated as pre/posttests, are conducted in at least two "waves." In the prewave the respondents are screened and interviews are conducted just before the advertising runs in a sample of markets where the product will be advertised and in a sample of comparable markets where there will be no advertising. In postwave, respondents are screened and interviews are conducted after the client and agency feel that the advertising has run long enough to have the desired effects (usually 3 months). The advertising is tested for changes in awareness, beliefs and attitudes, and sales.[9] Chevron used such campaigns to pretest and posttest its corporate advertising.

Figure 23.1 is an example of a pre/posttest that can be used to track attitude shifts in the soft-drink industry. The same test, requesting consumers to allocate a portion of a specific sum of money to the purchase of a number of listed brands, can be given in two waves.

A microcomputer-based model, PROD, helps forecast the performance of new products on the basis of inputs from tracking-survey data. For example, by means of the tracking data information, a manager can simulate alternative future levels of GRP's necessary to generate adequate awareness of advertising for the product among members of the target market.[10]

Tracking studies tend to be costly and time consuming. They do not provide early evaluations of what may be expensive mistakes. Questions are raised concerning their validity, particularly in terms of the samples used in the several waves. Nevertheless, tracking can help determine advertising effectiveness in various stages of the communication process. It provides continuous feedback on the creative process and may suggest the need for executional or appeal changes, reveal belief and attitude shifts, and indicate that a campaign is beginning to wear out.

---

[9]Lewis C. Winters, " . . . A Case History Comparing Pretesting and Posttesting of Corporate Advertising," *Journal of Advertising Research*, Vol. 23, No. 1 (February/March 1983), pp. 25–32.

[10]Fred S. Zufryden, "PROD II; A Model for Predicting from Tracking Studies," *Journal of Advertising Research* (April/May 1985), pp. 45–51.

FIGURE 23.1   Gathering Tracking Test Data

Constant Sum Allocation Pre & Post:

Indicate how you would distribute $10 among the brands on this list. The more you prefer a brand, the more dollars you should give it. You may assign as many or as few dollars—even no dollars—to each brand, but the total number of dollars must equal 10.

			Dollar Distribution
Cola:	A.	Coca-Cola	_____
	B.	Pepsi-Cola	_____
	C.	RC Cola	_____
	D.	Dr. Pepper	_____
	E.	Diet Pepsi	_____
	F.	Tab	_____
	G.	Some other cola brand	_____
Root Beer:	H.	Dads	_____
	I.	A&W	_____
	J.	Hires	_____
	K.	Barrelhead	_____
	L.	Shasta	_____
	M.	Some other root beer brand	_____
Lemon & Lime:	N.	Sprite	_____
	O.	7-Up	_____
	P.	Fresca	_____
	Q.	Some other lemon/ lime brand	_____
Other:	R.	Some other brand and flavor	_____
		TOTAL	$10

Source: from "Choosing the Right Attitude Measure," *McCollum/Speilman Topline,* Vol. 2, No. 2 (April 1, 1980). Reprinted by permission of McCollum-Speilman.

SUMMARY

Techniques for evaluating advertising can test the effectiveness of an individual advertisement or the effectiveness of an entire campaign. An appropriate test begins with a statement of the objectives. In testing individual advertisements (copy testing) several decisions are necessary; these include determining which variables to measure, when to conduct the test, and the conditions under which the ads are to be exposed to respondents.

Pretests include laboratory techniques which are used to eliminate verbal communication problems. However, they are conducted under the most artificial conditions, and it is sometimes difficult to interpret the responses.

Consumer jury tests examine the reactions of consumers to proposed advertisements. In print media these include order-of-merit tests, paired comparison tests, folio tests, and "tip-in" tests. For television, in-home projectors may be used as well as trailers or other interviewing sites located in malls or other areas. Interviewing centers and simulated driving tests are used to evaluate radio commercials.

Theater tests are conducted under forced viewing conditions and are designed to measure persuasion in the form of brand preference shifts. "On-air" testing offers the benefits of natural viewing conditions and indicates recall of a message on the assumption that recall is related to purchase intention.

Inquiry tests are useful for evaluating different advertisements during a campaign. Split-run tests are also conducted during a campaign, frequently as part of an inquiry test. Since the tested ads are run simultaneously in the same medium, this technique eliminates some of the variations due to time or media changes.

Posttests include recognition, recall, and scanner tests. Recognition is a form of posttest under natural conditions; that is, after the ads have appeared in the media. They mostly occur in print media and provide a measure of readership, which to the advertiser is an indication of interest. Recall, as a posttest, is designed to test the memorability of an advertisement. Recall provides more qualitative data than recognition and permits respondents to "play back" the parts of the advertisement.

Scanners are an emerging technology that can be used for pretests, tests during, and posttests. The basic advantage over other methods is that scanners provide a measure of sales, in terms of scanning consumers' purchases.

Market tests are usually conducted prior to the introduction of an advertising campaign for high-risk situations and can measure variables other than advertising. These may be in the form of matched market pairs (using test and control markets), controlled test markets (using one test area), and simulated market tests which offer a "simulated" shopping experience in a laboratory rather than in an actual market area.

Tracking studies are used to measure the cumulative effects of an advertising campaign, either during or after it has been run. Tracking studies are conducted in waves to determine the extent to which this goal was achieved.

QUESTIONS FOR DISCUSSION

1. In your opinion, why are there so many techniques available for copy testing?

2. What are the advantages and limitations of pretesting? posttesting?

3. Why are environmental conditions used to test advertising? Explain.

4. What is the basic philosophy in using "consumer jury" tests? What kinds of evaluative information are provided by such tests?

5. Describe the theater test and discuss its objectives.

6. Discuss the "recall" versus "persuasion" controversy. What is your opinion?

7. What methods are used to test advertisements during a campaign? What are their strengths and weaknesses?

8. How do the posttesting methods of recognition and recall differ? Which do you believe is more effective?

9. Discuss the use of scanners in copy testing in terms of their benefits and limitations.

10. How are market tests used to evaluate advertising effectiveness?

KEY TERMS

copy testing	theater tests
pretesting	simulated driving tests
posttesting	on-air testing
artificial environment	day-after recall
forced environment	inquiries
natural environment	hidden offer
consumer jury tests	sweetening the offer
order-of-merit method	split run
paired comparison	Starch Readership Service
folio tests	unaided recall
animatics	aided recall
photomatics	scanners
liveamatics	matched market pairs
in-home projector tests	tracking studies
trailer tests	

CASE

Posttesting

Video Storyboard Tests Inc. conducts an annual survey interviewing about 30,000 consumers as to the advertisements they consider the best during the previous year. Coca-Cola ranked number one in the survey for 1986 ads, based on reactions to both new Coke and Coca-Cola Classic (see the accompanying Table). Most frequently mentioned by consumers was the Max Headroom computer-generated character; however, few consumers associated Max Headroom with the new Coke.

As usual, heavy advertisers of fast food, soft drinks, beer, and wine coolers dominated the list of the 25 most outstanding commercials. However, third place went to the "I Heard it Through the Grapevine" commercial for California raisins, despite the relatively low expenditure by the California Raisin trade association.

Celebrities starred in 10 of the 25 campaigns, the most featured being Chicago Bears quarterback Jim McMahon. A public service ad by Adolph Coor Co. in which a bartender takes the car keys from his buddy who has had one too many beers was in the top 25.

The survey provides information on popularity ranking and cost efficiency. Cost efficiency mea-

Video Storyboard Poll

1986 Rank	1985 Rank	Brand (Agency)	1986 TV Spending* (In millions)	1986 Cost Efficiency
1	4	Coca-Cola (McCann-Erickson/SSC & B)	$ 48.3	$12.07
2	3	McDonald's (Leo Burnett)	321.2	64.67
3	—	California raisins (Foote, Cone & Belding)	5.8	N.A.
4	2	Miller Lite (Backer & Spielvogel)	70.9	42.89
5	1	Pepsi-Cola (BBDO)	42.1	10.92
6	14	Bartles & Jaymes (Hal Riney & Partners)	30.3	N.A.
7	7	Bud Light (DDB Needham)	52.3	42.99
8	5	Burger King (J. Walter Thompson)	165.2	43.40
9	8	Jell-O (Young & Rubicam)	44.5	N.A.
10	—	Isuzu (Dela Femina, Travisano)	29.1	N.A.
11	10	Kibbles'n Bits (J. Walter Thompson)	10.0	23.13
12	—	Levi's (Foote, Cone & Belding)	18.1	7.47
13	15	Snuggle (SSC&B)	22.0	N.A.
14	—	Coors (Foote, Cone & Belding)	72.1	73.00
15	—	Honda scooters (Wieden & Kennedy)	12.7	N.A.
16	6	Wendy's (DFS Dorland)	79.6	40.26
17	—	Seagram's wine cooler (Ogilvy & Mather)	23.6	N.A.
18	—	Taco Bell (Tracy-Locke)	50.2	102.76
19	17	Huggies (Ogilvy & Mather)	20.2	N.A.
20	—	Sprite (Lowe Marschalk/Carden & Cherry)	24.0	34.40
21	23	French's mustard (J. Walter Thompson)	2.1	N.A.
22	16	Acutrim (Ally Gargano/MCA)	8.3	N.A.
23	9	Pizza Hut (Chiat/Day)	71.3	53.52
24	18	Kodak (J. Walter Thompson)	43.4	N.A.
25	—	Hefty (Wells, Rich, Greene)	10.5	N.A.

*Source: Broadcast Advertisers Reports

Source: Ronald Alsop, "New Coke Is a Smash Success With Consumers in This Poll," *The Wall Street Journal* (February 26, 1987), p. 25.

CASE

Scanner Testing

Scanners have been around since the early 1970s, when Kroger installed the first experimental unit in one of its Cincinnati outlets. Recent technological advancements, however, have invested scanners with new, sweeping capabilities. Scanner-equipped stores acounted for more than half of commodity sales by supermarkets in 1986, and that figure is expected to reach 62 percent by 1989.

The greater timeliness of scanner data will provide advertisers with the ability to monitor their advertising agencies more closely. Scanner reports give a fast readout of the success or failure of a particular promotion. However, there may be an excess of data, some of it not usable, from scanners. Moreover, close scrutiny of these data is required, since some promotional activity, such as coupons, may have a big impact on short-term sales.

Richardson-Vicks, a health and beauty aid company, tested a new shampoo, Crystal Spring, and a new cream formulation—a line extension for Oil of Olay—using BehaviorScan. The service offers its customers a choice of eight test market cities, installs scanners in all the chosen city's supermarkets (sometimes drugstores as well) and recruits a panel of 2500 households. The panelists give cashiers an ID card to record what they've bought every time they make a purchase.

Richardson-Vicks tested its two products in two cities each for a year. Advertising was done via cable television. The cost of the service is high; typically customers can spend up to a quarter of a million dollars on a one-year, two city study. However, the combination of UPC scanners and the panel allows BehaviorScan to keep track not only of total share data but of trial and repeat purchases by panel members.

Richardson-Vicks has not released the results of this study, but declare they were satisfied not only with the test results but with the testing medium as well.

DISCUSSION QUESTIONS

1. How does scanner testing differ from other advertising evaluation techniques?
2. What are the advantages and disadvantages of scanner testing?
3. As an advertiser under what circumstances would you used scanner testing?

Sources: "The great scanner face-off," S & MM (September 1986), pp. 43–46, and Leslie Brennan, "All in the Timing," S & MM (March 1985), p. 88.

---

sures the price an advertiser pays to be noticed by 1000 people who use its product. Taco Bell, for example, spent $102.76 for every 1000 taco buyers who remembered its ads; Levi's spent $7.47 for every 1000 jeans buyers who recalled its ads.

DISCUSSION QUESTIONS

1. Discuss this advertising research technique describing the environment in which it was conducted and the response measured.
2. As one of the advertisers listed in this poll what would be the significance of these results to you?
3. What suggestions for future advertising campaigns would the test results indicate?

24

Advertising a Service: The "I Love New York" Campaign

In 1969 Virginia introduced its "Virginia Is for Lovers" campaign, the first effort using advertising to lure tourists. Alaska found that most Americans living outside the state perceived it as a cold wasteland with a few recreational activities. Its advertising campaign shows the Anchorage skyline at night and declares "Once You've Gone to Alaska, You Never Come All the Way Back."

Much of the discussion in Part II on advertising campaign development and implementation focused on promotion of a product. The procedures for advertising a service, while similar, may require specialized efforts.

SERVICE ADVERTISING

Services are activities, benefits, or satisfactions that are offered for sale.[1] Several characteristics that distinguish them from products can be stressed in advertising. Most services are *intangible;* they cannot be held, displayed, or packaged; however, some consumers perceive as tangible the physical facilities where a service is provided and its personal and physical representations, such as plastic credit cards or bank statements.[2] Promotional activities may simulate tangible characteristics through, for example, the use of slogans or taglines: "You're in Good Hands with Allstate," or "Don't Leave Home Without It," (your credit card).

Services are characterized by *heterogeniety,* their performance varies from producer to producer, from customer to customer, and from day to day. Advertising of services can emphasize a quality corporate image to suggest consistency. Furthermore, since the type of customer may vary, promotional communication should adjust its language for different customers.[3]

Services are *inseparable;* they cannot exist without the source being present. Advertising can promote the respect, consideration, and friendliness of contact personnel as well as the trustworthiness and honesty of the company.

Finally services are *perishable* and therefore cannot be reused or stored. A service company's product comes in the form of people and their talents. Advertising can display these talented people effectively and offer a differential advantage that can be remembered and used as reference.

NEW YORK STATE'S TRAVEL AND TOURISM INDUSTRY CAMPAIGN[4]

In 1976 New York State's travel and tourism industry was declining. Its Department of Commerce and Wells, Rich, Greene, Inc., an advertising agency, prepared a promotional campaign to aid New York in reversing this trend.

Situation Analysis

As with most advertising campaigns the first step in this effort was a careful analysis of the situation. Research data secured through situation analysis revealed the following information.

---

[1]Philip Kotler, *Marketing Management, Analysis, Planning, and Control,* 5th ed. (Englewood Cliffs, NJ: Prentice-Hall, Inc., 1984), p. 465.

[2]A. Parasuraman, Valerie A. Zeithaml, and Leonard L. Berry, "A Conceptual Model of Service Quality and Its Implications for Future Research," *Journal of Marketing,* Vol. 49 (Fall 1985), pp. 41–50.

[3]Ibid., p. 47.

[4]Courtesy of Wells, Rich, Greene Inc., New York, NY, and New York State Department of Commerce.

Market and Market Trends

Travel and tourism in the United States was a growing industry, with services available from every state. For New York State, travel and tourism was a huge, income-producing industry and a significant source of needed jobs, business development, and tax revenues. It represented the second-largest industry in the state.

In 1976 New York State was facing a significant decline in its share of the tourism industry—from a 6.7 percent share in 1972 to 5.5 percent in 1976. At this rate the share of American travel dollars for New York State was projected at 4.8 percent for 1981. New York State's advertising budget for the promotion of tourism in 1976 was approximately $200,000; this represented an expenditure of 3 cents per traveler and placed New York last among all the states in promotion-spending per traveler.

Problems

Potential visitors to New York City declared the Number One problem to be the feeling that the city was too crowded and congested. Research conducted among New York residents indicated that they were more likely to spend their money on travel somewhere other than New York State.

Advertising Opportunities

New York State was an "outdoor" state, and its lakes and mountains were rated highly by vacationers. It also had a unique attraction in terms of its Broadway shows.

Target Market

The best prospects for drawing tourists to New York resided in the six surrounding states plus Ontario and Quebec. These areas accounted for 76 percent of all vacationers. Research among 1800 men and women from these areas, who had made vacation trips in the past three years, revealed the following characteristics of travel and tourism "users."

1. Demographic Segments. Travelers to New York generally constituted a mass market. There was some segmentation on the basis of state and city vacationers. Travelers to New York State were mostly couples and families with children; visitors to New York City were more likely to be couples with no children or singles.

2. Psychographic Segments. "Lifestyle" research was conducted to provide insights to the activities and interests and opinions of vacationers. Four basic psychographic segments emerged:
   outdoor enthusiasts liked the attractions of upstate New York,
   young fun-lovers liked New York City,
   sun resorters liked its mountains and the lakes, and
   culture-oriented vacationers liked sight-seeing.

3. Benefit Segments. The benefits sought by vacationers varied. For those who visited the Upstate area the primary attribute was the beautiful scenery. The primary benefit for those visiting New York

How to Sell
a Service —
How to Sell
a State
The
I ❤ NY
Campaign

I LOVE NEW YORK
New York City
VISITORS GUIDE
AND MAP

New York in Spring

New York City Tour Package Directory

CLIENT: New York State Department of
Commerce
AGENCY: Wells, Rich, Greene, Inc.

The Campaign Objective

The I Love NY campaign was designed to sell travel and tourism. Prior to its start, research showed that there were really two different services to be advertised: travel and tourism in Upstate New York, and travel and tourism in the Big Apple.

Creative Strategy for the New York City Campaign

The targets of this campaign were couples with no children and singles, identified by researchers as "young fun-lovers" or "culture-oriented vacationers." The primary appeal was the "unique selling proposition" that New York City offered—its theaters and night life.

Broadway and nine other ways to love New York.

1. The Great White Way:
The lights and the music! The laughter and the tears! There's only one Broadway, and New York's got it. That's why many of our 300 affordable "I Love New York City" vacation packages include theater tickets. You'll love New York-Broadway, or any way.

2. The Romantic Way:
How about a second honeymoon, with champagne and breakfast in bed? Two days and one night in a deluxe hotel costs as little as $157 for the two of you. And don't forget to take a romantic hansom cab ride through Central Park.

3. The Gourmet Way:
Entrecôte au poivre in an elegant French restaurant? Or pastrami on Delancey where the prices still ain't fancy? You'll find all the world's kitchens cooking in New York. And a delicious dinner is included in the price of many packages.

4. The Scenic Way:
Pick a package with a sightseeing tour built in, or go exploring on your own. $12 takes you around Manhattan on the Circle Line. A quarter buys a round trip on the Staten Island Ferry. And a walk across the Brooklyn Bridge is free.

5. The Sporting Way:
Watch the Rangers skate at the Garden, or do it yourself at Rockefeller Center. Catch the Yankees or the Mets. Or check the racing at Aqueduct. New York is a sports lover's mecca. So there's always something to cheer about.

6. The Shopper's Way:
From Bloomingdale's, head west to FAO Schwarz, Tiffany, Trump Tower, and all the fashionable stores down Fifth Avenue. At 34th Street, it's west again to Macy's and Gimbels, and then south to the avant-garde shops in SoHo and the bargain markets on Canal Street.

7. The Cultural Way:
Art? Madison Avenue has more galleries than ad agencies. Museums? There's the Metropolitan, the Modern, the Whitney and 77 more. And for you symphony and ballet lovers, only New York has Carnegie Hall, Lincoln Center, and the Brooklyn Academy of Music.

8. The Midnight Way:
New York doesn't roll up its sidewalks after dark. Jazz trios vamp through the wee hours at elegant midtown supper clubs. Dixieland bands play at the latenight spots in Greenwich Village. And yes, places like The Stork Club, The Rainbow Room, The Cotton Club and The Copacabana really do exist.

9. The Affordable Way:
Believe it or not, for as little as $35 each, Mom and Dad can spend a night and two days in a junior suite with a fully-equipped kitchenette, where kids under 12 can share your room free.

10. Your Way:
The best way to pick the package that's best for you is to read our I LOVE NEW YORK CITY GUIDE AND TOUR PACKAGES brochure and then see a Travel Agent. Advice from a Travel Agent is absolutely free, and so is the brochure. To get one, just call us at 1-800-554-3600. Or send the coupon. You'll love New York—Broadway and every way.

Photography by Judy Lawne.

Come to New York and See the World.

If you're looking for the place that has everything, there's only one place to visit. And that's New York. It's a whole world in a city.

The World Of Theater: All of New York is a stage. And it begins with Broadway. Where else can you find so many hit shows in one place? Only in New York!

The World Of Music: Spend an evening with Beethoven at Lincoln Center. Swing to the great jazz of Greenwich Village. Or rock yourself silly at the hottest dance spots found anywhere.

The World Of Art: From Rembrandt to Picasso. From Egyptian tombs to Indian teepees. Whatever kind of art you fancy, you'll find it in New York.

The World Of Fine Dining: Whether it's roast duck Peking in Chinatown, lasagna in Little Italy, or the finest French coq au vin found anywhere, there's a world of great taste waiting for you in New York.

The World Of Sights: What other city has a Statue of Liberty? A Rockefeller Center? Or a Bronx Zoo? Where else can you take a horse drawn carriage through Central Park, then sip champagne 107 stories up in the air? You guessed it...only in New York!

Find out all the affordable ways you can enjoy the five boroughs of New York. Send for our free I LOVE NEW YORK CITY VISITORS GUIDE AND MAP and the I LOVE NEW YORK TOUR PACKAGE DIRECTORY, or see a Travel Agent. To get

our brochure, simply call **1-800-637-8800.** Or send the coupon.

Execution

The technique of mood creation was used to present the benefits of the city. To create awareness of the excitement of visiting the "capital of entertainment," song-and-dance commercials, featuring Broadway celebrities, were used.

New York State Department of Commerce   60-seconds

(MUSIC IN)

(MUSIC IN)

(MUSIC UNDER) VO:
There's only one Broadway
. . . It's in New York . . .

(CAST OF "A CHORUS
LINE" SINGING I LOVE
N.Y.)

(CAST OF "THE WIZ"
SINGING I LOVE N.Y.)

(CAST OF "GREASE"
SINGING I LOVE N.Y.)

(CAST OF "THE KING AND
I" SINGING I LOVE N.Y.)

(CAST OF "ANNIE"
SINGING I LOVE N.Y.)

VO: Introducing "I Love
New York"

Broadway Show Tours
(CAST OF "CHAPTER TWO")

. . . 16 specially priced
packages of shows and
hotels.

For a free booklet, see your
travel agent or
(CAST OF "THE GIN GAME")

call toll free, 800 331-1000.
(CAST OF "THE MAGIC
SHOW")

DRACULA: I Love New York
. . . especially in the evening.

(MUSIC OUT)
(SUPER: I LOVE NEW YORK
BROADWAY SHOW TOURS)

Creative Strategy for the New York State Advertising Campaign

The New York State campaign wanted to reach families with children and couples, identified as "outdoor enthusiasts" and "sun resorters." The basic appeals were New York State's attributes—its lakes, mountains, and resort areas. Anglers, skiers, hikers, boaters, and nature lovers would respond to these attractions.

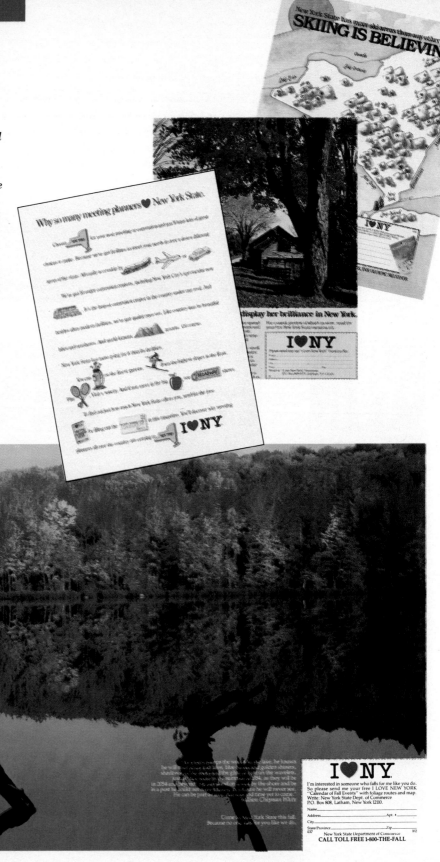

Execution

Noncelebrity personalities from other regions of the country were used to describe and emphasize the state's attributes. These average spokespeople, featured in television commercials, declared their enthusiasm for the state's exciting offerings.

New York State Department of Commerce

60 seconds

ANNCR: This vacation if you can't do what you love in New York, it probably can't be done. SINGERS: C'mon and see New York. . .

and ski New York. . .

C'mon and climb New York. . .

and raft New York. . .

HE SAYS: I Love New York.

SINGERS: C'mon and stroll New York. . .

and bike New York. . .

C'mon and fish New York. . .

and swim New York. . .

SHE SAYS: I Love New York.

ANNCR: Call 800-554-3800. Our activities number. . . .

whatever your family loves to do, we'll tell you where to do it. . .

with free vacation brochures.

SINGERS: C'mon and ride New York. . .

and drive New York. . .

and dive New York. . . . ANNCR: You'll love New York vacations.

SHE SAYS: I Love New York! SINGERS: I Love New York.

Supplementary Media and Sales Promotion

Although campaign strategy emphasized advertising, sales promotion and supplementary media proved memorable. Outdoor and transit advertising proclaimed the benefits of the city and state on streets and highways; trade shows developed the theme; and people everywhere wore buttons on their lapels and plastered bumper stickers on their cars. Graphic designer and illustrator Milton Glaser, who was instrumental in campaign development, created the I ♥ NY logo. He also produced an impressive series of posters to promote New York State festivals.

The campaign theme has been so successful it is
still going strong and has even been expanded. The
piece on the next page, created by SSC&B and run
in a recent issue of Fortune, advertises business in
New York State.

If you think New York State goes all out for a birthday, you should see what we do for business.

In terms of size and success, the celebration was uniquely New York.

And New York State can offer those same dimensions to your business. What other state has more capital? Or more Fortune 500 companies?

For that matter, what state has more colleges, museums, plays? Millions of acres of wilderness and parklands? Even spectacular sports teams? All for an unsurpassed quality of life.

What's more, New York State is continuing to cut taxes by billions of dollars. Combined with unequalled loans and financial assistance, our business benefits are one-of-a-kind.

And that's something to celebrate.

City was nightlife glamour as personified by Broadway. The conclusions from these data were that New York State offered two different "products"—Upstate New York State (excluding New York City) and the city itself. Each of these contained characteristics desired by different tourist segments.

Advertising Objectives

On the basis of the foregoing research two advertising campaigns with similar objectives were designed to reach two different tourist segments. For both the Upstate and New York City campaigns the objectives were the following:

1. To increase awareness of the site as a tourism and vacation resort.
2. To increase tourism to this site by describing its benefits and appeals, and by providing information on how to plan a vacation in this area.

Creative Strategy

The color booklet on the campaign, following p. 518, illustrates the advertising strategy for the I Love New York Campaign. Despite the similar advertising objectives, the creative strategy for the New York City and New York State advertising campaigns differed. These variations resulted from the difference in target markets.

The target for the New York City campaign consisted mainly of couples with no children, singles, and young "fun lovers." The primary appeal was the unique selling proposition the city offered—its theaters and nightlife. The execution technique used to present this benefit was primarily "mood creation" designed to promote awareness. Specifically, the unique characteristics of New York City were presented in "Song and Dance" commercials using Broadway celebrities (i.e. the Dracula commercial following p. 518). To meet the objective of increasing tourism by providing information on how to plan a vacation, print media presented information on the low cost of packages—which included hotel accommodations, dinner, and theater tickets. The ads also described music, restaurants, and shopping and included coupons for obtaining brochures for more information. This newspaper ad combines the descriptive approach with the attractive use of celebrity spokespersons (see Exhibit 24.1).

The target market for the Upstate campaign consisted of outdoor enthusiasts and sun resorters. The basic appeals of this campaign were New York State's natural attributes—its lakes, mountains, and islands—and its resort areas (see Exhibit 24.2). Its execution incorporated the use of noncelebrity personalities from other regions of the country featured in television commercials. Print media reinforced these concepts and presented details for obtaining information on vacation planning, much the same as the city campaign. To reinforce the emotionally

Incredible, Affordable New York.

New York reaches out to you with 104 skyscrapers, 23,400 restaurants, 410 theaters, 106,000 hotel rooms. That's incredible! Hundreds of package tours filled with stars, half price theater tickets, designer clothes at discount prices. That's affordable!

Fitzgerald wrote about it, Frank Sinatra sang about it, and you can enjoy it. The romance, the glamour and the spirit make New York unique. It's incredible, it's affordable, it's the heartbeat of the world.

To help remember all our special New York secrets, save this piece as a reference.

Getting To The Most Glorious City In The World Is As Easy As 1, 2 ...

Three and you're here. Child's play, really. Any major airline can book you here. Often at low excursion fares. Some cities have shuttle service every hour. Or your travel agent is equipped to arrange every step in a dazzling package. Last year New York welcomed 17,000,000 visitors who came by plane, train, boat or car to see and feel and fall in love with New York. This year, we'd love to welcome you. So come on along.

Where to stay, you ask? What is it that you want? Sparkling new hotels or majestic old ones. New York can offer an intimate European atmosphere or a traditional Japanese one. Whether it's a penthouse suite or an offbeat hideaway, your travel agent will know them all. From a 829.50 one night stay to a 8700 suite at the Plaza, there's really no end to the variety.

How will you get around? If you don't want to miss a beat, bring your most comfortable shoes, and stroll along to the rhythm of New York. The Whitney and Metropolitan Museums are just seven blocks apart. And Bloomingdale's, Bergdorf's, Bendel's and Tiffany's are all in a six block radius. But no compass is needed. The city streets are logically numbered so you can't get lost, no matter how excited you get. The streets are full of cabs. The Manhattan Yellow Pages are full of limo services. The Gray Line Tour will show you around town. And what a town it is.

"Exciting. Vital. Dramatic. I Feel More Alive When I'm In New York."

Everybody can feel it. East Side, West Side, all around the town. The spectacular variety of restaurants, stores, galleries, museums. It's the center of it all. Come to New York to rediscover your roots. Tour the world without leaving the city.

Chinatown, Little Italy, Yorkville and Harlem are only part of the history New York has to offer. In Chinatown, even the telephone booths look like pagodas. In Little Italy, you can walk from Milan to Sicily in five minutes. Yorkville has brought the spirit of Munich across the Atlantic. In Harlem, see some of the most beautiful churches in the world.

Shakespeare's always in town and there are always sporting events going on at Madison Square Garden. New York is an endless celebration of the individual. New York is, well... New York.

"There's A Front Row Seat Waiting For You In One Of New York's 410 Theaters— Some At Half Price."

That's how much New York wants you to be there at show time. *TKTS* is a special place on 47th St. and Broadway dedicated to slicing ticket prices in half. Explore the array of theatrical tastes—from Broadway's legendary musicals to the classics. Did you know that for the price of a movie ticket, you can watch up-and-coming artists in an Off Broadway Theater? *New York Magazine* can help. What's available, what's hot and what's not, it's all in the theater section. Movies are all around town—the best of the old and the best of the new. Broadway sparkles and glitters. It's a gold mine of talent. It all adds up to the magic of New York.

Artists Love New York Because New York Loves The Performing Arts.

It's in the air. Symphony, Opera, Ballet. New York is an art lover's paradise. The famed Lincoln Center is proof of that. Wander through 122 museums and 425 art galleries. Make curtain time at 410 theaters On and Off Broadway. Dance in all forms, the American Ballet Theatre, Joffrey and City Ballet call this city their home. The Dance Theatre of Harlem, Alvin Ailey and Martha Graham add even more movement. The Rockettes at Radio City Music Hall, Vivaldi at Carnegie Hall, Chopin at Avery Fisher Hall, Gilbert and Sullivan at the Light Opera of Manhattan—New York has it all. There's all-night jazz and rhythm & blues. There's foot-stomping country & western, discoing at Xenon, waltzing at Roseland.

There's so much to New York nights that we made up a special brochure—we've called it "I Love New York At Night Packages." It makes everything so simple. Hotel rooms, meals, theater tickets, sightseeing. Just pick your package, decide on the date and your travel agent will do the rest. Come watch a city reawaken after dark when New York's night crowd comes alive. You can always sleep at home!

"Buy The Best In New York. If You Can't Find It Here, It Probably Doesn't Exist."

New York brings out the passion in every shopper. Thirty tantalizing department stores, including the largest one in the world—Macy's. Spend some time in Bloomingdale's... Queen Elizabeth did. See the best of American fashion in the home of greats like Bill Blass, Calvin Klein and Halston. They all made it in New York! There's also haute couture from France, hand-made knits from Italy and crisp cottons from England.

Seventh Avenue features the world's most distinguished architects of fashion. It's really a fashion extravaganza. That's why Seventh Avenue is also called Fashion Avenue. Come and see why New York men and women always look "just right."

Browse through the best book shops. Go back in time in some of Madison Avenue's antique shops. Go bargain hunting on Orchard and Delancey Streets and find big designer names at small prices. Seek out the works of soon-to-be-famous artists in New York's Left Bank—Soho.

Splurge on famed Fifth Avenue or search for the exotic on the Upper West Side. *The Underground Shopper*—it's a guide that tells great shopping secrets. All you need is a little adventure. New York has everything else.

"All My Favorite Restaurants Are In New York— All 23,400 Of Them..."

Authentic family-style restaurants in Chinatown. Exotic curries in New York's "Little India." Foot-long hot dogs at Central Park Zoo. The most elegant Nouvelle Cuisine. Caviar bars. Sophisticated wine bars. Hot pretzels and chestnuts you buy on the street.

The fastest way to see all of New York is over cocktails—107 stories up at Windows On The World. It's one of New York's famed restaurants in the sky. Whether you want to dress up for blanquette de veau or dress down for a toasted bagel, you can in New York. No wonder New York bookstores carry dozens of different restaurant guides. *The Underground Gourmet* is especially useful for discovering wonderful dinners at wonderfully affordable prices.

And should you come on a package tour, delicious meals are often included. No other city can boast of such international fare. Sample the best of France, Italy, Pakistan, Greece, Israel and the Ukraine...Spain, Hungary, Ireland, Japan and Korea...did we leave out Brazil? Come to New York and go back to the old country to eat.

Million Dollar Tips For Free

Some Helpful Numbers To Keep With You:

NYC Convention and Visitors Bureau is for general information: **(212) 397-8222**

Big Apple Report gives you an hourly update on what's up in New York: **(212) 976-2323**

Lincoln Center gives all the information for the entire Lincoln Center complex: **(212) 877-1800**

Madison Square Garden Sporting Events are all under one number: **(212) 564-4400**

Ticketron is where you can charge Broadway or other entertainment to your credit card: **(212) 977-9020**

Jazzline gives you an up-to-date report on all the jazz around town: **(212) 423-0488**

Our "I Love New York City Travel Guide" and "I Love New York At Night Packages" tell you what's available. Just fill in the coupon below and we'll rush you—free—these helpful brochures. They tell about the best night life in the world. They're yours for the asking. See your Travel Agent or write:

New York State Department of Commerce, P.O. Box 808-U55, Latham, New York 12110

Please send me the "I Love New York City Travel Guide" and "I Love New York At Night Packages" brochures.

Name _____

Address _____

City _____

State _____

Province _____ Zip _____

I ♥ NY®

Whatever you do, just don't miss incredible, affordable New York. Wait and see, you'll love it too.

EXHIBIT 24.1
Print Ad for New York City

involving mood of the campaign, the now-familiar "I Love New York" slogan accompanied every ad, whether in print or set to music in broadcast commercials, and for both the city and state campaigns.

Media Plan and Strategy

An efficient media plan requires selection of the appropriate media, determination of the media budget and the development of a media schedule. The overall media strategy for this campaign was designed to reach potential users of travel and tourism services.

— Target Description: Research among potential users of travel and tourism services revealed relatively few distinctions in demographic characteristics, suggesting that this is a mass market. Moreover, although there were some variations in life styles among potential users of New York City versus Upstate services, many of their requirements were similar.

— Media Strategy: Based on the characteristics of the target market, advertising, which reaches large numbers of people with one message, was selected as the primary promotional effort. Sales promotion and supplementary media were added to provide support.

— Media Selection and Budget: The media budget was increased significantly. The amount spent on space, time, and production costs in 1977 through 1982 was the following:

Year	Media and Production Costs
1977/78	$3.3 million
1978/79	7.5
1979/80	6.1
1980/81	6.0
1981/82	7.0

The specific media selected for the advertising campaigns were the following: Consumer advertising was done on television, radio, in magazines, newspapers, and Sunday supplements, along with trade advertising in magazines; sales promotion and supplementary media was done at trade shows, meetings and conventions, and specialty advertising was used.

— Media Schedule: The media schedule listed the various media used and the time periods for insertions. Research disclosed that most vacation decisions were made one-and-a-half months prior to the actual vacation period and the schedule was designed accordingly.

Flighting was used for consumer advertising, since consumers generally made vacation decisions on a seasonal basis. The key season was summer, which provided 67 percent of the total tourism activity. *Continuous* advertising was used for the trade, to

EXHIBIT 24.2
Print Ad for New York State

The copy strategy for print media was to emphasize the basic benefits of New York State and how these benefits served tourists' needs.

keep travel agents aware of New York State as a potential vacation resort, and to stimulate the local and private sectors' involvement in tourism and tourism-related capital investment.

— Coordinating Promotional Efforts: Various promotional efforts were included in the "I Love New York" campaign. These techniques ranged from trade shows and festivals to specialties in the form of "bumper stickers" and "I Love New York" buttons. A schedule coordinating these efforts in the 1982/83 campaign is presented in Figure 24.1.

Evaluating Advertising Effectiveness

The "I Love New York" campaign included extensive research to evaluate the effectiveness of both individual advertisements and the entire campaign. Several techniques described in Chapter 23 were used for this purpose.

Copy Testing

Prior to their commitment to media many advertisements for this campaign were subject to copy tests. One of the methods most frequently used for this purpose was the Burke "Day-After-Recall" test. For example, a test was conducted to measure the communications effectiveness of the "I Love New York at Night" commercial. Over 200 program viewers were questioned by telephone the day after the commercial appeared during a television movie. The commercial generated recall from 53 percent of the respondents. This level of recall is more than twice as high as the Burke norm for 60-second commercials (24 percent). In addition the commercial achieved the highest scoring execution in terms of overall memorability based on 52 tests conducted among women for two years. Recall of the sales message was at a 50 percent level compared to the Burke norm of 22 percent for message recall.

Evaluating the Campaign Effectiveness

The objectives of the campaign were twofold—to create awareness and to increase travel to New York. To determine the extent to which the campaign achieved these objectives, tracking studies to examine trends were conducted.

Tracking Awareness   Research was conducted periodically to determine the "top-of-mind awareness" of vacation destinations (the first place that comes to mind) of those surveyed. For those respondents who were aware of the "I Love New York" advertising, "top-of-mind" awareness more than doubled. For those who were not aware of the advertising there was no significant statistical difference in top-of-mind awareness.

Increase in Sales   The most important measure of effectiveness was the extent to which travel activity to New York State increased. After the introduction of the "I Love New York" campaign the following

FIGURE 24.1 New York State Dept. of Commerce I Love New York Program Scheduling

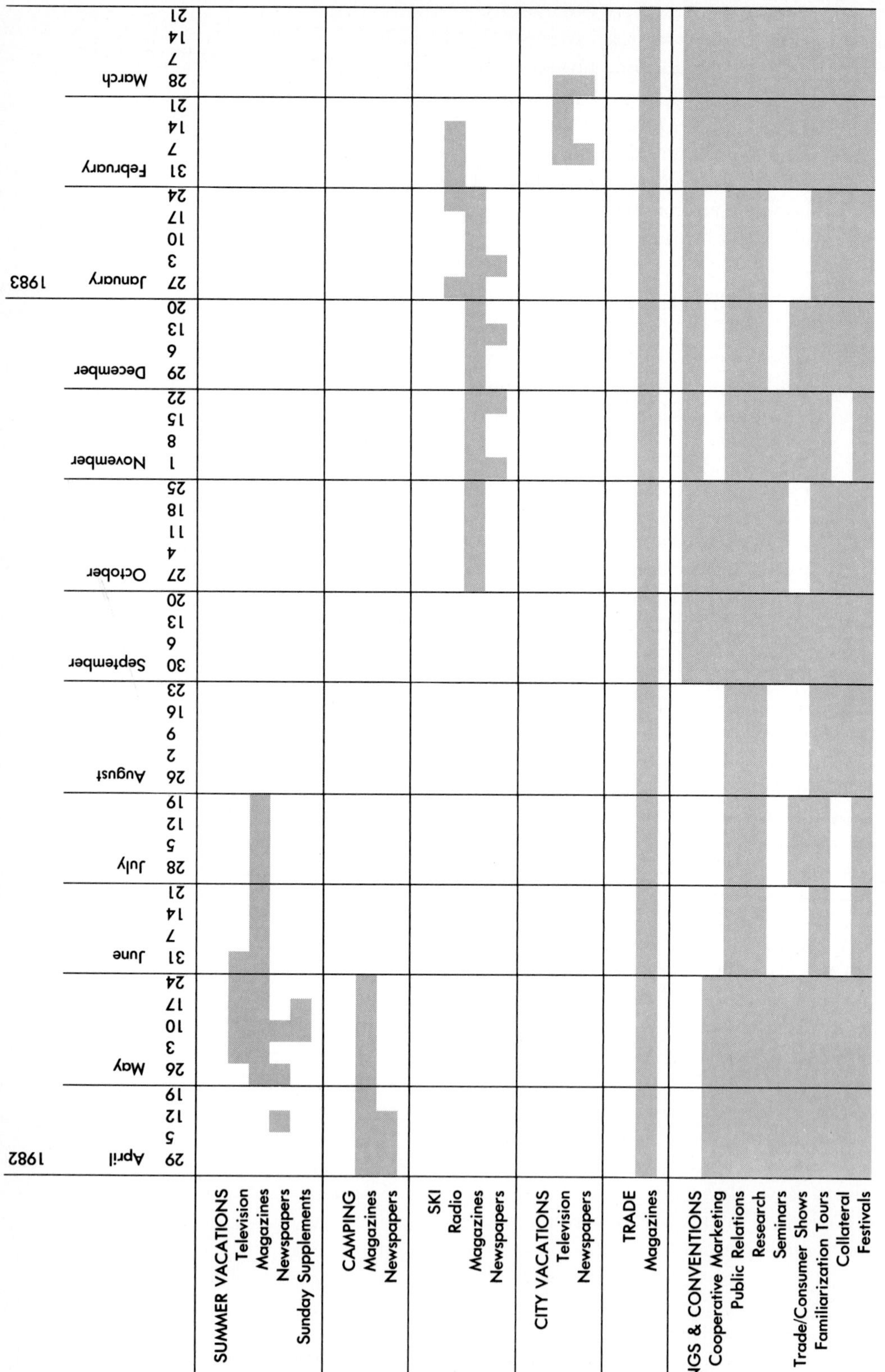
1982
1983
April 29 5 12 19
May 26 3 10 17 24
June 31 7 14 21
July 28 5 12 19
August 26 2 9 16 23
September 30 6 13 20
October 27 4 11 18 25
November 1 8 15 22
December 29 6 13 20
January 27 3 10 17 24
February 31 7 14 21
March 28 7 14 21
SUMMER VACATIONS
Television
Magazines
Newspapers
Sunday Supplements
CAMPING
Magazines
Newspapers
SKI
Radio
Magazines
Newspapers
CITY VACATIONS
Television
Newspapers
TRADE
Magazines
MEETINGS & CONVENTIONS
Cooperative Marketing
Public Relations
Research
Seminars
Trade/Consumer Shows
Familiarization Tours
Collateral
Festivals

Source: from "I Love New York Program Scheduling." Reprinted by permission of the New York State Department of Commerce.

trends were evident from 1976 to 1981:[5] New York doubled its travel receipts; reversed its declining share of the American travel market; more than doubled its theater ticket sales; and increased hotel occupancy rates.

Creative Effectiveness   The "I Love New York" campaign won 11 major awards including a special Tony award. The "I Love New York" music has become the official New York State song.

New York is continuing to reap the rewards of its campaign. About $3.8 billion of the $66.6 billion spent by people visiting New York State the past seven years is believed to be a direct result of the advertising drive, and the State estimates it has added 102,000 workers to accommodate the influx of tourists to both the state and New York City since 1977. However, because of inflation in production and media costs, it is estimated that New York will have to spend $2 million to $3 million more each year to maintain its current level of advertising buying. Moreover, as a result of strong competition from other states, tourism in New York has plateaued for the last two or three years.

SUMMARY

This chapter described the steps in an advertising campaign. In analyzing the situation relevant to the decline in New York State's travel and tourism industry, the market and market trends were examined; problems and opportunities were determined; and demographic, psychographic, and benefit segments were evaluated. Advertising objectives included an increase in awareness of New York as a vacation resort as well as an increase in tourism to the state. Campaigns for New York City appealed to love of theaters and night life; those for New York State praised its attributes as a vacation site. The basic theme "I Love New York," appeared in all advertisements.

Media were selected on the basis of the demographic characteristics of the target market, and a detailed media schedule was prepared using mostly television, radio, magazines, and newspapers. Sales promotion and supplementary media in the form of trade shows and specialty advertising were also used.

Copy testing was conducted through "day-after recall tests" and campaign effectiveness was evaluated through tracking studies. The campaign was considered a significant success and many states began using advertising campaigns to encourage tourism to their areas.

---

[5]"Tourists Don't Just Bite at Big Apple," *Advertising Age*, (May 20, 1985), p. 88E.

QUESTIONS FOR DISCUSSION

1. What characteristics distinguish services from products?
2. How can these characteristics be incorporated in service promotion?
3. What did an analysis of New York State's tourism industry in 1976 reveal?
4. How was this information used in the creation of the tourism advertising campaign?
5. How did the campaign for New York City differ from that of New York State? Why was this done?
6. What techniques were used to evaluate the campaign's effectiveness?
7. How did the New York State Tourism campaign apply the distinguishing service characteristics?
8. What suggestions would you give New York State to meet the tourism advertising competition emanating from other states?

AD PRACTICE

Contact the state tourism office in your state and determine what kind of promotional campaigns it uses to encourage tourism. Provide recommendations to improve this campaign.

25

Special-Purpose
Advertising Campaigns

Levi Strauss & Co. had difficulty entering the Japanese market probably because of the resistance of the Japanese to Western-style dress, and spent extensive funds with little success. The company finally decided to capitalize on the Japanese propensity for hero worship by developing a campaign using some of America's most famous movie stars to endorse the Levi brand. The idea had major problems since the top film stars whose personalities were compatible with Levi's brand (for example, Robert Redford, Jane Fonda) didn't do endorsements. A decision was made to use legendary stars such as John Wayne, Marilyn Monroe, and James Dean. The concept involved using outtakes of films in which each had appeared wearing Levi jeans (for example, Monroe in "The Misfits"). Three-and-a-half years after the campaign was introduced brand awareness soared from 6 percent to 75 percent, giving Levi Strauss the highest brand preference scores in the market.

Most advertising campaigns can be constructed using the format described in the previous chapters. Special considerations, however, are required in the creation of campaigns designed to reach nontypical consumer markets.

CHAPTER OBJECTIVE

— To discuss some of the characteristics and strategies that distinguish advertising campaigns in the following categories: international advertising, retail advertising, and business advertising

INTERNATIONAL ADVERTISING

Increasing competition in both local and foreign markets has generated growing interest in international advertising, advertising beyond a firm's national borders. An international advertising campaign encompasses a series of steps similar to those discussed in previous chapters; however, it involves additional concerns and is subject to restraints that may vary from country to country.

United States agencies remain the dominant force in international advertising, but inroads currently are being made by foreign agencies, who are increasing their international expansion through acquisition.[1] In response American agencies are engaging in acquisitions and joint ventures abroad. There are, however, American firms which used to dominate their markets who must now fight for market share with European and Japanese competitors. In automotive, chemicals, electronics-appliances, metal manufacturing, and commercial banking the number of American firms that are among the world's largest has declined in recent years.[2]

Situation Analysis

An advertiser wishing to capture a share of an international market must examine variations in that market very carefully. Despite numerous opportunities and research efforts there have been an abundance of international business blunders. It is easy, for example, to be misled by the apparent similarities between Japanese and American marketing situations and to overlook significant differences. When similarities do occur they are mainly because of the universal impact of economic factors. Differences stem largely from cultural consideration. It is apparent that the cross-cultural setting creates situations in which marketers must decide whether they should extend their standard marketing strategy to all countries or adjust their ways of doing business in foreign markets.[3]

Recently there has been an assertion of a "global market," suggesting that adjustment may not always be necessary. According to Theodore Levitt, "The world's needs and desires have been irrevocably homogenized" so that manufacturers can offer globally standardized items which are functional, reliable, and low-priced. Furthermore, he states, technologies, such as satellites and cables, are encouraging commonality, and their ability to reach many markets simultaneously are encouraging the development of new techniques for cross-cultural communications.[4]

---

[1]"How Pan-European Brands Stack Up," *Advertising Age* (July 11, 1985), p. 19.

[2]Nizam Aydin, Vern Terpstra, and Attila Yaprak, "The American Challenge in International Advertising, *Journal of Advertising*, Vol. 13, No. 4 (1984), pp. 49–59.

[3]Jagdish N. Sheth, "Cross-Cultural Influences on Buyer Seller Interaction/Negotiation Process," *Asian Pacific Journal of Management*, Vol. 1, No. 1 (September 1983), pp. 46–55.

[4]Theodore Levitt, "The Globalization of Markets," *Harvard Business Review* (May/June 1983), pp. 92–102.

This thesis has generated some controversy. Philip Kotler of Northwestern University supports advertising that is tailored to a local culture. He observes that there appears to be no evidence that consumers everywhere are becoming more alike. Jerry Wind of the Wharton School indicates that as people around the globe get better educated and more affluent their tastes actually diverge.[5]

Nonetheless several agencies are redesigning their organization structures, and large agencies are merging into larger groups to accommodate the global view. Britain's Saatchi & Saatchi acquired a number of American agencies to become the largest agency worldwide. Young and Rubicam has entered into a joint venture with Dentsu, Japan.[6] However few clients are positioning all their products globally; some are developing portfolios of products positioned globally, regionally, and locally. Even with global marketing, the advertising campaign may not look identical from country to country.[7]

International Marketing Intelligence and Research

According to James A. Thwaites, president of International Operations of 3M Company, good foreign market intelligence is critical for companies considering an entry into international marketing.[8] Several areas require specific investigation.

Language and Culture

Language barriers are considered one of the biggest deterrents to global advertising strategies. There are approximately 3000 different languages in the world, and when differences in dialects are included, this estimate may be as high as 10,000.[9] Translations, even when carefully considered, sometimes result in faux pas or failures. For example, "Body by Fisher" was translated as "Corpse by Fisher" and Pepsi's "Come Alive" was interpreted as "Come out of the grave."[10] An airline company from the United States lost customers after advertising its rendezvous lounges on flights to Brazil. *Rendezvous* in Portugese means "a place to have sex."[11] To avoid such blunders advertisers should engage in "back" translation; that is, someone familiar with the language of the country in which the message is to appear translates the foreign version back into English.

[5]Anne B. Fisher, "The Ad Biz Gloms onto 'Global'," *Fortune* (November 12, 1984), pp. 77–80.

[6]Nizam Aydin, Vern Terpstra, and Attila Yaprak, "The American Challenge in International Advertising" *Journal of Advertising*, Vol. 13, No. 4 (1984), pp. 49–59.

[7]Valerie Mackie and Dennis Chase, "Global Marketing: One Year Later," *Advertising Age* (June 24, 1985), p. 39.

[8]"Global Marketing Success Is Contingent on a Solid Bond of Foreign Market Intelligence," *Marketing News* (December 23, 1983), p. 1.

[9]Vern Terpstra and Kenneth David, *The Cultural Environment of International Business*, (Cincinnati, Ohio: South-Western Publishing Co.), 1985, p. 20.

[10]S. Watson Dunn, "Effect of National Identity on Multinational Promotions in Europe," *Journal of Marketing*, 40 (October 1976), pp. 50–57.

[11]Ann Helming, "Culture Shocks," *Advertising Age* (May 17 1982), pp. M-8, M-9.

Even if groups of countries employ the same language or speak languages that are mutually understandable, they do not have the same culture. The major cultural factors that tend to limit standardization, in addition to language, are literacy, the use of symbolism, attitudes toward women, and consumer consumption and shopping patterns. An understanding of the customs of the various countries is necessary in preparing a multinational advertising campaign. For example, a firm trying to introduce its mouthwash in Thailand promoted its product through an ad that displayed a young couple holding hands. Local customs in Thailand consider public display of physical contact between members of the opposite sex as unacceptable and offensive. Sales increased when two girls were selected to appear in the same scene.[12] Research to uncover potential problems should be conducted prior to introducing new campaigns.

Occasionally the custom of a country may offer marketing opportunities. Although some countries prohibit the use of alcoholic beverages, this provides an opportunity, as evidenced by the recent successful launch of several nonalcoholic beers in some Middle Eastern countries.[13]

Products and Product Usage

A survey of marketing executives from major American corporations indicated that they thought industrial and high technology products such as computer hardware, airlines, and photographic equipment were most appropriate for global marketing.[14] Such strategies also appeared to be effective for automobiles: the Datsun is now called Nissan as a global tactic. General Motors' advertising campaign presents individual cars, large and in color, with vague backgrounds to suggest no specific terrain. Comfort, luxury, and technology are the main themes. Because of the different cultures and religions each print advertisement must face, no human models are used. Instead the advertisements feature engineering-style line-drawings and "graph-paper" overlays to demonstrate a particular feature (see Exhibit 25.1).

It is important that a distinction be made between products and brands. While a global product may be standardized or sold with only minor modifications, positioning and promotion may have to reflect local conditions.[15] For example, the perceived importance of an automobile's characteristics may vary from country to country. Volvo has applied this concept successfully in the international markets. The company emphasizes economy, durability, and safety in America; status and leisure in France, performance in Germany, and safety in Switzerland. Price is

[12]Jonathan R. Slater, "The Hazards of Cross-Cultural Advertising," *Business America* (April 2, 1984), pp. 20–23.

[13]Morten M. Lenrow, "Mapping New Strategy for WorldBrands," *Advertising Age* (November 1, 1984), pp. 40–42.

[14]Nancy Giges, "Executives Say Global Strategies Are Limited," *Advertising Age* (June 3, 1985), p. 56.

[15]Alice Randolph, "Standardization Is Not Standard for Global Markets," *Marketing News* (September 27, 1985).

EXHIBIT 25.1
Global Automobile Advertising

The headline for this ad translates to "Chevrolet Corvette. Its advanced five-link control arm suspension is just one indication of its sophistication." Though written here in Arabic, it's suitable to appear in Spanish, Dutch, German, or French versions as well.

considered to be a critical variable to Mexican customers, and quality is of more importance to Venezuelans.[16]

The manner in which a product is used in various countries may require different positioning strategies. General Foods acknowledges such variations in product usage by positioning its Tang as a breakfast drink in the United States. However, in France, where orange juice is not usually consumed at breakfast, Tang is positioned as a refreshment.

Media Availabilities

Most countries have media similar to the United States—television, radio, newspapers, magazines, outdoor, and direct mail. The use of television, however, may be restricted due both to governmental restraints and the extent of television ownership within some populations.

Opportunities to advertise in magazines in international markets occur through American publishers, such as Time Inc. and Scientific American, who circulate international editions of their magazines abroad. Ads placed in foreign magazines can be placed individually or in a network of foreign countries through the service of organizations such as McGraw-Hill.

Outdoor advertising is available in most countries. Even in China, where advertising plays a minor role, an obvious visual barometer of how much the country has changed in recent years is that advertisements have replaced Chairman Mao's ideological statements on the outdoor boards of the cities (see Exhibit 25.2).

The major choice for advertisers in most countries is print media, since many restrictions are directed at broadcast media. The restrictions on television amount to a total ban of all advertising in the Scandinavian

---

[16]David A. Ricks, *Big Business Blunders, Mistakes in Multinational Marketing*, (Homewood, Ill.: Dow Jones, Irwin, 1983), p. 60.

EXHIBIT 25.2
Outdoor Advertisement for Sony in Beijing, China

countries or to limiting the available time in Finland, which allows only 12 minutes per channel per day.

Where advertising on television is permitted, there may be bans on advertising specific products such as tobacco, alcohol, pharmaceuticals, and health-aid products. Furthermore regulations vary from country to country—France bans advertising tourism and supermarket chains on television and does not allow auto ads to state the potential speed of a car; Britain prohibits advertising undertakers, the Bible, matrimonial agencies, and private detectives.[17]

J. Walter Thompson Company prepared a demonstration to show how a commercial broadcast in the United States and Britain for Kellogg's Corn Flakes would have to be adjusted to accommodate local customs and regulations in other countries.[18] Because France doesn't allow children to endorse products, the word Kellogg's on the child's T-shirt would be removed. Austria would eliminate his brothers and sisters as well since that nation forbids the use of children for commercials. (Advertisers there use midgets, provided they are more than 16 years of age.) West Germany is sensitive about competitive claims so the reference to "only Kellogg's makes the best flakes" would have to be removed. What would be left of the commercial would be a handful of film frames and a few isolated bars of jingle.

Advertising to children is subject to many restrictions in foreign countries.[19] For example, children cannot be used as endorsers of child-

[17]Laurel Wentz, "Local Laws Keep International Marketers Hopping," *Advertising Age* (July 1985), p. 20.

[18]Fred Rotherberg, "Retailoring U.S. Ads for Export," *Newsday* (November 6, 1983), Part II, p. 31.

[19]J. J. Boddewyn, "Advertising to Children" Regulation and Self-Regulation in 40 Countries, International Advertising Association, Inc. (April 1984).

related products in Australia, Finland, Ireland, Denmark, and France. In many more countries children cannot be used as presenters or commentators for products about which they cannot be expected to have any direct knowledge. A number of products or services cannot be advertised to children including alcohol, tobacco, and medicinal products.

The use of television is also limited by restrictions on the use of foreign television commercials overseas. In Australia, for example, foreign ad content in television advertising must remain at 20 percent.[20]

At this writing efforts are being made to provide greater standardization in regulations in international markets. The European Economic Committee has been pressing for relatively unregulated advertising on TV broadcasts across European borders.[21] Limitations would still exist, however; for example, advertising duration would be limited to 20 percent of total broadcasting time, products such as tobacco may be banned, and advertising for alcoholic beverages would be subject to "codes of conduct" in order to prevent abuse. Nevertheless standardization of advertising regulations will eliminate the need to vary campaigns from country to country and ease the preparation of cross-European campaigns.

Creative Strategy

Marketing research and intelligence can reveal similarities and differences among countries. Such information aids the advertiser in choosing between a standardized campaign and one that can be adapted to foreign needs.

Standardizing Advertising

Many companies have found significant benefits in standardizing their international approach to marketing. These benefits include increased effectiveness, reduced costs, and the ability to deal consistently with consumers worldwide. Such consistency in product style, packaging, brand name, and advertising may heighten the appropriate image companies want to project to their customers. McCann-Erickson Advertising Agency claims to have saved $90 million in production costs over twenty years by producing worldwide Coca-Cola commercials.[22] Victor Kiam, chairman of Remington Products, makes his own commercials in his Bridgeport, Connecticut, office and uses the same pitch in 15 languages. Since he started this five years ago Remington's unit sales have increased 60 percent in Great Britain and 140 percent in Australia.[23]

---

[20]Mary McKinney, "Australia Fighting Foreign Ads," *Advertising Age* (March 25, 1985), p. 60.

[21]Gary Yerkey, "Deregulate Ads, EEC Panel Favors Open Airwaves," *Advertising Age* (January 28, 1985), p. 60.

[22]John A. Quelch and Edward J. Hoff, "Customizing Global Marketing," *Harvard Business Review* (May-June 1986), p. 62.

[23]Anne B. Fisher, "The Ad Biz Gloms onto 'Global'," *Fortune* (November 12, 1984), pp. 77–80.

ROMANCE: A UNIVERSAL MOTIVE

A simple "boy meets girl" love story is used as the theme for Impulse's global TV advertising. A woman is seen leaving a confined space (a telephone booth or cab). A young man enters the same confined space and is instantly intrigued by the lingering fragrance. He grabs a bunch of flowers and chases after the woman, following the fragrance. He then presents her with the flowers, and she realizes that it is because she is wearing Impulse.

In some countries there are slight changes. In Italy, for example, the girl gets a single flower, since giving a whole bunch of flowers is viewed as a "pick up" in that country.

Impulse now dominates the body-spray market worldwide and claims a substantial share of the total deodorant market in many countries.

Source: Braina Olover, "A Little Romance Puts Impulse on Global Path," *Advertising Age,* June 24, 1985, p. 39.

A standardized campaign may be desirable when the company is well known and accepted as a leader. Although IBM uses some foreign advertising agencies, the basic theme featuring a Charlie Chaplin character is adapted in all European markets. Although its new American campaign uses M*A*S*H characters, Charlie Chaplin will continue to appear overseas. Pepsi, however, which is not as accepted or as well-known in Europe as Coca-Cola, uses different campaigns for its European markets.

Similar marketing strategies for more than one country are possible when buyers buy for the same reasons, when there are no overriding cultural factors in the product's marketing (ideas of beauty, taste and habit), and when there are no national regulations affecting a product's

composition and distribution.[24] Focusing on the similarities among nations can provide a fertile field for the international advertiser. Even if differences in language, diet, norms, and customs exist from country to country, motivations may be the same. For example, the desire to cook and prepare tasty meals for the family, the wish to be beautiful, and the desire for romance may exist in all cultures.

The "Manhattan Landing" commercial for British Airways has global recognition, and the same television "outer space" spots—unchanged except for voiceovers—ran in 45 countries. Even though the name of the "brand" or company did not appear for the first 70 seconds of the commercial—contrary to standard executions—the commercial was a success (see Exhibit 25.3).[25]

Efforts to determine commonalities across countries can focus on similarities in consumer response patterns.[26] Research should be designed to determine whether a set of benefits which make sense in one culture also make sense in other cultures. In cross-cultural advertising testing situations, it is best to test the basic premise and/or selling idea

EXHIBIT 25.3
British Airways Campaign

The "Manhattan Landing" TV spot shows New York hovering above a London street, then shifts to control room and landing—in all, 70 seconds before a voiceover is heard.

[24]Robert F. Roth, "Calling the Shots," *Advertising Age* (May 17, 1982), pp. M10–M11.

[25]Fred Danzig, "Selling an Airline at $10,000 a Word," *Advertising Age* (December 12, 1983), p. M-4.

[26]John U. Farley, "Are There Truly International Products—and Prime Prospects for Them?" *Journal of Advertising Research*, Vol. 26 (Oct./Nov., 1986), p. 18.

first, to be sure that it has some relevance for the target audience.[27] If the idea is relevant further testing can be conducted to determine whether these benefits are effectively presented.

Wherever the campaign is run, three basic communications questions should be answered.[28] Was the intended message delivered? Was any message not intended delivered? How did the potential customers evaluate the message, the characters, the setting, and the tone?

Slight variations are made in some advertisements to make them more relevant to the countries in which they appear. "Oil of Olay" has successfully advertised its product in countries all over the world using local women who wish to appear young and attractive. The widely acclaimed "Mean Joe Greene" ad for Coca-Cola substitutes an Asian athlete and a Brazilian soccer player for the famous athlete who tosses his jersey to an awe-struck young fan.

The Problems in International Advertising

As noted earlier, international advertisers have made significant blunders in the past by not being sensitive enough to cultural differences. Companies may acquire undesirable publicity and unfavorable reputations for their marketing programs in developing countries. The Nestlé Company was the target of such criticism for its marketing practices in Malaysia and the Philippines. It used "milk nurses" to visit new mothers, provide them with gifts and advice, and leave samples of a powdered baby formula. According to INFACT (the Infant Formula Action Coalition, an organization developed to counteract this program), the formula was excessively costly for the mothers in these areas and potentially harmful to the babies because of the scarcity of pure water and the lack of knowledge of sterilizing procedures. Nestlé defended its activities, but INFACT instituted a boycott of the product.

In 1981 the United Nations World Health Organization adopted a marketing code for instant formula due, in large part, to INFACT demands for curbs against marketing practices they felt were designed to wean mothers away from breastfeeding. The WHO code recommends the cessation of all advertising and promotion of infant formula directed at the general public, restricts the inclusion of certain material such as pictures of babies on product labels, and requires health warnings about using formula and a statement about the superiority of breastfeeding on labels.

Nestlé agreed to comply with the international marketing code and established a Nestlé Infant Formula Audit Commission to monitor the company's marketing practices. In 1983 the Commission reported that Nestlé had stopped giving away samples and improved health warnings on its labels.[29] In 1984 the boycott was lifted in the United States. How-

[27]Joseph T. Plummer, "The Role of Copy Research in Multinational Advertising," *Journal of Advertising Research,* Vol. 26 (Oct./Nov. 1986), p. 15.
[28]"Global advertisers should pay heed to contextual variations," *Marketing News* (Feb. 13, 1987), p. 18.
[29]"Audit Commission Mediates Infant Formula Disputes," *Marketing News* (November 11, 1983), p. 6.

ever, while Nestlé has been making significant inroads in adhering to the code, there are many other sellers of infant formula in the developing countries that are not.

American campaigns may be inappropriate for foreign countries because of differences in symbolic interpretations. For example, using the Marlboro Country theme with the grizzled American cowboy was a colossal failure in Hong Kong. There was an apparent clash between the "Marlboro Man" image and the dominant Chinese culture. The younger population did not relate to an older man, and cattle connoted rice paddies and "coolies."[30] To relate the ad to Chinese culture the older cowboy was replaced with a younger man wearing a white hat and riding a white horse. He was shown leading a group of ranchhands on a cattle drive, leaving the impression that he owned, not just worked on, the ranch. He was never shown alone, since Chinese are considered sociable people. Sales increased 40 percent after the new commercials were shown.

The Customized Approach

Many products and services cannot be sold with "one sound, one sight" worldwide. Variations in attitudes toward women in advertising suggest campaigns specifically tailored to some countries' requirements. Saudi Arabia prohibits photos of women so line art must be used in ads; in Pakistan women can be shown only in black shrouds. Even in more modern Malaysia, female models must have their shoulders covered to avoid any hint of nudity (see Exhibit 25.4).

Shopping patterns vary widely among countries. Advertising a specific price may be difficult. This is particularly true in those countries where bargaining is common, and, in fact, is considered a source of satisfaction.

Consumption patterns may also encourage a nonstandardized approach. McDonalds finds resistance to fast-food dining in some countries.[31] In Germany, for example, such an eating style is viewed as too "plastic." In an effort to improve its image, McDonald's has designed a corporate campaign for Germany. One ad shows a well-dressed man preparing to eat a bowl of soup, but the tip of his necktie has fallen into the bowl. The caption reads: "Every culture's eating style has its little tricks," and points out that even gourmets don't eat at fancy restaurants every day (see Exhibit 25.5).

Kotler proposes a customization index, which measures a product, buyer-behavior, and environmental dissimilarities between the source and target countries to indicate discrepancies. The index allows a manager to decide whether the discrepancies are significant enough to require customization.[32]

EXHIBIT 25.4
Meeting Foreign Ad Requirements

[30]Dennis Chase, "The Cowboy Gets Worked Over in the East," *Advertising Age* (January 31, 1983), p. M19.

[31]Dagmar Mussy, "McDonald's Image Gets Polished in German Ads," *Advertising Age* (July 8, 1985), p. 38.

[32]Alice Rudolph, "Standardization Is Not Standard for Global Marketers,". . .

EXHIBIT 25.5
Adapting to Foreign Culture

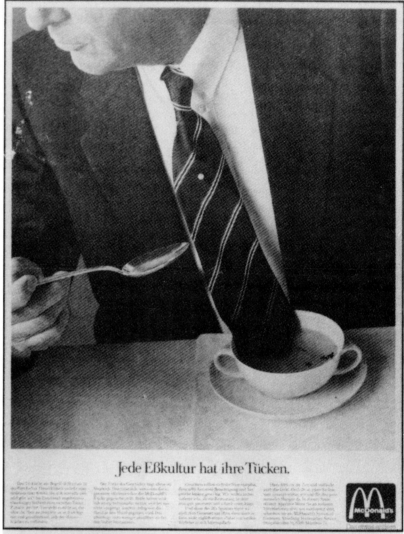

McDonald's first corporate campaign in Germany.

Evaluating Advertising Effectiveness

International campaigns require continual monitoring, particularly since blunders may cause extensive damage to the advertiser. Their effectiveness, similar to all advertising campaigns, must be judged on the basis of their objectives. The techniques for evaluating advertising effectiveness, discussed in earlier chapters, are applied to international advertising campaigns as well.

Research conducted by the Compton Advertising Agency had found that, although British Airways was carrying more passengers to more continents than any other airline, Pan Am was most frequently mentioned as the largest carrier. Consumers usually related "bigness" to advertising visibility and awareness.[33] Moreover, consumers stated they had not seen much advertising for British Airways.

The basic objective of the British Airways campaign was to attract awareness. The "Manhattan Landing" commercial was designed to overcome this problem and was shown in 40 countries throughout the world. Tracking studies revealed that the ad, which resembled "Close Encounters of a Third Kind," created a significant increase in awareness. In addition British Airways sold twice as many package tours as it had before the campaign started.

RETAIL ADVERTISING

Retail advertising is often called *local advertising*, since the target market is frequently local in nature; however, institutions that may advertise locally, such as banking, financial services, and real estate organizations, are not considered part of the retail trade by the Bureau of the Census. Moreover, some retailers such as Sears, Roebuck and J. C. Penney advertise on a national basis. This *retail advertising* specifically refers to communications disseminated by retail institutions.

Advertising by retailers is designed to perform several functions: selling products, encouraging store traffic, announcing sales, and creating and communicating a store image or "personality." While some retailers make use of advertising agencies, more frequently a retailer's advertising department is responsible for the promotional effort. The department is generally more familiar with the local market and its needs, and more flexible in adapting to local conditions (for example, a sudden snowstorm or a special local event).

Standard methods are used for determining the advertising appropriation. Budget classifications incorporate specific retailing requirements, and, for example, may include divisions and departments, as well as time intervals. Advertising expenditures by retail institutions frequently take on flighted characteristics; that is, they are increased significantly in periods such as back-to-school and Christmas time.

Media Choice

Practically all media can carry a retailer's message; however, newspapers carry the bulk of retail advertising. This is understandable since newspapers appear daily and are current. Moreover, many consumers consult newspapers for their shopping trips and use newspaper ads to compare prices. Sunday newspapers carry multiple-page inserts where retailers feature their products and offer coupons and discounts. Some newspapers even provide research efforts to retailers.

---

[33]Fred Danzig, "Selling an Airline at $10,000 a Word," *Advertising Age* (December 12, 1983), p. M-4.

Magazines are used less frequently. They tend to be more costly than newspapers for advertising and result in waste circulation since many of their readers may be located beyond a local market. Nevertheless, retailers place ads in magazines to create prestigious images, and chain stores that are geographically dispersed find magazines useful. Fashion merchandise can be displayed more effectively in magazines because of the reproduction limitations in newspapers.

The local character of radio stations and the relatively inexpensive cost of such advertising offer many opportunities for retailers. The kind of radio station selected depends on the trading area reached and the characteritistics of the radio listeners. Retailers may draw consumers from beyond an immediate area, and radio stations can be selected that attract these groups.

While retailers have used local television in recent years large chains have invested heavily in network television. Sears has become the fourth largest advertiser in the United States, spending a large portion of its advertising budget on television.[34]

Direct mail is part of most retailing advertising campaigns. Such mailers range from postcards announcing sales, to extravagant brochures with fine paper and expensive color photographs, to 100-page Christmas catalogs.

Video technology may provide an important communication medium for retailers in the future. Interactive computers have been placed in stores to provide catalog information, department location, and availability of products. Currently Channel 2000 and Qube offer Videotex, an in-home shopping medium. Future adoption of this interactive technology by retailers may provide a new channel for disseminating information to consumers.[35]

Creating Retail Advertising

While the objective of retail advertising may be the same as that for national advertising, a number of characteristics differentiate these efforts. The time span for preparing and implementing retailing advertising is shorter, limiting the ability to test and review advertisements. The feedback period also is shorter, permitting retail advertisers to adapt to changes more rapidly than national advertisers. Since retailers are close to target markets and must constantly monitor and adapt to changes in local conditions, they tend to use house agencies or media services in the preparation of their advertisements rather than employing advertising agencies.

---

[34]"100 Leading Advertisers by Primary Business," *Advertising Age* (September 4, 1986), p. 160.

[35]Joel E. Urbany and W. Wayne Talarzyk, "Videotex: Implications for Retailing," *Journal of Retailing*, Vol. 59 (Fall 1983), pp. 76–90.

EXHIBIT 25.6
Department Store "Personalities" in
Retail Ads

In general, the structure of retail ads contains the same elements as national advertising; however both the emphasis and manner of presentation may differ. In retail advertising the primary emphasis is on the close and the copy frequently stresses the urgency to "buy now." Unlike national ads, the body copy of retail advertisements contains more specific information such as price, variations of the item that are available, location of the store, and so on.

Despite their differences retailers can adopt some of the strategic approaches of national advertisers such as situation analysis designed to encompass information about the store, the community, and the marketplace; and establishing objectives and developing strategic approaches for their advertising campaigns. Since much retail advertising involves stores, one strategy particularly useful for retailers is the creation of store "personalities" which evolves from many factors—their ambience, prices, services, customers, and neighborhood. These same personalities can then be reflected in their advertisements through the copy used in ads, the manner in which it is presented, and in the creation of a logo or a slogan. Recently stores have employed celebrities who embody elements of the established personalities (see Exhibit 25.6).

BUSINESS-TO-BUSINESS ADVERTISING

Advertising rarely dominates the promotional budgets of organizations that sell to business units. Nevertheless, business-to-business advertising is widespread and may take the form of industrial advertising, trade advertising, and professional advertising.

Industrial Advertising
According to the Industrial Marketing Review Board *industrial goods* are "goods which are used in producing consumers' goods, other business or industrial goods, and services." Industrial advertising promotes

these goods which are classified as capital items, materials, parts, supplies, and services.

Capital items consist of installations and fixed equipment, and require top level purchasing decisions. *Materials* can either be raw materials such as farm products, natural products such as iron ore, or manufactured items. *Parts* are items added to finished products with no further changes in form (radios or tires added to cars). *Supplies*, such as typing paper or brooms, are similar to consumer convenience goods and are usually purchased with a minimum effort. *Services* include maintenance and repair services and are frequently purchased on the basis of the supplier's reputation and personnel.

Trade Advertising

Trade advertising is frequently conducted in conjunction with consumer advertising campaigns and is designed to encourage wholesalers and retailers to carry and sell an advertisers' product. Some trade ads are similar in appearance to consumer advertising; however, the targets differ as does the media in which the ads appear. Procter & Gamble, for example, anticipating an increase in the decaffeinated coffee market, prepared a trade advertisement, which appeared in restaurant trade magazines, encouraging restaurants to serve brewed decaffeinated (see Exhibit 25.7).

Professional Advertising

Many firms offer their goods and services to professional groups such as doctors and dentists. Drug companies sell to this target mainly through "detail" people; that is, salespeople visit professionals and try to interest them in a company's products and services. This personal selling effort is particularly effective, since the "detail" representative can seek out the professional, respond to his or her questions, and offer samples for trial.

Professional advertising is part of the promotional mix and refers to ads generally appearing in professional journals. However, such ads are subject to FDA restrictions—they may not overclaim and must state contraindications of the drug offered (see Exhibit 25.8).

The Business Market

The number of potential customers in the business market is much smaller than the consumer market. Business customers buy in larger quantities and tend to be more informed than consumers.

Information concerning the business market is available from many sources. The Standard Industrial Classification (SIC) compiled by the U. S. Office of Management and Budget provides a listing of business customers. There are eight general classifications:[36] agricultural, for-

---

[36]Substantial data relating to SIC classifications are available from publications such as the Bureau of Industrial Economics' *Industrial Outlooks, Dun & Bradstreet's Middle Market Directory* and Sales & Marketing Management's Survey of *Industrial & Commercial Buying Power.*

EXHIBIT 25.8
Drug Advertisement

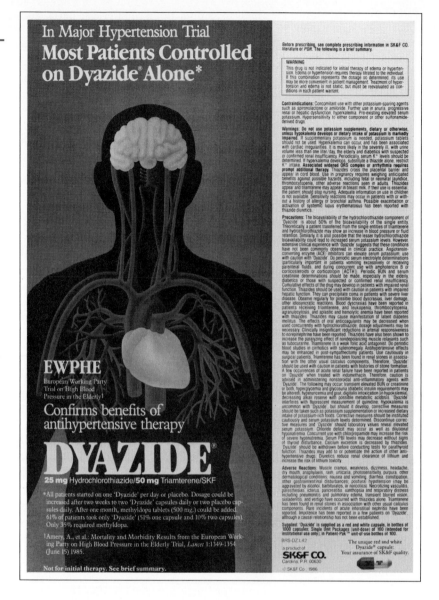

estry, and fishing; mining; construction; manufacturing; transportation, communication; electric, gas, and sanitary services; wholesale and retail trade; and finance, insurance, and real estate services.

Purchasing requirements differ among businesses, suggesting the need for variations in promotional appeals, rather than a standardized message. For these reasons personal selling is the dominant element in promotional efforts directed towards business targets. However, trade shows are also widely used in selling to business. Originally they were considered a means of generating goodwill; more recently these shows have been used more aggressively to sell products.[37] Catalogs offering

---

[37]Thomas V. Bonoma, "Get More Out of Your Trade Shows," *Harvard Business Review* (January/February 1985), p. 83.

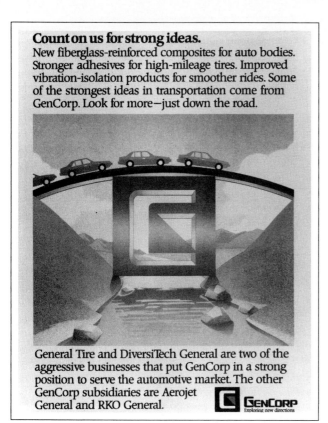

EXHIBIT 25.9
Promoting Products and Plans

illustrations and detailed descriptions of the merchandise are used by many businesses as a means of selling their wares.

While advertising represents a relatively smaller portion of the business promotional budget it can create awareness, generate leads, and develop a company's image (see Exhibit 25.9). Bethlehem Steel, for example, prepared a campaign that promoted the strength of its low-cost sheet steel used in car bumpers. At the same time it conducted a corporate campaign to indicate that it was making changes and was, in fact, a "good company".[38]

Advertising Budgets

Business advertisers can use the same methods in arriving at their budgets as consumer advertisers do. Although industrial advertisers used mainly the arbitrary method in the early 1970s, they have turned to the objective-and-task method in recent years.[39] Nonetheless industrial advertisers can still develop more efficient budgeting methods. This requires increasing sophistication in budgeting techniques, as well as the elimination of many nonadvertising items from the industrial budget.

---

[38]"Industrial Advertisers, Start Your Engines," *S&MM* (April 25, 1983), p. 42.

[39]Vincent J. Blasko & Charles H. Patti, "The Advertising Budgeting Practices of Industrial Marketers," *Journal of Marketing*, Vol. 48 (Fall 1984), pp. 104–10.

Business Publications

The greatest amount of business-to-business advertising occurs through the business press; traditional consumer media, including television and direct mail, are also used for selling to business units. Business publications date back to the early 1800s; more than thirty of the publications launched before the Civil War are still being published, including the *Daily News Record* and the *Architectural Record*. These publications serve a specific field and provide a specific function. With rare exception, they are not sold on newsstands and are directed to readers only by subscriptions. The average circulation for business publications is approximately 50,000; however, there are some that have a circulation over 500,000. Despite their relatively small circulation the audiences have enormous buying power; thus a large proportion of the average business-to-business advertising budget is allocated to advertising in business publications.

Kinds of Business Publications

The American Business Press, created in the 1960s, is a trade association concerned with business publication developments and the future of the business press. It provides data on business-to-business advertising, sets standards for publication (such as those for the use of color), and acts as a strong voice for the industry in such issues as fighting for equity in postal rates.[40] Business publications fall into several categories: industrial publications, trade publications, and professional publications (see Exhibit 25.10).

Industrial Publications

The audience for industrial publications consists mainly of people in manufacturing industries. Advertising in such publications are designed to reach the person who directly or indirectly influences the purchasing decision. Since the cost of an industrial sales call is extremely high, and getting higher, advertising may be an efficient means of either creating awareness, creating preference, or motivating a purchaser to seek out an advertising firm.

Industrial publications are divided into two types. *Horizontal publications* reach a specific category or job function across many different industries. *Industry Week*, for example, declares it reaches 1.5 million management readers. *Vertical publications* reach various groups within the same industry. *Dairy Extra* is a vertical publication that may reach many segments of the dairy industry.

Professional Publications

Professional publications are designed to reach the various professions such as doctors, lawyers, architects, accountants, and engineers. Profes-

---

[40]Charles S. Mill, "American Business Press," *Advertising Age* (May 11, 1981), p. S–9.

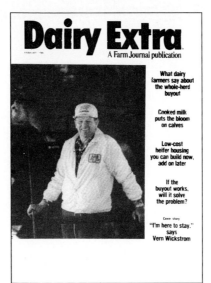

EXHIBIT 25.10
Business Publications

sional advertising is particularly important because it reaches the group that is influential in making ultimate decisions for many clients or patients.

Trade Publications

Trade publications are those publications that reach the various institutions in channels of distribution such as wholesalers and retailers. These publications are usually specific to a "trade," or business, for example, *Progressive Grocer* and *Children's Business*. The advertising is designed to encourage wholesalers and retailers to stock and "push" the merchandise they carry.

Buying Space in Business Publications

Information concerning the costs of business publications may be found in the SRDS' *Business Publications Rate and Data Book*. Rates for business publications are quoted in a manner similar to that of consumer magazines.

Many business publications use reader service cards, commonly known as "bingo cards." Their purpose is to stimulate inquiries by making it easy for readers to request more information. Readers merely have to circle the numbers listed on the cards that correspond to the advertised products and services in which they are interested.

Circulation

There are basically only two kinds of business magazine circulation—paid and free. Which method of circulation is best is the subject of much discussion. Each has its advantages: paid circulation assumes "wantedness," free circulation provides a larger audience but may not reach the most interested target group.

One variation of the free method is *controlled circulation*, officially called *qualified circulation*. Controlled circulation is secured through the development of a list of people who have certain qualifications or characteristics. These people are then offered a specially edited publication at no cost. The publisher relies totally upon advertising for income. Thus controlled circulation provides free delivery but seeks out the appropriate target market. In the final analysis the best method is the one that is applicable to a given industry.

Creative Strategy

Business units tend to require information, and rational copy appeals are more likely to provide such data. Advertising in business publications tends to be more informative than that in consumer publications. However, advertisers still need to pay attention to the creative aspects of their messages. Illustrations can be designed to attract attention, arouse curiosity, and show comparisons.

There has always been general acknowledgment that marketing the same product to industrial and consumer markets required different promotional efforts. (see Exhibit 25.11). Recently, however, there has been a growing awareness of similarities between these two activities.[41] In industrial advertising, for example, it is useful to stress "owner benefits" rather than design qualities. The fact that a knife made of chromium-vanadium steel is of good quality is mainly of interest to other designers

---

[41]Edward F. Fern & James R. Brown, "The Industrial/Consumer Marketing Dichotomy: A Case of Insufficient Justification," *Journal of Marketing*, Vol. 48 (Spring 1984), pp. 68–77.

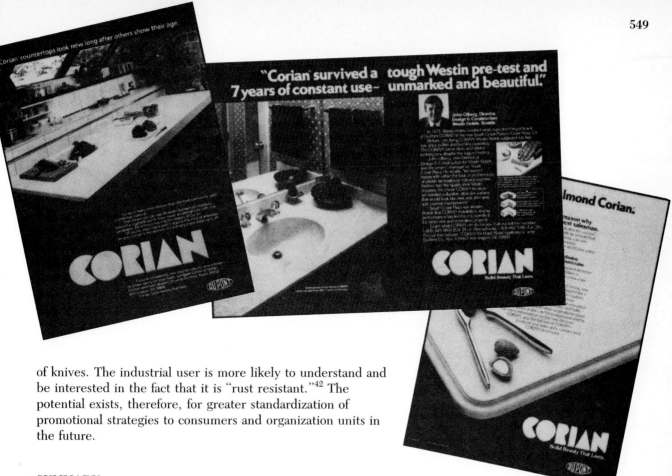

of knives. The industrial user is more likely to understand and be interested in the fact that it is "rust resistant."[42] The potential exists, therefore, for greater standardization of promotional strategies to consumers and organization units in the future.

EXHIBIT 25.11
Different Approaches in Consumer, Hotel, Motel, and Trade Ads for the Same Product

SUMMARY

Advertising campaigns that go beyond national borders, that are conducted by retailing institutions or designed for business customers, may involve special considerations. In international advertising there have been suggestions that emergence of a "global" market calls for the creation of standardized advertising campaigns that can be used worldwide. However, a global approach is not always desirable, particularly where there are significant cultural differences among countries.

Preparing an international campaign requires research into language variations, product or product usage differences, and cultural distinctions.

Standardized advertising may be effective where ideas of beauty, taste, and habit are similar, and where no national regulations affect a product's composition and distribution. Limits to standardization include language variations, literacy, the use of symbols, attitudes toward women, and consumer consumption and shopping patterns.

Retail advertising forms the major portion of a retailer's promotional mix. Such advertising can sell products, encourage store traffic, announce sales, and create and communicate a store image.

---

[42]Herbert L. Kahn, "Your own brand of advertising for nonconsumer products," *Harvard Business Review* (Jan./Feb., 1986), p. 26.

Newspapers are used most widely for retail advertising, although local radio and television are also available, and network television is used extensively by large retail chains. Direct mail is important, and videotex technology offers an advertising medium that may be significant in future retailing.

The time span for preparing retail advertising is short; however the feedback period is also short, permitting retailers to adapt to changing conditions. Retail advertising may merely feature "item and price," although retailers have begun to adopt some of the strategic approaches of national advertisers and are developing store personalities in their ads.

Business-to-business advertising encompasses industrial advertising, trade advertising, and professional advertising. Most firms selling to business place their heaviest promotional efforts in personal selling. Trade shows and catalogs are also widely used. Business-to-business advertising is employed to create awareness, generate leads, and develop a company's image.

Business units require information, necessitating rational copy appeals. However, business-to-business ads may also incorporate creative aspects to attract attention and arouse curiosity.

QUESTIONS FOR DISCUSSION

1. What are the advantages of global marketing?
2. What are some of the barriers that may prevent effective global advertising?
3. What are the restrictions to media use in foreign markets?
4. Under what circumstances is a standardized advertising campaign effective? When should the campaign be customized?
5. Discuss the media used for retail advertising, noting their special capabilities for retailers.
6. How are retail ads different from general consumer ads?
7. What kinds of business publications are used for business-to-business advertising?
8. What is meant by a *horizontal publication*? a *vertical publication*?
9. What is the purpose of a bingo card?
10. What is meant by "controlled circulation"?

KEY TERMS

global market

international advertising

industrial advertising

trade advertising

capital items

professional advertising

horizontal publications

vertical publications

controlled, or qualified, circulation

AD PRACTICE

Find ads in the following categories for a single product: consumer advertising, international advertising, retail advertising, and business advertising. Discuss differences among these ads in terms of the publications they appeared in, their basic appeals, the use of illustrations, and the manner of presentation.

CASE

Global Advertising

Procter & Gamble has performed miserably since introducing its products in Japan in 1973, losing in the process an estimated quarter of a billion dollars. Some of the mistakes made by P & G involved their advertising strategies.

In the late 1970s Japanese housewives voted Procter & Gamble's Cheer ads the least liked on television because they were repulsed by a hard sell that stressed product benefits and user testimonials. Commercials for Procter & Gamble's Camay soap were also disliked. In one commercial in the late 1970s, a man meeting a woman for the first time immediately compares her skin to that of a fine porcelain doll. The Japanese were insulted. Japanese ad executives warned that for a Japanese man to say something like that to a Japanese woman would indicate he was either unsophisticated or rude; P & G, however, went ahead with the commercial.

Another mistake was Procter & Gamble's global policy of advertising the brand and not the company. Japanese people like to have a relationship with a manufacturer. It took some time before Procter & Gamble flashed the company's name at the end of its commercials, a practice usually found in Japanese advertisements.

DISCUSSION QUESTIONS

1. Describe Procter & Gamble's international marketing strategy.
2. What are some of the problems they encountered?
3. What recommendations would you make for helping them to prepare effectively for their Japanese advertising campaigns?

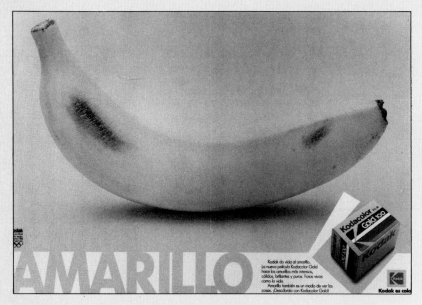

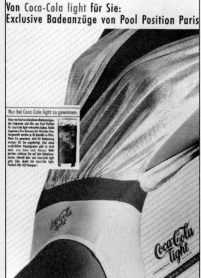

Kodak and Coca-Cola have developed global marketing and advertising strategies. Although the companies have made some product modifications to accommodate international tastes, both have reached their target markets with their advertising.

Source: Andrew Tanzer, "They Didn't Listen to Anybody," *Forbes* (December 15, 1986), pp. 168–69.

CASE

Standardizing and Customizing International Advertising

The two largest auto companies in the world use diametrically op posed strategies for advertising in world markets. General Motor uses a single agency, McCann-Erickson Worldwide, on a variety of assignments in 37 countries. Although major markets such as Western Europe run independently, much of GM's overseas car advertising is created in Detroit. For example, a print ad running in several Middle East and African markets would be prepared and translated by McCann in Detroit, shipped to local McCann branches for idiomatic translation by local personnel, and returned to the United States for production.

Ford uses 24 different agencies—21 outside the United States—although J. Walter Thompson Co. is most widely used. Each local Ford sales arm directly controls its own advertising agency, and there is no attempt to create a unified advertising theme. However, J. Walter

Thompson's VP-international worldwide client-service director coordinates Ford's international advertising. He views hundreds of commercials and print ads and travels hundreds of thousands of miles yearly, showing local agencies what other agencies are doing. He tries to nurture a "Ford feel" that doesn't clash with the message in other markets.

DISCUSSION QUESTIONS

1. Explain the different international advertising strategies used by GM and Ford.
2. Discuss the advantages and disadvantages of each strategy.
3. Which do you believe is most effective? Why?

Source: Jesse Snyder, "Global Ads Hit Snags," *Advertising Age* (March 24, 1986), p. 80.

IV

Advertising: A Macro View

P_{ART} IV examines advertising from a macro perspective. It studies the nature and role of advertising within an entire economic system with special emphasis on its aggregate performance. Specifically, it examines the effects of advertising in our socioeconomic system, as well as the efforts designed to regulate and control this promotional activity.

26

The Social Aspects of Advertising

In 1986 several well-known dermatologists strongly objected to a series of advertisements using as spokesperson Dr. Christiaan Barnard, the South African surgeon who conducted the first successful human heart transplant. Dr. Barnard promoted a face cream that "can make older skin behave and look like younger skin." The doctor who no longer practices medicine because of severe arthritis, defended his participation in the ad campaign, saying that, in laboratory tests, the active ingredient in the cream had the ability to cause rejuvenation of cells. He also said that he needed the money he was paid for the endorsement.

There was nothing illegal about this endorsement. However, the dermatologists objected to the ads since they suggest, without substantiation, that the line of skincare products (called Glycel) would make old skin young again. They also criticized Dr. Barnard for his portrayal in the advertisements as an expert in a field, dermatology, that was not his specialty.

An evaluation of advertising from a macro perspective requires an examination of its aggregate effects on society and the economy. These two areas are closely interrelated. Social issues, however, focus on advertising's impact on the public, rather than the business economy.

SOCIAL CRITICISMS AND DEFENSES OF ADVERTISING

Social accusations have been directed at advertising in such pungent, imaginative, and descriptive terms that they appear to emanate from talents as creative as those within the advertising community. Advertising is said to destroy the finer things of life. It is described by some as vulgar, idiotic, degrading, shrill, noisy, blatant, and aggressive. It is said to exalt lower values, glorify mediocrity, and good taste.[1]

A number of humanities and social science scholars view advertising as intrusive and environmental and its effects as inescapable and profound. They see it as reinforcing materiality, cynicism, irrationality, selfishness, anxiety, social competitiveness, sexual preoccupation, powerlessness and loss of self respect.[2]

These are strong indictments. They imply that advertising is a powerful force. However, the history of advertising is replete with failures of advertising campaigns, difficulties in proving advertising effectiveness, and indications that only a small percentage of advertising is actually noticed.

In Defense of Advertising

Socially, defenders of advertising note that it has a beneficial effect on several basic areas:[3]

— *Information:* Advertising aids in the education of the general public; facilitates the exercise of free choice and free will; and subsidizes mass communication providing essential services to the public.

— *Values and Life-Styles:* Advertising contributes to improvement in the standard of living; contributes to the sharing of opulence among the masses; and represents an essential factor in the economies of abundance.

— *Creative Experience:* Advertising adds new and interesting experiences to life.

However, some observers declare that advertising may contain misinformation and be excessively persuasive, that the values and life-styles promoted through advertising are unacceptable, and that the new and interesting experiences are often objectionable. While none of the critics tend to argue that advertising alone is responsible for these conditions it is appropriate for researchers to take assertions about advertising's

---

[1]Claude Robinson, "Are People Mad at the Hidden Persuaders?" *The Role of Advertising*, ed. C. H. Sandage and Vernon Fryburger (Homewood, Ill.: Richard D. Irwin, Inc., 1960), p. 294.

[2]Richard W. Pollay, "The Distorted Mirror: Reflections on the Unintended Consequences of Advertising," *Journal of Marketing*, Vol. 50 (April 1986), p. 18.

[3]C. J. Firestone, *The Economic Implications of Advertising* (Toronto: Metheun Publications, 1967), pp. 16–17.

unintended consequences seriously and examine these issues. Such an inquiry does not require researchers to believe that advertising will be absolved of all charges as much as it requires having faith that the institutions of advertising have a potential for self-correction.[4]

Advertising and Information

Advertising can perform a socially useful function by educating the public about product qualities so that consumers can exercise free choice and free will in the marketplace.[5] Moreover, retail advertising, catalog advertising, and much industrial advertising provide a substantial amount of information. A study by Aaker and Norris of prime-time television commercials suggests that even television advertising is perceived as informative by substantial groups of people.[6]

Robert Steiner notes the consumer ignorance prevailing in industries that don't use advertising and suggests that this prevents the shopping public from intelligently comparing the attributes of competing brands or even from recognizing as identical the same brand on sale in different outlets.[7] Critics concede that because of brand advertising there is a wide assortment of goods within each performance or quality grade, although some critics assert this variety is excessive.

Advertising and Free Choice

Critics declare that the information provided in advertising may manipulate people to buy things they don't really need. They point to the example of Gerald Lambert of the Lisertine company who took the word "halitosis" and through intensive repetition in widespread advertising infected Americans with the fear of bad breath—making up to $20,000,000 in the process. Critics also declared that the old Lifebuoy ads shouting "Body Odor," caused the psychologically insecure and inadequate to become uncomfortable and apprehensive, so that if "they detected nothing else they did smell their own primitive fears, guilt feelings and insecurities . . . ."[8]

It is claimed that motivational researchers have studied man's unconscious needs and then put a dangerous manipulative tool in the hands of advertisers. Messages may be sent below our threshold of consciousness and still affect us. We are being brainwashed by hidden persuasion.

---

[4]Richard W. Pollay, "The Distorted Mirror: Reflections on the Unintended Consequences of Advertising," *Journal of Marketing*, Vol. 50 (April 1986), p. 33.

[5]Phillip Nelson, "Advertising as Information," *Journal of Political Economy*, Vol. 81, No. 4 (July/August 1974), pp. 729–54.

[6]David A. Aaker and Donald Norris, "Characteristics of Television Commercials Perceived as Informative," *Journal of Advertising Research* (February 1982).

[7]Robert L. Steiner, "Judging the Welfare Performance of Manufacturers' Advertising," *Journal of Retailing* (1981), pp. 3–13.

[8]Milton Rokeach, "The Consumer's Changing Image," in *Marketing and the Behavioral Sciences*, edited by Perry Bliss, 2nd ed. (Boston: Allyn and Bacon, Inc., 1967), p. 87.

There is some justification to the idea of effective persuasion through advertising. In fact, much advertising is designed to be persuasive. Persuasive advertising is used primarily as a type of propaganda. The essence of propaganda is that it conditions people to act in a way that is favorable toward the product being advertised.[9] There is no doubt that we have, largely on the basis of improved knowledge in the various disciplines of psychology, sociology, and anthropology, developed increasingly refined and effective means of persuasion. However, just as the persuaders become more sophisticated, so do those who are to be persuaded.[10]

Does Advertising Persuade People to Buy Things They Do Not Need?

Advertising is said to create excessive demand, sometimes for unnecessary goods. According to John Kenneth Galbraith,

> . . . *Along with bringing demand under substantial control,* . . . *[the management of demand] provides, in the aggregate, a relentless propaganda on behalf of goods in general. From early morning until late at night, people are informed of the services rendered by goods—of their profound indispensability. Every feature and facet of every product having been studied for selling points, these are then described with talent, gravity and an aspect of profound concern as the sources of health, happiness, social achievement, or improved community standing. Even minor qualities of unimportant commodities are enlarged upon with a solemnity which would not be unbecoming in an announcement of the combined return of Christ and all the apostles. More important services, such as the advantages of white laundry, are treated with proportionately greater gravity.*[11]

While advertising is designed to accelerate changes in tastes, swings in fashion, and minor product differentiation, it can only be effective if it is noticed and needed. Consumers are not passive, but selective (see Exhibit 26.1), they are exploratory and receptive to new ideas.

Subliminal Persuasion

In the 1950s there was much publicity and interest focused upon the effects of subliminal, or subthreshold, communications. *Subliminal (beneath the limin,* which in Latin means *threshold) communication* refers to "the sending, reception, and effects of physically weak visual or aural messages which people receive in a physiological sense, but of which they are not consciously aware."[12]

---

[9]Edmund D. McGarry, "The Propaganda Function in Marketing," in *Marketing and Its Environment: Some Issues and Perspectives*, p. 305.

[10]Raymond A. Bauer, "Limits of Persuasion," in *The Role of Advertising*, p. 230.

[11]*The New Industrial State*, 3/E by John Kenneth Galbraith. Copyright © 1967, 1971, 1978 by John Kenneth Galbraith. Reprinted by permission of Houghton Mifflin Company and Andre Deutsch, Ltd.

[12]"Subliminal Communication," a report prepared by the Institute of Practitioners in Advertising, London (July 1958), p. 7.

EXHIBIT 26.1
Does Advertising Persuade People to
Buy Things They Do Not Need?

DESPITE WHAT SOME PEOPLE THINK, ADVERTISING CAN'T MAKE YOU BUY SOMETHING YOU DON'T NEED.

Some people would have you believe that you are putty in the hands of every advertiser in the country.

They think that when advertising is put under your nose, your mind turns to oatmeal.

It's mass hypnosis. Subliminal seduction. Brain washing. Mind control. It's advertising.

And you are a pushover for it.

It explains why your kitchen cupboard is full of food you never eat.

Why your garage is full of cars you never drive.

Why your house is full of books you don't read, TV's you don't watch, beds you don't use, and clothes you don't wear.

You don't have a choice. You are forced to buy.

That's why this message is a cleverly disguised advertisement to get you to buy land in the tropics.

Got you again, didn't we? Send in your money.

ADVERTISING
ANOTHER WORD FOR FREEDOM OF CHOICE.
American Association of Advertising Agencies

Public interest was aroused by reports of the 1957 experiment in a New Jersey theater where the Subliminal Projection Company flashed the words *Drink Coke* and *Eat Popcorn* on the screen so quickly that they were below the conscious awareness of average movie viewers. It was alleged that the sales of Coke and popcorn were markedly increased by the use of this subthreshold technique.

A committee established in Great Britain to study the issue concluded, "Present evidence shows little if any effect from subliminal communication in the fields of selling and persuasion."[13] In the United States the Federal Communications Commission stated that because so-

---

[13]"Subliminal Communication," a report prepared by the Institute of Practitioners in Advertising (London, July 1958), p. 7.

called "subliminal" advertising was not used by television stations, and was frowned upon by that industry, the Commission had not found it necessary to adopt any covering rules and regulations.

However, in 1973 the FCC, after being notified by some parents that a 60-second television commercial for Husker-Do, a children's game, contained the subliminal message "Get it," issued the following public notice:[14]

> *We believe that the use of subliminal perception is inconsistent with the obligations of a licensee and therefore we take this occasion to make clear that broadcasts employing such techniques are contrary to the public interest. Whether effective or not, such broadcasts clearly are intended to be deceptive.*

By the late seventies, several books by Wilson B. Key, a Canadian journalism professor, popularized the notion that subliminal sexual images were widely used in advertising. In *Subliminal Seduction, Media Sexploitation,* and *The Clam-Photo Orgy,* Key noted that speed-photography and airbrushing are among the techniques used in ads to hide subtle appeals to subconscious sex drives (see Exhibit 26.2). Thus, Key postulated, Ritz crackers had the word *sex* baked into them, and a Gilbey's gin ad contained microscopic erotica.[15]

According to Timothy E. Moore, who reviewed the literature on subliminal advertising, whether erotic imagery has been deliberately planted in a product or ad is not relevant to a consideration of the imagery's alleged effects. He declares that "holding advertisers responsible for one's erotic musings is analogous to accusing Rorschach of insinuating particular themes into the inkblots."[16] Moore concludes that while subliminal perception is a bona fide phenomenon, the effects obtained are subtle. Moreover, there is little empirical documentation for strong subliminal effects, such as inducing particular behaviors or changing motivation.

There is no clear evidence that subliminal advertising is in current use. Charles F. Adams, speaking for the American Association of Advertising Agencies in 1981 declared, "We are convinced there is no subliminal advertising in America today. Advertising people learned long ago that the best way to say a thing is to *say* it—up front, on top, and above board—where it belongs."[17]

Advertising's Influence on Values and Life-Styles

Historian David Potter declares that "the most important effects of this powerful institution (advertising) are not upon the economies of our dis-

---

[14]FCC 74-78 08055 (January 24, 1975).

[15]Timothy E. Moore, "Subliminal Advertising: What You See Is What You Get," *Journal of Marketing,* Vol. 46 (Spring 1982), pp. 38–47.

[16]Timothy E. Moore, "Subliminal Advertising: What You See Is What You Get," pp. 38–47.

[17]Jane E. Brody, "Is Subliminal Persuasion a Menace? Evidently Not," *The New York Times* (August 17, 1982), pp. C1, C2.

EXHIBIT 26.2
Are There Subliminal Sexual Images Used in Ads?

PEOPLE HAVE BEEN TRYING TO FIND THE BREASTS IN THESE ICE CUBES SINCE 1957.

The advertising industry is sometimes charged with sneaking seductive little pictures into ads.

Supposedly, these pictures can get you to buy a product without your even seeing them.

Consider the photograph above. According to some people, there's a pair of female breasts hidden in the patterns of light refracted by the ice cubes.

Well, if you really searched you probably *could* see the breasts. For that matter, you could also see Millard Fillmore, a stuffed pork chop and a 1946 Dodge.

The point is that so-called "subliminal advertising" simply doesn't exist. Overactive imaginations, however, most certainly do.

So if anyone claims to see breasts in that drink up there, they aren't in the ice cubes.

They're in the eye of the beholder.

ADVERTISING
ANOTHER WORD FOR FREEDOM OF CHOICE.
American Association of Advertising Agencies

tributive system; they are upon the values of our society."[18] He compares advertising to schools and churches in the magnitude of its social influence. His major criticism is that, unlike school or church, advertising does not have as a goal the betterment of the individual.

Other historians, however, note that advertising does not oppose our value system, it reflects it (see Exhibit 26.3). Otis Pease, who has been exploring trends of the social content of advertisements since the early 1900s declares that, at least until the 1950s, ". . . the values conveyed in advertising regarding high consumption were ambivalent, even conservative, and tended to reflect rather than accelerate changes in the

---

[18]David M. Potter, *People of Plenty: Economic Abundance and the American Character* (Chicago: The University of Chicago Press, 1954), p. 188.

EXHIBIT 26.3
Does Advertising Influence or Reflect Tastes?

traditional structure of values that were taking place."[19] He notes, however, that advertisements convey social messages that have some potential for affecting social values, and recommends that historians conduct further studies to chart the continuing impact of advertising. The more that is known about changes in social values and attitudes and the actual impact of advertising in shaping them, the more likely it is that advertisers and the consuming public will be able to respond intelligently to these issues.[20]

---

[19]Otis A. Pease, "Teaching Americans to Consume: A Reappraisal of Advertising as a Social Force," in *Advertising and the Public*, Sandage Symposium II, ed. Kim B. Rotzoll; Symposium conducted by the University of Illinois Urbana-Champaign, June 17–19, 1979, p. 14.

[20]Otis A. Pease, "Teaching Americans to Consume . . .", p. 14.

EXHIBIT 26.4
Dreams Come True—Through Gambling

Advertising and Life-Style

One of the most frequently quoted social defenses of advertising is that it raises the standard of living by disseminating information concerning innovative technological advancements in goods and services. Critics immediately counter, citing the difficulties involved in proving a causal relationship. They then note that, if advertising is to be credited with changing the standard of living, the resulting improvement appears only on a material level. They concede that advertising may have raised the level of living—by creating greater desires for, and increasing the consumption of, material wants—but they declare that from an ethical, moral, or social viewpoint living standards have not improved. They state that advertising promotes the wrong goods (with extensive built-in obsolescence features) at the wrong price.

Both the accolades and the blame may arise from a false assumption about advertising's power. Advertising does not lure fish into hitherto uninhabited waters. Its power is akin to casting in a stream when the fish are biting.[21] In other words, advertising by itself cannot create demand for a product. It can accelerate the acceptance of a product where the potential demand already exists. Nor can advertising manipulate people so that their wants become distorted into asocial desires for material acquisitions. Rather, society has assigned to advertising the job of presenting a case for an abundant material life since there is no other institution that accepts this function to a significant degree. Bauer and Greyser, writing in *Harvard Business Review,* note that criticism of a materialist society appears to be a criticism of the extent to which people spend their resources of time, energy, and wealth on the acquisition of material things, rather than pursuing more important nonmaterial goals. They point out, however, that the distinctive feature of our society is that material goods are used to attain the *nonmaterial* goals of ego enhancement, psychic security, and social status.[22] In reality, advertising projects both traditional and alternative life-styles (see Exhibits 26.5 and 26.6).

Advertising Is Said to Emphasize Inappropriate Behavior

Critics point to ads endorsing activities such as drinking and gambling (see Exhibit 26.4). Anheuser-Busch's Michelob and Somerset's Johnny Walker Red ads are denoted as "highly supportive of a heavy drinker's daily drinking style." There are suggestions that other brands as well either appeal to heavy- or problem-drinkers by presenting alcohol as "the key to unwinding, coping with problems, and staying ahead."[23] However, some advertisers have designed campaigns to limit inappropriate behavior. Coors, for example, discourages drinkers from driving (see Exhibit 26.7).

---

[21]Clarence C. Walton, "Ethical Theory, Societal Expectations, and Marketing Practices," in *Speaking of Advertising,* edited by John S. Wright and Daniel S. Warner (New York: McGraw-Hill Book Co., Inc., 1963), p. 370.

[22]Raymond A. Bauer and Stephen A. Greyser, "The Dialogue That Never Happens," *Harvard Business Review,* Vol. 45 (November/December 1967), p. 6.

[23]"Pertschuck's Plea: Turn FTC Loose," *Advertising Age* (April 25, 1983), p. 69.

EXHIBIT 26.5
A Traditional Life-Style

EXHIBIT 26.6
An Alternative Life-Style

Does Advertising Create Stereotypes?

Advertising has been said to create or reinforce stereotypes. These criticisms extend to ethnic characterizations as well as to the ways in which men, women, and children are portrayed.

Stereotyping Ethnic Groups   Significant inroads have been made in eliminating the stereotypical ads involving blacks. Black agencies now specialize in preparing ads for the black target market, and black celebrities are often used as spokespersons. Flip Wilson advertises Tender Vittles, Bill Cosby improves E. F. Hutton's image, and William "The Refrigerator" Perry appears in ads for Kraft, Coca-Cola, McDonald's, Levi Strauss, Alberto Culver, and Duke thermal underwear.[24] Mr. T is

---

[24]Pat McGeehan, "An Appliance That Sells 'Fridge' Perry Snares Star Presenter Honors," *Advertising Age* (April 28, 1986), p. 38.

EXHIBIT 26.7
Discouraging Drunk Driving

used in public service announcements for fair housing in New York. Advertising and packaging for Aunt Jemima brands has changed dramatically over the years.

Stereotyping Women   A frequent criticism of advertising is its stereotypical or sexist presentations of women. Several organizations periodically monitor ads and point out those they consider objectionable. Women Against Pornography, for example, gave its Plastic Pig Award to Calvin Klein's women's underwear ads and Kimberly-Clark's Huggies disposable diapers ads which were considered unacceptable.[25] However, they applauded Jockey underwear's "Jockey for Her" print campaign for showing underwear on a model without making her look too provocative (see Exhibit 26.8).

While such criticisms frequently result in changing strategies (see Exhibit 26.9), advertisers sometimes continue their campaigns. The Maidenform ads, where models appeared in public places wearing only underwear and a bra, were defended on the basis of the fact that males in the ad never looked in the direction of the scantily clad female.

Criticism can result, however, in more awareness and enforcement. In France, for example, laws have been passed which give women's rights groups a legal base to sue for any ad deemed sexist or damaging to the image of women. The Socialist French Minister of Women's Rights would like to ban ads for Buffalo jeans, showing women in skin-tight jeans with their torsos tied with ropes.

Advertising and Children

Advertising's effect on children has been the subject of numerous studies and continuing debates. Some of the issues raised include:

1. Children, particularly those between the ages of 5 and 6, cannot differentiate between the commercial and the program. This inability to differentiate between fantasy and reality results in confusion between right and wrong.
2. Young children are vulnerable to advertising and may be manipulated by advertising because they are too young to understand.
3. Children have limited experience, and while they are not mature enough to make purchase decisions, they may do so on the basis of the ads.
4. Advertising causes children to become surrogate salespersons.

Defenders of advertising to children offer the following positive effects:

1. Advertising gives product information to the child that assists him or her in making decisions (see Exhibit 26.10).
2. Children are developing skills through advertising and will be more independent and make better selections among products targeted toward them.

EXHIBIT 26.8
A Nonprovocative Underwear Ad

_____

[25]"Ads Slapped for Porno Pig Tales," *Advertising Age*, March 4, 1985, p. 8.

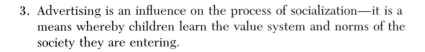

EXHIBIT 26.9
A More Realistic Portrayal of Women

As the sound track plays "Put on Your Red Dress Momma," a young mother searches frantically for her dress and finally finds it on her little girl who is playing "dress up." The mother shakes her head, smiles, and dumps the dress into the washing machine, using Colgate-Palmolive's Fresh Start laundry detergent. The dress launders beautifully, and a few hours later the wife leaves with her husband for an evening out.

3. Advertising is an influence on the process of socialization—it is a means whereby children learn the value system and norms of the society they are entering.

The extent to which advertising to children should be controlled is a subject of continuing controversy. Because the FTC has jurisdiction over deceptive advertising—to children or any other segment of the public—consumer advocate groups such as ACT (Action for Children's Television) have continually encouraged it to take action against other advertising to children that, while not deceptive, is considered unacceptable. Specific criticisms have been directed at the cereal industry for its excessive advertising of sugar-coated, ready-to-eat cereals.

In the late 1970s the FTC proposed a rule restricting children's advertising. This raised a public outcry from advertisers and their agencies. The FTC was accused of being a "National Nanny," and recommendations were made to restrict its activities. In 1980 Congress passed an FTC Improvement Act which imposed a number of restrictions on the FTC's rulemaking. It prohibited the FTC from promulgating a children's advertising rule on the basis of unfairness in commercial advertising. It did permit the establishment of future proceedings in children's advertisements if they were based on deception. Currently, however, the FTC has discontinued its efforts toward developing a rule concerning children's television advertising.

The Public View of Advertising

Although it is not difficult to find the economist's and sociologist's viewpoint about advertising, such is not the case if one wants to examine the public's viewpoint. In some respects this is understandable, because the public's viewpoint generally does not emerge from either a scientific or a professional analysis. Consumers do not provide adequate documentation of the economic significance or the social consequence of advertising.

Numerous surveys have taken place over the past 50 years. While it is difficult to make rigorous comparisons among these surveys because

"FRANKLY, I'D RATHER HAVE AN ORANGE."

EAT FRUIT. SNACK SMART.

EXHIBIT 26.10
Children's Advertising as a Positive Influence

The Department of Agriculture prepared an advertising campaign designed to reach 6 to 12-year-olds emphasizing the use of fruit as a snack.

of the methodological differences, several trends were noted.[26]

From the 1930s to the 1950s few surveys were conducted, and they reflected relatively stable attitudes toward advertising. Although some criticism was present, the American public seemed basically satisfied and content.

In 1964, the American Association of Advertising Agencies and the Harvard Business School combined forces to provide a comprehensive examination of public attitudes toward advertising. They found that the public's opinion toward ads and toward advertising were preponderantly favorable. An interesting insight into advertising's effectiveness revealed that *the average American adult [was] aware of 76 advertisements a day in the major media.*[27] (Although advertising folklore suggests that the average person is exposed to 1500–3000 advertisements a day, this number represents the *opportunity* for exposure; the counter technique used in the study required conscious action.) Nonetheless, of the 76 advertisements that were counted as engaging the attention, only 16 percent of these were further categorized as creating a particularly favorable or unfavorable impression. Of the 16 percent of the advertisements that were further categorized, 72 percent (9 ads) were given favorable ratings (enjoyable or informative) and 28 percent (3 ads) unfavorable ratings (annoying or offensive).

In a 1974 study fewer people agreed that advertising resulted in "better products for the public," that "it helped raise our standard of living," or that "in general, advertising resulted in lower prices."[28] There was an increase in the number of people who felt that advertising often "persuaded people to buy things they should not buy," and that most advertising "insulted the intelligence of the average consumer."

Some of the reasons that attitudes and opinions changed toward advertising included:[29]

— the rise in the amount of advertising;
— the increased use of television as an advertising medium with its attendant "intrusiveness";
— the rise in commercial clutter;
— the decline of *caveat emptor* ("let the buyer beware") and the higher standard of social responsibility forced on advertisers by the public, who were more likely to criticize deceptive and unsavory advertising practices; and
— the rise and institutionalization of consumerism.

---

[26]Eric Zanot, "Public Attitudes Toward Advertising," in *Advertising in a New Age,* ed. H. Keith Hunt, Proceedings of the Annual Conference of the American Academy of Advertising (Provo, Utah, 1981), pp. 142–46.

[27]Raymond A. Bauer and Stephen A. Greyser, *Advertising in America: The Consumer View* (Boston: Harvard University Press, 1968), p. 176 (italics in original).

[28]Rena Bartos and Theodore F. Dunn, *Advertising and Consumers, New Perspectives* (New York: American Association of Advertising Agencies), p. 44.

[29]Eric Zanot, "Public Attitudes Toward Advertising," p. 142.

TABLE 26.1 Purchase Behavior / Attitudes Toward Television Commercials

Sampling Population	509 People	102 Teens
Have you ever bought a specific brand, assuming you needed a product in that category anyway, because you *liked* the advertising for that brand?	19%	38%*
Have you ever decided *not* to buy a specific brand because you *disliked* a television commercial for that brand?	25%	20%

*Significant at .95 level of confidence

Source: from "A Study to Evaluate Consumer Attitudes Toward Television Commercials," No. 7. Reprinted by permission of Lowe Marschack Co.

Negative and Positive Characteristics of Advertising

Advertisements have been the focus of numerous complaints as well as various studies to examine consumers' likes and dislikes. Some of the negative and positive ingredients of ads as perceived by consumers are the following:

Negative Ingredients
Insults intelligence
In poor taste, offensive, overly sexual
Childish, silly, stupid
Exaggerated and phony, misleading and false
Repetitive
Manipulative

Positive Ingredients
Provides information
Humorous, funny, amusing

In a study of 524 prime time network commercials a number of copy characteristics or advertising approaches were found to either increase or decrease irritation.[30] Irritation levels were higher when commercials emphasized a sensitive product, an unbelievable situation, a put-down person, a threatened relationship, a graphic portrayal of physical discomfort, tension, an unattractive or unsympathetic character, a suggestive scene, or poor casting. Irritation levels were lower when the commercial included or conveyed a happy mood, a warm mood, a credible spokesperson, humor, or useful information.

In a study conducted by Marschalk Company to evaluate purchase behavior and attitudes toward television commercials, there appeared to be a great distaste for television commercials and a relatively high resolve not to purchase brands with irritating commercials (see Table 26.1). This attitude was particularly prevalent among teenagers; teenag-

[30]David A. Aaker & Donald E. Bruzzone, "Causes of Irritation in Advertising," *Journal of Marketing*, Vol. 49 (Spring 1985), p. 57.

ers, however, were more likely to buy a specific brand because they liked the advertising.

Another survey conducted by Home Testing Institute for Warwick, Walsh & Miller advertising agency indicated that 55 percent of those surveyed said they avoided buying products whose ads they found objectionable and annoying. Of particular significance was the fact that they did so without contacting broadcasters, broadcasting stations, or marketers.

Improving the Public's View of Advertising

The advertising industry has long been concerned with negative perceptions of consumers relevant to advertising. Improving the public's perception of advertising is presumed to provide benefits not only for the industry, but for the brand image and reputation of those who advertise.

The American Association of Advertising Agencies has engaged in a number of programs to improve advertising's image. It has prepared a number of advertisements designed to explain advertising's role in the economy and society, and has asked its member advertising agencies to aid in getting these ads published in various media (see Exhibit 26.11). The Four A's has also prepared a campaign to discourage drug abuse that will place the equivalent of $1.5 billion in messages before the public during the next three years.[31]

One suggested approach for incorporating social concerns in marketing strategies is to build a parallel between the organization's problems and the problems of an average family.[32] The central values used by the family to solve family problems provide a benchmark for developing values within a marketing organization. Appropriate statements of core social values for the organization that can be applied to advertising strategies may be as follows:[33]

— Treat customers with respect, concern, and honesty, the way you yourself would want to be treated or the way you would want your family to be treated.
— Make and market products you would feel comfortable and safe having your own family use.
— Treat the environment as though it were your own property.

This approach is socially desirable; however, it cannot minimize the requirements of business to provide economic goods and services efficiently.

[31]Daniel Kaha, "Advertising Agencies Plan Anti-Drug Media Campaign," *Newsday* (May 16, 1986), p. 43.
[32]Donald P. Robin & R. Eric Reidenbach, "Social Responsibility, Ethics, and Marketing Strategy; Closing the Gap Between Concept and Application, *Journal of Marketing*, Vol. 51 (January 1987), p. 44.
[33]Ibid., p. 45.

EXHIBIT 26.11
Improving Public Views of Advertising

THIS AD IS FULL OF LIES.

LIE #1: ADVERTISING MAKES YOU BUY THINGS YOU DON'T WANT.

Advertising is often accused of inducing people to buy things against their will.

But when was the last time you returned home from the local shopping mall with a bag full of things you had absolutely no use for? The truth is, nothing short of a pointed gun can get *anybody* to spend money on something he or she doesn't want.

No matter how effective an ad is, you and millions of other American consumers make your own decisions. If you don't believe it, ask someone who knows firsthand about the limits of advertising. Like your local Edsel dealer.

LIE #2: ADVERTISING MAKES THINGS COST MORE.
Since advertising costs money, it's natural to assume it costs *you* money. But the truth is that advertising often brings prices down.

Consider the electronic calculator, for example. In the late 1960s, advertising created a mass market for calculators. That meant more of them needed to be produced, which brought the price of producing each calculator down. Competition spurred by advertising brought the price down still further.

As a result, the same product that used to cost hundreds of dollars now costs as little as five dollars.

LIE #3: ADVERTISING HELPS BAD PRODUCTS SELL.
Some people worry that good advertising sometimes covers up for bad products.

But nothing can make you like a bad product. So, while advertising can help convince you to try something once, it can't make you buy it twice. If you don't like what you've bought, you won't buy it again. And if enough people feel the same way, the product dies on the shelf.

In other words, the only thing advertising can do for a bad product is help you find out it's a bad product. And you take it from there.

LIE #4: ADVERTISING IS A WASTE OF MONEY.
Some people wonder why we don't just put all the money spent on advertising directly into our national economy.

The answer is, we already do.

Advertising helps products sell, which holds down prices, which helps sales even more. It creates jobs. It informs you about all the products available and helps you compare them. And it stimulates the competition that produces new and better products at reasonable prices.

If all that doesn't convince you that advertising is important to our economy, you might as well stop reading.

Because on top of everything else, advertising has paid for a large part of the magazine you're now holding.

And that's the truth.

ADVERTISING.
ANOTHER WORD FOR FREEDOM OF CHOICE.
American Association of Advertising Agencies

SUMMARY

The social role of advertising is subject to widespread criticisms. Advertising does influence many critical social areas; however, it has less impact in these dimensions than the strongly worded indictments would seem to indicate.

Defenders note that advertising provides information which aids consumers in their search for goods and services. Critics declare advertisements may be persuasive rather than informative. However, advertising alone cannot make people buy things they do not need—it is only one of the sources of stimulation for purchase. There are limits to advertising's persuasive capabilities. It does not "brainwash" people nor can it make them conforming robots. Advertising does not have extensive power to influence nor does it create widespread corruption of editorial independence.

While critics state advertising molds values (some of which are questionable), defenders declare it merely reflects them. The desire for material acquisitions cannot be laid at advertising's door—it is part of the current-day life-style of the consumer which is created in a high-consumption economy.

Advertising is said to create or reinforce stereotypes, especially those of ethnic groups and women. Advertising's effect on children is a subject of continuing concern. Young children may be confused or manipulated by advertising, and encouraged to make or request undesirable purchases. Defenders declare advertising helps to prepare children for their adult roles in society and helps to develop their skills in decision making. Regulatory activities in the late seventies, designed to curtail advertising to children, are currently in abeyance.

Over the years the public's perceptions of advertising has become increasingly negative. Suggestions for improving the public's perception of advertising include development of research projects to pinpoint problem areas, public relation's efforts to improve the image of advertising, and the inclusion of social concerns in the firm's marketing strategies.

QUESTIONS FOR DISCUSSION

1. Which social criticisms of advertising do you think are most justified? Why?
2. Do you believe advertising molds our cultural values or reflects them? Explain.
3. Can advertising persuade you to purchase something you do not wish to purchase? Explain.
4. What is your reaction to the use of subliminal perception?
5. Should advertising to children be limited? Discuss.
6. Describe some stereotypes that are created or reinforced by advertising.
7. Select a magazine and examine the manner in which women are portrayed in the advertisements. Discuss.
8. As a consumer, what is your attitude toward advertising?
9. What recommendations would you make to improve the consumer's perception of advertising?
10. What suggestions would you offer for increasing the social benefits of advertising?

KEY TERM

subliminal persuasion

AD PRACTICE

Select four ads you consider acceptable from a societal perspective and four ads you do not. Explain the reasons for your choices.

27

The Economics of Advertising

In 1986 General Foods allocated $24 million to advertise and promote its latest entry in the "wholesome snack" market—Fruit Corners' Fruit Wrinkles, a coffee-bean shaped, processed-fruit product designed to compete directly with Sunkist Fun Fruits, a pellet-shaped product introduced in 1985 by Unilever's Thomas J. Lipton, Inc. The $24 million in support for Fruit Wrinkles was the largest budget General Mills had ever allocated to an item in its Fruit Corners line.

While business firms see advertising as an important competitive tool, many critics complain about the role of advertising in our economic system. More than 200 bills were introduced in state legislatures in 1986 seeking to ban, regulate, or tax advertising. Expenditures on advertising are a constant object of conflicting criticisms and defenses from an economic perspective.

ADVERTISING'S ROLE: THE ECONOMIC VIEW

Early economic theorists paid little attention to advertising's role in the economic environment; however, in the late nineteenth and early twentieth centuries, advertising became more widespread and could no longer be ignored. In his book, *Industry and Trade*, Alfred Marshall divided advertising into two categories, constructive and combative.[1] *Constructive* (or informative) advertising was considered useful because it provided information about products to society; *combative* (or competitive) advertising was considered persuasive and wasteful as it merely shifted demand from one producer to another.

Advertising and Information

Advertising's informational role is generally accepted even by its detractors. Nonetheless this informational capacity must be emphasized because of the tendency to overlook its importance. As L. G. Telser declares:

> *Advertising is a necessary adjunct to a volatile economy and a high consumption society. In a static economy it would not be necessary to continually inform people about new goods, new services, new market intermediaries, new terms of sale, new styles. . . . Information would not become obsolete and people would continue to use the same things in the same way. To the extent that advertising conveys pertinent information about change it facilitates economic growth.[2]*

Exhibit 27.1 illustrates the informational role of advertising.

Advertising and Competition

The case for competitive advertising is not presented as easily, nor is there as much consensus on the verdict. The opinion of economists on the effects of competitive advertising range from the viewpoint that it is a social waste to the conclusion that it is a natural accompaniment of a free and democratic system. Nicholas Kaldor presents the economic case against advertising and argues that because advertising has no positive price, but is offered jointly with goods and services, consumers are forced to pay more for advertising than they want. Consumers, therefore, become unwilling accomplices to a waste of resources.[3] Paul A. Samuelson criticizes the "self-cancelling" effect of competitive advertising which merely tends to shift demand from one good to another and back again (see Exhibit 27.2).[4]

EXHIBIT 27.1
Informational Advertising—How to Protect Your Business

---

[1]Alfred Marshall, *Industry and Trade* (London: The Macmillan Co., 1919), p. 395.

[2]From "Some Aspects of the Economics of Advertising" by L. G. Telser, *The Journal of Business*, Vol. 41 (April 1967). Copyright © 1968 The University of Chicago Press. Reprinted by permission.

[3]Nicholas Kaldor, "The Economic Aspects of Advertising," *The Review of Economic Studies*, 1949–50, Vol. 18, No. 45, p. 6.

[4]Paul A. Samuelson, *Economics, An Introductory Analysis* (New York: McGraw-Hill Book Co., Inc., 1955), p. 169.

EXHIBIT 27.2
Competitive Advertising—Shifting Demand

F. W. Tausig feels that although we cannot clearly delineate the benefits of advertising's competitive role, its elimination may have adverse effects:

> *The incessant vaunting has a sort of indirect or preventive productiveness, analogous to that of the police [officer] and the criminal courts; directly they contribute nothing but without them things would not go smoothly and uninterruptedly. Apparently the advertising must be there in order that effective production shall be continually maintained.*[5]

---

[5]F. W. Tausig, *Principles of Economics*, 4th ed. (New York: The Macmillan Co., 1946), p. 235.

The Consumer Model

Different judgments of advertising's role emerge to some extent from different views of the consumer model. The early economists viewed the consumer as an economic person making a rational choice among alternatives in the marketplace. George Katona, who has made numerous studies in the field of consumer behavior, describes this thesis in terms of a norm: the way rational people seek a maximization of profits or of utilities, on the assumption that they have full knowledge and control over all means of achieving the postulated economic end.[6] Therefore, advertising which presents economic information is consistent with the concept while advertising which presents persuasive and emotional appeals is not.

However traditional economics, according to one economist, is not quite in keeping with today's realities.

> *Modern psychological research makes clear that the postulates of traditional demand theory, derived from the model of perfect competition with known wants and static supply conditions, are irrelevant. Information is an ambiguous concept in consumer behavior, since to be effective it must have elements of persuasion, which to its critics is often its antithesis.*[7]

In other words, in today's economy the consumer is a person who does not have full knowledge and control, and, therefore, needs more than pure information. Bauer and Greyser suggest that when businesspeople and critics view the consumer world they see different models.[8] Their different perceptions arise from their different interpretations of the following words:

1. *Competition*—Critics think of competition as strictly price competition, while businesspeople consider competition in terms of product differentiation, either through physical product developments or promotional themes.
2. *Product*—Critics see product as having a primary identifiable function only (for example, an automobile as transportation only). Businesspeople consider the secondary function (the horsepower of an automobile) in their definitions of the product since this may be the only way of providing differentiation.
3. *Consumer Needs*—According to critics, consumer needs correspond to a product's primary function; businesspeople see needs as any consumer levers they can use to differentiate a product.

---

[6]George Katona, *The Powerful Consumer* (New York: McGraw-Hill Book Co., Inc., 1960), p. 7.

[7]From "The Economic Aspects of Advertising" by Peter Doyle, *The Economic Journal* (September 1968). Copyright © 1968 by the Royal Economic Society. Reprinted by permission of Basil Blackwell Ltd.

[8]Raymond A. Bauer and Stephen A. Greyser, "The Dialogue That Never Happens," *Harvard Business Review*, Vol. 45 (November-December 1967), p. 3.

ECONOMIC DEFENSES AND CRITICISMS OF ADVERTISING

Over the years, defenses and criticisms of the economic aspects of advertising have emanated from various sources. Frequently these judgments are cited as two sides of the same coin:

> Advertising (adds, does not add) utility.
> Advertising (raises, lowers) costs.
> Advertising (raises, lowers) prices.
> Advertising (widens, narrows) consumer choice.
> Advertising (promotes, retards) competition.

Many of these conflicting conclusions arise from the difficulties in isolating the advertising variable from the total marketing complex and pinpointing its effect accurately. They also emerge from differences in theoretical approach and differences in judgmental viewpoints concerning advertising's economic role.

Which of these judgments are closer to the mark? This section examines these issues and attempts to evaluate them.

Advertising (Adds, Does Not Add) Utility

An evaluation of the utility-creating abilities of advertising depends upon how one defines and perceives utility. Utility and value have often been used interchangeably. However, in economic literature *value* is expressed in monetary terms and is often synonymous with *price*, while *utility* refers to the want-satisfying qualities of products.[9] However the added value of advertising is frequently examined in terms of the added satisfaction to consumer wants that extends beyond a products' primary functions; therefore the utility-adding and value-adding function of advertising will be discussed as though they are synonymous.

Advertising and Form Utility

Modern advertising offers an element of form utility, that is, value which emanates from the design of a product. Prior to embarking on an advertising campaign, most large advertisers engage in marketing research to secure data on consumer preferences which ultimately will aid in the creation of the most effective advertising appeals. Frequently the research uncovers ways to improve products to meet marketplace needs, and the products are therefore modified accordingly. While it is true that market research alone might uncover these desirable attributes, it is also true that much of this research is currently initiated and conducted under the auspices of advertising.

---

[9]Vincent Norris, "Advertising and Value Added," in *The Role of Advertising*, edited by C. H. Sandage and Vernon Fryburger (Homewood, Ill.: Richard D. Irwin, Inc., 1960), p. 151.

EXHIBIT 27.3
Emphasizing Physical Utilities While Implying Psychological Utilities

Psychological Considerations

Defenders of advertising argue that advertising adds value in goods and increases the utility either by calling attention to attributes consumers otherwise would have been unaware of, or by creating a psychic value that increases users' perceptions of utility (see Exhibit 27.3).[10] The first part of this defense is consistent with the informational role of advertising; the second concerns advertising's psychological aspects. Economists have generally accepted advertising as a means of providing consumers with information upon which to base rational choices, but they are less willing to validate its relationship to satisfying psychological wants.

Nevertheless psychological considerations as well as economic factors must be considered in determining the total utility consumers secure from their purchases. As one modern economist declares:

---

[10]Ralph Harris and Arthur Seldon, *Advertising in a Free Society* (London: Institute of Economic Affairs, 1959), pp. 45–46.

There is no psychological justification for viewing the consumer as a simple metabolic mechanism with clearcut desires for want satisfaction. Rather we economists should consider the consumer as a complex mass of emotions with an infinite capacity to absorb a variety of both physical and psychological utilities.[11]

Current behavioral research discloses that consumers are not motivated by economic considerations alone, but by prestige, status, approval, acceptance, belonging, recognition, and a host of other factors which influence choice. For example, in the purchase of an expensive automobile it is reasonable to assume that the prestige value may be as important as the transportation value. Since the prestige value was at least partly created by advertising, the selling cost as well as the production cost for this item satisfies a human want, and, therefore, both are creating utility.

Support for the psychological utility of advertising emerged from a study by Laric and Sarel concerning the use of seals of approval.[12] Results indicated consumers believed that a product with a Good Housekeeping Seal of Approval was better than one without it. Moreover readers of *Good Housekeeping* magazine indicated significant usage of the Good Housekeeping Seal of Approval in their information search and evaluation process.

Companies apparently believe in the utility value of advertising. Products are presented for sale with the statement "as advertised in *Time (New Yorker, Life)*."

Advertising and Utility: The Legal Viewpoint

The legal determination of whether advertising creates utility has not been clearly defined. In two cases that deal only indirectly with advertising, the Supreme Court made significant and somewhat contradictory judgments concerning the economic value of advertising. In a decision on the use of brand names, the Supreme Court upheld a contention by the Federal Trade Commission that "labels do not differentiate products for the purpose of determining grade or quality," noting, however, that "one label may have more customer appeal and command a higher price in the marketplace from a substantial segment of the public."[13]

The case concerned itself with price discrimination as interpreted under the Robinson-Patman Act. The Borden Company attempted to justify price differentials between nationally branded milk under the Borden label and physically identical and equal quality milk sold under private labels. Borden contended that "consideration should be given to all commercially significant distinctions which affect market value

---

[11]From "An Economist Defends Advertising" by John W. Lowe, *Journal of Marketing*, Vol. 27 (July 1963). Copyright © 1963 American Marketing Association. Reprinted by permission.

[12]Michael V. Laric and Dan Sarel, "Consumer (Mis)Perceptions and Usage of Third Party Certification, 1972 and 1980: Did Public Policy Have An Impact?" *Journal of Marketing*, Vol. 45 (Summer 1981), pp. 135–42.

[13]*Federal Trade Commission* v. *The Borden Co.*, 86 S.Ct. 1092 (1966).

whether they be physical or promotional." The Court used an essentially economic yardstick and rejected the premise that promotional considerations add value to physically identical products.

However, Mr. Justice Stewart, who was joined by Mr. Justice Harlan in the dissenting opinion, applied a psychological yardstick, declaring that:

> *Although it is undisputed that the physical attributes and chemical constituents of Borden's premium and private label brands of evaporated milk are identical . . . nonetheless . . . the product purchased by a consumer includes not only the chemical components that any competent laboratory can itemize, but also a host of commercial intangibles that distinguish the product in the market place.*

Although the Supreme Court applied an economic yardstick in its decision on the branding of physically identical products, it appears to have used a psychological criterion in its decision upholding the obscenity conviction of Ralph Ginzburg, publisher of *Eros* and other similar literature.[14]

Control over obscenity had been limited by the difficulties involved in providing precise distinctions between freedom of expression of an art form and legally identifiable obscene material. In the Ginzberg case the Supreme Court not only examined the specific material, but also inspected the images and pictures created through the advertising that attempted to promote this material. Mr. Justice Brennan held that, although accused publications might not themselves be obscene, convictions could be sustained in view of evidence of the defendant's pandering in production, sale, and publicity with respect to publication, thus the Court declared that a finding of "titillating" advertising (in the form of provocative names of post offices from which the magazine was mailed) could be part of the proof that the advertised material was obscene. This finding caused Dr. Ernest Dichter, Director of the Institute of Motivational Research, to note that the Court had accepted the long-standing claim of advertisers that the image of the product produced by advertising and promotion is part of the product itself.[15]

Advertising (Raises/Lowers) Costs

One of the criticisms most frequently directed at advertising is that it raises the costs and, ultimately, the prices of goods and services. Obviously, the cost of advertising must be included in the costs of production and distribution of goods and services, but whether the final tally is larger or smaller because of the inclusion of advertising is uncertain.

From an economic viewpoint, the cost of informational advertisements is generally considered acceptable. However even this information function has been questioned.

---

[14]*Ralph Ginzburg et al., Petitioners* v. *U.S.*, 86 S.Ct. 942 (1966).
[15]*New York Sunday Times*, March 27, 1966, Sec. 4, p. 1.

The most comprehensive attempt to resolve the issue of advertising and costs through the analysis of quantitative data culminated in "The Economic Effects of Advertising" published in 1947.[16] This study, which still remains the most extensive ever undertaken in this area, was unable to provide conclusive evidence about the effect of advertising on costs. The study declared:

> *No answer was possible to the question of whether advertising has tended to increase distribution costs as a whole. The distribution cost picture is obscured by the fact that advertising and distribution cost data of business concerns related to numerous combinations of products and of functional services and these combinations are subject to constant shifting. The overall effects of advertising on total distribution costs cannot be traced.*[17]

As for production costs, the study also states: ". . . the question of advertising's effects . . . is indeterminate."[18]

Economies of Scale

Frequently the costs of advertising are weighed against the economies of scale resulting from advertising expenditures. These economies of scale may occur in two areas: production and distribution. Economies of scale in production imply that the large advertisers increase demand, which in turn permits them to increase their production close to the optimum level, at which point their unit costs of production will be lowered. In order for this lower cost to provide economic justification for advertising expenditures, the resultant savings must be passed on to consumers.

Several studies have indicated that advertising has resulted in large national markets which allow large-scale production and lower manufacturing costs. Studies by Steiner in the toy industry and Benham in the eyeglass industry provided support for this theory; however, few other empirical studies have attributed these cost savings to advertising.[19]

Despite the difficulties in attempting to justify advertising's role in economies of scale and resultant benefits in consumer prices, there is evidence that advertising has been efficient in this area. For example, today's television sets and radios are much less expensive than in the past, despite higher costs of labor and material. In part, these lower prices can be attributed to advertising, which was a significant factor in creating widespread demand, leading to improved mass productive techniques (see Exhibit 27.4).

---

[16]Neil H. Borden, *The Economic Effects of Advertising* (Chicago, Ill.: Richard D. Irwin, Inc., 1947), p. 854.

[17]Neil H. Borden, *The Economic Effects of Advertising*, p. 854.

[18]Neil H. Borden, *The Economic Effects of Advertising*, p. 854.

[19]Robert L. Steiner, "Does Advertising Lower Consumer Prices?" *Journal of Marketing* (October 1973), pp. 19–26. Lee Benham, "The Effect of Advertising on the Price of Eyeglasses," *Journal of Law & Economics*, Vol. 15 (October 1972), pp. 337–52.

Social and Legal Issues in Advertising

A television spot, "The Deficit Trials," for W. R. Grace & Company, prepared by Aliens *and* Blade Runner *director Ridley Scott, never made it to the networks. It was considered to present a controversial issue and, as such, may have triggered the Fairness Doctrine. This would have required the networks to provide advertising time for opposing viewpoints to this issue. Recently, the FCC abolished the Fairness Doctrine, and therefore, controversial ads may be presented on the networks in the future. However, Congress has indicated they may reinstate the doctrine. Do you believe that broadcasters should be required to provide broadcasting time to both sides of an issue?*

"THE DEFICIT TRIALS" GXCP 5602   60 SECONDS

OLD MAN: I've already told you, it was all going to work out somehow.

There was even talk of an amendment. But no one was willing to make the sacrifices.

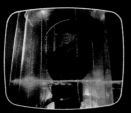

I'm afraid you're much too young to understand.

BOY: Maybe so. But I'm afraid the numbers speak for themselves.

By 1986, for example, the national debt

had reached 2 trillion dollars.

Didn't that frighten you?

ANNCR VO: No one really knows what another generation

of unchecked federal deficits will bring.

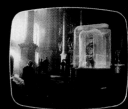

OLD MAN: This frightens me.

BOY: No more questions.

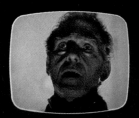

OLD MAN: I have a question. Are you ever going to forgive us?

ANNCR VO: But we know this much.

You can change the future. You have to.

AT W.R. Grace, we want all of us to stay one step ahead of a changing world.

Public service advertising often makes strong statements no other kind of advertising can make so clearly. The American Cancer Society has long been active in disseminating lung cancer prevention messages. Today's messages are derived from current research and are even harder hitting for some people— pregnant women in particular.

With some of its slicker entries, ACS has taken on other types of cancer. This ad acknowledges the sun worshipper's quest for beauty but urges her to think below the surface.

Kids deserve a better teacher than experience.

Two-thirds of the sexually-active teens in America don't use birth control or don't use it consistently. Some of them take the risk because they think it can't happen to them (until it does).

But the vast majority don't even know what the real risks are. Which is why a million teens will get pregnant this year. Unintentionally.

Aware of this tragedy, most Americans (over 85%, according to a recent Harris Poll) want schools to give our kids the facts. Yet only two states and the District of Columbia require sex education in schools.

Why the failure? Because local school boards have been pressured by a vocal minority of parents convinced that ignorance is bliss. They want to deny the facts of life not only to their own kids but to everyone else's. And because school administrators and school boards haven't heard from the rest of you, they give in.

Of course, research shows that the more teens know, the more likely they are to say "no." In fact, the less they know, the more likely they are to learn the hard way.

Which is why Planned Parenthood thinks the only thing wrong with sex education is there's not enough of it.

All caring parents convey their values at home. But if you think your kids get the facts at school, think again. Then get involved. (See coupon.)

Because sex education should never take a back seat in our schools. Or anywhere else.

Teen pregnancy is everybody's problem. I want to help:

☐ Please send me information about Planned Parenthood's POWER (Parents Organized to Win Educational Rights) Campaign so I can make a difference where I live.

☐ Send me a copy of the booklet, "How to Talk with Your Child about Sexuality" (one dollar enclosed).

☐ Here's my tax-deductible contribution to support all of Planned Parenthood's programs encouraging responsible decisions by teens and adults:
☐ $25 ☐ $35 ☐ $50 ☐ $75 ☐ $150 ☐ $500 or: $_____
Send your check to 810 Seventh Avenue, New York, NY 10019

NAME

STREET/CITY/ZIP

Planned Parenthood®
Federation of America

Who Says There's No Place In Society For Drunk Drivers?

MADD
Mothers Against Drunk Driving

Planned Parenthood uses a strong fear appeal to encourage awareness of the social problem of teenage pregnancy, while Mothers Against Drunk Driving (MADD) uses an even stronger approach to combat dangerous and illegal behavior.

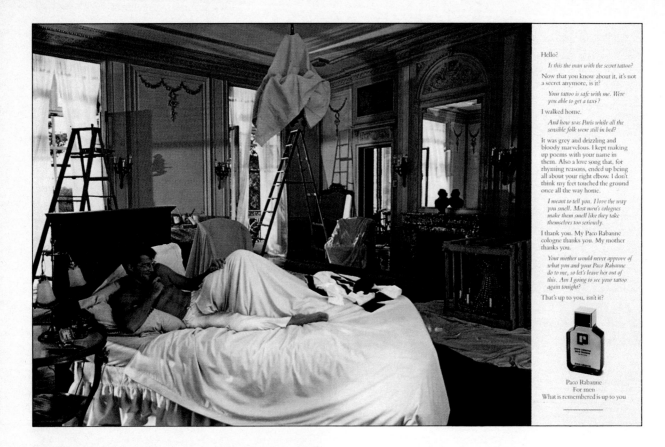

Hello?

Is this the man with the secret tattoo?

Now that you know about it, it's not a secret anymore, is it?

Your tattoo is safe with me. Were you able to get a taxi?

I walked home.

And how was Paris while all the sensible folk were still in bed?

It was grey and drizzling and bloody marvelous. I kept making up poems with your name in them. Also a love song that, for rhyming reasons, ended up being all about your right elbow. I don't think my feet touched the ground once all the way home.

I meant to tell you. I love the way you smell. Most men's colognes make them smell like they take themselves too seriously.

I thank you. My Paco Rabanne cologne thanks you. My mother thanks you.

Your mother would never approve of what you and your Paco Rabanne do to me, so let's leave her out of this. Am I going to see your tattoo again tonight?

That's up to you, isn't it?

Paco Rabanne
For men
What is remembered is up to you

Sex and sensuality in advertising have been with us for some time, from cheesecake posters of the 1930s and 1940s to today's sophisticated messages. If there is a rule of thumb, it must be that taste and true relevance to a product are necessary. For example, fragrances and underclothing may be advertised successfully and appropriately with sensual approaches, while garage doors or shoes may not.

Paco Rabanne print advertisements have become well-known as original, highly sensual ad messages that are appropriate to the product. Regarding the shoe ad, do you find the approach irrelevant or distracting from brand recall? Or does the ad pique your interest in the shoes?

HOW A WOMAN RESPONDS TO SAX.

Even if it's the first time, most women love Sax.

Because Saxon™ Soothing After Shave is a pleasure to smell. And it makes your face a pleasure to touch.

Sax is different from high alcohol after shaves. It's cool and refreshing. But there's no sting—even if you're razor-sensitive.

The special Saxon conditioners soothe irritation, relieve redness, protect against dryness all through the day. And the distinctive fragrance lasts into the night.

Of course, you can't base a relationship on Sax. But it can make a difference.

Discover the Joy of Sax.

In Woodspice and Golden Musk
SAXON SOOTHING AFTER SHAVE

The sexual double entendre can be very daring.

wear it well into the night.

pierre cardin · man's musk

Is this advertisement sensual or sexually explicit?

"I'll do a lot for love, but I'm not ready to die for it."

"I never thought having an intimate relationship with someone could be a matter of life or death. But with everything I hear about AIDS these days, I'm more than uncomfortable. I'm afraid."

AIDS isn't just a gay disease, it's everybody's disease.

And everybody who gets it dies.

AIDS is transmitted from one sexual partner to another, often by a mate who has contracted the disease without even knowing it.

But what we find so alarming about this terrible disease is that people are doing so little to try to prevent it.

Especially since the Surgeon General recently stated, "The best protection against infection right now, barring abstinence, is use of a condom."

It's for this reason that we at LifeStyles® say that the proper use of a LifeStyles Brand Condom can greatly reduce the chances of you or your partner contracting AIDS.

Because a LifeStyles condom acts as a shield that helps prevent the transfer of the AIDS virus. So the likelihood of getting this disease is dramatically diminished. And LifeStyles Brand Condoms, when properly used, help prevent other sexually transmitted diseases like herpes and gonorrhea.

LifeStyles condoms are manufactured by Ansell International, America's largest manufacturers of condoms, Totona Falls, NJ 07774 © Ansell, Inc. 1987

LifeStyles®

The appearance of condom advertising is increasing due to AIDS. There is controversy surrounding the ideas of information versus persuasion. Is it responsible to let the public know of the availability of contraceptive products and their role in disease prevention? Or do you believe such advertising may be encouraging people to engage in casual sex, believing condoms make it safe?

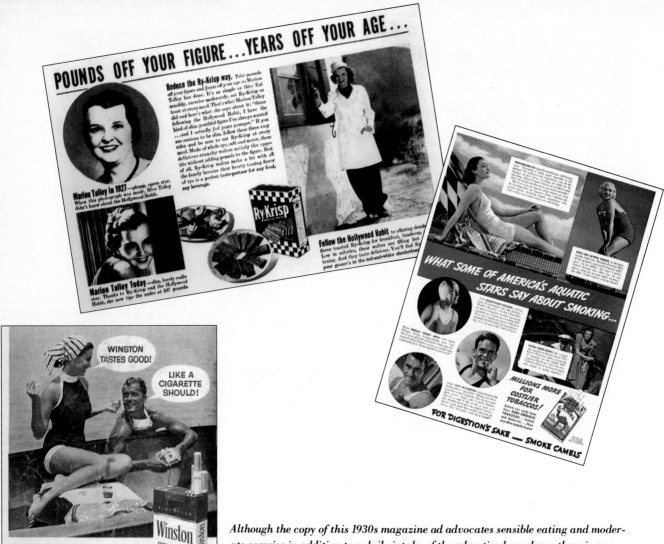

Although the copy of this 1930s magazine ad advocates sensible eating and moderate exercise in addition to a daily intake of the advertised crackers, there is an implied claim that the consumer will be physically improved by the product. Advertising regulation today calls for substantiation of such a claim. Association of a low-calorie product with a healthful life-style is fine, but any implication that the product itself provides a health benefit may be subject to investigation by the regulatory agencies.

Today, cigarette advertising is still well populated with people having fun socially, but well-known athletes are never among the crowd, as they are in this 1937 ad. Nor is it permissible to imply that cigarettes improve vitality, are easy on the throat, or calm nerves. In fact, ads for cigarettes now usually contain very little copy, making their points with imagery and mood-setting rather than words.

The famous tag line, "Winston Tastes Good Like a Cigarette Should," is grammatically incorrect and was criticized as such during the campaign's run in the 1950s. Wendy's restaurant's "Ain't No Reason to Go Anyplace Else" is an example from this decade. Is bad grammar in advertising merely a reflection of the way people really talk; is it poetic license; or is it simply wrong? Do you feel that advertising as a communication function owes its audience responsible treatment of the language?

Although this ad was not found to be in violation of any regulations, it came under fire from a group of dermatologists who objected to the endorsement of a skincare product by a famous heart surgeon. How do you feel about a claim made by a person who is not an authority in this field? Also, is the inclusion of the chemical formula convincing to you?

Another celebrity endorser who came under fire was Cybill Shepherd. Although she does believe in an occasional hamburger as she stated, the Beef Council received reports that she did not eat much red meat.

There is no question that prunes are rich in fiber, and that adequate fiber intake has been medically linked with cancer prevention. However, Kellogg's All Bran campaign was deemed controversial. The campaign appeared very soon after the American Cancer Society published data on the fiber connection, and it was feared that consumers would perceive too direct a link between one product and cancer-free health. The regulatory agencies have since indicated approval of this ad. Should natural foods be advertised as providing a health benefit?

Promoting responsible behavior is what Coors had in mind with its "Gimme the Keys" TV spot and others like it in their recent campaign. Liquor companies have found that acknowledging their social responsibility has not hurt their businesses. How do you feel about this?

CLIENT: ADOLPH COORS COMPANY
PRODUCT: COORS LIGHT

TITLE: "GIMME THE KEYS"
COMM'L NO.: YCPL4623
LENGTH: :30 TV

(SFX: SHUFFLE BOARD GAME)...

...

ROB: Mike, are you alright?
MIKE: Yeah, fine -- I'm just a little tired.

ROB: You've had two beers, right?

MIKE: I had two beers here.

ROB: (STARES AT MIKE WITH DISAPPOINTMENT)
Gimme the keys.

MIKE: What?
ROB: Gimme your keys.

Arnie'll take you home.

ARNIE: Sure, I'd be happy...
MIKE: Arnie, forget it.

ROB: Mike, I'm serious.

MIKE: What is your problem, Rob?

ROB: The problem is that you've had too much to drink.

And you're my friend. So, what else do you wanna know?

MIKE: (HANDS ARNIE HIS KEYS)

MIKE (VO): Where am I parked?

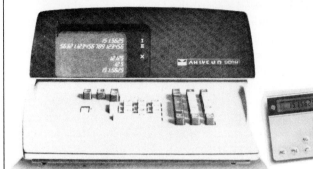
EXHIBIT 27.4
Advertising's Effect on Cost and Price

Advertising (Raises/Lowers) Prices

The question of advertising's effect on prices is partially related to the other issues of cost and utility. If advertising creates economies of scale, then it should not cause higher prices (assuming the savings from these economies are passed on to the consumer). If it does not result in economies, then costs are higher because of advertising, and prices must be higher to recoup these costs. However, if as implied in the discussion of advertising and utility, advertising has value to consumers, then the higher price they are paying is offset by the value received.

It should be noted that, as a tool of nonprice competition, advertising is designed to make prices more stable and not as sensitive to supply and demand. Professor Borden, in "The Economic Effects of Advertising" study discussed earlier, noted that the manufacturers' prices of many products had been relatively insensitive because of the establishment of brand preferences for these products. Nonetheless he concluded: "When sellers of differentiated products have attempted to secure a price difference for their brands which consumers have deemed too high, demand has flowed toward the lower-price products."[20] From a competitive viewpoint the higher price of a branded product may permit the entrance of new firms with merchandise at lower prices, sought out by customers to whom savings are important. This effect occurred in an advertising campaign in which Datril declared it was essentially the same product as Tylenol at a lower price. Shortly after the campaign was aired Tylenol reduced its prices to Datril's level.

A recent investigation into the impact of advertising on the price of consumer products focused on two opposing doctrines that ascribe different roles to advertising in our economy:[21]

1. *Advertising is persuasion.* It raises consumer price by differentiating products, decreasing consumers' price sensitivity, and creating barriers to entry; by establishing brand loyalty it creates market power.
2. *Advertising is information.* It lowers consumer prices by informing consumers and increasing their price sensitivity, thus reducing brand loyalty and monopoly power.

Researchers agree that both theoretical roles are plausible and both have some empirical support. They note, however, that further research is necessary to properly evaluate the impact of advertising on the price of consumer products.

Advertising (Widens/Narrows) Consumer Choice

One step into a modern supermarket with over 14,000 different varieties on display, most of which have been presold through advertising, would appear to support the idea that advertising has been instrumental in presenting consumers with multiple choices. However, a closer look may reveal that instead of many varieties there are merely a proliferation of brands of one specific product. Moreover, advertising has, to some extent, reduced consumer choice in product fields where brand preferences have been established by limiting consumers' selections to these brands.

In general, advertising has helped to widen consumer choice by increasing the variety of goods marketed and by providing consumers with information about these goods. It is not enough, however, to state this

---

[20]Neil Borden, "The Economic Effects of Advertising," p. 603.
[21]Mark S. Albion and Paul W. Farris, *The Advertising Controversy: Evidence on the Economic Effects of Advertising* (Boston: Auburn House, 1980).

**Drive yourself today
and tomorrow you may not have to.**

EXHIBIT 27.5
This ad supports the "work ethic," but critics may point to the ultimate goal as "undesirable" material acquisition.

without answering the related issue of whether advertising improves consumer welfare by increasing these choices. This response requires an evaluation of advertising's influence in several areas: the effects on the standard of living, the rate of innovation, and the control of quality.

Does Advertising Improve the Standard of Living?

It is extremely difficult to isolate advertising as a marketing variable, and trace its individual repercussions in the marketplace. Accordingly, the extent to which advertising may be credited for improvements in the standard of living is debatable. There is general agreement that advertising has at least made people aware of better living standards and may have contributed to the widespread adoption of such comforts as central heating and air conditioning. However, there is less agreement about an appropriate "standard" of living, particularly in terms of material acquisitions (see Exhibit 27.5).

Expressions of varying judgments can be seen in the different views on material acquisitions presented by Arnold Toynbee and William Lazer. Although Toynbee agrees that advertising stimulates consumption he feels it is of the wrong kind and states:

> *Working for this obviously worthwhile purpose . . . to supply the elementary needs of the poverty-stricken three-quarters of the human race . . . would bring us much greater satisfaction than working under the stimulus of advertising, in order to consume goods that we do not need and do not genuinely want . . . Advertising deliberately stimulates our desires, whereas experience, embodied in the teaching of religions, tells us that we cannot be good or happy unless we limit our desires and keep them in check.*[22]

A contrary view is expressed by Lazer who states:

> *Moral values are not vitiated as many critics seem to think by substantial material acquisitions. In reality the improvement of material situations can lead to a greater recognition of intrinsic values, the lifting of general tastes, the enhancement of a moral climate and the direction of more attention to the appreciation of art and aesthetics.*[23]

Does Advertising Increase Innovation?

Supporters of advertising note that small firms, who are often product innovators, are able to enter a market dominated by large firms through advertising (see Exhibit 27.6). However innovative progress depends on elements other than advertising: the pressure to innovate (that is, competitive pressure), capacity to innovate (large firms have advantages in finance and technical skills), and the opportunities.[24] Product innovators who build up acceptance for products through extensive advertising may eventually find themselves in competition with product imitators who spend little or no money on research and product development, may incur very little advertising expenditures in launching their products and may charge lower prices.

Does Advertising Improve Quality Control?

The claim that advertising causes uniformity of product and improves quality control can be considered reasonably valid. Today's manufacturers sell more than one product. Moreover, these products are frequently sold under a national brand such as Ford or Chrysler. Since the same

---

[22]Arnold Toynbee, "Is Advertising Morally Defensible?" in *The Environment of Marketing Behavior,* by Robert J. Holloway and Robert S. Hancock (New York: John Wiley & Sons, Inc., 1964), p. 136.

[23]William Lazer, "Life Style Concepts and Marketing," in *Marketing and Its Environment: Some Issues and Perspectives,* by Richard A. Scott and Norton E. Marks (California: Wadsworth Publishing Co., Inc., 1968), p. 161.

[24]O. J. Firestone, *The Economic Implications of Advertising,* p. 180.

EXHIBIT 27.6
Advertising Supports Innovation

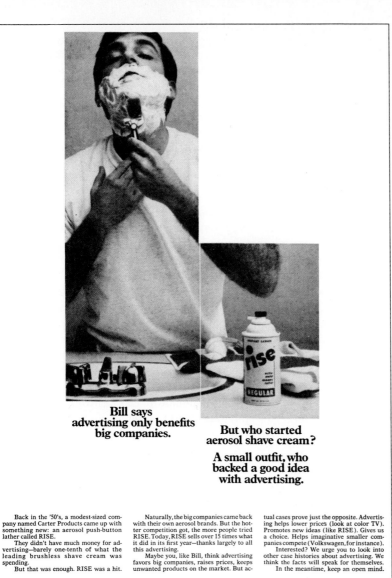

**Bill says
advertising only benefits
big companies.**

**But who started
aerosol shave cream?**

**A small outfit, who
backed a good idea
with advertising.**

Back in the '50's, a modest-sized company named Carter Products came up with something new: an aerosol push-button lather called RISE.

They didn't have much money for advertising—barely one-tenth of what the leading brushless shave cream was spending.

But that was enough. RISE was a hit.

Naturally, the big companies came back with their own aerosol brands. But the hotter competition got, the more people tried RISE. Today, RISE sells over 15 times what it did in its first year—thanks largely to all this advertising.

Maybe you, like Bill, think advertising favors big companies, raises prices, keeps unwanted products on the market. But ac-

tual cases prove just the opposite. Advertising helps lower prices (look at color TV). Promotes new ideas (like RISE). Gives us a choice. Helps imaginative smaller companies compete (Volkswagen, for instance).

Interested? We urge you to look into other case histories about advertising. We think the facts will speak for themselves.

In the meantime, keep an open mind.

brand name is used to cover a variety of products, it becomes extremely important for manufacturers to maintain an acceptable quality for all their products (see Exhibit 27.7).

Professor Marshall Goldman, taking "Some Lessons from Soviet Experience," declared the use of product differentiation, through brand names, for example, obviated the need for as extensive a governmental inspection and administration system as would otherwise be required.[25]

---

[25]Marshall Goldman, "Product Differentiation and Advertising: Some Lessons from Soviet Experience," *Journal of Political Economy*, Vol. 68 (August 1960).

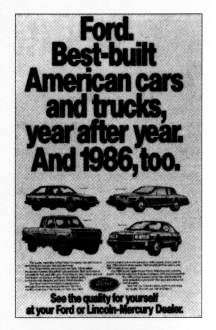

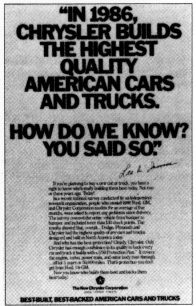

EXHIBIT 27.7
Advertising Emphasizing Quality Control

Ford fires a new shot in its "best-built" battle with Chrysler based on an updated survey that includes 1986 model cars.

As Theodore Levitt reported:[26]

A few years ago several Russian factories manufactured identical 17-inch TV sets. On more than one occasion, even though consumers were clamoring for more sets, many simply were not bought. Inventories piled up. After a good deal of fruitless and wasteful searching for an explanation, the answer came. Because the public could not identify the factory source of any one 17-inch set, and one factory habitually produced "lemons," soon sales of all 17-inch TV sets fell. This refusal to buy was the public's one way to protect itself.

Shortly after this experience Soviet trademarks began to appear, initially as a means of identifying the factory source for the convenience of the authorities, but ultimately, to reward quality and efficiency and punish shoddiness and waste. Quality producers sold their products because consumers had developed confidence in their trademarks. It appeared consumers had learned that "You can be sure if its Westinghouski."[27]

It should be noted, however, that despite consumers' perceptions, brand names do not ensure quality. Rather they tend to provide purchasers with reasonable anticipation that firms are likely to be concerned about quality and willing to stand behind their products. Where products such as Audi have been questioned for inferior quality or lack of safety features, companies have engaged in widespread efforts incorporating advertising to restore and maintain quality control as a means of protecting their brands' reputations (see Exhibit.27.8).

Advertising (Promotes/Retards) Competition

To the extent that advertising promotes competitive offerings it fosters competition. Attention has been focused on whether advertising inhibits competition by helping companies to secure excessive market control, providing barriers to market entry, and offering a means by which companies can secure discriminatory allowances.

Advertising and Market Control

Advertising, in some measure, is designed to create a monopolistic condition for an advertiser. It attempts to develop strong consumer preference for a good, together with the illusion that an advertiser is the sole supplier of this good. There is, however, competition from other advertisers and a wide range of potential substitutes available which limit an advertiser's control of the market (see Exhibit 27.9).

Advertising and "Monopoly Rewards"   Advertising is said to result in excessive control of the market through exceptionally high prices which

---

[26]Theodore Levitt, "Branding on Trial," *Harvard Business Review*, Vol. 44 (March-April 1966), p. 28.
[27]Theodore Levitt, "Branding on Trial," *Harvard Business Review*, p. 28.

EXHIBIT 27.8
Restoring a Firm's Reputation

Sometimes adversity is the mother of invention.

The invention is the Automatic Shift Lock.

From the beginning, we were confident it could help prevent unintended acceleration in our cars.

Now the National Highway Traffic Safety Administration (NHTSA) has asked us to install it on 250,000 1978-86 Audi 5000s.

Audi owners have also been urged by the NHTSA to have the Shift Lock installed as the best safeguard against unintended acceleration.

Not only have we complied with the government's request, but we will also seek to set a new industry standard for owner participation in a recall.

To that end, we are initiating a program which makes available at participating dealers up to 1,000 Audis to be used by as many of our customers as possible while their Automatic Shift Locks are being installed.

Our responsibility has always been to our customers. Our compliance with this recall, and our effort to develop and install the industry's only real safeguard against unintended acceleration, should satisfy any doubts about Audi.

As the automotive press and thousands of loyal owners attest, the Audi 5000 has been and continues to be one of the finest cars in the world.

may have resulted in "monopoly rewards." A study by Comanor and Wilson on the effects of advertising on market structure noted that "industries with high advertising outlays tended to earn profit rates which were about 50 percent higher than those which did not undertake a significant effort . . . (and concluded) . . . on the basis of these empirical findings, it is evident that for industries where products are differentiable investment in advertising is a highly profitable activity."[28]

[28]William S. Comanor and Thomas A. Wilson, "Advertising, Market Structure and Performance," *The Review of Economics and Statistics*, Vol. 49 (November 1967), p. 437.

EXHIBIT 27.9
Using Advertising to Limit Control of Large Companies

MCI's new campaign touting long-distance rates lower than AT&T included this take off on a familiar Bell spot (right). In the MCI version, the mother is crying not because her son called to say he loved her, but because her phone bill is too high.

The conclusions in this study have been criticized for relying on limited data; and inferring, by relating profits to advertising expenditures, that advertising has more power and is more effective than the advertising world itself has ever implied.

Trademarks and Market Control   One method by which a company may attempt to strengthen its control of the market is through the adoption and promotion of a trademark which cannot be used by other companies. The use of a trademark is not considered in restraint of trade, because a competitor may easily enter the market with a similar product with perhaps an improved feature or at a lower price.

Some manufacturers, by use of a trademark, have been able to build up a near-monopoly in the mind of consumers for a short period of time, but not a monopoly of supply. Such names as Frigidaire, Victrola, and Kodak were at one time almost considered names of a product class rather than a specified brand and, as such, came close to securing monopoly attributes for their respective companies. Competitors, however, were able to break this hold on consumer attitudes through their own use of advertising.

Advertising as a Barrier-to-Entry

The issue of advertising's potential contribution to barriers-to-entry has long been the concern of economists. There are two ways in which such barriers may be created:[29]

1. *Cost Advantage.* High levels of advertising may create costs for potential entrants greater than those faced by existing firms when they entered. Furthermore the need to obtain funds for advertising places an additional, risky capital requirement upon entering firms, since advertising is not a tangible asset with resale value.

2. *Economies of Scale.* If economies of scale exist in advertising, potential entrants must either incur higher advertising costs per unit of output than existing firms or increase output. Economies of scale can also evolve from lower prices for large advertisers because of prevailing quantity discounts.

The evidence supportive of a barriers-to-entry hypothesis consists largely of a significant correlation between profit rates and advertising insensitivity for important segments of the manufacturing industry.[30] The belief that advertising leads to cost advantage and acts as a barrier to market-entry may be based on the erroneous accounting assumption that advertising is a revenue expense, when, in fact, it should be treated as a capital investment. A British study of 250 leading advertisers corrected this "error," illustrating that advertising results in a normal return on capital used and, in fact, provides a means of competing, rather than preventing competition.[31] In fact, advertising is a cost-effective method of ensuring a voluntary exchange of information between seller and buyer.

Relatively little empirical evidence is available to substantiate the economies-of-scale effect of increasing advertising expenditures. A number of studies examining the relationship between advertising and sales have been conducted in the cigarette industry, since sales and advertising data by brand are available in this industry and price competition, which may distort results is relatively limited. One such study found that there were decreasing returns to scale for heavy advertising and declared if there were increasing returns it would be more productive for firms to push old brands than to engage in their continuing practice of introducing new brands.[32]

A more recent study found decreasing average costs to advertising and other indications that barriers to entry were created by advertising

---

[29]William S. Comanor and Thomas A. Wilson, *Advertising and Market Power* (Cambridge: Harvard University Press, 1974).

[30]Harold Demsetz, "Accounting for Advertising as a Barrier to Entry," *Journal of Business*, Vol. 52, No. 3 (1979), pp. 345–60.

[31]W. Duncan Reekie, "Advertising, Consumer Welfare and Profits," *Admap* (August 1980), pp. 358–63.

[32]Yoram Peles, "Economies of Scale in Advertising Beer and Cigarettes," *Journal of Business*, Vol. 44 (January 1971), pp. 32–37.

EXHIBIT 27.10
Cooperative Advertising

Cooperative advertising is used by a variety of firms, from shirt manufacturers to automobile producers.

in the cigarette industry. However, these findings also indicated that as brands got older, the returns to advertising capital fell.[33]

An alternative hypothesis suggests advertising, rather than acting as a barrier-to-entry, positively affects competition.[34] A high level of repeat purchase is not brand loyalty but may merely reflect the lack of information about alternatives. Since advertising provides information, it may be a way to solve the problem and increase competition. In a comprehensive review of studies in this area, no conclusive evidence could be found to determine whether advertising as a competitive weapon is pro-competitive or anti-competitive.

Promotional Allowances and Competition

Many manufacturers offer cooperative advertising funds to their resellers to encourage them to engage in promotional efforts (see Exhibit 27.10).

The Robinson-Patman Anti-Discrimination Act, which was passed in 1936 as an amendment to the Clayton Act, prohibits the discrimination of price between different purchasers "of commodities of like grade and quality . . . where the effect of such discrimination may be substantially to lessen competition."[35] Specifically, the Act prohibits the provision of promotional allowances unless they are offered to all purchasers "on proportionally equal terms." Therefore, by law, if manufacturers adopt a cooperative advertising program they are required to offer promotional allowances to all sellers, although it is generally to their advantage to provide these funds to large resellers who can use them most effectively. Moreover, large resellers are in the best positions to insist on cooperative advertising funds from manufacturers. Small resellers neither have the power to insist on funds nor the ability to make effective use of them. Cooperative funds are usually limited to approximately two percent of sales and carry with them the requirement that resellers must pay fifty percent of the cost of the advertising in order to be eligible. The amount small resellers receive may therefore be negligible, or they may feel that the additional advertising expenditure may be too large for their needs or their purse.

The questions of whether promotional allowances limit competition are not easily resolved. Many manufacturers would like to discontinue this practice because of the cost and legal problems involved but are forced to provide promotional allowances as long as other competing manufacturers are doing so. This, then, tends to suggest that it fosters competition.

---

[33]Randall S. Brown, "Estimating Advantages to Large-Scale Advertising," *The Review of Economics and Statistics*, Vol. 60 (August 1978), pp. 428–37.

[34]Thomas T. Nagle, "Do Advertising Profitability Studies Really Show That Advertising Creates a Barrier to Entry?" *Journal of Law & Economics*, Vol. 24 (October 1981), pp. 333–49.

[35]49 Stat. 1526; 15 U.S.C.A., sec. 13, as amended.

ECONOMIC CONTROLS

Control over advertising's potential to inhibit competition or create a monopoly may be of two kinds: limitations on advertising expenditures and fiscal controls.

Any recommendations to restrict advertising immediately raises implicit issues of freedom of speech. There are also questions as to whether limitations to the amount of space and time which mass media could devote to advertising, or constraints on the maximum amount of advertising expenditures for the firm, would be effective. These latter measures may in fact favor the larger firm and increase the difficulties of new firms seeking entry.

Fiscal controls could be in the form of a tax on advertisers. Recently, the Florida legislature extended the scope of the state sales tax to cover all service transactions, including advertising, media purchases, and agency's services. The 5 percent tax effects not only Florida advertisers but national advertisers who enter the state. Representatives of various advertising organizations are fighting this tax arguing that the tax will not only be detrimental to Florida's advertising community, but to the state's economic growth and tax revenues as well.

EVALUATING ADVERTISING'S ECONOMIC EFFECTS—FUTURE RESEARCH DIRECTIONS

Numerous opinions have been offered about advertising's benefits to an economy and to the well-being of a society. Nicosia and Jacobson, who have studied this area extensively, note that research on the subject has barely begun. They identify four research questions:[36]

1. Does advertising of a specific brand or product contribute to sales in some meaningful economic way?
2. Does advertising contribute to sales of a product or product class in an industry?
3. How does advertising affect market structure in terms of prices, level and quality of output, barriers-to-entry, and so on?
4. What are the macroeconomic effects of advertising; that is, what is the relationship between all advertising expenditures and various measures of aggregate demand in the economy?

According to Nicosia and Jacobson future research should emphasize the macroeconomic effects of advertising. They note the principal crite-

---

[36]Franco M. Nicosia and Robert Jacobson, "Advertising Consumers, and Public Policy, The Macroeconomic Effects of Advertising," in *Advertising and the Public,* ed. Kim B. Rotzoll, Department of Advertising, University of Illinois, 1980, p. 52.

ria that research in this area must satisfy in order to provide reliable information. These include selection of appropriate data, selection of appropriate variables and their functional relationships, and selection of the appropriate inference techniques.

It is evident additional research concerning the economic effects of advertising is necessary. Perhaps the most potent indictment is that advertising misallocates resources by directing them toward inconsequential efforts rather than toward the solution of the serious economic problems of nations. To some extent this indictment remains justified, for in conjunction with large and extensive expenditures on banal and repetitive advertising, we find evidences of poverty and hunger within our affluent society.

However, advertising alone cannot be faulted for this condition, and there are suggestions that it might be more widespread if it were not for advertising's impetus in creating a more productive economy. Nonetheless it is evident that large sums of money continue to be expended on advertising food to a portion of the population that scarcely can eat much more, while another segment of the population goes hungry. It appears to be the responsibility of all concerned citizenry, including the advertising community, to take steps to eliminate obvious disparities and to provide more equitable allocation of resources.

SUMMARY

From an economic viewpoint advertising has become the object of conflicting criticisms and defenses. Economists tend to view its role as informative and/or competitive. While advertising's information role is generally accepted, many economists note that competitive advertising merely shifts demand from one good to another and raises price in doing so. Others declare that even competitive advertising may add utility.

Advertising is said to cause a number of economic deficiencies which, due, in part, to the difficulties involved in securing adequate and reliable data, have neither been proven nor disproven. It is said to raise costs since the price of advertising must be recouped. However the economies of scale resulting from advertising expenditures may decrease costs. Although advertising may widen the range of consumer choice, it is criticized for stimulating a desire for material acquisitions and excessive consumption.

Advertising has been criticized as retarding competition through creating excessive market control and barriers-to-entry. Studies have offered conflicting evidence. To evaluate the numerous criticisms and defenses, future research efforts are required, particularly those focusing on the macroeconomic effects of advertising.

QUESTIONS FOR DISCUSSION

1. What are the major differences between "the economic person's" model of the consumer and the "businessperson's" model?
2. What are the functions of advertising under each of these concepts?
3. What kinds of utility can be created by advertising?
4. Does advertising raise the costs of goods and services? Explain.
5. Do you believe advertising raises the prices you pay for goods and services? Explain.
6. How does advertising affect the range of goods available for consumers?
7. Does advertising improve the standard of living? Explain.
8. Does advertising create barriers-to-entry?
9. How may a small firm use advertising to enter a market?
10. What are the economic benefits of brand or trademark advertising?

KEY TERMS

consumer model
utility
form utility

AD PRACTICE

Select advertisements that offer useful information, show psychological utility, and enhance the competitive environment. Discuss these ads as a critic and then as a defender of advertising.

28

Advertising Regulation and Control

CHAPTER OBJECTIVES

— To examine the means by which federal, state, and local governments exert control over advertising

— To discuss the self-regulatory groups and the mechanisms they use for controlling advertising abuse

To demonstrate the superiority of plate glass over plain glass in car windows, Libby-Owens-Ford prepared a commercial showing two automobile windows. For the plain glass presentation, vaseline was streaked over the window and the resulting view indicated obvious distortions; for the plate glass presentation, the view was photographed with the window rolled down. Although the consequences for the companies were relatively minor (they were told not to engage in these practices again) the legal impact for false advertising may be much more serious.

In 1985 Jartran, a truck-and-auto rental company, ran a series of print ads comparing its prices and equipment with its rival, U-Haul. The ads were so effective that the campaign won a Golden Effie Award from the American Marketing Association. U-Haul, however, instituted a suit for false advertising, declaring the data used to show Jartran's superiority were false. A federal court, ultimately upheld by an appeals court, levied what is believed to be a record-setting false advertising fine of $40 million against Jartran to be awarded to U-Haul.

The legal aspects of advertising cover a broad and complex area for the advertising decision-maker. From a public policy perspective control over advertising is designed to protect business by preventing unfair methods of competition. For the consumer, advertising controls prevent unfair or deceptive practices which include false and misleading advertising.

Control over advertising is maintained through governmental regulation and self-regulation. Although no precise set of standards has evolved in eliminating advertising abuse, there exist numerous control mechanisms with which advertisers should familiarize themselves.

GOVERNMENT REGULATION OF ADVERTISING

Government control over advertising emanates from various federal, state, and local agencies through laws, judicial precedent, rules, and guides. By far the greatest force is exerted by the federal segment.

FEDERAL LAWS AFFECTING ADVERTISING

For some time the federal government has attempted to eliminate and control deceptive advertising practices. Control activities did not emerge from a stated policy, generally, the government applied preventive measures to combat specific advertising abuses as they arose. However, several federal laws have been passed that have a significant impact on advertising.

Federal Trade Commission Act (1914)

The Federal Trade Commission Act which created the federal authority most active in controlling advertising abuse was originally passed to implement the antitrust concept, one of a series of laws that attempted to restrain monopolistic practices and unfair methods of competition. It contained no statement about advertising.

A consumer movement developed in 1933 to counteract the deficiencies in both the Federal Trade Commission Act and the Food and Drug Act which had been passed in 1906. In 1937 two bills were formulated, one bestowing on the Federal Trade Commission the power to regulate all advertising in the public interest and the other granting the Food and Drug Administration similar broad powers with respect to the sale and labeling (but not advertising) of food, drugs, and cosmetics. Critics mounted an opposition to the bills, but in the fall of 1937, at a crucial stage in the proceedings, action was precipitated by a tragedy. Dr. Samuel Massengell, a prominent druggist from Bristol, Tennessee, having found a method of packaging sulfanilamide in a liquid form, bottled nearly 500 gallons of the mixture and proceeded to sell it as a patent medication called Elixir Sulfanilamide. He had not tested the mixture for toxicity, nor had he bothered to test its effects even on animals. The use of the patent medicine ultimately caused 73 deaths in 7 states. Under the existing law the Food and Drug Administration was unable to hold Massengell responsible, and it was only through a technicality that it could legally seize the drug. Ultimately Massengell was fined $200 for having misbranded a drug product.[1] By the end of the year all opposition from reputable drug manufacturers collapsed, and Congress delayed no longer in passing the acts in question, which took effect in June, 1938. The Food and Drug Administration under the Federal Pure Food, Drug, and Cosmetic Act was given added power over the labeling

---

[1]For a comprehensive examination of these conflicts, see Otis Pease, *The Responsibility of American Advertising: Private Control and Public Influence, 1920-1940* (New Haven: Yale University Press, 1958), p. 124.

of food, drugs, and cosmetics, and the Federal Trade Commission was given the power to regulate the advertising of these same commodities in the Wheeler Lea Amendments to the Federal Trade Commission Act.

Wheeler Lea Amendments (1938)

The Wheeler Lea Amendments seemed to broaden the Commission's power over advertising when the important Section 5 of the Federal Trade Commission Act was rewritten to read: "Unfair methods of competition in commerce, and unfair or deceptive acts or practices are hereby declared to be unlawful." The addition of the phrase *unfair or deceptive acts or practices* was designed to indicate that if there were injury to the public as well as to competitors the Commission was empowered to act.

The amendments also specified that false advertising of foods, drugs, cosmetics, and devices was an unfair or deceptive act or practice. This did not add much as all false advertising was held to be deceptive, but Section 15 (a) was helpful in defining the term *false advertising*:

> . . . *'false advertising' means an advertisement other than labeling, which is misleading in a material respect; and in determining whether any advertisement is misleading, there shall be taken into account (among other things) not only representations made or suggested by statement, word, design, device, sound, or any combination thereof but also the extent to which the advertisement fails to reveal facts material in the light of such representations or material with a respect to consequences which may result from the use of the commodity to which the advertisement relates under conditions prescribed in said advertisement, or under such conditions as are customary or usual.*

In subsequent years a number of acts were passed that related to advertising and labeling, but enforcement of these was placed under the FDA or FTC. For example, the Public Health Smoking Act of 1970 banned cigarette advertising on radio and television and the Comprehensive Smokeless Tobacco Health Education Act of 1986 placed a similar ban on the broadcast advertising of smokeless tobacco products. The FTC is required to report annually to Congress on the effects of cigarette advertising and promotion and has designed warning notices to appear in print advertisements for smokeless tobacco.

The Federal Food, Drug and Cosmetic Act (1938)

A flood of popular writings describing evils in the food and drug industry descended upon the public in the first years of the twentieth century. Magazine articles by the dozens, together with several popular books began to devote themselves to "muckraking." Finally, the revelations of the extraordinary unhygienic conditions in the meat packing industry by Upton Sinclair in *The Jungle* aroused great public clamor, and President Theodore Roosevelt supported a Food and Drug Bill.

Although the passage of the Federal Pure Food and Drug Act in 1906 made some strides against the elimination of dangerous products, still no action could be taken against advertising. The case of Radithor (a radioactive drinking water which caused a number of deaths) was indicative of the problem. Radithor's labeling said "Certified Radioactive Water, Contains Radium and Mesothorium in Triple-Distilled Water"— exactly what it was! However its advertising made extravagant claims of curative worth for some 160 afflictions.[2] The subsequent Federal Food, Drug, and Cosmetic Act, passed in 1938, did not provide jurisdiction over advertising with the exception of prescription-legend drugs. Nonetheless, control over "misbranding and mislabeling" as vested in the Food and Drug Administration necessarily covered some aspects of promotion. Moreover, the courts have upheld the FDA's contention that accompanying literature is to be considered as labeling.

With the passage of time the Food and Drug Administration found itself unable to cope with several problems under the existing law. In 1962, the Kefauver-Harris Drug Amendments were passed to assure a greater degree of safety, effectiveness, and reliability in prescription drugs, and to strengthen new drug clearance procedures.[3] These amendments place severe restrictions on certain aspects of drug advertising. The regulations forbid employment of "fanciful" proprietary names for drugs or ingredients; featuring inert or inactive ingredients in order to create an impression of value greater than a true functional role, and use of proprietary names which, because of the similarity of spelling or pronunciation, may lead to confusion with the established names of other drugs.

The Lanham Act (1947)

The Lanham Act, which provides protection for trademarks also encompasses false advertising. Section 43 (a) of the Act prohibits "any false description or representation including words or other symbols tending falsely to describe or represent the same." While the FTC Act does not provide individual advertisers with the opportunity to sue for deception, under the Lanham Act such suits are permitted. Relatively few advertisers had instituted suits for false advertising in the past. With the increase in the use of comparison advertising, advertisers have begun to seek such protection under the Lanham Act as in the Jartran case discussed at the beginning of this chapter.

Recently, Maybelline won a preliminary injunction against competitor Noxell Corporation's advertising and packaging for Clean Lash mascara. The judge ruled that the advertising violated the Lanham Act in claiming that the mascara was waterproof and "laughs at tears."[4] Testimony from cosmetic industry experts indicated that Clean Lash washed off in the shower and during swimming. The judge ordered Noxell to stop waterproof claims and send letters to distributors instructing them to stop selling the product "under the present deceptive packaging."

---

[2]Ruth deForest Lamb, *American Chamber of Horrors* (New York: Farrar & Rinehart, 1936), p. 79.

[3]Public Law 87–781.

[4]Pat Sloan, "Judge Hits Noxell over Mascara Ads," *Advertising Age* (September 1, 1986), p. 31.

Magnuson-Moss Warranty—Federal Trade Commission Improvements Act (1975)

In 1975 a two-section act considerably expanded the FTC's authority. The Magnuson-Moss Warranty section was designed to enable consumers to make "valid and informed comparisons of warranties for similar products," and gave the FTC the power to promulgate rules for any product warranted in writing with an actual cost to the consumer exceeding five dollars.

The FTC Improvements section of the act broadened the scope of the FTC's activities to cover practices that "affected commerce" rather than only those designated as "in commerce," and permitted the Commission to order restitution to consumers. Most importantly it empowered the FTC to promulgate trade regulation rules that specify unfair or deceptive acts or practices and authorized penalties for violations of these rules.

In keeping with its expanded jurisdiction the FTC proposed and promulgated a number of trade regulation rules. These generated significant controversy, particularly since many of them were based on "unfair" rather than "deceptive" practices, and critics claim that "unfairness" was a nebulous concept and could not be precisely defined. The most controversial of these rules was a proposed trade regulation rule to limit children's television advertising based on the fact that some of this advertising was unfair.

The 1980 FTC Improvements Act

The 1980 FTC Improvements Act appropriated funds for the Commission. However, in response to what some critics viewed as the FTC's "overly broad" use of unfairness, a provision was included that prohibited the FTC from using unfairness as a basis for designing any trade regulation rules on advertising. This provision is to be reconsidered in the next appropriations bill, which has not been passed at this writing.

FEDERAL AGENCIES THAT CONTROL ADVERTISING

Currently numerous federal agencies have some responsibility for advertising regulation. Of all the federal authorities the Federal Trade Commission has, by far, the widest jurisdiction over advertising and has exercised the greatest efforts toward the control of advertising abuse. The responsibility of most of the other federal authorities is limited to the advertising of particular products or services, or to certain types of media, as noted in Table 28.1.

Federal Trade Commission

There is overlapping jurisdiction in the control of advertising practices but the Federal Trade Commission is considered the principal regulatory agency. Many of the other federal authorities refer their advertising problems to the Federal Trade Commission (for example, the Federal

TABLE 28.1   Control over Advertising Practices by Federal Authorities

Federal Authority	Area of Responsibility
Independent Regulatory Commissions	
Federal Trade Commission	All media, all products and services except for meat packing, banking, and common carriers
Federal Communications Commission	Broadcast media
Securities and Exchange Commission	Securities
Civil Aeronautics Board	Airlines
Interstate Commerce Commission	Carriers
Federal Energy Regulatory Commission	Public utilities
Environmental Protection Agency	Pesticides
Divisions of Executive Departments	
Post Office	Mail
Department of Health and Human Services: Food and Drug Administration	Prescription drugs and labeling of foods, drugs, cosmetics, and devices
Treasury Department: Bureau of Alcohol, Tobacco and Firearms	Alcohol, tobacco, and firearms
Department of Agriculture: Grain Division	Seed
Department of Agriculture: Bureau of Animal Husbandry	Meat packing
Department of Commerce: Bureau of Standards	Commercial standards of various products
Department of Energy	Energy
Department of Interior	Lands within jurisdiction, and Indian arts and crafts
Department of Justice	American flag
Treasury Department	Money, coins, and bonds
Others	
Customs Bureau	Some imported products
Narcotics Bureau	Narcotics
Patent Office	Registers trademarks
Farm Credit Administration	Federal farm loans
Library of Congress	Protects copyrights

Communications Commission refers cases of misleading commercials).

The primary methods used by the Commission to end deceptive practices are the halting of illegal business practices, through the issuance of complaints and cease-and-desist orders, and the encouragement of business people to abide voluntarily by the trade practice laws. Voluntary compliance is achieved by the Commission's industry guidance program under which it issues advisory opinions and industry guidelines. Trade regulation rules now have the force and effect of law.

What Is Unfair and Deceptive Advertising?

The terms *deception* and *unfairness* have not been precisely defined; however, they have acquired meaning. This is particularly true of *deception,* as there are years of precedent which have helped establish criteria for the Commission's actions in protecting consumers from deceptive practices. In legal terminology deception is "having the capacity or tendency to deceive." Under the current administration a new definition has emerged and the FTC has declared that a finding of deception will occur where there is "a representation, omission, or practice that is likely to mislead the consumer acting reasonably in the circumstances to the consumer's detriment." FTC activities and court decisions indicate the kinds of questions to be raised by advertisers in determining whether their ads will be considered deceptive.

Who Is the Target of the Ad?

The target groups in whose interest advertising is regulated have been referred to as the public, the purchasing public, the consuming public, the consumer, the average consumer, the customer, the buyer, the individual, and the average individual. Moreover, the mind and intelligence of these individuals are subject to close scrutiny. According to the courts, the public may include the "trusting as well as the suspicious," as well as "that vast multitude which includes the ignorant, the unthinking, and the credulous."[5] The Commission, however, has noted that it would not hold an advertiser liable for misconceptions "among the foolish or feebleminded."[6]

The current FTC which added the phrase "consumers acting reasonably" to a finding of deception has declared the consumer will be the average individual, except in cases where the ads are targeted at the elderly, children, or the terminally ill. In these cases the Commission will consider a reasonable member of that group.

Is the Representation (Claim) True?

Attempts are made to determine the truth of an advertisement by examining the claim (also called the representation, the promise, and the benefit). The claim may occur in any part of an advertisement or in an accompanying promotional material. It may be presented pictorially, in the copy, or by affixing trade names and trademarks.

Objective Claims   In determining the falsehood of an objective claim, the FTC will generally consider a statement deceptive where a standard exists for determining the truth of the representation and where there is sufficient knowledge to establish its falsity. Of course, the difficulty arises in deciding which standards to use as yardsticks against which representations are measured. The Commission may use dictionary definitions, government definitions or specifications, general usage, and ex-

---

[5]*FTC* v. *Standard Education Society,* 302 U.S. 112 (1937).
[6]*Continental Wax Corp.* v. *FTC,* 5 Trade Reg. Rep. #71,090 (CA-2, 1964).

pert opinion as its authoritative standard and in recent years has used consumer surveys.

Proof of the falsity of an objective claim may be accomplished with relative simplicity as, for example, in an ad which claimed that the user of the denture adhesive Poligrip could eat problem foods such as apples and corn-on-the-cob without embarrassment or discomfort. In fact, dentures are usually constructed with front teeth that are virtually useless for biting, with or without Poligrip, and only serve cosmetic purposes.[7] Claims which are clearly and objectively false are relatively infrequent in the Commission's recent caseload.

Subjective Claims   Subjective or opinion claims are difficult to prove false, especially since "trade puffery" is generally considered beyond the scope of the Commission. A *puff* has been defined as a statement that "probably would not be taken too seriously by the ordinary reader."[8] Such claims are often considered as incapable of proof or disproof, not because of inadequate knowledge, but because the applicable criterion is so personal and individual that it defies objective measurement. Thus, statements that a toothpaste "will beautify your smile" and a sewing machine "is almost human" are considered by the courts as "puffing."

Nevertheless, when superlatives are used that can be objectively disproved, these may be considered deceptive. For example, the FTC has ordered companies to stop advertising safety helmets as "finest, safest, or best,"[9] or batteries as "trouble free for five years."[10]

Implied Claims   The courts have ruled that in assessing the meaning of a communication the FTC must look at the impression that is likely to be created. "Deception by innuendo" may occur, for example, through the use of certain words or phrases. The FTC issued a cease-and-desist order to a debt-collection agency noting the use of the word *Letegram* in its mailing to various people misrepresented the immediacy of any action the agency might take against a debtor.[11]

Uniqueness Claim   When a company indicates that its product is the only one to possess a particular attribute, it is using a uniqueness claim. If such a claim is made for a characteristic of a product that exists in competitive products, the uniqueness claim may be considered misleading and deceptive. An ad for Cope stated "Cope looks different, is different. Besides a powerful pain reliever, Cope give you a gentle relaxer. The others don't . . . A unique formula for really effective relief of nervous tension headache. And you get it only in Cope." The FTC declared that the ads that portrayed Cope as unique were false and misleading.[12]

---

[7]In re Block Drug Co., Inc. 3 Trade Reg. Rep. #21,360 (1977).
[8]Necchi Sewing Machine Sales Corp., 53 FTC 1040 (1957).
[9]In re Lew Siegler, Inc., 3 Trade Reg. Rep. #20,412 (1973).
[10]National Dynamics Corp., 82 FTC 488 (1973).
[11]In re Capax, Inc., et al., 3 Trade Reg. Rep. #21,427 (1978).
[12]In re Sterling Drug Inc., Dancer-Fitzgerald-Sample, Inc. and Lois Holland Callaway, Inc., FTC Docket No. 8919, Trade Regulation Reports No. 604 (July 19, 1983).

The Claim with Two Meanings   An advertisement that is capable of two meanings, one of which is false, is misleading.[13] The Commission issued a cease-and-desist order prohibiting the National Commission on Egg Nutrition from advertising the statement: "There is no scientific evidence that eating eggs increases the risk of . . . heart disease." NCEN appealed the order on the grounds that the statement is true. The topic is controversial—some medical experts believe that existing evidence indicates that increased consumption of dietary cholesterol, including that in eggs, may increase the risk of heart disease; others, however, do not believe in this relationship. A court of appeals upheld the Commission order declaring that where an advertisement conveys more than one meaning, one of which is false, the advertiser is liable for the misleading variation.[14]

Is the Claim Adequately Substantiated?

Much of the FTC's recent activity relates to claims which are not adequately substantiated. According to the FTC, it is illegal to advertise an affirmative claim for a product without having a reasonable basis. The requirement to substantiate advertising claims relates to those made regarding a product's safety, performance, efficacy, quality, or comparative price.

The substantiation requirements emerged from a program introduced by the Commission in the 1970s and were crystallized in an FTC decision in which the Commission stated that it was unfair to advertise a claim without having a reasonable basis to support it, even if the claim was true and the product ultimately performed as advertised.[15] This unfairness, according to the Commission, resulted from imposing on the consumer the economic risk that a product may not perform as advertised if a manufacturer did not have a reasonable basis for belief in the product claim. Advertised claims that had been considered to be inadequately substantiated range from a beauty product that claimed it removed wrinkles to automobile tires that were designated as "safe."[16] Recently, the FTC ordered Thompson Co. to cease making efficacy claims for its topical analgesic Aspercreme unless it had conducted at least two well-controlled, clinical studies of its product.[17]

Has Material Information Been Omitted?

Not only what is said but what is not said may constitute a deceptive act. According to the current commission a material representation is one which is likely to affect a consumer's conduct regarding the choice of a product. Where a material representation is omitted it is an indication that an injury to the consumer is likely to exist ("consumer detriment" will occur). Certain categories of information are considered ma-

[13]*Rhodes Pharmacol Co., Inc.* v. *FTC*, 208 F.2d 382 (7th Cir. 1953).
[14]*National Commission on Egg Nutrition, et al.*, 570 F.2d 157, 162 (7th Cir. 1977).
[15]In re Pfizer Inc., 3 Trade. Reg. Rep. #20,056 (July 1972)
[16]Dorothy Cohen, "The FTC's Advertising Substantiation Program," *Journal of Marketing*, 44 (Winter 1980), pp. 26–35.
[17]*Thompson Medical Co., Inc.* v. *FTC*, CCH #67,103 (CA-DC May 1986).

terial, including expressed claims and information which the seller knew or should have known an ordinary consumer would need to evaluate a product or service. Information concerning health, safety, and the central characteristics of a product is generally considered to be material.

If an ad makes claims and omits material facts that may relate to these claims this may "trigger" affirmative disclosure requirements in future ads. For example, Fresh Horizons bread was highly touted for its fiber content. According to the FTC the presence of wood in the bread was a material fact and in a consent order agreement required the ads to state "The source of this fiber is wood" or "Contains fiber derived from the pulp of trees."[18] In the Aspercreme case mentioned earlier the FTC required the company to disclose in all advertising and labeling that Aspercreme did not contain aspirin.

Unfair Advertising

The precedents for a finding of unfairness are much less developed than those concerning deception. In 1972, the Supreme Court encouraged the Commission to apply unfairness in protecting consumers.[19] Nevertheless, in most of its case-by-case adjudications the Commission continued to use unfairness only in conjunction with deception.

The FTC has complained of unfairness in advertising to children in several recent cases, expressing its concern for ads that may have the tendency or capacity to influence children to engage in unsafe behavior. Hudson Pharmaceutical agreed not ot use a hero figure such as Spiderman in its vitamin advertising because such advertising could induce children to take excessive amounts of vitamins.[20] General Foods agreed not to depict Euell Gibbons picking and eating certain wild plants since some plants may be harmful if eaten.[21] Mego agreed to discontinue an ad for its Cher doll showing a little girl, seated next to a sink full of water, using an electric hair dryer to dry the doll's hair.[22]

The 1980 FTC Act prohibited the FTC from promulgating trade regulation rules on the basis of unfairness in advertising and indicated that this prohibition would be reevaluated when the next FTC Appropriations Bill was passed. It did not prevent the FTC from proceeding against unfair advertising on a case-by-case basis; however, there has been relatively little activity in this area. The FTC has issued a policy statement providing a more detailed sense of definition and limits of unfairness. The basic criterion is that the unfairness must cause *substantial consumer injury*, outweighed by any countervailing benefits, and the injury must be one the consumer cannot reasonably avoid. Passage of an FTC Appropriations Bill will no doubt provide clarification of this area.

---

[18]In re ITT Continental Baking Co., Inc., 3 Trade Reg. Rep. #21,546 (1979).
[19]*FTC* v. *Sperry & Hutchinson Co.*, 405 U.S. 233 (1972).
[20]In re Hudson Pharmaceutical Corp., 3 Trade Reg. Rep. #21,191 (1976).
[21]In re General Foods Corp., 3 Trade Reg. Rep. #20,928 (1975).
[22]In re Mego Int'l, Inc., 3 Trade Reg. Rep. #21,399 (July 1978).

Remedies for Unfair and Deceptive Advertising

The FTC was not established to resolve private disputes, but to end illegal practices. Its objective was to restrain future violators, not punish violators for past misconduct. In fact, the FTC was not empowered to require penalties for unfair and deceptive practices. Its basic remedy was to issue a cease-and-desist order; penalties were imposed only if a firm continued to commit the prohibited acts in violation of that order. Nevertheless, the scope and impact of these remedies have increased in recent years.

An alleged violation may come to the attention of the Commission in a number of ways: through a complaint about a competitor's ad, a consumer complaint, from government agencies upon referral by the courts, or through the Commission itself.

A Cease-and-Desist Order

The earliest remedy available to the FTC for ending false advertising is the *cease-and-desist order*, which is issued after the Commission investigates the alleged violation, serves a formal complaint, and receives no reply. If a reply is made, a formal hearing is held before a trial examiner who issues an initial decision. Unless this decision is appealed by either side, or unless the Commission places it on its own docket for review, the initial decision becomes the final decision of the Commission. This decision may incorporate an order to cease and desist from the practice which was the subject of the complaint.

A Consent Order

At any stage in the proceedings before the hearing, a settlement may be negotiated between the FTC and the advertiser. When both sides agree, a consent order is prepared. The order contains a statement that signing is for settlement purposes only and does not constitute an admission by a firm that it has violated the law. However, the firm agrees not to engage in the activities which were the subject of the complaint.

Penalties

Until 1973, the maximum penalty for a single violation of an FTC cease-and-desist order was $5000; after 1973 it was raised to $10,000. Moreover such penalties can take on significant proportions.

When *Reader's Digest*, in violation of an FTC order prohibiting the use of simulated checks or bonds, mailed approximately 14 million simulated "travel checks" and over 4 million simulated "bonds" in connection with its promotional efforts, the FTC requested the court to impose civil penalties of $1,750,000.[23] The FTC contended that *Reader's Digest* distributed a total of almost 18 million individual mailings containing checks or bonds and was, therefore, guilty of approximately 18 million separate violations. Although the total maximum penalty for these items could have amounted to more than $89 billion, the FTC requested a fine of $1.75 million.

---

[23]*United States v. Reader's Digest Association*, 5 Trade Reg. Rep. #64,431 (1980).

Reader's Digest ultimately appealed to the Supreme Court, declaring that the ruling set a precedent for imposing a fine on each item mailed and could have a "chilling effect" on publishers and advertisers. The Supreme Court, however, refused to set aside the fine of $1.75 million, supporting the FTC's interpretation for computing violations.

Affirmative Disclosure

Affirmative disclosure requires that a company disclose in its advertising the deficiencies or limitations of a product or service so that a consumer may be aware of the negative, as well as the positive, attributes of an item. The most widespread use of affirmative disclosures are the cautionary requirements in cigarette advertising.

Corrective Advertising

Corrective advertising is designed to overcome the continuing effects of inaccurate information in prior deceptive advertising. While it is similar to affirmative disclosure its objectives are somewhat broader and include (1) dispelling the residual effects of prior deceptive advertising, (2) restoring competition to the stage that prevailed before the unfair practice, and (3) depriving firms of falsely obtained gains to which deceptive advertising may have contributed. In addition corrective advertising specifically addresses the misinformation previously offered; affirmative disclosure adds information that was not previously offered.

The "marbles in the soup" case was the first in which such a remedy was suggested. While shooting an ad Campbell Soup Company was alleged to have placed marbles in a soup bowl to force the solid ingredients to the surface, creating the false impression that there was more stock than actually existed. A group of law students, designating themselves SOUP (Stamp Out Unfair Practices) recommended that the Commission require Campbell to use corrective advertisements; however the FTC accepted a consent agreement from Campbell in which Campbell agreed to change its advertising in the future. Although the Commission did not consider the corrective order appropriate in this case, they did use it in a number of subsequent cases.

In the first litigated order (the firm appealed to the courts) involving corrective advertising the FTC declared that since 1921 Listerine advertisements had fostered the belief that Listerine was effective in the treatment and prevention of colds and sore throats. Accordingly, the FTC required Warner-Lambert to spend an amount equal to the average Listerine annual advertising budget—which has been estimated at $10 million—on a corrective advertising campaign. The Commission ordered Warner-Lambert to place the corrective statement "Listerine will not help prevent colds or sore throats or lessen their severity" in its ads. The Supreme Court upheld this order and Warner-Lambert conducted the campaign.

The effectiveness of corrective advertising as a remedy has been questioned by researchers. Proposals to increase the efficiency of this remedy include suggestions that the FTC stress consumer responses during a campaign and provide advertisers with incentives to seek effective corrective communication.[24]

Redress of Consumer Injury

The Magnuson-Moss Act authorizes the Commission to bring civil actions to redress consumer injury. This may include rescission of contracts, refund of money, return of property, and payment of damages. The court, however, may not award exemplary or punitive damages.

The Commission can bring such actions only if there has been a violation of a trade regulation rule, or if there is violation of a cease-and-desist order and where a reasonable man would have known under the circumstances that the act was dishonest or fraudulent. In 1981 Horizon Corporation, one of the largest sellers of undeveloped real estate in the Southwest, was ordered to pay $14.5 million to purchasers who bought land because of the company's false and misleading claims.

The FTC has also engaged in activities designed to notify consumers of redress capabilities. In 1981 Ford Motor Company ran the first repair-information advertising ordered by the FTC. The Commission had charged that Ford was repairing cars powered by four-cylinder engines that were inadequately lubricated; by quietly fixing a widespread problem only for those who complained, Ford was providing a "secret warranty." Ford was ordered to run black-and-white, one-page ads in magazines such as *Newsweek, Reader's Digest, Time, Sports Illustrated,* and *U.S. News & World Report*. The headlines stated, "Ford Motor Co. introduces the customer information system. It makes greater after-sales service even better."[25]

The Federal Communications Commission

Congress gave the FCC the responsibility of encouraging proper standards of radio and television transmission.[26] One of its activities is the general regulation of both visual and aural broadcasting.

The FCC has been concerned with the excessive time and excessive number of commercials, as well as with commercial content. However, control in these areas has been left to self-regulatory mechanisms, particularly radio and television codes established by the National Association of Broadcasters. The Federal Communications Commission has, however, disapproved, on moral and ethical grounds, advertising by physicians, clergy, those offering advice on marriage and family matters, and the advertising of lotteries and hard liquor.

---

[24]William L. Wilkie, Dennis McNeill, and Michael B. Mazis, "Marketing's Scarlet Letter: The Theory and Practice of Corrective Advertising," *Journal of Marketing,* Vol. 48 (Spring 1984), p. 28.

[25]"Ford to Run FTC-Ordered Ads in 1981," *Advertising Age* (October 27, 1980), p. 28.

[26]48 Stat. 1064 (1934), 47 USC 151 (1952).

Regulation of false and misleading advertising in broadcasting has been accomplished by referring such activities to other regulatory agencies specializing in such matters. Under a cooperative arrangement with the FTC, the Federal Communications Commission notifies stations of broadcast advertising cited by the Federal Trade Commission, so that these stations may take any necessary action consistent with their obligations to operate in the public interest.

Equal Time
The equal-time provisions of the Federal Communications declare that if a legally qualified candidate secures broadcast advertising time, equal time has to be provided to opposing candidates. However, such equal time must be requested by the opposing candidate, and it must also be paid for.

The Fairness Doctrine and Counter-Advertising
The fairness doctrine requires that broadcasters provide for the expression of opposing viewpoints. Designed to strike a balance among the interests competing for broadcasting it has even been supported by the Supreme Court.[27]

Prior to the passage of the Public Health Cigarette Smoking Act which barred the advertising of cigarettes on electronic media, broadcasters were ordered by the FCC to provide counter-advertisements which indicated the hazards of cigarette smoking. This form of advertising influenced several organizations to apply to the FCC for counter ads for alcoholic beverages, drugs, and even automobiles. Ultimately the courts declared that commercial speech, such as advertising, does not trigger the fairness doctrine. Where political speech is involved, such as in advocacy advertising, the broadcasters can determine whether to provide time for a controversial issue. Currently, counter-advertising is almost nonexistent, but suggestions for its use in public welfare issues are raised periodically.

Broadcasters have the right to accept or reject advertising involving controversial issues. Under the fairness doctrine, if they choose to put on the air one side of what they consider to be a controversial view, they must provide sufficient coverage of the opposing view and must take affirmative action to secure such coverage. However they can decide on the spokesperson and do not have to provide the exact amount of time or the same format as the initial presentation.

This action requirement has led some networks to reject ads such as television spots prepared by W. R. Grace & Co. about the federal deficit. The commercials present a fictitious trial in the year 2017 in which a young prosecutor questions an elderly witness about why no one did anything about the deficit in 1986. The witness ends his testimony by asking the prosecutor, "Are you ever going to forgive us?"

---

[27]Recently, the FCC repealed the Fairness Doctrine; however, Congress may reinstate it.

The Post Office Department

The U. S. Post Office is a major advertising medium essentially under government control. Regulations by the Post Office over advertising encompass two areas: those concerned with second-class mailing privileges and those affected by the lottery, fraud, and obscenity statutes.

Originally it seemed as though the Post Office had strong regulatory powers over publications through revocation of special mailing rights. Although revocation of second-class mailing privileges is a potentially powerful sanction, the limitations imposed by the judiciary and the reluctance on the part of the Post Office to impose this restriction have made it of minimal effectiveness in advertising regulation. Of somewhat more effectiveness has been the Postmaster General's powers to exclude nonmailable matter, to issue fraud orders, and to impose penal sanctions for the fraudulent use of mails.

The fraud order under postal laws has been used more frequently in an attempt to control deceptive advertising. Action has been taken against deceptive business opportunities, dance studio lessons, medical cures, and work-at-home jobs. The Post Office's control over obscene material is limited by the difficulties involved in identifying legally obscene matter. To combat the effect of advertisements which are not legally obscene but may shock the families who receive them, a law has been passed designed to curb these "pandering advertisements."[28] The individual mail patron is the sole judge of whether an advertisement is offensive to him or her.

The Food and Drug Administration

The Food and Drug Administration is now under the jurisdiction of the Department of Health and Human Services. It is actively involved in setting rules for labeling and for drug packaging. In some procedural aspects the Food and Drug Administration has greater authority than the Federal Trade Commission, because the FDA can seize food and drugs on charges of false and misleading advertising.

Over $200 million worth of advertising for drugs appears in leading medical journals in one year.[29] The FDA has criticized as inappropriate advertisements of drugs before they are approved, the increasing use of comparative ads in which deficiencies of competing brands are cited, as well as the growing tendency to make promotional claims that may be considered excessive, and is taking steps to correct such abuses. Recently, for example, a drug company advertised a heart medicine, and, according to the FDA, the ad was "false and misleading in its overall message, and by misrepresenting important warnings, increased the risk of serious adverse reactions to patients." The FDA ordered the company to revise its promotional material, send letters to all physicians who

---

[28]Prohibition of Pandering Advertisements in the Mail, Public Law 90-206, Title III, 39 U.S. Code #4009.

[29]"Medicine, Excess Marks the Spot, The FDA Blows the Whistle on Abuses in New Drug Ads," *Time* (September 27, 1982).

might have received the original literature, and publish "remedial advertisements" in two issues of several publications. The FDA has told companies who make anti-aging claims for their cosmetic products, that if they wish to continue making such claims, they will have to seek approval of their products as drugs instead of cosmetics.

Bureau of Alcohol, Tobacco, and Firearms

The Bureau of Alcohol, Tobacco, and Firearms, established in 1972, is an agency within the Treasury Department. It combines functions involving law enforcement, industry regulation, and tax collection. Ever since Prohibition was repealed in 1933 the liquor industry has been one of the most tightly controlled and self-restricted in the United States. In part this is because of a fear of pre-Prohibition abuses and even greater government restrictions.

EXHIBIT 28.1
Ad Prohibited by New BATF Rules

BATF has extremely broad powers over liquor advertising. It not only has the customary authority to act against deceptive and misleading advertising, but can also require informative advertising. The regulations are very specific about the mandatory information required on advertising and the prohibited statements that may not appear. The labeling requirements are even more detailed, and statements in the advertising which may be inconsistent with statements on the labeling are prohibited.

BATF rules require that ads for alcoholic beverages should not convey the impression that the use of the product is conducive to athletic skill or prowess. In the past this has been interpreted as prohibiting the use of currently active athletes in alcohol ads. Recently the Bureau declared that athletes could endorse a beer as long as they weren't shown consuming it. However the broadcasting networks have indicated they will not permit the use of active athletes in beer ads.

A recent rule declares if a product contains less than 0.5-percent alcohol it cannot be called beer; furthermore, the term *alcohol-free* cannot be used on nonalcoholic beer brands. This ruling creates problems for companies such as Guiness Import who advertize Kaliber, a nonalcoholic beer from Ireland as a "great imported beer without alcohol (see Exhibit 28.1).[30] The BATF has also imposed a prohibition against the use of subliminal advertising in all liquor ads, despite protestations by the alcohol industry that it does not use this technique.

The agency is empowered to apply strong sanctions for advertising infractions. It issues permits to distillers and vinters, can suspend, revoke, or annul these permits for violations, including those relating to advertising.

Other Federal Controls

All of the institutions listed in Table 28.1 have some jurisdiction over advertising in their respective fields. For example, the Civil Aeronautics

---

[30]Pat Winters, "BATF Rules on 'Alcohol-Free' Ad Claims," *Advertising Age*, January 27, 1986, p. 35.

Board and the Federal Energy Regulation Commission regulate the economic aspects of airlines and public utilities, respectively. These Commissions provide stringent rules for rates in their specific areas and presumably regulate the advertising of these rates. They do not concern themselves to any significant extent with the general field of advertising abuse.

The Library of Congress enforces copyright laws which grant authors and creators of artwork the exclusive right to multiply and sell copies of works from their intellectual productions for a number of years. For advertisers the copyright laws provide some protection for their advertisements. It is relatively simple to secure such protection by applying to the Library of Congress and indicating in an ad that it is copyrighted.

Advertising and Freedom of Speech

A statement by the Supreme Court, "casual and almost offhand" to the effect that commercial advertising is not protected by the First Amendment, served as a standard in advertising regulation for over 34 years.[31] In 1976 the Supreme Court overturned this doctrine by declaring that freedom of speech did relate to commercial advertising.[32] The case involved restrictions in the advertising of prescription drugs, and the initial impact of the decision was to eliminate a ban on such advertising. The Court declared that in concluding that commercial speech is protected, it does not hold that it never can be regulated in any way. In subsequent decisions the Supreme Court ruled that restrictions designed to deprive consumers of accurate information about products or services legally offered for sale were invalid in cases concerning lawyers' services, contraceptives, abortions, and housing.

In 1986 the Supreme Court, for the first time, upheld a ban on truthful advertising for a legal product or service. The court approved state restrictions on local advertising inviting Puerto Rico residents to visit casinos.[33] In writing the majority opinion in the Posados case, Justice Rehnquist declared that if it is constitutional for the government to totally ban a product or activity, it is constitutional for the government to take the less restrictive course of forbidding the stimulation of demand for that product or activity through advertising. Using the four-pronged test developed in an earlier case the Supreme Court ruled in a five-to-four decision that the Puerto Rico legislature had the power to ban advertising of casino gambling to local residents.

Although the Posados ruling is limited to the advertising of casinos to local residents of Puerto Rico it suggests new directions for a Su-

[31]Dorothy Cohen, "Advertising and the First Amendment," *Journal of Marketing* (July 1978), pp. 58–68.

[32]*Virginia State Board of Pharmacy and Virginia Citizens Consumer Council, Inc.*, U.S. 96 S.Ct. 1817 (1976).

[33]*Posados de Puerto Rico Associates a/k/a Condado Holiday Inn* v. *Tourism Co. of Puerto Rico*, U.S. (No. 84-1903, July 1, 1986).

TEST FOR FIRST AMENDMENT PROTECTION OF COMMERCIAL SPEECH

1. Is the activity unlawful and/or the speech misleading or fraudulent?
2. Is the government interest in restricting such speech substantial?
3. Do the challenged restrictions on commercial speech "directly advance" the government's interest?
4. Are the restrictions on commercial speech no more extensive than necessary to serve the government's interest?

Source: *Central Hudson Gas & Electric Corp.* v. *Public Service Commission of New York,* 447 U.S. 557 (1980).

preme Court that has been expanding the doctrine of First Amendment protection of commercial speech, and creates concerns for advertisers of products such as alcohol and tobacco.

STATE AND LOCAL CONTROLS

Many states have accumulated a large number of civil and criminal statutes concerned with the advertising of a specific product, service, or profession. Many of these involve limitations based on considerations of good taste and morality rather than on the dangers of deception. A number of states have adopted "little FTC acts" that more or less parallel the proscription against unfair or deceptive practices contained in the FTC Act.

The extent to which consumers are protected under federal law depends upon the FTC's willingness to act. Many states, however, expressly provide that consumers may sue those engaged in prohibited practices to recover double or triple actual damages or obtain other relief. Moreover, state regulation of advertising has been substantially increased with the passage of civil remedial statutes enforced by state attorneys general. With the federal deregulation movement, state attorneys general who formerly deferred to the FTC are beginning to exercise their jurisdiction over false advertising claims. In New York, for example, the state attorney general required Campbell Soup to discontinue advertising "Soup Is Good Food," because the ads failed to reveal the high sodium content that could be harmful to some consumers. Attorneys general in three states asked McDonalds Corp. to stop advertisements that tout its food as nutritional, charging that they are deceptive.[34]

Consumer fraud divisions have been established in a few large cities to proceed against major instances of false advertising. For example, a regulation that is unique is enforced in New York City. It requires mer-

---

[34]Robert Johnson, "Three States Charge McDonald's Ads on Its Foods Nutrition Are Deceptive," *The Wall Street Journal* (April 27, 1987), p.14.

chants who sell merchandise in *excess* of the manufacturer's suggested list or retail price, if one exists, to disclose the manufacturer's recommended price on the tag or label of each item. This requirement is designed to provide protection to foreign tourists and low-income consumers who may be unfamiliar with comparison shopping techniques or the usual values of consumer items, and consequently vulnerable to excessive or exorbitant prices.[35]

CONTROL OVER ADVERTISING: SELF-REGULATION

Control over advertising is maintained through self-regulation and government regulation. For years the advertising industry has fostered self-regulation in order to promote "truth and taste in advertising," and at the same time offset the possibility of more stringent government controls. Nonetheless, when the industry felt it necessary, the advertising associations encouraged the development of governmental legislation and were instrumental in the passage of the Federal Trade Commission Act and the Wheeler Lea Amendments to the Act. Today the advertising industry, through voluntary controls, promotes adherence to the laws, encourages "taste" in advertising, and is concerned with preventing the passage of punitive legislation which would place limitations on advertising or tax advertising.

There is no business area which has a longer history or wider range of self-regulatory work than advertising. Self-regulation emanates from advertisers, both as individuals and as part of an industry group, from advertising trade associations, and from advertising media.

The Better Business Bureau

The Better Business Bureau is a nonprofit corporation financed entirely by membership dues or subscriptions voluntarily paid to it by responsible business and professional firms. It is not limited to one specific industry, but, in performing its main task, which is "to protect business by building an environment of public confidence in which companies can operate peacefully and profitably," the association actively promotes fair advertising and selling practices in all industries.

There are 164 bureaus in the United States and they operate to secure voluntary observance by business of reasonable standards of practice governing advertising and selling. The BBB aids in establishing standards and then acts as a compliance agency to determine if the standards are observed. Compliance is secured through "moral suasion"; however, if fraudulent practices are disclosed, the BBB refers those to the appropriate legal authorities. The Bureau also provides a complaint service and tries to work out satisfactory adjustments between buyers and sellers. To provide information to businesspeople, the Association of Better Business Bureaus publishes a "Guide for Retail Advertising

---

[35]David G. Samuels, "Consumer Law," *New York Law Journal* (August 17, 1981).

and Selling" and the National Better Business Bureau publishes the "Do's and Don'ts on Advertising Copy."

The National Advertising Division (NAD) was created by the Council of Better Business Bureaus and initiates investigations, determines issues, collects and evaluates data, and negotiates settlements. Its objective is to sustain high standards of truth and accuracy in national advertising. If the NAD fails to resolve a controversy, an appeal can be made to a five-member panel of the National Advertising Review Board (NARB).

As a self-regulatory agency the NAD has no force of law, but uses moral suasion and industry cooperation to encourage compliance. If an advertiser refuses to participate in this process and is engaging in some questionable activities, the NAD may file a complaint with an appropriate law enforcement agency.

The NAD has a Children's Advertising Review Unit (CARU) and offers guidelines for child-directed advertisements. Generally a large proportion of its activities relate to determining whether claims in advertising are substantiated.

NAD conducts systematic monitoring of national television, radio, and print advertising—this is the largest single source of cases for investigation. Other sources include competitors' challenges, referrals from BBBs, and consumer complaints. Following a complaint from the Can Manufacturers Institute, for example, the NAD found that TV and print ads, themed "New Ragu Pasta-Meals—fresh taste you don't get from a can," presented statements that could be misleading to consumers about the quality of metal packaging. Chesebrough-Pond, producers of Ragu, said they would consider NAD's concerns in future ads for the brand.[36]

Beech-Nut Nutrition Company modified claims for its Stages Baby Foods after a review by the NAD. A print ad declared "Stages is the only leading baby food to remove chemically modified starch from all products and replace it with more real foods." In a television spot the company posed the question: "If you made your own baby food, would you add chemically modified starch as a filler?" Although Beech-Nut provided a study supporting its claim that chemically modified starch can be hard on a baby's digestive system, the NAD did not accept this as adequate substantiation and declared that the net impression of these claims would misrepresent the wholesomeness of widely accepted food ingredients used in competitor's products. Beech-Nut discontinued the campaign for reasons unrelated to the challenge and declared future advertising would take NAD's concerns into account.[37]

Trade Association Self-Regulation

A number of trade associations have introduced advertising self-regulation programs. These include organizations representing the alcohol industry—American Wine Association, Wine Institute, Distilled Spirits

[36]"Ragu Pasta Jar Ads a Pain in the Can," *Advertising Age* (September 15, 1986), p. 12.

[37]"Beech-Nut stages ad modification," *Advertising Age*, (January 19, 1987), p. 12.

Association, and United States Brewers Assocation—and drugs—Pharmaceutical Manufacturers Association and Proprietary Association. Other programs emanate from the Bank Marketing Association, National Swimming Pool Institute, Toy Manufacturers Association, and Motion Picture Association of America.[38]

The Motion Picture Association of America, for example, requires prescreening of advertisements to ensure that they comply with code standards. Each commercial is evaluated to determine whether it conforms to the MPAA advertising code of ethics. A rating is assigned (G, PG, R, X) which indicates the minimum age requirement for the commercial's audience. The rating of the commercial determines whether it can be shown on television or in a theater where children might be in the audience.[39]

Self-Regulation by Advertising Industry Groups

Throughout the years the advertising industry and the various groups that represent it have been proponents of self-regulation. There are numerous associations in the advertising industry, but there are three that are most actively concerned with advertising regulation.

1. The American Advertising Federation is composed of advertisers, advertising agencies, media, and numerous advertising clubs. The objectives of the organization have widened to cover education and public service as well as work in the legislative field. In the latter area, the AAF actively opposes proposed punitive legislation, such as regulation that would limit or tax advertising.

2. The American Association of Advertising Agencies is the national association of advertising agencies. The goals of the AAAA are to foster, strengthen, and improve the agency business, to advance the cause of advertising as a whole, and to give service to members. The AAAA has established standards of practice for its member organizations which include a creative code designed to persuade members to obey the legal regulations pertaining to advertising and to "broaden the application of high ethical standards." This code is endorsed by numerous other advertising associations including the Association of National Advertisers. The Four A's also issue guidelines for specific types of advertising (see the box on p. 618).

3. The Association of National Advertisers is comprised of large corporate advertisers and operates a committee in conjunction with the AAAA for the Improvement of Advertising Content. The concern of this committee is not false and misleading advertising, which the government regulates, but advertising which is not quite illegal but may be considered objectionable on the grounds of taste and opinion.

---

[38]Priscilla A. LaBarbera, "Analyzing and Advancing the State of the Art of Advertising Self-Regulation," *Journal of Advertising*, Vol. 9, No. 4 (1980), p. 30.

[39]Priscilla A. LaBarbera, "Analyzing and Advancing the State of the Art of Advertising Self-Regulation," p. 30.

Self-Regulation by Advertising Media

The checking and screening of advertising by the media in which it appears is one of the oldest forms of self-regulation. Most media exercise some control over advertising abuse.

Newspapers and Magazines

Individual newspapers draft their own set of advertising requirements, a practice considered both a right and duty by most publishers. Magazine ethical requirements include limitations about what products may be advertised. The *Reader's Digest* will not accept tobacco advertising; the *New Yorker* will not accept advertising of any feminine hygiene products. The variations in advertising restrictions among magazines result from the existence of numerous specialized audiences attracted by the variety of special interest magazines. As a result, advertising restrictions among these specialized media go beyond the requirements of truth and taste and evolve out of the needs and character of their readers and the personal convictions of their publishers.

Television and Radio

In 1937 the National Association of Broadcasters established a radio code; in 1952 it promulgated a television code. Both codes prohibit the advertising of certain products and services, such as hard liquor, fortune-telling, occultism, astrology, phrenology, palm-reading, numerology, tip sheets, racetrack publications, and lotteries. They provide standards for the presentation of advertising which include the manner in which products involving health considerations are presented and the placement of commercials in or near programs designed for children. The codes are specific in their time standards for nonprogram material, which includes billboards, all credits in excess of 30 seconds, and promotional announcements as well as commercials.

As noted previously, the Justice Department considered the time standards in this code to be in restraint of trade. In a consent order the NAB agreed to discontinue these restrictions. Subsequently the NAB suspended all of its code provisions. While there are indications that some of these will be revised and reinstated, the codes still remain suspended. Individual broadcasters continue to enforce many of the code provisions, nevertheless the major networks recently agreed to accept lingerie ads featuring live models, a practice that had been prohibited by the NAB television code.

Each of the major television networks has its own clearance process. ABC's Advertising Standards and Guidelines, for example, range from absolute prohibitions in some product categories, such as the advertising of liquor and handguns, to guidelines concerning techniques such as endorsements and judgments regarding matters of personal tastes (how personal hygiene sprays are depicted).[40]

---

[40]Eric Zanot, "Unseen but Effective Advertising Regulation: The Clearance Process," *Journal of Advertising*, Vol. 14, No. 4 (1985), p. 47.

AMERICAN ASSOCIATION OF ADVERTISING AGENCIES GUIDELINES FOR THE USE OF COMPARATIVE ADVERTISING

1. The intent and connotation of the ad should be to inform and never discredit or unfairly attack competitors, competing products or services.
2. When a competitive product is named, it should be one that exists in the market as significant competition.
3. The competition should be fairly and properly identified but never in a manner or tone that degrades the competitive product or service.
4. The advertising should compare related or similar properties or ingredients of the product, dimension to dimension, feature to feature.
5. The identification should be for honest comparison purposes and not simply to upgrade by association.
6. If a competitive test is conducted, it should be done by an objective testing source, preferably an independent one, so that there will be no doubt as to its validity.
7. In all cases the test should be supportive of all claims made in the advertising based on the test.
8. The advertising should never use partial results or stress insignificant differences to cause the consumer to draw an improper conclusion.
9. The property being compared should be significant in terms of value or usefulness to the consumer.
10. Comparatives delivered through the use of testimonials should not imply that the testimonial is more than one individual's thought unless that individual represents a sample of the majority viewpoint.

Source: from "Slugging It Out Fairly in Comparative Advertising" by Leonard S. Matthews, *Advertising Age* (July 11, 1983). Copyright © 1983 Crain Communications, Inc. Reprinted with permission from Advertising Age. All Rights Reserved.

Direct Mail

The Direct Marketing Association has established guidelines of ethical business practice for members of its association which includes requirements for the way in which merchandise is sold as well as advertised. If members violate these standards, they are requested, by letter, to make corrections. Failure to cooperate may result in expulsion from the organization.

Outdoor Advertising

The Outdoor Advertising Association of America, Inc., is a national trade association of the standardized outdoor medium and represents outdoor plant members that operate more than 90 percent of the medium's facilities in the country. It has established a code of practices that includes requirements for the location, building, and maintenance of structures as well as standards for truth and morality in advertising.

Benefits and Limitations of Self-Regulation

Self-regulation and government regulation in advertising complement each other. Self-regulation, however, has certain characteristics which set it apart from the vast machinery of government controls.

1. Self-regulation is faster, cheaper, and more effective (flexible and up-to-date) than government regulations.[41]
2. It is voluntary and generally entered into without compulsion or threat of penalties.
3. It encourages the development of individual, company, and industry standards which are higher than those imposed by law.
4. It deals with matters of public taste, welfare, and interest which are beyond the proper scope of legislation.
5. It promotes obedience to the law itself.
6. Peer pressure is effective in improving standards.
7. Company credibility and message effectiveness are bolstered by advertising self-regulation to a greater extent than government regulation.
8. In self-regulation advertisers are subject to less adverse publicity when a case is processed through a self-regulating body instead of a government agency.[42]

There are serious limitations, both procedural and legal, to self-regulation. A major problem is that of enforcement of self-regulatory codes. Strong enforcement techniques involving coercion and restraint are subject to antitrust inquiries. More frequently, the problem is weak enforcement or the absence of serious restraints.

Another problem is to convince all the interests involved in any one activity to agree on a specific remedy. Moreover the funds necessary for self-regulatory activities are usually large and not easily forthcoming. It may impair business competition and innovation because of self-serving restraints on the part of the associations; for example, many advertising bodies have opposed comparison advertising. Finally industry rarely begins an active program of self-regulation before it feels the threat of some kind of government control.

THE FUTURE OF ADVERTISING CONTROLS

It appears as though future control over advertising will continue to be exercised through the combined efforts of self-regulation and government legislation. The limitations against censorship and the freedoms inherent in the marketplace operate to restrict the growth of government controls. Self-regulation cannot operate alone as a control device because of the weakness of imposed sanctions, and the self-regulatory agencies have admitted that one of their strongest weapons in achieving compliance is the threat of government controls. Nonetheless,' the FTC has indicated that the self-regulatory efforts of groups such as the NAD have been significant in reducing the amount of advertising abuse.

---

[41]J. J. Boddewyn, "Advertising Self-Regulation: Private Government and Agent of Public Policy," *Journal of Public Policy & Marketing,* Vol. 4, editor Thomas C. Kinnear, The Division of Research, Graduate School of Business Administration, The University of Michigan, 1985, p. 131.

[42]Priscilla A. LaBarbera, "The Diffusion of Trade Association Advertising Self-Regulation," *Journal of Marketing* (Winter 1983), Vol. 47, pp. 58–67.

Current activities are directed at deregulation. This is a reversal of the trend in the seventies when additional regulatory mechanisms were introduced to provide more governmental control of advertising abuses.

Changes may occur in the future in the design of the control mechanisms rather than in the agencies that enforce them. For example, with the growth of current research in the behavioral sciences, new theories of consumer behavior have evolved, and these concepts may have significance in setting standards for protection from advertising abuse. In keeping with these concepts as well as with the current "back-to-basics" regulatory movement, it is useful to refer to a statement made by Senator Newlands, principal sponsor of the FTC bill. Although it was made in 1914, the following statement has particular relevance for today's marketplace:[43]

> *We are entering now upon a new field of inquiry as to what constitutes unfair competition. This Commission, and ultimately the courts, will be called upon to make nice distinctions with reference to this matter for the purpose of determining what set of facts and circumstances constitute unfair competition . . . . We went through this instrumentality not to punish but to secure higher standards of conduct, by rules that will be laid down by this Commission and sustained by the court, and which will have an educational effect upon the commerce of the country.*

---

[43]63rd Congress, 2d Sess., 1914.

QUESTIONS FOR DISCUSSION

1. Briefly describe the federal laws concerned with advertising.
2. Describe deceptive advertising; unfair advertising.
3. How would you describe the consumer you believe should be protected from advertising abuse.
4. What criteria are used to determine deception in an ad?
5. Discuss the remedies for advertising abuse used by the FTC. Which do you consider most effective and why?
6. What is meant by *equal time? The Fairness Doctrine?*
7. Can counter advertising be effective in limiting the use of undesirable products? Explain.
8. Discuss the kinds of organizations involved in self-regulation of advertising.
9. What is the current status of First Amendment protection for commercial speech?
10. Do you think self-regulatory control or government control over advertising should be expanded? Explain.

KEY TERMS

cease-and-desist order	puffing
equal time	unfair advertising
The Fairness Doctrine	consent order
counter advertising	affirmative disclosure
deceptive advertising	corrective advertising

AD PRACTICE

Contact your state attorney general's office and determine what kinds of protection are available for advertising abuse. How do these rules and regulations compare to those of the Federal Trade Commission?

CASE

Tobacco Advertising

The extent to which a total ban should be placed on tobacco advertising is a controversial issue. Currently cigarettes and little cigars cannot be advertised on radio or television and health warnings must appear in other advertisements for these products. Recently print advertisements for smokeless tobacco products were required to contain one of the following three warnings: "WARNING: THIS PRODUCT MAY CAUSE MOUTH CANCER," WARNING: THIS PRODUCT MAY CAUSE GUM DISEASE AND TOOTH LOSS," or "WARNING; THIS PRODUCT IS NOT A SAFE ALTERNATIVE TO CIGARETTES."

Proponents of the total ban on tobacco advertising stress the harmful effects both to smokers and non-smokers emanating from tobacco use and declare that advertising encourages such use. Tobacco advertisers state that they do not encourage consumers to smoke, but merely offer their brand to those who already are smokers.

While there is some question concerning whether or not a total ban on the advertising of a

legally salable product such as tobacco would be justified under the First Amendment, a number of groups are trying to secure such a ban. A bill to ban all tobacco advertising and promotion has been introduced to Congress. It is supported by the many health and consumerist groups as well as the American Medical Association. In opposition to this bill are a number of advertising associations. The New York State Bar Association introduced a resolution urging the American Bar Association to initiate and support legislation prohibiting tobacco advertising. The Illinois State Bar submitted a counter resolution to the ABA stating that "legislation prohibiting truthful advertising of lawful products

would compromise basic First Amendment values and would represent a dangerous and ill-advised attempt to control behavior through censorship." At this writing the American Bar Association has not agreed to support legislation eliminating tobacco advertising.

FTC Chairman Daniel Oliver stated that the information benefits to the consumer from advertisements free of government control are too important to surrender. He declared "Advertising of cigarettes conveys two useful pieces of information—one about the low-tar and nicotine, the other the Surgeon General's health warning. I think it would be a mistake to deprive the consumer of his ability to acquire that useful information."

DISCUSSION QUESTIONS

1. Discuss the pros and cons concerning a ban on advertising tobacco products, from a social, economic, and legal viewpoint.
2. What would your recommendations be in reference to this issue?

Source: Virginia Reilly, "Meeting of the American Bar Association," *The 4A's Washington Newsletter* (February 1987), American Association of Advertising Agencies, Washington, D. C., p. 4. Steven W. Colford "FTC chief opposes ad limits," *Advertising Age* (November 17, 1986), p. 103.

CASE

Children's Advertising

Criticism of advertising and programming directed to children has been ongoing for years. The FTC so-called "Kid-Vid" rulemaking proceeding issued a report in February 1978 asserting that "Many young children—including an apparent majority of those under the age of eight—are so naive that—they cannot perceive the selling purposes of television advertising or otherwise comprehend or evaluate it and tend . . . to view commercials simply as a form of information programming." The FTC's attempt to limit advertising on television to young children ended in 1981, after months of hearings that did not disclose evidence of harm which would be sufficient to overcome First Amendment protection afforded to advertising.

Despite the outcome of these hearings consumer groups such as ACT (Action for Children's Television) still hold the position that young children are manipulated by the advertising and programming they see on the air and continues to petition for government action and intervention into the broadcast area. In 1985 the FCC denied an ACT request for adoption of a rule requiring broadcasters to insert inaudible electronic signals around children's advertising to automatically turn the set off during advertising.

While both the FTC and the FCC have established standards of advertising relating to children, neither have ever supported the attempt to ban advertising that is truthful about products lawful to sell to children. The Supreme Court has recognized the government's interests in protecting young children from hearing obscene speech. They upheld the FTC's censure of Station WBAI for broadcasting George Carlin's "Dirty Words" monologue in a time period in which many children could be expected to hear a string of obscene words. According to the Court, "Government's interest in the well-being of its youth and in supporting parents' claim to authority in their own household justified the regulation of otherwise protected expression."

DISCUSSION QUESTIONS

1. What kinds of legal protection are offered to advertising as speech? What is the test for First Amendment protection of commercial speech?
2. What social, economic, or legal criticisms can be directed at children's advertising?
3. To what extent do you believe the federal regulatory agencies should attempt to control advertising and programming directed toward children? Explain.

Primary Business	Rank	Company	U.S. Ad Spending 1985	U.S. Sales 1985	Advertising as Percent of U.S. Sales 1985
Airlines	81	AMR Corp.	$105,412	N/A	N/A
	88	Delta Air Lines	94,020	N/A	N/A
	91	Eastern Air Lines	89,700	N/A	N/A
	62	UAL Inc.	145,000	N/A	N/A
Automotive	65	American Motors Corp.	126,000	N/A	N/A
	22	Chrysler Corp.	393,400	$18,767,200	2.1
	7	Ford Motor Co.	614,600	43,526,000	1.4
	5	General Motors Corp.	779,000	89,099,000	0.9
	55	Honda Motor Co.	156,475	N/A	N/A
	58	Goodyear Tire & Rubber Co.	149,305	6,437,300	2.3
	85	Mazda Motors of America	101,743	N/A	N/A
	49	Nissan Motor Co.	162,566	N/A	N/A
	45	Toyota Motor Corp.	172,035	N/A	N/A
	67	Volkswagen of America	123,100	N/A	N/A
Chemicals & Petroleum	31	American Cyanamid Co.	266,189	2,489,100	10.7
	82	Dow Chemical Co.	105,000	5,211,000	2.0
	75	E.I. du Pont de Nemours & Co.	112,184	20,301,000	0.6
	40	Mobil Corp.	195,262	16,601,000	1.2
	90	Monsanto Co.	92,885	4,451,000	2.1
	77	Union Carbide Corp.	110,000	6,371,000	1.7
Electronics & Office Equipment	94	Apple Computer	83,859	1,490,396	5.6
	97	Canon Inc.	81,201	1,500,600	5.4
	35	Eastman Kodak Co.	247,300	7,392,000	3.3
	24	GE/RCA	373,336	35,060,300	1.1
	27	International Business Machines	327,834	28,511,000	1.1
	92	Matsushita Electric Industrial Co.	86,000	3,700,00	2.3
	41	Tandy Corp.	186,861	N/A	N/A
	64	Xerox Corp.	128,898	N/A	N/A
Entertainment & Communications	98	Capital Cities/ABC	72,247	N/A	N/A
	39	CBS Inc.	208,000	4,201,000	5.0
	63	Walt Disney Co.	140,000	N/A	N/A
	95	Gulf & Western	82,101	2,991,000	2.7
	86	MCA Inc.	98,360	1,786,257	5.5
	56	Time Inc.	156,205	N/A	N/A
	66	Warner Communications	124,165	1,881,725	6.6
Food	6	Beatrice Cos.	684,000	8,662,000	7.9
	38	Campbell Soup Co.	215,059	3,344,702	6.4
	70	CPC International	120,000	1,765,000	6.8
	13	Dart & Kraft	489,349	7,316,900	6.7
	14	General Mills	484,146	N/A	N/A
	32	H.J. Heinz Co.	261,541	2,764,815	9.5
	100	George A. Hormel & Co.	70,702	N/A	N/A
	46	IC Industries	171,000	3,943,900	4.3
	25	Kellogg Co.	364,299	2,074,900	17.6
	9	McDonald's Corp.	550,000	2,863,826	19.2

Primary Business	Rank	Company	U.S. Ad Spending 1985	U.S. Sales 1985	Advertising as Percent of U.S. Sales 1985
	28	Nestle SA	319,254	N/A	N/A
	17	Pillsbury Co.	473,220	5,373,700	8.8
	36	Quaker Oats Co.	245,997	N/A	N/A
	12	Ralston Purina Co.	508,365	N/A	N/A
	3	RJR/Nabisco	1,093,000	12,557,000	8.7
	29	Sara Lee Corp.	285,956	6,631,000	4.3
	72	Wendy's International	115,000	N/A	N/A
Gum & Candy	71	Hershey Foods Corp.	118,990	N/A	N/A
	30	Mars Inc.	275,504	N/A	N/A
	96	Wm. Wrigley Jr. Co.	81,536	444,038	18.4
Miscellaneous	69	American Dairy Assn.	121,000	N/A	N/A
	47	American Express Co.	169,868	9,434,000	1.8
	84	Greyhound Corp.	102,604	N/A	N/A
	33	U.S. Government	259,050	N/A	N/A
Pharmaceuticals	21	American Home Products Corp.	399,516	3,636,900	11.0
	78	Bayer AG	108,000	4,177,000	2.6
	26	Bristol-Myers Co.	344,293	3,380,200	10.2
	20	Johnson & Johnson	401,217	3,989,900	10.1
	53	Pfizer Inc.	158,463	2,342,600	6.8
	48	Schering-Plough Corp.	169,383	1,123,700	15.1
	37	Sterling Drug	224,940	1,143,575	19.7
	18	Warner-Lambert Co.	469,339	1,670,000	28.1
Retail	99	Cotter & Co.	71,670	N/A	N/A
	8	K mart Corp.	567,000	N/A	N/A
	15	J.C. Penney Co.	478,892	13,228,000	3.6
	4	Sears, Roebuck & Co.	800,000	N/A	N/A
Soaps & Cleaners	79	Clorox Co.	107,105	N/A	N/A
	34	Colgate-Palmolive Co.	253,495	2,169,988	11.7
	61	S.C. Johnson & Sons	146,146	N/A	N/A
	1	Procter & Gamble	1,600,000	10,243,000	15.6
	19	Unilever U.S.	413,623	4,188,000	9.9
Soft Drinks	23	Coca-Cola Co.	390,000	4,909,000	7.9
	16	PepsiCo Inc.	478,372	7,105,000	6.7
Telephone	11	American Telephone & Telegraph	521,318	N/A	N/A
	57	GTE Corp.	153,606	13,563,000	1.1
	59	ITT Corp.	149,000	12,253,000	1.2
Tobacco	51	American Brands	160,000	3,150,000	5.1
	44	Batus Inc.	175,420	N/A	N/A
	43	Grand Metropolitan plc	176,749	2,269,900	7.8
	54	Loews Corp.	156,918	N/A	N/A
	2	Philip Morris Cos.	1,400,000	11,496,000	12.2
Toiletries & Cosmetics	42	Beecham Group plc	186,322	1,007,500	18.5
	52	Chesebrough-Pond's	159,792	2,084,982	7.7

Primary Business	Rank	Company	U.S. Ad Spending 1985	U.S. Sales 1985	Advertising as Percent of U.S. Sales 1985
	68	Cosmair Inc.	122,149	N/A	N/A
	50	Gillette Co.	161,000	1,024,800	15.7
	80	Noxell Corp.	106,128	327,781	32.4
	60	Revlon Group	147,215	1,830,000	8.0
Toys	73	Hasbro Inc.	114,849	965,038	11.9
	93	Mattel Inc.	85,092	765,010	11.1
Wine, Beer & Liquor	10	Anheuser-Busch Cos.	522,900	N/A	N/A
	87	Brown-Forman Co.	94,260	N/A	N/A
	83	Adolph Coors Co.	104,981	N/A	N/A
	76	Jos E. Seagram & Sons	110,183	1,739,000	6.3
	74	Stroh Brewery Co.	113,000	N/A	N/A
	89	Van Munching & Co.	93,388	N/A	N/A

NOTE: Dollars in thousands.

"100 Leading Advertisers by Primary Business," *Advertising Age*, September 4, 1986. Copyright © 1986 Crain Communications, Inc. Reprinted with permission from Advertising Age.

GLOSSARY

A

Account executive Advertising agency representative who is the service and contact person for a specific client account or accounts; performs all supervision and liaison work between client and agency services./85

Advertising budget Plan for use of all funds set aside for advertising expenditures; entire financial design for the advertising program./105

Advertising elasticity Relative change in quantity of a good sold in proportion to relative change in the advertising budget./111

Advertising plan Statement developed by a company to direct its advertising effort; guides decision making, suggests implementation and coordination, and provides control devices./75

Advertising research Application of marketing research to advertising; consumer behavior research and pure research aimed at developing theoretical approaches to creation of advertising strategies./146

Advocacy advertising Advertising directed to discussion and clarification of social issues of public concern; often takes a controversial approach in the interest of the advertiser./12

Affirmative disclosure FTC requirement that a company must disclose in its advertising the deficiencies or limitations of its product or service./607

Agate-line Older measurement of newspaper ad space; a unit of space column (2¹⁄₁₆ inches) wide and ¹⁄₁₄-inch deep./373

AIDA Acronym for a model of the four steps required in the objectives of advertising: attention, interest, desire, and action./133

Aided recall A research technique that determines the effectiveness of an ad message by asking a volunteer to recall the message when given a name, shown an ad, or presented with another clue./504

Àla carte services Services offered to order to a client by an agency; creative and media services are frequently purchased this way./89

Answer print Final, client-approved TV commercial print; still needs color and timing correction prior to release./333

Appeal The selling message in advertising; what an ad has to say to a consumer./201

Arbitron Research company specializing in measuring local broadcast audiences./348

Audience The number of people reached by a medium or a vehicle; computed differently for different media./405

Audimeter Electronic device developed by A.C. Nielsen for measuring the number of TV sets tuned in in a given area./405

B

Balance Visual weight distribution in an advertising layout; see Optical center./276

Barter Exchange of advertising space or time for the advertiser's products or services./398

Ben Day process Shading in a line engraving; dot pattern./310

Billboard (broadcast) Sponsor identification messages at the beginning and end of TV programs./436

Billings Amount of client money an agency spends an advertising activities and media expenditures (compare to gross income)./83

Body copy Text of a printed advertisement, as opposed to headlines./263

Boutique Agency used as a creative consultant, specializing in concepts and strategy development and execution./89

Brand manager Manager in an agency or a company with marketing and advertising responsibilities for a specific brand./69

Brand name Name by which the manufacturer identifies its goods and services, distinguishing them from those of its competitors; may or may not be the same as the company's trade name./234

Broadsheet Standard size newspaper, such as *The New York Times* or *The Wall Street Journal.*/368

Buried position In newspaper advertising, ad position placed between other ads; undesirable for the advertiser./375

Business-to-business advertising Advertising directed to industrial users, resellers, and professionals./8

C

Caption Brief copy that accompanies a photograph in a print ad./261

Cease-and-desist order Legal order by the FTC to an advertiser to stop an ad that is thought to be unfair or deceptive pending determination of the legitimacy of the claim; advertiser is first served a formal complaint which it must ignore in order to be presented with a cease-and-desist order./606

Centralization Organization of the advertising function within a firm so that one unit services the entire organization./61

Channels of distribution Paths markers use to distribute merchandise; may be direct or indirect (through intermediaries)./47

Classified advertising Printed advertising divided into classes (auto, real estate, rentals); short message for products or services available or wanted; the "want ads."/369

Claymation Animation technique in which clay figures are designed, created, positioned, and photographed to create the effect of movement, similar to animation done with drawings or photos./317,330

Closing date The last date advertising materials will be accepted by a publication./314

Closure Perceptual organization technique whereby the perceiver closes gap in presentation with his or her own assumption of completeness./176

Cold type Generic name for typesetting without "hot metal;" may be photocomposition, strike-on setting, or even hand lettering./306

Color separation Division by photographic color filters of a full-color original image into four-color parts (primaries and black); the color negatives each make a separate printing plate, which is inked on the press by its own color./313

Column inch Newspaper space one column (2¹⁄₁₆ inches) wide and one inch deep; unit of measurement for determining ad sizes./373

Combination rate Special rate for advertising in two or more media vehicles owned by the same organization./373

Commercial advertising Advertising by manufacturers and producers for a product or service, and by retailers, resellers, and wholesalers./6

Communication process Along with the persuasion process, the steps of information processing that ad messages take: source, message, channel, receiver, and destination./479

Comparative advertising Advertising that compares specific product attributes with those of competititors' brands; can be controversial./12

Competition-oriented pricing Pricing based on keeping tabs on competitors' prices./45

Competitive parity Percentage-of-sales approach to determining the advertising budget combined with analysis of the competitive environment./114

Comprehensive Detailed presentation of a rough layout; looks more like the finished ad./275

Consent order Order prepared when both sides reach an agreement in an FTC proceeding to stop unfair or deceptive advertising./606

Consumer advertising Advertising designed to reach anyone who does not remake or resell a product; advertising to the ultimate consumer./8

Consumer jury test Method of testing ads by presenting them to consumer respondents and asking them to rank the ads, compare them to other ads, state what they recall about them, and give their opinions about them./493

Consumer model The way consumers are thought to behave in the marketplace, whether influenced by competition, how the product is defined, or their own needs and wants./577

Consumer stimulants Sales promotion directed at stimulating consumers to buy products; includes use of coupons, free samples, and premiums./454

Continuous advertising Media timing strategy in which the advertiser purchases space in both the purchase cycle and nonpurchase times; consumer is continually reminded of the product or service; media discounts are available to advertiser./352

Controlled (qualified) circulation Circulation of business publications to a specially interested target market at no cost to the consumer./548

Controls Within a corporation, devices supported by organizational structure and budgetary decisions that ensure performance standards set by management are met./78

Cooperative advertising Advertising as a joint effort between the producer and reseller, retailer, or wholesaler of a good or service./49

Copy All reading matter in print advertising; all written and spoken words in broadcast advertising. /253

Copy testing Research testing to evaluate the communication effectiveness of an ad by measuring consumers' responses./490

Cooperative advertising Advertising of company itself, rather than its produce or services./9

Corporate advertising campaign Campaign that treats the company as a product, positioning it and clearly differentiating it from other companies./67

Corrective advertising Advertising mandated by the FTC to remedy prior false or misleading claims; advertising designed to overcome the continuing effects of inaccurate information in prior deceptive advertising./607

Cost-based pricing Pricing according to a computation of costs plus profit./45

Cost per inquiry In direct-response advertising, the cost to generate an inquiry for a product or a service; the total cost of advertising divided by the number of responses to it./434

Cost per thousand (CPU) Quantitative criteria for media choice in which the cost of sending an ad message to one thousand people is determined./353

Cost plus/fixed fee Billing procedure in TV commercial advertising that tabulates the cost of the work plus a given fee; cost of production data is available through a professional association./324

Counter advertising Advertising that takes the opposing view in a controversial issue; required by the FCC Fairness Doctrine in political candidacy advertising./609

Coverage The portion of the broadcast audience that is reached one or more times by a given advertising schedule./403

Creativity The ability to produce new, useful ideas; originality, imagination, or the capacity to join elements to form a new unity or purpose./195

Creative strategy in advertising In the campaign, the development of the appeal, or what is to be said, and the executive, or how it is to be said./200

Creative strategy research Advertising research geared to determining a product's market or target group; includes motivation, attitude, and psychographic research./473

Cumes (accumulated or unduplicated audience) The number of different persons or households in a broadcast audience during a specific time period. /423

Cumulative effects of advertising Objective of research to determine the effects of advertising over a long period of time; includes use of data on sales trends, price structures, sales promotion expenditures, and advertising schedules./118

Cutting or taking TV production optical technique in which scenes are changed with a quick switch from one picture to another./329

D

Dailies (rushes) In TV production, the unedited film that is obtained after a day's shooting./333

DAGMAR Acronym for defining advertising goals for measured advertising results, a model for selecting and qualifying advertising goals./113

Day-after recall test On-air copy test for determining how many consumers who were exposed to an ad can recall its content the next day./496

Dayparts Parts of the TV broadcast day./399

Dealer and distributor stimulants Sales promotion methods directed to dealers and distributors to increase purchasing action; *e.g.*, trade shows, point-of-purchase displays, premiums, and samples./52

Decay constant Projected rate of sales loss in the absence of advertising./117

Decentralization Organization of the advertising function within a firm so that each department carries out its own advertising functions./63

Deceptive advertising Advertising defined by the FTC as occurring where there is a "representation, omission, or practice that is likely to mislead the consumer acting reasonably in the circumstances, to the consumer's detriment."/602

Demand-oriented pricing Pricing based on calculation of what the target market will accept./45

Demographic segmentation Market segmentation that classifies consumers by sex, age, geographic location, county size, education, employment, household income, race, marital status, or the presence of children./149

Departmentalized agency Agency organized by function rather than client, for example, media, writing, TV production./84

Depth interview In advertising research, a one-on-one interview between a consumer and a trained researcher, often a psychologist, to determine consumer motives, perceptions, and thought and behavior processes./183

Direct costs In establishing a fee for agency services, the salaries of the personnel directly involved in the advertiser's account./96

Direct mail advertising All forms of promotional messages sent throughout the Post Office and private delivery firms to individuals and organizations./429

Direct lithography Lithographic printing through which the printing plate is in direct contact with the paper (compare to offset lithography)./295

Discount pricing Pricing low to encourage consumption; a major promotional strategy./46

Display ad Full-size newspaper advertising; accounts for the largest portion of a newspaper's ad revenue./369

Dissolve Optical technique used in TV production to change scenes through which one picture fades out as the next comes into clearer focus./329

Duplicated audience Amount of a total audience that is reached by more than one media vehicle at the same time./423

E

Electrical spectacular Outdoor display that is a large, custom-produced sign usually used in areas of high urban traffic; puffs of smoke, moving parts, or special lighting effects are characteristic./438

Em Unit of measurement for type specification equaling the square of the body of a typeface; derived from the letter M, which is as wide as it is high./303

Equal time Provision of the FCC Fairness Doctrine that states the necessity of providing the same amount of broadcast time to an opposing political candidate as was provided to the initial political advertiser./609

Exclusive distribution Tight limitation of outlets that carry a product; designed to capitalize on a product's image and secure attention for the product and its services./48

Eye tracking In advertising research, method of testing viewers' interest by studying the movement of their eyes when looking at an ad; a film of the eye movement is superimposed over the ad to chart the areas of interest./481

F

Fairness Doctrine A legal requirement of the FCC that states broadcast stations must allow "reasonable opportunity for a discussion of conflicting views on issues of public importance;" equal time for political candidates is mandated under the Fairness Doctrine./609

Family brand Product name used for a group of a company's products; may be company name, subsidiary name, or specially developed name./236

Figure-and-ground differentiation From of perceptual organization in which a part (or parts) of a visual image is emphasized by how it is technically presented to the eye./176

Fixed-sum-per-unit method Method of determining the advertising budget based on the premise that a specific amount of advertising is related to the marketing cost of each unit produced rather than total sales volume./113

Flat rate Standard rate for amounts of media space or time./373

Flighting Media timing strategy in which heavy advertising occurs in certain time periods and little or no advertising appears in others; attracts attention, presents a unified campaign./353

Focus group interview Motivation research technique in which a small number of representative consumers (6–12) work with a leader to provide opinions, generate ideas, and evaluate advertisements./183

Four Ps Basic ingredients in a marketing mix: product, price, place (distribution), and promotion./40

Frame of reference Perceptual organization technique that relates a product to a familiar or desirable setting./177

Franchised position Magazine ad position that is regularly sold to the publication's steady advertisers./384

Frequency Average number of times an individual or household is exposed to a media vehicle or entire media schedule within a time period./354

Full position Newspaper display ad position at the top of a column and alongside reading matter./375

Full-service agency Agency that performs the full range of services for the advertiser; includes research, creative, and media services, as well as participation in the client's entire marketing process./87

G

Galvanometer testing Study of viewers' responses to a message based on changes in respiration, heartbeat, and perspiration; detects strong feelings without regard to positive or negative impact./481

Gatefolds and dutch doors Gatefolds: double and triple pages in magazines that fold out for one advertisement; Dutch doors: pages that partially cover each other and fold out./385

Guaranteed circulation figure Magazine rate structure computed on a circulation figure guaranteed to advertisers./387

Gaze motion Directon of the reader's attention to follow the looks of the people or animals in an ad./279

Generic brand Products without national or private brand labels./236

Global market Concept of the worldwide marketing of items that are standardized and functional, reliable, and low priced./528

Gravure (intaglio) Printing process that uses cut or etched plates to hold ink; used to reproduce fine tones and strong color./296

Gross impressions Total number of people or households delivered by a media schedule without duplication; reach times frequency./354

Gross income Amount of client money an agency receives (compare to billings)./83

Gross rating points (GRPs) Percentage of people reached by a media schedule times the frequency of reach; used to compute costs and determine the effectiveness of a medial schedule./356

Gutter Inside margin of a page in a newspaper or magazine./373

H

Halftone Engraving made by photographing through a screen; the image is broken up into small dots of varying intensities so that shading is visible in reproduction./310

Hierarchy-of-effects theory Model of consumer behavior based on the causal or predictive relationship between changes in a person's knowledge or attitude about a product or service and changes in his or her purchase of that product or service./133

Horizontal publications Business publications that reach people of a specific job category or function across many different industries./546

Hot composition (hot metal) Older, traditional method of typesetting in which molten metal is used to cast letters in a type font; in typesetting copy, lettes are moveable through the use of a keyboard./89

I

Image advertising Corporate advertising designed to highlight the superiority or desirable characteristics of the sponsoring corporation./10

Individual brand Product brand name given just to one product; Tide, Cheer, Gleem, Crest./238

Industrial advertising Advertising of raw materials, semimanufactured goods, equipment, supplies, and services to the agricultural, extractive, and manufacturing industries./8

Inquiries Responses by consumers to coupons, hidden offers, sweetened offers; provide copy testing measures./498

Insert Special section printed by an advertiser and shipped to a newspaper or magazine to be bound or slipped into the publication./369

Intensive distribution Use of as many outlets as possible in placing a product./48

Interlock First version of a TV commercial presented for client approval./333

International advertising A firm's advertising efforts beyond its national borders./528

Island position In newspaper advertising, ad position isolated from other ads and surrounded by reading matter; highly desirable./375

L

Lanham Act Federal statute passed in 1946 that established trademark law./246

Layout Physical arrangement of the elements in a print advertisement so that its mental idea may be effectively presented./273

Leader pricing Pricing strategy through which some

items in a store are priced lower to increase store traffic./46

Leading Insertion of space between lines of type; derived from hot metal type composition in which metal strips (leads) were inserted between the lines of formed metal characters./303

Letterpress Printing process in which ink is stamped onto the paper; inked plates with raised, backward letters print through contact with the paper on the press./294

Lifestyle analysis Type of psychographic segmentation to determine a target profile based on studies of the overall manners in which people spend their time and money./159

Lithography Printing process in which the ink is transferred from a flat surface onto paper; the image areas on the printing plate are treated to accept oil-based substances (ink), the nonimage area to repel them./294

Local advertising Advertising serving the needs of a particular area; may be municipal or regional./7

Logotype (logo) Presentation of the company name, brane name, or trademark in a distinctive form or style./235

M

Macromarketing Marketing means through which a company adapts itself to uncontrollable factors within the environment./39

Make goods Other times slots offered to the advertiser if guaranteed program ratings fall short, if commercials are omitted, or if commercials do not meet reasonable standards of reproduction./426

Marginal analysis Method of setting the advertising budget by determining the point at which an additional dollar spent on advertising equals additional profit./109

Market segment A group of buyers who have similar needs and may respond to similar marketing efforts./43

Market segmentation Division of the total market into well-defined consumer groups that can be reached by one marketing plan./43

Marketing information system (MIS) Formalized method of gathering and analyzing data continually for information that will help marketing managers make decisions./146

Marketing mix A firm's own unique combination of marketing activities, policies, and procedures; basically made up of the Four Ps: product, price, place, and promotion./40

Marketing research Systematic gathering, recording, and analyzing of data about problems relating to the marketing of goods and services (AMA definition)./146

Master tape Final version of a radio commercial upon which the narration and dialog tapes are mixed with the music tape; duplicates are made for distribution./338

Matte shot Shot in TV production of a product through a cut-out, or matted form, placed in front of the camera; gives the impression of looking through a window or keyhold./329

Mechanical (paste-up) Final working stage of layout from which the art elements can be photographed for film and platemaking./275

Media buying services Organizations that consult with and buy media for an advertiser but perform no other agency functions./89

Media concentration theory In media scheduling, the advertiser buys space in one medium only; develops strength by concentration./352

Media dominance theory In media scheduling, the advertiser buys a large amount of space in one medium, and after building coverage and frequency, shifts to do the same in another medium./352

Media plan A firm's detailed plan for use of media to carry its advertising messages./343

Medium and vehicle Medium: channel or system of communication such as newspapers or radio; Vehicle: specific carrier within that channel./343

Merchandising the advertising Promoting a firm's advertising program to the sales force and hence to distributors./466

Micromarketing Internal activities a firm uses to react controllably to external forces; includes setting objectives, selecting target markets, developing marketing plans, and controlling the marketing effort./39

Milline rate Computation of costs of sending one agate line of advertising in a newspaper to a million people./376

Motivation research Research based on psychological theories that attempt to determine how and why consumers behave as they do./181

Movement (sequence) Directional flow in advertising layout guiding the reader's eye naturally from one element to another./278

N

Narrowcasting Broadcasting to audiences with special interests; used in cable./410

National advertising Advertising on a national scale; indicates a manufacturer's brand./7

National brand Product brand name owned by manufacturer that may be distributed nationally, regionally, or locally; for example, Kraft cheese, Jell-o gelatin dessert./235

Network Group of affiliated broadcast stations carrying the same programming supplied by a central broadcasting company; for example, ABC, CBS, NBC, or PBS./396

Nielsen rating Measure of TV audience size based on research by A.C. Nielsen company; the percentage of households tuned to a program during a minute of its airtime./405

Noncommercial advertising Advertising that promotes ideas or institutions, including political candidates and advertising by religious and philanthropic organizations, labor unions, and government./6

O

Odd pricing Pricing based on the assumption that a price ending with an odd number ($3.99 instead of $4) will attract consumers who want to spend less./46

Off pricing Pricing lower to appeal to higher income groups; distinguished from discounting by its use in pricing quality merchandise, usually well-known, nationally branded items./46

Offset lithography Printing process through which the image from a printing plate is transferred to a rubber (blanket) cylinder and then onto the paper; advantage is that rubber can more easily print on many different qualities of paper surface and still allow fine details; used in printing most advertisements./296

On-air tests Testing method for recall that presents broadcast commercials in a natural setting, that is, amid programming and other commercials./496

Optical center Central point in an advertisement to which the reader's eye is directed; fulcrum or balancing point./276

Opticals Camera techniques for smooth transitions in scene changes in broadcast commercials; cutting, dissolving, wiping./329

Out-of-home advertising Any advertising message delivered outside the home, most notably outdoor displays and transit cards./435

Outdoor advertising Advertising messages placed on stationary outdoor structures; the audience moves past the structure./436

Overhead In establishing a fee for agency services, computation of salaries of those indirectly involved in an advertiser's account (accountants, managers, traffickers), as well as rent, depreciation, and utilities./96

P

Painted bulletin Outdoor display composed of an advertising message painted directly on a wood frame, or bulletin./437

Participation Sharing of a specific amount of broadcast advertising time by several advertisers./416

Percentage-of-sales Method of determining the advertising budget based on the firm's anticipated sales for a given year; sales figures are usually derived from past years' performances and growth projections./111

Perceived risk Nature and amount of risk a consumer perceives he or she is taking by buying a product; may be functional or psychosocial./177

Penetration pricing strategy Pricing low in a product's early stage to gain increased market share./44

Personal selling Selling through direct, face-to-face contact between buyer and seller./49

Persuasion process Along with the communication process, the steps in information processing that advertising messages take: exposure, emotional response, encoding, acceptance, and behavior (purchase)./479

Photoanimation Use of still photographs in animation./330

Photoboards Photographed versions of TV commercials kept as records by agency and client./333

Photocomposition Computer typesetting./307

Photoengraving Engraved (relief) printing plate made photochemically; also the process of photoengraving./308

Photoplatemaking Process used to convert original

art material (drawings, photographs, reproducible typography in pasted-up format) into printing plates or other image carriers required to print ads./308

Pica Unit of measurement for type specification and printing; six picas equal one inch./303

Picture window Conventional layout format for a print ad layout in which the picture is usually placed at the top of the page and the copy placed below. /281

Point A small unit of measurement for type specification; seventy-two points equal one inch./301

Point-of-purchase advertising (P.O.P.) Advertising display material located at the retail store; may be banners or window displays as well as counter and floor displays./463

Poster panel Outdoor display bulletin upon which posters are pasted to compose a complete ad message./436

Posttesting Copy testing after an ad has appeared in the media./490

Preemptible rate Rate for purchasing TV spots that is low enough to be preempted by another advertiser wanting to spend more to purchase the spot; advertiser buying at the preemptible rate gambles to save money on the spot./401

Preemption of an idea Creative strategy that advertises a product *as if* it has a unique selling proposition./205

Preferred position Position in a newspaper or magazine thought to attract the most reader attention; for example, the back cover of a magazine./375

Premium An item of merchandise offered free or at a low cost as a bonus to purchasers of a product./455

Prestige pricing Pricing higher to make the product more desirable./46

Pretesting Copy testing prior to placing an ad in the media./490

Primary demand advertising Advertising geared to demand for the generic product (compare to selecti e demand)./10

Private brand Product brand owned by wholesaler or retailer that may be distributed nationally, regionally, and locally; for example, Kenmore (Sears)./236

Product differentiation Practice intended to influence demand for a product through developing and promoting differences./43

Product life cycle Stages of a product's market acceptance: introduction, growth, maturity, and sales decline./46

Product management Advertising system within a firm that has specific products or brands managed by single managers./69

Product positioning A brand's placement among its competitors as perceived by its consumers./43

Product related segmentation Market segmentation based on research into targeted consumers uses of a product or service or their attitudes toward what the product or service may offer; includes volume segmentation, benefit segmentation, and counter segmentation (which recombines smaller groups)./162

Professional advertising Advertising designed to reach professional groups such as doctors, dentists, and pharmacists who may use the advertiser's equipment or products in servicing their patients or clients./8

Progressive proofs Set of proofs used in checking four-color printing which show each color plate separately and in combination./313

Public relations advertising Corporate advertising focusing on public interest but maintaining a relationship to the corporation's products or services./10

Public service advertising Advertising designed to operate in the public interest and promote public welfare./11

Publicity Practice of securing placement of information about a product, service, or idea in the media; form of public relations./51

Puffing, puffery A subjective claim in advertising that may seem to exaggerate a product's benefits but that cannot be disproven and is not illegal./603

Pulsing Media timing strategy in which advertising appears in regular intervals, not necessarily in seasonal patterns./353

Pupilometrics In advertising research, study of the relationship between a viewer's pupil dilation and the interest value of visual stimuli./480

Psychographic segmentation Market segmentation by classifying consumers on the basis of psychological characteristics initially determined by standardized tests./159

Q

Qualitative research Research techniques that emphasize the quality of meaning of consumer perceptions, attitudes, or past behavior; for example, depth interviews and focus group interviews./182

Quantitative research Research techniques that emphasize measurement of incidence of consumer trends within the population./182

R

Rate card Card issued by an advertising vehicle that gives it particular rates, requirements, and other information./347

Rating point In television, one percent of all television households in a given area reached one time; in radio, one percent of all households in a given area reached one time./357

Reach The number of individuals of households exposed at least once to a particular media vehicle or an entire media schedule within a time period./354

Reference groups Social groups that have significance to an individual in terms of selfidentification; include membership or associative groups, anticipatory or aspiration groups, and negative or dissociative groups./172

Residuals Compensation to TV commercial actors that is tabulated each time the commercial is run. /327

Retail advertising Local advertising originating from a retail store./7

Rotoscoping Film technique through which an editor adds drawings to previously shot live-action film footage./330

Rough Sketch of an ad, evolving from an earlier thumbnail sketch, that gives more detail and can be presented for analysis, criticism, and approval of layout./274

Rought cut Intermediate step in commercial TV production in which dailies, or unedited film, are roughly edited together, without voiceover or music./333

Run-of-press, run-of-book Any location for a print ad the publisher chooses./349

S

Sales promotion Marketing activities that stimulate consumer purchasing and dealer effectiveness other than personal selling, advertising, and publicity; includes trade and consumer stimulants./451

Sales-response function The effect of advertising on sales./117

Scene setting Technique in radio production that uses realistic sounds (auto engines, sirens) to simulate background and foreground noises./336

Selective demand advertising Advertising designed to cover a particular manufacturer's brand (compare to primary demand)./10

Selective distribution Limited placement of a product in outlets; creates "shopping goods," or products consumers will shop for./48

Semiotics Theories and symbolism used in researching names for products and services./246

Set solid Lines of type set closely together, without leading, or space, between them./303

Scanners Electronic research technology placed in supermarkets to record consumer purchases./505

Silk screening (serigraphy) Stencil printing that uses a screen to block out areas of an image; ink is forced through the screen onto the printing surface./296

Situation analysis Gathering and evaluation of information as the first step in the advertising campaign; immediate objective is the identification of the target group./144

Skimming strategy Pricing high in a product's early stage for a quick return on investment./44

Soft sell Advertising copy designed to create a mood rather than use strong emotional stimuli./260

Specialty advertising Type of advertising in which products bearing the name of the advertiser are gifted to prospective customers./460

Split run Capability of print media to offer advertisers a run of different ads in alternate copies of the same vehicle; useful in copy testing different versions of the same ad./499

Spot announcements Individual advertising messages interspersed in a TV or radio program./398

Spot radio or television In media placement, time slots in geographic broadcast areas; time is purchased on a market-to-market basis rather than through a network./345, 397

Spread In print media, an advertisement that spreads across two facing pages./381

Standard Advertising Unit System (SAUS) System of standard sizes for newspaper ads developed by the American Newspaper Publishers Association./373

Standard Rate and Data Service (SRDS) Service

that publishes up-to-date information on rates, requirements, closing dates and other information necessary for ad placement in media./347

Starch scores Three measurements that result from Starch recognition testing: noted, or the percent of readers who saw the tested ad; associated, or the percent of readers who associated the ad with the advertiser; and read-most, or the percent of readers who read half or more of the copy./502

Starch Readership Service A research organization (Starch INRA Hooper) that conducts studies of magainze readership using a recognition technique; provides the ad's rank in issue, Starch scores, and comparison to the issue's median ad./501

Stop motion Photographic technique that speeds up or slows down objects separately from the natural motion of the film; animates inanimate objects./330

Storyboard Blueprint for a TV commercial; paneled presentation of images and script./321

Strategic planning In marketing, the process of planning to achieve the optimum fit between the organization and the marketplace./71

Structural motion Direction of the reader's attention to follow a mechanical pattern, such as an S shape or a pointed finger./279

Subliminal persuasion Sending, reception, and effects of subtle visual or aural messages that are supposedly perceived psychologically but not consciously./559

Super (superimposition) In TV production, imposing one image over another./321

Supplement (Sunday supplement) Special feature section in a newspaper that usually appears on Sunday./367

Supplementary media Those vehicles other than the mass media that disseminate messages for promotional purposes; for example, specialty advertising, motion picture advertising, directory advertising, and point-of-purchase advertising./460

Syndicated television program Program airing in more than one market that is sold directly to a station by its producer or representative./398

T

Tabloid Newspaper about half the size of a regular newspaper./368

Tachistoscope testing Advertising research technique that measures a viewer's perception of an ad according to the speed of recognition of the ad's elements under conditions of different lighting and exposure./482

Tag line Slogan; phrase in an ad designed to be repeated and remembered./265

Target group Group of people who are the best prospects for purchase of a product or service./148

Teaser campaign Advertising campaign designed to provoke interest for a new product or a product modification; not a complete ad campaign, rather a precampaign./132

Theater testing Test method for advertising effectiveness in which a randomly selected audience is measured for attitude shifts after viewing commercials./495

Thumbnail sketch Simple, often small, drawing that shows basic visualization of an ad./274

Time compression Broadcast production technique that electronically deletes length from TV commercials; useful in fitting more copy into 30-second spots, but somewhat controversial./324

Tracking studies Research designed to monitor advertising's effects over time./510

Trade advertising Advertising directed at a products resellers rather than its reusers; for example, advertising to sell coffee to restaurants./8

Trade character Distinctive people, cartoon characters, animals, or puppets used as trademarks; for example, the Jolly Green Giant, the Pillsbury Dough Boy./242

Trade name Name under which a company conducts its business; for example, General Motors Corporation, the Borden Company./234

Trade stimulants Sales promotion directed at stimulating dealers and distributors to carry a manufacturer's merchandise and to effectively handle and sell it./45

Trademark A distinguishing word, emblem, symbol, or device used to indicate and identify a manufacturer or distributor of a product./234

Transit advertising Advertising messages that appear on transit vehicles: trains, taxicabs, subway cars, and buses./444

Type font The complete assortment of capital and lower case letters and characters in a given typeface. /301

Typeface Design for printed letters to be set into

words; this book's typeface is called Caledonia./297

Typography Specification (by designer) and setting (by compositor or typesetter) of type in a printed piece./297

U

Unaided recall A research technique in which a volunteer is asked to recall ad messages without any clues or prompting./504

Unfair advertising Advertising as defined by the FTC that causes substantial consumer injury, not outweighed by countervailing benefits, that the consumer could not have reasonably avoided; not often seen separately from deceptive advertising./605

Unique selling proposition Creative strategy that stresses a specific and often unusual product benefit that the competition does not offer and that is strong enough to gain new customers./202

Unity Design principle that requires all elements in an ad to make sense together, to be welded into a pleasant, compact composition./280

Utility and form utility Utility: the want-satisfying qualities of a product; Form utility: the value that emanates from the design of a product./578

V

VALS (SRI Values and Lifestyles Program) Type of psychographic segmentation that divides consumers by their values, lifestyles, and demographics into three main groups and nine subgroups to pinpoint a target market./161

Vertical publications Business publications that reach people within the same industry (compare to Horizontal publications)./546

Visualization The process of "seeing" the advertising piece based on what the concept is and how it is supposed to work./273

Voice-pitch analysis (VOPAN) In advertising research, computerized method of analyzing a respondent's voice for his or her feelings and attitudes about an ad./482

Voiceover Announcer's vocal presentation in a TV commercial./323

W

Wave theory of media scheduling Advertiser purchases space in various media and moves in and out in waves; sacrifices continuity to build up coverage and/or frequency./352

White charges Expenses for items known to be legitimately part of the advertising budget, such as media, artwork, or agency fees./107

White space Part of the print advertisement's space that is not occupied by elements; does not have to be white in color./280

Wipe TV production optical technique that changes scenes by using one picture to literally wipe or push another one off the frame./329

Word painting Highly descriptive use of words to evoke images in writing radio copy; attempts to place the listener in the middle of an imaginary scene./336

CREDITS

Chapter 13

254 ©Pioneer Electronics (USA) Inc. 255 Nike Inc. 256 Clinique Laboratories 257 Courtesy of Eastman Kodak Company 261 ©Schieffelin & Co. 264 Courtesy of Eastman Kodak Company 269 Philip Morris, Inc.

Chapter 14

276 Courtesy The Dannon Company 277 Carillon Importors, Ltd 279 Best Foods CPC International Inc. 280 Hershey Foods Corporation 282 Wamsutta Home Products 284L NYNEX Corporation 286 Beiersdorf Inc. 287 Saatchi & Saatchi Compton, Inc. 291 ©Great Waters of France, Inc.

Chapter 16

318 California Raisin Advisory Board 320 ©Procter & Gamble Company 332 Hershey Foods Corporation 341L Courtesy of International Business Machines Corporation 341R William Grant & Sons, Inc.

Chapter 17

356 DDB Needham World Wide

Chapter 18

385 Transamerica Corporation

Chapter 19

394L General Motors 394R General Motors 404 A. C. Nielsen Co.

Chapter 20

431 Reproduced with permission of Kimberly-Clark Corp. & Lionel Kalish, artist. 436 Northwest Orient Airlines 438T Institute of Outdoor Advertising 438B Institute of Outdoor Advertising 439 Nike Inc. 440(all) St. Mary's Medical Center

Chapter 21

456 ©Philip Morris, Inc. 457 Sunkist Growers, Inc. 458 George Hormel & Co. 462 ©Universal City Studios, Inc. 463 Point of Purchase Advertising Institute, Inc. 464L Point of Purchase Advertising Institute, Inc. 464R Point of Purchase Advertising Institute, Inc. 470R Hyundai Motor America 471L ITT Corporation 471R ©N.A.P. Consumer Electronics Corp.

Chapter 22

481 Perception Research Services, Inc.

Chapter 23

505 Information Resources, Inc. 514L California Raisin Advisory Board 514R ©American Honda Motor Co. Inc.

Chapter 24

520 N. Y. State Dept. of Commerce 522 N. Y. State Dept. of Commerce

Chapter 25

532 Lafont/Sygma 535 British Airways 541L ©Sears, Roebuck & Co. 541R ©J. C. Penney Co. Inc. 542 ©Procter & Gamble Company 544 ©SK & F Co.

Part IV ©Jay Freis/The Image Bank

Chapter 26

564 Caesars Boardwalk Reagency 565 Chrysler Corporation 566T ©Adolph Coors Company 566B ©Jockey International

Chapter 27

576 ©Kraft, Inc. 579 ©Toyota Motor Sales U.S.A. Inc. 585 Time Inc., All rights reserved. 589 ©Audi 590BL ©MCIC 590R Courtesy A. T. & T.

What's Old, What's New in Advertising

following page 6
1–3(all) The Coca-Cola Company 4–5(all) ©Procter & Gamble Company 6TR Hershey Foods Corporation 6M Colgate-Palmolive 6B Miles Laboratories 7 Volkswagen of America, Inc. Reprinted with permission. 8TL ©1952 United Feature Syndicate, Inc. Metropolitan Life Insurance Company 8TR ©1987 Warner Bros Inc. Used with permission 8BL ©1978 United Feature Syndicate, Inc. 8BR Unisys

The Advertising Business: Inside and Outside an Agency

following page 70
1 Karen Hirsch/Foote, Cone & Belding 2L Gabe Palmer/The Stock Market 2R Jim Pickerell/Click/Chicago Ltd. 2B Scott, Foresman 3T Gabe Palmer/After-Image 3C Karen Hirsch/Foote, Cone & Belding 3B Gabe Palmer/The Stock Market 4L Christopher Springman/After-Image 4R Brownie Harris/The Stock Market 4B Richard Gross/The Stock Market 5L Craig Hammell/The Stock Market 5R Craig Hammell/The Stock Market 5B Frank Siteman/After-Image 6T Ted Kawalerski/The Image Bank

6C Mark Godfrey/Archive Pictures Inc.   6B Donald Dietz/Stock Boston   7L J. Freis/The Image Bank   7R Peter Fonk/Click/Chicago Ltd.   7B Roy Morsch/The Stock Market   8T Craig Hammell/The Stock Market   8B Richard Gross/The Stock Market

Ads That Hit Their Targets

following page 166

1 Suzanne DeLyon   2T Cliff Notes, Inc.   2C ©Maybelline Co.   2B ©Jockey International   3TL Precor   3TC ©Reebok International   3TR CNA Insurance Companies   3BL ©Jockey International   3BR With permission from Denny's Restaurants & Foote, Cone & Belding   4 Courtesy Burrell Advertising, Inc.   4B J.P. Martin Associates, Inc.   5TL U. S. Army Photo   5TR Norwegian Cruise Lines   5BC Courtesy A. T. & T.   5BR General Electric   6TL Bulgari   6TC Piaget Watch Corporation   6TR Cadillac Division of GM   6BC ©Bill Blass Inc.   6BR Karastan Rug Mills   7TL Ritz-Carlton   7TR Spiegel   7BL Courtesy Burrell Advertising, Inc.   7BC American Floral Marketing Council   7BR Colgate-Palmolive   8TL ©Pioneer Electronics (USA) Inc.   8TR Benetton   8BL ©American Express Travel Related Services Company, Inc. Reprinted with permission.   8BR ©Revlon Inc.

Creative print Production Process

following page 262

Entire essay: Kameny Communications

Advertising Award Winners

following page 454

1 Frankenberry, Laughlin & Constable   2–3(all) Courtesy Foote, Cone & Belding   4TL Citizen Watch

Company of America   4TR ©1986 Citizen Watch Company of America. From the concept in the book *Hanimals* by Mario Mariotti, copyright ©Fatatrac S.p.A. 1982.   4B ©National Potato Board   5 North Carolina Division of Travel and Tourism   6L ©Anheuser-Busch, Inc.   6R Della Femina, Travisano and Partners   7 Tracy-Locke, Dallas   8–9 (all) Courtesy Chiat/Day   10T ©Procter & Gamble Company   10BL Scali, McCabe, Sloves   10BR Widen & Kennedy   11 BBDO, New York   12T Livingston & Company   12B Institute of Outdoor Advertising   13 Institute of Outdoor Advertising   14–15 (all) Courtesy Hal Riney & Partners   16 BBDO, New York

How to Sell a Service–How to Sell a State The "I Love New York" Campaign

following page 518

1T Milton Glaser   1B N. Y. State Dept. of Commerce   2,3,4,5,8 (all) N. Y. State Dept. of Commerce   6T N. Y. State Dept. of Commerce   6B & 7 (all) Milton Glaser

Social and Legal Issues in Advertising

following page 582

1 W. R. Grace & Company   2 American Cancer Society   3L Planned Parenthood   3R MADD   4T Paco Rabanne Parfums   4B HipOppoTamus   5TL Saxon   5TR Pierre Cardin   5B LifeStyles   6TL Ry-Krisp   6BL R. J. Reynolds & Co.   6R ©Philip Morris, Inc.   7L Alfin Fragrances   7TR ©Beef Industry Council & Beef Board   7BR Courtesy Hal Riney & Partners   8 ©Adolph Coors Company

NAME INDEX

SUBJECT INDEX